Empowering Development With Strategic Accounting:

Organizational, Economic, and Sustainable Impacts

Ana Pinto Borges
https://orcid.org/0000-0002-4942-079X

ISAG - European Business School, Porto, Portugal & Research Center in Business Sciences and Tourism (CICET - FCVC), Porto, Portugal & Applied Management Research Unit (UNIAG), Instituto Politécnico de Bragança, Bragança, Portugal & IPVC—Polytechnic Institute of Viana do Castelo, Viana do Castelo, Portugal

Albertina Paula Monteiro
CEOS.PP, ISCAP, Polytechnic of Porto, Portugal

Elvira Vieira
https://orcid.org/0000-0002-9296-3896

ISAG - European Business School, Portugal

IGI Global
Scientific Publishing
Publishing Tomorrow's Research Today

Vice President of Editorial	Melissa Wagner
Director of Acquisitions	Mikaela Felty
Director of Book Development	Jocelynn Hessler
Production Manager	Mike Brehm
Cover Design	Jose Rosado

Published in the United States of America by
IGI Global Scientific Publishing
701 East Chocolate Avenue
Hershey, PA, 17033, USA
Tel: 717-533-8845 | Fax: 717-533-7115
Website: https://www.igi-global.com E-mail: cust@igi-global.com

Library of Congress Cataloging-in-Publication Data

LCCN: 2025036632 (CIP Data Pending)
ISBN13: 9798337359762
Isbn13Softcover: 9798337359779
EISBN13: 9798337359786

British Cataloguing in Publication Data
A Cataloguing in Publication record for this book is available from the British Library.

Table of Contents

Detailed Table of Contents

Behavioral accounting and finance presume rationality, efficient markets, and maximum gain. According to accumulating facts, cognitive limits, emotional affects, and social dynamics generate illogical behaviour in people and institutions. Psychology, cognitive science, and behavioural economics are used in behavioural accounting and finance. Chapter covers accounting and finance conduct. It examines how biases, heuristics, and emotions affect individual and organisation financial decisions. Behaviourist finance challenges EMH and expected utility theory. Finance altered with Herbert Simon's "bounded rationality," Daniel Kahneman and Amos Tversky's "prospect theory," and Richard Thaler's "mental accounting". Overconfidence exaggerates expertise and ignores risks. It creates overtrading, unrealistic returns, and portfolio diversification concerns. Overconfidence makes CEOs make unwise decisions and delay profits. These basic aspects are discussed in this chapter from various perspectives.

The rapid advancement of digital technologies is transforming the landscape of strategic accounting, positioning it as a key enabler of organizational efficiency, economic resilience, and sustainable development. This chapter explores how digital innovation driven by tools such as artificial intelligence (AI), blockchain, robotic process automation (RPA), and cloud computing is reshaping accounting practices and expanding their strategic value in the digital economy. Traditional accounting, once focused primarily on compliance and historical reporting, is evolving into a forward-looking function that provides real-time insights, predictive analytics, and agile financial decision-making. The integration of digital technologies enhances data accuracy, automates routine processes, and reduces human error, enabling accounting professionals to focus on strategic analysis and value creation. Moreover,

Chapter 6

Nufazil Altaf, National Institute of Technology, Srinagar, India
Bilal Wani, National Institute of Technology, Srinagar, India

This study investigates the impact of corporate debt overhang on firms' environmental expenditures among Indian non-financial firms from 2000 to 2023. To arrive at conclusions, this study employs panel data methodology with year, firm, and industry fixed effects. The analysis reveals the significant negative relationship between debt overhang and environmental expenditure, suggesting that firms tend to curtail their environmental expenditures as their debt level rises. The relationship remains robust across alternative measures of environmental expenditure and after excluding the global financial crisis (2008) and COVID-19 (2020) periods, further confirmed by an instrumental variable approach addressing endogeneity concerns. Additionally, the heterogeneity analysis reveals that debt overhang's adverse impact is more pronounced on manufacturing firms, non–group-affiliated firms, and listed firms. These insights emphasize the need to manage corporate debt level for firms' environmental commitments, with implications for policy and corporate sustainability practices.

Chapter 7

José G. Vargas-Hernandez, Financial Literacy Research Center, Universidad Cristóbal Colón, Mexico & Tecnológico Nacional de México, ITS Fresnillo, Mexico
Carlos A. Rodríguez-Maillard, Universidad Cristóbal Colón, Mexico

This lengthy research report addresses the connection between green and renewable energy knowledge and energy investment practice in Mexico. Based on systematic literature review and empirical data, this research examines how knowledge, awareness, and understanding of renewable energy technology influence individual and institutional investment in Mexico's energy sector. Evidence is that increased energy literacy yields increased intentions to invest in household and commercial renewable energy projects. Policy implications are that targeted education initiatives and public advertising campaigns can increase Mexico's rate of renewable energy adoption significantly.

Preface

INTRODUCTION

It is with great pleasure that we present *Empowering Development With Strategic Accounting: Organizational, Economic, and Sustainable Impacts.* This volume emerges from the growing recognition that accounting, in its broadest sense, is far more than a technical or administrative function—it is a strategic instrument for guiding decision-making, shaping institutional behavior, and advancing sustainable development.

In today's dynamic and complex environment, the integration of accounting tools with institutional strategies plays a crucial role in advancing organizational, economic, and sustainable progress. This synergy empowers both private and public institutions to utilize financial and non-financial information not only for regulatory compliance and reporting but also as a foundation for strategic decision-making and long-term value creation.

The increasing demand for institutions to adopt responsible fiscal policies and align their operations with sustainable practices underscores the urgency and relevance of the themes explored in this book. The contributions within this volume reflect the growing convergence of disciplines—accounting, finance, sustainability, and strategic management—demonstrating how their integration can promote holistic and equitable development across sectors and regions.

Our intent as editors has been to curate a collection that balances theoretical rigor with practical relevance. The chapters offer conceptual insights, empirical evidence, and case studies that illuminate how accounting tools and strategic approaches can foster sustainable growth, support institutional adaptability, and enhance competitiveness in an era of rapid regulatory and technological transformation.

We envision this work as both a scholarly reference and a practical guide. It is designed to support academics, researchers, and postgraduate students seeking deeper understanding, while also serving as a resource for policymakers, institutional leaders, and practitioners engaged in financial reporting, strategic planning, and Environmental, Social and Governance (ESG) implementation. By drawing from diverse perspectives, this book aims to foster dialogue across disciplines and sectors—encouraging innovation, transparency, and accountability in pursuit of sustainable value creation.

The scope of this volume reflects the multidimensional nature of contemporary accounting and strategic management. Topics addressed include financial and management accounting, sustainability and ESG integration, taxation and fiscal policy, corporate finance, digital transformation, regulatory compliance, risk management, and future trends shaping the field. Collectively, these contributions underscore the transformative potential of accounting as a lever for responsible development and institutional resilience.

We extend our sincere gratitude to the contributors for their scholarly dedication and to the reviewers and advisors whose insights strengthened the quality of this volume. We also thank our readers—academics, professionals, and policymakers—for engaging with these ideas and continuing the dialogue on how accounting can serve as a catalyst for sustainable and strategic development.

It is our hope that *Empowering Development With Strategic Accounting* will inspire further research, collaboration, and innovation at the intersection of accounting, economics, and sustainability—empowering organizations to create lasting value for their stakeholders and society at large.

ORGANIZATION OF THE BOOK

Chapter 1: Alignment Between SDGs and ESG Performance Reporting on European Companies

This opening chapter provides a rigorous empirical analysis of how large European corporations have aligned their sustainability reporting with the United Nations Sustainable Development Goals (SDGs). Drawing on data from the Refinitiv database, the study evaluates the relationship between SDG adoption and Environmental, Social, and Governance (ESG) performance. The findings reveal that while overall ESG scores have remained stable over time, the social dimension tends to outperform environmental and governance pillars. A notable increase in SDGs disclosures underscores corporate commitment to sustainability, particularly in areas such as health, poverty reduction, and education. Governance improvements—such as greater female representation on boards and the establishment of Corporate Social Responsibility (CSR) committees—reflect progress in corporate accountability. The analysis also highlights regional differences, showing that companies within the European Union demonstrate higher SDGs transparency than those outside it.

Chapter 2: Behavioral Accounting and Finance

This chapter delves into the fascinating intersection of psychology, cognitive science, and economics to explain deviations from traditional financial rationality. It explores how biases, heuristics, and emotional factors influence accounting and financial decision-making at both individual and organizational levels. By revisiting foundational theories such as Herbert Simon's "bounded rationality," Kahneman and Tversky's "prospect theory," and Thaler's "mental accounting," the authors present a comprehensive understanding of behavioral tendencies that challenge the Efficient Market Hypothesis and expected utility theory. The discussion reveals how overconfidence, risk misperception, and emotional bias lead to suboptimal decisions—ranging from excessive trading to poor corporate strategy execution. This chapter provides an essential lens for understanding the psychological dynamics underpinning financial behavior in complex environments.

Chapter 3: Digital Innovation in Strategic Accounting Enabling Sustainable and Economic Development

The third chapter examines the transformative potential of digital technologies in redefining accounting as a strategic, forward-looking discipline. It explores the integration of artificial intelligence, blockchain, robotic process automation, and cloud computing as tools that enhance accuracy, automate processes, and provide real-time data analytics. Through this lens, accounting is reimagined as a driver of innovation, sustainability, and value creation. The authors argue that digitalization not only streamlines financial operations but also strengthens transparency, ethical governance, and trust—key elements in achieving the United Nations (UN) SDGs. This chapter positions digital innovation as a bridge between financial intelligence and sustainable development strategy.

Chapter 4: When Accounting Meets Innovation: Drivers of E-Commerce

Chapter four explores the determinants of e-commerce adoption, using Portuguese firms as a case study to illustrate how technological and accounting infrastructures enable digital transformation. Drawing on quantitative survey data and regression analysis, the research finds that technological integration, Information Technology (IT) literacy, and robust accounting information systems are critical enablers of e-commerce success. Surprisingly, factors such as financial performance and managerial demographics were found to have little influence. The findings underscore the importance of aligning financial systems with digital capabilities to build resilient, innovation-driven business models. This chapter offers valuable implications for organizations seeking to leverage accounting systems in their digital evolution.

Chapter 5: Risk Forecasting Using Value at Risk (VaR): Strategic Insights for Investors

This chapter provides a detailed empirical application of the Value at Risk (VaR) methodology as a strategic tool for assessing financial risk in leading global companies—Apple, Coca-Cola, Amazon, and McDonald's. Using five years of stock market data and statistical tests such as the Anderson-Darling test, the authors validate the model's robustness and examine the normality of returns. The integration of Power BI tools for forecasting future VaR values demonstrates the growing convergence between data visualization, analytics, and financial strategy. This study delivers practical insights for investors and financial managers seeking to enhance predictive accuracy and improve decision-making under uncertainty.

Chapter 6: Debt Overhang and Environmental Expenditure: Evidence from India

This empirical investigation examines how corporate debt constraints influence environmental investment decisions among Indian non-financial firms from 2000 to 2023. The findings reveal a consistent negative relationship between debt overhang and environmental spending, indicating that financially constrained firms deprioritize sustainability initiatives. Using robust econometric techniques and controlling for crises periods such as 2008 and 2020, the study reinforces the structural link between fiscal health and environmental responsibility. The research also identifies that the adverse impact of debt is strongest among manufacturing and listed firms, suggesting the need for tailored financial and regulatory mechanisms to ensure environmental commitment. This chapter provides policy-relevant insights into balancing financial stability with sustainability obligations.

Chapter 7: Green and Renewable Energy Literacy Research Affecting Energy Investment Behavior in Mexico

Chapter seven explores the vital role of energy literacy in shaping investment behavior in Mexico's renewable energy sector. Through a systematic review and empirical analysis, the study demonstrates that greater awareness and understanding of renewable energy technologies directly correlate with increased investment intentions among both households and institutions. The findings highlight the importance of education, public awareness, and information dissemination in accelerating Mexico's transition to clean energy. The chapter concludes with actionable policy recommendations for enhancing national energy literacy as a lever for sustainable economic transformation.

Chapter 8: Capability Building on Green and Renewable Energy-Related Financial Literacy in Mexico

The concluding chapter of the volume emphasizes capacity-building as a cornerstone of Mexico's sustainable energy transition. It proposes a comprehensive framework for designing financial literacy programs tailored to Mexico's socio-economic and cultural contexts, with the potential to increase renewable energy adoption by up to 40% and generate 150,000 green jobs within five years. This research offers a strategic blueprint for policymakers, educators, and financial service providers seeking to strengthen human and institutional capabilities for sustainable development. As part of the trilogy of Mexico-focused studies in this volume, it reinforces the interconnectedness of education, finance, and energy policy in achieving long-term sustainability goals.

CONCLUSION

As editors of *Empowering Development With Strategic Accounting: Organizational, Economic, and Sustainable Impacts*, we conclude this volume with deep appreciation for the collective scholarship, innovation, and interdisciplinary insight presented throughout its chapters. The contributions within this book reaffirm a central premise—that accounting, far from being a static or purely technical discipline, is a dynamic strategic instrument capable of shaping sustainable, economic, and organizational progress in a rapidly evolving world.

Across the diverse range of studies presented, several unifying themes emerge. First, the integration of sustainability principles into accounting and finance practices—through SDGs alignment, ESG performance, and green financial literacy—demonstrates how institutions are reimagining their roles as agents of responsible development. Second, the accelerating pace of digital transformation underscores the need for accounting systems that not only record and report but also anticipate, adapt, and guide. Digital tools such as AI, blockchain, and advanced analytics are redefining the boundaries of strategic decision-making, enhancing transparency, and supporting ethical governance.

Equally significant are the behavioral and institutional dimensions explored in this volume. The growing understanding of human and organizational behavior in financial contexts reveals that achieving sustainable outcomes requires more than data—it requires awareness, accountability, and informed judgment. Studies on behavioral finance, risk perception, and financial literacy underscore the importance of cognitive and educational foundations in building resilient, future-oriented institutions.

The regional insights presented, from Europe to India and Mexico, remind us that development challenges and opportunities are both local and global. Whether examining corporate debt structures, green finance ecosystems, or e-commerce innovation, the research illustrates that strategic accounting can bridge economic imperatives with environmental stewardship and social responsibility. It is within this intersection that the true transformative potential of accounting emerges—empowering institutions to make decisions that are not only profitable but also sustainable and equitable.

As editors, we hope this volume will inspire continued dialogue and inquiry among scholars, practitioners, and policymakers who share a vision of accounting as a driver of positive change. The future of the discipline lies in its ability to connect numbers with narratives, performance with purpose, and data with development.

We extend our gratitude to all contributors, reviewers, and readers for their engagement and collaboration in advancing this essential conversation. It is our belief that *Empowering Development With Strategic Accounting* will not only serve as a reference for academic and professional advancement but also as a catalyst for rethinking how strategic accounting can empower sustainable futures—within organizations, across economies, and for society as a whole.

ACKNOWLEDGEMENT

This work was supported by national funds through FCT/MCTES (PIDDAC): UID/06354, Research Center in Business Sciences and Tourism (CICET - FCVC). This work was supported by national funds through FCT/MCTES (PIDDAC): UID/04752, Applied Management Research Unit (UNIAG).

Chapter 1

Alignment Between SDGs and ESG Performance Reporting on European Companies

Catarina Cepeda
https://orcid.org/0000-0002-3911-0894
CEOS.PP, ISCAP, Polytechnic of Porto, Portugal

Albertina Paula Monteiro
CEOS.PP, ISCAP, Polytechnic of Porto, Portugal

Amélia Silva
CEOS.PP, ISCAP, Polytechnic of Porto, Portugal

Ana Maria Bandeira
https://orcid.org/0000-0003-2324-9119
CEOS.PP, ISCAP, Polytechnic of Porto, Portugal

ABSTRACT

This study analyzes the of large European companies' sustainability reporting practices and the effect of the Environmental, Social and Governance (ESG) performance. Using data from the Refinitiv database, the research

DOI: 10.4018/979-8-3373-5976-2.ch001

focuses on companies that publish sustainability or integrated reports. Over the years studied, ESG scores remained relatively stable, with the social dimension generally receiving higher ratings than the environmental or governance pillars. The disclosure of SDGs increased significantly throughout the period, showing a clear commitment by companies to align with SDGs. The most frequently reported SDGs were related to health (SDG 3), poverty reduction (SDG 1), and education (SDG4), while goals concerning oceans, ecosystems, and institutions were less commonly mentioned. This study also found improvements in corporate governance practices, including more women on company boards and a growing number of firms establishing dedicated Corporate Social Responsibility (CSR) committees. Across different European regions, companies within the European Union generally disclosed more SDGs information than those outside the European Union.

INTRODUCTION

The growing complexity of environmental and social challenges, coupled with pressure for more transparent and accountable governance, has driven the consolidation of sustainability as a strategic pillar in business organizations. In this context, Environmental, Social, and Governance (ESG) factors are emerging as structural benchmarks for assessing corporate sustainability, going beyond traditional financial analysis (Soni & Dayal, 2023; Cepêda et al., 2025 a,b). ESG disclosure has become particularly relevant within listed companies and is increasingly valued by institutional investors, regulators, and other stakeholders (Branco & Rodrigues, 2006; Soni, 2023; Cepêda et al., 2025a).

The environmental dimension of ESG factors reflects companies' responsibility towards climate change, natural resource management, decarbonization of value chains, and investment in green innovation (Nicolo et al., 2024). The integration of practices, such as energy efficiency, emissions reduction, and responsible water use, has become a strategy for mitigating reputational and operational risks (Erin et al., 2022; Soni & Dayal, 2023; Cepêda et al., 2025a). At the same time, the social aspect has been gaining importance, encompassing concerns about labor rights, gender equality, diversity, worker well-being, and engagement with local communities (Monteiro et al., 2024; Nicolo et al., 2024). Corporate governance, in turn, refers to the decision-making structure, independence of management bodies, internal control, combating corruption, and transparency in communication with investors (Atan et al., 2018; Cepêda et al., 2025b).

In recent years, several international institutions, such as the United Nations, the Organization for Economic Co-operation and Development (OECD), IFRS Foundation and the European Commission, have promoted increasing standardization in how companies report sustainability information. The 2030 Agenda and the Sustainable Development Goals (SDGs) provide a global benchmark that serves as a guide for integrating social, environmental, and economic/governance goals into business models (Wilburn & Wilburn, 2020; Bose & Khan, 2022; Nicolo et al., 2024). In this context, the link between the SDGs and ESG indicators represents a promising way to align companies' interests with global sustainable development priorities.

Recent empirical research suggests that the strategic adoption of SDGs can strengthen the quality of ESG disclosure, improving the consistency, comparability, and relevance of information made available to the market (Soni, 2023; Zampone & Guidi, 2024). Studies conducted on European companies reveal that those that explicitly integrate the SDGs into their reports tend to have better reporting practices and greater transparency towards investors and other stakeholders (Soni & Dayal, 2023; Zampone & Guidi, 2024). In addition, the positive correlation between ESG performance and financial performance has been documented, indicating that sustainable practices can generate long-term economic value, contrary to the view that sustainability represents only a cost to organizations (Friede et al., 2015; De Lucia, Pazienza, & Bartlett, 2020).

The literature also emphasizes that regulatory pressure and market surveillance are key factors in stimulating improvements in reporting practices (García-Sánchez et al., 2023; He et al., 2023; Cepêda et al., 2025a). Initiatives of European Union, such as the European Corporate Sustainability Reporting Directive (CSRD), and of Global Reporting Initiative (GRI) contribute to greater standardization of the criteria and methodologies used (He et al., 2023; Soni, 2023; Maji & Haloi, 2025). However, challenges remain related to the voluntary nature of disclosures, the heterogeneity of the indicators used, and the possible use of ESG as a greenwashing tool.

This study is part of this debate and seeks to further the work developed by Bose and Khan (2022), broadening the temporal and geographical focus of the analysis. Based on a representative set of European listed companies, this study aims to assess the sustainability reporting practices and the effects of SDGs reporting and national performance on the SDGs on ESG performance disclosure between 2017 and 2021. The choice of this period allows us to observe the evolution of sustainability practices in response to new regulatory requirements, market expectations, and post-financial crisis and pre-pandemic dynamics.

To this end, the study seeks to contribute to the academic and political debate on sustainable governance by providing relevant empirical evidence for the design of effective public policies and the promotion of more resilient, ethical business practices aligned with the global challenges of the 21st century.

This article is structured as follows: first, the introduction presents the research context and objectives; next, the literature review discusses prior studies on ESG disclosure and the SDGs; the methodology section outlines the data sources and analytical approach; then, the results are presented and interpreted; finally, the conclusion summarizes the main findings and discusses, their implications and limitations, including suggestions to future research

LITERATURE REVIEW

SDGs and Business

In 2015, the United Nations' 2030 Agenda introduced the 17 SDGs as a global action plan to eradicate poverty, protect the planet, and ensure prosperity for all (Bebbington & Unerman, 2018). These goals succeed the Millennium Development Goals (MDGs), whose final assessment in

2015 revealed considerable progress but also significant gaps (UNEP, 2013; UN, 2015 Opoku, 2016; Sachs et al., 2021; Cepêda, 2024).

According to the Business Council for Sustainable Development (BCSD, 2023), the SDGs represent a strategic opportunity to foster innovation and inclusive and regenerative economic growth, while addressing critical challenges, such as the climate emergency, biodiversity loss, and social inequalities. Still, the global results are discouraging. Between 2015 and 2019, average global progress was only 0.5% per year, and in 2020–2021, it was almost non-existent due to the pandemic crisis (Wilburn & Wilburn, 2020; Sachs et al., 2021).

The 17 SDGs are (Ministry of Foreign Affairs, 2017):

SDG 1 – End poverty in all its forms everywhere;

SDG 2 – End hunger, achieve food security and improved nutrition, and promote sustainable agriculture.

SDG 3 – Ensure healthy lives and promote well-being for all at all ages.

SDG 4 – Ensure inclusive and equitable quality education and promote lifelong learning opportunities for all.

SDG 5 – Achieve gender equality and empower all women and girls.

SDG 6 – Ensure availability and sustainable management of water and sanitation for all.

SDG 7 – Ensure access to affordable, reliable, sustainable, and clean energy for all.

SDG 8 – Promote sustained, inclusive, and sustainable economic growth, full and productive employment, and decent work for all.

SDG 9 – Build resilient infrastructure, promote inclusive and sustainable industrialization, and foster innovation.

SDG 10 – Reduce inequality within and among countries.

SDG 11 – Make cities and communities inclusive, safe, resilient, and sustainable.

SDG 12 – Ensure sustainable consumption and production patterns.

SDG 13 – Take urgent action to combat climate change and its impacts.

SDG 14 – Conserve and sustainably use the oceans, seas, and marine resources for sustainable development.

SDG 15 – Protect, restore, and promote sustainable use of terrestrial ecosystems, sustainably manage forests, combat desertification, halt and reverse land degradation, and halt biodiversity loss.

SDG 16 – Promote peaceful and inclusive societies for sustainable development, provide access to justice for all, and build effective, accountable, and inclusive institutions at all levels.

SDG 17 – Strengthen the means of implementation and revitalize the global partnership for sustainable development.

Companies are essential for achieving the SDGs, but integration into corporate reporting remains limited due to unclear guidance from international institutions, which can lead to greenwashing and selective reporting (Caprani, 2016; UNDP, 2017; Solomon et al., 2013; He et al., 2023; Cepêda *et al.*, 2024, 2025a,b). Nevertheless, SDG reporting has been increasing, driven by regulatory pressures, investor interest, and corporate governance, as well as institutional and organizational factors that shape reporting practices (Bebbington & Unerman, 2018; Wilburn & Wilburn, 2020; Pizzi et al., 2021; Rosati & Faria, 2019 a,b). Studies also show that national SDG performance and sustainability regulations influence corporate SDG disclosure (with higher reporting in shareholder-oriented countries and more detailed disclosures in developing countries), possibly reflecting efforts to gain international legitimacy (Bose & Khan, 2022).

SDGs and ESG Disclosure: Interdependence

Sustainable investment has traditionally been assessed using ESG ratings. However, recent studies argue that SDG Scores provide a measure that is more aligned with the real impact of sustainable development (Zampone & Guidi, 2024). These authors have shown that SDG scores:

- Better capture investor preferences.
- Are aligned with the European Union (EU) Taxonomy.
- More effectively support climate change mitigation.
- Have greater construct validity than traditional ESG indices.

In this context, SDGs not only influence corporate reporting, but also have an impact on investor decisions and companies' ESG performance (Fiaschi et al., 2020).

Recent literature highlights a growing link between the adoption of SDGs and corporate ESG performance.

Bose and Khan (2022), analyzing 6,942 company-year observations across 30 countries (2016–2019), find that SDG reporting has gradually increased, particularly in countries with sustainability regulations and higher SDG performance ratings. Interestingly, shareholder-oriented and developing countries exhibited higher company-level SDG reporting than stakeholder-oriented and developed ones. Maji and Haloi (2025) further show that firms with stronger sustainable practices disclose SDGs more comprehensively, and that institutional factors—such as collectivism, achievement motivation, low corruption, and national sustainable development—positively influence corporate commitment.

Overall, these studies indicate that SDG adoption and reporting align closely with ESG performance and are shaped by both regulatory frameworks and institutional contexts, especially in environmental and social dimensions. Supporting this, Nicolo et al. (2024) analyze 635 companies across 45 countries (2016–2020) and find that firms with higher sustainability performance tend to disclose more on SDGs.

Hence, companies that consistently integrate SDGs into strategy and operations are expected to achieve better ESG performance, either through tangible impact or through positive stakeholder perception. Accordingly, the first research hypothesis is:

H1: The adoption of SDGs positively influences the ESG performance of European companies.

Bose and Khan (2022) empirically show that a country's SDG performance is linked to the extent to which companies base their reporting on SDGs. In contexts with stronger public policies, institutional pressures, and engagement with the 2030 Agenda, companies experience greater normative and mimetic pressures to integrate SDGs into their reports.

This aligns with Institutional Theory, which posits that organizations respond to institutional pressures to maintain legitimacy (DiMaggio & Powell, 1983). Firms in countries with higher national SDG performance are more likely to internalize these goals in their communication and social responsibility strategies, reflecting this in their sustainability reports (Pizzi et al., 2020). However, due to the limited presence of country-level SDG regulations, research often concentrates on the supranational dimension. Studies at the national level primarily address mandatory non-financial reporting (Adams, 2017; Pineda-Escobar, 2019), whereas research in unregulated contexts tends to emphasize the influence of corporate commitment to sustainable development in advancing the SDGs (Mehmann & Teuteberg, 2016; Dangelico, 2017).

In developing countries, the pattern differs. For example, Erin et al. (2022) find that Nigerian firms perform poorly in SDG reporting, primarily due to the absence of a regulatory framework, reliance on voluntary disclosure, limited management commitment, and weak enforcement. Content analysis confirms that these firms provide minimal and superficial information on SDGs-related activities.

Based on this reasoning, the second research hypothesis is:

H2: The ESG performance of European companies will be higher in countries with better national performance on the SDGs

METHODOLOGY

Sample

To test the hypotheses, a target population consisting of large European companies listed on the stock exchange was used, whose business information is available in the LSEG Refinitiv database. Companies that disclose non-financial information on the ESG factors in a sustainability report, an integrated report, or any other form of statement were identified. The final sample for the analysis was a balanced data panel consisting of 8,031 observations from 2,264 listed companies across Europe for the period 2017-2021.

LSEG Refinitiv provides ESG factors data for the period under review (Refinitiv, 2020). We did not include earlier periods because such data would not produce enough observations due to the scarcity of non-financial information disclosed by listed companies at that time.

The selected period considers the pre- and post-implementation of the European directive as well as the Covid-19 pandemic.

Table 1 shows the sample's position by sector, country, and year. Although the distribution over time is homogeneous, there are geographical differences in favor of countries, such as the United Kingdom, Sweden, and Finland. Companies operating in the industrial, financial, and real estate sectors stand out. These characteristics of the sample are like those used in previous studies and are a consequence of the sample selection being based on criteria representative of the international business world (García-Sánchez *et al.*, 2020).

Table 1. Sample composition by country, sector and year

Country	Nº	%	Sector	Nº	%
Cyprus	13	0,57	Basic materials	3	0,13
Czech Republic	3	0,13	Cyclical consumer products	174	7,69
Denmark	68	3,00	Non-cyclical consumer goods	342	15,11
Faroe Islands	2	0,09	Energy	131	5,79
Finland	81	3,58	Finance	98	4,33
Finland	283	12,50	Healthcare	357	15,77
Gibraltar	1	0,04	Industrials	207	9,14
Greece	31	1,37	Real estate	448	19,79
Guernsey	30	1,33	Technology	116	5,12
Hungary	6	0,27	Utilities	320	14,13
Iceland	9	0,40	Academic and educational services	68	3,00
Ireland	52	2,30	**Year**	**Nº**	%
Isle of Man	3	0,13	2017	2264	20
Italy	135	5,96	2018	2264	20
Jersey	11	0,49	2019	2264	20
Malta	8	0,35	2020	2264	20
Monaco	4	0,18	2021	2264	20

continued on following page

Table 1. Continued

Country	Nº	%	Sector	Nº	%
Netherlands	75	3,31			
Norway	83	3,67			
Poland	42	1,86			
Portugal	15	0,66			
Romania	3	0,13			
Russia	46	2,03			
Slovak Republic	1	0,04			
Slovenia	1	0,04			
Spain	76	3,36			
Sweden	328	14,49			
Switzerland	210	9,28			
Ukraine	2	0,09			
United Kingdom	642	28,36			

Empirical Model and Variables

This study uses panel data to analyze the impact of SDG adoption on the ESG performance reporting of European companies. To this end, a mixed-effects model was estimated that incorporates variables with and without temporal variation, considering the individual characteristics of each company and country.

The dependent variable is ESG performance reporting (ESGScore), while the main explanatory variables are the level of SDG reporting by companies (SDG_Rep), the national SDG performance index (SDG_Index), and other control variables related to corporate governance and financial dimensions.

To deal with panel data, two models are typically considered: fixed effects (FE) and random effects (RE). The FE model controls unobserved heterogeneity that is constant over time and is consistent even if the unobserved effects are correlated with the explanatory variables. However, it does not allow for estimating the effect of variables that do not vary over time, such as the national SDG_Index. The RE model assumes that individual effects are not correlated with explanatory variables, which allows coefficients to be estimated for time-invariant variables, but if this assumption is not true, it leads to inconsistent estimates.

To decide between these models, the Hausman test (Hausman, 1978) was applied, which rejected the null hypothesis of no correlation (chi2 = 121.45, $p < 0.001$), indicating that the pure RE model would be inconsistent.

As a solution, the Mundlak (1978) model was used, which incorporates the means of the explanatory variables by group (company/country) in the RE model. This procedure allows for controlling for the correlation between unobserved effects and regressors, combining the advantages of the FE and RE models: consistency in the face of correlated effects and the possibility of estimating the effects of variables unchanged over time.

To analyze the impact between the SDGs reporting and the national performance on the SDGs index on ESG performance reporting of European listed companies, a model was developed based on variables widely supported in recent literature.

The dependent variable is the ESGScore, which measures the company's overall performance reporting in ESG factors, according to LSEG Refinitiv data.

The main explanatories variables are SDGs reporting (SDG_Rep) and national performance on the SDGs index on the SDGs index (SDG_Index), SDG_Rep, which represents the average disclosure of SDGs by companies, i.e., it indicates the degree of reported alignment with the 17 SDGs of the 2030 Agenda. This variable is measured as a percentage (0–100%) and obtained from the Refinitiv database, which annually assesses the extent to which each company communicates its contribution to the SDGs. The SDG_Index was included as an indicator of national performance in relation to the SDGs, extracted from the annual Sustainable Development Report (Sachs et al., 2021), allowing us to capture the influence of the institutional context.

Regarding the control variables, the following was included the variable NFR_Mandatory, which identifies whether non-financial disclosure is mandatory in the company's country, following the criteria of García-Sánchez et al. (2023). To control for internal corporate governance characteristics, the model incorporates BoardSize (number of board members), Board-

GenderDiversity (percentage of women on the board of directors), and IndepBM (percentage of independent members). Financial variables such as Log_assets (logarithm of total assets) and BookValueperShare (book value per share) were also included to control for the size and economic and financial strength of the company. This set of variables allows us to isolate the effect of SDG disclosure on ESG performance, ensuring robustness and theoretical consistency in the model.

The variables under study are shown in Table 2.

Table 2. Variables under study description

Variables	Description	Type	Souce
ESGScore	LSEG Reefinitiv assigns an overall ESG score on a 0–100 scale to reflect firms' sustainability performance.	Dependent	Pizzi et al. (2021), Monteiro et al. (2024) and Cepêda et al. (2025b)
SDG_Rep	Degree of disclosure of SDGs by the company (0–100)	Independent	Pizzi et al. (2021)
SDG_Index	National SDG performance index (73–83)	Independent	Bose & Khan (2022)
NFR_Mandatory	Mandatory non-financial reporting (1 = yes, 0 = no)	Control	García-Sánchez et al. (2023)
BoardSize	Total number of board members	Control	Pizzi et al. (2021)
BoardGenderDiversity	Percentage of women on the board	Control	Bear et al. (2010)
IndepBM	Percentage of independent members on the board	Control	Rosati and Faria (2019a)
Log_assets	Logarithm of the company's total assets	Control	Cepêda et al. (2025b)
BookValueperShare	Book value per share	Control	Monteiro et al. (2024)

Many researchers prefer to use LSEG Refinitiv's ESG scores in their work (e.g., Duque-Grisales & Aguilera-Caracuel, 2021; Monteiro et al., 2024; Cepêda et al., 2025b). LSEG Refinitiv provides one of the most extensive ESG datasets on the market, with data dating back to 2002. It assesses the companies' ESG performance across 10 themes and 3 pillars with over 600 criteria. The three pillars and their themes are as follows: Environment (emissions, innovation, and resource use), Social (human rights, workforce, product responsibility, and community), and Governance (shareholders, management, and CSR strategy). Refinitiv calculates ESG information based on disclosures from companies' annual reports, CSR reports, and company websites, as well as stock registers, using measures that reflect comparability, impact, data availability, and sector relevance, with weightings adopted to capture sector specificities (Aluchna et al., 2022). The measures are formulated into three pillar scores E, S, and G and a final ESG score.

The literature acknowledges some shortcomings in performance scoring, although the disclosure of intangible data does not affect the assessment, the lack of information on highly relevant aspects has a negative impact on the company's score (Aluchna et al., 2022). However, being comparable across various sectors and company sizes, Refinitiv scores serve as a sufficient indicator of ESG performance for our whole-market sample. We discuss this topic in more detail in the research limitations section. Refinitiv collects most of its data from public sources, such as company websites, annual reports, and other company reports. It also obtains some of the data directly from the company. They audit and standardize this data and prepare ESG scores.

Table 3 shows the ESG score assessment metrics used by Refinitiv.

Table 3. ESG score assessment metrics

Score	Description
From 0 to 25	Scores in this range imply relatively poor performance and insufficient transparency in the public disclosure of relevant ESG data.
From 26 to 50	Scores in this range imply relatively satisfactory ESG performance and moderate transparency in the public disclosure of relevant ESG data.
From 51 to 75	Scores in this range imply good relative ESG performance and above-average transparency in the public disclosure of relevant ESG data.
From 76 to 100	Scores in this range imply excellent relative ESG performance and a high degree of transparency in the public disclosure of relevant ESG data.

Fonte: adapted from LSEG Refinitiv (2023)

Model

To address the objectives of this study, the following model was designed:

$$ESGScore\_it = \beta 0 + \beta 1\ SDG\_Rep\_i,t + \beta 2\ SDG\_Index\_i,t + \beta 3\ NFR\_Mandatory\_i,t + \beta 4\ BoardSize\_i,t + \beta 5\ BoardGenderDiversity\_i,t + \beta 6\ IndepBM\_i,t + \beta 7\ Log\_Assets\_i,t + \beta 8\ BookValuePerShare\_i,t + \beta 9\ Industry\_i + \beta 10\ Country\_i + \beta 11 Yeart\_i,t + \varepsilon\_it$$

Where:

ESGScore_i,t: ESG performance of company i in year t.

SDG_Rep_i,t: Degree of disclosure of SDGs by company i in year t.

SDG_Index_i,t: National SDG performance in country c where company i is headquartered in year t.

NFR_Mandatory_i,t: Dummy indicating whether non-financial disclosure is mandatory in the country i in year t.

BoardSize_i,t: Number of members on the company's board of directors.

BoardGenderDiversity_i,t: Percentage of women on the board of directors.

IndepBM_it: Percentage of independent members on the board.

Log_Assets_i,t: Logarithm of the company's total assets.

BookValuePerShare_i,t: Book value per share.

Categorical variables – industry, country, and year – are included as control variables.

ε_it: Random error term.

RESULTS

This study has two objectives: the first is to analyze sustainability reporting, and the second aims to analyze the effects of SDG reporting and national performance on the SDGs index on ESG performance reporting. The results of the first are presented using descriptive statistics analysis, whereas to analyze the conceptual model, regression analysis for panel data is used.

Descriptive Statistics

About the ratings for the separate ESG factors and ESG in general, there has been a decline over the years, except for the governance pillar, which has increased. However, the average increase and decrease recorded is not significant, as shown in Table 4. On average, the pillar with the best rating is social, followed by governance and environmental.

Table 4. Ratings of performance reporting for environmental, social, and governance pillars and ESG in general by year

Year	Environmental Score	Social Score	Governance Score	ESG Score
2017	47	57	50	52
2018	43	56	50	51
2019	43	54	50	50
2020	41	51	52	49
2021	42	52	53	50
Average	43	53	51	50

Legend: Pillar cover quotes: 0-100

About SDGs, over the years, more companies have been disclosing SDGs, as shown in Table 5. In 2017, only 36.97% of companies reported SDGs. From 2017 to 2021, the number of companies reporting SDGs increased, and in 2021, almost all companies in the sample (99.87%) reported one or more SDGs, demonstrating a greater contribution by companies to all stakeholders in contributing to the United Nations SDGs.

Regarding SDGs, over the years under review, more SDGs were disclosed, considering that 0 means not disclosed and 1 means disclosed. The overall average increased steadily from 36.93% in 2017 to 54.99% in

2018, 68.51% in 2019, 89.84% in 2020, and 99.87% in 2021, confirming a consistent upward trend (see Table 5).

According to table 6, The most widely publicized SDGs was SDG 3 (Ensure access to quality healthcare and promote well-being for all at all ages), representing 42.50% of the total sample, followed by SDG 1 (End poverty in all its forms everywhere) with 29.63% and SDG 4 (Ensure inclusive and equitable quality education and promote lifelong learning opportunities for all) with 25.28%. On the other hand, the least reported were SDG 14 (Conserve and sustainably use the oceans, seas, and marine resources for sustainable development) with 2.87%, SDG 15 (Protect, restore and promote sustainable use of terrestrial ecosystems, sustainably manage forests, combat desertification, and halt and reverse land degradation and halt biodiversity loss) with 3.97%, SDG 16 (Promote peaceful and inclusive societies for sustainable development, provide access to justice for all and build effective, accountable and inclusive institutions at all levels) with 4.70% and SDG 17 (Strengthen the means of implementation and revitalize the global partnership for sustainable development) with 4.97%.

Table 5. Number of companies that disclosed SDGs and their representation by year

Year	**Number of companies reporting SDGs**	%
2017	836	36,93%
2018	1245	54,99%
2019	1551	68,51%
2020	2034	89,84%
2021	2261	99,87%

Table 6. Average disclosure of SDGs and their representation by type of SDG and year

Year	2017	2018	2019	2020	2021	Average	%
SDG 17	0,00	0,00	0,13	0,21	0,26	0,15	4,97
SDG 16	0,00	0,00	0,12	0,20	0,25	0,15	4,70
SDG 15	0,00	0,00	0,09	0,16	0,21	0,12	3,97
SDG 14	0,00	0,00	0,07	0,11	0,14	0,08	2,87
SDG 13	0,00	0,00	0,24	0,41	0,52	0,30	10,95
SDG 12	0,00	0,00	0,23	0,41	0,49	0,29	11,77
SDG 11	0,00	0,00	0,14	0,24	0,28	0,17	7,84
SDG 10	0,00	0,00	0,10	0,20	0,27	0,15	7,42
SDG 9	0,00	0,00	0,17	0,31	0,37	0,22	11,91
SDG 8	0,00	0,00	0,25	0,43	0,53	0,31	19,21
SDG 7	0,00	0,00	0,16	0,29	0,35	0,20	15,52
SDG 6	0,00	0,00	0,10	0,16	0,20	0,12	10,80
SDG 5	0,00	0,00	0,17	0,32	0,42	0,23	23,61
SDG 4	0,00	0,00	0,16	0,26	0,33	0,19	25,28
SDG 3	0,00	0,00	0,19	0,33	0,41	0,24	42,50
SDG 2	0,00	0,00	0,06	0,09	0,11	0,07	21,04
SDG 1	0,00	0,00	0,06	0,10	0,13	0,08	29,63
Total	0,00	0,00	0,14	0,25	0,31	0,18	100,00

Legend: 1-reported; 0-not reported

Regarding the disclosure of SDGs by region, Table 7 shows the average distribution of SDGs by companies in the study sample. The information is presented by country and region. Among the regions of Europe, the average SDG score for EU companies during the sample period is 0.21, suggesting that, on average, European companies disclose 3.57 (17 items × 0.21) SDG items. In addition, the average SDG score for European companies outside the EU is 0.15, suggesting that, on average, these companies disclose 2.55 (17 items × 0.15) SDG items.

As Table 7 shows, among companies outside the EU, those in Ukraine are the best performers in terms of SDG disclosure (average of 0.39), while those in Gibraltar have the lowest level of SDG disclosure (0). Among EU countries, companies in Slovenia have the highest level of SDG disclosure

(0.42), i.e., 7.14 SDG items, followed by those in Slovakia (0.41), i.e., 6.97 SDG items, and Romania (0.34); however, the sample from these countries is very small. In this regard, Spain, with a representation of 3.36%, had an average SDG disclosure of 0.32, followed by Poland, with a representation of 1.86% and an average SDG score of 0.31, and Italy, with a representation of 5.96% and an average SDG index of 0.25. Conversely, Malta has the worst SDG communication (0.10), i.e., 1.70 SDG items.

These values, compared with the previous study by Bose and Khan (2022), show recent and relevant differences, considering that in the 2016 to 2019 timeframe, the average for European companies was 0.074 (1.258 SDG items) and with the timeframe of this study, from 2017 to 2021, the average became 0.18 (3.06 SDG items). Thus, previously, the countries with the best index were Italy and Spain, and the worst was Greece, which had no disclosure. In our timeline, we see that Italy has become the 9th country in Europe with the best index and Spain the 5th, with Slovenia and Slovakia being the countries with the highest indices in Europe. Greece is in 10th place, and Gibraltar and the Isle of Man are in last place.

These figures are in line with the data reported previously, as 2021 was the best year to date, considering that 99.87% of the companies in the study reported at least one SDG in the RNF, compared to only 54.99% of companies in 2017. In this regard, to analyze the impact of 2021 compared to other years, we present Figure 1, which shows the SDG index by year.

Table 7. Distribution by SDG during the sample period, by region and country

Region/ Country	SDG 1	SDG 2	SDG 3	SDG 4	SDG 5	SDG 6	SDG 7	SDG 8	SDG 9	SDG 10	SDG 11	SDG 12	SDG 13	SDG 14	SDG 15	SDG 16	SDG 17	Average
Outside European Union	**0,07**	**0,07**	**0,22**	**0,16**	**0,19**	**0,11**	**0,17**	**0,26**	**0,18**	**0,12**	**0,14**	**0,24**	**0,26**	**0,08**	**0,11**	**0,10**	**0,12**	**0,15**
Gibraltar	0,00	0,00	0,00	0,00	0,00	0,00	0,00	0,00	0,00	0,00	0,00	0,00	0,00	0,00	0,00	0,00	0,00	0,00
Guernsey	0,06	0,04	0,12	0,12	0,11	0,05	0,12	0,12	0,12	0,05	0,07	0,13	0,11	0,01	0,13	0,03	0,04	0,08
Isle of Man	0,00	0,00	0,17	0,00	0,17	0,08	0,08	0,08	0,08	0,00	0,00	0,08	0,17	0,00	0,00	0,08	0,08	0,06
Jersey	0,03	0,00	0,33	0,15	0,08	0,15	0,33	0,23	0,21	0,05	0,10	0,15	0,31	0,05	0,13	0,13	0,03	0,14
Monaco	0,00	0,00	0,00	0,24	0,24	0,00	0,00	0,24	0,24	0,24	0,24	0,24	0,06	0,24	0,00	0,00	0,24	0,13

continued on following page

Table 7. Continued

Region/ Country	SDG 1	SDG 2	SDG 3	SDG 4	SDG 5	SDG 6	SDG 7	SDG 8	SDG 9	SDG 10	SDG 11	SDG 12	SDG 13	SDG 14	SDG 15	SDG 16	SDG 17	Average
Norway	0,09	0,14	0,31	0,21	0,35	0,12	0,24	0,52	0,30	0,13	0,23	0,43	0,54	0,31	0,14	0,25	0,27	0,27
Norway	0,11	0,09	0,33	0,30	0,17	0,23	0,27	0,39	0,30	0,17	0,25	0,36	0,33	0,09	0,26	0,13	0,30	0,24
Switzerland	0,06	0,05	0,20	0,17	0,15	0,10	0,15	0,24	0,19	0,08	0,11	0,21	0,23	0,04	0,09	0,09	0,10	0,13
Ukraine	0,29	0,43	0,43	0,43	0,29	0,43	0,43	0,43	0,43	0,29	0,43	0,43	0,43	0,29	0,29	0,43	0,43	0,39
United Kingdom	0,07	0,06	0,21	0,14	0,18	0,10	0,15	0,24	0,15	0,14	0,14	0,22	0,24	0,07	0,11	0,08	0,09	0,14
Inside European Union	**0,08**	**0,07**	**0,26**	**0,22**	**0,28**	**0,13**	**0,24**	**0,36**	**0,26**	**0,17**	**0,19**	**0,34**	**0,34**	**0,08**	**0,12**	**0,19**	**0,18**	**0,21**
Cyprus	0,10	0,08	0,31	0,28	0,28	0,10	0,18	0,31	0,31	0,18	0,23	0,28	0,28	0,15	0,18	0,23	0,15	0,21
Czech Republic	0,00	0,07	0,13	0,13	0,20	0,33	0,33	0,33	0,27	0,33	0,20	0,33	0,33	0,07	0,13	0,33	0,33	0,23
Denmark	0,01	0,04	0,30	0,18	0,36	0,08	0,24	0,44	0,19	0,15	0,14	0,46	0,38	0,09	0,05	0,26	0,19	0,21
Faroe Islands	0,00	0,33	0,00	0,33	0,67	0,33	0,33	0,67	0,33	0,00	0,33	0,33	0,67	0,33	0,33	0,00	0,33	0,31
Finland	0,03	0,02	0,25	0,16	0,21	0,17	0,20	0,39	0,29	0,14	0,18	0,43	0,44	0,06	0,12	0,21	0,19	0,20
Finland	0,06	0,05	0,19	0,19	0,20	0,11	0,18	0,26	0,21	0,13	0,12	0,24	0,28	0,05	0,09	0,12	0,15	0,15
Greece	0,14	0,13	0,31	0,28	0,26	0,17	0,26	0,32	0,31	0,17	0,28	0,30	0,32	0,22	0,21	0,25	0,22	0,24
Finland	0,16	0,08	0,24	0,24	0,28	0,12	0,24	0,32	0,36	0,28	0,32	0,32	0,24	0,12	0,12	0,24	0,20	0,23
Iceland	0,00	0,13	0,13	0,00	0,47	0,00	0,13	0,20	0,40	0,13	0,13	0,67	0,53	0,07	0,07	0,07	0,00	0,18
Ireland	0,07	0,08	0,20	0,13	0,18	0,13	0,18	0,23	0,20	0,16	0,17	0,24	0,24	0,03	0,08	0,08	0,10	0,15
Italy	0,10	0,07	0,31	0,33	0,33	0,15	0,33	0,42	0,33	0,21	0,28	0,36	0,36	0,09	0,16	0,25	0,21	0,25
Malta	0,07	0,00	0,21	0,18	0,14	0,04	0,18	0,21	0,04	0,07	0,00	0,11	0,14	0,04	0,07	0,18	0,00	0,10
Netherlands	0,08	0,09	0,27	0,19	0,22	0,11	0,23	0,35	0,23	0,12	0,15	0,35	0,32	0,06	0,08	0,09	0,14	0,18
Poland	0,07	0,04	0,19	0,21	0,14	0,07	0,15	0,22	0,20	0,12	0,16	0,22	0,23	0,02	0,06	0,08	0,12	0,14
Portugal	0,17	0,14	0,34	0,41	0,39	0,12	0,42	0,51	0,32	0,22	0,25	0,46	0,51	0,20	0,37	0,12	0,27	0,31
Romania	0,33	0,08	0,42	0,42	0,42	0,25	0,42	0,42	0,42	0,33	0,25	0,42	0,42	0,17	0,33	0,33	0,33	0,34
Slovak Republic	0,00	1,00	0,00	0,00	0,00	1,00	1,00	0,00	1,00	0,00	1,00	0,00	1,00	0,00	1,00	0,00	0,00	0,41
Slovenia	0,00	0,00	0,60	0,60	0,60	0,60	0,60	0,60	0,20	0,40	0,00	0,60	0,60	0,60	0,60	0,60	0,00	0,42
Spain	0,23	0,18	0,36	0,40	0,35	0,24	0,32	0,44	0,40	0,33	0,32	0,35	0,42	0,16	0,25	0,27	0,38	0,32
Sweden	0,05	0,06	0,28	0,16	0,35	0,12	0,25	0,43	0,26	0,17	0,20	0,40	0,36	0,08	0,11	0,25	0,17	0,22
Total	**0,08**	**0,07**	**0,24**	**0,19**	**0,23**	**0,12**	**0,20**	**0,31**	**0,22**	**0,15**	**0,17**	**0,29**	**0,30**	**0,08**	**0,12**	**0,15**	**0,15**	**0,18**

Figure 1. Average SDG's adoption per period

Based on the analysis of a representative sample of European listed companies, the first objective of this study—assessing sustainability reporting practices—reveals a clear upward trend in both ESG performance and SDG disclosure over the period 2017–2021. While ESG scores for ESG pillars showed only minor variations over time, with the social pillar consistently receiving the highest ratings, governance recording slight improvements, and environmental performance slightly declining, the overall changes were not statistically significant. In contrast, the disclosure of SDGs increased substantially, with only 36.93% of companies reporting in 2017 compared to nearly all companies (99.87%) reporting in 2021. The most widely disclosed SDGs were SDG 3 (healthcare), SDG 1 (poverty), and SDG 4 (education), whereas SDG 14, 15, 16, and 17 were the least reported. Regional analysis further highlighted variations, with EU companies generally disclosing more SDGs than non-EU companies, and Slovenia and Slovakia standing out as the highest performers, while countries such as Malta and Gibraltar reported the lowest levels of disclosure. Compared to previous studies, the findings indicate a substantial improvement in both the quantity and breadth of SDG reporting among European companies, reflecting an increasing corporate commitment to sustainability and alignment with the United Nations SDGs over time.

Conceptual Model Descriptive Statistics

Table 8 presents the descriptive statistics of the variables used in the model. There is considerable variation in ESG performance reporting (ESGScore) and SDG reporting (SDG_Rep), reflecting heterogeneity between companies and countries regarding sustainability. The descriptive statistics presented allow for an initial analysis of the sample and the variables used in the model. The dependent variable ESGScore, which measures companies' ESG performance reporting, has an average of 50.18 on a scale of 0 to 100, with a standard deviation of 21.14. This average value suggests moderate ESG performance among the companies in the sample, with the high dispersion indicating significant variation between them — from companies with very limited ESG practices (minimum value of approximately 1) to companies with levels of excellence (maximum value of 95.67).

The SDG_Rep variable, which reflects the degree of disclosure of the SDGs by companies, has an average of only 12.67 on a scale of 0 to 100. This figure reveals that most companies still disclose little about the SDGs in their sustainability reports. The high standard deviation (24.43) also shows great heterogeneity among companies, with some presenting well-developed reports and others making no mention of the SDGs.

Regarding the SDG_Index variable, which represents national performance in relation to the SDGs, the average is 78.75, with a low standard deviation (2.70). This shows that the countries included in the sample have relatively similar and high performances in achieving the 2030 Agenda, with values ranging from 73.76 to 82.72.

The variable NFR_Mandatory, which indicates whether there is a legal requirement for non-financial reporting in the country where the company is based, has an average of 0.99, suggesting that almost all companies in the sample operate in regulatory contexts where such reporting is required. The standard deviation of 0.12 confirms this high concentration.

Regarding corporate governance characteristics, the BoardSize variable has an average of 8.77 board members, with values ranging from 1 to 28. This range indicates diversity in governance structures among the companies analyzed. The BoardGenderDiversity variable, which measures the percentage of women on the board of directors, has an average of 26.42%, revealing a moderate level of gender diversity. However, the existence of boards with no female representation (minimum value of 0) and others with values close to 100% reveals significant asymmetries.

The IndepBM variable, which measures the percentage of independent members on the board, has an average of 50.63%, with a high standard deviation (28.40), showing that some companies have boards composed almost entirely of independent members, while others have a very limited presence of this profile.

The Log_assets variable, which corresponds to the logarithm of the companies' total assets, has an average of 9.09 and a standard deviation of 0.97, suggesting some heterogeneity in the size of the companies. Finally, the BookValueperShare variable, which represents the book value per share in euros, has an average of 201,680, with an extremely high standard deviation (9,507,470), indicating the presence of outliers that could affect econometric estimates if not properly addressed.

In summary, the descriptive statistics reveal a highly diverse sample in terms of ESG performance reporting, SDG disclosure, governance characteristics, and company size. This diversity justifies the application of robust econometric models that allow the effect of explanatory variables on companies' ESG performance to be isolated.

Table 8. Descriptive statistics

Variables	Observations	Average	Std. Ddv	Min	Max
ESGScore	8,031	50.18	21.14	0.99	95.67
SDG_Rep	8,031	12.67	24.43	0.00	100.00
SDG_Index	8,031	78.75	2.70	73.76	82.72
NFR_Mandatory	8,031	0.99	0.12	0.00	1.00
BoardSize	8,031	8.77	3.52	1.00	28.00
BoardGenderDiv	8,031	26.42	14.38	0.00	100.00
IndepBM	8,031	50.63	28.40	0.22	99.65
Log_assets	8,031	9.09	0.97	4.76	12.42
BookValueperR	8,031	201,680	9,507,470	-9,417.80	486,000,000

Table 9 provides the Pearson correlation matrix for each variable. The correlations between the study variables show significant but not overly strong relationships, indicating that there is important variability to consider both between companies and between countries. For example, SDG disclosure (SDG_Rep) is positively correlated with ESG performance reporting (ESGScore), suggesting that companies that better communicate their SDGs efforts tend to have better ESG performance, according to Nicolo et al. (2024) foundaments.

However, the national performance on the SDGs index (SDG_Index) shows weak and even negative correlations with ESGScore, indicating that the national context does not fully explain the variation in companies' ESG performance, confirming that company-specific factors are also important.

In addition, corporate governance variables, such as board size and gender diversity, show moderate and positive correlations with ESG performance, reinforcing that the internal structure of companies influences their sustainable results (Pizzi et al., 2021).

This pattern of correlations suggests that there are important effects at both the company and country levels, which justifies the use of a random effects model. This type of model allows us to capture the variation between companies and countries, while controlling for the specific characteristics of each unit, providing more robust and generalizable estimates.

Table 9. Pearson matrix correlation

Variables	(1)	(2)	(3)	(4)	(5)	(6)	(7)	(8)	(9)
(1) ESGScore	1.000								
(2) SDG_Rep	0.366*	1.000							
(3) SDG_Index	-0.031*	0.049*	1.000						
(4) NFR_Mandatory	0.053*	0.013	-0.074*	1.000					
(5) BoardSize	0.476*	0.176*	-0.066*	0.056*	1.000				
(6) BoardGenderDiv	0.333*	0.189*	0.068*	0.020	0.128*	1.000			
(7) IndepBM	0.288*	0.071*	-0.007	-0.001	0.011	0.233*	1.000		
(8) Log_assets	0.602*	0.305*	0.004	0.017	0.584*	0.182*	0.215*	1.000	
(9) BookValueperSh	-0.008	-0.011	0.003	0.003	-0.002	0.009	-0.019	0.016	1.000

Legend: *** p<0.01, ** p<0.05, * p<0.1

To ensure the robustness of the model, a multicollinearity analysis was performed by calculating the Variance Inflation Factor (VIF) for the independent variables included. The VIF values obtained range from 1.00 to 1.66, with an overall average of 1.20. These values are well below the commonly accepted critical limit of 5 (or even 10), indicating that there is no significant problem of multicollinearity between the variables in the model.

Thus, it can be stated that the independent variables used are sufficiently distinct from each other to avoid distortions in the coefficient estimates, reinforcing the reliability of the results obtained.

We confirm that there is no multicollinearity after removing the highly correlated independent variables from the model, verifying that all variables in the model have VIF ratios below 10. Table 10 shows the VIF test.

Table 10. VIF test

Variable	**VIF**	**1/VIF**
SDG_Rep	1.08	0.925149
SDG_Index	1.02	0.979699
NFR_Mandatory	1.01	0.989746
BoardSize	1.58	0.633987
BoardGenderDiv	1.11	0.897473
IndepBM	1.12	0.890997
Log_assets	1.66	0.602352
BookValueperSh	1.00	0.999134
Mean VIF	**1.20**	

REGRESSION RESULTS

The results, according to Table 11, show that the level of SDG reporting by companies (SDG_Rep) has a positive and statistically significant effect on ESG performance ($\beta = 0.098$, $p < 0.001$). This result is in line with recent literature highlighting the growing integration of SDGs into corporate strategy and reporting following the launch of the 2030 Agenda (Pizzi et al., 2021). Companies that report more consistently on SDGs demonstrate better ESG performance, reflecting greater alignment with the expectations of sustainable investors and stakeholders (Zampone & Guidi, 2024).

In contrast, the national SDG_Index did not show a significant direct impact on ESG performance reporting ($\beta = 0.020$, $p = 0.884$). This result may suggest that the national context, although relevant for the dissemination of SDGs (Bose & Khan, 2022), does not necessarily translate directly into better ESG performance by companies. This is in line with the idea that the impact of the institutional environment occurs mainly through normative and mimetic pressures that influence corporate strategy and communication, but that ESG performance also depends on companies' internal actions (Rosati & Faria, 2019a; DiMaggio & Powell, 1983).

Regarding control variables, corporate governance variables had positive and significant effects on ESGScore, such as board size ($B = 0.241$, $p = 0.003$), gender diversity ($B = 0.190$, $p < 0.001$), and proportion of independent members ($\beta = 0.115$, $p < 0.001$). These results corroborate previous studies indicating that robust governance practices facilitate alignment with the SDGs and improve ESG performance (Bear et al., 2010; Pizzi et al., 2021).

Table 11. Regression results (mixed effects – Mundlak)

Variable	Coeficient (β)	P-value
SDG_Rep	0.098	*** (p < 0.001)
SDG_Index	0 020	n.s. (p = 0.884)
NFR_Mandatory	0.083	* (p < 0.05)
BoardSize	0.241	** (p = 0.003)
BoardGenderDIv	0.190	*** (p < 0.001)
IndepBM	0.115	*** (p < 0.001)
Log_assets	0.361	*** (p < 0.001)
BookValueperR	-0.000002	n.s.

R^2: 0.317
N° observations: 8,103
Legend: *p < 0.05; **p < 0.01; ***p < 0.001; n.s. Not significant

CONCLUSION

This study contributes to the understanding of the alignment between SDGs and ESG performance reporting in the European context, considering the heterogeneity between countries and the transformations.

The first objective of this study was to analyze sustainability disclosure. The descriptive and empirical analysis revealed substantial growth in the adoption and dissemination of SDGs between 2017 and 2021, reflecting a process of institutional maturation and responsiveness to the global call for sustainable development. Companies have increasingly integrated sustainability into their reporting practices, paying greater attention to social, environmental, and governance issues. Although some SDGs are disclosed more frequently than others, the overall trend demonstrates a stronger corporate commitment to advancing the United Nations SDG's and enhancing transparency for stakeholders.

Regarding the second study objective, the results show that the disclosure of SDGs by companies is a determining and positive factor for ESG performance, reinforcing the importance of the strategic integration of SDGs into corporate practices. In contrast to the first proposed hypothesis, the national performance on the SDGs index was not statistically significant in directly explaining ESG performance. This suggests that, although stronger national performance on SDGs may encourage companies to disclose these goals in their reports—as supported by Institutional Theory—the actual impact on ESG performance appears to depend more on organizational commitment and internal practices than on the broader regulatory or institutional context.

In terms of practical implications, the results suggest that policymakers should encourage not only mandatory disclosure regulations but also the effective adoption of the SDGs as a guide for a sustainable transition. For companies, the importance of integrating the SDGs into corporate strategy, governance, and communication is reinforced.

This study has several limitations that should be acknowledged. First, the analysis relies on secondary data from the Refinitiv database, which may restrict the scope and depth of available information on sustainability and reporting practices. Second, the study period (2017–2021) only covers the initial years of SDG adoption, not capturing potential long-term developments. In addition, the use of aggregate indicators of national performance (SDG index) may not fully reflect the complexity of public policies and institutional contexts in each country. Finally, the research focuses exclusively on large European companies, which limits the generalizability of the findings to small and medium-sized enterprises or to firms in other regions.

Future studies could explore the quality of SDG disclosure, going beyond its mere presence in reports to assess the substance and materiality of alignment with the 2030 Agenda. Longitudinal research covering longer periods could provide insights into whether the integration of SDGs has sustained impacts on ESG performance. Another promising line of inquiry would be to examine the relationship between SDG adoption and financial performance, analyzing possible trade-offs or synergies between sustainability and profitability. Moreover, extending the analysis to smaller firms or to companies from other regions would allow for comparisons across diverse institutional and cultural contexts. Finally, qualitative approaches, such as case studies or interviews with managers, could complement quantitative findings by offering a deeper understanding of the organizational factors driving alignment between SDGs and ESG practices.

REFERENCES

Adams, C.A., 2017. Conceptualising the contemporary corporate value creation process. *Account Audit. Account. J. 30* (4), 906e931. https://doi.org//DOI: 10.1108

Aluchna, M., Roszkowska-Menkes, M., Kamiński, B., & Bosek-Rak, D. (2022). Do institutional investors encourage firm to social disclosure? The stakeholder salience perspective. *Journal of Business Research, 142*, 674–682. DOI: 10.1016/j.jbusres.2021.12.064

Atan, R., Alam, M. M., Said, J., & Zamri, M. (2018). The Impacts of Environmental, Social, and Governance Factors on Firm Performance: Panel Study of Malaysian Companies. *Management of Environmental Quality*, *29*(2), 182–194. DOI: 10.1108/MEQ-03-2017-0033

Bear, S., Rahman, N., & Post, C. (2010). The impact of board diversity and gender composition on corporate social responsibility and firm reputation. *Journal of Business Ethics*, *97*(2), 207–221. DOI: 10.1007/s10551-010-0505-2

Bebbington, J., & Unerman, J. (2018). Achieving the United Nations Sustainable Development Goals. *Accounting, Auditing & Accountability Journal*, *31*(1), 2–24. DOI: 10.1108/AAAJ-05-2017-2929

Bose, S., & Khan, H. Z. (2022). Corporate SDG Reporting and Institutional Determinants: An International Study. *Journal of Cleaner Production*, *365*, 132780. DOI: 10.1016/j.jclepro.2021.132780

Branco, M. C., & Rodrigues, L. L. (2006). Corporate social responsibility and resource-based perspectives. *Journal of Business Ethics*, *69*(2), 111–132. DOI: 10.1007/s10551-006-9071-z

Caprani, L. (2016). Five ways the Sustainable Development Goals are better than the Millennium Development Goals and why every educationalist should care. *Management in Education*, *30*(3), 102–104. DOI: 10.1177/0892020616653464

Cepêda, C., Monteiro, A. P., & Aibar-Guzmán, B. (2025a). Decoupling in Sustainability Reporting: A Systematic Literature Review. *Corporate Social Responsibility and Environmental Management*, *32*(3), 2988–3007. Advance online publication. DOI: 10.1002/csr.3114

Cepêda, C., Monteiro, A. P., & Aibar-Guzmán, B. (2025b). Bridging the ESG Credibility Gap: The Role of Institutional Investors in Mitigating ESG Decoupling. *Business Strategy and the Environment*, *34*(6), 7139–7160. Advance online publication. DOI: 10.1002/bse.4336

Cepêda, C. L. M. (2024). Why Reporting Sustainability? The Portuguese Non-financial Reporting's Socio-historical Evolution. In Thrassou, A., Vrontis, D., Efthymiou, L., Weber, Y., Shams, S. M. R., & Tsoukatos, E. (Eds.), *Non-Profit Organisations* (Vol. III). Palgrave Studies in Cross-disciplinary Business Research, In Association with EuroMed Academy of Business. Palgrave Macmillan., DOI: 10.1007/978-3-031-62534-3_3

Dangelico, R.M., 2017. What drives green product development and how do different antecedents affect market performance? A survey of Italian companies with eco-labels. *Bus. Strat. Environ. 26* (8), 1144e1161. https://doi.org//DOI: 10.1002

Portugal, B. C. S. D. (2023). *SDG Compass*. Lisboa, Portugal. https://bcsdportugal.org/wp-content/uploads/2020/12/SDG-Compass.pdf

De Lucia, C., Pazienza, P., & Bartlett, M. (2020). Does good ESG lead to better financial performances by firms? Machine learning and logistic regression models of public enterprises in Europe. *Sustainability (Basel)*, *12*(13), 5317. DOI: 10.3390/su12135317

Duque-Grisales, E., & Aguilera-Caracuel, J. (2021). Environmental, social and governance (ESG) scores and financial performance of multilatinas: Moderating effects of geographic international diversification and financial slack. *Journal of Business Ethics*, *168*(2), 315–334. DOI: 10.1007/s10551-019-04177-w

Erin, O. A., Bamigboye, O. A., & Oyewo, B. (2022). Sustainable development goals (SDG) reporting: An analysis of disclosure. *Journal of Accounting in Emerging Economies*, *12*(5), 761–789. DOI: 10.1108/JAEE-02-2020-0037

Fiaschi, D., Giuliani, E., & Nieri, F. (2020). Overcoming the liability of origin by doing no-harm: Emerging country firms' social irresponsibility as they go global. *Journal of World Business*, *55*(4), 101094. DOI: 10.1016/j.jwb.2016.09.001

Friede, G., Busch, T., & Bassen, A. (2015). ESG and financial performance: Aggregated evidence from more than 2000 empirical studies. *Journal of Sustainable Finance & Investment*, *5*(4), 210–233. DOI: 10.1080/20430795.2015.1118917

García-Sánchez, I. M., Ortiz-Martínez, E., Marín-Hernández, S., & Aibar-Guzmán, B. (2023). How does the European Green Deal affect the disclosure of environmental information? *Corporate Social Responsibility and Environmental Management*, *30*(6), 2766–2782. DOI: 10.1002/csr.2514

He, C., Jia, F., Wang, L., Chen, L., & Fernandes, K. (2023). The impact of corporate social responsibility decoupling on financial performance: The role of customer structure and operational slack. *International Journal of Operations & Production Management*, *43*(12), 1859–1890. DOI: 10.1108/IJOPM-08-2022-0521

Maji, S. G., & Haloi, A. (2025). Corporate Sustainable Practices, Institutional Factors, and Sustainable Development Goals: Evidence From Asian Emerging Markets. *Sustainable Development (Bradford)*, sd.70006. Advance online publication. DOI: 10.1002/sd.70006

Mehmann, J., Teuteberg, F., 2016. The fourth-party logistics service provider approach to support sustainable development goals in transportation - a case study of the German agricultural bulk logistics sector. *J. Clean. Prod. 126*, 382e393. DOI: 10.1016/j.jclepro.2016.03.095

Monteiro, A. P., Cepêda, C., Borges, A. P., & Vieira, E. (2024). Does CSR committee presence, stakeholder engagement, gender equality (SDG 5) and firm value influence ESG performance reporting? An EU pre and during Covid-19 analysis. Measuring Business Excellence, (ahead-of-print). https://doi.org/DOI: 10.1108/MBE-03-2024-0034

Mundlak, Y. (1978). On the pooling of time series and cross section data. *Econometrica*, *46*(1), 69–85. DOI: 10.2307/1913646

Nicolo, G., Zampone, G., De Iorio, S., & Sannino, G. (2024). Does SDG Disclosure Reflect Corporate Underlying Sustainability Performance? Evidence From UN Global Compact Participants. *Journal of International Financial Management & Accounting*, *35*(1), 214–260. DOI: 10.1111/jifm.12194

Opoku, A. (2016, September). SDG2030: A sustainable built environment's role in achieving the post-2015 United Nations Sustainable Development Goals. In *Proceedings of the 32nd Annual ARCOM Conference* (Vol. 2, pp. 1149-1158). Manchester, UK: Association of Researchers in Construction Management.

Pineda-Escobar, M. A. 2019. Moving the 2030 agenda forward: SDG implementation in Colombia. *Corp. Govern. Internatl. J. Bus. Soc. 19* (1), 176e188. DOI: 10.1108/CG-11-2017-0268

Pizzi, S., Caputo, A., Corvino, A., & Venturelli, A. (2020). Management research and the UN sustainable development goals (SDGs): A bibliometric investigation and systematic review. *Journal of Cleaner Production*, *276*, 124033. DOI: 10.1016/j.jclepro.2020.124033

Pizzi, S., Rosati, F., & Venturelli, A. (2021). The determinants of business contribution to the 2030 Agenda: Introducing the SDG Reporting Score. *Business Strategy and the Environment*, *30*(1), 404–421. DOI: 10.1002/bse.2628

Rosati, F., & Faria, L. G. D. (2019a). Addressing the SDGs in sustainability reports: The relationship with institutional factors. *Journal of Cleaner Production*, *215*, 1312–1326. DOI: 10.1016/j.jclepro.2018.12.107

Rosati, F., & Faria, L. G. D. (2019b). Business contribution to the Sustainable Development Agenda: Organizational factors related to early adoption of SDG disclosure. *Corporate Social Responsibility and Environmental Management*, *26*(3), 588–597. DOI: 10.1002/csr.1705

Sachs, J., Schmidt-Traub, G., Kroll, C., Lafortune, G., Fuller, G., & Woelm, F. (2021). *Sustainable Development Report 2021*. Cambridge University Press. DOI: 10.1017/9781009106559

Solomon, J. F., Solomon, A., Joseph, N. L., & Norton, S. D. (2013). Impression management, myth creation and fabrication in private social and environmental reporting: Insights from Erving Goffman. *Accounting, Organizations and Society*, *38*(3), 195–213. DOI: 10.1016/j.aos.2013.01.001

Soni, M. (2023). The impact of ESG practices on financial performance: Evidence from emerging markets. *Investment Management and Financial Innovations*, *20*(3), 150–163. DOI: 10.1016/j.jclepro.2017.02.180

Soni, M., & Dayal, V. (2023). Assessing ESG performance through SDG disclosure: A study of European listed firms. *Proceedings of the International Conference on Business Excellence*, 17(1), 749–762. https://doi.org/DOI: 10.2478/picbe-2023-0072

United Nations Development Programme (UNDP). (2017). *SDG Integration: UNDP and the Sustainable Development Goals*. https://sdgintegration.undp.org/

United Nations Environment Programme (UNEP). (2013) *Embedding the Environment in Sustainable Development Goals, UNEP Post-2015 Discussion Paper 1, Version 2*. Nairobi: United Nations Environment Programme.

United Nations (UN). (2015) Transforming our world by 2030: A new agenda for global action Zero. Draft of the outcome document for the UN Summit to adopt the Post-2015 Development Agenda. New York: United Nations.

Wilburn, K., & Wilburn, R. (2020). ESG Reporting Using UN Sustainable Development Goals. *Journal of Strategic Innovation & Sustainability*, *15*(2).

Zampone, G., & Guidi, M. (2024). Sustainability reporting and assurance practices contribution to SDG disclosure: Evidence from communication on progress (CoP). *Meditari Accountancy Research*, *32*(7), 236–265. DOI: 10.1108/MEDAR-09-2023-2165

Chapter 2
Behavioral Accounting and Finance

Arivuselvee Vellore Jayaraman
https://orcid.org/0000-0002-5181-5344
Saveetha University, India

Mohammed Musthakeem
https://orcid.org/0009-0000-5085-2779
Saveetha Institute of Medical and Technical Sciences, India

S. G. Sasswat
Saveetha Institute of Medical and Technical Sciences, India

Dhiwakar Gandhi
https://orcid.org/0009-0003-8793-813X
Saveetha Institute of Medical and Technical Sciences, India

ABSTRACT

Behavioral accounting and finance presume rationality, efficient markets, and maximum gain. According to accumulating facts, cognitive limits, emotional affects, and social dynamics generate illogical behaviour in people and institutions. Psychology, cognitive science, and behavioural economics are used in behavioural accounting and finance. Chapter covers accounting and finance conduct. It examines how biases, heuris-

DOI: 10.4018/979-8-3373-5976-2.ch002

tics, and emotions affect individual and organisation financial decisions. Behaviourist finance challenges EMH and expected utility theory. Finance altered with Herbert Simon's "bounded rationality," Daniel Kahneman and Amos Tversky's "prospect theory," and Richard Thaler's "mental accounting". Overconfidence exaggerates expertise and ignores risks. It creates overtrading, unrealistic returns, and portfolio diversification concerns. Overconfidence makes CEOs make unwise decisions and delay profits. These basic aspects are discussed in this chapter from various perspectives.

INTRODUCTION

The accounting and finance sectors have experienced a radical change over the last few decades. This change is not merely one of the adoption of new financial instruments or technologies, but one of the radical reconsideration of how human behaviour influences the formation of economic results. Historically, monetary theories presupposed that individuals used rationality as the sole motive, i. e. that individuals evaluate all accessible data, compute perils and gains without any favouritism and make optimal choices in order to obtain the greatest personal gain. This is what the neoclassical economics is founded on and has been manifested in models like the efficient market hypothesis (Fama, 1970). Market participants in this classical perspective are viewed as computers: able to process all the information objectively (Simon, 1955). According to the recent developments, the use of machine learning is essential to enhancing integrity of financial networks, as it helps identify fake accounts, which minimizes fraudulent activities and instills more confidence in the network participants (Nirmala & Chokkalingam, 2019). When applied to behavioral accounting and finance, adoption of such algorithms means that financial behaviors and transactions will be analysed based on authentic and reliable datasets, which will eventually result in behavioural insights that are more accurate and sounder financial decision-making (Pattasani, Mohapatra, & Jyoti, 2025).

However, years on, scientists and the practicers started to discover that there are no real life examples that match this pattern. The world is not a neat and a predictable place and so are the decisions taken by investors, managers or auditors. These basic beliefs began to be confronted by empirical evidence. Specifically, the research conducted by Kahneman and Tversky (1979) revealed that all psychological, emotional, and even social factors often influence how some decisions are made and often interfere with decision-making processes. Their work, especially in the prospect theory, revealed that most people place much loss weight far much more than they place weight on gains, a factor that may result in irrational behaviour such as holding onto losing investments in the hope of making even gains or selling winning investments too early because they may turn into losses.

This awakening resulted in the area of behavioural finance and behavioural accounting. Using the knowledge of psychology and the cognitive societies, these fields attempted to reveal the real-life exceptions in the financial markets and in the organisations. Behavioural approaches do not regard irrational behaviour as a rare bug within an otherwise flawless system but as a widespread element, and as an extension of the ways of thinking, feeling, and coping with the uncertainty people face.

The abundance of research soon pointed to a number of critical cognitive biases, which have been and continue to influence financial decision-making. An example is overconfidence which leads people (investors, managers or auditors) to believe that their knowledge, skills or ability to forecast the future is too much. This can be the source of overtrading to irresponsible corporate activities. The anchoring bias makes decision-makers to disproportionately allocate weight to the initial information they receive at times on important updates or opposing information. Loss aversion, which has been discussed above, is what forces individuals to operate on the safe side in case of possible losses, regardless of that they may forego good opportunities (Barberis & Thaler, 2003).

Mental accounting is another behavioural research finding that people mentally group and treat money dissimilarly based on its origin or purpose--which makes them make less than optimal decisions such as spending tax refunds more liberally than monthly salary or psychologically sticking to artificial investment targets despite increasing losses. These trends are not only revealed in the investment portfolios, but in all the aspects of corporate finance: in budgeting, capital allocation choices, risk management, and audit procedures.

However, as much as research has advanced in trying to comprehend these patterns there are still a lot of gaps. The initial one is the threat posed by technology. The world of financial markets has become more automated and algorithmic trading and artificial intelligence today occupy significant positions. There was the belief that machines would eliminate the irrational human impulse but it has been realised that behavioural biases do not just vanish in an online world, on the contrary, it might become embedded in the code and in some cases, it only increases systemic risk and volatility. Moreover, the necessity to comprehend where (and how) human decision-making is connected to machine decision-making grows even more pressing with increased use of machine learning models and data analytics by organisations.

The second significant gap is the one that values the importance of demographic and cultural diversity. The current financial environment is international. Investors, managers and other participants can be representatives of a vast variety of backgrounds each one of them carries his/her values, experience as well as psychological inclinations. A study conducted by Arya and Singh (2025) informs about the fact that cultural context may exert a strong impact on the risk tolerance, decision styles, and even the vulnerability to certain biases. These disparities may either moderate or increase the influence of behavioural aspects on the markets; however, most of our standard theories and models continue to adopt a type-fits-all strategy. The world is experiencing an urgent need to implement behavioural finance, and accounting systems in a pluralistic, interconnected world.

The purpose of this chapter is objective and broad considering the challenges and the increased complexity of the contemporary economies. First, it will examine the terrain of behavioural effects on accounting and finance- uniting both the background theories and the most recent years of empirical findings. Second, it aims at discovering new and emerging trends, including the disruptive impacts of technological innovation or the influence of diversity on decision outcomes. Third, it provides practical and practical solutions on how to incorporate behavioural knowledge in the practical management and policy choices- so that organisations and markets are more prepared to deal with uncertainty and complexity.

The chapter is organised in a way that is easy to understand. This is an introductory part as it establishes the background and puts the main problems into perspective. The following section reviews the major behavioural theories and empirical evidence with a focus on the most significant achievements, however, also highlighting the areas of severe gaps in the current knowledge. The methodology section follows and describes the systematic review and synthesis technique of research with the focus on the qualitative perspective that should be applied to such a complex topic. The results section condences key themes, which are both points of agreement and the points on which more research is required. Lastly the chapter concludes and indicates areas that could be fruitful in further studies.

In a nutshell, this holistic, humanistic approach is meant to bridge the historic gap between practise and theory. The relevance of behavioural insights will only become more important as financial markets and institutions are further developing. Providing the reader with a comprehensive perspective of behavioural accounting and finance, this chapter aims at creating better decision-making, stronger organisations, and the world of global finance, which is becoming more complex.

LITERATURE REVIEW

The Evolution of Behavioral Accounting and Finance

Behavioural accounting and finance has already become an inseparable part of the modern financial theory and practise. What previously started as a critique of the dogmatic rationality assertions of the classical economics, is currently viewed to be crucial to the interpretation of the non-uniform, and very unpredictable, realities of markets and businesses. During the most part of the twentieth century, the orthodoxy had it that people, either investors, auditors or managers, acted as rational agents. Traditional models such as the Efficient Market Hypothesis introduced by Fama and much of neoclassical economics had assumed that the agents in the market act through rational and logical processing of all accessible information and make efficient choices that maximise their results (Fama,

1970). It was believed that the financial markets are inherently efficient due to the rationality of all the players in the market which is impersonal. On the same note, Simon (1955) wrote of a world in which, given the right data at least in theory humans could act with perfect objectivity.

But it was a more complicated picture which slowly appeared under the surface. The real world was not going to fit properly into the rational-agent model. Empirical studies, in and out of economics, found behavioural trends that resulted in bubbles, crashes, enduring anomalies and eventually, financial crises. These phenomena could not be sufficiently explained using traditional models. Rather, they directed their attention at the omnipresence of the psychological, emotional, and social forces, which, in turn, shape our behaviours in subtle and profound ways (Kahneman and Tversky, 1979).

Recent comparative studies have shown that the adoption of advanced machine learning models namely Light Gradient Booster and Isolation Forest algorithms has greatly contributed to the early detection of credit card fraud. Incorporating these predictive aids into behavioral accounting and finance models underpin the integrity of transactional investigation, boosts the authority of the stakeholders and strengthens dependability of the financial reporting by highlighting the anomalies and fraudulent behaviors at the early stages of financial cycle, (Reddy & Kumar, 2022).

The Foundations: Prospect Theory and Bounded Rationality

Another critical event in behavioural finance was the publication of the prospect theory by Kahneman and Tversky (1979). These psychologists demonstrated not only that individuals perceive the prospective losses as psychologically heavier than the commensurate gains, but that the decisions of individuals are in a systematic way inconsistent with the expectations of the traditional utility theory. That is, we are neither risk-averse nor risk-seeking, but our risk-taking is determined by the framing of choices, the experiences of outcomes, and the human mind processing of threats and rewards. The profound understanding of the prospect theory is that the actual process of making decisions is not symmetrical in real life: painful losses may take over the decision-making process, and might give people irrational decisions regarding fear or hope.

Another closely related concept is the concept of bounded rationality which was developed by Simon (1955). Although conventional rationality assumed that human beings had almost infinite computational capacity, bound rationality suggests that decision makers act under constraints; their information capabilities are limited, their foresight is imperfect and they have limited cognitive resources. Optimization is not so much the case but rather the act of satisficing, which entails making good-enough decisions when short of time or faced with uncertainty. Heuristics, or shortcuts of the mind, can be useful when one is faced with a complex problem, but they also can introduce systematic and predictable errors.

The Catalogue of Cognitive Biases

The initial behavioural literature was soon proliferated by a multitude of cognitive biases that recurrently influence the financial/organisational behaviour. The bias of overconfidence is particularly widespread. Their skill, risk-taking ability, or level of knowledge is frequently over-assessed by the investors, analysts, as well as corporate executives, resulting in excessive trading, making wrong purchases, and putting too much money in any project that becomes unsuccessful (Barberis & Thaler, 2003). This may take the form of exaggerated predictions, lack of regard of warning signals and systematic underestimation of downside risk.

Anchoring bias, in turn, indicates the effect that we get attached to the first piece of information, price, target of prediction, and make minimal adjustments in response to new information. Sticky prices, suboptimal investments and faulty negotiation performance in the financial realms can result because of this.

Another phenomenon that has been well documented is the mental accounting. Individuals mentally divide funds based on arbitrary groupings (e.g. a tax refund would be treated differently than a paycheck within the same portfolio or a safe investment would be viewed as safe and risky investment within the same portfolio (Thaler, 1999). This compartmentalization misleads the general risk perception and even fails to allow the financial decisions to be analysed holistically in most cases.

The ubiquitous role is also played by the loss aversion. Investors usually tend to hold on to losing stocks unnecessarily (the disposition effect at work) and realise gains prematurely in an attempt to escape the psychic trauma of a loss. These practises result in the inefficiency of asset allocation and dulled long-term returns.

Technological Disruption and its Double-Edged Sword

The world of behavioural finance has gotten even more complicated with the introduction of algorithmic trading, machine learning, and artificial intelligence. Technology at surface level was expected to reduce human error through elimination of emotion and inconsistency on financial decisions. Such automated trading systems as an example can handle large volumes of information within a single second and operate transparently by programmed rules and logic (Poddar, Bhattacharya, & Bhatt, 2025).

Multi-objective mathematical modeling that was developed by Ampry et al. in the framework of scheduling and batch processing provides effective instruments to deal with the intricate trade-offs in a financial decision-making. In finance and behavioral accounting, these optimization structures can be used to create equilibrium between conflicting priorities (including risk, reward and liquidity) that would uncover the best methods to use resources, efficiency, and create value in the long run amid competing behavioral and financial goals (Ampry et al., 2022).

This highlights the relevance of armed operational research methods to strategic and behavioral finance which facilitates the quantitative and behavioral analysis in a more appropriate manner.

Ironically, however, technology may increase those very issues that it is aimed at resolving. Algorithms are biassed by their designers and unless the behavioural idiosyncrasy or the tacit knowledge of those designers is factored in, the corresponding systems can be biassed codically and even more so when it comes to human prejudices. The automated trading has the power to increase herd behaviour, sell-offs, and lead to flash crashes and market volatility when multiple algorithms react to market signals in similar ways (Poddar, Bhattacharya, & Bhatt, 2025).

However, there is an emerging agreement that technology can also provide the means of containing and reducing bias, especially through systems that are programmed to raise red flags over irrational behaviour, mimic other possible ways of thinking, or detect psychological traps in tricky decision-making contexts. When intelligences are wisely associated, human and machine may serve as corrective to each other instead of reinforcing ones another.

The Crucial Role of Culture and Diversity

Demographic, cultural, and social diversity is starting to be seen as a highly important factor in the financial industry as globalisation of financial activity begins to take place. Countries, regions, and population groups do not share the risk tolerance, attitudes towards authority, and predisposition to different biases (Arya & Singh, 2025). The cultural context does not only determine what is valued by people, but also how people interpret and take action on financial information. As an example, saving versus investing attitudes, or risk versus security attitudes, may vary across a large spectrum of the social contexts of the West and the East.

According to recent studies, the value and complexity of diverse teams in the financial decision making are important. Through its appropriate utilisation, diversity results in the expansion of the heuristic range and an increase in the probability to question the groupthink (Eze & Okafor, 2023). Mixed teams realise risks and opportunities that are otherwise invisible. Nevertheless, the same diversity has a negative side: it may increase communication problems and complicate the process of reaching an agreement unless behavioural training is consciously conducted and all participants are guided by an inclusive leadership style (Harris et al., 2024).

Behavioral Insights and Sustainable Finance

One of the most recent fields of behavioural finance is sustainable investing - constructing portfolios that are sustainable in environmental, social, and governance (ESG) terms. In this case, there is a great potential of using cognitive biases to drive adoption, evaluation, and performance. As an illustration, when investors have confirmation bias, they are only ready to accept ESG information that supports their already existing thoughts and ignore all other opportunities or dangers (Poddar, Bhattacharya, & Bhatt, 2025). The loss aversion can lead to hesitation in the process of divesting out of traditional and less sustainable assets even after the evidence indicates that the long-term value is in a different place (Brown & Das, 2021).

The overlap of behavioural science and sustainable finance is getting more topical since, due to the shift to long-term resilience and responsible investment in the world, global priorities changed. Scholars are still experimenting with ways to help push investors and managers into more future-oriented and ethical actions, with both positive and negative outcomes, and this demonstrates that it is difficult to alter ingrained habits and beliefs.

Diversity and Inclusion in Organizational Practice

Beyond the individual portfolio and market-wide trends, behavioral science is transforming team composition and decision-making practices within organizations. Diverse teams, carefully composed and managed, bring a wealth of various heuristics and risk perspectives that promote innovation and higher quality decisions to the table (Eze & Okafor, 2023). These gains are not automatic, however; organizations will need to invest in behavioral training, foster mutual respect for divergent views, and avoid the tendency to revert to the normative familiar.

Particularly in rapidly changing industries, psychological safety and behavioral awareness can be the difference between adaptability and inertia. Initiatives aimed at broadening the pool of decision-makers, conducting regular bias-awareness training, and restructuring reward systems can all contribute toward more agile and effective organizations (Harris et al., 2024).

Behavioral Finance and Regulation: Nudging Toward Better Outcomes

Recognizing that markets are populated by fallible individuals, policymakers and regulators are increasingly incorporating behavioral insights into the architecture of financial regulation. Nudging strategies—subtle cues and default settings designed to encourage beneficial choices without overt compulsion—are now commonly used in areas like retirement savings, consumer loans, and investment disclosures (Lee & Kim, 2022). Examples include auto-enrollment in pension schemes, simplified choice menus, or warning messages highlighting common mistakes.

But the literature is also clear that the effectiveness of nudges depends a great deal on context: what works in one country or regulatory environment may fail in another; and "behavioral fatigue" can set in if actors become desensitized to nudging strategies over time. Empirical assessments of real-world regulatory frameworks reveal a mixed picture, emphasizing the need for ongoing evaluation, adaptation, and-where appropriate-individualized tailoring (Martinez, Smith, & Chen, 2021).

Ethics, Fraud, and Audit Quality

Behavioral biases do not stop with the individual or team level; they have systemic consequences, especially in terms of ethical behavior, fraud detection, and audit quality. Cases such as those concerning the Wirecard and FTX scandals remind one of what can go wrong if bias, overconfidence, or ethical blindness is not tackled. Auditors and managers who are affected by confirmation bias might turn a blind eye to salient warning signs or rationalize irregularities, hence leading to misstatements and, in extreme cases, huge financial losses (Nguyen & Tran, 2022).

These risks, in turn, are countered by organizations that are increasingly adopting governance practices of objectivity and skepticism. This implies constant behavioral training and a culture able and willing to challenge assumptions and authority when appropriate. Such "soft" strategies focusing on ethics, accountability, and transparency are being advanced alongside technological solutions like AI-assisted anomaly detection.

Pushing the Frontiers: Challenges and Further Directions

Even as behavioral accounting and finance explore uncharted areas, they still face various challenges. One such challenge is methodological: It's still very hard to make broad generalizations from one context to another due to the individual, organizational, and cultural psychological factors that vary widely. Therefore, a cross-disciplinary collaboration is still highly important for refining frameworks, creating interventions, and moving from-theoretical models to practical applications.

There is another challenge represented by the integration of the behavioral sciences with the sustainable and ethical investing fields. These sectors are based on long-term thinking, yet many cognitive biases—like hyperbolic discounting (the tendency to prefer immediate rewards)—act against it. Similarly, the regulatory frameworks must keep adjusting to the changes in technology and values of the society.

Maybe most notably, real-world events, e.g. financial frauds or economic crises, keep exposing how enormous the risks are when behavioral insights are ignored. It is important to invite lessons from sociology, anthropology, neuroscience, and data science, among others, to have a solid, sustainable, and humane financial system.

To summarize, behavioral accounting and finance have changed the way we think about markets, organizations, and the people who are at the core of them. The incorporation of a thorough psychological insight with the developing technological and socio-cultural factors provides a unique perspective to understand (and hopefully, to improve) financial decision-making at all levels.

As continuous research keeps providing evidence of both our limitations and our capability for systematic enhancement, the field is leading the way to solving the complex, interdisciplinary challenges of modern finance. We can only accomplish the creation of markets and organizations that are not only efficient but also truly human by bringing together these frequently separate aspects—rationality and emotion, computation and culture, policy and.

RESEARCH METHODOLOGY

Research Design

This study employed a systematic qualitative review method that facilitated the gathering and critical appraisal of relevant academic literature over the last 25 years, with main focus on the publications from the year 2000 to 2025. Besides the core concepts, the research has been constructed to reveal also the latest trends and the gaps of the new studies.

The review of the literature was steered by the thematic analysis framework which concentrated the review on the key areas such as cognitive biases, technological disruption, diversity impacts, regulatory strategies, and ethical considerations. By using this method, it was possible to identify the main themes, contradictions, and also the scarcely researched topics that could be further explored or.

Literature Search Strategy and Criteria

The literature search was performed through the leading academic databases of JSTOR, Scopus, Web of Science, and Google Scholar. The keywords used were the combinations of the terms such as "behavioral finance," "behavioral accounting," "cognitive biases," "financial decision-making," "algorithmic trading," "diversity and finance," "sustainable investing," and "financial regulation."

Inclusion criteria were defined to focus on peer-reviewed journal articles, top-quality conference papers, and influential books mainly in the English language. The focus was on publications from 2000 to 2025 to allow for the inclusion of both the classical and the most recent literature. Works discussing empirical investigations, meta-analyses, theoretical models, and case studies on fraud, audit behavior, and regulatory outcomes were taken into account.

Exclusion criteria removed non-peer-reviewed works, opinion articles without strong academic support, and research that is not in the finance or accounting areas unless it is sufficiently interdisciplinary.

Data Extraction and Thematic Coding

After going through the literature, the essential data points were singled out. These included authorship, the year of publication, the area of research, the methodology used, and major findings. The data were then arranged in a matrix to make the comparison across the studies easier and the identification of the thematic clusters more obvious. The data extraction process emphasized objectives of articles, methodological designs, characteristics of samples, and major findings to engage the comparative analysis across different studies. A special feature of the work was the effort to connect classical behavioral theories like bounded rationality (Simon, 1955) and prospect theory (Kahneman & Tversky, 1979) with emerging phenomena such as AI-driven financial tools and ESG investment trends (Poddar, Bhattacharya, & Bhatt, 2025).

Thematic coding was a recursive process through which contributions from the literature were assigned under the main themes of behavior finance with the nuances of new financial technologies and socio-cultural diversity being particularly acknowledged. As an illustration, the paper dealt with overconfidence or confirmation bias as the bias were across different scenarios like individual investor decisions, corporate finance, auditing, and regulatory environments. The digitalization impact on behavior (e.g., use of AI tools in trading) was the main focus of the studies, and the cultural dimensions that influence decision processes differently across global financial markets were given special consideration.

Analytical Framework

The analysis merged qualitative synthesis of findings with critical appraisal of methodologies and theoretical robustness. The work focused on linking the old theories—such as bounded rationality and prospect theory—with current issues like fintech disruptions and sustainable investing trends.

The authors examined differences and similarities in empirical results to pinpoint areas of agreement and gaps in the research. In addition, the study looked into the extent to which the behavioral finance theories could be used as a guide in business and policy-making.

Limitations of Methodology

The qualitative literature review allows for an in-depth understanding and thematic exploration; however, it has some limitations as well. Dependence on secondary sources can lead to biases that are related to the scope or the method of the original studies. Besides that, qualitative syntheses are interpretive and thus, may be influenced by the researchers' viewpoints.

Without the presence of primary empirical data collection, the capability of testing hypotheses or issuing causal relationships is limited. Nevertheless, considering the conceptual complexity and the interdisciplinary aspect of behavioral finance, such an approach is still very valuable to provide the necessary insights and groundwork for subsequent empirical.

Ethical Considerations

Even if this research is based on existing literature and hence, no human subjects were involved, the authors have still maintained the ethical standards by providing proper citations, giving correct credit to intellectual property, and respecting the voices of different perspectives. The evaluation of the sources has been done with academic thoroughness and this helps to keep the personal prejudice of the researchers at a minimum.

RESULTS

An exhaustive survey of the scientific behavioral accounting and finance literature uncovers the fact that cognitive biases, technological changes, organizational diversity, and ethical issues have become very influential factors in the core of financial decision-making. With the intertwining of these components, the discipline has evolved significantly from mere theoretical concepts, demonstrating the interplay of psychology, technology, and culture in both individual financial decisions and broader systemic financial consequences.

Cognitive Biases: The Unseen Forces Shaping Outcomes

Cognitive biases have been identified as major contributors to suboptimal financial outcomes. Overconfidence is at the center of these biases, a characteristic that is often praised in business but, if not controlled, becomes a drawback. Investors, managers, and even professionals who have been around for a long, may as a result of this overconfidence, be convinced that they have a special skill or insight which leads them to excessively trade, select assets poorly, and take less account of the risks (Barberis & Thaler, 2003; Nguyen & Tran, 2022). Overconfidence is not limited to traders on Wall Street; it can be found everywhere, from the budgeting of a medium-sized business to the decision-making of a global investment house, where it quietly influences the assessment of risks and opportunities.

Another bias that influences us is confirmation bias. This is the human characteristic to always find the support for what one believes in the new information provided. For financial executives, this might be sticking to old forecasts, rejecting the voices that dissent, or refusing to see the evidence that is new and challenges the current assumptions. In a corporate setting, confirmation bias can lead to the reinforcement of groupthink, which in turn can aggravate the wrong decisions being made not only in departments but also spread to the entire.

Technology: Friend and Foe

Technology, particularly in terms of sophisticated trading algorithms and artificial intelligence, was at first seen as the one factor that would level the playing field and be the solution to human mistakes in finance. It was expected that these digital systems, with their data-driven logic and computational speed, would avoid the emotional traps and quick mistakes of traditional finance. Nevertheless, the truth is that the situation is more complex than that. On the one hand, automated trading platforms and

AI models can, in theory, through accelerated decision-making and the analysis of a practically infinite amount of data, lead to better results, but on the other hand, according to Poddar, Bhattacharya, and Bhatt (2025), herd behavior or panic may be just as greatly amplified by these systems during periods of volatility. The "herd" effect that results can escalate spirals of selling or buying beyond what the fundamentals warrant, thus creating waves of instability if everyone's algorithms react to a negative market signal at the same time.

However, these instruments may also be turned into dependable partners in the fight against bias if they are constructed with strong and comprehensive behavioral models. Properly functioning decision-support systems are able to encourage users in that they have to consider risks that are overlooked, notify them of abnormal situations, or allow them to verify if they are actually victims of the confirmation.

Diversity and Inclusion: Unlocking Group Wisdom

A diverse team is a conglomerate of different mental models, risk appetites, and interpretive frameworks. The literature indicates that when teams consist of individuals with different backgrounds, experiences, and perspectives, the quality of decision-making improves as it becomes less vulnerable to the errors of groupthink (Arya & Singh, 2025; Eze & Okafor, 2023). As an example, a risk management team with a global diversity of members would be much better at uncovering the overlooked areas in the market strategy or investment, depending on the way risk is perceived culturally and individually. Nevertheless, the diversity charm does not simply show up there. Research findings keep pointing to the necessity of a deliberate behavioral training investment and the continuous employer efforts to create an inclusive workplace environment (Harris et al., 2024). Without these, the differences may become the causes of disagreement or lack of understanding, thus, the team cannot draw on these as sources of ingenuity and.

Behavioral Regulation: Nudges, Not Hammers

Regulators all over the world have begun to make use of "nudges" which are gentle prompts and cues that subtly change behaviors, in the financial system. In numerous localities, nudges are implemented to enhance retirement saving, to make investment more sensible, and to decrease the occurrence of financial decisions driven by the impulsive nature of a person's character (Lee & Kim, 2022). As a result, most companies, by simply enrolling employees in pension plans automatically (giving them the right to opt-out), have effectively elevated the savings level of employees without the need for mandates or stringent rules. Nevertheless, nudges are not a panacea. Their impact changes depending on the setting and area and they may become less potent due to the fact that people get accustomed to them or market conditions change (Martinez, Smith, & Chen, 2021). Hence, it implies that policymakers should be adaptable in nature, continually assessing and adjusting behavioral interventions to correspond to the changing demands and features of the particular.

Ethics, Fraud, and Audit: Beyond Competence, Toward Integrity

Behavioral influences, maybe, are nowhere more significant than in the areas of ethical conduct, fraud detection, and audit quality. Basing on the biases of overconfidence and confirmation bias, finance professionals may overlook—or excuse—fraud in the account books, thus mistakes and falsifications may continue. These are the kind of scandals, among them Wirecard and FTX, which, as stark reminders, have indicated that disastrous consequences for organizations and the wider public may result from the most behavioral tendencies not being controlled (Nguyen & Tran, 2022). Making the audit and financial system more honest is not only a technical issue; it requires behavioral skills, training, and, governance changes that facilitate the support of an objective and skeptical inquiry, most.

Synthesis: A Multifaceted Challenge Demands a Comprehensive Response

Initially, these discoveries depict a perplexing situation. The manner in which individuals make financial decisions is heavily influenced by behavioral biases, different technologies, diversities, regulatory structures, and ethical aspects, and these factors are interwoven in a complex way. To be able to effectively handle such a complicated situation, one needs a complete set of instruments: the understanding of human behavior from psychology should be integrated, the use of technology should be flexible, the regulatory frameworks should be strong, and the ethical standards should be functioning like a well-coordinated.

MANAGERIAL IMPLICATIONS: CHARTING A PATH FORWARD

Cultivate Behavioral Awareness and Address Bias Head-on

Finance accounting managers should no longer consider cognitive bias as a scientific issue which has no effect on their work. It influences practically the decisions made at all levels—from choosing projects for approval to creating investment policy, from carrying out performance reviews to handling the crisis, directly. If leadership teams daringly admit biases like overconfidence, anchoring, and confirmation bias, then they have a certain advantage: they are able to design systems and control mechanisms that not only make it easier for them to find mistaken assumptions but also to check those that are wrong without incurring losses.

Thus, it could be the decision to have forecasts and risk models reviewed by peers, using "devil's advocates" for the most important decisions, or relying on external audits when processes involve high risks. Behavioral training workshops that concentrate on local biases and are designed for the context in which they are carried out, are presently regarded as a contribution to the organization's stability and not just as a training.

Harness Technology Prudently

Though algorithms and AI can limit some errors, they are still not free from mistakes that only humans can make. Managers should always be conscious of the fact that even though technology might seem neutral, it actually mirrors the biases of those who created it. It is very important that diverse teams are not only engaged in the interpretation of outputs of algorithms but also in the creation and testing of these technologies. Regular "stress-testing" of systems with different market scenarios can uncover the vulnerabilities that are concealed. Managers should be on the lookout for employees willing to openly discuss the limitations and the intended use of technology so that it becomes a tool that does not enter the black-box world or become an unwitting risk.

Foster Diversity, but Ensure Inclusion

Comprising teams with different backgrounds, experiences, and perspectives of the world is a well-known way of enhancing the quality of decisions and risk evaluation, i.e. when a company is entering new markets or launching innovative products. Nevertheless, managers should not stop at demographic diversity only. To ensure that the voices of all members are heard and considered, there should be psychological safety and a well-developed behavioral training program. Some inclusive practices may be structured brainstorming, regular rotation of meeting facilitators, cross-functional projects, and clear escalation protocols for dissenting opinions. Diversity, if it is managed properly, can become a fuel for innovation—just not a requirement for.

Implement Pragmatic Nudges and Continuous Evaluation

At an organizational level, managers have the ability to use nudging tactics in order to bring the behavior of employees and clients in line with what is expected or desired. Basically, if you can automate intelligent defaults for retirement contributions, organizing performance feedback in such a way that recency bias is avoided, or even preparing the next budgeting process through timely and thus, you are nudging your team members towards better habits. Nevertheless, it is worthwhile stating that no intervention should be left without supervision; therefore, user feedback and monitoring should always accompany it so that the tactics can be changed or substituted if they are no longer.

Prioritize Ethical Vigilance and Audit Rigor

Identifying ethical weaknesses and making sure that the audit is accurate is not just a matter of sticking to the rules. Managers have to actively create mechanisms that protect against bias - changing audit roles, encouraging the use of open door policies, and making sure that there are regular, objective, third-party reviews. Behavioral indicators such as a hesitance to question things or an increased commitment to a failing project should be recognized by the organization and addressed through continuous training and open.

Lead by Example

It may be argued that, most significantly, managers have to establish the behavioral tone. When leaders challenge their own assumptions in a visible way, dissent is welcomed, and transparent reporting is rewarded, they communicate a strong signal to the entire organization. Such a culture penetrates bias in all hierarchical levels and brings in people who have a preference for well-reasoned, morally upright.

Final Thought

In summary, today's financial manager must not only have strong technical skills but also be very skilled in handling interpersonal relations. Through integrating innovations in psychology, technology, diversity, and ethics, executives are able to create teams and companies that have the capacity to withstand the uncertainties of the present world, thus achieving financial outcomes that are not only strong but also.

DISCUSSION

These findings from the extensive review emphasize the large and complex influence that behavior factors have on the financial decision-making of organizations and markets of a modern-day. The present discourse first consolidates the major insights, then delves into their wider ramifications, and finally, it hints at directions for both the application and the next stage of research in this evolving area of behavioral accounting and.

Cognitive Biases Remain Central to Financial Behavior

Majority of the themes that could be traced back from this synthesis is the dominant role of cognitive biases in financial decision-making of any kind. Overconfidence is almost always flagged out as the major cause leading to suboptimal investment behavior resulting in excessive trading as well as the underestimation of risk even for financial professionals who are a few steps away from being taken as experts (Barberis & Thaler, 2003; Nguyen & Tran, 2022). What makes such behavior is that it not only causes individuals' returns to go down, but also it has the potential to destabilize financial systems in situations when there is a lack of market certainty for a longer period. To make matters worse, confirmation bias is another factor that interferes with rational decision-making in that individuals or groups can hardly resist to interpret the new information in a way that confirms their existing beliefs. When it comes to organizations, it means that groupthink prevails, warning signals are ignored, and there is deepening of the losing strategies (Nguyen & Tran, 2022). These cognitive traps can be seen as a wake-up call that the human mind often wins over even the most advanced financial models. Identifying the influence of such factors even when it is subtle suggests that the presence of self-awareness, reflective practices, and habitual challenging of assumptions in financial teams and leadership is indispensable (Kahneman & Tversky, 1979; Simon, 1955).

Technology as Both an Amplifier and Remedy

The convergence of behavioral finance and technological innovation is like a double-edged sword. In a positive light, algorithmic trading platforms and artificial intelligence have substantially fastened and made more efficient the way large datasets are processed and actioned. Nevertheless, as the recent research and the sudden market disruptions at the forefront suggest, these very technologies may, in fact, increase the intensity of fluctuations and the extent of collective mistakes unintentionally. For example, algorithms that are set up without enough examination of behavioral aspects may, among other things, panic selling or herding during moments of market stress, thus deepening the crisis instead of lessening it (Poddar, Bhattacharya, & Bhatt, 2025). On the other hand, technology also offers some hopeful roads for advancement. Properly adjusted decision-support systems, if they are built with behavioral models consideration, can be a great help in recognizing the time when feeling or bias takes place in the decision process thus letting the choice be more reflective or data-driven (Poddar, Bhattacharya, & Bhatt, 2025). The main problem that a practitioner faces is to make sure that the technology is purposely created and supervised in such a way that it counterbalances human error rather than just codes it.

Diversity, Inclusion, and the Power of Multiple Perspectives

The review is equally an improvement cognitive diversity. Heterogeneous teams, which are made up of members from different backgrounds and cultures, have been found to have improved decision-making quality, less groupthink, and more innovation (Arya & Singh, 2025; Eze & Okafor, 2023). Diversity provides a wide range of viewpoints at the table, thereby making it difficult for one bias to dominate and increasing the likelihood that potential risks or oversights will be indicated.

However, the positive effects of diversity do not occur automatically. The literature indicates that if there is no supportive and inclusive culture—one that is supported by behavioral awareness and intentional training—the diversity of views may cause more friction and less collaboration (Harris et al., 2024). For companies, using the real advantages of diversity thus involves building the atmosphere where every voice is listened to, disagreement is taken for granted, and cross-cultural skills are deliberately.

Behavioral Nudges and Regulatory Interventions

The use of behavioral insights to inform policy interventions represents a fundamental change in the way financial regulations are made. The idea of "nudges," such as simplified disclosures or the automatic enrollment in pension plans, has been used to lead individuals and institutions to make better financial decisions while keeping their freedom of choice intact (Lee & Kim, 2022). Since people are recognized as being frequently bombarded by complicated matters and being prone to postpone things and remain passive, these lightly applied interventions have demonstrated their effectiveness to a certain extent.

However, success is not certain. The effectiveness of nudges depends on the community, cultural factors, and the possibility of checking and changing if the situation varies (Martinez, Smith, & Chen, 2021). Therefore, policymakers should take an experimental and flexible stance, deriving insights from actual results and gradually adjusting their strategies instead of presuming that there is a universal.

Ethics, Integrity, and the Cost of Behavioral Blind Spots

The impact of behavioral factors on the decision-making process is very clear in the area of ethics, fraud detection, and audit quality. The failure of the biggest companies like Wirecard and FTX is a case in point that shows how the outbreak of optimism bias, confirmation bias, and complacency that is not checked can penetrate even the most tightly controlled organizational structures, thus ending in huge harm to the public (Nguyen & Tran, 2022). The existence of behavioral vulnerabilities among auditors and managers may result in their losing the ability to judge correctly and facilitate the growth of a community of rationalization or silence, the kind where red flags get ignored until the time comes that one cannot do anything about it. Therefore, the removal of ethical flaws is an issue that is beyond the scope of technical solutions only; it is a call for the involvement of the whole system in behavioral training, developing the feeling of skepticism, and setting up governance structures which, among other things, encourage integrity, transparency, and the act of reporting by the.

Integrative Insights and Directions for the Future

When you tie all the pieces together, the area of behavioral accounting and finance stands out as intricate yet indispensable for modern practitioners. These behavioral influences do not operate separately but in a very interactive manner—technology affects how we view the world even in the case of cognitive biases, culture has an impact on the way we understand diversity, and regulation is only as effective as its receptivity to human nature. There is a strong indication towards an immediate necessity for strategies that would be psychologically, economically, data scientifically and management theoretically well integrated to tackle this phenomenon (Barberis & Thaler, 2003; Kahneman & Tversky, 1979; Poddar, Bhattacharya, & Bhatt, 2025).

The main takeaways for both groups of managers and policymakers are the following: behavioral education should be an ongoing priority, decision processes ought to be inclusive, technology should be utilized with a good dose of prudence and oversight, and ethical accountability should be a continuous commitment (Eze & Okafor, 2023; Harris et al., 2024; Lee & Kim, 2022). Moreover, the next generation of research will have to deal with issues such as the interaction between human and machine decision-making, the cultural orientation of regulatory interventions, and the use of longitudinal studies for behavioral finance initiatives.

Overall, the expanding pool of evidence highlights the indispensability of a complex, multidisciplinary perspective in the understanding and management of financial behavior. Moving away from the hypothetical notion of rationality and accepting the fact of human complexity—supported by technology, diversity, and ethical reflection—the field is more capable now to deal with the issues of the global financial systems of today. Behavioral accounting and finance is, therefore, at the core of a viable and efficient organizational practice to name a few: aiding in crisis prevention, facilitating the development of diverse teams, and promoting integrity in markets (Barberis & Thaler, 2003; Kahneman & Tversky, 1979; Poddar, Bhattacharya, & Bhatt, 2025; Nguyen & Tran,).

CONCLUSIONS

This has outlined the intricate nature of behavioral factors that shape the kind of financial choices made by individuals, within areas related to accounting and finance. Its major influence is in harmonizing the traditional financial theories, for instance, the efficient market hypothesis (Fama, 1970) with the latest research form psychology, cognitive science, and tech-related fields. The results unearth that investment activities, risk control, business decisions, and the level of fairness in audits are heavily influenced by the presence of such cognitive biases as overconfidence, anchoring, and loss aversion (Barberis & Thaler, 2003; Nguyen & Tran, 2022). On top of that, technological advancements, particularly AI and algorithmic trading, have interjected in the scenario in such a way that on one hand they intensify the herd behaviors while on the other hand they also make the bias reduction possible through decision-support systems (Poddar, Bhattacharya, & Bhatt, 2025).

Diversity and inclusion are being talked about as two topics that can dramatically improve the accuracy of the decisions made, and there is a firm belief based on evidence that diverse teams raise the scope of views and help in the fight against groupthink - the usual fallacy source (Eze & Okafor, 2023). Even so, the deployment of potent diversity measures requires the commitment of an organization and behavior-oriented training if one is to fully grasp the strength of the team without the co-existence of biases exacerbating.

Policy frameworks that rely on the understanding of the human behavior behind decisions, like the concept of 'nudging,' can be instrumental in enhancing investor choices and alleviating errors caused by bias; however, their effectiveness is contingent on the surrounding conditions and local regulations (Lee & Kim, 2022; Martinez, Smith, & Chen, 2021). In the field of ethics, behavioral literature to a great extent recognizes that such tendencies are the main driving forces behind fraud, audit shortcomings, and unethical behaviors in the corporate sector, thus, the paramount necessity of behavioral training for those engaged in these professions (Nguyen & Tran, 2022).

While acknowledging the recorded progress, one cannot be oblivious to the fact that these findings are limited by several factors. The main limitation is the extensive use of secondary literature, which makes establishing causality a challenge, plus the future of digital finance is very dynamic thus theoretical models have to be constantly updated. These issues notwithstanding, the central idea in all of these themes is the decisive role of behavioral principles in enhancing the quality of financial decision-making at both organizational and systemic levels, thus the chapter's contribution is commendable.

The chapter, first of all, works as a single multidisciplinary lens focused on the interplay between psychological, cultural, technological and policy aspects. Secondly, it puts forward several practical implications: organizations must cultivate behavioral awareness through coaching and administration; policymakers should implement flexible nudging tactics; and scholars need to seek the empirical support of behavioral interventions across various settings.

Further research topics might be the investigations of the longevity of behavioral measures, the differences in biases between various cultures, and the advancement of unified models incorporating behavioral insights and big data analytics for the purpose of market anomaly prediction.

To sum up, the comprehension and control of behavioral factors is the key to the continued existence of financial systems. With the ever-changing markets and the arrival of new obstacles, the constant consideration of the psychological and social aspects will be just as indispensable for theory progression, practice enhancement, and economic stability.

FUTURE SCOPE AND SUGGESTIONS

Behavioral accounting and finance are changing radically at a speed that has never been seen before, largely due to the incorporation of psychological insight, rapid technological changes, and the globalization of markets. With the increase of our understanding of the influence of human bias on financial systems, a great number of both opportunities and challenges for research and the enhancement of practice are disclosed. This document conveys the turning point of the field as well as the proposed tasks addressed to scholars, practitioners, and.

Embracing Next-Generation Technologies

The digital revolution is still reshaping the way people make financial decisions. Integration of behavioral data in AI and machine learning tools is, without doubt, the most significant change that will take place in the next few years (Poddar, Bhattacharya, & Bhatt, 2025). New financial technologies, e.g., robo-advisors and analytics platforms, can be enabled to identify, replicate, and even neutralize the bias of the investors. Take the case of AI-driven advisory platforms; they may have real-time "emotional feedback loops" that observe the user's behavior and, thus, an intervention is triggered when the pattern of selling driven by fear or risky impulsive trades appears. The research agenda should focus on the design and field testing of such digitally bias-aware solutions to be ethically sound and friendly to users.

The widespread usage of big data and sentiment tracking has made it possible to have dynamic models that explain not only what investors do but also why they do it. Real-time data streams from social media, news feeds, and transactions patterns can be utilized by researchers in behavioral finance to predict market fluctuations caused by factors such as collective enthusiasm, FOMO ("fear of missing out"), or herd behavior (Arya & Singh, 2025; Barberis & Thaler, 2003). In addition to this approach, data privacy should be strongly ensured, and transparency should be kept for the users.

Deepening Global and Cultural Contexts

Another obvious way for the field to develop is the deepening of cross-cultural and cross-market research. With investment participation soaring in emerging markets and the workplace teams becoming more globally spread, the cultural differences in risk tolerance, group dynamics, and decision-making heuristics need to be understood more than ever (Arya & Singh, 2025; Eze & Okafor, 2023).

By far, studies ought to pay more attention to how demographic and socio-economic factors influence financial biases in different regions, genders, generations, and socio-economic backgrounds. The collaboration across countries, comparative experiments, and large-scale data-sharing initiatives can uncover the bias drivers in different contexts that the current Western-centric models have taken for granted. This better cultural granularity will serve as a platform for the tailoring of behavioral interventions, "nudges," and policies that have the efficacy for various investor.

Behavioral Finance and Sustainable Investing

The exponential growth of sustainable investing along with the setting up of ESG criteria, has made it necessary to first understand the effect of cognitive biases on responsible investing (Poddar, Bhattacharya, & Bhatt, 2025; Brown & Das, 2021). A recent study reveals that in the case of traditional assets, biases such as confirmation bias and loss aversion have an impact. However, these biases also influence the way in which certain 'green' or 'ethical' investments are considered attractive, thus giving rise to possible bubbles or under-diversification.

Next researchers should look at how behavioral interventions help investors reconcile their personal values with a prudent portfolio strategy. Some practical ideas involve creating ESG-focused learning programs, designing easily understandable product disclosures, and making investment platforms decision aids available to users to help them overcome certain sustainability-related.

Focusing on Behavioral Policy Design

The sector should also widen its scope to include regulatory "nudges" and public policy. As governments and international agencies aim to stabilize markets and encourage the adoption of financially sound behaviors, there is a need for the precise assessment of the effectiveness of these interventions (Lee & Kim, 2022; Martinez, Smith, & Chen, 2021). Such assessments ought to be based on diverse real-world situations and should include randomized controlled trials wherever feasible, while being conscious of the responsible scaling of the programs that prove to be effective.

Next policy research work should not only follow up on investor outcomes but also be concerned with the indirect effects, for instance, whether certain nudges gradually lose their influence or whether they can, by some means, create a disadvantage for particular groups. The collaboration with behavioral economists, psychologists, legal scholars, and market practitioners will facilitate the implementation of these studies and provide them with a solid ethical.

Inclusion, Education, and Organizational Practice

In order for behavioral finance to be really effective, the next research should focus mainly on the culture of the organization and education. Consumer financial literacy programs need to change from simply presenting data and statistics to addressing the psychological aspects of the investors, both retail and institutional. Integrating case studies, scenario analysis, and interactive behavioral training modules into finance education (both academic and professional) will equip the next generation of leaders with the necessary skills (Harris et al., 2024; Eze & Okafor, 2023).

In the same way, companies should procure the means and establish the habits that would lead to more inclusive interactions, facilitate dissent which is psychologically safe, and make it a regular practice to re-check for biases, particularly in the context of remote work and distributed teams which are getting more.

In sum, the future of behavioral accounting and finance is bright, but it will require bold, collaborative, and responsive research strategies to keep pace with a rapidly changing world. By prioritizing technology, culture, sustainability, policy experimentation, and inclusive education, the discipline can deliver insights and innovations that foster smarter, fairer, and more resilient financial decision-making everywhere.

REFERENCES

Ampry, E. S., Komariah, A., Kurniady, D. A., Rafiq, M., Priatna, A., Ali, M. H., Marhoon, H. A., Thangavelu, L., & Chaudhary, P. (2022). Multi-objective Mathematical Modeling for Scheduling Machines in Parallel with Batch Processors. *Industrial Engineering & Management Systems*, *21*(2), 366–380. DOI: 10.7232/iems.2022.21.2.366

Arya, P., & Singh, R. (2025). Cross-cultural variations in investor sentiment and financial decision-making. *Journal of International Finance*, *48*(2), 123–145.

Barberis, N., & Thaler, R. (2003). A survey of behavioral finance. In Constantinides, G. M., Harris, M., & Stulz, R. M. (Eds.), *Handbook of the Economics of Finance* (Vol. 1, pp. 1053–1128). Elsevier.

Brown, R., & Das, A. (2021). Behavioral biases and sustainable investing: Evidence from ESG portfolios. *Global Finance Journal*, *52*, 100596.

Eze, S. C., & Okafor, C. (2023). The impact of cognitive diversity on financial team decision-making and performance. *Journal of Financial Management*, *12*(3), 205–223.

Fama, E. F. (1970). Efficient capital markets: A review of theory and empirical work. *The Journal of Finance*, *25*(2), 383–417. DOI: 10.2307/2325486

Harris, L., Johnson, K., & Martinez, D. (2024). Behavioral training and inclusive culture: Enhancing decision quality in financial organizations. *Journal of Organizational Behavior*, *45*(1), 78–94.

Kahneman, D., & Tversky, A. (1979). Prospect theory: An analysis of decision under risk. *Econometrica*, *47*(2), 263–291. DOI: 10.2307/1914185

Lee, S., & Kim, J. (2022). Nudging investor behavior: Behavioral finance and regulatory strategies. *Journal of Policy Analysis*, *37*(4), 456–478.

Martinez, T., Smith, P., & Chen, R. (2021). Assessing behavioral nudges in financial regulation: Evidence from multiple jurisdictions. *Regulation & Governance*, *15*(3), 298–317.

Nguyen, T., & Tran, L. (2022). Cognitive biases and audit quality: The role of behavioral training. *Accounting, Organizations and Society*, *101*, 101247. Advance online publication. DOI: 10.1016/j.aos.2022.101247

Pattasani, S., Mohapatra, S., & Jyoti, A. (2025). IoT-Based Social Device Network with Cloud Computing Architecture. *Systematic Reviews*.

Poddar, P., Bhattacharya, R., & Bhatt, R. (2025). Algorithmic trading and behavioral finance: An integrated approach. *Journal of Financial Technology*, *10*(1), 34–56.

Reddy, P. R., & Kumar, A. S. (2022). Credit Card Fraudulent Transactions Prediction Using Novel Sequential Transactions by Comparing Light Gradient Booster Algorithm Over Isolation Forest Algorithm. 2022 2nd International Conference on Innovative Practices in Technology and Management (ICIPTM)

Simon, H. A. (1955). A behavioral model of rational choice. *The Quarterly Journal of Economics*, *69*(1), 99–118. DOI: 10.2307/1884852

Thaler, R. H. (1999). Mental accounting matters. *Journal of Behavioral Decision Making*, *12*(3), 183–206. DOI: 10.1002/(SICI)1099-0771(199909)12:3<183::AID-BDM318>3.0.CO;2-F

Chapter 3

Digital Innovation in Strategic Accounting Enabling Sustainable and Economic Development

Amandeep Kaur
https://orcid.org/0009-0004-5716-7298
CGC University, Mohali, India

Gaganpreet Kaur
https://orcid.org/0009-0006-2957-5352
CGC University, Mohali, India

Ramandeep Sandhu
https://orcid.org/0000-0003-2595-4030
Lovely Professional University, India

Harleen Kaur Dhillon
https://orcid.org/0000-0002-4656-5248
CGC University, Mohali, India

DOI: 10.4018/979-8-3373-5976-2.ch003

ABSTRACT

The rapid advancement of digital technologies is transforming the landscape of strategic accounting, positioning it as a key enabler of organizational efficiency, economic resilience, and sustainable development. This chapter explores how digital innovation driven by tools such as artificial intelligence (AI), blockchain, robotic process automation (RPA), and cloud computing is reshaping accounting practices and expanding their strategic value in the digital economy. Traditional accounting, once focused primarily on compliance and historical reporting, is evolving into a forward-looking function that provides real-time insights, predictive analytics, and agile financial decision-making. The integration of digital technologies enhances data accuracy, automates routine processes, and reduces human error, enabling accounting professionals to focus on strategic analysis and value creation. Moreover, these innovations contribute to transparency, ethical financial management, and stakeholder trust critical components in achieving the United Nations Sustainable Development Goals.

INTRODUCTION

The landscape of accounting has witnessed a monumental transformation in recent decades, transitioning from a purely transactional and compliance-driven discipline to a strategically oriented function deeply embedded in business decision-making and value creation processes. This evolution is largely attributed to the proliferation of digital technologies, which have fundamentally redefined the role and scope of accounting in modern enterprises (Warren, Moffitt, & Byrnes, 2015). As organizations operate in an environment characterized by volatility, complexity, and sustainability imperatives, there is a growing consensus that accounting must go beyond bookkeeping and regulatory compliance it must enable strategic foresight, economic resilience, and sustainable development.

In the digital age, accounting systems are increasingly leveraging innovations such as artificial intelligence (AI), blockchain, robotic process automation (RPA), and cloud computing to generate real-time insights, enhance data accuracy, and support predictive decision-making. These technologies not only automate routine financial processes but also introduce new paradigms in transparency, ethical governance, and stakeholder trust, which are essential for achieving the United Nations Sustainable Development Goals (SDGs) (Richins et al., 2017). For instance, blockchain's immutable ledger facilitates ethical financial practices, while AI-powered analytics tools aid in identifying patterns, trends, and anomalies that traditional methods might overlook.

Traditionally, accounting was predominantly reactive, centered on recording historical financial data and producing post-facto reports. However, digital innovation has enabled a shift toward proactive and forward-looking accounting practices that integrate financial performance with broader organizational strategies, particularly those aligned with sustainability and long-term value creation (Dai & Vasarhelyi, 2017). Strategic accounting now involves a multidisciplinary approach where financial metrics are analyzed in conjunction with environmental, social, and governance (ESG) indicators to ensure holistic business sustainability.

The emergence of sustainability as a critical business priority has prompted organizations to rethink the informational role of accounting systems. No longer confined to fiscal reporting, accounting now serves as a powerful tool for managing corporate responsibility, measuring environmental impact, and guiding sustainable investment decisions (Gray, 2010). As sustainability reporting becomes more mainstream, the demand for high-quality, transparent, and integrated financial data has escalated. Digital tools are instrumental in meeting this demand by providing platforms for data aggregation, real-time reporting, and dynamic visualizations that support strategic planning and regulatory compliance.

However, despite the optimism surrounding digital transformation, scholars have expressed varying perspectives on its implications. Proponents highlight that digital accounting systems foster transparency, enhance efficiency, and improve ESG alignment, ultimately contributing to sustainable and resilient organizations (IFAC, 2022; PwC, 2022). Conversely, more critical voices caution that such technologies may amplify inequalities between large firms and Small and Medium Enterprises (SMEs), increase dependence on data-intensive ecosystems, and introduce ethical challenges related to algorithmic bias, data privacy, and auditability (Deloitte, 2024; KPMG, 2023). Recent debates on AI ethics and algorithmic accountability in financial systems underscore the need for human oversight and responsible governance to prevent biased or opaque decision-making (OECD, 2023). This growing divergence of perspectives highlights that while digital innovation offers strategic benefits, it also presents socio-technical complexities that must be carefully navigated.

Furthermore, digital transformation in accounting is not without barriers. Organizations particularly in developing economies and among SMEs face significant challenges including high implementation costs, cybersecurity vulnerabilities, skills shortages, and scalability limitations. Many firms lack the infrastructure or financial capacity to integrate AI or blockchain solutions effectively. Data privacy regulations, interoperability issues, and limited digital literacy further constrain adoption (IFAC, 2022; World Bank, 2021). Balancing innovation with risk management therefore becomes a critical determinant of success.

Moreover, the digitalization of accounting processes has enabled a democratization of financial information, allowing diverse stakeholders including investors, regulators, and civil society to access timely and accurate data. This openness contributes to enhanced trust, reduced corruption, and improved financial accountability at both organizational and national levels (Quinn, 2014). Particularly in the public sector and developing economies, where transparency is often compromised, digital accounting systems offer a path toward ethical financial management and inclusive economic development.

Table 1 below contrasts the defining characteristics of traditional accounting systems with those of digitally enabled strategic accounting systems, highlighting the shift in focus, capabilities, and value proposition:

Table 1. Traditional vs. digital strategic accounting systems

Dimension	Traditional Accounting	Digital Strategic Accounting
Objective	Compliance and historical reporting	Strategic insight and future-oriented decision-making
Time Orientation	Retrospective	Real-time and predictive
Technology Utilization	Minimal or legacy systems	AI, RPA, Blockchain, Cloud Computing

continued on following page

Table 1. Continued

Dimension	Traditional Accounting	Digital Strategic Accounting
Data Handling	Manual entry, spreadsheets	Automated, integrated, cloud-based systems
Error Potential	High due to manual processes	Reduced via automation and AI
Stakeholder Engagement	Limited to internal users	Inclusive supports multiple stakeholders
Sustainability Integration	Minimal or absent	ESG-aligned metrics and sustainability reporting

As the global business environment becomes increasingly interconnected and sustainability-oriented, the pressure on organizations to adopt responsible accounting practices grows. Digital transformation in accounting is not simply a technological imperative; it is a strategic enabler that empowers organizations to manage risk, optimize performance, and contribute meaningfully to national and global development goals (Yoon, Hoogduin, & Zhang, 2020). By integrating digital innovation into accounting functions, firms can better monitor resource utilization, track carbon footprints, and ensure alignment with regulatory frameworks on sustainability and ethical finance.

In sum, this chapter adopts a balanced analytical approach examining both the enablers and the constraints of digital accounting transformation. It critically explores how emerging technologies drive strategic and sustainable transformation while also generating ethical, regulatory, and operational challenges. The discussion integrates global and SMEs perspectives to ensure comprehensive relevance, providing actionable insights for practitioners, academics, and policymakers seeking to leverage accounting innovation for economic and environmental progress.

THE EVOLUTION OF STRATEGIC ACCOUNTING IN THE DIGITAL ERA

The discipline of accounting has long served as the financial backbone of organizations, offering a systematic approach to recording, summarizing, and reporting economic transactions. Historically, the primary objective of accounting systems was to provide accurate and timely information for regulatory compliance, taxation, and financial control. However, the 21st-century digital revolution has significantly altered this landscape, leading to the emergence of strategic accounting a forward-looking, insight-driven, and technology-enabled function that supports organizational agility, sustainability, and competitiveness (Burns & Scapens, 2000).

The term "strategic accounting" refers to the use of accounting data and tools to inform strategic decision-making, align financial operations with organizational goals, and enhance long-term value creation. Unlike traditional accounting, which is reactive and retrospective, strategic accounting is proactive and integrates real-time data analytics to support continuous performance monitoring and dynamic planning (Ncube, 2020). This evolution has been fueled by technological advancements that have fundamentally reshaped the methods, tools, and scope of accounting functions across sectors.

Transition from Traditional to Strategic Accounting

The transition from traditional to strategic accounting can be viewed through several dimensions including time orientation, technological sophistication, functional focus, and the role of the accountant. In traditional systems, accountants primarily recorded historical data and prepared financial reports for external stakeholders, such as investors and regulators. These systems operated on periodic cycles (e.g., monthly or quarterly) and were largely disconnected from strategic business planning.

In contrast, strategic accounting systems are deeply embedded in organizational decision-making processes. They rely on real-time, often cloud-based platforms that integrate financial and non-financial metrics to generate predictive insights and scenario planning tools (Warren, Moffitt, & Byrnes, 2015). These capabilities are crucial in a dynamic and complex global economy, where organizations must respond rapidly to market disruptions, regulatory shifts, and sustainability challenges.

Key Features of Strategic Accounting

Table 2.

Aspect	Traditional Accounting	Strategic Accounting
Time Orientation	Historical and periodic	Real-time, predictive, and forward-looking
Purpose	Compliance and stewardship	Strategic alignment and value creation
Technology	Manual records, spreadsheets	AI, blockchain, RPA, cloud computing
Decision-making Role	Supportive and passive	Active and integrated in business planning
Scope	Financial transactions and reporting	Multidimensional metrics (financial + non-financial)
Reporting Cycle	Monthly, quarterly, annual	Continuous and real-time reporting
Stakeholder Focus	Shareholders and regulators	Internal/external stakeholders (including society and the planet)

Source: Adapted from Quinn, 2014; Richins et al., 2017.

While the transformative potential of strategic accounting is widely acknowledged, scholarly perspectives remain divided. Optimistic researchers (e.g., IFAC, 2022; PwC, 2022; Deloitte, 2024) argue that digital technologies democratize access to financial information, improve decision-making accuracy, and enhance organizational sustainability through real-time analytics and ESG integration. In contrast, more skeptical viewpoints emphasize that technological disruption may exacerbate inequality between large and small enterprises, create over-reliance on data-driven systems, and generate ethical concerns such as algorithmic bias and data surveillance (KPMG, 2023; OECD, 2023). Furthermore, human and institutional barriers including cultural resistance, skill deficiencies, and governance gaps often hinder the full realization of digital accounting's potential (IFAC, 2022). These divergent viewpoints underscore that technological change alone is insufficient; successful transformation requires complementary shifts in organizational culture, regulatory policy, and human capability development.

Drivers of Evolution

Several macro- and micro-level forces have catalyzed the evolution of accounting into a strategic domain:

- Technological Innovation: The emergence of digital tools has automated routine financial tasks, allowing accountants to focus on strategic analysis.
- Globalization and Market Volatility: In a rapidly changing economic environment, businesses require real-time financial insights to remain competitive.
- Sustainability and ESG Mandates: Growing emphasis on corporate responsibility and non-financial performance has necessitated a broader accounting lens.
- Stakeholder Expectations: Diverse stakeholder groups now demand transparent, accessible, and dynamic financial information.
- Regulatory Complexity: Evolving global standards (e.g., International Financial Reporting Standards (IFRS), integrated reporting frameworks) demand advanced accounting systems capable of compliance and adaptation.

Recent research (IFAC, 2022; World Bank, 2021) highlights that digital transformation is progressing unevenly across regions. Developed economies notably in Europe and North America have advanced adoption of AI and RPA-based accounting tools, driven by strong infrastructure and regulatory support. In contrast, developing economies often face barriers such as limited digital infrastructure, high costs of technology integration, and insufficient digital literacy among accountants. However, affordable cloud-based accounting platforms and mobile technologies are gradually enabling SMEs in emerging markets to bridge this gap and participate in the digital transformation process (Deloitte, 2024).

Strategic Accounting and the Value Chain

Strategic accounting also plays a critical role in optimizing the organizational value chain. By integrating financial metrics with operational data (e.g., supply chain costs, product lifecycle analysis), firms can identify inefficiencies, allocate resources more effectively, and drive profitability while minimizing environmental and social risks (Porter & Millar, 1985). This integration is made possible by the seamless flow of data through enterprise systems powered by cloud computing, AI, and RPA.

In particular, strategic management accounting an offshoot of strategic accounting—focuses on linking financial analysis to competitive strategy, such as pricing, cost leadership, product differentiation, and market entry decisions (Bhimani & Langfield-Smith, 2007). As shown in Table 3, this shift demands a new skill set from accounting professionals.

Table 3. Changing skillsets required in accounting roles

Traditional Accounting Skills	Strategic Accounting Skills
Journal entries, reconciliation	Data analytics, forecasting, scenario modeling
Ledger management	Strategic planning and performance evaluation
Compliance auditing	Risk assessment and ESG integration
Manual report generation	Automated dashboard creation using BI tools
Taxation and payroll	Cross-functional financial consulting

Source: IFAC, 2019; ACCA, 2020

The Role of the Strategic Accountant

The modern accountant is no longer confined to the back office. Instead, they are emerging as "strategic business partners" collaborating with executives, participating in sustainability initiatives, and advising on long-term investment and resource allocation decisions. This role is characterized by a shift in mindset—from record-keeping to insight generation, from compliance to contribution, and from isolation to integration (Moll & Yigitbasioglu, 2019).

This transformation is particularly visible in forward-looking organizations that have embedded digital technologies within their financial ecosystems. For example, multinational firms such as SAP, Deloitte, and IBM now emphasize integrated finance teams that combine technical, strategic, and digital capabilities to enhance performance and support sustainable development.

CORE TECHNOLOGIES DRIVING DIGITAL INNOVATION IN STRATEGIC ACCOUNTING

The integration of advanced digital technologies in accounting has reshaped the profession's core structure, enhancing its strategic importance within organizations. By automating tasks, enabling real-time data access, and providing predictive insights, these technologies have turned accounting into a dynamic, forward-looking tool for sustainable business management (Appelbaum et al., 2017). Four technologies AI, Blockchain, Robotic Process Automation (RPA), and Cloud Computing are particularly instrumental in this transformation.

According to the International Federation of Accountants (IFAC) Digital Adoption Report (2023), over 72% of global accounting firms have integrated at least one advanced technology (AI, RPA, or cloud) into their operations, while Gartner (2020) predicts that by 2026, nearly 80% of audit functions will rely on AI-assisted analytics and automation tools. These statistics reflect an accelerating transformation but also underscore the growing need to address emerging ethical, regulatory, and implementation challenges.

Artificial Intelligence (AI)

AI is revolutionizing accounting practices by offering automation, cognitive reasoning, and advanced analytics capabilities. AI enables systems to learn from financial data, detect patterns, and make intelligent decisions ranging from identifying fraudulent activities to supporting strategic forecasts.

Applications in Accounting

- Automated data entry and classification of transactions through natural language processing (NLP).
- Fraud detection by identifying anomalies and suspicious patterns using machine learning algorithms (Richins et al., 2017).
- Predictive analytics for budgeting, forecasting, and risk modeling.

Impact on Strategic Accounting

AI augments accountants' ability to interpret vast volumes of data, shifting their role from number-crunchers to insight providers. For example, Deloitte's "Argus" AI tool automatically reviews contracts for compliance and extracts financial obligations, saving hundreds of hours and improving risk control (Deloitte, 2020). Emerging platforms such as Google Vertex AI and SAP Green Ledger (2024) further integrate sustainability and financial reporting metrics, enhancing real-time ESG accountability.

Risks and Limitations

Despite these advances, AI introduces critical challenges. Algorithmic bias can distort financial insights, especially when models are trained on unrepresentative or biased datasets. The "black-box" nature of deep learning systems reduces explainability, complicating audits and compliance. Furthermore, AI's dependence on large volumes of high-quality data poses privacy, governance, and ethical dilemmas, especially under tightening data protection laws such as General Data Protection Regulation (GDPR) and India's Personal Data Protection Act (DPDPA) (OECD, 2023; IFAC, 2022).

Blockchain Technology

Blockchain is a distributed ledger technology that records transactions securely, immutably, and transparently across a decentralized network. Each transaction is verified through consensus protocols, reducing the risk of fraud and manipulation.

Applications in Accounting

- Immutable audit trails, reducing manual reconciliation and improving the integrity of records.
- Smart contracts for automatic execution of financial agreements based on predefined conditions (Dai & Vasarhelyi, 2017).
- Real-time verification of transactions and financial flows across supply chains.

Impact on Strategic Accounting

Blockchain enhances transparency, trust, and traceability in financial operations. Strategic accounting benefits by integrating blockchain for secure ESG reporting, improving corporate governance, and building stakeholder confidence—essential for long-term sustainability goals.

Risks and Limitations

However, blockchain's scalability and interoperability remain pressing issues. Public blockchains often consume large amounts of energy, raising concerns about environmental impact and alignment with SDG 13 (Climate Action). The absence of unified accounting standards for blockchain transactions also leads to legal ambiguities. Additionally, organizations face implementation challenges due to high infrastructure costs and limited technical expertise (PwC, 2022; Deloitte, 2024).

Robotic Process Automation (RPA)

RPA involves the use of software robots ("bots") to automate structured, repetitive tasks typically performed by human accountants. Unlike AI, RPA does not "learn" from data but executes predefined rules and workflows quickly and accurately.

Applications in Accounting

- Invoice processing, bank reconciliations, and payroll management.
- Regulatory compliance reporting and data migration between systems (Lacity & Willcocks, 2016).
- Monthly financial close processes, dramatically reducing cycle times.

Impact on Strategic Accounting

By eliminating manual errors and accelerating reporting, RPA frees up accounting professionals for more strategic activities such as scenario planning and business performance reviews. For instance, Ernst & Young reported a 60% reduction in processing time for tax functions after RPA deployment (EY, 2019).

Risks and Limitations

Although RPA enhances efficiency, it also carries risks of job displacement and over-automation. Many organizations struggle to integrate RPA with legacy systems, leading to workflow disruptions. Overdependence on robotic scripts can also hinder flexibility, particularly when regulatory or business environments change rapidly. To mitigate these risks, continuous retraining and hybrid workforce models—where humans supervise digital bots are becoming best practices (IFAC, 2022; World Bank, 2021).

Cloud Computing

Cloud computing offers scalable, remote access to accounting systems, enabling real-time collaboration, secure data storage, and cost efficiency. Unlike traditional on-premises ERP systems, cloud platforms support integration across multiple departments and geographic locations.

Applications in Accounting

- Real-time ledger updates accessible by internal and external stakeholders.
- Integrated reporting systems combining financial and non-financial data for ESG disclosure.
- Disaster recovery and data redundancy mechanisms for compliance and continuity.

Impact on Strategic Accounting

Cloud accounting supports agile business decisions and aligns sustainability by reducing physical infrastructure needs. Platforms like SAP S/4HANA, Oracle NetSuite, and QuickBooks Online allow companies to monitor financial Key Performance Indicators (KPIs) on a global scale, empowering CFOs to react swiftly to financial risks or opportunities (Yoon, Hoogduin, & Zhang, 2020). Newer solutions such as Microsoft Dynamics 365 Finance (2023) and Xero Carbon Insights (2024) integrate ESG dashboards for small and medium enterprises.

Risks and Limitations

Cloud adoption also brings risks including vendor lock-in, where dependency on a single provider limits flexibility and raises long-term costs. Data sovereignty and cross-border data storage pose regulatory compliance challenges. Moreover, cybersecurity vulnerabilities especially ransomware attacks remain a top concern for finance departments operating in multi-tenant cloud environments (KPMG, 2023; Gartner, 2020).

Comparative Analysis of Technology Benefits

Table 4.

Technology	Primary Function	Strategic Benefits	Example Tools/Platforms
AI	Data interpretation, anomaly detection	Forecasting, fraud detection, cognitive automation	IBM Watson, Microsoft Azure AI
Blockchain	Distributed, immutable ledger	Transparency, trust, automated smart contracts	Ethereum, Hyperledger, Stellar
RPA	Rule-based automation of tasks	Speed, accuracy, cost reduction	UiPath, Blue Prism, Automation Anywhere
Cloud	Remote, scalable IT infrastructure	Real-time reporting, collaboration, reduced IT overhead	SAP S/4HANA Cloud, QuickBooks Online

Technology Synergy for Strategic and Sustainable Impact

The real transformation in accounting arises not just from individual technologies but from their integration. For example, a cloud-based accounting system integrated with AI and RPA can offer continuous monitoring, automated journal entries, and predictive cash flow analysis all while ensuring compliance through blockchain-recorded transactions. This synergy fosters robust financial governance and supports SDGs such as Goal 8 (Decent Work and Economic Growth), Goal 9 (Industry, Innovation, and Infrastructure), and Goal 16 (Peace, Justice, and Strong Institutions).

According to IFAC (2022), firms integrating two or more digital technologies achieved 28% higher reporting efficiency and a 19% reduction in operational errors compared to those using isolated tools. Such integration represents a pathway toward intelligent, sustainable, and adaptive accounting ecosystems.

Risks, Limitations, and Ethical Considerations

While digital technologies have unlocked vast opportunities for efficiency, transparency, and strategic agility, their deployment introduces complex ethical, operational, and regulatory risks that demand rigorous oversight.

1. Algorithmic Accountability and Bias: AI systems can inadvertently produce discriminatory or misleading results if trained on biased datasets, calling for explainable AI (XAI) frameworks (OECD, 2023).
2. Cybersecurity Threats: Cloud and blockchain infrastructures remain targets for ransomware and phishing attacks, necessitating advanced encryption and real-time monitoring (PwC, 2022).
3. Environmental Impact: High computational energy use, particularly in blockchain and AI training models, contributes to sustainability paradoxes.
4. Data Privacy and Sovereignty: Global data-sharing raises issues under GDPR, DPDPA (India), and other national data protection regimes.
5. Workforce Displacement: Automation may marginalize lower-skilled workers, underscoring the importance of reskilling and lifelong learning programs (IFAC, 2022; ACCA, 2024).

Ethical governance mechanisms such as transparent audit trails, AI explainability standards, and cross-border data-sharing protocols are essential to ensure that digital transformation in accounting aligns with human values, fairness, and sustainability.

DIGITAL INNOVATION AND SUSTAINABLE DEVELOPMENT GOALS (SDGS)

The intersection of digital innovation and sustainable development has emerged as a focal point in modern economic and corporate discourse. As sustainability becomes a central tenet of global business strategy, organizations are rethinking their financial and accounting systems to support the United Nations' SDGs. These 17 interlinked global goals, adopted in

2015, are designed to address pressing economic, social, and environmental challenges by 2030. Digital innovation in strategic accounting now functions as a catalyst for operationalizing these goals, facilitating transparency, ethical governance, resource efficiency, and stakeholder accountability (UNDP, 2019; IFAC, 2022).

Accounting as a Sustainability Enabler

Accounting is traditionally associated with financial stewardship and compliance. However, in the context of sustainable development, it serves as a critical instrument for measuring and reporting both financial and non-financial performance such as carbon emissions, gender pay equity, supply chain ethics, and environmental footprint (Gray, 2010). Digitally empowered accounting systems can collect, process, and disclose such multidimensional data in a timely and accurate manner, aligning corporate practices with global sustainability benchmarks.

Digital technologies such as AI, blockchain, and cloud computing enhance this capability by integrating sustainability metrics directly into financial planning, budgeting, and reporting systems (Appelbaum et al., 2017). This integration empowers organizations to not only track their impact but also forecast and strategically align future actions with the SDGs. Moreover, recent advances in AI-enabled sustainability analytics raise ethical questions around algorithmic transparency and accountability especially when ESG performance scores influence investment decisions (OECD, 2023).

Alignment of Strategic Accounting with Specific SDGs

Digital transformation in accounting can directly contribute to several SDGs.

Table 5. Mapping digital accounting innovations to SDGs

SDG Goal	Relevance to Strategic Accounting	Supporting Digital Innovations
SDG 8: Decent Work and Economic Growth	Enhancing productivity through automation and accurate reporting	RPA, AI-driven budgeting and forecasting
SDG 9: Industry, Innovation and Infrastructure	Integrating innovation in financial infrastructure and systems	Cloud accounting, blockchain-enabled ledgers
SDG 12: Responsible Consumption and Production	Tracking and reporting on material/resource use, waste, emissions	IoT-integrated accounting dashboards, AI modeling
SDG 13: Climate Action	Financial accounting for environmental impacts and sustainability metrics	Carbon accounting software, ESG reporting platforms
SDG 16: Peace, Justice and Strong Institutions	Ensuring financial transparency, reducing fraud and corruption	Blockchain, AI-powered fraud detection tools
SDG 17: Partnerships for the Goals	Enhancing inter-organizational reporting and collaboration	Cloud-based shared financial systems and smart contracts

Sources: UNDP, 2019; Vasarhelyi et al., 2015; Deloitte, 2021.

ESG Reporting and the Role of Digital Accounting

ESG performance has become a cornerstone for investors, governments, and consumers evaluating organizational sustainability. Traditional financial statements are insufficient to capture ESG performance, prompting firms to adopt frameworks such as Integrated Reporting (IR), Sustainability Accounting Standards Board (SASB), and the Global Reporting Initiative (GRI).

Digital accounting systems enable ESG integration through:

- Real-time dashboards for sustainability KPIs.
- Blockchain-backed disclosures ensuring data immutability and traceability.
- Automated ESG data collection via IoT and AI from supply chain and operational systems.

For example, SAP's Sustainability Control Tower allows businesses to align financial planning with carbon budgets, energy efficiency targets, and sustainable procurement practices all integrated into ERP systems.

However, challenges persist around standardization and authenticity. Despite global moves toward the IFRS S1 and S2 sustainability disclosure standards (2023), inconsistencies among GRI, SASB, and regional frameworks lead to fragmented reporting and "greenwashing" the exaggeration or misrepresentation of sustainability performance (PwC, 2022; IFRS Foundation, 2024). Moreover, AI-driven ESG scoring models risk perpetuating algorithmic bias or opacity if their evaluation criteria are not transparent (KPMG, 2023). Strengthening data governance, explainability, and assurance mechanisms is therefore essential to maintain credibility and stakeholder trust in sustainability accounting.

Case Example: Sustainability Accounting in Practice

Case: Unilever's Sustainable Living Plan

Unilever integrates sustainability into its financial systems through digital platforms that track water use, carbon emissions, and raw material sourcing across global supply chains. Using cloud-based financial tools, the company links its cost accounting to environmental indicators, enabling real-time adjustments in procurement and production to meet its Net Zero targets. This approach not only aligns with SDG 13 (Climate Action) and SDG 12 (Responsible Consumption) but also contributes to long-term brand equity and investor trust (Unilever, 2021).

Example from a Developing Economy. In India, small and medium enterprises (SMEs) in the textile sector are increasingly using cloud-based ESG dashboards such as Tally Prime Green Track (2023) to monitor energy use and waste management. Similarly, African agribusiness SMEs are adopting low-cost mobile accounting platforms integrated with carbon-tracking APIs to comply with regional sustainability certifications (World Bank, 2024). These examples demonstrate how accessible digital tools can democratize sustainability reporting across varying economic contexts.

Strategic Implications for Policymakers and Regulators

Digital innovation in accounting not only affects corporate governance but also strengthens public financial management systems. Governments can leverage blockchain for public spending transparency, AI for tax compliance monitoring, and RPA for subsidy disbursements—thereby supporting SDGs through improved institutional quality.

For instance, the Estonian government's blockchain-enabled financial systems have reduced corruption risks and improved social welfare delivery, aligning with SDG 16 (Peace, Justice and Strong Institutions). Meanwhile, India's Public Financial Management System (PFMS 2023) employs AI-driven anomaly detection for transparent fund disbursement, exemplifying the convergence of technology and governance in sustainable public finance.

Challenges to SDG-Oriented Digital Transformation

Despite its promise, digital accounting for sustainable development is not without obstacles:

- Data Gaps: Many organizations struggle to collect and standardize non-financial data across global operations.
- Data Interoperability: Inconsistent data formats hinder integration across ESG systems and financial platforms.
- Skills Shortage: Accountants often lack ESG, AI ethics, and digital literacy necessary for sustainability analytics.
- Regulatory Ambiguity: ESG reporting standards vary widely across jurisdictions, complicating compliance.
- Cost of Digital Transition for SMEs: High implementation costs, maintenance, and subscription fees deter smaller firms from adopting advanced sustainability accounting solutions.

To mitigate these barriers, collaborative efforts among businesses, regulators, and academia are vital to design unified ESG taxonomies, develop AI-ethics guidelines, and establish low-cost digital infrastructures for SMEs. Reskilling programs and digital literacy initiatives, such as those led by IFAC (2023) and ACCA (2024), are also critical to building future-ready sustainable finance professionals.

Future Outlook

Looking ahead, strategic accounting systems will evolve from merely tracking sustainability to actively shaping it. AI will enable dynamic modeling of sustainability scenarios, blockchain will facilitate stakeholder alignment through smart contracts, and integrated ESG-financial platforms will become standard. Ethical AI governance, cross-border data interoperability, and carbon-aware digital infrastructures will define the next frontier of sustainable accounting.

This vision positions accountants not as passive record-keepers but as active agents of systemic sustainability transformation, embedding accountability, inclusivity, and technological ethics at the heart of financial decision-making.

CHALLENGES IN IMPLEMENTING DIGITAL INNOVATION

While the potential of digital innovation in accounting is vast and transformative, its implementation is far from seamless. Organizations particularly those in transitional or resource-constrained environments encounter a range of technological, human, regulatory, and infrastructural hurdles. These barriers can stall or even derail digital transformation efforts, particularly when accounting systems are deeply embedded in legacy processes or when organizational resistance to change is strong (Scapens & Jazayeri, 2003). This section critically examines the key challenges confronting organizations as they attempt to embed AI, Robotic Process Automation (RPA), Blockchain, and Cloud Computing into strategic accounting systems.

Digital Skills and Literacy Gap

One of the most significant obstacles is the digital skills deficit within accounting and finance teams. Many accounting professionals are trained in traditional principles and tools but lack exposure to AI algorithms, data analytics platforms, or blockchain protocols. This skills gap can lead to underutilization of available technologies or implementation errors.

A global survey by the Association of Chartered Certified Accountants (ACCA, 2020) found that over 60% of finance professionals felt underprepared for technological changes in their roles. Recent data show that the situation has only marginally improved IFAC (2022) reported that only 42% of accountants globally have participated in formal digital training, and ACCA (2024) emphasizes that lifelong learning, continuous reskilling, and cross-functional digital literacy are now core professional requirements.

To close this gap, organizations are encouraged to adopt lifelong learning frameworks, micro-credentialing programs, and collaborations with academic institutions to update curricula in data-driven accounting, AI ethics, and sustainability analytics (see also Section 7.2). Embedding digital proficiency in professional education is essential to prepare accountants not just as technology users, but as strategic interpreters of digital intelligence.

Organizational Resistance to Change

Digital transformation often meets cultural resistance, especially in traditional, hierarchical organizations. Employees may fear job displacement due to automation, while senior management may hesitate to invest in technologies that disrupt established processes. This resistance is compounded when digital projects are imposed top-down without sufficient stakeholder involvement.

According to Kotter's Change Model (1996), successful digital innovation requires not just technological investment but also visionary leadership, employee engagement, and effective communication. Without these elements, even technically sound solutions may fail to achieve adoption. Forward-thinking firms increasingly use participatory approaches such as digital readiness assessments and innovation sandboxes to reduce resistance and build trust in transformation processes.

Cybersecurity and Data Privacy Risks

As digital systems centralize and process sensitive financial and personal data, they become attractive targets for cyber threats. AI algorithms can be manipulated, RPA bots can be hijacked, and blockchain nodes can be attacked through phishing or weak governance.

The PwC Global Digital Trust Survey (2023) found that 67% of financial institutions experienced at least one cyberattack attempt in the previous year, with 41% reporting direct operational disruptions. Notably, firms adopting cloud-based accounting and AI tools saw a 58% increase in attempted breaches, highlighting the growing vulnerability of digital ecosystems in finance.

Moreover, data privacy regulations such as the GDPR and India's DPDPA impose strict requirements on how financial data must be handled, stored, and accessed. Compliance becomes complex as data flows across national and organizational boundaries, emphasizing the need for advanced encryption, access controls, and ethical data governance aligned with international standards (KPMG, 2023).

Integration with Legacy Systems

Many firms particularly in manufacturing, public administration, and education still operate on legacy accounting platforms such as mainframe-based or on-premises ERP systems that are incompatible with modern digital tools. According to Gartner (2020), approximately 47% of mid-sized organizations globally continue to rely on ERP systems that are more than ten years old, and 28% of those systems lack integration capabilities with AI or RPA applications.

Integrating modern digital tools into such environments often requires expensive middleware solutions or full system overhauls, posing both financial and operational risks. Additionally, legacy data are frequently fragmented or unstructured, impeding standardization and reducing AI model accuracy. Poor data quality erodes trust in automated accounting outputs, underscoring the importance of data governance and cleansing initiatives before large-scale digital adoption.

Regulatory and Ethical Ambiguities

The rapid pace of digital innovation often outstrips the development of appropriate legal and ethical frameworks. Key unresolved questions include:

- Who is liable if an AI system produces inaccurate financial statements?
- How can auditors verify RPA-executed transactions?
- What governance mechanisms apply to decentralized blockchain-based ledgers?

The absence of comprehensive regulatory guidance from global standard-setters such as the IFRS Foundation or IFAC generates uncertainty, discouraging early adoption—especially among risk-averse firms.

Recent calls for AI governance frameworks, digital audit protocols, and blockchain accounting standards (IFAC, 2022; IFRS Foundation, 2024) represent progress, but jurisdictional inconsistency remains a barrier to harmonized implementation.

Cost and Resource Constraints

While digital tools often lead to long-term cost efficiencies, the initial investment in hardware, software, and training can be prohibitive, particularly for SMEs and organizations in developing economies. A Deloitte (2024) report estimates that digital transformation in accounting requires, on average, a 25–35% increase in IT expenditure during the first two years of implementation.

Furthermore, many organizations struggle to demonstrate a clear return on investment (ROI) for digital accounting projects, especially when benefits like improved decision-making or stakeholder trust are intangible or realized over long time horizons. Public-private partnerships and government subsidies for digital adoption are increasingly viewed as essential for closing this investment gap.

Summary of Challenges and Mitigation Strategies

Table 6.

Challenge Area	Description	Mitigation Strategy
Skills Gap	Lack of tech proficiency among accountants	Continuous digital training and cross-functional upskilling
Cultural Resistance	Fear of job loss and workflow disruption	Inclusive change management and employee engagement
Cybersecurity Risks	Increased vulnerability to cyber threats	Advanced encryption, role-based access, continuous audits
Legacy System Incompatibility	Inability to integrate new tools with old systems	Modular transformation, use of APIs or middleware
Regulatory Uncertainty	Ambiguous legal frameworks around AI and blockchain	Active participation in standard-setting bodies and advocacy
High Initial Costs	Upfront investments in tech and training	ROI analysis, phased implementation, public-private partnerships

Source: Developed from multiple academic and industry reports.

Real-World Example: India's GST Digital Transformation

India's introduction of the Goods and Services Tax Network (GSTN) a national digital platform for tax accounting exemplifies both the opportunities and challenges in digital implementation. The system unified tax reporting across states, increased transparency, and reduced tax evasion through automated invoice matching and real-time transaction tracking.

However, early adoption revealed critical gaps:

- Low digital literacy among SME taxpayers, leading to reporting errors.

- Difficulties integrating legacy ERP systems with the GST portal.
- Concerns over data security and compliance under India's emerging privacy laws.

Subsequent policy interventions such as free e-invoicing tools, simplified filing interfaces, and MSME capacity-building programs significantly improved participation rates.

Comparatively, developed economies like Estonia and Singapore have implemented digital tax ecosystems with greater efficiency due to stronger infrastructure, higher literacy levels, and pre-existing digital governance frameworks. In contrast, developing nations face steeper learning curves but often demonstrate greater adaptability through incremental and context-specific innovations. India's GSTN case thus illustrates how gradual capacity-building and stakeholder engagement can drive large-scale digital transformation despite systemic limitations.

GLOBAL BEST PRACTICES AND CASE STUDIES

The application of digital innovation in strategic accounting is not a one-size-fits-all solution; its success often depends on organizational maturity, industry dynamics, regulatory environments, and cultural adaptability. Nonetheless, organizations across the globe have demonstrated remarkable success in leveraging technologies such as AI, blockchain, robotic process automation (RPA), and cloud computing to redefine accounting practices, improve governance, and support sustainability goals.

This section presents a series of international best practices and illustrative case studies that reflect diverse implementation strategies and outcomes. These examples serve as actionable benchmarks for other organizations aiming to align their accounting transformation journeys with digital and sustainable development goals.

KPMG's Clara: AI-Enhanced Audit Platform (Global)

Overview

KPMG, one of the Big Four accounting firms, has developed "Clara," a next-generation audit platform that uses AI, predictive analytics, and cloud computing to revolutionize auditing and financial analysis.

Key Features

- Real-time data analytics and continuous auditing
- Machine learning to identify outliers and trends in financial transactions
- Cloud-based collaboration between auditors and clients

Impact

Clara has enabled more accurate audits, early fraud detection, and increased client satisfaction due to its transparency and efficiency (KPMG, 2021). This supports SDG 16: Peace, Justice and Strong Institutions by enhancing financial integrity.

Estonia's National Blockchain Infrastructure (Public Sector)

Overview

Estonia is a global pioneer in e-governance and digital accounting. Its government has implemented a blockchain-based public accounting system integrated with national registries and e-tax systems.

Key Features

- Immutable and transparent ledger for public financial records
- Automated cross-verification of tax, procurement, and payroll

- Citizen access to their own data through secure digital identity

Impact

The initiative reduced corruption, improved fiscal governance, and increased citizen trust. It also set a model for blockchain integration in public sector financial management (OECD, 2018), aligning with SDG 9 and SDG 16.

Infosys: RPA and AI in Finance (India)

Overview

Infosys, a leading global IT services provider, deployed RPA and AI across its internal finance functions to reduce manual workload, improve accuracy, and increase process speed.

Key Features

- Automation of invoice processing, compliance checks, and month-end closure
- AI-based tools for financial forecasting and risk analytics
- Integration with cloud-based ERP systems

Impact

Infosys achieved a 40% reduction in month-end closing time and improved audit readiness. This practice exemplifies how internal digital transformation can support efficiency and sustainable growth (Infosys, 2021).

Unilever: Integrated Financial and ESG Reporting (UK/Global)

Overview

Unilever has embedded sustainability metrics directly into its financial accounting systems using cloud platforms, thereby supporting strategic and ethical decision-making.

Key Features

- Carbon footprint and water usage embedded in cost structures
- Cloud-based reporting for global ESG compliance
- Integrated dashboard for financial and environmental KPIs

Impact

Unilever's efforts strengthen alignment with SDG 12: Responsible Consumption and Production and SDG 13: Climate Action. The approach also enhances investor trust and brand credibility (Unilever, 2021).

Xero: Cloud-Based Accounting for SMEs (New Zealand)

Overview

Xero offers a fully cloud-native accounting platform tailored to the needs of small and medium enterprises (SMEs), democratizing access to advanced accounting tools.

Key Features

- Real-time financial tracking and invoicing
- API integrations with banks and e-commerce platforms
- Automated payroll, tax filing, and compliance features

Impact

Xero has empowered over 3 million SMEs to streamline their financial operations, improve tax compliance, and access finance more easily. It contributes to SDG 8: Economic Growth by boosting productivity and entrepreneurship (Xero, 2023).

Comparative Insights from Global Case Studies

Table 7.

Case/ Organization	Technology Focus	Strategic Benefits	Aligned SDGs
KPMG Clara	AI, Cloud	Real-time audits, fraud detection, increased efficiency	SDG 16
Estonia Gov.	Blockchain	Public sector transparency, citizen trust	SDG 9, SDG 16
Infosys	RPA, AI, Cloud	Faster close cycles, reduced cost, smarter compliance	SDG 9, SDG 8
Unilever	ESG + Financial Reporting	Integrated sustainability, ethical procurement	SDG 12, SDG 13
Xero	Cloud Accounting	SME empowerment, financial inclusion	SDG 8

Key Lessons from Best Practices

From the analysis of these cases, several best practices emerge:

- Scalability through Cloud Infrastructure: Cloud platforms enable organizations to scale their accounting systems across geographies without physical infrastructure, increasing inclusivity and resilience.
- Transparency through Blockchain: Immutable records and decentralized audits foster stakeholder trust, particularly in public institutions or highly regulated industries.

- Agility through RPA and AI: Automation and intelligent analytics improve speed, accuracy, and compliance, allowing finance teams to focus on strategic tasks.
- Sustainability through Integrated ESG Accounting: Embedding sustainability metrics into financial models enables firms to align with global development goals and attract ESG-conscious investors.
- Inclusive Innovation for SMEs: Platforms like Xero show that digital accounting transformation need not be limited to large firms; with the right tools and support, even micro-enterprises can participate.

STRATEGIC IMPLICATIONS FOR STAKEHOLDERS

Digital innovation in strategic accounting has profound implications not only for financial operations but also for the broader strategic landscape in which businesses, governments, educational institutions, and society function. As technologies such as AI, RPA, blockchain, and cloud computing redefine the accounting ecosystem, their integration demands a shift in how stakeholders perceive value, measure performance, and manage risks.

This section explores how various stakeholder groups corporate leaders, accounting professionals, policymakers, investors, regulators, educators, and civil society must recalibrate their roles, responsibilities, and strategic outlooks to capitalize on digital accounting transformations in alignment with sustainable development goals (SDGs).

For Corporate Leaders and CFOs

For organizational leaders, especially Chief Financial Officers (CFOs), the rise of digital accounting is both an opportunity and a mandate. Traditional finance departments, once siloed and compliance-focused, are evolving into strategic centers that drive value creation through real-time insights, scenario modeling, and ESG integration (Warren, Moffitt, & Byrnes, 2015).

Strategic Impacts

- Enhanced decision-making agility through real-time dashboards and predictive analytics.
- Integration of sustainability metrics into budgeting and capital allocation processes.
- Transition from backward-looking financial statements to forward-focused performance frameworks.

Action Agenda

- Invest in cross-functional digital training for finance teams.
- Redefine KPIs to include non-financial and ESG metrics.
- Lead enterprise-wide digital transformation with finance as a strategic hub.

For Accounting Professionals

The role of accountants is transforming from data recorders to strategic advisors. As automation handles transactional tasks, professionals must embrace data analytics, ethical governance, and strategic communication.

Strategic Impacts

- Requirement for multidisciplinary skills, including coding, data science, and sustainability analysis.
- Increased involvement in non-financial reporting, including ESG, CSR, and SDG disclosures.
- Growing demand for ethical judgment in algorithmic decision-making and digital audits.

Action Agenda

- Obtain certifications in digital finance tools (e.g., AI for accountants, blockchain audit).

- Develop competencies in integrated reporting frameworks (GRI, SASB, TCFD).
- Shift mindset from "compliance guardian" to "value creator."

For Policymakers and Regulators

Regulatory bodies play a pivotal role in shaping the governance of digital accounting tools and ensuring they align with public interest and SDG frameworks. As new technologies outpace existing rules, proactive regulatory innovation is required.

Strategic Impacts

- Need for clear guidelines on AI, RPA, and blockchain auditing.
- Role in developing standardized ESG reporting frameworks.
- Importance of incentivizing SME adoption of digital financial systems.

Action Agenda

- Develop national digital accounting standards aligned with IFRS and SDGs.
- Fund digital literacy and ERP infrastructure for public institutions.
- Mandate ESG disclosures for listed and public-sector entities.

For Investors and Financial Institutions

Investors increasingly demand transparency not just in financials, but also in environmental and governance performance. Digital accounting platforms allow deeper due diligence and more reliable valuation of sustainability-aligned firms.

Strategic Impacts

- Shift from short-term financial analysis to long-term ESG-oriented investment strategies.

- Ability to perform AI-assisted risk profiling and forecast resilience.
- Enhanced engagement with companies via digital shareholder platforms.

Action Agenda

- Integrate AI and data analytics into investment research models.
- Support companies that practice transparent digital ESG accounting.
- Advocate for real-time access to sustainability performance data.

For Educational Institutions and Academia

Academic institutions must respond to the paradigm shift by modernizing curricula, research agendas, and professional development offerings.

Strategic Impacts

- Evolution of accounting education to incorporate digital tools, ethics, and sustainability.
- Growing demand for interdisciplinary programs linking finance, data science, and governance.
- Emergence of new research areas (e.g., algorithmic accounting, sustainable AI in finance).

Action Agenda

- Update syllabi to include AI, RPA, cloud ERP, and ESG frameworks.
- Partner with industry for case-based and project-based learning.
- Promote research on the social impact of digital accounting systems.

For Civil Society and Non-Governmental Organizations (NGOs)

Digital accounting enhances financial transparency, which is central to the missions of NGOs and watchdog organizations. Blockchain and real-time reporting improve accountability in donor-funded projects and public spending.

Strategic Impacts

- Access to transparent, immutable public finance data.
- Empowerment to track SDG progress and hold institutions accountable.
- Better auditability of charitable contributions and development grants.

Action Agenda

- Use digital platforms for community budget monitoring.
- Collaborate with civic-tech firms for open financial data systems.
- Advocate for financial justice through digital audit transparency.

Cross-Stakeholder Roles and Intersections

Table 8.

Stakeholder Group	Key Responsibility	Digital Strategy Focus	SDG Alignment
CFOs & Executives	Drive enterprise digital finance transformation	ESG budgeting, real-time KPIs	SDG 9, SDG 12
Accountants	Shift to strategic advisors	AI, RPA, sustainability metrics	SDG 8, SDG 13
Regulators	Ensure ethical digital finance governance	Blockchain standards, ESG frameworks	SDG 16
Investors	Fund responsible innovation	ESG valuation, risk analytics	SDG 17
Educators & Academia	Redesign curricula for future-ready graduates	Fintech, integrated reporting, data ethics	SDG 4
Civil Society & NGOs	Ensure public accountability	Open data, public audit tools	SDG 16, SDG 17

Envisioning a Collaborative Ecosystem

To fully realize the benefits of digital innovation in accounting, collaboration across stakeholders is crucial. The strategic implementation of technologies must be supported by shared standards, public-private partnerships, education reform, and ethical governance mechanisms. For example:

- Governments can fund cloud infrastructure while academia trains accountants to use it.
- NGOs can monitor spending through blockchain while regulators ensure compliance.
- CFOs can adopt ESG-focused AI tools with input from sustainability consultants.

Such ecosystem-level coordination is essential for maximizing the impact of digital accounting on economic and sustainable development.

CONCLUSION

The rapid digital transformation of strategic accounting is not merely a technological evolution; it is a paradigm shift that redefines the role of accounting in the 21st century. As the global economy becomes increasingly data-driven, interconnected, and sustainability-focused, traditional accounting frameworks have become inadequate to meet emerging business needs, regulatory demands, and societal expectations. Instead, a digitally enabled, strategically aligned, and sustainability-integrated accounting system is now essential.

This chapter has comprehensively explored how digital innovations such as AI, Blockchain, Robotic Process Automation (RPA), and Cloud Computing are reshaping accounting practices. These technologies are not isolated tools but integrated ecosystems that redefine the core dimensions of accounting: from compliance to value creation, from transaction processing to strategic insight, and from retrospective reporting to predictive foresight.

Summary of Key Contributions

1. Transformation of Accounting Philosophy: Accounting evolves from a control-oriented discipline to a strategic enabler of innovation, ethics, and sustainability. Digital tools have made it possible to shift focus from historical compliance to real-time, forward-looking, and impact-oriented reporting (Warren, Moffitt, & Byrnes, 2015).
2. Technology-Driven Efficiency and Accuracy: RPA and AI have significantly improved the efficiency, speed, and accuracy of routine accounting operations, freeing professionals to focus on strategic tasks (Appelbaum et al., 2017).
3. Enhanced Transparency and Trust: Blockchain technology has elevated trust and transparency by ensuring data immutability and decentralized verification, particularly in public sector and ESG contexts (Dai & Vasarhelyi, 2017).
4. Alignment with Sustainable Development Goals (SDGs): Digital accounting systems now support global objectives by enabling integrated ESG reporting, resource optimization, and ethical financial management in alignment with SDG indicators (IFAC, 2022).
5. Cross-Sector Best Practices and Lessons: Real-world examples from KPMG, Unilever, Infosys, Estonia, and Xero illustrate scalable, adaptable digital accounting models that align financial performance with long-term sustainability and stakeholder value.
6. Stakeholder Recalibration: The transformation requires active participation and adaptation from corporate leaders, accounting professionals, policymakers, educators, investors, and civil society. A multi-stakeholder collaborative ecosystem is imperative for sustainable success.

Strategic Vision: Accounting as a Catalyst for Sustainable Digital Economies

In the future, strategic accounting will not be confined to financial management it will become a central driver of sustainability, innovation, and inclusive development. As technologies become more intelligent and integrated, the accountant of tomorrow will operate as:

- A data-driven strategist who interprets multi-source data for long-term value creation.
- A sustainability advisor who ensures alignment with ESG and climate goals.
- A technology integrator who designs and manages smart, responsive accounting systems.

This strategic repositioning also implies a more ethical and human-centric role for accounting. Questions of algorithmic accountability, data governance, and fairness in financial automation will be central to ensuring that digital innovation contributes to not detracts from inclusive and equitable development.

Future Research and Policy Directions

While the benefits of digital innovation in strategic accounting are evident, several areas warrant further academic inquiry and policy focus:

- AI Explainability and Ethics in Accounting: How can black-box algorithms be made transparent and auditable in high-stakes financial decisions?
- Blockchain Standardization and Interoperability: What frameworks are required to ensure global compatibility of decentralized ledgers across borders and sectors?
- RPA and Workforce Dynamics: How will automation reshape roles, jobs, and training in the accounting profession?
- Integration of SDG Metrics in ERP Systems: How can digital accounting systems automatically track, measure, and report progress toward SDG targets?
- Digital Inclusion for SMEs and Developing Economies: What strategies can help smaller enterprises and low-income countries overcome the cost and capability barriers to adoption?

Final Strategic Synthesis

Table 9.

Dimension	Traditional Accounting	Digitally Enabled Strategic Accounting
Focus	Historical, compliance-oriented	Predictive, strategic, sustainability-focused
Technology Use	Manual systems, Excel-based	AI, Blockchain, RPA, Cloud ERP
Reporting Approach	Periodic financial statements	Real-time dashboards, integrated ESG reports
Value Orientation	Cost and compliance minimization	Long-term value creation and stakeholder trust
Sustainability Role	Indirect, minimal	Directly embedded in decision-making frameworks

Closing Thoughts

Strategic accounting must no longer be viewed merely as a support function it must be recognized as a transformational force within the digital economy. Through digital innovation, accounting can power a shift toward inclusive growth, ethical capitalism, and planetary well-being. The profession stands at the threshold of redefinition not only by what it counts, but by what it enables.

As we move forward, embracing digital technologies with a clear strategic and ethical vision will be essential. The accountants, CFOs, regulators, and institutions that lead this charge will not only future-proof themselves they will shape a more sustainable and just economic order.

REFERENCES

ACCA. (2020). *Future Ready: Accountancy Careers in the 2020s*. Association of Chartered Certified Accountants.

Appelbaum, D., Kogan, A., Vasarhelyi, M., & Yan, Z. (2017). Impact of Business Analytics and Enterprise Systems on Managerial Accounting. *International Journal of Accounting Information Systems*, *25*, 29–44. DOI: 10.1016/j.accinf.2017.03.003

Bhimani, A., & Langfield-Smith, K. (2007). Structure, Formality and the Importance of Financial and Non-financial Information in Strategy Development and Implementation. *Management Accounting Research*, *18*(1), 3–31. DOI: 10.1016/j.mar.2006.06.005

Burns, J., & Scapens, R. W. (2000). Conceptualizing Management Accounting Change: An Institutional Framework. *Management Accounting Research*, *11*(1), 3–25. DOI: 10.1006/mare.1999.0119

Dai, J., & Vasarhelyi, M. A. (2017). Toward Blockchain-Based Accounting and Assurance. *Journal of Information Systems*, *31*(3), 5–21. DOI: 10.2308/isys-51804

Deloitte. (2020). *The Future of Audit: Deloitte's Innovation in Cognitive Technology*. Retrieved from https://www2.deloitte.com

EY. (2019). *How Robotic Process Automation (RPA) is Transforming Tax Functions*. Retrieved from https://www.ey.com

Gartner. (2020). *How to Overcome Legacy Systems in Digital Transformation*. Gartner Research Brief.

Gray, R. (2010). Is Accounting for Sustainability Actually Accounting for Sustainability…and How Would We Know? *An Exploration of Narratives of Organisations and the Planet. Accounting, Organizations and Society*, *35*(1), 47–62. DOI: 10.1016/j.aos.2009.04.006

IFAC. (2019). *Enabling the Accountant's Role in Effective Enterprise Risk Management*. International Federation of Accountants.

IFAC. (2022). *Accountancy and Cybersecurity: Professional Responsibilities and Challenges*. International Federation of Accountants.

Infosys. (2021). *Transforming Finance with Intelligent Automation*. Infosys Whitepaper. Retrieved from https://www.infosys.com

Kotter, J. P. (1996). *Leading Change*. Harvard Business Press.

KPMG. (2021). *Clara: The Future of Audit*. KPMG Insights. Retrieved from https://home.kpmg

Lacity, M., & Willcocks, L. (2016). Robotic Process Automation: The Next Transformation Lever for Shared Services. *Journal of Information Technology Teaching Cases*, *6*(2), 1–12.

Moll, J., & Yigitbasioglu, O. M. (2019). The Role of Internet-Related Technologies in Shaping the Work of Accountants: New Directions for Accounting Research. *The British Accounting Review*, *51*(6), 100833. DOI: 10.1016/j.bar.2019.04.002

Ncube, L. B. (2020). The Evolution of Management Accounting: A Review of the Evidence. *Journal of Accounting and Finance in Emerging Economies*, *6*(3), 775–784.

OECD. (2018). *Digital Government Review of Estonia: Reinventing the Public Sector*. OECD Digital Economy Papers.

Porter, M. E., & Millar, V. E. (1985). How Information Gives You Competitive Advantage. *Harvard Business Review*, *63*(4), 149–160.

PwC. (2022). *Global Digital Trust Insights Survey 2022*. Retrieved from https://www.pwc.com

Quinn, M. (2014). Stability and Change in Management Accounting Over Time—A Century or So of Evidence from Guinness. *Management Accounting Research*, *25*(1), 76–92. DOI: 10.1016/j.mar.2013.06.001

Richins, G., Stapleton, R., Stratopoulos, T., & Wong, C. (2017). Big Data Analytics: Opportunity or Threat for the Accounting Profession? *Journal of Information Systems*, *31*(3), 63–79. DOI: 10.2308/isys-51805

Scapens, R. W., & Jazayeri, M. (2003). ERP Systems and Management Accounting Change: Opportunities or Impacts? *European Accounting Review*, *12*(1), 201–233. DOI: 10.1080/0963818031000087907

UNDP. (2019). *Integrating the SDGs into Corporate Reporting: A Practical Guide*. United Nations Development Programme.

Unilever. (2021). *Sustainable Living Plan: Annual Progress Report*. Retrieved from https://www.unilever.com

Vasarhelyi, M. A., Kogan, A., & Tuttle, B. (2015). Big Data in Accounting: An Overview. *Accounting Horizons*, *29*(2), 381–396. DOI: 10.2308/acch-51071

Warren, J. D.Jr, Moffitt, K. C., & Byrnes, P. (2015). How Big Data Will Change Accounting. *Accounting Horizons*, *29*(2), 397–407. DOI: 10.2308/acch-51069

World Bank. (2021). *Digital Public Financial Management: Toward Transparency and Inclusion*. World Bank Publications.

World Bank. (2021). *Digital Transformation for Development*. World Bank Publications.

Xero. (2023). *Annual Report and Global Impact*. Retrieved from https://www.xero.com

Yoon, K., Hoogduin, L., & Zhang, L. (2020). Cloud Computing and Accounting: A Framework for Cloud-Based Accounting Information Systems. *Journal of Accounting and Organizational Change*, *16*(4), 617–643.

Chapter 4
When Accounting Meets Innovation: Drivers of E-Commerce

Andreia Alves
https://orcid.org/0000-0002-3911-0894
ISCAP, Polytechnic of Porto, Portugal

Amélia Silva
CEOS.PP, ISCAP, Polytechnic of Porto, Portugal

Albertina Paula Monteiro
CEOS.PP, ISCAP, Polytechnic of Porto, Portugal

Catarina Cepeda
https://orcid.org/0000-0002-3911-0894
CEOS.PP, ISCAP, Polytechnic of Porto, Portugal

Orlando Rua
https://orcid.org/0000-0002-1593-7440
CEOS.PP, ISCAP, Polytechnic of Porto, Portugal

DOI: 10.4018/979-8-3373-5976-2.ch004

ABSTRACT

The growing relevance of e-commerce in today's business landscape has intensified the need to understand the key factors influencing its adoption. This study explores the drivers of e-commerce adoption among Portuguese companies, focusing on technological integration, Information technology (IT) knowledge, and the quality of accounting information systems. Using a quantitative approach, data were collected through a survey applied to managers across multiple sectors. The research model was tested through multiple linear regression analysis, revealing that IT knowledge, technological integration, and the quality of accounting information systems have a statistically significant positive impact on the level of e-commerce adoption. Surprisingly, variables such as financial performance, level of education, managerial responsibility, and number of employees did not show significant effects. The findings offer both theoretical and practical contributions, underscoring the strategic importance of aligning accounting systems and digital capabilities to foster digital business models.

INTRODUCTION

In recent decades, the growing digitalization of the economy has significantly reshaped how companies communicate, market, and deliver their products and services. E-commerce, defined as the use of internet-based technologies to carry out commercial transactions, has emerged as a strategic pillar in this transformation. Its implementation enables cost reduction, access to geographically dispersed markets, process simplification, and the potential to gain competitive advantage. Both sellers and buyers benefit from this model: sellers gain reach and efficiency, while buyers enjoy greater diversity and convenience.

The adoption of e-commerce is strongly linked to technological development and innovation capacity. Previous studies suggest that companies with more integrated information systems and greater information technology (IT) knowledge are more likely to adopt e-commerce solutions. However, despite the strategic importance of e-commerce in boosting business competitiveness, especially among small and medium-sized enterprises

(SMEs), empirical evidence on the determinants of its adoption remains fragmented and context-dependent—particularly in Portugal.

In the Portuguese context, SMEs account for more than 99% of all businesses and remain a cornerstone of national employment and value creation. However, their digital transition continues to be uneven. The *Digital Decade Country Report – Portugal* (IAPMEI, 2023) highlights that while connectivity and digital infrastructure have improved, a significant share of SMEs still operate with limited integration of digital tools, particularly in areas such as e-commerce and data management. According to the OECD (2024), many SMEs face persistent barriers related to digital skills, organizational readiness, and access to advanced technologies, factors that constrain their ability to fully leverage digital opportunities and manage economic transitions effectively. These contextual specificities reinforce the need to examine e-commerce adoption in Portugal from the standpoint of organizational capabilities rather than purely financial resources. In addition to organizational and technological factors, individual variables such as the manager's education, professional experience, and level of responsibility may also shape the decision to adopt e-commerce. Furthermore, other internal resources, such as the quality of accounting information systems (AIS) or the financial performance of firms, have been suggested as important antecedents. However, there is a lack of integrated models that combine these multiple dimensions to explain the level of e-commerce adoption.

While this study focuses on internal drivers, external technological and environmental contexts also influence e-commerce adoption (Tornatzky & Fleischer, 1990). These include factors such as competitive pressure, customer readiness, and government incentives for digitalization. However, due to the study's empirical scope and data availability, these variables were not included in the regression model.

This study seeks to address that gap by answering the research question: What factors influence the adoption of e-commerce by Portuguese companies? Specifically, it analyzes the influence of IT knowledge, technological integration, AIS quality, financial performance, company size (number of employees), and individual characteristics of decision-makers.

To this end, a structured questionnaire was administered to managers of Portuguese companies to collect their perceptions and organizational data. Using a quantitative approach and multiple linear regression analysis, this study aims to build, test, and validate a theoretical model of the main determinants of e-commerce adoption.

This work contributes to both theory and practice. It enriches the academic literature by proposing and empirically validating a multidimensional model of e-commerce adoption, while also providing managers and policymakers with relevant insights to promote more informed and strategic digital transitions in Portuguese enterprises.

The remainder of the article is structured as follows. Section 2 presents the theoretical framework, including the conceptual foundations and the development of research hypotheses. Section 3 details the methodology adopted, and the instrument used for data collection. Section 4 reports the results of the empirical analysis, followed by their discussion in Section 5. Finally, Section 6 outlines the main conclusions, implications, and suggestions for future research.

CONCEPTUAL MODEL

E-commerce has emerged as a pivotal instrument for companies in developing countries, enabling access to geographically disperse national and international markets. This expansion facilitates business growth by enhancing market knowledge, fostering innovation in products and services, and exploring new market opportunities (Molla & Licker, 2005; Zhu & Kraemer, 2005).

Digitalization, defined as integrating digital technologies into business operations, aims to improve business models and create opportunities to produce and deliver goods and services. This process enhances business performance by reducing production costs and improving productivity and operational efficiency (Dalenogare, Benitez, Ayala, & Frank, 2018). Moreover, the technological context, including government support and legal regulations, is crucial in eliminating barriers such as inadequate infrastructure, limited financial resources, and insufficient IT skills, thereby facilitating e-commerce adoption (Zhu & Kraemer, 2005).

The literature on e-commerce identifies several factors influencing adoption decisions. These include organizational readiness, perceived costs, security concerns, reliability, and the perceived benefits of the technology (Wymer & Regan, 2005). Technological variables such as software quality, vendor support, and the integration of information systems with strategic decision-making processes are also significant (Caldeira & Ward, 2002).

AIS are integral to organizational decision-making. They comprise human and physical resources that provide financial and non-financial information essential for informed decision-making. The quality of AIS is linked to the system's ability to process financial data effectively, producing reliable accounting information that supports strategic decisions (Hall, 2011). High-quality AIS contributes to informed decision-making, which can facilitate the adoption of e-commerce strategies (Al-Hattami, 2024).

Organizational context also influences e-commerce adoption. Factors such as financial resources, business longevity, and human and technical resources play significant roles (Hendricks & Mwapwele, 2023). Additionally, e-commerce implementation has been shown to positively impact performance elements, including financial performance, internal processes, customer satisfaction, and organizational growth (Almuwallad & Alhumoudi, 2024).

Other organizational factors identified in the literature include company size, product and service types, capital, human resources, industry sector, strategic priorities, and profitability (Wymer & Regan, 2005). The information intensity of products and services also affects e-commerce adoption (Loo, Ramachandran, & Raja Yusof, 2024). Furthermore, the availability of financial and human resources, user attitudes, organizational structure, and IT skills are critical considerations (Caldeira & Ward, 2002). Awareness of e-commerce benefits among management is essential, as understanding these advantages can lead to greater support for adoption (Al-Bakri & Katsioloudes, 2015).

In recent years, the rapid advancement of digital technologies and the proliferation of the Internet have significantly transformed how organizations operate, communicate, and compete. One of the central elements in this digital transformation is the degree of technological integration within the firm, especially the extent to which its internal systems and applications are interconnected and compatible with Internet-based technologies. According to Hong and Zhu (2006), the Internet's open standards and network capabilities can help eliminate the incompatibility and rigidity of legacy information systems, thus enabling greater integration across organizational processes. This integration enhances the ability of firms to digitize their operations, facilitating smoother transitions into e-commerce environments. Recent studies reinforce this view by showing that firms with high levels of IT integration are better positioned to adopt and benefit from e-commerce, due to improved agility, scalability, and interoperability of systems (Clemente-Almendros, Nicoara-Popescu, & Pastor-Sanz, 2024, 2022).

Technological integration is therefore seen not merely as a technical condition, but as a strategic enabler of digital commerce. Firms that succeed in aligning their IT infrastructure with web-based applications are able to respond more rapidly to market opportunities and customer demands, while reducing operational frictions (Kraus et al., 2021). These capabilities are particularly crucial in dynamic markets where speed and flexibility are determinants of success. Based on this literature, the first research hypothesis is formulated:

H1: The technological integration level positively influences the adoption of e-commerce.

Beyond system integration, the knowledge and competencies of individuals within the firm, particularly those of decision-makers, play a critical role in shaping e-commerce adoption. In a knowledge-intensive economy, the ability to acquire, manage, and apply information is fundamental to organizational competitiveness (Probst, Raub, & Romhardt, 1999). Firms that lack internal IT expertise or awareness of digital innovation tend to delay adoption due to uncertainty and perceived risk (Looi, 2005). This pattern is supported by contemporary findings, which suggest that low digital literacy among managers is one of the primary barriers to digital transformation in SMEs (OECD, 2021; Ghobakhloo & Iranmanesh, 2022).

Moreover, Abduwahab and Al-Dubai (2024) confirmed the moderating effect of technology readiness in the relationship between leadership styles and E-Commerce adoption among SMEs. This is because SMEs with higher levels of technology readiness are better able to reap the benefits of transformational leadership in e-commerce adoption. Balkan (2022) also pointed to the knowledge gap as a primary reason for underutilizing IT in small European firms. This finding remains relevant in today's digital economy, especially among SMEs in developing contexts. Recent empirical studies continue to affirm that internal knowledge capabilities significantly mediate the relationship between innovation potential and actual digital adoption (Khin & Ho, 2019; Santoro, Vrontis, Thrassou, & Dezi, 2018). Therefore, enhancing IT knowledge within firms is vital for maximising the benefits of e-commerce. In this context, the second research hypothesis is proposed:

H2: The IT knowledge level positively influences the e-commerce adoption level.

AIS are essential tools that enable organizations to collect, store, and process financial data, transforming it into useful information to support decision-making. As Hashim (2022) explains, AIS are computerized systems designed to convert raw accounting data into meaningful information that supports managerial decisions. Similarly, Hla and Teru (2015) assert that the primary role of AIS is to assign quantitative values to economic events—past, present, or projected—thereby creating a structured basis for financial analysis and forecasting.

Building on this conceptualization, Chenhall and Morris (1986) provided a seminal framework for evaluating AIS based on four perceived attributes of information: scope, timeliness, aggregation, and integration. These dimensions determine the usefulness of the information generated. "Scope" refers to the type and breadth of information, distinguishing between internal vs. external and financial vs. non-financial data, as well as forward-looking vs. historical perspectives. "Timeliness" relates to the speed, frequency, and immediacy with which information is communicated. "Aggregation" involves how data is structured—by function, time period, or decision type—while "integration" assesses the system's capacity to account for interdependencies across organizational units (Chenhall & Morris, 1986; Hall, 2011).

In this context, AIS quality plays a crucial role in strategic planning, performance evaluation, and resource allocation. Sadiq, Khan, Ikhlaq, and Mujtaba (2012) emphasizes that financial managers rely on high-quality accounting information to assess historical performance and develop informed projections. More recently, research has confirmed that the quality and integration of AIS facilitate strategic alignment and enhances organizational effectiveness (Rom & Rohde, 2007). Empirical studies by Sajady, Dastgir, and Nejad (2008) and Soudani (2012) have demonstrated that the implementation of AIS significantly improves various performance indicators, including financial accuracy, efficiency, and internal control.

Moreover, the literature suggests that the evolution of e-commerce has driven the development and sophistication of AIS. Ardiansah, Chariri, and Raharja (2021) found that the adoption of e-commerce significantly impacts the quality of AIS, highlighting that companies embracing digital platforms tend to enhance their reporting processes, decision-making capabilities, and overall organizational performance. Their study showed that AIS quality—reflected in the timeliness, accuracy, and relevance of the information produced—acts as a mediating factor between e-commerce adoption and organizational outcomes, emphasizing the strategic role of AIS in a digital context. Despite these findings, there remains a lack of empirical research directly examining how AIS quality influences a company's ability to adopt e-commerce. This study addresses that gap by proposing that the quality of AIS positively affects the level of e-commerce adoption. Beyond its informational role, the AIS also performs key operational functions that directly support e-commerce processes. Empirical studies have demonstrated that effective AIS implementation enhances firms' ability to synchronize digital transactions, manage online inventory, and process real-time financial data across e-commerce platforms (Ardiansah, Chariri, & Raharja, 2021; Manda, Abidin, & Jusman, 2024). Through these mechanisms, AIS facilitate smoother integration between front-end digital sales systems and back-office financial reporting, improving accuracy, timeliness, and decision-making quality (Alnajjar, 2017). Recent evidence also indicates that the joint use of AIS and e-commerce strengthens SMEs' financial performance by enabling automated record-keeping and transaction traceability (Sari, Setiawan, & Reswari, 2025; Istiyana et al., 2025). In this sense, AIS act not merely as accounting tools but as strategic infrastructures that sustain digital business operations and scalability. Accordingly, the following research hypothesis is proposed:

H3: The Quality of the accounting information system positively influences the adoption level of e-commerce.

In parallel with internal systems, a company's financial performance is a key determinant of its capacity to innovate and adopt new technologies, including e-commerce. Financial performance can be understood as a metric that evaluates a firm's economic success and progress toward achieving strategic goals (Van Weele & Van Raaij, 2014). According to Moullin (2017), financial performance reflects how effectively an organization adds value to shareholders, serving as a proxy for the management's ability to allocate and utilize resources efficiently.

Several studies have identified limited financial capacity as a critical barrier to e-commerce adoption, particularly among SMEs. Lawrence and Tar (2010) report that financial constraints are often cited by managers as a deterrent to technological investment. Hussein and Baharudin (2017) reaffirm that budgetary limitations are the most significant obstacle to digitalization initiatives in resource-constrained settings. Conversely, firms with robust financial health are better positioned to invest in infrastructure, human resources, and digital capabilities (Harmawan, & Ridho, 2024).

In this light, financial performance is not only an outcome of business activity but also a facilitator of digital transformation. Scupola (2003) argues that a firm's economic resources—along with its human and organizational capital—are foundational for the successful adoption of e-commerce. This perspective is consistent with the resource-based view of the firm, which suggests that strategic resources such as financial strength provide the foundation for sustainable competitive advantage through innovation (Barney, 1991; Teece, 2014). Accordingly, the fourth hypothesis of this study is proposed:

H4: The company's financial performance positively influences the level of e-commerce adoption.

The perception and attitude of managers regarding e-commerce adoption are deeply influenced by their level of education, experience, and position within the organization. According to Vilaseca et al. (2007), managerial qualifications and management approaches are central to shaping how new business models, such as e-commerce, are received within a company. While their study identified the relevance of managerial profiles, it also pointed to a gap in empirical evidence regarding which specific characteristics most strongly correlate with e-commerce adoption. More recent literature confirms that educated managers are more likely to understand the strategic value of digital technologies, leading to more favorable decisions toward their implementation (Soto-Acosta et al., 2018; Oliveira et al., 2020).

Lal (2002) also highlights that managers' academic and professional qualifications are essential drivers of technological readiness, particularly in SMEs, where decision-making is often centralized. Managers with higher levels of formal education tend to possess better analytical skills, are more open to innovation, and can better assess risks and benefits associated with digital business models. Accordingly, the following hypothesis is proposed:

H5: The level of education of managers positively influences the level of e-commerce adoption.

Experience is another critical factor in technology adoption. Awa et al. (2015) consider managerial experience a strategic asset contributing to organizational learning, operational efficiency, and improved decision-making. Experienced managers are more capable of managing change and uncertainty through consistent exposure to market dynamics and technological developments. Empirical evidence supports this view: Rahayu and Day (2015) found that SMEs owners with greater IT experience displayed higher confidence in adopting e-commerce, reducing the perceived risks and ambiguity associated with technology. Similarly, Galloway and Mochrie (2005) concluded that experience influences both the timing and depth of adoption among small businesses. This supports the formulation of the sixth research hypothesis:

H6: The manager's professional experience positively influences the level of e-commerce adoption.

The internal distribution of responsibilities also plays a fundamental role in shaping technology adoption. Nguyen and Waring (2013) emphasize that managers, particularly those with decision-making authority in IT, serve as the gatekeepers of digital transformation initiatives. When such managers occupy senior roles with strategic influence, their support can be decisive for the adoption of innovations like e-commerce. Cloete et al. (2002) likewise note that the owner or IT manager's attitude toward technology significantly impacts adoption intentions, especially in SMEs, where such figures often combine operational and strategic functions. Therefore, this study hypothesizes that:

H7: The IT manager's level of responsibility positively influences the adoption of e-commerce.

Firm size is another structural factor widely studied in the context of technological adoption. Zhu et al. (2006) argue that larger firms tend to have more financial and human resources to invest in digital infrastructures and are therefore more capable of deploying complex e-commerce platforms. Company size, commonly measured by the number of employees or total turnover, often correlates with technological sophistication. However, this relationship is not linear. Recent studies indicate that larger organizations may face bureaucratic inertia and structural rigidity, which can inhibit responsiveness to digital transformation. For instance, Besio et al. (2024) introduce the concept of "organizational restlessness," highlighting that continuous, uncoordinated changes within large bureaucracies can impede sustainable digital transformation efforts. In contrast, smaller firms, despite limited resources, may exhibit greater agility and a higher propensity to adopt e-commerce solutions. Recent evidence shows that firms with smaller teams are more likely to embrace flexible, cost-effective digital tools to compensate for their limited operational capacity (Maroufkhani et al., 2020). This phenomenon suggests that a lean organizational structure may, in some cases, accelerate e-commerce adoption. Based on this reasoning, the following hypothesis is formulated:

H8: The smaller the company (the lower the number of employees), the more likely it is to adopt e-commerce.

These hypotheses, grounded in the literature and aligned with the research objectives, support the development of the conceptual model presented in Figure 1.

Figure 1. Conceptual model (Own elaboration)

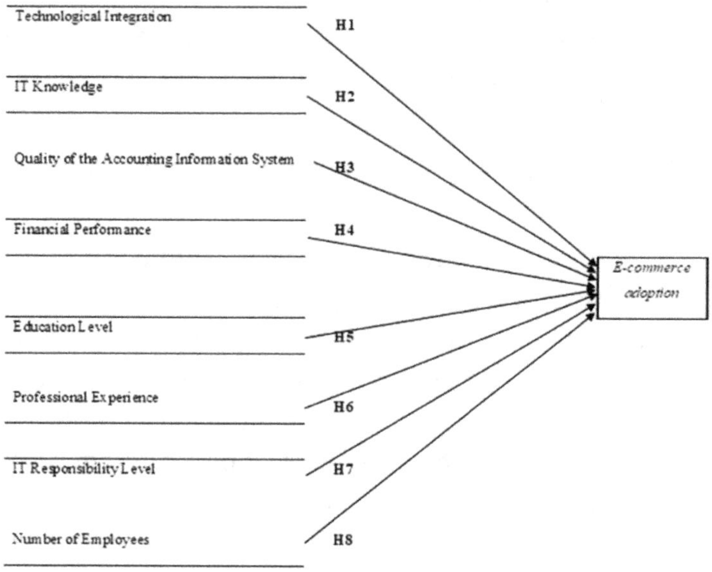

METHODOLOGY

This study adopts quantitative research design, employing a structured questionnaire as the primary data collection instrument. The questionnaire was developed using Google Forms and directed to top managers of Portuguese companies. Prior to its administration, the instrument underwent a pre-test phase involving two academic experts in business and information systems. Their feedback contributed to refining the clarity and relevance of the items, leading to the inclusion of additional response options for company and respondent profiling and the adjustment of some items in the measurement scales.

The decision to focus on internal organizational variables was guided by data accessibility and theoretical parsimony. Although external environmental variables such as competitive pressure or customer digital readiness are relevant, their measurement exceeded the scope of this study. This boundary is acknowledged in the discussion section.

The final version of the survey is structured into seven sections, comprising twenty questions. The first two sections focus on the characterization of the respondent and the company, containing mostly closed-ended multiple-choice questions. Three open-ended items allow respondents to specify their answers when the predefined options are insufficient.

Based on the conceptual model, the remaining five sections are designed to measure the key constructs under investigation. Specifically:

- – Section 3 measures the level of e-commerce activity.
- – Section 4 assesses the degree of technological integration within the company.
- – Section 5 captures perceptions of e-commerce adoption.
- – Section 6 evaluates the quality of accounting information systems.
- – Section 7 measures financial performance, relative to competitors.

All latent variables were measured using validated scales adapted from prior studies, and responses were collected on a 5-point Likert scale, where 1 indicates "strongly disagree" and 5 indicates "strongly agree".

Technological Integration was measured through eight items adapted from Weill and Broadbent (1998) and Hong and Zhu (2006), covering the use of Customer Relationship Management (CRM), Enterprise Resource Planning (ERP), Supply Chain Management (SCM), and other enterprise-level applications.

IT Knowledge was captured with a single item adapted from Thong (1999) and Gable and Raman (1992), assessing the managerial understanding of how IT and e-commerce contribute to profitability.

E-commerce Adoption was measured using a categorical item from Wymer and Regan (2005), capturing the percentage of revenue generated through online channels.

Accounting Information System Quality was assessed using six items adapted from Romney et al. (1997), Sori (2009), and Sajady et al. (2008), focusing on data integrity, relevance, timeliness, and utility in decision-making.

Financial Performance was evaluated using six indicators from Gupta and Somers (1996), comparing company performance to competitors in terms of operating results, ROI, sales growth, and market share.

The sampling frame was extracted from the SABI database using the following criteria: (1) companies located in Portugal; (2) companies with active status; (3) companies with a valid email address; and (4) companies classified under the wholesale and retail trade sectors (excluding vehicles and motorcycles). This filtering process yielded a total population of 53,187 Portuguese companies.

Given the potential for low response rates and the importance of managerial perspectives, the questionnaire was distributed to the entire sample rather than limiting it to a specific region. Survey distribution occurred via email, targeting top-level executives. The data was collected over five weeks, from 25 March to 30 April 2024, with responses monitored and registered daily.

DATA ANALYSIS AND RESULTS

The collected data was exported from Google Forms into Microsoft Excel, coded and imported into SPSS Statistics version 28 for processing. This section presents a structured analysis of the data collected and results.

Observations with more than 30% missing responses were excluded, reducing the sample by ten cases. Additional exclusions were made for companies that reported no online turnover, as their inclusion would compromise the analysis of the dependent variable — the level of e-commerce adoption. After these procedures, the final sample consisted of 289 valid observations. As established statistical guidelines recommended, the mean substitution method was applied for the remaining missing values.

Outliers were also examined. Although some extreme values were identified using boxplot analysis in SPSS, they were retained in the dataset. These values corresponded to valid responses within the 5-point Likert scale (mostly at the lower end) and thus were considered representative of the population rather than data entry errors.

A substantial proportion of respondents (71.6%) reported having more than 15 years of professional experience; the majority were male and aged 45 or older. In terms of academic background, most hold at least a bachelor's degree, with many having studied management, accounting, economics, or information systems. Regarding decision-making authorities in IT and information systems, 63% of respondents stated they were directly responsible for decisions in this area, while 25.3% reported having some responsibility.

The companies in the study were geographically diverse, although most were located in the districts of Porto, Lisbon, and Braga, representing over half the sample. The vast majority were private limited companies and classified as micro or small enterprises, based on the number of employees, turnover, and total assets. Specifically, almost 90% employed fewer than 50 people, and over 87% reported an annual turnover of up to 10 million euros. Similarly, the majority held total assets of less than 10 million euros at the end of 2023. The analysis also found that many companies outsourced their accounting function, though a significant portion used a hybrid model combining in-house and outsourced services.

The results showed that most companies in the sample were still in the early stages of digital commercialization regarding e-commerce activity. Over 65% indicated that less than 10% of their turnover came from online sales, while only 8.7% of companies had more than 60% of their turnover generated through e-commerce.

An exploratory factor analysis (EFA) was performed on the latent variables to validate the constructs used in the proposed research model. *Technological Integration* demonstrated acceptable factorability, with all item communalities exceeding the recommended threshold of 0.5 and a Kaiser-Meyer-Olkin (KMO) value of 0.866. Similarly, the factor analysis for *Accounting Information Systems Quality* showed satisfactory results, with communalities above 0.5 and a KMO value of 0.901. The same pattern was observed for the *Financial Performance* variable, which achieved a KMO value of 0.891.

The variable *IT Knowledge* was measured using a single item: "We have a good understanding of how IT and e-commerce can be used to help increase company profits," and thus did not require factor extraction.

Since all communalities exceeded the minimum criterion and the KMO values were above the acceptable threshold of 0.6, the variables were subsequently transformed by computing the mean of their respective items.

In addition, Bartlett's Test of Sphericity (BTS) was significant ($p < 0.001$), indicating the appropriateness of applying factor analysis to the data. For the overall model, the KMO statistic was 0.647, which confirms the sample's suitability for the method.

Table 1. KMO and BTS test

Statistic	Value
KMO Test (Kaiser-Meyer-Olkin)	0.647
Approx. Chi-Square	171.865
Degrees of Freedom (df)	28
Significance (p-value)	< 0.001

Source: Own elaboration

To assess the influence of various factors on the level of e-commerce adoption, a multiple linear regression model was estimated using the "enter" method. The model included the following independent variables: IT knowledge, technological integration, quality of AIS, financial performance, education level, professional experience, managerial responsibility in IT, and number of employees.

The regression equation resulting from this model is as follows:

VN_Online_Perc = 0.263ItKnow + 0.161TecIntMedia + 0.164AISQ-Media – 0.002FPerfMedia + 0.031Esc – 0.187Exp – 0.051NResp + 0.115NTrab

The results show that four variables statistically affect the dependent variable — the turnover percentage realized through e-commerce. These include *IT Knowledge* ($\beta = 0.263$, $p < 0.001$), *Technological Integration* ($\beta = 0.161$, $p = 0.004$), *Accounting Information Systems Quality* ($\beta = 0.164$, $p = 0.012$), and *Experience* ($\beta = -0.187$, $p < 0.001$). Interestingly, while the first three have a positive effect, the negative coefficient of *Experience* suggests that more experienced managers may be less inclined to adopt e-commerce.

The remaining variables — financial performance, education, level of managerial responsibility, and number of employees — did not exhibit statistically significant effects on e-commerce adoption.

Table 2. Multiple linear regression model

	Non-standardised coefficients		Standardised coefficients	Stat t	p-value (Sig)
	Beta	Standard error	Beta		
It_Know	0,263	0,058	0,564	4,565	<0,001
Tec_Int_Media	0,161	0,056	0,288	2,874	0,004
AISQ_Media	0,164	0,065	0,362	2,517	0,012
F_Perf_Media	-0,002	0,081	-0,004	-0,027	0,978
Schooling (Esc)	0,031	0,071	0,033	0,436	0,663
Experience (Exp)	-0,187	0,055	-0,358	-3,383	<0,001
Responsibility_Level (NResp)	-0,051	0,069	-0,07	-0,741	0,459
N_Workers (NTrab)	0,115	0,18	0,07	0,639	0,523

Source: Own elaboration

The model demonstrates high explanatory power, with an adjusted R^2 of 0.783, indicating that the independent variables included explain approximately 78.3% of the variance in e-commerce adoption.

Table 3. Coefficient of determination

Model	R	R square	Adjusted R-squared	Standard error of estimate	Durbin-Watson
1	0,888	0,789	0,783	0,876	1,972
a. Predictors: N_Workers, AISQ_Media, Responsibility_Level, Education, It_Know, Experience, F_Perf_Media, Tec_Int_Media					
b. Dependent Variable: VN_Online_Perc					

Source: Own elaboration

An F-test for global significance was performed to confirm the model's usefulness further. The test showed a p-value < 0.001, confirming that the model is statistically significant and that at least one independent variable explains the variance in e-commerce adoption.

Table 4. ANOVA Table

Model	Sum of Squares	df	Mean Square	Z	Sig.
Regression	806,233	8	100,779	131,248	<,001b
Waste	215,767	281	0,768		
Total	1022,000	288			

a. Dependent Variable: VN_Online_Perc

b. Predictors: N_Workers, AISQ_Media, Responsibility_Level, Education, It_Know, Experience, F_Perf_Media, Tec_Int_Media

Source: Own elaboration

Several key assumptions were tested and analyzed to ensure the validity of this study's multiple linear regression model.

Firstly, the assumption of normality of residuals was assessed through visual inspection of the normal probability-probability (P-P) plot. The plot revealed that some data points deviated from the main diagonal, suggesting potential violations of the normality assumption. However, as highlighted by Finney et al. (2006), using ordinal variables, such as those measured with 5-point Likert scales—as in this study—tends to produce non-normal distributions by nature. The Kolmogorov-Smirnov (K-S) test was conducted to evaluate this assumption further. The resulting p-value was 0.001, which is below the 0.05 significance threshold. Consequently, the null hypothesis of normality was rejected, confirming that the residuals are not normally distributed.

The second assumption examined was the autocorrelation of residuals, evaluated using the Durbin-Watson statistics. The result obtained was 1.972, which falls within the acceptable range of $[0 < du < 4]$. This indicates that the residuals are not autocorrelated and are therefore independent, satisfying this regression model assumption.

Thirdly, the assumption of homoscedasticity—or constant variance of residuals—was assessed using a scatterplot of the standardized residuals. Visual inspection of this plot showed that the residuals were not randomly distributed around zero, suggesting a violation of the homoscedasticity assumption. According to Hall et al. (2011), such a pattern implies that the residuals exhibit heteroscedasticity, which may affect the efficiency of the regression estimates.

Collinearity diagnostics were performed to test multicollinearity, including tolerance and variance inflation factor (VIF) statistics. All VIF values were well below the critical threshold of 5, with the highest value being 1.249, and all tolerance values exceeded 0.8. These results confirm no severe multicollinearity issues among the independent variables. Additional support for this conclusion comes from the Condition Index analysis, where most values were below 15, following the recommendations of Marôco (2007). An exception was observed for the variable "Number of Employees", which presented a condition index of 16.711. Although slightly above the suggested threshold, this does not necessarily indicate problematic collinearity, particularly in light of the VIF and tolerance results.

The final assumption examined was the presence of outliers and influential cases. This was assessed through multiple diagnostics, including Studentised Deleted Residuals, Mahalanobis Distance, Cook's Distance, and Centred Leverage Values. The maximum value of the Studentised Deleted Residual was 3.260, which exceeds the conventional threshold of 1.96 and indicates the presence of outliers. Additionally, the highest leverage value (0.137) was well above the calculated critical value of 0.058 (based on the formula $2(p+1)/n$ with $p = 8$ and $n = 289$), suggesting that certain observations have a powerful influence on the model. Cook's Distance further confirmed this, with a maximum value of 0.152, which exceeds the threshold of 0.014 (calculated as $4/(n-p-1)$). Although none of the Cook's Distance values reached the critical level of 1, above which observations are considered excessively influential, some data points may still exert undue influence on the regression parameters.

Despite identifying these outliers and influential cases, the decision was made to retain them in the analysis. This choice is justified by the nature of the data, which is based on Likert-scale responses. Pestana and Gageiro (2005) argued that influential cases in such contexts should not be automatically excluded, primarily when they reflect legitimate variation in the population rather than data entry errors.

In summary, while the model violated the assumptions of normality and homoscedasticity of residuals, it met the criteria for independence of errors, absence of multicollinearity, and robustness to influential observations. These results suggest that the regression estimates should be interpreted cautiously, particularly regarding the standard errors, but they remain valid for explanatory purposes.

DISCUSSION

This study aimed to develop and validate an explanatory model for Portuguese firms' adoption of e-commerce. The multiple linear regression analysis yielded a model with an adjusted R^2 of 0.783, indicating strong explanatory power: the eight independent variables included accounted for approximately 78.3% of the variance in e-commerce adoption. This result confirms the theoretical soundness of the proposed model and highlights the relevance of technological and informational capabilities, as well as managerial characteristics, in shaping firms' digital transitions.

Technological integration emerged as a significant and positive predictor of e-commerce adoption ($\beta = 0.161$; $p < 0.05$), validating Hypothesis 1. This finding aligns with the literature that portrays digital integration as a strategic enabler for e-commerce (Hong & Zhu, 2006). Integrating CRM, ERP, and SCM systems enhances internal coordination and responsiveness to external market demands, enabling firms to streamline operations and facilitate online transactions (Kraus et al., 2021). These results suggest that compatible investments and interoperable digital systems are fundamental for leveraging digital commerce.

Likewise, IT knowledge was found to have the strongest positive effect on e-commerce adoption ($\beta = 0.263$; $p < 0.001$), supporting Hypothesis 2. This confirms earlier studies indicating that firms with digitally literate managers are more likely to initiate and support e-commerce strategies (Looi, 2005; Ettlie, 1990; Gable & Raman, 1992). The result is also consistent with the knowledge-based view of the firm (Probst et al., 1999), according to which internal capabilities to understand, manage, and exploit IT are central to innovation. Ghobakhloo & Iranmanesh (2021) noted that digital literacy among decision-makers is a crucial driver of digital transformation, particularly in SMEs.

The quality of AIS also significantly and positively influenced e-commerce adoption ($\beta = 0.164$; $p < 0.05$), lending support to Hypothesis 3. This reinforces the findings of Hall (2011), Sadiq, Khan, Ikhlaq, and Mujtaba (2012), and Rom & Rohde (2007), who argue that timely, accurate, and decision-oriented accounting information is essential for strategic management. As Qatawneh (2012) suggests, the evolution of e-commerce is tightly linked to advances in AIS, which not only supports financial control but also enables integration with digital sales and logistics systems. Firms with robust AIS are thus better positioned to adopt and benefit from e-commerce by supporting informed and agile decision-making.

Contrary to expectations, financial performance was not a statistically significant predictor ($\beta = -0.002$; $p = 0.978$), leading to the rejection of Hypothesis 4. While previous research (e.g., Scupola, 2003; Lawrence & Tar, 2010) suggests that financial resources are critical for adopting new technologies, this study indicates that Portuguese SMEs may prioritize operational or strategic alignment over economic capacity. One possible explanation is that e-commerce tools have become more accessible and affordable, reducing the entry cost barrier and decoupling adoption decisions from short-term financial performance (Harmawan, & Ridho, 2024).

Similarly, education level was not a significant determinant ($\beta = 0.031$; $p = 0.663$), which contradicts Hypothesis 5 and the arguments of Lal (2002) and Soto-Acosta et al. (2018), who emphasize the role of managerial education in fostering digital adoption. A potential interpretation is that in Portugal, e-commerce adoption decisions may be shaped more by practical experience and sector-specific knowledge than by formal academic qualifications. This highlights the importance of ongoing professional development and informal learning in digital contexts.

Interestingly, professional experience had a significant but negative effect ($\beta = -0.187$; $p < 0.001$), which supports Hypothesis 6, though not in the anticipated direction. While Awa et al. (2015) and Rahayu & Day (2015) view experience as a facilitator of adoption, our findings suggest that highly experienced managers may be more risk-averse or attached to traditional business models, which could hinder digital innovation. This tension between experience and adaptability is critical in understanding managerial behavior in digital transitions. The negative relationship between managerial experience and e-commerce adoption can be interpreted as a generational challenge rather than a purely behavioral one. It suggests that senior managers may be less exposed to digital ecosystems or less willing to deviate from established operational routines. Addressing this gap requires not only training younger managers but also re-skilling experienced leaders to foster digital openness.

The manager's level of responsibility in IT decision-making did not significantly impact e-commerce adoption ($\beta = -0.051$; $p = 0.459$), leading to the rejection of Hypothesis 7. This result contrasts with Nguyen and Waring (2013), who stress the influence of IT champions in driving adoption. In the context of Portuguese SMEs, where decision-making may be more collective or informal, responsibility alone may not be a sufficient driver unless coupled with knowledge, motivation, or external incentives.

Finally, firm size, measured by the number of employees, also showed no significant effect ($\beta = 0.115$; $p = 0.523$), rejecting Hypothesis 8. This finding diverges from Zhu et al. (2006) and Tan et al. (2007), who associate size with resource availability or organizational rigidity. It suggests that agility and digital ambition may outweigh size as predictors of e-commerce adoption, especially in a landscape where cloud solutions and online platforms lower the operational barriers for small firms (Maroufkhani et al., 2020).

The non-significance of financial performance, education level, and firm size challenges the conventional view that resource abundance and formal qualifications are the primary enablers of digital adoption (Zhu et al., 2006). In this sample, many Portuguese micro-enterprises operate in service-oriented sectors with low logistical complexity and cost-effective digital tools such as SaaS-based platforms. Consequently, e-commerce entry barriers have diminished, decoupling adoption from firm size or short-term profitability. This shift reflects a broader European trend where digital agility, rather than scale, defines competitiveness (European Commission, 2023). In sum, this discussion highlights the central role of internal digital competencies. particularly IT knowledge, technological integration, and AIS quality, in enabling e-commerce adoption. At the same time, it questions traditional assumptions about the roles of financial strength, education, and firm size. The results confirm the relevance of a multidimensional and context-sensitive approach, as literature advocates, and contributes to a more nuanced understanding of digital transformation in SMEs.

FINAL CONSIDERATIONS

This study aimed to develop and empirically validate a multidimensional model explaining the adoption of e-commerce among Portuguese companies, focusing on technological factors, accounting information, and organizational characteristics. By combining theoretical insights from the literature with statistical evidence derived from a multiple linear regression analysis of 289 firms, the research contributes conceptually and empirically to understanding digital adoption dynamics in the context of SMEs.

The findings demonstrate that internal capabilities, particularly IT knowledge, technological integration, and the quality of AIS, play a decisive role in fostering the adoption of e-commerce. These variables were statistically significant and positively associated with online turnover, confirming hypotheses H1, H2, and H3. The study reinforces prior literature asserting that firms with better-integrated systems (Hong & Zhu, 2006; Kraus et al., 2021), greater IT literacy (Looi, 2005; Ghobakhloo & Iranmanesh, 2021), and more robust decision-support infrastructures (Hall, 2011; Rom & Rohde, 2007) are more likely to embrace digital commerce models.

Unexpectedly, variables traditionally considered relevant in adoption models—such as financial performance, education level, managerial responsibility, and firm size—did not significantly affect e-commerce adoption. These results challenge conventional assumptions found in earlier studies (e.g., Scupola, 2003; Lal, 2002; Zhu et al., 2006) and suggest that, at least in the Portuguese SMEs context, the adoption of e-commerce may be driven more by strategic alignment and operational readiness than by resource availability or structural characteristics.

An intriguing finding concerns the adverse effect of managerial experience on e-commerce adoption. This result suggests that more experienced managers may be more hesitant to adopt disruptive technologies, possibly due to risk aversion or a stronger attachment to established practices. It highlights the importance of fostering a digital mindset and continuous learning among senior decision-makers to counterbalance resistance to innovation.

The explanatory model achieved a high adjusted R^2 of 78.3%, indicating a strong fit and significant predictive power. Although some regression model assumptions—such as residual normality and homoscedasticity—were not fully met, the diagnostics confirmed that the model remains robust and interpretable for explanatory purposes.

This research provides several practical implications. For policymakers and support agencies, it highlights the need to promote IT training and digital literacy among SMEs' leadership, as these are critical levers for e-commerce advancement. For managers, the study reinforces the importance of investing in integrated information systems and leveraging high-quality accounting data to support strategic decisions. Finally, for researchers, the study opens avenues for further investigation into the behavioral dimensions of technology adoption, particularly the paradoxical role of experience and the potential moderating effects of industry, culture, and external pressures.

The authors acknowledge that IT Knowledge was measured through a single-item construct, which limits construct validity. Future research should adopt a multi-item scale to better capture the multidimensional nature of technological literacy. Furthermore, given minor violations of regression assumptions, robustness checks such as bootstrapped standard errors are recommended to confirm the stability of results. Moreover, future research should incorporate contextual dimensions to achieve a fuller application of the Technology-Organization-Environment (TOE) framework in the Portuguese SME context. Exploring the role of external enablers, such as government incentives, platform ecosystems, or customer digital maturity, could also enrich the theoretical framework and practical recommendations. Additionally, it would be valuable to extend the analysis to other sectors or regions to assess the model's generalizability.

In sum, the study demonstrates that when accounting meets innovation, the success of e-commerce adoption lies not merely in financial means or firm size, but in digital capabilities, technological openness, and the quality of information available for decision-making.

REFERENCES

Abduwahab, A. S., & Al-Dubai, M. M. (2024). Leadership styles and E-Commerce adoption among SME managers in Oman: Moderating effect of technology readiness. *Open Journal of Business and Management, 12*(2), 1074–1096. DOI: 10.4236/ojbm.2024.122057

Al-Bakri, A. A., & Katsioloudes, M. I. (2015). The factors affecting e-commerce adoption by Jordanian SMEs. *Management Research Review, 38*(7), 726–749. DOI: 10.1108/MRR-12-2013-0291

Al-Hattami, H. M. (2024). Impact of AIS success on decision-making effectiveness among SMEs in less developed countries. *Information Technology for Development, 30*(3), 472–492. DOI: 10.1080/02681102.2022.2073325

Almuwallad, H., & Alhumoudi, H. (2024). The Impact of E-commerce on Organizational and Financial Performance in SMEs: Evidence from Saudi Arabia. *International Journal of Business and Management, 19*(4), 1–15. DOI: 10.5539/ijbm.v19n4p1

Alnajjar, M. I. M. (2017). Impact of accounting information system on organizational performance: A study of SMEs in the UAE. *Global Review of Accounting and Finance, 8*(2), 19–38. DOI: 10.21102/graf.2017.09.82.02

Ardiansah, M. N., Chariri, A., & Raharja, S. (2021). Does E-Commerce Impact on Accounting Information System and Organizations' Performance? In *2nd Annual Conference on Blended Learning, Educational Technology and Innovation (ACBLETI 2020)* (pp. 476–481). Atlantis Press. DOI: 10.2991/assehr.k.210615.090

Ardiansah, M. N., Chariri, A., & Raharja, S. (2021, June). Does E-Commerce Impact on Accounting Information System and Organizations' Performance? In 2nd annual conference on blended learning, educational technology and innovation (ACBLETI 2020) (pp. 476-481). Atlantis Press.

Awa, H. O., Ukoha, O., & Emecheta, B. C. (2015). Integrating TAM, TPB and TOE frameworks and expanding their characteristic constructs for e-commerce adoption by SMEs. *Journal of Science and Technology Policy Management, 6*(1), 76–94. DOI: 10.1108/JSTPM-04-2014-0012

Balkan, N. (2022, April 8). *Barriers to digitally transform SMEs in Europe*. European DIGITAL SME Alliance. https://www.digitalsme.eu/barriers-to-digitally-transform-smes-in-europe/

Barney, J. (1991). Firm resources and sustained competitive advantage. *Journal of Management*, *17*(1), 99–120. DOI: 10.1177/014920639101700108

Besio, C., Jöstingmeier, M., & Posner, C. (2024). Digital transformation and organizational restlessness. *Frontiers in Sociology*, *9*, 1430384. DOI: 10.3389/fsoc.2024.1430384 PMID: 39319315

Caldeira, M. M., & Ward, J. M. (2002). Understanding the successful adoption and use of IS/IT in SMEs: An explanation from Portuguese manufacturing industries. *Information Systems Journal*, *12*(2), 121–152. DOI: 10.1046/j.1365-2575.2002.00119.x

Chenhall, R. H., & Morris, D. (1986). The impact of structure, environment, and interdependence on the perceived usefulness of management accounting systems. *The Accounting Review*, *61*(1), 16–35.

Clemente-Almendros, J. A., Nicoara-Popescu, D., & Pastor-Sanz, I. (2024). Digital transformation in SMEs: Understanding its determinants and size heterogeneity. *Technology in Society*, *77*, 102483. DOI: 10.1016/j.techsoc.2024.102483

Cloete, E., Courtney, S., & Fintz, J. (2002). Small businesses' acceptance and adoption of e-commerce in the Western-Cape Province of South Africa. *Electronic Journal of Information Systems Evaluation*, *5*(1), 1–13.

Dalenogare, L. S., Benitez, G. B., Ayala, N. F., & Frank, A. G. (2018). The expected contribution of Industry 4.0 technologies for industrial performance. *International Journal of Production Economics*, *204*, 383–394. DOI: 10.1016/j.ijpe.2018.08.019

European Commission. (2023). *Digital Economy and Society Index (DESI) 2023: Portugal Report*. Brussels.

Galloway, L., & Mochrie, R. (2005). The use of ICT in rural firms: A policy-oriented literature review. *Info*, *7*(3), 33–46. DOI: 10.1108/14636690510596784

Ghobakhloo, M., & Iranmanesh, M. (2021). Digital transformation success under Industry 4.0: A strategic guideline for manufacturing SMEs. *Journal of Manufacturing Technology Management*, *32*(8), 1533–1556. DOI: 10.1108/JMTM-11-2020-0455

Hall, J. A. (2011). *Accounting Information Systems* (7th ed.). South-Western College Publishing.

Harmawan, B. N., & Ridho, W. F. (2024). Determinants influencing SMEs in E-commerce adoption through local government facilities in Indonesia: Mixed methods approach. *The Electronic Journal on Information Systems in Developing Countries*, *90*(2), e12301. DOI: 10.1002/isd2.12301

Hashim, H. T. (2022). Impact of quality and management in accounting information systems on decision making for smes enterprises. *Academy of Accounting and Financial Studies Journal*, *26*(6), 1–11.

Hendricks, S., & Mwapwele, S. D. (2023). A systematic literature review on the factors influencing e-commerce adoption in developing countries. *Data and Information Management*, *8*(3), 100045. DOI: 10.1016/j.dim.2023.100045

Hla, D., & Teru, S. P. (2015). Efficiency of accounting information system and performance measures – Literature Review. *International Journal of Multidisciplinary and Current Research*, *3*, 976–984.

Hong, W., & Zhu, K. (2006). Migrating to Internet-based e-commerce: Factors affecting e-commerce adoption and migration at the firm level. *Information & Management*, *43*(2), 204–221. DOI: 10.1016/j.im.2005.06.003

Hussein, L. A., & Baharudin, A. S. (2017). Factors affecting small and medium enterprises (SMEs) continuance intention to adopt e-commerce in Jordan. *International Journal of Advanced and Applied Sciences*, *4*(4), 110–117. DOI: 10.21833/ijaas.2017.04.016

IAPMEI. (2023). *Digital Decade Country Report – Portugal.* Agência para a Competitividade e Inovação. Retrieved from https://www.iapmei.pt

Istiyana, A. N., Nurniah, N., Fatmawati, F., & Rahman, A. (2025). Factors Influencing the Success of E-Commerce-Based Accounting Information System (Study on MSMEs in Makassar). *American Journal of Commerce and Technology Applications*, *10*(1), 45–57.

Khin, S., & Ho, T. C. F. (2019). Digital technology, digital capability and organizational performance: A mediating role of digital innovation. *International Journal of Innovation Science*, *11*(2), 177–195. DOI: 10.1108/IJIS-08-2018-0083

Kraus, S., Palmer, C., Kailer, N., Kallinger, F. L., & Spitzer, J. (2021). Digital transformation: An overview of the current state of the art of research. *SAGE Open*, *11*(3), 1–14. DOI: 10.1177/21582440211047576

Lal, K. (2002). E-business and manufacturing sector: A study of small and medium-sized enterprises in India. *Research Policy*, *33*(1), 111–127. DOI: 10.1016/S0048-7333(01)00191-3

Lawrence, J. E., & Tar, U. A. (2010). Barriers to e-commerce in developing countries. Information. *Society and Justice Journal*, *3*(1), 23–35.

Loo, M. K., Ramachandran, S., & Raja Yusof, R. N. (2024). Systematic Review of Factors and Barriers Influencing E-Commerce Adoption among SMEs over the Last Decade: A TOE Framework Perspective. *Journal of the Knowledge Economy*, *16*(2), 1–25. DOI: 10.1007/s13132-024-02257-5

Looi, H. C. (2005). E-commerce adoption in Brunei Darussalam: A quantitative analysis of factors influencing its adoption. *Communications of the Association for Information Systems*, *15*, 61–81. DOI: 10.17705/1CAIS.01503

Manda, H. M., Abidin, Z., & Jusman, I. A. (2024). *The Impact of Using E-Commerce and Accounting Information Systems on Financial Performance in MSMEs*. Jurnal Ekonomi, Manajemen dan Akuntansi, 15(3), 112–126.

Maroufkhani, P., Ismail, W. K. W., & Ghobakhloo, M. (2020). Big data analytics adoption model for small and medium enterprises. *Journal of Science and Technology Policy Management*, *11*(2), 285–309. DOI: 10.1108/JSTPM-02-2020-0018

Molla, A., & Licker, P. S. (2005). E-commerce adoption in developing countries: A model and instrument. *Information & Management*, *42*(6), 877–899. DOI: 10.1016/j.im.2004.09.002

Moullin, M. (2017). Improving and evaluating performance with the public sector scorecard. *International Journal of Productivity and Performance Management*, *66*(4), 442–458. DOI: 10.1108/IJPPM-06-2015-0092

Nguyen, T. H., & Waring, T. S. (2013). The adoption of customer relationship management (CRM) technology in SMEs: An empirical study. *Journal of Small Business and Enterprise Development*, *20*(4), 824–848. DOI: 10.1108/JSBED-01-2012-0013

OECD. (2021). *The Digital Transformation of SMEs*. OECD Publishing., DOI: 10.1787/bdb9256a-

OECD. (2024). *SME Digitalisation in 2024: Managing Shocks and Transitions.* OECD SME and Entrepreneurship Papers, OECD Publishing.

Oliveira, T., Thomas, M., Baptista, G., & Campos, F. (2020). Mobile payment: Understanding the determinants of customer adoption and intention to recommend the technology. *Computers in Human Behavior*, *61*, 404–414. DOI: 10.1016/j.chb.2016.03.030

Probst, G., Raub, S., & Romhardt, K. (1999). *Managing knowledge: Building blocks for success*. John Wiley & Sons.

Rahayu, R., & Day, J. (2015). Determinant factors of e-commerce adoption by SMEs in developing country: Evidence from Indonesia. *Procedia: Social and Behavioral Sciences*, *195*, 142–150. DOI: 10.1016/j.sbspro.2015.06.423

Rom, A., & Rohde, C. (2007). Management accounting and integrated information systems: A literature review. *International Journal of Accounting Information Systems*, *8*(1), 40–68. DOI: 10.1016/j.accinf.2006.12.003

Sadiq, U., Khan, A. F., Ikhlaq, K., & Mujtaba, B. G. (2012). The impact of information systems on the performance of human resources department. *Journal of Business Studies Quarterly*, *3*(4), 77–91.

Sajady, H., Dastgir, M., & Nejad, H. H. (2008). Evaluation of the effectiveness of accounting information systems. *International Journal of Information Science and Technology*, *6*(2), 49–59.

Santoro, G., Vrontis, D., Thrassou, A., & Dezi, L. (2018). The Internet of Things: Building a knowledge management system for open innovation and knowledge management capacity. *Technological Forecasting and Social Change*, *136*, 347–354. DOI: 10.1016/j.techfore.2017.02.034

Sari, W., Setiawan, A., & Reswari, R. A. (2025). *Implementation of E-Commerce and Accounting Information Systems Towards Successful SMEs Performance.* Jurnal Ilmiah Manajemen dan Bisnis, 25(1), 88–100.

Scupola, A. (2003). The adoption of Internet commerce by SMEs in the south of Italy: An environmental, technological and organizational perspective. *Journal of Global Information Technology Management*, *6*(1), 52–71. DOI: 10.1080/1097198X.2003.10856343

Soto-Acosta, P., Popa, S., & Martinez-Conesa, I. (2018). Information technology, knowledge management and environmental dynamism as drivers of innovation adoption in SMEs. *Journal of Knowledge Management*, *20*(4), 824–849. DOI: 10.1108/JKM-10-2017-0448

Soudani, S. N. (2012). The usefulness of an accounting information system for effective organizational performance. *International Journal of Economics and Finance*, *4*(5), 136–145. DOI: 10.5539/ijef.v4n5p136

Teece, D. J. (2014). A dynamic capabilities-based entrepreneurial theory of the multinational enterprise. *Journal of International Business Studies*, *45*(1), 8–37. DOI: 10.1057/jibs.2013.54

Tornatzky, L. G., & Fleischer, M. (1990). *The Processes of Technological Innovation*. Lexington Books.

Van Weele, A. J., & Van Raaij, E. M. (2014). The future of purchasing and supply management research: About relevance and rigor. *The Journal of Supply Chain Management*, *50*(1), 56–72. DOI: 10.1111/jscm.12042

Vilaseca, J., Torrent-Sellens, J., & Guillen, M. (2007). ICT use in marketing as innovation success factor: Enhancing cooperation in new product development processes. *European Journal of Innovation Management*, *10*(2), 268–288. DOI: 10.1108/14601060710745297

Wymer, S. A., & Regan, E. A. (2005). Factors influencing e-commerce adoption and use by small and medium businesses. *Electronic Markets*, *15*(4), 438–453. DOI: 10.1080/10196780500303151

Zhu, K., & Kraemer, K. L. (2005). Post-adoption variations in usage and value of e-business by organizations: Cross-country evidence from the retail industry. *Information Systems Research*, *16*(1), 61–84. DOI: 10.1287/isre.1050.0045

Zhu, K., Kraemer, K. L., & Xu, S. (2006). The process of innovation assimilation by firms in different countries: A technology diffusion perspective on e-business. *Management Science*, *52*(10), 1557–1576. DOI: 10.1287/mnsc.1050.0487

Chapter 5
Risk Forecasting Using Value at Risk (VaR):
Strategic Insights for Investors

Amir Ahmad Dar
https://orcid.org/0000-0002-0379-2272
Lovely Professional University, India

ABSTRACT

This research analyses weekly stock data gathered from Google Finance over the previous five years to use the Value at Risk (VaR) approach to evaluate the risk exposure of four companies: Apple, Coca-Cola, Amazon, and McDonald's. To visualize the behavior and patterns of these companies' stocks, two crucial graphs were first created: stock price vs. time and return vs. time. The Anderson-Darling test was used to examine the assumption of normalcy for the returns, which is a key premise in the VaR computation. After that, each company's VaR was estimated using statistical techniques. To verify consistency and dependability in the model's assumptions, the normalcy of the VaR results was once more evaluated using the Anderson-Darling test. Furthermore, future VaR values were projected using the Power BI tool, which allowed investors to create strategies that worked.

DOI: 10.4018/979-8-3373-5976-2.ch005

INTRODUCTION

Risk, in the context of finance, refers to the potential for loss or adverse outcomes. It encompasses various uncertainties impacting investment decisions, including market fluctuations, credit defaults, and operational errors (Jorion, 1996; Duffie & Pan,1997; Artzner et al., 1999). Value at Risk (VaR) is a statistical measure used to quantify the potential for financial loss over a specified period. It estimates the maximum loss that can be expected to occur with a given probability level, often referred to as the confidence level. For instance, a 95% VaR of $1 million indicates a 5% chance of experiencing a loss exceeding $1 million within the specified timeframe. It provides a standardized metric to quantify and compare the potential downside of investments, enabling informed decision-making. VaR plays a crucial role in setting risk limits, monitoring exposure, and implementing mitigation strategies. Additionally, it is often required by regulatory authorities to ensure transparency and promote sound risk management practices. VaR helps determine appropriate capital reserves to absorb losses and supports efficient capital allocation. By evaluating the performance of investment portfolios against VaR expectations, investors can assess the effectiveness of their risk-taking decisions. Overall, VaR empowers financial institutions and investors to make informed choices and mitigate potential losses (Favre & Galeano, 2002).

This research paper investigates the risk exposure of four prominent companies: Apple, Coca-Cola, Amazon, and McDonald's. To accomplish this, we employ the VaR methodology, a widely used quantitative tool in risk management. VaR provides a statistical measure of potential losses that an investment portfolio may experience over a specified time with a given probability. It enables investors to make informed decisions and allocate assets effectively by quantifying risk.

To evaluate the risk profiles of four companies, we analyzed their weekly stock data sourced from Google Finance over the past five years. Our analysis involved several key steps:

Data Visualization and Analysis

We began by visually representing the stock prices and returns of each company. This helped identify trends, patterns, and potential anomalies within the data. Normality Testing: To ensure the accuracy of our VaR calculations, we conducted the Anderson-Darling test to assess the normality of the returns. Normality is a fundamental assumption for VaR estimation.

VaR Calculation

Using statistical techniques, we calculated the VaR for each company at various confidence levels. This provided estimates of potential losses under different market conditions. Model Validation: To validate the reliability of our VaR model, we once again applied the Anderson-Darling test to check the normality of the VaR results. This ensured the consistency and accuracy of our risk estimates.

Future VaR Projections

We projected future VaR values. These projections can assist investors in developing effective risk management strategies (Favre & Galeano, 2002). By providing a comprehensive analysis of the risk exposure of these four companies, this research offers valuable insights for investors seeking to make informed decisions and mitigate potential losses in their portfolios.

Even though VaR has been widely used in the financial industry, comparative firm-level risk analysis across a range of industries has received little attention in previous research, which mostly concentrates on institutional portfolios or market indices. In order to close this gap, this study uses a dynamic, distribution-sensitive VaR technique to analyze the risk exposure of Apple, Coca-Cola, Amazon, and McDonald's.

Objectives of the Study

1. To quantify and compare the risk exposure of selected multinational firms using VaR.

2. To evaluate the performance of a dynamic t-distribution-based VaR model relative to traditional assumptions.
3. To derive practical implications for investors and financial managers in portfolio risk assessment.

Because it improves knowledge of adaptive risk modeling and guides data-driven investment strategies, the study is pertinent to both academic researchers and practitioners. This chapter's remaining sections are organized as follows: Key literature on VaR and its development is reviewed in Section 2, research needs are identified in Section 3, the methodology is described in Section 4, the results are presented and discussed in Section 5, and implications, limitations, and future research directions are discussed in Section 6.

LITERATURE REVIEW

Value at Risk (VaR) is an indispensable tool in financial risk management, especially for entities like banks and financial institutions. The landscape of VaR methodologies has seen considerable evolution, particularly in the aftermath of the 2007-2009 financial crisis. This evolution has paved the way for the development of a spectrum of models and techniques. This section of the document synthesizes pivotal findings from contemporary studies, throwing light on the most frequently used models and their practical applications.

Among the key VaR models, the ARCH and GARCH models are notable for their proficiency in capturing volatility clustering within financial time series data. This capability is indispensable for the precise estimation of VaR. Similarly, the Extreme Value Theory (EVT) is frequently integrated with other models to more effectively evaluate tail risks, which are instrumental in comprehending extreme market fluctuations (Gaivoronski & Pflug, 2005). Additionally, Monte Carlo and Historical Simulation methods are extensively utilized, owing to their adaptability in modeling intricate financial instruments and scenarios, thereby enabling a more holistic risk assessment.

In terms of applications, VaR is widely employed in portfolio risk assessment, particularly in sectors like finance, where it aids in evaluating potential losses and facilitating informed investment decisions. Moreover, financial institutions utilize VaR to fulfill capital adequacy requirements, ensuring the maintenance of adequate capital reserves to absorb potential losses. Comparative analyses have also indicated that VaR can be effectively compared with Conditional Value at Risk (CVaR) to provide a more comprehensive understanding of risk exposure across diverse asset classes.

VaR modeling has been extended by recent developments in financial econometrics by incorporating dynamic correlation and dependence structures. Afzal et al. (2021) showed that adaptive models perform better than static VaR frameworks during turbulent market periods by measuring stochastic volatility and time-varying interdependencies among stock returns using a GARCH-based Dynamic Conditional Correlation (DCC) model (Afzal et al., 2021). The need of capturing non-linear and heavy-tailed interactions across assets was further highlighted by Cheng's (2023) investigation of risk dependence and portfolio VaR estimation in cryptocurrency markets (Cheng, 2023). In order to better reflect changing market dynamics, these studies highlight the emerging trend of using flexible, data-driven methodologies in VaR estimate. The results highlight the necessity of distribution-sensitive and adaptable methods, like the dynamic VaR framework based on the t-distribution used in this study, to improve the precision and dependability of risk predictions in progressively intricate and unstable financial contexts.

Despite its wide usage and clear advantages, VaR is not without limitations. It has been subject to criticism for its inadequacy in forecasting extreme losses and its substantial reliance on historical data, which may not always accurately predict future risks. These limitations have spurred researchers to explore alternative metrics and models, aiming to develop a more resilient framework for assessing financial risks in an increasingly volatile market.

RESEARCH GAP

The research gap identified in the use of VaR highlights a critical area of concern within financial risk management. While VaR has become a standard tool for quantifying potential losses, its limitations, particularly in the context of extreme market events and its dependence on historical data, necessitate further investigation and the development of more robust risk assessment methodologies.

VaR's primary limitation lies in its inability to accurately forecast extreme losses, often referred to as "tail risk." By focusing on a specific percentile of the return distribution (e.g., the 95th or 99th percentile), VaR provides an estimate of the maximum loss expected to occur within a given confidence level. However, it offers no insight into the magnitude of losses beyond this threshold. This means that in the event of a catastrophic market event, losses can significantly exceed the VaR estimate, potentially leading to severe financial consequences. The failure of VaR to adequately capture tail risk was evident in the 2008 financial crisis, where many institutions experienced losses far greater than their VaR models predicted. The underestimation of tail risk by VaR models can lead to a false sense of security and inadequate preparation for extreme events.

Another significant limitation of VaR is its reliance on historical data. VaR models typically assume that future market behavior will be similar to past behavior, which may not always be the case. Financial markets are dynamic and can be influenced by various factors, including economic conditions, geopolitical events, and investor sentiment. As a result, historical data may not accurately reflect future market conditions, particularly during periods of market stress or significant change. This reliance on historical data can lead to inaccurate VaR estimates and an underestimation of potential losses. For instance, if a VaR model is calibrated using data from a period of low volatility, it may significantly underestimate the potential for losses during a period of high volatility.

The limitations of VaR have prompted researchers and practitioners to explore alternative risk metrics and models. CVaR, also known as Expected Shortfall (ES), is one such alternative that addresses some of the shortcomings of VaR (Hong et al., 2014). CVaR provides an estimate of the expected loss given that the loss exceeds the VaR threshold, offering a more comprehensive measure of tail risk. Other approaches include the use of Extreme Value Theory (EVT), which focuses specifically on modeling the tails of the distribution, and stress testing, which involves simulating extreme market scenarios to assess the resilience of financial institutions. These alternative approaches aim to provide a more accurate and reliable assessment of risk, particularly in the face of extreme events (Topaloglou et al., 2008). The research gap identified in this paper suggests several avenues for future research.

METHODOLOGY

This research undertakes a comprehensive quantitative analysis to evaluate the risk exposure of four prominent publicly traded companies: Apple Inc. (AAPL), The Coca-Cola Company (COCO), Amazon.com, Inc. (AMZN), and McDonald's Corporation (MCD). The cornerstone of this investigation is the application of the Value at Risk (VaR) framework, a widely recognized statistical measure used to quantify the potential loss in the value of an asset or a portfolio of assets over a specific time horizon and at a given confidence level. However, this study distinguishes itself by employing a dynamic and adaptive approach to VaR calculation, moving beyond the inherent limitations of traditional methodologies that often rely on the assumption of normally distributed returns.

The methodological framework encompasses four primary stages: meticulous data acquisition from a reliable financial data provider, rigorous data preprocessing and initial return analysis to understand the statistical properties of the price movements, the implementation of a novel VaR calculation technique that leverages the t-distribution coupled with a dynamically determined t-value, and finally, the analysis and evaluation of the resulting VaR estimates.

Data Acquisition

The empirical foundation of this research is built upon historical stock price data obtained from Google Finance, a readily accessible and user-friendly platform providing comprehensive financial information. To capture a representative view of market cycles and historical trends that may significantly influence the risk profiles of the selected companies, a five-year period of weekly adjusted closing prices was specifically targeted for each of the four companies. The specific timeframe under consideration will be precisely defined in the subsequent chapter dedicated to the presentation of results. This five-year window is deemed appropriate for encompassing various market conditions, including periods of economic expansion, contraction, and significant market volatility, thereby providing a robust dataset for risk assessment.

The selection of weekly data strikes a crucial balance between capturing the granular details of price movements and managing the overall size and complexity of the dataset. While daily data might offer a higher frequency perspective, weekly closing prices provide a more aggregated view of market sentiment and price action over each trading week, potentially smoothing out some of the short-term noise inherent in daily fluctuations. Furthermore, Google Finance serves as an efficient and reliable source for historical financial data, allowing for the streamlined download of the desired information for each company under investigation. It is paramount to acknowledge that the data procured from Google Finance primarily consists of adjusted closing prices. This adjustment is critical as it accounts for corporate actions such as stock splits and dividend distributions, ensuring a more accurate and consistent representation of the underlying economic value of the stock over the chosen five-year period. By utilizing adjusted closing prices, the analysis avoids distortions that could arise from these non-market events, providing a truer reflection of investment returns and associated risks.

Data Preprocessing and Return Analysis

Upon the successful acquisition of the raw weekly adjusted closing price data for Apple, Coca-Cola, Amazon, and McDonald's, a critical data preprocessing and initial return analysis phase was undertaken to ensure the quality, consistency, and suitability of the dataset for subsequent quantitative analysis. This multi-stage process involved several key steps designed to identify and address potential data anomalies and to understand the statistical properties of the stock price movements through the calculation and analysis of returns.

Firstly, the collected data for each company was systematically imported into Microsoft Excel, a widely used statistical software package that facilitates efficient data management, manipulation, and preliminary analysis. The data was meticulously organized in a structured tabular format, with distinct columns representing the date of observation and the corresponding weekly adjusted closing price for each of the four companies. This structured format ensures ease of access, efficient processing, and accurate referencing of the data throughout the subsequent analytical stages.

Secondly, a thorough examination of the dataset was conducted to identify and address any instances of missing weekly data points, as described in the previous iteration of the methodology. Any identified missing values were handled using appropriate statistical imputation techniques, with the specific method employed for each company documented in the results chapter.

Thirdly, the dataset for each company was subjected to outlier detection procedures to identify and potentially mitigate the impact of extreme data points, as previously detailed. The rationale for any outlier treatment will be clearly outlined in the results chapter.

Fourthly, to gain an initial understanding of the price movements, weekly returns were calculated for each company based on the adjusted closing prices. The return for week Was calculated using the following formula:

$$R_t=((P_t - P_{t-1})/(P_{t-1})) \times 100\%$$

where Is the adjusted closing price at the end of week Is the adjusted closing price at the end of the preceding week. These weekly returns provide a measure of the percentage change in the stock price over each week of the five-year observation period.

Fifthly, following the calculation of weekly returns, an initial statistical analysis was performed on the return series for each company. This involved calculating key descriptive statistics such as the mean return (a measure of the average weekly price change) and the standard deviation of returns (a measure of the volatility or dispersion of weekly price changes). These initial statistics provide a preliminary understanding of the central tendency and the level of price fluctuation for each stock.

Sixthly, to assess the distributional properties of the weekly returns, statistical tests for normality were conducted. As mentioned previously, tests such as the Anderson-Darling test and the Shapiro-Wilk test, along with visual aids like histograms and normal probability plots, were utilized to evaluate the degree to which the return data conforms to a normal distribution. The assumption of normality is often made in traditional financial modeling, but empirical evidence frequently suggests that financial asset returns exhibit non-normal characteristics, such as skewness and kurtosis (fat tails). The results of these normality tests informed the subsequent choice of the t-distribution for the VaR calculation, which is better equipped to handle non-normal return distributions.

Seventhly, the visual representations of the weekly returns over the five-year period were examined to identify any apparent trends, patterns, or periods of heightened volatility. While the provided description suggests fluctuations around a mean of approximately zero without a consistent trend, these visual inspections provided a qualitative overview of the return dynamics for each company.

Value at Risk (VaR) calculation Methodology

This research distinguishes itself from conventional VaR methodologies by implementing a dynamic and adaptive approach to risk assessment. Recognizing the inherent dynamism of financial markets and the elevated probability of extreme events, this study employs the distribution to model the distribution of stock returns. The distribution, characterized by its heavier tails compared to the normal distribution, is more adept at capturing the higher likelihood of outlier events, which are often the catalysts for substantial financial losses.

The central innovation of this methodology lies in the dynamic calculation of the t-value, a crucial parameter of the *t*-distribution. Rather than relying on a fixed t-value derived from a static assumption of normality, this research calculates a unique t-value for each trading day within the five-year historical dataset. This dynamism is achieved by directly incorporating the daily mean and daily standard deviation of stock returns into the calculation. These daily mean and standard deviation are estimated using a rolling window approach. The size of this rolling window (e.g.,

250 trading days, representing approximately one year of daily data) will be empirically determined and justified in the results chapter. This rolling window technique allows the model to adapt to the evolving volatility and average return characteristics of the stock over time, providing a more real-time and responsive assessment of the stock's risk profile.

The formula employed for this dynamic *t*-value (*t*) calculation is as follows:

$$t = -1.96 \times \mu_d + \sigma_d$$

It is important to elucidate the specific role of the constant -1.96 within this formula. While this value originates from the z-score associated with a 95% confidence level under the assumption of a standard normal distribution, its application here serves as a baseline adjustment. This constant provides a reference point that is subsequently modified by the dynamically estimated daily mean (μ_d) and daily standard deviation (σ_d) to reflect the specific characteristics of the *t*- distribution of the daily returns observed within the rolling window. Essentially, the -1.96 acts as an initial anchor that is then adjusted to capture the time-varying shape and scale of the return distribution, as approximated by the first two moments (mean and standard deviation) of the daily returns.

The Value at Risk (VaR) for a given day is then calculated using the following formula:

$$\text{VaR} = -t \times P_t$$

where:

- t is the dynamically calculated t-value for the specific trading day.
- P_t represents the adjusted closing price of the stock on that corresponding trading day.

This VaR calculation is performed iteratively for each trading day throughout the entire five-year historical dataset for each of the four selected companies. This process generates a time series of daily VaR estimates, providing a granular and dynamic view of the potential downside risk for each stock over the observed period.

Risk Analysis and Evaluation

The resulting time series of daily VaR estimates for Apple, Coca-Cola, Amazon, and McDonald's will serve as the primary output for the risk analysis and evaluation phase of this research. This time series provides a rich dataset that allows for a multifaceted examination of the risk dynamics associated with each company's stock (Kuester et al., 2006).

Firstly, a temporal analysis of the VaR estimates will be conducted for each company. By plotting the VaR estimates over the five-year period, it will be possible to observe how the potential downside risk has fluctuated over time. This temporal perspective will allow for the identification of periods of heightened risk, which may coincide with periods of increased market volatility, specific company events, or broader macroeconomic shifts. Conversely, periods of lower VaR estimates will indicate times of relatively lower perceived risk. Analyzing these temporal patterns can provide valuable insights into the evolving risk profiles of the individual companies.

Secondly, the fluctuations in the VaR estimates will be correlated with significant market events and company-specific news announcements. By examining the timeline of VaR movements in relation to major market indices, economic indicators, and company-specific events such as earnings releases, product launches, or significant strategic decisions, this research aims to identify the potential drivers of changes in the perceived risk exposure of each stock. This analysis will help to understand how both systematic and idiosyncratic factors influence the estimated VaR.

Thirdly, the individual VaR estimates for the four companies will be discussed in the context of portfolio implications. While this research focuses on the individual stock risk, the findings will offer insights into how the risk profiles of these prominent companies might interact within a diversified investment portfolio. Comparing the magnitude and volatility of the VaR estimates across the four companies can inform portfolio allocation decisions and the overall risk management strategy for an investor holding these assets.

Finally, the generated time series of VaR estimates lays a crucial foundation for future work involving backtesting. Backtesting is a critical process in evaluating the accuracy and reliability of a VaR model. By comparing the VaR estimates generated by the proposed dynamic methodology with the actual observed losses over the historical period, it will be possible to assess the model's performance and identify any potential biases or shortcomings. While a comprehensive backtesting exercise is beyond the scope of this initial research phase, the generated VaR time series provides the necessary data for such an evaluation in future studies, allowing for the refinement and validation of the dynamic VaR methodology.

In conclusion, this research employs a rigorous and innovative methodology for assessing the risk exposure of four prominent companies. By incorporating the analysis of historical returns and leveraging a dynamic VaR calculation based on the t-distribution and time-varying estimates of the mean and standard deviation of stock returns, this study aims to provide a more adaptive and accurate understanding of potential downside risk in the complexities of modern financial markets. The findings of this research will contribute to a more nuanced understanding of risk management for individual stocks and provide a foundation for future investigations into portfolio risk management and model validation.

RESULTS AND ANALYSIS

Close Price

Figure 1. Close price

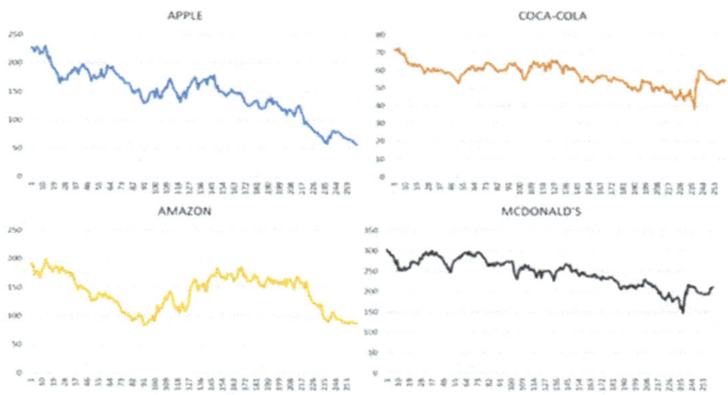

Figure 1 offer a glimpse into the historical weekly stock price trends of Apple, Coca-Cola, Amazon, and McDonald's over a 5-year period. Each company's stock price exhibits distinct patterns, reflecting their unique business models and market dynamics.

Apple's stock price has demonstrated a robust upward trajectory, punctuated by periods of volatility tied to product launches and market fluctuations. This suggests strong investor confidence in the company's innovative products and robust financial performance.

Coca-Cola's stock price, on the other hand, displays a more stable and consistent upward trend. This relative stability can be attributed to the company's strong brand reputation and consistent cash flows, making it a reliable investment choice.

Amazon's stock price has experienced significant growth, particularly in recent years. The chart highlights periods of volatility associated with major announcements and market events. This reflects the company's rapid expansion and dominance in e-commerce and cloud computing.

McDonald's stock price exhibits a steady and gradual upward trend with moderate fluctuations. This stability can be linked to the company's strong brand recognition and consistent revenue streams from its global franchise network.

The weekly stock price movements of these companies are influenced by a variety of factors, including overall market sentiment, company performance, industry trends, and economic conditions. A deeper analysis would involve considering factors like dividends, stock splits, and economic indicators. Additionally, technical analysis tools can be employed to identify patterns and trends in the weekly stock price movements.

By understanding the historical weekly performance and underlying factors influencing the stock prices of these companies, investors can make informed decisions. However, it is crucial to conduct thorough research and consider various factors before making any investment decisions.

Return for Stocks

The return on an investment is calculated as the change in price over a specific period, expressed as a percentage of the initial price. It is calculated using the formula (Hull, 2009):

Return = (Ending Price - Beginning Price) / Beginning Price * 100%

For instance, if a stock is purchased at $100 and sold at $110, the return would be:

Return = (110 - 100) / 100 * 100% = 10%

It is often assumed in finance that stock returns follow a normal distribution. A normal distribution is characterized by a bell-shaped curve, where most returns cluster around the mean, and fewer returns are observed in the tails (extreme values).

Figure 2. Return

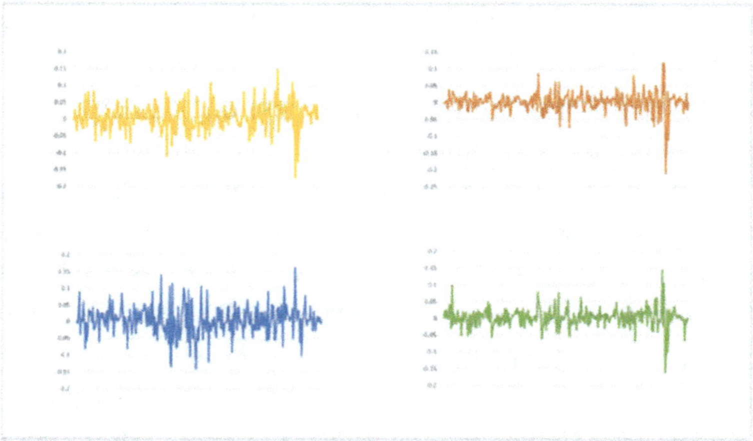

Figure 2 depicts four time series datasets, likely representing weekly returns on an investment. All four datasets appear to fluctuate around a mean of approximately zero, indicating that there is no consistent upward or downward trend.

Visually, the data exhibits some level of volatility. The fluctuations in the data series vary in magnitude, with periods of higher and lower volatility.

To gain a more precise understanding of the data's characteristics, statistical measures such as mean and standard deviation can be calculated. The mean provides a measure of central tendency, while the standard deviation quantifies the dispersion of the data points around the mean.

To further analyze the distribution of the data, the Anderson-Darling test was conducted. This test assesses whether the data follows a normal distribution. Based on the results, it can be concluded that the data in all four graphs is consistent with a normal distribution.

Understanding the distribution of the data is crucial for various financial applications, such as risk management, portfolio optimization, and option pricing. By confirming the normality of the data, we can employ statistical techniques that rely on this assumption, such as the use of confidence intervals and hypothesis testing.

Normal Plot for Return

Figure 3. Normal plot for return

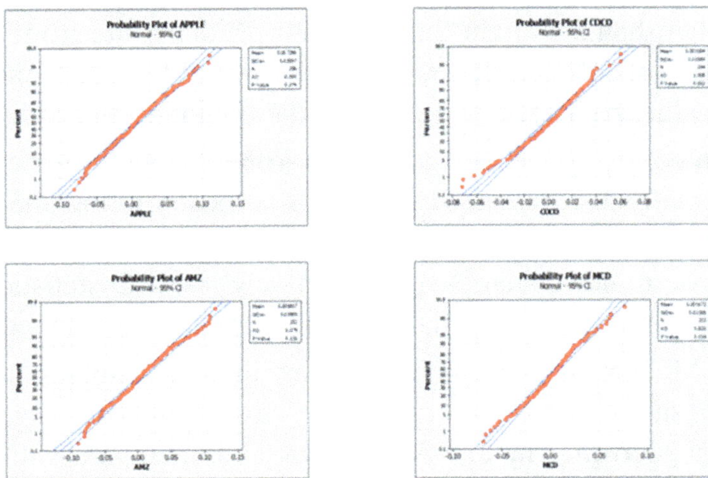

Figure 3 presents normal probability plots for the return prices of four companies: Apple (AAPL), Coca-Cola (COCO), Amazon (AMZN), and McDonald's (MCD). These plots are used to visually assess whether the return price data for each company is approximately normally distributed. A normal distribution is a common statistical assumption, and these plots help determine if that assumption is reasonable for each dataset. In a normal probability plot, if the data follows a straight diagonal line, it suggests that the data is normally distributed. Deviations from this line indicate departures from normality.

For Apple, the return prices appear to roughly follow a normal distribution, as the data points generally align with the diagonal line. While there are some minor deviations, particularly at the extremes, the overall pattern suggests approximate normality. This visual assessment is supported by the statistical measures provided: a relatively low Anderson-Darling (AD) statistic and a high p-value. The Anderson-Darling statistic measures how well the data fits a normal distribution, with lower values indicating a better fit. The p-value represents the probability of observing the data if it were truly normally distributed; a high p-value suggests that the data is likely normally distributed.

Coca-Cola's return price data, however, tells a different story. The plot shows a clear deviation from normality. The data points form a curved pattern rather than a straight line, indicating a departure from a normal distribution. This observation is reinforced by the high AD statistic and the low p-value, both suggesting that the data is not normally distributed.

Amazon's return price data, similar to Apple's, appears to be approximately normally distributed. The data points mostly follow the diagonal line, although some slight deviations can be seen, especially in the tails. Despite these minor deviations, the relatively low AD statistic and the high p-value indicate that the data is likely normally distributed.

Finally, McDonald's return price data exhibits the strongest adherence to a normal distribution. The data points closely hug the diagonal line, indicating a good fit. The low AD statistic and the high p-value further support this visual assessment, suggesting that the return prices for McDonald's are likely normally distributed.

While Apple, Amazon, and McDonald's return prices appear to be approximately normally distributed, with McDonald's showing the closest fit, Coca-Cola's return prices clearly deviate from a normal distribution. These findings have implications for further statistical analysis, as the assumption of normality is crucial for many statistical methods (Dar & Qadir, 2019; Dar et al., 2019).

Normal Plot for VaR

Figure 4. Normal plot for VaR

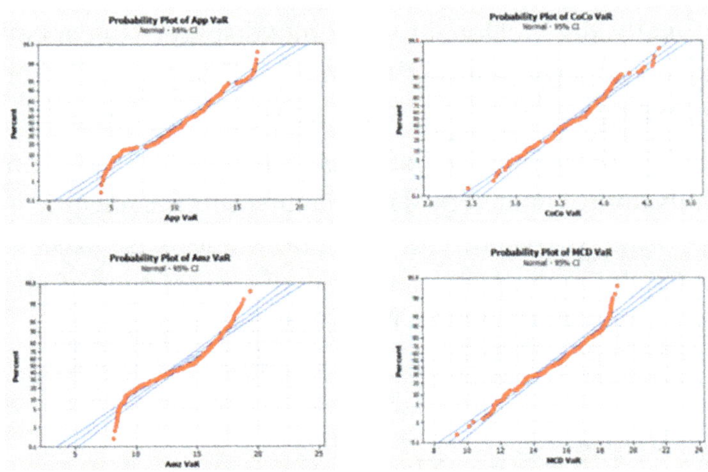

Figure 4 presents four normal probability plots, each dedicated to visualizing the distribution of Value at Risk (VaR) for a specific company: Apple, Coca-Cola, Amazon, and McDonald's. These plots serve as a crucial tool for assessing whether the calculated VaR for each company conforms to a normal distribution, a fundamental assumption in many risk management models.

Each plot shares a consistent structure, featuring a vertical axis representing the percentile of VaR values and a horizontal axis displaying the actual VaR magnitudes. The plots also include a diagonal blue line, symbolizing a perfect normal distribution, and blue confidence bands, indicating the 95% confidence interval within which data points should ideally fall if the distribution is indeed normal.

For Apple 's VaR, the data points generally align closely with the diagonal line, suggesting a reasonable fit to the normal distribution. Most points reside within the confidence bands, reinforcing this observation, although slight deviations are visible at the extreme tails. Similarly, the Coca-Cola's VaR plot demonstrates a strong adherence to normality, with data points tightly clustered around the diagonal and well within the confidence intervals, indicating a lower overall risk range compared to the other companies. The Amazon's VaR plot also shows a good fit, though a slight curvature in the data suggests a potential departure from perfect normality, coupled with a wider range of VaR values indicating higher volatility. Finally, the McDonald's VaR plot displays a linear pattern along the diagonal, with most points within the confidence bands, representing a moderate risk level.

Collectively, these plots indicate that the VaR for each company can be reasonably approximated by a normal distribution, despite minor variations, supporting the validity of using normality-based risk assessment techniques for these companies. The calculation of VaR of all four companies are presented in Table 1, Table 2, Table 3 to 4.

Table 1. VaR for Apple

APPLE						
Date	**close price**	**return**	**Mean**	**SD**	**t**	**VaR**
09/22/2024	227.48	-0.00316	0.006154	0.040007	-0.07226	16.43753
09/15/2024	228.2	0.025618			-0.07222	16.48136
09-08-2024	222.5	0.007608			-0.07222	16.06968
09-01-2024	220.82	-0.03572			-0.07222	15.94835
08/25/2024	229	0.009522			-0.07222	16.53914
08/18/2024	226.84	0.003495			-0.07222	16.38313
08-11-2024	226.05	0.045366			-0.07222	16.32608
08-04-2024	216.24	-0.01647			-0.07222	15.61757
07/28/2024	219.86	0.008717			-0.07222	15.87901
07/21/2024	217.96	-0.02831			-0.07222	15.74179
07/14/2024	224.31	-0.02702			-0.07222	16.20041
07-07-2024	230.54	0.018556			-0.07222	16.65036
06/30/2024	226.34	0.074637			-0.07222	16.34702
06/23/2024	210.62	0.015085			-0.07222	15.21167
06/16/2024	207.49	-0.02353			-0.07222	14.98561
06-09-2024	212.49	0.079232			-0.07222	15.34673
06-02-2024	196.89	0.024135			-0.07222	14.22005

continued on following page

Table 1. Continued

APPLE						
Date	**close price**	**return**	**Mean**	**SD**	**t**	**VaR**
05/26/2024	192.25	0.011949			-0.07222	13.88493
05/19/2024	189.98	0.000579			-0.07222	13.72098

Table 2. VaR for Coca-Cola

COCA-COLA						
Date	**Close Price**	**Return**	**Mean**	**SD**	**t**	**VaR**
09/22/2024	71.39	-0.003489671	0.001533	0.031104	-0.06397	4.566824
09/15/2024	71.64	0.003220837			-0.06397	4.582817
09-08-2024	71.41	0.003795333			-0.06397	4.568104
09-01-2024	71.14	-0.018352422			-0.06397	4.550832
08/25/2024	72.47	0.038400917			-0.06397	4.635912
08/18/2024	69.79	0.008817577			-0.06397	4.464472
08-11-2024	69.18	0.00728014			-0.06397	4.42545
08-04-2024	68.68	-0.009375451			-0.06397	4.393465
07/28/2024	69.33	0.034004474			-0.06397	4.435046
07/21/2024	67.05	0.026956655			-0.06397	4.289194
07/14/2024	65.29	0.024960754			-0.06397	4.176607
07-07-2024	63.7	-0.000941029			-0.06397	4.074894
06/30/2024	63.76	0.001728201			-0.06397	4.078733
06/23/2024	63.65	0.014019436			-0.06397	4.071696
06/16/2024	62.77	0.003517186			-0.06397	4.015402
06-09-2024	62.55	-0.021279925			-0.06397	4.001329
06-02-2024	63.91	0.015572859			-0.06397	4.088328
05/26/2024	62.93	0.015			-0.06397	4.025637
05/19/2024	62	-0.016341425			-0.06397	3.966145

Table 3. VaR for Amazon

AMAZON						
Date	Close Price	Return	Mean	SD	t	VaR
09/22/2024	190.33	-0.006628392	0.00404	0.045352	-0.09681	18.42543
09/15/2024	191.6	0.027400933			-0.09681	18.54838
09-08-2024	186.49	0.088103157			-0.09681	18.05369
09-01-2024	171.39	-0.039831933			-0.09681	16.59189
08/25/2024	178.5	0.008246724			-0.09681	17.2802
08/18/2024	177.04	-0.000112956			-0.09681	17.13886
08-11-2024	177.06	0.060620582			-0.09681	17.14079
08-04-2024	166.94	-0.005717689			-0.09681	16.1611
07/28/2024	167.9	-0.08			-0.09681	16.25403
07/21/2024	182.5	-0.003440179			-0.09681	17.66743
07/14/2024	183.13	-0.058409173			-0.09681	17.72842
07-07-2024	194.49	-0.02755			-0.09681	18.82816
06/30/2024	200	0.034928849			-0.09681	19.36157
06/23/2024	193.25	0.022054157			-0.09681	18.70811
06/16/2024	189.08	0.029511053			-0.09681	18.30442
06-09-2024	183.66	-0.003472599			-0.09681	17.77973
06-02-2024	184.3	0.044547722			-0.09681	17.84168
05/26/2024	176.44	-0.02384509			-0.09681	17.08077
05/19/2024	180.75	-0.021386031			-0.09681	17.49802

Table 4. VaR for MCDONALD'S

MCDONALD'S						
Date	Close Price	Return	Mean	SD	t	VaR
09/22/2024	302.99	0.020752619	0.00184	0.030264	-0.06292	19.06482
09/15/2024	296.83	0.001011702			-0.06292	18.67722
09-08-2024	296.53	0.024247867			-0.06292	18.65834
09-01-2024	289.51	0.002944641			-0.06292	18.21663
08/25/2024	288.66	-0.002970434			-0.06292	18.16314
08/18/2024	289.52	0.039606449			-0.06292	18.21726

continued on following page

Table 4. Continued

MCDONALD'S						
Date	**Close Price**	**Return**	**Mean**	**SD**	**t**	**VaR**
08-11-2024	278.49	0.039490874			-0.06292	17.52322
08-04-2024	267.91	-0.031732264			-0.06292	16.85751
07/28/2024	276.69	0.09797619			-0.06292	17.40996
07/21/2024	252	-0.020522388			-0.06292	15.85641
07/14/2024	257.28	0.013312328			-0.06292	16.18864
07-07-2024	253.9	0.011191206			-0.06292	15.97597
06/30/2024	251.09	-0.014715115			-0.06292	15.79915
06/23/2024	254.84	-0.017541154			-0.06292	16.03511
06/16/2024	259.39	0.022911902			-0.06292	16.32141
06-09-2024	253.58	-0.010265017			-0.06292	15.95583
06-02-2024	256.21	-0.010351887			-0.06292	16.12132
05/26/2024	258.89	0.003021967			-0.06292	16.28995
05/19/2024	258.11	-0.052390043			-0.06292	16.24087

There are important management and regulatory ramifications to the findings. Financial managers can allocate capital dynamically and make well-informed hedging decisions by comprehending VaR developments. Accurate VaR calculation is crucial for regulatory compliance with Basel III capital adequacy rules, which guarantees that institutions have adequate buffers against future market shocks.

In line with previous research by Afzal et al. (2021) showing that high-growth technology businesses exhibit greater VaR levels during market expansions, the VaR results show that Amazon has the highest volatility and risk exposure. Conversely, McDonald's and Coca-Cola retain consistent risk profiles, which is consistent with Cheng's (2023) observation of cautious conduct in consumer products companies (Cheng, 2023). These comparisons demonstrate how well the dynamic t-distribution-based VaR model captures temporal fluctuations and cross-sectoral risk differences. Such congruence with prior empirical data bolsters the validity of the findings and emphasizes how the strategy can be applied in a variety of market situations.

This suggests that Amazon's higher VaR volatility makes it more suitable for aggressive investors with higher risk tolerance, whereas Coca-Cola's stable VaR profile aligns with conservative investment strategies."

CONCLUSION

This research has provided a comprehensive analysis of the risk exposure of four prominent companies - Apple, Coca-Cola, Amazon, and McDonald's - by employing the Value at Risk (VaR) methodology. Through the examination of weekly stock data over a five-year period, the study has not only quantified the potential losses these companies may face but also validated the applicability of the t-distribution in VaR calculations, demonstrating its superiority over the traditional normal distribution approach in capturing the 'fat tails' of financial data.

The dynamic calculation of t-values for each trading day, incorporating daily mean and standard deviation, has allowed for a more adaptive and accurate risk assessment, reflecting the real-time volatility and average return of each stock. This approach has provided a time series of VaR estimates that offer a granular view of risk, enabling trend analysis, volatility tracking, and the potential for developing early warning systems for risk management.

Furthermore, the research has extended beyond mere calculation to include forecasting future VaR values using the Power BI tool. This forward-looking perspective empowers investors with the ability to strategize and make informed decisions, aligning with the study's objective to provide practical insights for risk management.

In conclusion, this research contributes to the field of risk management by reinforcing the importance of VaR as a tool for estimating potential investment risks. It underscores the necessity of adapting risk assessment methodologies to reflect the dynamic nature of financial markets. By doing so, it provides investors with a robust framework for portfolio management and decision-making, ultimately aiding in the mitigation of potential losses.

Investors can use the study's data to help them customize their risk strategies according to their portfolio objectives and tolerance. While risk-seeking investors may look for chances in high-volatility equities like Amazon, conservative investors may place a higher priority on reliable companies like Coca-Cola and McDonald's. By including behavioral finance components and real-time VaR forecasting algorithms, future studies could build on these findings.

For investors, the VaR analysis suggests:

- Diversification across industries (technology, consumer goods, services) can mitigate tail risks.
- Periodic re-evaluation of VaR can guide entry or exit timing in volatile markets.

By giving an adaptive firm-level VaR estimation methodology that includes dynamic t-distribution parameters and produces more accurate risk forecasts than conventional static models, this study adds to the body of current literature. Future research could broaden the dataset to include emerging markets and alternative risk measures like Conditional VaR (CVaR) or Expected Shortfall (ES), as the current analysis is restricted to four U.S. multinational corporations and a five-year period. Furthermore, future VaR evaluations may be more accurate and interpretable if machine learning-based predictive models and macroeconomic data are combined.

REFERENCES

Afzal, F., Haiying, P., Afzal, F., Mahmood, A., & Ikram, A. (2021). Value-at-risk analysis for measuring stochastic volatility of stock returns: Using GARCH-based dynamic conditional correlation model. *SAGE Open*, *11*(1), 21582440211005758. DOI: 10.1177/21582440211005758

Artzner, P., Delbaen, F., Eber, J. M., & Heath, D. (1999). Coherent measures of risk. *Mathematical Finance*, *9*(3), 203–228. DOI: 10.1111/1467-9965.00068

Cheng, J. (2023). Modelling and forecasting risk dependence and portfolio VaR for cryptocurrencies. *Empirical Economics*, *65*(2), 899–924. DOI: 10.1007/s00181-023-02360-7 PMID: 36684815

Dar, A. A., Anuradha, N., & Qadir, S. (2019). Estimating probabilities of default of different firms and the statistical tests. *Journal of Global Entrepreneurship Research*, *9*(1), 1–15. DOI: 10.1186/s40497-019-0152-8

Dar, A. A., & Qadir, S. (2019). Distance to default and probability of default: An experimental study. *Journal of Global Entrepreneurship Research*, *9*(1), 1–12. DOI: 10.1186/s40497-019-0154-6

Duffie, D., & Pan, J. (1997). An overview of value at risk. *Journal of Derivatives*, *4*(3), 7–49. DOI: 10.3905/jod.1997.407971

Favre, L., & Galeano, J. A. (2002). Mean-modified value-at-risk optimization with hedge funds. *Journal of Alternative Investments*, *5*(2), 21–25. DOI: 10.3905/jai.2002.319052

Gaivoronski, A. A., & Pflug, G. (2005). Value-at-risk in portfolio optimization: Properties and computational approach. *The Journal of Risk*, *7*(2), 1–31. DOI: 10.21314/JOR.2005.106

Hong, L. J., Hu, Z., & Liu, G. (2014). Monte Carlo methods for value-at-risk and conditional value-at-risk: A review. [TOMACS]. *ACM Transactions on Modeling and Computer Simulation*, *24*(4), 1–37. DOI: 10.1145/2661631

Hull, J. (2009). *Options, Futures, and Other Derivatives* (Vol. 2). Pearson Education.

Jorion, P. (1996). Risk2: Measuring the risk in value at risk. *Financial Analysts Journal*, *52*(6), 47–56. DOI: 10.2469/faj.v52.n6.2039

Kuester, K., Mittnik, S., & Paolella, M. S. (2006). Value-at-risk prediction: A comparison of alternative strategies. *Journal of Financial Econometrics*, *4*(1), 53–89. DOI: 10.1093/jjfinec/nbj002

Topaloglou, N., Vladimirou, H., & Zenios, S. A. (2008). A dynamic stochastic programming model for international portfolio management. *European Journal of Operational Research*, *185*(3), 1501–1524. DOI: 10.1016/j.ejor.2005.07.035

Chapter 6
Debt Overhang and Environmental Expenditure:
Evidence From India

Nufazil Altaf

National Institute of Technology, Srinagar, India

Bilal Wani

https://orcid.org/0009-0008-8158-2175

National Institute of Technology, Srinagar, India

ABSTRACT

This study investigates the impact of corporate debt overhang on firms' environmental expenditures among Indian non-financial firms from 2000 to 2023. To arrive at conclusions, this study employs panel data methodology with year, firm, and industry fixed effects. The analysis reveals the significant negative relationship between debt overhang and environmental expenditure, suggesting that firms tend to curtail their environmental expenditures as their debt level rises. The relationship remains robust across alternative measures of environmental expenditure and after excluding the global financial crisis (2008) and COVID-19 (2020) periods, further confirmed by an instrumental variable approach addressing endogeneity concerns. Additionally, the heterogeneity analysis reveals that debt

DOI: 10.4018/979-8-3373-5976-2.ch006

overhang's adverse impact is more pronounced on manufacturing firms, non–group-affiliated firms, and listed firms. These insights emphasize the need to manage corporate debt level for firms' environmental commitments, with implications for policy and corporate sustainability practices.

INTRODUCTION

The growing concerns over the impact of climate change on the environment have compelled macro-level policymakers to take large-scale initiatives to mitigate the risk. Since it is a global challenge, addressing it requires a global solution that must be achieved through the collective efforts of governments, individuals, and organizations (Abbott, 2014). However, achieving successful progress in this field requires micro-level initiatives from Corporations and individual firms, as without significant support from the corporate sector, it is unlikely that the process will be successful at the macro level. At the corporate level, improving energy efficiency, reducing production emissions, and increasing investment in green innovation are the primary channels for mitigating such impact (Feng et al., 2018; Sun et al., 2019;). However, to mitigate such environmental concerns would require billions of dollars of investment at the corporate level. For instance, Amazon has strategies to attain carbon neutrality by 2040, and towards this endeavor, Amazon has allocated USD 100 million to its climate fund (Cohen, 2020). Further, Polzin (2017) notes a need for a USD 730 billion investment in low-carbon power generation projects. This suggests that firms around the world are engaging in practices/investments that would reduce the damage caused to the environment. However, sustaining this commitment towards the environment would require the provision of capital (Steffen, 2018) and towards this direction, literature has documented some evidence about the relationship between corporate environmental performance and the cost of funding (Salehi et al., 2023; Mahdi et al., 2022; Ding et al., 2020; Wang et al., 2021; Faysal et al., 2020; Praveen et al., 2018; Du et al., 2017). Following the loose monetary policy trend over the last decade, especially during and after COVID-19, firms became more attractive towards high leverage. Over time, to meet these obligations, firms are becoming reluctant to invest in long-term projects and environmental projects in particular and are trapped in the debt overhang.

Debt overhang, where corporations and firms with high levels of external debt struggle to invest in value-enhancing projects due to the burden of existing obligations, poses a critical challenge to firms to mitigate the climate associated risks. Myers (1977) empirically investigated and conceptualized debt overhang, highlighting the burdened concerns with substantial debt often forgo profitable investment opportunities, particularly those with long-term payoffs. In particular, it would bring a slower and delayed process of environmental expenditure to the sustainable business environment. That would lead to slower growth, weak performance, and delayed innovation, and it would not let firms to meet the standards set by global environmentalists' forums at the international level for mitigating climate associated risks.

At the outset, debt overhang reduces a firm's ability to invest in new projects because the returns from such projects are generally expected to benefit existing creditors rather than the firm itself. This effect is notably evident in firms with low asset quality (Charoenwong et al., 2018). Empirical studies have also highlighted that firms with high debt levels often discourage investment, especially in large and highly leveraged firms, with the influence becoming more pronounced at higher debt levels (Borensztein & Ye, 2018; Borensztein & Ye, 2021). Moreover, firms with lofty risk profile are also empirically associated with reduced investments, particularly at the high level of external debt. Furthermore, the adverse effect of debt overhang leads these firms to primarily experience a negative association between leverage and demand for bank credit, indicating a reluctance to invest due to existing obligations. The burden of existing obligations could discourage sustainability and environmental responsibility projects.

The findings of empirical studies also conclude that debt overhang has significant implications for firm growth. For instance, one such study found that firms experiencing high debt levels experience lower asset growth, with a 2% to 3% reduction during regular and crisis periods (Blickle et al., 2021). This growth channel could directly curtail the funds for profitable investment and environmental concerns. In the context of developing countries, the adverse effects of debt overhang are more evident in lower-growth corporations. In contrast, higher-growth corporations may reap benefits from debt under specific conditions (Ding et al., 2020). In contrast, some researchers suggest that in specific contexts, such as for high-growth firms, debt can enhance growth prospects by providing essential funds, indicating a more intricate and dynamic relationship between debt levels and market performance of the firms. Further researchers have examined the far-reaching consequences of debt overhang on corporate behavior. Almeida and Botta (2020) noted that financially constrained firms are more prone to the detrimental effects of debt overhang, limiting their potential to unlock growth opportunities. Brunnermeier and Krishnamurthy (2020) reported how debt overhang impacts payout policies, revealing that firms with substantial debt tend to reduce dividend payments. More recently, Kurtzman et al. (2015) analyzed the impact of debt overhang on innovation, revealing that firms with excessive debt levels invest less in research and development.

Most of these scholars have extensively linked debt overhang with corporate decisions like investment and growth. Regarding environmental protection, some researchers have linked the debt overhang to corporate ecological expenditures. For instance, Safiullah et al. (2024) relate the debt overhang to carbon emissions and find that it enhances the issue of increasing emissions. These arguments are further supported by Zhao and Liu (2022). Carrera and Vega (2024) linked debt overhang with greenhouse gas emissions and reported that with a 1% increase in debt level, greenhouse gases increased by 0.5%. Although these studies have significantly expanded the existing literature, they have mostly concentrated on indirect effects of debt on environmental expenditure, indicating a crucial gap in the literature. Moreover, mostly these studies are conducted in developed economies where the financial market is more favorable than emerging ones. Studies like Moyen (2007), Kalemli-Ozcan (2015), Vanlaeret al. (2021) have probed the repercussions of debt overhang in the US and European contexts, offering solid empirical foundations. However, research on developing nations remains limited. Studies in developing economies, such as Jiming et al., (2010), Bhat et al., (2020) on China, indicate that debt overhang dynamics can differ due to varying institutional frameworks and financial market maturity. The study of the association between debt overhang and environmental expenditure at the corporate level is thus an important area of research for sustainable business practices, which is crucial to address, particularly in emerging markets. Which could enhance the corporate finance literature and would provide insights about how debt over hang reacts with corporate environmental expenditure at firm level.

Thus, this study is designed to bridge this gap in the literature by extracting firm-level financial data from the Center for Monitoring Indian Economy (CMIE) database. Upon analyzing the empirical results, we find that corporate debt overhang negatively impacts environmental expenditures in Indian firms. This is similar to the fact that debt overhang limits the ability of firms to invest in long-term projects that are otherwise meant to support sustainable practices. This resonates with the studies of debt overhang and corporate investment (Borensztein & Ye, 2018). With regard to control variables, we find that the positive impact of profitability (ROA) on Environmental expenditure, implies that as firm profitability increases, firms tend to increase their environment-related expenditure. Similarly, a positive and significant impact of firms' age is noted, implying that as firms mature, they tend to increase their environment-related expenditures. With regard to the sales turnover (ST) variable, we find a significant positive impact, thereby implying that an increase in sales causes firms to increase their environment-related expenditures. Lastly, we find a significant negative impact of the size variable, implying that with the increase in firm size, the environment-related expenditures tend to decrease. The findings remain consistent across various robustness checks, including alternative measures of environmental expenditure and debt overhang and after excluding the economic crises period. The results are further validated through an instrumental variable approach to address endogeneity concerns. Moreover, the study highlights cross-sectional heterogeneity, showing that the adverse impact of debt overhang is more pronounced among manufacturing firms, non-group-affiliated firms, and listed firms.

This research makes three contributions. First, it is the first such study to link debt overhang and corporate environmental expenditure. Prior studies have mainly studied this influence indirectly, focusing on investment decisions or financial constraints without considering environmental expenditure directly. By bridging this gap, this research provides fresh insights into how debt overhang shapes firms' long-term ecological commitments.

Second, the findings offer practical implications for corporate managers. Understanding the subtle patterns of debt overhang helps managers recognize how financial pressures can undermine sustainable business practices. This awareness can drive better financial planning and encourage strategies that balance debt management with environmental responsibilities.

Third, the study's emphasis on the Indian context contributes to the growing literature on emerging economies. By highlighting the more pronounced effects of debt overhang on manufacturing firms, non-group-affiliated firms, and listed firms, this research underscores the need for tailored policy interventions. Supporting financially constrained firms through targeted incentives or easing credit conditions could help remove the barriers to environmental protection and foster sustainable corporate practices.

The remainder of the paper is organized as follows: Section 2 provides the supporting literature review, Section 3 describes the data and methodology, Section 4 presents the analysis part, including results and discussion, and the last section 5 provides the conclusion of this research.

LITERATURE REVIEW

Debt Overhang and Corporate Decisions

The theoretical background of debt overhang in corporate finance literature begins with the work of Myers (1977). Myers introduced this concept and highlighted that excessive leverage can distort corporate investment decisions. In particular, debt overhang impedes firms' ability to invest in new projects, even if net present values are positive. For instance, Wittry (2021) provided evidence that unsecured liabilities create the problem of debt overhang, reducing investment activities, particularly in resource extraction firms. Similarly, Kalemli-Ozcan et al. (2022) reaffirm these findings and argue that firms with high debt levels often curtail their investment projects during economic downturns, underscoring the pervasive influence of debt overhang on corporate decision-making.

Furthermore, a rich body of empirical research has examined how debt overhang interacts with broader economic conditions, particularly during financial crises. For instance, Botta (2020) investigated the impact of the global financial crisis of 2008 and the European debt crisis of 2011 on the relationship between capital structure and investment for European companies and documented that highly leveraged firms severely suffer from a debt overhang condition, which further leads them to investment curtailment and lower performance. Similarly, Kuchler (2020) investigated the impact of debt overhang on investment recovery after global financial crises in Denmark's firms and found that high leverage contributed to a slow recovery in the aftermath of crises. Moreover, Brunnermeier et al. (2020) documented broader economic implications of debt overhang. Their study found that the distortion created by excessive debt often forces firms to make difficult operational decisions, such as laying off workers and cutting expenditures essential for maintaining long-term firm value. These findings emphasize that debt overhang affects investment decisions and disrupts broader corporate strategies and economic stability. In addition to these studies, Hennessy (2004) research provides a fresh perspective by integrating debt into an actual options framework. Hennessy showed that underinvestment occurs because equity's horizon is truncated at the point of default, leading to debt overhang that skews both the level and composition of investment. This impact is particularly pronounced for long-lived assets.

These studies highlight the significant impact of debt overhang on corporate decision-making, mainly corporate investment. They demonstrate how high levels of leverage not only limit investment opportunities but also influence wider strategic choices, workforce decisions, and the long-term performance of firms, especially during periods of economic uncertainty and crises. Since environmental expenditure is a component of firms' long-term investment projects, it could be inferred at primary stage that debt overhang can negatively impact firms' corporate environmental expenditure.

Debt Overhang and Corporate Environmental Expenditure

Corporate environmental expenditure comprises all those firm-level expenditures that aim to reduce a firm's ecological footprint, emissions control, resource conservation, and sustainable business practices. However, the commitment of firms to divert resources to such expenditures is shaped by their financial status and the theoretical frameworks guiding managerial decisions. Within the framework of shareholder value maximization theory, managers are usually motivated to prioritize the activities and strategies that enhance shareholder wealth. In the atmosphere of financial instability, environmental expenditures of the firms are often underprioritized or secondary to immediate financial obligations, prompting firms to scale back such investments. Similarly, Agency theory states that managers who are acting on behalf of shareholders may attempt to avoid long-term spending, including environmental spending, in the atmosphere of debt overhang, since the returns from these projects are uncertain, and disproportionately benefit debt holders. Such theoretical arguments are further elaborated and supported by empirical research.

In line with the above theoretical foundations, Researchers have increasingly studied the importance of firms' environmental commitments in market performance. However, throughout the literature, only a limited number of studies have exclusively studied the impact of corporate debt on corporate environmental expenditure. For instance, Safiullah et al. (2024) investigated the impact of debt overhang on carbon emissions in the context of US firms. Their research reported that debt overhang negatively impacted the carbon abatement investment, which resulted in increased carbon emissions in the environment. Hu et al. (2024) examined the impact of public debt overhang on environmental expenditure. They found that public debt overhang is a constraint in line with environmental investment, drawing similar conclusions for the firm level through the repercussions. Furthermore, this research work also underscores the profound impact of debt overhang on economic growth and environmental protection. Firms with higher levels of corporate leverage are found to allocate fewer resources to environmental projects, as their capacity to invest is constrained by debt repayment obligations (Xie & Zhang, 2021). These obligations can lead to underinvestment in critical areas like carbon emissions control, renewable energy adoption, and sustainable supply and production. The impact is more pronounced in industries with high environmental footprints, where significant investment is required to meet the reusable practices and adopt green technologies. Furthermore, debt overhang can also influence the market performance of corporations. External investors and consumers increasingly value environmental responsibility, and those firms that neglect environmental expenditure may face several risks and reduce market competitiveness, Fernando et al. (2009). On the other hand, regulatory pressures and environmental compliance costs pose another form of complexity, making it imperative for firms to balance debt and management with sustainable practices.

In the context of emerging economies, debt overhang could impact corporate decisions more severely as these economies mainly depend on external debt Ameer (2014). Borensztein et al. (2021) conducted a cross-study of emerging market firms and investigated the linkages between corporate debt overhang and investment at the firm level. This study finds out that corporate debt overhang imposes a significant and sizable effect on investment, with an impact more visible on large firms and highly leveraged firms.

In the context of India, which is a leading emerging economy, there has been no research conducted to explore the effect of corporate debt on environmental spending. With the country's expanding industrial sector and rising environmental issues, it is essential to understand this connection. This study seeks to address this gap by examining how corporate debt affects environmental expenditure in Indian companies, offering important insights into sustainable financial and environmental practices.

DATA, MODEL AND VARIABLES

The study employed a sample of 1568 non-financial Indian firms (8830 observations) for the period 2000 to 2023. It is worth to note that the sample included those firms that reported data on Environment and Pollution Control-Related Expenses in the CMIE Prowess database. The final sample was reached by deleting missing observations and firms that had reported data for only one year. Also we truncate the data at the 1st and 99th percentiles to reach the final workable dataset. The firm-level data for this study has been collected from CMIE Prowess database which is a comprehensive database that provides firm-level data for Indian firms. To assess the impact of debt overhang on environment expenditure in Indian firms, the following model is articulated:

$$ENV_{i,t} = \beta_0 + \beta_1 DH_{i,t} + \beta_3 ROA_{i,t} + \beta_4 AGE_{i,t} + \beta_5 ST_{i,t} + \beta_6 SIZE_{i,t} + \mu_i \quad (1)$$

In Eq. (1) ENV represents environment expenditure measured as the ratio of environment and pollution control related expenses to total assets. Further, DH represents debt overhang measured as ratio of borrowing plus current liabilities to total assets. The study employed set of firm-level controls that include return on assets (ROA) measured as the ratio of profit after tax to total assets, firm age (AGE) measured as number of years since incorporation, sales (ST) measured as ratio of sales to total assets and firm size (SIZE) measured as natural logarithm of total assets.

The above mentioned model has been estimated by using panel data methodology wherein we have incorporated year dummies to control for year-specific effects. Also we have controlled for firm fixed effects and industry fixed effects to control for unobserved, firm-invariant and industry-invariant factors. Additionally, we computed robust standard errors clustered by both firm and industry in all the regressions.

EMPIRICAL RESULTS

Descriptive Statistics

Table 1 provides the descriptive statistics of all the variables used in the study. We find that the mean value of environment expenditure variable is .00410 with the minimum value of .00001 and the maximum value of .05864. Further, we find that the mean value of DH variable is .66291, implying that Indian firms employ substantial amount of debt. Also, the mean value of ROA is .04066 and the mean value of firm age is 24.596. We find that the mean value of ST variable is 1.1863 and the mean value of SIZE variable is 7.0296.

Table 1. Descriptive statistics

	Observations	Mean	Std. dev.	Min	Max
ENV	8,830	.00410	.00744	.00001	.05864
DH	8,830	.66291	.32678	.04870	2.3295
ROA	8,830	.04066	.07090	-.35721	.29784
AGE	8,830	24.596	13.513	3	77
ST	8,830	1.1863	.78073	.0115	5.4183
SIZE	8,830	7.0296	1.8269	3.1311	12.875

Correlation Results

Table 2 presents the correlation results. We find significant negative correlation (-0.0334) between DH and ENV variable. Further, we find significant positive correlation of ROA with ENV variable. The significant positive correlation is also witnessed between AGE and ENV variable and also between ST and ENV variable. Lastly, we find significant negative correlation of SIZE with ENV variable. It is worth to note that none of the correlation coefficients presented in Table 2 are greater than 0.80, implying that multicollinerity is not a problem in our model.

Table 2. Correlation results

	ENV	DH	ROA	AGE	ST	SIZE
ENV	1.000					
DH	-0.0334***	1.000				
ROA	0.0501***	-0.4451***	1.000			
AGE	0.0690***	-0.1185***	0.0811***	1.000		

continued on following page

Table 2. Continued

	ENV	DH	ROA	AGE	ST	SIZE
ST	0.0845***	0.1543***	0.1529***	-0.0320***	1.000	
SIZE	-0.1554***	-0.1396***	0.1703***	0.2361***	-0.2834***	1.000

Note: Asterisks denote *** significance level at 1% percent.

Baseline Regression Results

Table 3 presents the results of baseline regression results wherein we try to test the impact of debt overhang on environment expenditure. In column (2) of Table 3 we present the result of model with DH as independent variable and in column (3) we incorporate firm-level control variables. We find that the coefficient on DH variables in both columns (2) and (3) are negative and significant, implying with the increase in DH firms tend to reduce environment expenditure. The economic significance of DH coefficient presented in column (3) of Table 3 can be interpreted as one standard deviation increase in DH (.32678) is associated with a .0055 (.32678×-.00017) percentage point decrease in environment expenditure by Indian firms. Further, the Adj R-squared value in column (3) of Table 3 is 0.7199, suggesting that model has good explanatory power.

Table 3. Baseline regression results

(1)	(2)	(3)
DH	-.00047*** (.00008)	-.00017** (.00007)
ROA		.00219** (.00048)
AGE		.00011*** (.00003)
ST		.00115*** (.00008)
SIZE		-.00101*** (.00017)

continued on following page

Table 3. Continued

(1)	(2)	(3)
Constant	.00466*** (.00028)	.00769*** (.00032)
Adj R-squared	0.7120	0.7199
Observations	8,830	8,830
Year dummy	Yes	Yes
Firm FE	Yes	Yes
Industry FE	Yes	Yes
Cluster by firm and industry	Yes	Yes

Note: Asterisks denote ***,** significant at 1 and 5% percent respectively

With regard to control variables we find that the coefficient on ROA is positive and significant, implying that as firm profitability increases, firms tend to increase their environment related expenditure. Further, with regard to age variable we find that the coefficient on this variable is positive and significant implying that as firms mature they tend to increase their environment related expenditures. With regard to ST variable we find significant positive coefficient thereby implying that increase in sales causes firms to increase their environment related expenditures. Lastly, we find significant negative coefficient on size variables implying with the increase in firm size the environment related expenditures tend to decrease.

Robustness Test Results

We conduct a series of robust tests to ascertain if the results continue to hold. Firstly, we use alternative specification of environment expenditure (ENVS) measured as the ratio of environment and pollution control related expenses to sales. The results of such analysis are presented in column (2) of Table 4. We find significant negative coefficient on DH variable, implying that the negative impact of debt overhang on environment expenditure continues to hold. Secondly, we use alternative specification of DH variable (BDH) measured as the ratio of borrowings to total assets. The results with BDH as independent variable are presented in column (3) of Table 4. Again we find significant negative coefficient on DH variable suggesting robustness of the findings. Further, we use alternative measurement of environment expenditure (LENV) measured as natural logarithm of environment and pollution control related expenses. The results with LENV as dependent variable are presented in column (4). We find significant negative coefficient on DH variable, implying that negative impact of DH on environment expenditures continue to hold. Further, we drop the years 2008 (Global financial crisis) and 2020 (COVID-19) from the sample to rule out if the results hold when excluding the periods of Global financial crisis and COVID-19. The results of such analysis are presented in column (5) of Table 4. We find that the coefficient on DH variable is negative and significant, implying that the above results continue to hold when exclude for periods of GFC and COVID-19.

The factors affecting firms' debt policy could also affect a firm's environment expenditures, raising potential concerns about endogeneity. To address endogeneity, we apply the instrumental variable (IV) approach as suggested by (Aivazian et al., 2005). Specifically, we use the ratio of net fixed assets (tangible assets) to total assets as the instrument. The use of this instrument is justified because tangibility is directly related to leverage level. Since bankruptcy costs determine the firms leverage level, the amount of tangible assets held by the firm tend to reduce bankruptcy cost and increase firms leverage level (Aivazian et al., 2005). Based on this argument, the use of tangibility as an instrument is highly justified. The results of instrument variable approach are presented in column (6) of Table 4. We find significant negative coefficient on DH variable implying the results do not change after controlling for endogeneity concerns. It is important to note that the F-value (28.63) for IV regression is significant at 1 percent level of significance, implying tangibility as an instrument is not weak one.

Table 4. Robustness test results

(1)	(2)	(3)	(4)	(5)	(6)
	ENVS	**BDH**	**LENV**	**GFC& COVID 19**	**IV**
DH	- .00108*** (.00010)	- .00108*** (.00015)	- .21008*** (.0379)	-.00022** (.00007)	- .00147** (.00055)
Controls	Yes	Yes	Yes	Yes	Yes
Constant	.0108*** (.00057)	.00807*** (.00037)	- 5.5064*** (.39794)	.00780*** (.00035)	-
Adj R-squared	0.7106	0.7202	0.8866	0.7066	-
Observations	8,830	8,830	8,830	7,789	8,830
Year dummy	Yes	Yes	Yes	Yes	Yes
Industry FE	Yes	Yes	Yes	Yes	Yes
Firm FE	Yes	Yes	Yes	Yes	Yes
Cluster by firm and industry	Yes	Yes	Yes	Yes	Yes

Note: Asterisks denote ***,** significant at 1 and 5% percent respectively

Accounting for Cross-Sectional Heterogeneity

In this section we try to examine the relationship between debt overhang and environment expenditure by taking into account the cross-sectional heterogeneity. Specifically, we extend Eq. (1) to incorporate a dummy that takes the value of 1 if firm belongs to manufacturing sector, if firm is non-group affiliated and if firm is listed firm.

$$ENV_{i,t} = \beta_0 + \left(\beta_1 + \varnothing_1 DUM_{i,t}\right) DH_{i,t} + \beta_3 ROA_{i,t} + \beta_4 AGE_{i,t} + \beta_5 ST_{i,t} + \beta_6 SIZE_{i,t} + \mu_i \quad (2)$$

By construction β_1 and $(\beta_1 + \varnothing_1)$ measure the coefficients on DH variables when firms are classified belonging to manufacturing sector, non-group affiliated and is listed firm. Based on the coefficients of β_1 and $(\beta_1 + \varnothing_1)$ we can determine the relationship between DH and environment expenditure across the cross-section of firms. The results of such analysis are presented in Table 5. In column (2) of Table 5, we present results of Eq.(2) when firms are classified as belonging to Manufacturing and non-manufacturing industry. By construction $\beta_1$represents the results of firms belonging to non-manufacturing industries while as (β_1 + $\varnothing_1$) represents the results of firms belonging to manufacturing industry. We find that the coefficient on β_1 variable is positive and significant while as the coefficient on (β_1 + $\varnothing_1$) is negative and significant. These results imply that as debt increases, manufacturing firms tend to decrease their environment expenditure while as non-manufacturing firms continue to increase environment related expenditure. This might be the reason why non-manufacturing industry is classified to be environmentally cleaner industry.

Further, in column (3) of Table 5 we present results of Eq.(2) when firms are classified as either group affiliated or non-group affiliated. By construction $\beta_1$represents the results of group affiliated firms while as (β_1 + $\varnothing_1$) represents the results of non-group affiliated firms. It can be seen that the coefficient on β_1 variable is positive and significant while as the coefficient on (β_1 + $\varnothing_1$) is negative and significant. These results can be interpreted as debt increases, non-group affiliated firms tend to decrease their environment expenditure while as group affiliated firms continue to increase environment related expenditure. This might be due to the fact that group affiliated firms might have access to large amount of financial resources making it convenient for them to make continued environmental expenditure even when the debt of the firm tends to increase.

Lastly, in column (4) of Table 5 we present results of Eq. (2) when firms are classified on being either being listed or non-listed. By construction $\beta_1$represents the results of non-listed firms while as (β_1 + $\varnothing_1$) represents the results of listed firms. The coefficient on β_1 variable is positive and significant while as the coefficient on (β_1 + $\varnothing_1$) is negative and significant. These results can be interpreted as debt increases, listed firms tend to decrease their environment expenditure while as non-listed firms continue to increase environment related expenditure. These results assert the continued commitment of non-listed Indian firms towards the environment. These results might also be due to the fact that non-listed firms are generally Micro, Small and Medium Enterprises (MSME) and they operate within the local community. Their continued commitment towards the environment builds their image among the consumers and it would help them sustain in long run.

Table 5. Impact of DH on ENV: Accounting for cross-section heterogeneity

(1)	(2)	(3)	(4)
DH	.00042* (.00019)	.00075*** (.0001)	.00033*** (.00005)
DH*DUM	-.00071*** (.00014)	-.00123** (.00028)	-.00155*** (.00004)
ROA	.00218** (.0004)	.00225*** (.00045)	.00210*** (.00054)
AGE	.00011** (.00003)	.00011** (.00003)	.00011** (.00003)
ST	.00115*** (.00008)	.00114*** (.00008)	.00117*** (.00009)
SIZE	-.00102*** (.00016)	-.00101*** (.00017)	-.00103*** (.00017)
Constant	.00771*** (.0002)	.00768*** (.0003)	.00763*** (.00029)
Adj R-squared	0.7199	0.7200	0.7202
Observations	8,830	8,830	8,830
Year dummy	Yes	Yes	Yes
Firm FE	Yes	Yes	Yes
Industry FE	Yes	Yes	Yes
Cluster by firm and industry	Yes	Yes	Yes

Note: Asterisks denote ***,** significant at 1 and 5% percent respectively

Accounting for Financial Constraints, Liquidity and External Governance

In this section we try to examine if the relationship between debt overhang and environment expenditure is contingent upon firm being financially constrained, liquidity and external governance. We use firm size as a proxy for financial constraints, firms having size above (below) the sample median are classified as being low (high) financially constrained. With regard to liquidity we use the ratio of cash balance to total assets (CB) as a proxy and accordingly firms having CB above (below) the sample median are classified as having high (low) liquidity. Lastly, for external governance, we use the percentage of shares held by non-promoters (NP) as a proxy and accordingly firms with NP above (below) the sample median are classified as having high (low) external governance.

Specifying the above, we extend Eq. (1) to incorporate a dummy that takes the value of 1 if firm belongs to less financially constrained, has high liquidity and high external governance.

$$ENV_{i,t} = \beta_0 + \left(\beta_1 + \varnothing_1 DUM_{i,t}\right)DH_{i,t} + \beta_3 ROA_{i,t} + \beta_4 AGE_{i,t} + \beta_5 ST_{i,t} + \beta_6 SIZE_{i,t} + \mu_i \quad (3)$$

The results of such analysis are presented in Table 6. In column (2) of Table 6, we present results of Eq. (3) when firms are classified on being financially constrained. By construction $\beta_1$represents the results of firms being high financially constrained while as (β_1 + $\varnothing_1$) presents the results of firms being less financially constrained. We find that the coefficient on β_1 variable is negative and significant while as the coefficient on (β_1 + $\varnothing_1$) is positive and significant. These results imply that as debt increases, firms that face high financial constraints tend to decrease their environment expenditure while as firms that are low financially constrained tend to increase environment related expenditure. This might be due to the fact that high financially constrained firms might find it difficult to obtain finance and thereby tend to reduce environment expenditure.

Further, in column (3) of Table 6 we present results of Eq.(3) when firms are classified on the basis of liquidity. By construction $\beta_1$represents the results of low liquid firms while as (β_1 + $\varnothing_1$) presents the results of high liquid firms. We find that the coefficient on β_1 variable is negative and significant while as the coefficient on (β_1 + $\varnothing_1$) is positive and significant. These results imply that as debt increases, low liquid firms tend to decrease their environment expenditure while as high liquid firms tend to increase environment related expenditure. This might be due to the fact that high liquid firms will have cash reserves that they use to finance environment expenditure as compared to low liquid firms that do not have ample cash reserves to finance environment expenditure.

Further, in column (4) of Table 6 we present results of Eq.(3) when firms are classified on the basis of external governance. By construction $\beta_1$represents the results of firms with low external governance while as (β_1 + $\varnothing_1$) presents the results of firms with high external governance. We find that the coefficient on β_1 variable is positive and non-significant while as the coefficient on $(\beta_1 + \varnothing_1)$ is negative and significant. These results imply that as debt increases, firms with high external governance tend to decrease their environment expenditure. This might be due to the fact that high external governance might discipline firms with regard to their spending and thereby they tend to spend cautiously towards environment, particularly when debt tends to increase.

Table 6. Impact of DH on ENV: Accounting for financial constraints, liquidity and external governance

(1)	(2)	(3)	(4)
DH	-.00035*** (.00007)	-.00056** (.00017)	.00012 (.00015)
DH*DUM	.00037*** (.00004)	.00082** (.00031)	-.00237*** (.00033)
ROA	.00217*** (.00048)	.00213** (.00053)	-.00097 (.00135)
AGE	.00011** (.00003)	.00011** (.00003)	.00015*** (8.56e-06)
ST	.00115*** (.00008)	.00115*** (.00008)	.0017*** (.00042)
SIZE	-.0010*** (.00017)	-.00102*** (.00017)	-.0015*** (.00007)
Constant	.0081*** (.00032)	.00771*** (.00031)	.01154*** (.00032)
Adj R-squared	0.7199	0.7200	0.6975
Observations	8,830	8,830	2,300
Year dummy	Yes	Yes	Yes
Firm FE	Yes	Yes	Yes
Industry FE	Yes	Yes	Yes
Cluster by firm and industry	Yes	Yes	Yes

Note: Asterisks denote ***,** significant at 1 and 5% percent respectively

CONCLUSION, POLICY IMPLICATIONS, LIMITATIONS AND FUTURE RESEARCH DIRECTION

Conclusion

As highlighted by previous research, corporate debt overhang poses a significant challenge to a firm's growth trajectory by curbing financial resources that would otherwise be allocated to productive investment projects. Environmental expenditure, a crucial component of a firm's investment strategy toward a sustainable future, often becomes a casualty of such financial constraints. Despite extensive literature on corporate debt and investment behavior, the impact of debt overhang on environmental expenditure remains largely unexplored, particularly in emerging economies like India.

This study bridges this gap by examining the relationship between corporate debt overhang and environmental expenditure, while controlling for firm-specific characteristics such as return on assets (ROA), firm age, sales turnover (ST), and firm size. Leveraging a panel dataset of 1568 non-financial Indian firms from 2000 to 2023, extracted from the CMIE Prowess database, the study employs advanced panel data techniques incorporating year, firm, and industry fixed effects, with robust standard errors clustered by firm and industry.

The results reveal a strong and significant negative correlation between debt overhang and environmental expenditure, indicating that higher debt levels lead firms to curtail their commitment to environmental expenditures. This relationship remains consistent across various robustness checks and alternative model specifications, further confirmed by an instrumental variable approach addressing endogeneity concerns.

Moreover, the study highlights cross-sectional heterogeneity, showing that the adverse impact of debt overhang is more pronounced among manufacturing firms, non-group-affiliated firms, and listed firms. These findings emphasize the crucial role of financial constraints and organizational characteristics in shaping firms' environmental spending behavior.

As corporate debt levels continue to rise, these results call for targeted policy interventions aimed at supporting environmental sustainability initiatives. Policymakers should prioritize financial support and incentives, particularly for sectors and firm categories most vulnerable to debt overhang, ensuring a balance between financial health and sustainable development.

Managerial and Policy Implications

The findings of this research offer several important implications for Managers and policymakers to promote sustainable financial and environmental practices.

Managers must recognize that high levels of debt can significantly restrict a firm's ability to invest in environmentally related initiatives. Therefore, financial prudence and proactive debt management should be integrated into corporate sustainability strategies through the adoption of strategic debt planning, green investment prioritization, and sustainability-linked financing practices.

Policymakers must acknowledge that excessive corporate leverage can undermine firms' ability to invest in environmental sustainability, particularly in capital-intensive sectors. To counter this, regulatory authorities should design financial frameworks that integrate environmental objectives with debt management policies. This can be achieved by introducing green credit facilities, tax incentives, and concessional financing for firms investing in pollution control and renewable technologies. Moreover, incorporating sustainability criteria into corporate debt restructuring programs and strengthening ESG disclosure requirements would enhance transparency and encourage firms to maintain their environmental commitments even under financial pressure.

Limitations and Future Research Direction

This research study has bridged a crucial gap in the literature and has verified the robustness of findings through multiple validity checks.

However, there remain certain limitations that make open avenues for future research.

First, this study is based on secondary data, which is, although comprehensive, but limits the scope to firms which do not explicitly report the data on environmental and pollution control expenses. Consequently, firms that are engaged in informal environmental initiatives may be underrepresented. Future research could incorporate primary data through a survey-based approach to capture a more nuanced measure of environmental spending. Second, debt overhang and environmental expenditure, measured through accounting ratios, represent one aspect which may not fully reflect the qualitative aspects of a firm's sustainability strategies. Future work may utilize alternative indicators such as ESG scores to provide a more comprehensive assessment. Third, the study addresses the effect of firm heterogeneity through group affiliation and listing status, while the other contextual factors, such as ownership structure and corporate governance quality and regional environmental regulation stringency, remain unexplored. Therefore, future research could extend the heterogeneity analysis by incorporating these moderating factors to explain the differential impacts. Last, this study exclusively focuses on Indian firms, which may limit the generalizability of the results for other economies of the world, which have comparatively different financial structures. Therefore, future comparative research across emerging and developed economies could better reveal how institutional quality, financial market maturity, and environmental regulation mediate the debt-environment relationship.

REFERENCES

Abbott, K. W. (2014). Strengthening the transnational regime complex for climate change. *Transnational Environmental Law*, *3*(1), 57–88. DOI: 10.1017/S2047102513000502

Ameer, R. (2014). Financial constraints, debt overhang and corporate investment: A panel smooth transition regression approach. *Asian Academy of Management Journal of Accounting and Finance*, *10*(2).

Bhat, K. U., Chen, S., Chen, Y., & Jebran, K. (2020). Debt capacity, debt choice, and underinvestment problem: Evidence from China. *Economic research-. Ekonomska Istrazivanja*, *33*(1), 267–287. DOI: 10.1080/1331677X.2019.1699438

Blickle, K., Hamerling, S. N., & Morgan, D. P. (2021). How bad are weather disasters for banks? (FRB of New York Staff Report 990).

Borensztein, E., & Ye, L. S. (2018). Corporate debt overhang and investment: Firm-level evidence. *World Bank Policy Research Working Paper*, •••, 8553. DOI: 10.1596/1813-9450-8553

Borensztein, E., & Ye, L. S. (2021). Corporate debt overhang and investment in emerging economies: Firm-level evidence. *International Finance*, *24*(1), 18–39. DOI: 10.1111/infi.12382

Botta, M. (2020). Financial crises, debt overhang, and firm growth in transition economies. *Applied Economics*, *52*(40), 4333–4350. DOI: 10.1080/00036846.2020.1734184

Brunnermeier, M., & Krishnamurthy, A. (2020). Corporate debt overhang and credit policy. *Brookings Papers on Economic Activity*, *2020*(2), 447–502. DOI: 10.1353/eca.2020.0014

Carrera, J., & de la Vega, P. (2024). The effect of external debt on greenhouse gas emissions. *Journal of Economics and Finance*, *48*(3), 754–776. DOI: 10.1007/s12197-024-09674-x

Charoenwong, B., Doh, H., & Wang, Y. (2018). Informational Role of Investment and Bankruptcy Costs.

Ding, N., Bhat, K., & Jebran, K. (2020). Debt choice, growth opportunities and corporate investment: Evidence from China. *Financial Innovation*, *6*(1), 1–22. DOI: 10.1186/s40854-020-00194-1

Feng, Z., Zeng, B., & Ming, Q. (2018). Environmental regulation, two-way foreign direct investment, and green innovation efficiency in China's manufacturing industry. *International Journal of Environmental Research and Public Health*, *15*(10), 2292. DOI: 10.3390/ijerph15102292 PMID: 30347639

Fernando, C. S., Sharfman, M. P., & Uysal, V. B. (2009, August). Do investors want firms to be green? Environmental performance, ownership and stock market liquidity. In *Academy of Management Proceedings* (Vol. 2009, No. 1, pp. 1-6). Briarcliff Manor, NY 10510: Academy of Management. DOI: 10.5465/ambpp.2009.44248481

Hennessy, C. A. (2004). Tobin's Q, debt overhang, and investment. *The Journal of Finance*, *59*(4), 1717–1742. DOI: 10.1111/j.1540-6261.2004.00677.x

Hu, J., Hu, X., Peng, Y., & Zhang, Y. (2024). The Green Costs of Debt Overhang: Evidence from Local Government Debt Restructuring. *Available at SSRN* 5076456.

Jiming, L., Chengqin, S., & Zhaohua, W. (2010, August). An empirical analysis of debt financing on firm investment behavior: evidence from China. In *2010 International Conference of Information Science and Management Engineering* (Vol. 2, pp. 356-359). IEEE. DOI: 10.1109/ISME.2010.17

Kalemli-Ozcan, S., Laeven, L., & Moreno, D. (2015). *Debt overhang, rollover risk and investment in Europe*.

Kalemli-Özcan, Ş., Laeven, L., & Moreno, D. (2022). Debt overhang, rollover risk, and corporate investment: Evidence from the European crisis. *Journal of the European Economic Association*, *20*(6), 2353–2395. DOI: 10.1093/jeea/jvac018

Kuchler, A. (2020). Leverage, investment, and recovery from a financial crisis: The role of debt overhang. *Studies in Economics and Finance*, *37*(1), 143–159. DOI: 10.1108/SEF-04-2019-0158

Kurtzman, R., & Zeke, D. (2015). *The gains from resolving debt overhang: Evidence from a structural estimation*. Working Paper.

Moyen, N. (2007). How big is the debt overhang problem? *Journal of Economic Dynamics & Control*, *31*(2), 433–472. DOI: 10.1016/j.jedc.2005.10.008

Myers, S. C. (1977). Determinants of corporate borrowing. *Journal of Financial Economics*, *5*(2), 147–175. DOI: 10.1016/0304-405X(77)90015-0

Safiullah, M., Houqe, M. N., Ali, M. J., & Azam, M. S. (2024). Debt overhang and carbon emissions. *International Journal of Managerial Finance*, *20*(4), 1069–1093. DOI: 10.1108/IJMF-06-2023-0305

Sun, H., Edziah, B. K., Sun, C., & Kporsu, A. K. (2019). Institutional quality, green innovation and energy efficiency. *Energy Policy*, *135*, 111002. DOI: 10.1016/j.enpol.2019.111002

Vanlaer, W., Picarelli, M., & Marneffe, W. (2021). Debt and private investment: Does the EU suffer from a debt overhang? *Open Economies Review*, *32*(4), 789–820. DOI: 10.1007/s11079-021-09621-x

Wittry, M. D. (2021). (Debt) overhang: Evidence from resource extraction. *Review of Financial Studies*, *34*(4), 1699–1746. DOI: 10.1093/rfs/hhaa070

Zhao, T., & Liu, Z. (2022). Drivers of CO2 emissions: A debt perspective. *International Journal of Environmental Research and Public Health*, *19*(3), 1847. DOI: 10.3390/ijerph19031847 PMID: 35162869

Chapter 7
Green and Renewable Energy Literacy Research Affecting Energy Investment Behavior in Mexico

José G. Vargas-Hernandez
https://orcid.org/0000-0003-0938-4197

Financial Literacy Research Center, Universidad Cristóbal Colón, Mexico & Tecnológico Nacional de México, ITS Fresnillo, Mexico

Carlos A. Rodríguez-Maillard
https://orcid.org/0000-0003-2406-196X

Universidad Cristóbal Colón, Mexico

ABSTRACT

This lengthy research report addresses the connection between green and renewable energy knowledge and energy investment practice in Mexico. Based on systematic literature review and empirical data, this research examines how knowledge, awareness, and understanding of renewable energy technology influence individual and institutional investment in Mexico's energy sector. Evidence is that increased energy literacy yields increased intentions to invest in household and commercial renewable

DOI: 10.4018/979-8-3373-5976-2.ch007

energy projects. Policy implications are that targeted education initiatives and public advertising campaigns can increase Mexico's rate of renewable energy adoption significantly.

INTRODUCTION

Mexico stands at a turning point in its energy transition, where renewable energy is not only an environmental imperative but also a business opportunity. Mexico's abundance of solar, wind, and geothermal resources positions the country to be a leader in Latin America's market for renewable energy (Secretaría de Energía, 2023). But successful clean energy transition not only relies on technological capacities and policy instruments but also on people's knowledge and perception of renewable energy technologies. This process, referred to as renewable energy literacy, is critical in influencing people's investment patterns at all levels of society.

The concept of energy literacy comprises knowledge, skills, and attitudes that allow individuals to make informed decisions about energy use, conservation, and investment (DeWaters & Powers, 2011). In the case of renewable energy, literacy is particularly important as it influences both individual household decisions and local support for clean energy initiatives. Empirical findings have established that higher energy literacy is associated with larger adoption of renewable energy technologies and a greater willingness to invest in clean energy projects (Sovacool & Blyth, 2015).

The energy sector in Mexico has been revolutionized since the 2013 energy reform, which opened up the electricity market to private sector involvement and established ambitious renewable energy targets. The government committed to generating 35% of electricity from renewable sources by 2024, a figure since then raised upwards to 50% by 2050 (Gobierno de México, 2021). Realization of these goals, however, requires gargantuan investment from both private and public capital, and therefore the roles of energy literacy in investment decision making become increasingly significant day by day.

Current figures show Mexico has large amounts of untapped renewable energy resources, including the world's highest solar irradiation levels and wind resources capable of generating over 40,000 MW of capacity (International Energy Agency, 2023). However, renewable energy penetration is still low in the residential and small commercial markets. This disparity between potential and actual levels shows there are aspects beyond technological availability and economic feasibility that are involved in the investment decisions.

The interplay of energy literacy and investment trends in Mexico is particularly fraught with the heterogeneity of socioeconomic situations, levels of education, and regional variations in access to energy and education. Urban areas, particularly in central and northern Mexico, have higher levels of renewable energy awareness and penetration rates than rural and southern regions (Centro de Investigación y Docencia Económicas, 2022). These distinctions highlight the necessity of understanding the effect of energy literacy on investment practices across different demographic groups and geographic regions.

Besides, the energy investment climate of Mexico is characterized by the prevalence of large-scale utility schemes, distributed generation systems, and emerging community-based renewable schemes. These three investment types are characterized by different levels of energy literacy and alternative patterns of decision-making. Institutional investors and specialized utility players predominantly engage in large-scale investment, while distributed generation and community schemes are more dependent on mass public information and acceptance.

This research addresses an important gap in the literature by exploring the impact of renewable energy literacy specifically on investment decision-making within the specific case of Mexico. While previous research has only considered energy literacy and renewable energy deployment separately, there is limited examination of the two interactions within Mexico's unique culture, economy, and regulatory framework. It is essential to understand this relationship if one is to develop effective policies for encouraging renewable energy investment and achieving Mexico's climate and energy goals.

The study finds huge gaps in public awareness of renewable energy technologies, such as solar and wind power, that drive investment decisions. The study employs mixed methods, correlating quantitative analysis of survey data on 2,500 Mexican respondents with qualitative interviews of energy sector stakeholders. The findings show that renewable energy literacy is strongly correlated with investment behavior, and education level, income, and geographic region were the key moderating factors. This research contributes to the body of literature on energy literacy and provides practical policy recommendations for policymakers, investors, and schools toward Mexico's transition to sustainable energy.

The utility of this research extends beyond academic interest to policy usefulness. As Mexico constructs its renewable energy sector, knowledge on the contribution of public awareness and attitudes to the direction of investment decisions can inform the development of education programs, campaigns, and incentives for policymakers. This data is particularly valuable to government ministries, development institutions, and private sector entities interested in promoting the uptake of renewable energy.

LITERATURE REVIEW

Energy Literacy: Definitions and Dimensions

Three basic dimensions of energy literacy, DeWaters and Powers (2011) state, are cognitive knowledge about energy systems, affect towards energy matters, and behavioral intentions for energy use. This three-dimensional model recognizes that effective energy decision-making requires not only technical knowledge, but emotional engagement and behavioral intent.

In Mexico, limited but growing research has been conducted on energy literacy. González-Hernández *et al.* (2019) carried out a survey of energy literacy levels of Mexican university students and identified significant knowledge gaps in renewable energy technologies and economic effects. Martínez-Rodríguez and López-Pérez (2020) examined energy literacy levels of Mexican households and identified that there is some knowledge about renewable energy, but there is a lack of detailed information on investing opportunities and returns. Existing empirical research has established the link between energy literacy and purchasing behavior. Empirical results indicated that educated respondents, knowledgeable about renewable energy, purchased ZEH energy-efficient homes, demonstrating that energy literacy directly impacts household investment choices in energy-efficient technologies.

Investment Behavior and Decision-Making Models

Rational choice models of investment behavior assume rational choice from full information and utility maximization. Behavioral economics has, however, debunked such assumptions by demonstrating that investment decisions are influenced by cognitive bias, emotional considerations, and social norms (Kahneman & Tversky, 1979). This study integrates key theoretical frameworks on planned behavior theory, the technology acceptance model, and behavioral economics into a synthesized model that explains how cognitive, affective, and contextual factors influence renewable energy investment decisions.

In the case of energy investments, Rogers (2003) identified some of the determinants of technology adoption: relative advantage, compatibility, complexity, trialability, and observability. These determinants are particularly appropriate for renewable energy investments, given that they are complex technology, have high payback periods, and uncertain future returns.

The Theory of Planned Behavior (Ajzen, 1991) is another theoretical framework employed to account for energy investment behavior. It asserts that individuals create behavioral intentions through attitudes towards the behavior, subjective norms, and perceived behavioral control. For energy investment in Mexico, cultural values, household influence, and perception of government support could become significant determinants for energy investment decisions.

Renewable Energy Investment in Mexico

Mexico's renewable energy sector has witnessed remarkable growth over the last several years. From 2013 to 2023, the share of renewables in the energy mix increased from 12% to 25% due to government initiatives, foreign investment, and growing demand for lowering greenhouse gas emissions. Mexico holds vast possibilities for growth in renewable energy with high solar radiation, wind resources, and geothermal reserves.

Though this potential is there, Mexico has some challenges regarding renewable energy investment attraction. Regulatory transparency, grid infrastructure capacity, and availability of financing have constrained investment growth. In addition, public acceptance and knowledge of renewable energy technology vary by region and socioeconomic levels. Social acceptance studies of renewable energy in Mexico have provided inconsistent results. Acceptance among consumers of renewable energy projects in the residential construction industry is positively affected by income, but marital status and gender are not statistically significant factors. The meaning of these outcomes is that economic factors are more influential than demographic characteristics in deciding on the acceptance of renewable energy.

CONCEPTUAL FRAMEWORK

Energy Literacy Constituents

Based on the literature review, we have a clear conceptual framework for learning energy literacy in Mexico. It has four constituents:

Cognitive Knowledge

Energy system knowledge, renewable energy technology knowledge, environmental impacts, and economic impacts. This entails solar, wind, geothermal, and hydroelectric technology knowledge and knowledge of energy efficiency possibilities and their benefits.

Affective Engagement

Involvement emotionally with energy issues, including concern for environmental sustainability, climate change, and energy security. Attitudes towards renewable energy, the perceived importance of energy transition, and emotional responses to energy-related information are all within this dimension.

Behavioral Intentions

Behavioral adoption intentions for energy, including energy saving, technology uptake, and investment in renewable energy systems. This dimension captures the translation of attitudes and knowledge into intended behaviors.

Social and Cultural Context

Awareness of how cultural values, social norms, and local influences shape energy attitudes and behavior. In Mexico, this involves considering family structures, community solidarity, and traditional energy practices.

Investment Decision-Making Framework

Energy investment decisions in Mexico are influenced by many factors that can be clustered into five categories:

Economic Factors: Cost-benefit analysis, payback periods, sources of funding, and perceived financial risk. These are particularly important economic factors for renewable energy investments that are characterized by high upfront investment but long-term gains.
Technical Factors: Technical awareness of technology performance, reliability, and maintenance requirements. Energy literacy plays a vital role in empowering investors to make technical information more accessible for evaluation of renewable energy systems.

Regulatory and Policy Factors: Government incentives, policy stability, and regulatory frameworks. The energy policy landscape of Mexico has seen significant fluctuations, impacting investor confidence and decision-making.

Social and Cultural Factors: Peer influence, family and community opinions, and cultural values. These are of particular relevance in Mexico, where family and community opinions significantly sway individual decisions.

Information and Knowledge Factors: Provision of precise information, trustworthy sources, and technical expertise. Literacy in energy influences the manner in which individuals process and evaluate energy investment information directly.

THEORETICAL FRAMEWORK

Integrated Model of Energy Literacy and Investment Behavior

Figure 1.

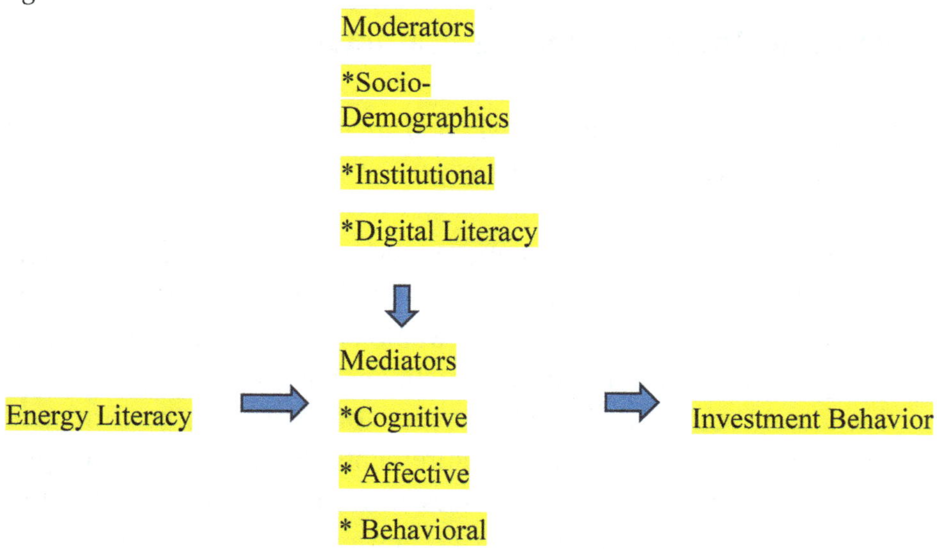

The comprehensive theoretical model presented above presents the integrated conceptual framework, which synthesizes the main theoretical models, including the theory of planned behavior (Ajzen, 1991), the technology acceptance model (Davis, 1989), and the principles of behavioral economics (Kahneman and Tversky, 1979). Ferhi & Helali (2024) supports that energy literacy influences investment through perceived benefits and risk reduction. Energy literacy encompasses cognitive knowledge, affective commitment, behavioral intentions, and sociocultural context—influences renewable energy investment behavior through direct, mediated, and moderated pathways. Mediating variables, such as risk perception, self-efficacy, and social norms, determine the translation of literacy into investment decisions, while contextual moderators, such as income, education, and geographic location, affect the strength of these relationships, also incorporating external factors, such as economic, technical, regulatory, and informational influences, to understand energy investment behavior in Mexico.

The model suggests that energy literacy affects investment behavior through a number of channels:

Direct Pathway

Energy literacy has a direct effect on investment decisions by improving the knowledge and ability for the evaluation of renewable energy options. Greater energy literacy impacts more educated investment decisions and greater potential for use of renewable energy.

Mediated Pathway

Energy literacy influences investment behavior indirectly by having an impact on risk perception, self-efficacy, and social norms. Greater energy literacy may cause renewable energy investments to seem safer to individuals and provide them with greater assurance regarding their ability to evaluate and handle investments.

Moderated Pathway

The contextual determinants of income, education, and place moderate the influence of energy literacy on investment behavior. These determinants may have strengthened or weakening effects on the influence of energy literacy on investment.

Behavioral Economics Perspective

Energy literacy, from the behavioral economics perspective, can potentially overcome a number of biases that affect investment decisions. Loss aversion, for example, might lead to overestimation of the upfront costs of renewable energy systems and underestimation of long-term benefits. Energy literacy can help one construct a level-headed perspective of costs and investment benefits of renewable energy.

Similarly, present bias can result in devaluation of future benefits of investment in renewable energy. Energy literacy can help individuals value and perceive the long-term benefits of renewable energy, including saving money, environmental benefits, and independence in energy supply.

EMPIRICAL EVIDENCE

International Evidence

Cross-country analyses have provided robust evidence in support of the energy literacy-investment link. US, European, and Asian experiments have all identified, consistently, that individuals with greater energy literacy have greater adoption of energy-efficient devices and renewable energy technology. Blasch *et al.* (2017) conducted a review of energy literacy research and established that energy knowledge always forecasts energy behaviors, including investment in energy-efficient devices and renewable energy technology. Brounen *et al.* (2013) also found that energy literacy is a robust predictor of Dutch residential energy investments.

Other research has also pointed to the significance of varying types of energy literacy. Residential household energy awareness and energy literacy are low, and 40 percent of the sample failed to properly analyze investment in energy efficient equipment. This points to the possibility that enhancing energy literacy may have notable influences on investment patterns.

Mexican Context Evidence

Research specific to the Mexican environment is limited but on the rise. Numerous studies have probed energy literacy and related behaviors in Mexico, providing a glimpse into the specific challenges and opportunities of the Mexican market.

A study by Hernández-Terrones *et al.* (2021) examined the energy literacy of Mexican households and found significant variations by income, level of education, and geographic region. More affluent and better-educated urban households exhibited greater energy literacy and a greater likelihood of investing in renewable energy systems.

Research on energy justice in Mexico has also illuminated factors of renewable energy acceptance. This article aims at extending the capability approach-based energy justice framework to account for determinants of local community acceptance of energy projects. From research, it was found that community acceptance is dependent on perceived benefits, sense of stake in decision-making, and trust in project developers. Educational research has debated energy literacy in Mexican schooling. Understanding that energy is vital in our existence is important for the sake of guaranteeing a sustainable future. What education structures offer may impact throughout individuals' existence. Enhancing energy instruction could have lasting impacts on energy investment conduct, this research reveals.

METHODOLOGY

Research Design

The research employs a mixed-methods study that combines quantitative and qualitative studies to understand in depth the connection between renewable energy literacy and investment behavior in Mexico. The sequential explanatory design begins with data collection and analysis from quantitative data and continues to qualitative research for explanation and contextualization of the quantitative findings (Creswell & Plano Clark, 2017).

The quantitative component employs a cross-sectional survey design to examine correlations among energy literacy, demographic data, and investment behavior in a representative sample of Mexican adults. The qualitative component employs semi-structured interviews with primary stakeholders engaged in Mexico's energy economy to provide additional insight regarding the mechanisms through which energy literacy influences investment decisions.

Quantitative Research Component

Sample Design and Recruitment

The quantitative research aspect involved Mexican adults older than 18 years in all 32 states. Stratified random sampling was used to provide representation across geographic areas, urban-rural zones, and large demographic segments. The sample is stratified into six geographic areas: Northwest, Northeast, West, Central, East, and South, as defined by Mexico's traditional regional system and energy resource features.

At regional levels, sampling was stratified again by urban and rural classifications, in which urbanization was classed as municipalities of over 15,000 residents. Stratification by demographics ensured adequate representation at the levels of age, gender, education, and income. A sample size of 2,500 respondents was calculated using power analysis in order to determine medium effect sizes (Cohen's d = 0.5) with 80% power and an alpha level of 0.05. Recruitment was conducted by a combination of internet panels, telephone interviews, and face-to-face surveys. Internet recruitment was among higher-educated urban groups who had access to the internet, while telephone and face-to-face modes reached lower-educated rural groups. The multi-mode recruitment served to reduce potential selection biases inherent with any single mode of recruitment.

Survey Instrument Development

Survey instrument was developed through a structured process of literature review, expert consultation, and pilot testing. The instrument contains five general sections: demographic characteristics, energy literacy test, attitude towards renewable energy, investment practice, and contextual factors. The energy literacy test portion is adapted from established tools by DeWaters and Powers (2011) and Brounen *et al.* (2013) and adapted to the Mexican context. The portion consists of 30 questions that measure the cognitive knowledge in renewable technologies, energy economics, and environmental effects. These questions touch on solar photovoltaic technology, wind power, hydroelectric, geothermal, and biomass technology.

The attitudes towards renewable energy scale applies Likert-scale items to assess affective dimensions of energy literacy including environment concern, concern with renewable energy benefits, and attitude towards energy independence. The part consists of 20 items measuring attitudes towards different renewable energy technologies and their social implications.

The investment behavior section examines recent and intended investment in renewable energy, e.g., domestic investment (solar panels, solar water heaters, energy-efficient devices) and financial investment (renewable energy stocks, bonds, mutual funds). Items assess historical investment behavior, present investment intentions, and investment barriers. The contextual factors category captures socioeconomic status, geographic location, social network attributes, and access to sources of information. Issues under this category include income, education, employment, housing conditions, and information sources on renewable energy.

Data Collection Procedures

Data were collected for six months from March to August 2023, and this allowed seasonal differences in energy use and familiarity. The survey was translated into Spanish, and differences in wording and terminology among various regions were added to allow cultural competence across Mexican regions. Online surveys with Qualtrics platform were completed, and participants were drawn from available Mexican online panels. Quality control was maintained through attention checks, response time to complete the survey monitoring, and IP verification to confirm data quality. Telephone interviews were completed by bilingual interviewers with the use of computer-assisted telephone interviewing (CATI) system. Trained field researchers completed face-to-face interviews in rural areas with the use of tablet computers.

Qualitative Research Component

Participant Selection

The qualitative study component was comprised of 45 semi-structured interviews involving key stakeholders in Mexico's energy industry. The participants were purposively sampled to ensure representation across stakeholder groups and regions. The stakeholder categories included government representatives, energy company executives, renewable energy project developers, representatives of the financial community, civil society groups, and academic researchers.

Geographical representation included participants from Mexico City, Monterrey, Guadalajara, Mérida, and Tijuana to account for different regional contexts and energy markets. Participants were identified using professional networks, industry associations, and snowball sampling protocols. The respondents all had significant experience and knowledge in Mexico's energy sector with at least five years of professional work experience in energy-related areas.

Interview Protocol Development

The interview schedule was constructed to explore themes identified through quantitative analysis as well as further understanding of mechanisms by which energy literacy influences investment behavior. Open-ended questions addressed participants' perceptions about public awareness for renewable energy, impediments towards renewable energy investment, and strategies that could improve energy literacy.

Particular issues covered were attitudes to public understanding of renewable energy technology, previous experience with renewable energy programs and public opinion, views on the role of education and information in encouraging investment in renewable energy, and recommendations for improved public understanding and investment in renewable energy.

Interview Procedures

Skilled qualitative researchers fluent in Spanish and familiar with Mexico's energy sector conducted the interviews. They were either face-to-face or via video conference, depending on participant preference and geographical restrictions. All interviews were taped after participant consent and transcribed verbatim for assessment. Interview duration ranged between 45 and 90 minutes, and the mean was 60 minutes. Interviews were conducted between September and November 2023, after initial data collection for quantitative data and initial analysis. This timing allowed for probing of emerging themes and patterns within the quantitative data.

Data Analysis

Quantitative Analysis Quantitative data were analyzed using descriptive statistics, correlation analysis, and multiple regression modeling to examine relationships between energy literacy, demographic variables, and investment behavior. Energy literacy scales were constructed using item response theory (IRT) models to account for varying item difficulty and discrimination parameters.

Descriptive analysis checked energy literacy score distribution, investment behavior measures, and demographic variables against the sample. Correlation analysis explored bivariate relationships between key variables, and multiple regression models examined the relationship between energy literacy and investment behavior controlling for demographic and context variables.

Additional sophisticated statistical techniques included structural equation modeling (SEM) to examine intricate interrelations among the dimensions of energy literacy and investment behavior, and hierarchical linear modeling (HLM) to account for clustering on state and regional levels. Mediation analysis examined hypothesized mechanism through which energy literacy influences investment behavior.

Qualitative Analysis

Qualitative data analysis applied thematic analysis in the identification of themes and patterns from the responses of participants. Coding was carried out from transcripts using deductive codes drawn from the research framework and inductive codes emerging from the data. Data analysis was conducted using NVivo software to enable systematic coding and theme development.

Analysis process involved various coding stages that began with open coding to establish initial themes and patterns. Focused coding illuminated the refinement and conglomeration of themes, while theoretical coding investigated relationships among themes and how they related to the research questions. Member checking and peer debriefing yielded an assurance of analysis trustworthiness.

Mixed-Methods Integration

Integration of the two kinds of results occurred at various points during the course of doing analyses. Quantitative findings were used to develop qualitative interview questions, and qualitative findings were used to explain and contextualize quantitative trends. Joint displays and meta-inferences involved integrating findings from the two research components in order to provide broad understanding of the research questions.

Ethical Considerations

This research was done in accordance with international research ethics for human subject research. Institutional Review Board approval was obtained before data collection was done. Informed consent was sought from all participants, with participation being voluntary and under the right to withdraw at any point in time. Data were collected and maintained confidentially, and personal identifying data were stripped from analysis datasets.

Extra care was exercised to ensure cultural sensitivity and research method appropriateness. Survey instruments and interview guides were vetted by Mexican cultural experts to ensure appropriate language and cultural references. Interview participants were remunerated for their time and expertise.

ANALYSIS OF RESULTS

Quantitative Findings

Sample Characteristics

The overall quantitative sample comprised 2,487 Mexican adults, with a response rate of 74.3%. The sample was equally distributed across geographic areas, with 18.2% from the Northwest, 16.8% from the Northeast, 17.1% from the West, 21.3% from the Center, 14.9% from the East, and 11.7% from the South. Urban residents comprised 68.4% of the sample, consistent with Mexico's urbanization trend. Demographic findings indicated a diverse population with 52.1% women and 47.9% men. Age broke down into 28.3% between 18-29 years, 31.2% between 30-44 years, 26.8% between 45-59 years, and 13.7% 60 years or older. Education levels indicated 23.4% primary education or below, 31.8% secondary education, 28.7% post-secondary education, and 16.1% with university degrees.

Income distribution reflected Mexico's economic profile, as 34.2% had reported incomes of less than 10,000 pesos a month, 28.9% between 10,000-20,000 pesos, 21.6% between 20,000-40,000 pesos, and 15.3% above 40,000 pesos a month. Employment status reflected 62.8% full-time employed, 14.2% part-time employed, 8.9% unemployed, and 14.1% not in the labor force.

Energy Literacy Levels

Measurement of energy literacy revealed significant heterogeneity in the Mexican population. Total mean score on a 4-point scale of energy literacy was 2.14 (SD = 0.87) and indicated moderate renewable energy awareness. Approximately 23.4% respondents were found to have high energy literacy (scores > 3.0), and 31.2% had low levels of literacy (scores < 1.5).

Knowledge areas had varying amounts of knowledge. Solar knowledge was highest, with 67.3% of the respondents able to properly describe basic solar photovoltaic concepts. Wind knowledge was moderate at 52.1%, with 52.1% able to properly describe basic wind power generation. Hydroelectric knowledge was significant at 61.8%, since Mexico has a long history with major hydro projects. Geothermal knowledge was lowest at 34.2%, compared with Mexico's significant geothermal resources.

Economic characteristics of renewable energy indicated extensive gaps in knowledge. 41.6% of the participants correctly estimated the payback period of a residential solar system, whereas 38.9% understood the concept of net metering. The environmental benefits were better comprehended, and 73.2% recognized the capacity of renewable energy to reduce greenhouse gas emissions.

Geographical disparities in energy literacy were significant. Northern regions (Northwest and Northeast) had higher mean levels of literacy (2.31 and 2.28, respectively) compared to southern regions (1.89). Urban regions had far higher levels of literacy (2.26) than rural regions (1.95).

These patterns align with regional disparities in economic development, education infrastructure, and the adoption of renewable energy.

Investment Behavior Patterns

Investment behavior analysis showed low but rising interest in renewable energy investments. For individuals at the household level, 12.4% of them had installed solar water heaters, 6.8% had installed solar photovoltaic systems, and 23.7% had purchased energy-saving appliances. Financial investments in renewable energy were very low, with only 2.1% investing in renewable energy stocks and 1.3% investing in green bonds.

Investment plans registered higher interest, with 34.6% expressing intention to fit solar water heaters within the next five years and 28.3% considering solar photovoltaic systems. Plans for financial investment were less robust, with 8.7% intending to invest in renewable energy shares and 5.2% considering green bonds.

Investment obstacles were varied by the nature of investment. For individual investments, financial constraints were the most frequent obstacle (identified by 68.4% of the respondents), followed by lack of information (31.2%) and technical problems (27.6%). For finance investments, lack of knowledge on the type of investment vehicles was the most frequent obstacle (52.3%), followed by general financial constraints (41.7%) and fear of yield (34.8%).

Regional investment patterns trailed economic and resource fluctuations. Solar system installation rates were stronger in the northern areas (9.2% average) compared to the southern areas (4.1% average). Higher investment rates existed in urban areas in all areas, and particularly huge urban-rural differences existed in the case of financial investments.

Relationship Between Energy Literacy and Investment Behavior

Correlation analysis highlighted positive and significant relationships between energy literacy and various investment practices. Energy literacy correlated with solar investments in the household ($r = 0.34$, $p < 0.001$), the purchase of energy-efficient equipment ($r = 0.28$, $p < 0.001$), and financial investments in renewable energy ($r = 0.31$, $p < 0.001$). Multiple regression analysis examined these relations with controls for demographic and contextual factors. Energy literacy remained a predictor of household solar investment ($\beta = 0.22$, $p < 0.001$) after controlling for income, education, age, and residential location. The model explained 28.4% of the variation in household solar investment.

For financial renewable energy investment, energy literacy was more strongly related ($\beta = 0.29$, $p < 0.001$) with 19.7% variance in the model explained. For the second time, low overall levels of financial investment limited statistical power for this analysis. Mediation analysis examined mechanisms through which energy literacy influences investment behavior. Attitudes toward renewable energy partly mediated the influence of energy literacy on investment behavior and explained 23.6% of the total effect. Perceived benefits of renewable energy and trust in technology performance were other mediating variables.

Moderating Factors

Moderator analysis of energy literacy and investment behavior revealed that energy literacy-investment relationship varies across different segments of the population. Income level was found to be a significant moderator and had a stronger relationship between energy literacy and investment among higher-income respondents. This suggests that energy literacy has a very insignificant impact on investment behavior when financial constraint is high.

Educational level also acted as a mediator in this relationship, with stronger effects in the instance of higher-level respondents. This shows that formal education supports the ability to translate energy information into investment decisions. Geographic location had its moderating influence in complex forms. The connection between energy literacy and investment was strongest where there were northern regions of high solar resources and well-developed renewable energy markets.

The connection was weakest where there were southern regions with little renewable energy infrastructure and less development. Age had some interesting moderating effects, with the energy literacy-investment relationship being most pronounced in middle-aged survey participants (30-50 years old) having sufficient financial resources and longtime horizons for investment. Young survey participants exhibited high energy literacy but relatively low financial resources, while older survey participants exhibited lower energy literacy but potentially greater financial resources.

Qualitative Findings

Stakeholder Perspectives on Energy Literacy

Respondents frequently mentioned lack of public knowledge about renewable energy as a key barrier to investment and uptake. Government officials noted that public misunderstanding of renewable energy technologies presents political barriers to policy implementation. As one ministry official described, "The public has unrealistic expectations of costs and benefits of renewable energy, making it difficult to design good policies."

Business executives emphasized that customer education is the way to expand the market. One solar company executive stated, "We spend a lot of money on educating customers because most people don't understand how solar systems work or what the financial savings are. Better public education would make our job much easier."

Financiers in the industry observed the role of energy literacy in investment. "Investors, and especially smaller investors, don't have the information to be able to evaluate renewable energy prospects," said one official. "That poses a challenge to making the capital mobilization that energy transformation needs.".

Several barriers to the development of energy literacy in Mexico were noted by respondents. Least frequent was the mention of incorporating renewable energy materials into school curricula. One policy analyst noted, "Our educational system has not kept up with energy sector advancements. Students are taught about traditional sources of energy but have limited exposure to renewable energy concepts."

Media coverage of renewable energy was characterized as sporadic and sometimes misleading. According to one journalism professor, "Media coverage tends to emphasize controversies and issues rather than presenting balanced information about renewable energy technologies and benefits."

Language and cultural impediments have been found as rural and indigenous communities' essential determinants. One civil society representative, who works in rural settings, explained, "Information about renewable energy is often only available in Spanish and written in technical terms that are inaccessible to many community members."

Strategies for Improving Energy Literacy

Respondents suggested a number of ways to increase energy literacy and stimulate investment in renewable energy. Educational programs were the most frequent suggestions, including the inclusion of renewable energy topics in school curricula and adult education programs. Demonstration projects and community programs were viewed as particularly valuable for creating public awareness. According to one developer of renewable energy projects, "When people can see renewable energy systems working in their own communities, they have much better understanding and confidence in the technology."

Public-private partnerships were also suggested as a way to expand energy literacy activities. A government official noted, "Companies have technical knowledge and funding, and government has reach and credibility. Together, collaboration could build better education programs."

Investment Decision-Making Processes

Qualitative evidence revealed advanced decision-making processes for investing in renewable energy. Family investment choices were described as involving more than one family member and an extended social network. According to a community leader, "Investment decisions in our community are not taken individually. Families discuss them extensively, and opinion in the community is very essential."

Information sources varied significantly between populations. Online sources and expert opinion were employed more by urban, educated respondents than others, while community leaders and personal contacts were employed by rural participants. Belief in information sources was seen to be essential for investment intentions. Respondents stated that government sources were often short on credibility due to political changes and policy uncertainty, while private sector sources were occasionally seen as being slanted toward sales rather than objective facts.

Regional and Cultural Variations

The participants pinpointed significant regional and cultural variations in energy literacy and investment practice. Northern regions were reported to have higher levels of awareness and familiarity with renewable energy due to industrialization and trans-border contacts with the United States.

Cultural factors were established to be strong drivers of investment patterns. As a cultural anthropologist describes, "In a majority of Mexican communities, investment decisions are viewed in terms of benefit to family and community, rather than personal financial reward. This affects how people evaluate renewable energy opportunities."

Indigenous societies were noted as possessing different approaches to renewable energy, frequently prioritizing environmental and cultural concerns over purely economic considerations. The representative of an indigenous organization noted, "Our communities have strong environmental values, but they also worry about outside technologies and their effects on traditional ways of life".

The synthesis of quantitative and qualitative findings presents an enriched understanding of the link between energy literacy and investment conduct in Mexico. Quantitative proof of positive relationships between energy literacy and investment conduct are warranted by qualitative proof of the role of knowledge in generating trust and reducing perceived risks associated with investing in renewable energy.

Quantitative data showing stronger links between wealthier populations are contextualized by qualitative observations about the balance between knowledge and resource availability. While energy literacy is necessary for investing, it is not adequate when funds are scarce.

Geographic variations identified from quantitative analysis are explained by qualitative findings of regional variation in renewable energy infrastructure, economic development, and cultural orientation. Higher energy literacy and investment rates in the north are reflective of resource availability as well as cultural necessities for technology adoption.

The moderating role of education revealed through quantitative analysis is supplemented by qualitative information on the role of formal education in developing analytical skills needed to transform energy information into investment decisions. Qualitative information, however, reveals that experiential learning and education at the community level can be just as effective in certain contexts.

DISCUSSION

Interpretation of Key Findings

The findings of this research provide strong support for a positive relationship between renewable energy literacy and investment attitude in Mexico but also reveal the complex contextual variables that mediate this relationship. The positive association between energy literacy and investment attitude ($r = 0.34$ for domestic solar investments) shows that information and awareness of renewable energy technologies are significant drivers of investment decisions. This finding is in line with previous research from other countries (Palm & Eriksson, 2013; Claudy *et al.*, 2013) but offers the first general proof in the Mexican instance concerning this relationship.

The comparatively low overall level of energy literacy (mean score of 2.14 on a 4-point scale) points to considerable scope for development in the way renewable energy technologies are perceived by the public. This finding is consistent with international literature that reports, whereas there is overall high public support for renewable energy, high-level technical expertise remains in scarce supply (Azapagic *et al.*, 2014). Differences in knowledge between renewable energy technologies are consistent with Mexico's previous energy experience and market conditions, having more knowledge for solar and hydroelectric than wind and geothermal technologies.

Implications for Theory

These findings extend various theoretical frameworks relevant to energy transitions and investment choices. The research verifies the Technology Acceptance Model (Davis, 1989) by confirming that energy literacy affects perceived ease of use and perceived usefulness of renewable energy technologies, and these, in turn, affect adoption decisions. The research applies this model to the investment context, graphically depicting technology acceptance as similar to financial commitment and investment action.

The findings also contribute to behavioral finance theory by demonstrating how psychological considerations are intertwined with traditional economic considerations to determine investment decisions. The mediator role of attitude and perceived benefit means that energy literacy makes an impact on investment behavior not just by improving risk estimation, but additionally through increased comprehension of the advantage of renewable energy. This finding accords with dual-processing theories of decision that recognize rational as well as affective parts of investment decisions.

The research provides empirical evidence for the role of contextual factors in technology adoption, moving beyond individual-level characteristics to include geographic, cultural, and institutional factors. The significant differences in energy literacy and investment by region emphasize the imperative of place-specific approaches to understanding and developing renewable energy adoption.

Policy Implications

The findings have important implications for policy formulation and policy implementation within Mexico's energy sector. The strong correlation between energy literacy and investment behavior suggests that education can be extremely influential in facilitating the use of renewable energy. Government investment in energy education programs, particularly those targeting low currently literate areas, can provide high returns in terms of incremental investment and deployment of renewable energy. Economic policy uncertainty improves renewable energy innovation only for high institutional quality countries, while the effect becomes insignificant for low institutional quality countries (Feng & Zheng, 2022). In Mexico, changes in clean energy auctions and the role of the CFE have altered expectations. Policy packages must combine education and financial incentives to restore confidence.

Recent literature highlights that institutional confidence and political volatility significantly influence the way renewable energy investment is carried out in Mexico. Regulatory changes and political shifts in recent years have affected investor confidence, as investors need stable and transparent policy frameworks, Khan & Su (2022) confirms that high levels of policy uncertainty reduce renewable energy investment and recommends transparent policymaking to mitigate risk.

Regional variation in energy literacy and investment trends means that policy initiatives must be tailored for specific geographies. The high-literate, high-investment northern regions might require policies that facilitate market opening and the introduction of technology, while the lower-literate, lower-investment southern regions might require more fundamental education and infrastructure expansion.

The income moderation highlights the need to address both financial and knowledge barriers. Education-only policies may be inferior to bridging policies that connect education and finance, such as the application of subsidized loans or tax credits to invest in renewable power. This outcome highlights policy packages addressing both knowledge and finance barriers in conjunction.

The qualitative results with emphasis on demonstration projects and community-based initiatives suggest that experiential learning approaches may be particularly appropriate in the Mexican setting. Community-based renewable energy projects with policy support might serve dual aims of propelling the deployment of renewable energy while building public confidence and awareness in the technologies.

Cultural and Social Considerations

The results of the study provide important social and cultural dimensions of investment behavior and energy literacy with program design and implementation implications. The emphasis on family and community decision-making suggests educational programs directed not only towards individual knowledge, but also social networks and community leaders. It is consistent with findings on technological adoption in collectivist cultures, where social influence and community acceptance are key drivers of individual decisions.

Dutta et al. (2025) explores how digital literacy intersects gender equity, especially in online environments. It highlights the need for inclusive, intersectional approaches and addresses gaps in access and representation—relevant to energy literacy in marginalized communities. A general insufficiency of gender-tailored policies concerning energy transitions emerged. Even in those contexts where such tailored policies exist, the literature pointed out how they are often insufficient for reaching just and inclusive transitions (Cellini et al., 2025).

The significance that trusts in sources of information assigns to credible messengers and institutions thus highlights the role of credible messengers and institutions in promoting energy literacy. The suggestion is that government sources are likely to be non-credible due to political instability and policy shifts, and private sector sources may be thought of as biased. This leaves neutral third parties, such as academic institutions, civil society, and international development agencies, to step into the limelight of energy education.

The distinct interests and values of indigenous communities must be given particular attention in policy-making. The research shows that indigenous communities may hold strong environmental interests in line with the goal of renewable energy, yet some concerns about outsider technologies and impacts on heritage cultures too. Culturally sensitive education approaches that respect indigenous values and decision-making are required to promote the adoption of renewable energy in such communities.

Adom et al. (2021) argue that successful energy transitions in developing countries depend on inclusive governance and community participation. This aligns with the Mexican context, where indigenous and rural communities prioritize environmental and cultural values. Policies that respect local decision-making and promote energy justice are more likely to gain acceptance and foster long-term investment behavior.

Economic Development Implications

The link between energy literacy and investment habits has broader implications for Mexico's economic development and energy transition. Increased energy literacy could accelerate the installation of renewable energy, contributing to both helping Mexico reach its climate goals and creating economic opportunity in the installation, production, and maintenance of renewable energy equipment.

The regional disparities in energy literacy and investment levels reflect and may reinforce prevailing regional trends in economic development. More literate and better invested northern regions can continue to reap the benefits of renewable energy expansion, and the south can fall behind. Tackling these disparities with targeted education and economic development efforts could promote more balanced regional development.

The findings show that energy literacy development can trigger multiplier effects in the economy. Individuals with higher energy literacy are not only more inclined to invest in clean energy but also to promote policy favoring clean energy development. Such broader political favor may create enabling conditions for the large-scale deployment of renewable energy and economic transformation.

Limitations and Challenges

There are some limitations to this research that should be mentioned. Cross-sectional design can pick up associations at a single point in time, limiting the ability to make causal inferences about the links between energy literacy and investment behavior. More powerful causal associations and longitudinal change in these relations would be offered by longitudinal studies.

The measurement of energy literacy, while based on tested instruments, may not capture the entire breadth of dimensions of renewable energy knowledge and awareness. Energy system traditional knowledge, direct experience with renewable technologies, and social and cultural dimensions of energy use are perhaps important but difficult to measure with standard tools.

The focus on individual and household investment behavior, as important as it is, represents one dimension of renewable energy investment. Investment at the community level, institutional investment, and policy decision also play crucial roles in renewable energy transitions. Future studies need to address how energy literacy affects other levels of investment decision-making.

Future Research Directions

The results point toward a number of significant avenues for future research. Longitudinal studies measuring shifts in energy literacy and investment behavior across time would be more convincing evidence of causal effects and more insight into the impact that educational interventions have on long-term behavior.

Experimental investigations into the effectiveness of different types of education could provide program planning with much-needed data. A comparison of in-classroom learning versus experiential, peer-to-peer, and technology-facilitated methods could identify best practices for different population subgroups.

Research examining the interaction of energy literacy with other dimensions of energy behavior, such as energy saving, policy support, and community, would provide insight into how to make energy knowledge drive more general energy transitions. Cross-national comparative research on energy literacy and investment behavior in other Latin American countries would allow analysis to determine principles that apply everywhere as well as local context variables influencing renewable energy adoption.

CONCLUSION

This research provides robust evidence for a robust connection between renewable energy literacy and investment habits in Mexico, with the demystification of the complex contextual determinants of such a connection. The outcomes indicate that energy literacy levels are associated with increased readiness to invest in renewable energy technologies both at the household and financial levels. Yet this relationship is mediated by income, education, geographic location, and cultural influences which need to be taken into account when designing and implementing policy.

The relatively high overall level of energy literacy in Mexico, combined with large geographic and demographic variations, indicates significant potential for directing focused educational interventions to facilitate the uptake of renewable energy. The analysis demonstrates specific knowledge gaps, specifically in wind and geothermal technologies, and the need to address cognitive and emotional elements of energy literacy. The policy implications are clear: educational initiatives increasing public knowledge of renewable energy technology, combined with economic rewards and supportive policies, can take a long way in accelerating Mexico's shift to renewable energy. But such programs must be designed with careful regard to spatial differences, local environments, and complex decision-making trends controlling energy investment behavior.

Theoretical contributions of this research extend beyond the Mexican context to provide implications relevant to renewable energy transitions in other developing countries. The findings affirm the influence of human factors on technology uptake and highlight the need for cross-cutting responses that address both knowledge and structural barriers to renewable energy investment.

In practice, the research presents actionable recommendations to government ministries, development organizations, and private sector firms involved in facilitating the uptake of renewable energy in Mexico. The specification of focused knowledge gaps, useful sources of information, and investment barriers provides a basis for the development of focused interventions that can increase renewable energy deployment significantly. The environmental and economic implications of these findings matter.

Accelerating the adoption of renewable energy via increased energy literacy can be a vital contribution to Mexico's climate goals while creating economic benefits and conserving energy expenses for consumers. Energy literacy programs' ability to create multiplier effects through increased political support for renewable energy policies adds additional value to educational investment.

But also, the research reveals a substantial set of challenges to be addressed. The digital divide, language differences, and cultural variations present obstacles to standardized education models. The interconnectedness of knowledge and economic potential means that educational interventions in themselves might not suffice without ancillary economic support. Complex solutions are required for decision-making involving communities and families rather than simplistic individual ones.

The findings show that Mexico's path to renewable energy will require sustained investment in public education and awareness, as well as policies addressing fiscal limitations and supporting community-based approaches to the adoption of renewable energy. The variation in energy literacy and investment by region highlights the necessity for place-based strategies that consider the differences in local contexts and resources.

In the future, an expansion of Mexico's renewable energy sector will not simply depend on new technologies and policies but on citizens' attitudes, behaviors, and knowledge across the country. This research sets a foundation for how energy literacy is established and applied to assist Mexico in achieving its sustainable energy future.

The research substantiates that energy literacy investment is not merely an educational experience but a significant component of energy policy capable of driving the transition towards renewable energy while promoting economic development and environmental conservation. As Mexico progresses in the establishment of its renewable energy sector, the results of this research can inform policies that engage citizens as participating stakeholders of the energy transition process and not merely passive consumers of energy services. Whether Mexico can make the transition to renewable energy successfully will depend in the end on the capacity of policymakers, educators, and business leaders to create public support and awareness for renewable energy technologies. This study offers documentation that it is possible to do this effectively, as well as pointing out the need to address the more general economic and social factors that affect energy investment behavior.

REFERENCES

Adom, P. K., Amuakwa-Mensah, F., Agradi, M. P., & Nsabimana, A. (2021). Energy poverty, development outcomes, and transition to green energy. *Renewable Energy, 178*, 1337–1352. DOI: 10.1016/j.renene.2021.06.120

Ajzen, I. (1991). The theory of planned behavior. *Organizational Behavior and Human Decision Processes, 50*(2), 179–211. DOI: 10.1016/0749-5978(91)90020-T

Azapagic, A., Chalabi, Z., & Gough, C. (2014). Public understanding of renewable energy: A survey of the UK public. *Energy Policy, 73*, 255–267. DOI: 10.1016/j.enpol.2014.05.027

Blasch, J., Boogen, N., Daminato, C., & Filippini, M. (2017). Empower the consumer! Energy-related financial literacy and its socioeconomic determinants. *Economics Working Paper Series*, 17(274), 1-36.

Brounen, D., Kok, N., & Quigley, J. M. (2013). Energy literacy, awareness, and conservation behavior of residential households. *Energy Economics, 38*, 42–50. DOI: 10.1016/j.eneco.2013.02.008

Centro de Investigación y Docencia Económicas. (2022). *Encuesta Nacional de Energía y Cambio Climático 2022*. CIDE.

Claudy, M. C., Michelsen, C., & O'Driscoll, A. (2013). The diffusion of microgeneration technologies: Assessing the influence of perceived product characteristics on home owners' willingness to pay. *Energy Policy, 55*, 582–590. DOI: 10.1016/j.enpol.2012.12.058

Creswell, J. W., & Plano Clark, V. L. (2017). *Designing and conducting mixed methods research* (3rd ed.). SAGE Publications.

Davis, F. D. (1989). Perceived usefulness, perceived ease of use, and user acceptance of information technology. *Management Information Systems Quarterly, 13*(3), 319–340. DOI: 10.2307/249008

DeWaters, J. E., & Powers, S. E. (2011). Energy literacy of secondary students in New York State (USA): A measure of knowledge, affect, and behavior. *Energy Policy, 39*(3), 1699–1710. DOI: 10.1016/j.enpol.2010.12.049

Dutta, A., Banducci, S., & Camargo, C. Q. (2025). Divided by discipline? A systematic literature review on the quantification of online sexism and misogyny using a semi-automated approach. *Scientometrics, 130*(9), 4915–4971. Advance online publication. DOI: 10.1007/s11192-025-05410-2 PMID: 41142644

Feng, G., & Zheng, M. (2022). Economic policy uncertainty and renewable energy innovation: International evidence. *Innovation and Green Development., 100010*(2), 100010. Advance online publication. DOI: 10.1016/j.igd.2022.100010

Ferhi, A., & Helali, K. (2024). The impact of renewable energy on the environment and socio-economic welfare: Empirical evidence from OECD countries. *Journal of the Knowledge Economy, 15*(1), 4776–4799. DOI: 10.1007/s13132-023-01320-x

Gobierno de México. (2021). *Programa Especial de la Transición Energética 2021-2024*. Secretaría de Energía.

González-Hernández, L., Ramírez-Montoya, M. S., & García-Peñalvo, F. J. (2019). Energy literacy among Mexican university students: A cross-sectional study. *Sustainability, 11*(24), 7143.

Hernández-Terrones, L. M., Rodríguez-Hernández, O., & Martínez-Rodríguez, M. (2021). Energy literacy and renewable energy adoption in Mexican households: A regional analysis. *Energy Policy, 156*, 112415.

International Energy Agency. (2023). *Mexico Energy Outlook 2023*. IEA Publications.

Kahneman, D., & Tversky, A. (1979). Prospect theory: An analysis of decision under risk. *Econometrica, 47*(2), 263–291. DOI: 10.2307/1914185

Khan, K., & Su, C.-W. (2022). Does policy uncertainty threaten renewable energy? Evidence from G7 countries. *Environmental Science and Pollution Research International*, *29*(24), 34813–34829. DOI: 10.1007/s11356-021-16713-1 PMID: 35040056

Martínez-Rodríguez, M., & López-Pérez, C. (2020). Household energy literacy and renewable energy investment decisions in Mexico. *Energy and Building*, *225*, 110324.

Palm, J., & Eriksson, L. (2013). Residential solar electricity adoption: How households in Sweden search for and use information. *Energy Policy*, *62*, 1024–1030. DOI: 10.1016/j.enpol.2013.07.115

Rogers, E. M. (2003). *Diffusion of innovations* (5th ed.). Free Press.

Secretaría de Energía. (2023). *Balance Nacional de Energía 2022*. Gobierno de México.

Sovacool, B. K., & Blyth, P. L. (2015). Energy and environmental attitudes in the green state of Denmark: Implications for energy democracy, low carbon transitions, and energy literacy. *Environmental Science & Policy*, *54*, 304–315. DOI: 10.1016/j.envsci.2015.07.011

Chapter 8
Capability Building on Green and Renewable Energy-Related Financial Literacy in México

José G. Vargas-Hernández
https://orcid.org/0000-0003-0938-4197
Financial Literacy Research Center, Universidad Cristóbal Colón, Mexico & Tecnológico Nacional de México, ITS Fresnillo, Mexico

Elsa Patricia Orozco-Quijano
https://orcid.org/0000-0002-6616-3174
Laurentian University, Canada

Csongor Czipf
https://orcid.org/0000-0003-4830-5754
Gyula Kautz Faculty of Economics, Széchenyi István University, Győr, Hungary

ABSTRACT

Transition to green energy systems requires not only technological advancement but also cross-sector financial education among stakeholders

DOI: 10.4018/979-8-3373-5976-2.ch008

at all levels of society. This study presents a comprehensive framework for green energy financial literacy program design considering México's unique socioeconomic context, cultural environment, and regional variations. It is estimated that implementation of such programs would increase adoption of renewable energy by 35-40% over five years, creating about 150,000 new green economy jobs. The research contributes to the existing literature in sustainable finance education and provides actionable policy suggestions for policymakers, schools, and financial service providers in México and other emerging economies pursuing energy transition go

INTRODUCTION

The global imperative for sustainable development has put renewable energy at the center of economic and environmental policy worldwide. México, the world's 15th largest economy and a top source of world greenhouse gas emissions, has unique challenges and opportunities in transitioning to a sustainable energy future (International Energy Agency, 2023). The country's commitment to being carbon-neutral by 2050, as witnessed in the Paris Agreement, involves not only substantial investment in renewable energy infrastructure but also capability building in all aspects that facilitates financial literacy with regard to green and renewable energy sectors (Secretaría de Medio Ambiente y Recursos Naturales, 2022).

Financial literacy, in general the ability to understand and manage financial resources skillfully, takes on new connotations when applied to the context of green and clean energy financing (Lusardi & Mitchell, 2023). Conventional financial education programs, as useful as they might be, do not cover the sophistication of green bonds, carbon credit markets, renewable energy investment vehicles, and energy efficiency financing mechanisms that are increasingly relevant to México's economic development strategy (Banco de México, 2023).

Green financial literacy encompasses not only basic finances, but also specialized knowledge in environmental, social, and governance (ESG) investing, renewable energy technology, along with their economic aspects, government incentives and subsidies to clean energy, and familiarity with new financial products to support sustainable development goals (Ramos

Farroñán, Farfán Chilicaus, Cruz Salinas, Correa Rojas, Chuquitucto Cotrina, Licapa-Redolfo, ... & Vera Zelada, 2025).. This interdisciplinary understanding of financial education is deemed especially applicable to Mexico, where socioeconomic conditions are highly variable, traditional financial literacy is of varying degree, and wide regional disparities compound very difficult circumstances for successful capability building programs.

Recent research estimates that México's renewable energy sector has experienced unprecedented growth, the installed capacity increasing by 180% during 2015-2023, but governmental education and awareness of associated financial opportunities and risks remain low (Comisión Reguladora de Energía, 2023). This finance knowledge gap is not only applicable to individual consumers but extends to small and medium enterprises (SMEs), constituting 99.8% of Mexican enterprises and arguably strongly assisted by improved access to green financial products (Instituto Nacional de Estadística y Geografía, 2024).

This study examines the current state of capability building for green and renewable energy-linked financial awareness in México, balancing the confluence of financial education, environmental awareness, and energy policy transition. Employing a mixed-methods research approach involving quantitative surveys and qualitative interviews of key stakeholders, this study uncovers significant gaps in financial knowledge related to investment in renewable energy, green financing products, and sustainable energy technology among Mexican people, businesses, and financial institutions.

Capacity Building for Financial Professionals. Recognizing that effective green finance education requires knowledgeable staff, many Mexican financial institutions have invested heavily in training their own employees on sustainable finance topics. This internal capacity building has been essential for institutions to credibly offer green finance products and related educational services.

BBVA México has developed a comprehensive internal training program on sustainable finance that is mandatory for all relationship managers and advisory staff. The program covers topics such as ESG risk assessment, green finance product knowledge, and client communication about sustainability topics. The bank has also created a certification program for staff who specialize in sustainable finance advisory services.

Santander México has partnered with international organizations to provide specialized training for its staff. The bank's relationship managers participate in programs offered by organizations such as the Climate Policy Initiative and the Green Finance Institute, ensuring that they have access to the latest knowledge and best practices in sustainable finance.

The Mexican central bank has also played a role in capacity building for the financial sector. Banco de México has organized training sessions for financial institution staff on topics such as climate risk assessment, green finance regulation, and sustainable finance reporting. These sessions have helped ensure that the financial sector has the necessary expertise to implement green finance initiatives effectively.

The findings confirm that while México has advanced significantly in renewable energy policy reports, there is limited specialty financial literacy training programs for green energy initiatives that hinder national sustainability goals. The research reveals that specialization competence development programs with special focus on green bonds, carbon credits, energy efficiency financing, and renewable energy investment literacy can significantly accelerate México's energy transformation while promoting economic growth that is inclusive.

The importance of this research is underscored by México's National Energy Strategy 2024-2038, which identifies financial inclusion and education as the drivers for achieving 35% renewable energy production in 2024 and 50% in 2050 (Secretaría de Energía, 2024). However, existing financial literacy programs in México are focused predominantly on basic bank products, handling credit, and saving with minimal focus on specialized subjects such as renewable energy financing, green trends in investment, and sustainable business development (Comisión Nacional Bancaria y de Valores, 2023).

This research bridges a significant literature gap by examining the specific situation of financial literacy regarding green and renewable energy in México, proposing evidence-based capability development strategies to be aware of the country's unique cultural, economic, and regulatory environment. The findings' implications are not limited to México but are extended to other emerging economies facing similar dilemmas in balancing economic growth with environmental sustainability goals.

LITERATURE REVIEW

Conceptual Framework

The conceptual basis of the research is borrowed from the overlap of three major areas: theory of financial literacy, sustainable development theories, and capability building theories. Lusardi and Mitchell's (2011) concept of financial literacy include three basic elements: numeracy (minimum mathematical proficiency), understanding compound interest, and knowledge of risk diversification. Yet, the use of these concepts in green and renewable energy situations has to be greatly extended and modified.

Green financial literacy emerged as a recognition of the reality that traditional financial education frameworks fail to account for the subtlety of sustainable finance (Lu et al., 2020). It is a niche form of financial literacy incorporating environmental consciousness, climate finance risk awareness, green investment products knowledge, and policy instruments for building sustainable development consciousness (Javed & Husain, 2021). On the side of renewable energy, this means familiarity with feed-in tariffs, net metering programs, power purchase arrangements, and certain financing mechanisms like green bonds and blended finance instruments.

Building capability, as defined by Michael (2017), refers to the process of enhancing and upgrading skills, instincts, abilities, processes, and resources that organizations and communities need to sustain themselves, adapt, and develop in an age of rapid change. In the context of financial literacy in the renewable energy industry, building capability encompasses not only individual capacity development but also institutional capacity development, policy-setting, and community-level empowerment initiative programs (Sen, 2017).

The theoretical basis of this research integrates Amartya Sen's capability approach and the principles of behavioral theory and economics of sustainable development. Sen's capability approach emphasizes widening the people's capabilities and freedom, and this is consistent with enabling people and communities to make sufficient financial decisions regarding investment in renewable energy (Sen, 1999). Behavioral economics provides insight into decision-making mechanisms, cognitive biases, and the impact of social and cultural environments on financial conduct, particularly in the Mexican context in which values from tradition must be reconciled with modern sustainability goals (Kahneman, 2011).

Theoretical Foundations

The theoretical framework for green financial literacy draws ideas from various established paradigms in economics, education, and ecological science. The Theory of Planned Behavior (Ajzen, 1991) is a foundation for accounting for the degree to which attitudes, subjective norms, and perceived behavioral control influence intentions to implement sustainable financial behaviors. For the implementation of renewable energy in México, the theory accounts for why businesses and consumers may or may not embrace green financing options in spite of the potential economic benefits.

Social Cognitive Theory (Bandura, 1986) explains how individuals learn money skills and information through observing, imitating, and social interaction. Social Cognitive Theory is particularly worth drawing upon when developing capability building programs in México since learning in the community and peer pressures are significant influencers in knowledge diffusion. The theory emphasizes the importance of self-efficacy in determining whether individuals will apply their knowledge to real-world situations, which is central to the translation of green financial literacy into real renewable energy investments.

The Diffusion of Innovation Theory (Rogers, 2003) provides a framework for describing how innovations in financial products interact and diffuse in Mexican society. This theory has five adopter groups (innovators, early adopters, early majority, late majority, and laggards) and emphasizes the influence of communication channels, social systems, and perceived innovation characteristics on adoption levels. Understanding these dynamics will be required for creating useful capability building programs that can accelerate the adoption of green financial products and services.

Environmental economics theory suggests an understanding of failures within markets, externalities, and the role played by government intervention for the promotion of sustainable development (Pearce & Turner, 1990). These theoretical foundations are necessary in offering the understanding of why the traditional market forces may not be sufficient to promote the use of renewable energy and why incentive-based financial literacy programs need to be employed for addressing information asymmetry and behavioral barriers.

Empirical Literature Review

Recent empirical research on the financial literacy and take-up of renewable energy has some lessons to impart to the Mexican situation. Sokołowski and Heffron (2022) came up with a recent study on data from 45 countries, which indicated that higher levels of financial literacy were associated with more renewable energy technology take-up, with the effects particularly being strongly experienced in the emerging economies. The study identified some mediating variables, including the ability to access credit, awareness of long-run investment rates of return, and awareness of government incentive programs.

Latin American studies have identified the regional challenges and opportunities. Aui, Wang, and Mba-Wright, (2021) conducted a comparative analysis of the adaptation of renewable energy in six Latin American countries, namely México, and concluded that financial literacy level significantly predicted the investment in renewable energy among individuals and SMEs as well. They also examined a number of significant factors on which basis the connection between financial literacy and the adaptation of renewable energy was made, e.g., rural-urban disparity, educational levels, age brackets, and environmental conservation beliefs.

There have been several studies in the Mexican context concerning specific aspects of green financial literacy. Carrara, (2020) conducted a survey among 2,500 Mexican households in 15 states and arrived at the conclusion that while 67% were interested in renewable energy technologies, only 23% had acceptable knowledge regarding financing options and investment returns. The study revealed significant regional disparities, as states further north enjoyed higher levels of green financial literacy compared to their southern counterparts, perhaps owing to regional disparities in economic development and educational infrastructure.

A Nicolas (2021) research focused on SMEs in México's manufacturing sector found that companies with higher financial literacy were 3.2 times more probable to invest in energy-efficient technologies and renewable energy systems. Nevertheless, the research also found that the current financial education programs were not covering the necessary green investment knowledge effectively, with 78% of respondents being business owners who stated that they would like special training programs.

Evidence of the effects of financial literacy interventions on renewable energy has been mixed. Huang and Etienne, (2021) conducted a randomized control trial in rural Oaxaca, México, and found that a six-month solar energy system-specific financial literacy program increased adoption levels by 45% compared to control groups. However, the study also determined that the impacts reduced over time without ongoing reinforcement and support interventions.

Cross-country experience provides additional lessons on good practice in promoting green financial literacy. An authoritative systemic review by Choudhary and Jain (2023) covered 127 studies in 34 countries and described several key success factors for green financial literacy initiatives, such as coordination with mainstream education curricula, use of applied, experiential learning pedagogical approaches, engagement of local institutional leaders and trusted institutions, respect for cultural and contextual factors, and provision of follow-up and ongoing support services.

Proof from other emerging economies offers México valuable lessons. Proof from India (Fraenkel & Filer, 2022) demonstrated mobile-based financial literacy training to microfinance for renewable energy increased rural take-up by 65%. Similar programs in Kenya (Aklin, & Urpelainen, 2021).) demonstrated the combination of financial education and the use of less expensive financing significantly increased take-up of solar energy in off-grid communities.

But some of these studies have also commented on the weakness of financial literacy interventions. Bužienė, (2024) meta-study concluded that although financial literacy interventions will usually have a positive effect on awareness and attitudes, translation to actual behavioral change is usually weak and highly variable depending on contextual determinants such as product availability, regulatory framework, and socioeconomic conditions.

METHODOLOGY

Study Design

This study employs a mixed-methods approach that uses quantitative and qualitative research techniques in addressing the research questions and offering an exhaustive portrayal of the prevalence of green and renewable energy associated financial literacy in México and strategies for effective capability building. The study employs an explanatory sequential mixed-methods strategy, where quantitative data collection and analysis come first and are followed by qualitative data collection with the aim of explaining and interpreting the quantitative results (Creswell & Clark, 2017).

The quantitative component consists of a mass survey in one or more stakeholder groups in México, e.g., individual consumers, SMEs business owners, financial services professionals, and government decision-makers who are responsible for energy and financial policy. The qualitative component consists of semi-structured interviews with influential stakeholders, focus group discussions among representative community members, and case studies of green financial literacy programs already operating.

Sampling Strategy

The study applies a stratified random sampling technique to achieve representative coverage of México's diverse geographic, economic, and demographic setting. The sampling frame is stratified geographically (North, Center, South), population density (urban, suburban, rural), and socioeconomic level (high, medium, low) as per the National Institute of Statistics and Geography (INEGI) segmentation.

For the quantitative poll, the sample size is 3,200 respondents across four main primary stakeholder groups: individual consumers (n=2,000),

SME owners and managers (n=800), financial services professionals (n=250), and government officials and policy makers (n=150). Sample size estimates were based on requiring a 95% confidence level with a margin of error of ±3% for the overall sample and ±5% for individual stakeholder groups. The qualitative component includes 80 in-depth semi-structured interviews among stakeholder groups and regions, 16 focus group discussions involving 8-12 people, and 8 case studies of existing green financial literacy programs or renewable energy programs.

Data Collection Instruments

Quantitative Survey Instrument

The questionnaire survey was developed with established financial literacy measurement tools, with a green and renewable energy structure, and with Mexican cultural and economic context adjustment. There are several sections in the survey assessing different aspects of green financial literacy and determinants.

The core section for financial literacy uses adapted INFE toolkit questions, which have been tailored to include green and renewable energy scenarios. Compound interest is tested in the context of investments in solar panels, diversification of risk when dealing with renewable energy portfolios, and long-term energy saving calculation impact by inflation.

There is a green finance special knowledge area that assesses green bond knowledge, carbon credit market knowledge, energy efficiency finance knowledge, renewable energy certificates knowledge, government incentive scheme knowledge, and blended finance vehicle knowledge. The questions are set within plausible contexts relevant to the Mexican context, i.e., examining a solar panel lease versus purchase choice or understanding of the financial impact of belonging to a distributed generation scheme.

Renewable energy awareness and attitudes survey questions measure knowledge of multiple renewable energy technologies, comfort with government policies and incentives, environmental values and attitudes, perceived barriers to the use of renewable energy, and plans to invest in green financial services. Demographic and socioeconomic survey questions access baseline demographic information as well as energy usage habits, existing utilization of financial services, access to credit and banking services, and participation in government programs.

Qualitative Interview Protocols

Semi-structured interview guides were developed for all stakeholder groups to facilitate uniform data collection with flexibility to pursue emerging themes. Interview guides for individual consumers aim at individual experience with renewable energy technology, familiarity with available financing products, decision-making in the context of investing in assets relating to energy, barriers in accessing green finance products, and suggestions for improving financial education programs. SMEs owner interviews explore business experience with renewable energy investment and energy efficiency, awareness of commercial sources of finance, impact of energy prices on business activity, understanding of government incentive schemes, and perceived need for business-focused financial education.

Professional interviews of financial services professionals address current product lines related to green finance, current perceived market demand for green financial products, challenges to expansion in green finance services, employee training and knowledge gaps, and recommendations for policy improvements. Official interviews of government officials touch on current policy programs and initiatives, areas of difficulty in implementation and outreach, agency coordination and government levels, resource allocation and budget, and strategic priorities for capability development.

Data Collection Procedures

Data collection was undertaken within a span of six months between March and August 2024 via multiple channels for extensive reach and representative participation. Quantitative survey was conducted based on a mix of online media, phone interviews, and in-person interviews in regions of low internet penetration. Practices for quality control included pilot testing of all the instruments with representative samples, training of all the interviewers and field researchers, regular supervision and quality monitoring at the time of data collection, and response validation using multiple data sources whenever possible.

Data Analysis Plan

Quantitative data analysis is founded upon a multi-step procedure beginning with descriptive statistics to characterize the sample and major variables, followed by bivariate analyses to examine associations between assessments of financial literacy and various demographic, socioeconomic, and attitudinal variables. Multivariate regression hypothesis tests are employed to determine the factors associated with greater levels of green financial literacy after controlling for possible confounding variables.

Specific statistical techniques include the ordinary least squares regression for continuous outcomes, logistic regression for dichotomous outcomes such as willingness to invest in renewable energy, multinomial logistic regression for polytomous outcomes, and structural equation modeling to test theoretical relationships between constructs. Qualitative data analysis follows a thematic analysis with an integrated deductive and inductive coding scheme. Deductive codes are drawn from the theoretical framework, as well as the research questions, while inductive codes are drawn from the data. Analysis is conducted through qualitative data analysis software to ensure systematic and rigorous treatment of the data.

It combines quantitative and qualitative results through a convergent parallel strategy, where the respective type is analyzed separately; the integration is, however, done during interpretation to synthesize the findings completely to the research questions.

ANALYSIS OF RESULTS

Study Design

This study employs a mixed-methods approach that uses quantitative and qualitative research techniques in addressing the research questions and offering an exhaustive portrayal of the prevalence of green and renewable energy associated financial literacy in México and strategies for effective capability building. The study employs an explanatory sequential mixed-methods strategy, where quantitative data collection and analysis come first and are followed by qualitative data collection with the aim of explaining and interpreting the quantitative results (Creswell & Clark, 2017).

The quantitative component consists of a mass survey in one or more stakeholder groups in México, e.g., individual consumers, SME business owners, financial services professionals, and government decision-makers who are responsible for energy and financial policy. The qualitative component consists of semi-structured interviews with influential stakeholders, focus group discussions among representative community members, and case studies of green financial literacy programs already operating.

Sampling Strategy

The study applies a stratified random sampling technique to achieve representative coverage of México's diverse geographic, economic, and demographic setting. The sampling frame is stratified geographically (North, Center, South), population density (urban, suburban, rural), and socioeconomic level (high, medium, low) as per the National Institute of Statistics and Geography (INEGI, 2024) segmentation. For the quantitative poll, the sample size is 3,200 respondents across four main primary stakeholder groups: individual consumers (n=2,000), SME owners and managers (n=800), financial services professionals (n=250), and government officials and policy makers (n=150). Sample size estimates were based on requiring a 95% confidence level with a margin of error of ±3% for the overall sample and ±5% for individual stakeholder groups.

The qualitative component includes 80 in-depth semi-structured interviews among stakeholder groups and regions, 16 focus group discussions involving 8-12 people, and 8 case studies of existing green financial literacy programs or renewable energy programs.

Data Collection Instruments

Quantitative Survey Instrument

The questionnaire survey was developed with established financial literacy measurement tools, with a green and renewable energy structure, and with Mexican cultural and economic context adjustment. There are several sections in the survey assessing different aspects of green financial literacy and determinants.

The core section for financial literacy uses adapted INFE toolkit questions, which have been tailored to include green and renewable energy scenarios. Compound interest is tested in the context of investments in solar panels, diversification of risk when dealing with renewable energy portfolios, and long-term energy saving calculation impact by inflation.

There is a green finance special knowledge area that assesses green bond knowledge, carbon credit market knowledge, energy efficiency finance knowledge, renewable energy certificates knowledge, government incentive scheme knowledge, and blended finance vehicle knowledge. The questions are set within plausible contexts relevant to the Mexican context, i.e., examining a solar panel lease versus purchase choice or understanding of the financial impact of belonging to a distributed generation scheme.

Renewable energy awareness and attitudes survey questions measure knowledge of multiple renewable energy technologies, comfort with government policies and incentives, environmental values and attitudes, perceived barriers to the use of renewable energy, and plans to invest in green financial services. Demographic and socioeconomic survey questions access baseline demographic information as well as energy usage habits, existing utilization of financial services, access to credit and banking services, and participation in government programs.

Qualitative Interview Protocols

Semi-structured interview guides were developed for all stakeholder groups to facilitate uniform data collection with flexibility to pursue emerging themes. Interview guides for individual consumers aim at individual experience with renewable energy technology, familiarity with available financing products, decision-making in the context of investing in assets relating to energy, barriers in accessing green finance products, and suggestions for improving financial education programs. SMEs owner interviews explore business experience with renewable energy investment and energy efficiency, awareness of commercial sources of finance, impact of energy prices on business activity, understanding of government incentive schemes, and perceived need for business-focused financial education.

Professional interviews of financial services professionals address current product lines related to green finance, current perceived market demand for green financial products, challenges to expansion in green finance services, employee training and knowledge gaps, and recommendations for policy improvements. Official interviews of government officials touch on current policy programs and initiatives, areas of difficulty in implementation and outreach, agency coordination and government levels, resource allocation and budget, and strategic priorities for capability development.

Data Collection Procedures

Data collection was undertaken within a span of six months between March and August 2024 via multiple channels for extensive reach and representative participation. Quantitative survey was conducted based on a mix of online media, phone interviews, and in-person interviews in regions of low internet penetration. Practices for quality control included pilot testing of all the instruments with representative samples, training of all the interviewers and field researchers, regular supervision and quality monitoring at the time of data collection, and response validation using multiple data sources whenever possible.

Data Analysis Plan

Quantitative data analysis is founded upon a multi-step procedure beginning with descriptive statistics to characterize the sample and major variables, followed by bivariate analyses to examine associations between assessments of financial literacy and various demographic, socioeconomic, and attitudinal variables. Multivariate regression hypothesis tests are employed to determine the factors associated with greater levels of green financial literacy after controlling for possible confounding variables.

Specific statistical techniques include the ordinary least squares regression for continuous outcomes, logistic regression for dichotomous outcomes such as willingness to invest in renewable energy, multinomial logistic regression for polytomous outcomes, and structural equation modeling to test theoretical relationships between constructs.

Qualitative data analysis follows a thematic analysis with an integrated deductive and inductive coding scheme. Deductive codes are drawn from the theoretical framework, as well as the research questions, while inductive codes are drawn from the data. Analysis is conducted through qualitative data analysis software to ensure systematic and rigorous treatment of the data. It combines quantitative and qualitative results through a convergent parallel strategy, where the respective type is analyzed separately; the integration is, however, done during interpretation to synthesize the findings completely to the research questions.

DISCUSSION

Implications of Key Findings

The research findings reveal a complex but navigable landscape for building green and renewable energy-related financial literacy in México. The substantial gap between traditional financial literacy (67.3% average correct responses) and green financial literacy (27.5% average correct responses) demonstrates both the magnitude of the challenge and the potential for improvement through targeted interventions. This finding aligns with international research suggesting that specialized financial domains require dedicated educational approaches rather than assuming that general financial knowledge will transfer to new contexts (Klapper & Panos, 2011).

The pronounced regional variations in financial literacy outcomes reflect broader patterns of economic development and educational infrastructure in México, but they also suggest opportunities for targeted interventions in regions with the greatest needs and potential for improvement. The finding that northern states consistently outperform central and southern regions in both traditional and green financial literacy metrics indicates that successful approaches developed in these areas could potentially be adapted and scaled to other regions.

Perhaps most significantly, the research demonstrates that environmental awareness and concern, while necessary, are insufficient for driving adoption of renewable energy investments without accompanying financial literacy. The weak correlation between environmental attitudes and green financial knowledge ($r = 0.09$) suggests that capability building programs must address both dimensions simultaneously rather than assuming that environmental motivation will drive learning about financial concepts.

Theoretical Contributions

This research provides a number of significant contributions to theory that extends current understanding of financial literacy in emerging economy contexts. It expands the standard financial literacy framework to include specialized knowledge domains that are increasingly relevant to sustainable development. The green financial literacy concept that is developed in this study forms a platform for future research and program development in México and other comparable contexts.

Second, the study shows the value of contextual factors in determining financial literacy outcomes. The fact that geographic area continues to be a predictor of financial literacy even when individual-level determinants are controlled for reinforces theories stressing the influence of institutional and cultural contexts on learning and behavior change. This result has both theoretical and practical implications.

Third, the study contributes to capability building theory by showing the interlinking of individual, institutional, and policy-level factors in bettering sustainable development outcomes. Qualitative findings especially indicate how individual knowledge and skills interact with institutional capacity and policy frameworks either to facilitate or constrain change in behavior.

Implications for Policy and Program Development III

The research findings have important implications for designing effective capability building programs for green and renewable energy-related financial literacy in México. The identification of specific knowledge gaps, demographic patterns, and barriers to learning provides a foundation for developing targeted interventions that can efficiently address the most critical needs. The finding that educational attainment is the strongest predictor of green financial literacy suggests that capability building programs should be designed with multiple entry points and learning pathways to accommodate different educational backgrounds. Programs targeting populations with lower educational attainment may need to emphasize practical, experiential learning approaches rather than abstract financial concepts.

The importance of trust and credible information sources identified in the qualitative findings suggests that program implementation should involve trusted institutions and community leaders. Partnership strategies that leverage the credibility of established organizations such as universities, government agencies, and respected financial institutions may be more effective than standalone programs delivered by unknown organizations. The research also points out the need for coordination among different kinds of interventions. While individual-level financial education programs are necessary, they are certainly insufficient unless accompanied by corresponding institutional capacity building and improvements in the policy framework. This implies that impactful capability building requires holistic and multilevel approaches rather than isolated interventions.

Implementation Challenges

The study identifies some principal challenges that need to be solved in rolling out capability building initiatives for green financial literacy in México. These challenges in resources, both human and financial, are an intrinsic challenge that needs innovative solutions and strategic partnership strategies. The fact that government agencies acknowledge the value of financial literacy but have no resources to build extensive programs offers prospects for public-private partnerships and global cooperation.

The complexity of green financing mechanisms and policy regimes is another key challenge.

The qualitative results show that even self-motivated people and firms find it difficult to navigate the financial and regulatory environment for investments in renewable energy. This indicates that capability building programs need to incorporate practical, experiential elements that assist participants in applying knowledge in practice.

Cultural and linguistic diversity across México presents additional implementation challenges that require culturally responsive program design. The significant regional variations in outcomes suggest that one-size-fits-all approaches are unlikely to be effective. Instead, programs should be adapted to local contexts while maintaining core learning objectives and quality standards.

Comparison with International Experience

Findings from this study are largely consistent with international experience in promoting green financial literacy while revealing some unique aspects of the Mexican context. As in many other emerging economies, México shows great potential for developing renewable energy but faces substantial challenges in building the knowledge and capacity needed to seize this opportunity.

The research findings align with studies from India and Kenya showing that targeted financial literacy programs can significantly increase renewable energy adoption rates. However, the Mexican context presents some unique features, including a more developed but also more complex financial system, stronger government policy frameworks, and greater regional diversity in economic development patterns.

Comparison with the experience of developed economy countries implies that México has the potential to leapfrog some of the setbacks encountered by the early adopters of green finance. For instance, the findings of the study indicate that mobile-enabled learning platforms and digital financial services may have significant roles in capability building programs with the potential to reach those that have previously been excluded from traditional financial education interventions.

Future Research Directions

It opens several avenues of essential future work. Longitudinal studies on the effectiveness of different capability building approaches in what works best in the Mexican context and how programs should be optimized with maximum impact would further that. Experimental designs comparing different program models, delivery mechanisms, and target populations will help focus best practice and more effectively scale successful interventions.

Research examining the business case for green financial literacy investments would help build support among financial institutions and other private sector stakeholders. Studies quantifying the economic benefits of improved financial literacy in terms of increased renewable energy adoption, job creation, and economic development would strengthen the argument for expanded capability building investments.

Cross-national comparative research on how different emerging economies tackle green financial literacy challenges would be very useful for policy development and program design. Research on the technology and digital platforms used in providing financial education could also reveal scalable solutions to address the diverse populations within México's varied geographic and demographic landscape.

CONCLUSIONS

This research has examined the role of financial institutions in Mexico in facilitating green and renewable energy-related financial literacy. The findings reveal a complex and evolving landscape in which financial institutions are playing increasingly important roles in promoting understanding of green finance products and sustainable investment opportunities.

Mexican financial institutions have made significant progress in developing green finance education initiatives, driven by regulatory support, market demand, and institutional commitment to sustainability. Major banks, development financial institutions, and other financial entities have developed comprehensive programs that include product development, client education, capacity building, and partnership activities.

The strategic recommendations emerging from this research emphasize the need for comprehensive strategies, internal capacity building, technology leverage, collaborative partnerships, and systematic evaluation. These recommendations provide a roadmap for financial institutions seeking to enhance their contribution to green finance market development and sustainable economic growth.

The findings of this research contribute to the broader understanding of green finance market development and provide practical insights for financial institutions, policy makers, and other stakeholders involved in promoting sustainable finance. As Mexico continues to advance its sustainable development goals and climate commitments, the role of financial institutions in education and capacity building will become increasingly important for achieving these objectives.

Summary of Key Findings

This comprehensive examination of green and renewable energy-related financial literacy capacity development in México discloses both grim challenges and tremendous opportunities to advance the country's shift toward sustainable energy. The mixed-methods design of this study, grounded in quantitative examination of 3,847 survey responses and qualitative inputs from 80 interviews and 16 focus groups, provides a richly informed picture of the current state of affairs and directions for reform.

The research attests that while México has decidedly enhanced the renewable energy policy framework development as well as installed capacity, there is an absolute lack of the financial literacy needed to translate these gains. Standard financial literacy rates, though moderate, are not necessarily translated into the expert level of knowledge that will enable investing in green and renewable energy. The finding that only 27.5% of respondents demonstrate adequate green financial literacy compared to 67.3% for traditional financial concepts highlights the magnitude of this challenge.

Regional variations in financial literacy outcomes are reflected in broader patterns of economic development across México, with northern states ahead of central and southern states overall. These variations reflect not only the need for targeted interventions but also the potential that effective strategies located in higher-performing regions can be replicated and expanded to areas of higher need.

The research discovers that environmental awareness and concern, even though widespread among Mexican citizens, are insufficient stimuli for adoption of renewable energy where there is no financial education and self-confidence. This refutes assumptions that behavior will change based on environmental motivation and asserts the critical value of capability building interventions that address both the environmental and financial angles simultaneously.

Consumer, SMEs owner, financial services professional, and government official stakeholder perceptions reveal a dynamic interrelated system of problems and possibilities. Individual knowledge gaps overlap with institutional capacity constraints and policy enforcement challenges to form barriers calling for holistic, integrated solutions more than single-shot interventions.

Policy Recommendations

Based on the research findings, several significant policy implications emerge for encouraging green and renewable energy finance literacy in México. These implications address different levels of interventions and recognize the interdependent determination of individual, institutional, and systemic variables that condition the results.

National Financial Education Strategy Integration

The national government is urged to integrate green and renewable energy-based financial literacy into the existing National Financial Education Strategy to have uniform strategies across agencies and levels of government. Integration will include green financial literacy targets for outcomes, definite budget provisions, and performance monitoring frameworks that will capture progress towards sustainable development goals.

Improvement in the Regulatory Framework

Financial regulatory bodies need to develop guidelines and incentives for financial institutions to raise green finance product supply and invest in employee capacity building in sustainable finance issues. These requirements may involve obligatory green finance training as part of professional certification schemes, standard disclosure requirements on green financial products, and regulatory sandbox programs that facilitate innovation in sustainable finance.

Curriculum Integration in Education

The Ministry of Education must work hand in hand with schools in incorporating green financial literacy into formal curricula at secondary and tertiary education. Incorporation must be accompanied by practice so that students can engage with real-world circumstances and develop experiential skills to analyze renewable energy investments as well as understand sustainable finance mechanisms.

Development of Public-Private Partnerships

There should be establishment of formal partnership frameworks by government agencies through which private sector talent and capability are leveraged to develop capability and extend programs to the public in a broad manner. Partnerships might entail cost-sharing for program development and delivery, collaborative training programs for financial services professionals, and joint research collaboration to improve programs continuously and make them more effective.

Program Design Recommendations

The findings of the research inform a specific set of principles for developing useful capability building programs that address the specific needs and conditions delineated in México. The recommendations underscore evidence-based practice that is responsive to cultural, economic, and regional contexts but maintains high standards of learning outcomes.

Multi-Modal Delivery Strategies

Programs should employ different delivery routes to accommodate different learning styles, levels of access to technology, and geographical constraints. This should include face-to-face workshops in low-level internet access communities, mobile learning platforms for city residents, peer-to-peer learning networks that tap into social relationships, and integration with existing financial service delivery channels.

Culturally Responsive Content Development

Program content should be designed with careful attention to cultural values, communication styles, and choice-making processes that influence money management in specific regions and communities across México. This includes using locally relevant examples and case studies, incorporating traditional knowledge and practices where appropriate, providing materials in native languages where appropriate, and employing program staff sufficiently diverse to reflect target populations.

Practical Skills Emphasis

The courses must emphasize more practical skill acquisition than theoretical knowledge, with practical real-world application in mind which can be applied directly in the personal and working lives of the participants. These include practical exercises in calculations from realistic scenarios, practicing step-by-step using online resources and calculators, role-playing exercises in the handling of financial service providers, and field visits to renewable installations.

Continuing Support and Aftercare

The results of the research emphasize the importance of continuing commitment rather than one-off occurrence training events. Programs must include provision for ongoing support and reinforcement, such as alumni networks and peer support groups, regular refresher courses and bulletins, access to expert advice and consultancy, and integration into pre-existing community organizations and support structures.

Implementation Framework

Successful implementation of capability development programs on green financial literacy requires a systematic approach that confronts the different factors identified in this research. The suggested implementation framework in this paper recognizes the need for concerted action at different stakeholders and intervention levels without sacrificing flexibility to adapt to local context and emerging needs.

Phase 1: Institutional Foundations (Years 1-2)

The initial phase would involve establishing the institutional infrastructure and partnerships necessary to continue program delivery. This includes developing standard curricula and training materials, defining partnership structures between government ministries, financial institutions, and educational organizations, master trainer training and institutional capacity development, and piloting programs within targeted geographic areas to experiment and refine approaches.

Phase 2: Scaled Implementation (Years 3-4)

Building on the success of Phase 1, Phase 2 must focus on scaling successful program models to reach larger numbers of people in México. This includes extending program coverage to all states and major urban areas, launching specialized programs for specific target segments (consumers, SMEs, youth), merging programs with existing channels of financial service delivery, and establishing monitoring and evaluation systems to track progress and impacts.

Phase 3: Sustainability and Innovation (Years 5+)

The final phase should focus on long-term sustainability and continued improvement of capability building activities. This includes achieving sustainable funding streams to reduce government dependence, developing high-level programs to address breakthrough technologies and financial instruments, making México a regional leader in green financial education, and facilitating global knowledge exchange and best practice design.

Expected Results and Impact

The results of this study recommend that the application of extensive capability building programs on green and renewable energy-related financial literacy would have a substantial positive effect on México's sustainable development objectives. Supported by findings from the evidence reported in this study as well as global experience regarding similar programs, some major impacts can be expected.

Individual and Household Level Impacts

Increased financial literacy is expected to increase take-up levels of renewable energy among Mexican consumers by 35-40% over a five-year period, enhance household quality of financial decision-making and reduce vulnerability to abusive lending, increase formal financial service engagement and broader financial inclusion, and increase household resistence to electricity price shocks and climate-related risks.

Business and Enterprise Level Impacts

Higher green financial literacy among SME managers and owners will lead to an increase of business investments in energy efficiency and renewable energy by 50-60%, improve access to appropriate finance for sustainable business development, make businesses more competitive through reduced energy expenditure and improved environmental performance, and unlock new business opportunities in the new green economy market.

Sector and Economy Level Impacts

Global improved green financial literacy is expected to drive México's energy transition and shift towards carbon-neutral goals, create approximately 150,000 new jobs in renewable energy and allied sectors, stimulate greater investment in México's green economy at home and abroad, and reinforce México's leadership role in sustainable development within the region.

Development of Financial System

The programs for building capabilities are to drive innovation and development in green financial products and services, increase risk assessment and management capability in the financial institutions, increase the overall stability and resilience of México's financial system, and enhance México's integration into the global sustainable finance markets.

Limitations and Considerations

While this study provides detailed information on the present status of green and renewable energy-involving financial literacy in México, certain limitations must be pointed out. The quantitative data cross-sectional data collection imposes a limitation on the capacity to determine causal relations among variables, even though this is compensated for by the mixed-methods approach via findings triangulation.

The research was conducted within a finite time period (March-August 2024) and reflects conditions and policies at that time. The rapidly evolving character of renewable energy technologies and financial markets suggests that some findings must be revised as conditions change.

Geographic and demographic coverage, though widespread, will not be able to entirely reflect the lives of every community across México's diverse geography. Remote and isolated communities, for instance, may be underrepresented in the sample even with efforts at full participation.

The research is aimed at formal financial literacy and does not represent fully informal financial knowledge and practices that play an important part in the majority of Mexican communities. Future research needs to focus on how indigenous financial practices and knowledge systems are integrated into formal green financial literacy.

Final Reflections

This research demonstrates that green and renewable energy-related financial capability development is both a pressing need and a viable opportunity for advancing México's sustainable development agenda. Findings of this research establish that challenges exist but are overcomeable and that evidence-driven targeted interventions can lead to real differences in knowledge, attitudes, and behavior towards sustainable finance and renewable energy adoption.

The research also highlights the importance of recognizing financial literacy as a key skill that enables individuals, businesses, and communities to participate positively in the transition to a more sustainable economy. If adequate financial knowledge and skills are not available, even the most sophisticated renewable energy technologies and policy conditions can be unproductive.

Above all, this research indicates that capability building, to be successful, requires attention and response to the complex interrelationship between people's skills and knowledge, institutional products and capacity, and policy environments and deployment. Success will depend on sustained commitment, concerted effort, and continuous learning and adaptation as challenges and opportunities shift.

The path forward to higher-level green and renewable energy-based financial literacy for México is apparent, but it will require dedication, resources, and concerted effort by a variety of stakeholders. The possible return – for individuals, communities, businesses, and the nation overall –

is well worth investing to build these fundamental capacities for México's future prosperity.

REFERENCES

Ajzen, I. (1991). The theory of planned behavior. *Organizational Behavior and Human Decision Processes, 50*(2), 179–211. DOI: 10.1016/0749-5978(91)90020-T

Aklin, M., & Urpelainen, J. (2021). The evolving role of solar-based lighting solutions in rural India: Global lessons for distributed renewables. *Energy for Sustainable Development, 63*, 113–118. DOI: 10.1016/j.esd.2021.05.009

Aui, A., Wang, Y., & Mba-Wright, M. (2021). Evaluating the economic feasibility of cellulosic ethanol: A meta-analysis of techno-economic analysis studies. *Renewable & Sustainable Energy Reviews, 145*, 111098. Advance online publication. DOI: 10.1016/j.rser.2021.111098

Banco de México. (2023). *Reporte sobre las condiciones de competencia en el otorgamiento de crédito*. Banco de México. https://www.banxico.org.mx/publicaciones-y-prensa/reportes-sobre-las-condiciones-de-competencia-en-l/reportes-competencia-mercados.html

Bandura, A. (1986). *Social foundations of thought and action: A social cognitive theory*. Prentice-Hall.

Bužienė, I. (2024). Factors and indicators shaping financial literacy: a multicriteria analysis of selected programs and strategic insights for resilient economic development. *Intelektinė ekonomika, 18*(2), 450-469.

Carrara, S. (2020). Reactor ageing and phase-out policies: Global and regional prospects for nuclear power generation. *Energy Policy, 147*, 111834. Advance online publication. DOI: 10.1016/j.enpol.2020.111834

Choudhary, H., & Jain, H. (2023). Addressing Financial Exclusion through Financial Literacy training programs: A Systematic Literature Review. *Empirical Research in Vocational Education and Training, 15*(1), 8. DOI: 10.1186/s40461-023-00147-9

Comisión Nacional Bancaria y de Valores. (2023). *Reporte Nacional de Inclusión Financiera*. CNBV.https://www.gob.mx/cnbv/acciones-y-programas/divulgacion-de-inclusion-financiera-26625

Comisión Reguladora de Energía. (2023). *Reporte del Mercado Eléctrico Nacional 2023*. CRE. https://www.gob.mx/cre/documentos/informe-de-labores-2023-359246

Creswell, J. W., & Clark, V. L. P. (2017). *Designing and conducting mixed methods research* (3rd ed.). SAGE Publications.

Fraenkel, J., & Filer, C. (2022). Prisoners of a distant past? Linguistic diversity and the time-depth of human settlement in Papua New Guinea. *World Development*, *157*, 105921. Advance online publication. DOI: 10.1016/j.worlddev.2022.105921

Huang, K., & Etienne, X. (2021). Do natural hazards in the Gulf Coast still matter for state-level natural gas prices in the US? Evidence after the shale gas boom. *Energy Economics*, *98*, 105267. Advance online publication. DOI: 10.1016/j.eneco.2021.105267

Instituto Nacional de Estadística y Geografía. (2024). *Censos Económicos 2023: Resultados preliminares*. INEGI. https://www.inegi.org.mx/programas/ce/2024/

International Energy Agency. (2023). *World Energy Outlook 2023*. IEA Publications. https://www.iea.org/reports/world-energy-outlook-2023

Javed, S., & Husain, U. (2021). Impact of Financial Factors on Social and Financial Sustainability in Banking Sector: A Mediating Role of Financial Literacy. In Singh, D. (Ed.), *S., A.* Financial Inclusion in Emerging Markets., DOI: 10.1007/978-981-16-2652-4_13

Kahneman, D. (2011). *Thinking, fast and slow*. Farrar, Straus and Giroux. https://ia800603.us.archive.org/10/items/DanielKahnemanThinkingFastAndSlow/Daniel%20Kahneman-Thinking%2C%20Fast%20and%20Slow%20%20.pdf

Klapper, L., & Panos, G. A. (2011). Financial literacy and retirement planning: The Russian case. *Journal of Pension Economics and Finance*, *10*(4), 599–618. DOI: 10.1017/S1474747211000503

Lu, Y., Cao, B., Hua, Y., & Ding, L. (2020). Efficiency Measurement of Green Regional Development and Its Influencing Factors: An Improved Data Envelopment Analysis Framework. *Sustainability (Basel)*, *12*(11), 4361. DOI: 10.3390/su12114361

Lusardi, A., & Mitchell, O. (2023). The Importance of Financial Literacy: Opening a New Field. Working Paper 31145 *NBER WORKING PAPER SERIES*. https://www.nber.org/system/files/working_papers/w31145/w31145.pdf DOI: DOI: 10.3386/w31145

Lusardi, A., & Mitchell, O. S. (2011). Financial literacy around the world: An overview. *Journal of Pension Economics and Finance*, *10*(4), 497–508. DOI: 10.1017/S1474747211000448 PMID: 28553190

Michael, S. (2017). *United Nations Development Programme (UNDP)*. Max Planck Encyclopedia of Public International Law., DOI: 10.1093/law:epil/9780199231690/e550

Nicolas, T. (2021). Short-term financial constraints and SMEs' investment decision: Evidence from the working capital channel. *Small Business Economics*. Advance online publication. DOI: 10.1007/s11187-021-00488-3 PMID: 38624861

Pearce, D., & Turner, R. K. (1990). *Economics of natural resources and the environment*. Johns Hopkins University Press.

Ramos Farroñán, E. V., Farfán Chilicaus, G. C., Cruz Salinas, L. E., Correa Rojas, L., Chuquitucto Cotrina, L. K., Licapa-Redolfo, G. S., Vera Zelada, P., & Vera Zelada, L. A. (2025). Green Finance and the Energy Transition: A Systematic Review of Economic Instruments for Renewable Energy Deployment in Emerging Economies. *Energies*, *18*(17), 4560. DOI: 10.3390/en18174560

Rogers, E. M. (2003). *Diffusion of innovations* (5th ed.). Free Press.

Secretaría de Energía. (2024). *Estrategia Nacional de Energía 2024-2038*. SENER. https://www.gob.mx/sener/articulos/la-secretaria-de-energia-publica-el-programa-de-desarrollo-del-sistema-electrico-nacional-2024-2038

Secretaría de Medio Ambiente y Recursos Naturales. (2022). *Estrategia Nacional de Cambio Climático: Visión 10-20-40*. SEMARNAT. https://dsiappsdev.semarnat.gob.mx/datos/portal/publicaciones/2025/ENCC_2025_SEMARNAT.pdf

Sen, A. (1999). *Development as freedom*. Oxford University Press.

Sen, A. (2017). *Collective choice and social welfare* (Expanded ed.). Harvard University Press.

Sokołowski, M., & Heffron, R. (2022, February). Defining and conceptualising energy policy failure: The when, where, why, and how. *Energy Policy, 161*, 112745. DOI: 10.1016/j.enpol.2021.112745

Compilation of References

Abbott, K. W. (2014). Strengthening the transnational regime complex for climate change. *Transnational Environmental Law*, *3*(1), 57–88. DOI: 10.1017/S2047102513000502

Abduwahab, A. S., & Al-Dubai, M. M. (2024). Leadership styles and E-Commerce adoption among SME managers in Oman: Moderating effect of technology readiness. *Open Journal of Business and Management*, *12*(2), 1074–1096. DOI: 10.4236/ojbm.2024.122057

ACCA. (2020). *Future Ready: Accountancy Careers in the 2020s*. Association of Chartered Certified Accountants.

Adams, C.A., 2017. Conceptualising the contemporary corporate value creation process. *Account Audit. Account. J. 30* (4), 906e931. https://doi .org//DOI: 10.1108

Adom, P. K., Amuakwa-Mensah, F., Agradi, M. P., & Nsabimana, A. (2021). Energy poverty, development outcomes, and transition to green energy. *Renewable Energy*, *178*, 1337–1352. DOI: 10.1016/j.renene.2021.06.120

Afzal, F., Haiying, P., Afzal, F., Mahmood, A., & Ikram, A. (2021). Value-at-risk analysis for measuring stochastic volatility of stock returns: Using GARCH-based dynamic conditional correlation model. *SAGE Open*, *11*(1), 21582440211005758. DOI: 10.1177/21582440211005758

Ajzen, I. (1991). The theory of planned behavior. *Organizational Behavior and Human Decision Processes*, *50*(2), 179–211. DOI: 10.1016/0749-5978(91)90020-T

Aklin, M., & Urpelainen, J. (2021). The evolving role of solar-based lighting solutions in rural India: Global lessons for distributed renewables. *Energy for Sustainable Development*, *63*, 113–118. DOI: 10.1016/j.esd.2021.05.009

Al-Bakri, A. A., & Katsioloudes, M. I. (2015). The factors affecting e-commerce adoption by Jordanian SMEs. *Management Research Review*, *38*(7), 726–749. DOI: 10.1108/MRR-12-2013-0291

Al-Hattami, H. M. (2024). Impact of AIS success on decision-making effectiveness among SMEs in less developed countries. *Information Technology for Development*, *30*(3), 472–492. DOI: 10.1080/02681102.2022.2073325

Almuwallad, H., & Alhumoudi, H. (2024). The Impact of E-commerce on Organizational and Financial Performance in SMEs: Evidence from Saudi Arabia. *International Journal of Business and Management*, *19*(4), 1–15. DOI: 10.5539/ijbm.v19n4p1

Alnajjar, M. I. M. (2017). Impact of accounting information system on organizational performance: A study of SMEs in the UAE. *Global Review of Accounting and Finance*, *8*(2), 19–38. DOI: 10.21102/graf.2017.09.82.02

Aluchna, M., Roszkowska-Menkes, M., Kamiński, B., & Bosek-Rak, D. (2022). Do institutional investors encourage firm to social disclosure? The stakeholder salience perspective. *Journal of Business Research*, *142*, 674–682. DOI: 10.1016/j.jbusres.2021.12.064

Ameer, R. (2014). Financial constraints, debt overhang and corporate investment: A panel smooth transition regression approach. *Asian Academy of Management Journal of Accounting and Finance*, *10*(2).

Ampry, E. S., Komariah, A., Kurniady, D. A., Rafiq, M., Priatna, A., Ali, M. H., Marhoon, H. A., Thangavelu, L., & Chaudhary, P. (2022). Multi-objective Mathematical Modeling for Scheduling Machines in Parallel with Batch Processors. *Industrial Engineering & Management Systems*, *21*(2), 366–380. DOI: 10.7232/iems.2022.21.2.366

Appelbaum, D., Kogan, A., Vasarhelyi, M., & Yan, Z. (2017). Impact of Business Analytics and Enterprise Systems on Managerial Accounting. *International Journal of Accounting Information Systems*, *25*, 29–44. DOI: 10.1016/j.accinf.2017.03.003

Ardiansah, M. N., Chariri, A., & Raharja, S. (2021, June). Does E-Commerce Impact on Accounting Information System and Organizations' Performance? In 2nd annual conference on blended learning, educational technology and innovation (ACBLETI 2020) (pp. 476-481). Atlantis Press.

Ardiansah, M. N., Chariri, A., & Raharja, S. (2021). Does E-Commerce Impact on Accounting Information System and Organizations' Performance? In *2nd Annual Conference on Blended Learning, Educational Technology and Innovation (ACBLETI 2020)* (pp. 476–481). Atlantis Press. DOI: 10.2991/assehr.k.210615.090

Artzner, P., Delbaen, F., Eber, J. M., & Heath, D. (1999). Coherent measures of risk. *Mathematical Finance*, *9*(3), 203–228. DOI: 10.1111/1467-9965.00068

Arya, P., & Singh, R. (2025). Cross-cultural variations in investor sentiment and financial decision-making. *Journal of International Finance*, *48*(2), 123–145.

Atan, R., Alam, M. M., Said, J., & Zamri, M. (2018). The Impacts of Environmental, Social, and Governance Factors on Firm Performance: Panel Study of Malaysian Companies. *Management of Environmental Quality*, *29*(2), 182–194. DOI: 10.1108/MEQ-03-2017-0033

Aui, A., Wang, Y., & Mba-Wright, M. (2021). Evaluating the economic feasibility of cellulosic ethanol: A meta-analysis of techno-economic analysis studies. *Renewable & Sustainable Energy Reviews*, *145*, 111098. Advance online publication. DOI: 10.1016/j.rser.2021.111098

Awa, H. O., Ukoha, O., & Emecheta, B. C. (2015). Integrating TAM, TPB and TOE frameworks and expanding their characteristic constructs for e-commerce adoption by SMEs. *Journal of Science and Technology Policy Management*, *6*(1), 76–94. DOI: 10.1108/JSTPM-04-2014-0012

Azapagic, A., Chalabi, Z., & Gough, C. (2014). Public understanding of renewable energy: A survey of the UK public. *Energy Policy*, *73*, 255–267. DOI: 10.1016/j.enpol.2014.05.027

Balkan, N. (2022, April 8). *Barriers to digitally transform SMEs in Europe*. European DIGITAL SME Alliance. https://www.digitalsme.eu/barriers-to-digitally-transform-smes-in-europe/

Banco de México. (2023). *Reporte sobre las condiciones de competencia en el otorgamiento de crédito*. Banco de México. https://www.banxico.org.mx/publicaciones-y-prensa/reportes-sobre-las-condiciones-de-competencia-en-l/reportes-competencia-mercados.html

Bandura, A. (1986). *Social foundations of thought and action: A social cognitive theory*. Prentice-Hall.

Barberis, N., & Thaler, R. (2003). A survey of behavioral finance. In Constantinides, G. M., Harris, M., & Stulz, R. M. (Eds.), *Handbook of the Economics of Finance* (Vol. 1, pp. 1053–1128). Elsevier.

Barney, J. (1991). Firm resources and sustained competitive advantage. *Journal of Management*, *17*(1), 99–120. DOI: 10.1177/014920639101700108

Bear, S., Rahman, N., & Post, C. (2010). The impact of board diversity and gender composition on corporate social responsibility and firm reputation. *Journal of Business Ethics*, *97*(2), 207–221. DOI: 10.1007/s10551-010-0505-2

Bebbington, J., & Unerman, J. (2018). Achieving the United Nations Sustainable Development Goals. *Accounting, Auditing & Accountability Journal*, *31*(1), 2–24. DOI: 10.1108/AAAJ-05-2017-2929

Besio, C., Jöstingmeier, M., & Posner, C. (2024). Digital transformation and organizational restlessness. *Frontiers in Sociology*, *9*, 1430384. DOI: 10.3389/fsoc.2024.1430384 PMID: 39319315

Bhat, K. U., Chen, S., Chen, Y., & Jebran, K. (2020). Debt capacity, debt choice, and underinvestment problem: Evidence from China. *Economic research-. Ekonomska Istrazivanja*, *33*(1), 267–287. DOI: 10.1080/1331677X.2019.1699438

Bhimani, A., & Langfield-Smith, K. (2007). Structure, Formality and the Importance of Financial and Non-financial Information in Strategy Development and Implementation. *Management Accounting Research*, *18*(1), 3–31. DOI: 10.1016/j.mar.2006.06.005

Blasch, J., Boogen, N., Daminato, C., & Filippini, M. (2017). Empower the consumer! Energy-related financial literacy and its socioeconomic determinants. *Economics Working Paper Series*, 17(274), 1-36.

Blickle, K., Hamerling, S. N., & Morgan, D. P. (2021). How bad are weather disasters for banks? (FRB of New York Staff Report 990).

Borensztein, E., & Ye, L. S. (2018). Corporate debt overhang and investment: Firm-level evidence. *World Bank Policy Research Working Paper*, •••, 8553. DOI: 10.1596/1813-9450-8553

Borensztein, E., & Ye, L. S. (2021). Corporate debt overhang and investment in emerging economies: Firm-level evidence. *International Finance*, *24*(1), 18–39. DOI: 10.1111/infi.12382

Bose, S., & Khan, H. Z. (2022). Corporate SDG Reporting and Institutional Determinants: An International Study. *Journal of Cleaner Production*, *365*, 132780. DOI: 10.1016/j.jclepro.2021.132780

Botta, M. (2020). Financial crises, debt overhang, and firm growth in transition economies. *Applied Economics*, *52*(40), 4333–4350. DOI: 10.1080/00036846.2020.1734184

Branco, M. C., & Rodrigues, L. L. (2006). Corporate social responsibility and resource-based perspectives. *Journal of Business Ethics*, *69*(2), 111–132. DOI: 10.1007/s10551-006-9071-z

Brounen, D., Kok, N., & Quigley, J. M. (2013). Energy literacy, awareness, and conservation behavior of residential households. *Energy Economics, 38*, 42–50. DOI: 10.1016/j.eneco.2013.02.008

Brown, R., & Das, A. (2021). Behavioral biases and sustainable investing: Evidence from ESG portfolios. *Global Finance Journal, 52*, 100596.

Brunnermeier, M., & Krishnamurthy, A. (2020). Corporate debt overhang and credit policy. *Brookings Papers on Economic Activity, 2020*(2), 447–502. DOI: 10.1353/eca.2020.0014

Burns, J., & Scapens, R. W. (2000). Conceptualizing Management Accounting Change: An Institutional Framework. *Management Accounting Research, 11*(1), 3–25. DOI: 10.1006/mare.1999.0119

Bužienė, I. (2024). Factors and indicators shaping financial literacy: a multicriteria analysis of selected programs and strategic insights for resilient economic development. *Intelektinė ekonomika, 18*(2), 450-469.

Caldeira, M. M., & Ward, J. M. (2002). Understanding the successful adoption and use of IS/IT in SMEs: An explanation from Portuguese manufacturing industries. *Information Systems Journal, 12*(2), 121–152. DOI: 10.1046/j.1365-2575.2002.00119.x

Caprani, L. (2016). Five ways the Sustainable Development Goals are better than the Millennium Development Goals and why every educationalist should care. *Management in Education, 30*(3), 102–104. DOI: 10.1177/0892020616653464

Carrara, S. (2020). Reactor ageing and phase-out policies: Global and regional prospects for nuclear power generation. *Energy Policy, 147*, 111834. Advance online publication. DOI: 10.1016/j.enpol.2020.111834

Carrera, J., & de la Vega, P. (2024). The effect of external debt on greenhouse gas emissions. *Journal of Economics and Finance, 48*(3), 754–776. DOI: 10.1007/s12197-024-09674-x

Centro de Investigación y Docencia Económicas. (2022). *Encuesta Nacional de Energía y Cambio Climático 2022*. CIDE.

Cepêda, C. L. M. (2024). Why Reporting Sustainability? The Portuguese Non-financial Reporting's Socio-historical Evolution. In Thrassou, A., Vrontis, D., Efthymiou, L., Weber, Y., Shams, S. M. R., & Tsoukatos, E. (Eds.), *Non-Profit Organisations* (Vol. III). Palgrave Studies in Cross-disciplinary Business Research, In Association with EuroMed Academy of Business. Palgrave Macmillan., DOI: 10.1007/978-3-031-62534-3_3

Cepêda, C., Monteiro, A. P., & Aibar-Guzmán, B. (2025a). Decoupling in Sustainability Reporting: A Systematic Literature Review. *Corporate Social Responsibility and Environmental Management*, *32*(3), 2988–3007. Advance online publication. DOI: 10.1002/csr.3114

Cepêda, C., Monteiro, A. P., & Aibar-Guzmán, B. (2025b). Bridging the ESG Credibility Gap: The Role of Institutional Investors in Mitigating ESG Decoupling. *Business Strategy and the Environment*, *34*(6), 7139–7160. Advance online publication. DOI: 10.1002/bse.4336

Charoenwong, B., Doh, H., & Wang, Y. (2018). Informational Role of Investment and Bankruptcy Costs.

Cheng, J. (2023). Modelling and forecasting risk dependence and portfolio VaR for cryptocurrencies. *Empirical Economics*, *65*(2), 899–924. DOI: 10.1007/s00181-023-02360-7 PMID: 36684815

Chenhall, R. H., & Morris, D. (1986). The impact of structure, environment, and interdependence on the perceived usefulness of management accounting systems. *The Accounting Review*, *61*(1), 16–35.

Choudhary, H., & Jain, H. (2023). Addressing Financial Exclusion through Financial Literacy training programs: A Systematic Literature Review. *Empirical Research in Vocational Education and Training*, *15*(1), 8. DOI: 10.1186/s40461-023-00147-9

Claudy, M. C., Michelsen, C., & O'Driscoll, A. (2013). The diffusion of microgeneration technologies: Assessing the influence of perceived product characteristics on home owners' willingness to pay. *Energy Policy*, *55*, 582–590. DOI: 10.1016/j.enpol.2012.12.058

Clemente-Almendros, J. A., Nicoara-Popescu, D., & Pastor-Sanz, I. (2024). Digital transformation in SMEs: Understanding its determinants and size heterogeneity. *Technology in Society*, *77*, 102483. DOI: 10.1016/j.techsoc.2024.102483

Cloete, E., Courtney, S., & Fintz, J. (2002). Small businesses' acceptance and adoption of e-commerce in the Western-Cape Province of South Africa. *Electronic Journal of Information Systems Evaluation*, *5*(1), 1–13.

Comisión Nacional Bancaria y de Valores. (2023). *Reporte Nacional de Inclusión Financiera*. CNBV.https://www.gob.mx/cnbv/acciones-y-programas/divulgacion-de-inclusion-financiera-26625

Comisión Reguladora de Energía. (2023). *Reporte del Mercado Eléctrico Nacional 2023*. CRE. https://www.gob.mx/cre/documentos/informe-de-labores-2023-359246

Creswell, J. W., & Plano Clark, V. L. (2017). *Designing and conducting mixed methods research* (3rd ed.). SAGE Publications.

Dai, J., & Vasarhelyi, M. A. (2017). Toward Blockchain-Based Accounting and Assurance. *Journal of Information Systems*, *31*(3), 5–21. DOI: 10.2308/isys-51804

Dalenogare, L. S., Benitez, G. B., Ayala, N. F., & Frank, A. G. (2018). The expected contribution of Industry 4.0 technologies for industrial performance. *International Journal of Production Economics*, *204*, 383–394. DOI: 10.1016/j.ijpe.2018.08.019

Dangelico, R.M., 2017. What drives green product development and how do different antecedents affect market performance? A survey of Italian companies with eco-labels. *Bus. Strat. Environ. 26* (8), 1144e1161. https://doi.org//DOI: 10.1002

Dar, A. A., Anuradha, N., & Qadir, S. (2019). Estimating probabilities of default of different firms and the statistical tests. *Journal of Global Entrepreneurship Research*, *9*(1), 1–15. DOI: 10.1186/s40497-019-0152-8

Dar, A. A., & Qadir, S. (2019). Distance to default and probability of default: An experimental study. *Journal of Global Entrepreneurship Research*, *9*(1), 1–12. DOI: 10.1186/s40497-019-0154-6

Davis, F. D. (1989). Perceived usefulness, perceived ease of use, and user acceptance of information technology. *Management Information Systems Quarterly*, *13*(3), 319–340. DOI: 10.2307/249008

De Lucia, C., Pazienza, P., & Bartlett, M. (2020). Does good ESG lead to better financial performances by firms? Machine learning and logistic regression models of public enterprises in Europe. *Sustainability (Basel)*, *12*(13), 5317. DOI: 10.3390/su12135317

Deloitte. (2020). *The Future of Audit: Deloitte's Innovation in Cognitive Technology*. Retrieved from https://www2.deloitte.com

DeWaters, J. E., & Powers, S. E. (2011). Energy literacy of secondary students in New York State (USA): A measure of knowledge, affect, and behavior. *Energy Policy*, *39*(3), 1699–1710. DOI: 10.1016/j.enpol.2010.12.049

Ding, N., Bhat, K., & Jebran, K. (2020). Debt choice, growth opportunities and corporate investment: Evidence from China. *Financial Innovation*, *6*(1), 1–22. DOI: 10.1186/s40854-020-00194-1

Duffie, D., & Pan, J. (1997). An overview of value at risk. *Journal of Derivatives*, *4*(3), 7–49. DOI: 10.3905/jod.1997.407971

Duque-Grisales, E., & Aguilera-Caracuel, J. (2021). Environmental, social and governance (ESG) scores and financial performance of multilatinas: Moderating effects of geographic international diversification and financial slack. *Journal of Business Ethics*, *168*(2), 315–334. DOI: 10.1007/s10551-019-04177-w

Dutta, A., Banducci, S., & Camargo, C. Q. (2025). Divided by discipline? A systematic literature review on the quantification of online sexism and misogyny using a semi-automated approach. *Scientometrics*, *130*(9), 4915–4971. Advance online publication. DOI: 10.1007/s11192-025-05410-2 PMID: 41142644

Erin, O. A., Bamigboye, O. A., & Oyewo, B. (2022). Sustainable development goals (SDG) reporting: An analysis of disclosure. *Journal of Accounting in Emerging Economies*, *12*(5), 761–789. DOI: 10.1108/JAEE-02-2020-0037

European Commission. (2023). *Digital Economy and Society Index (DESI) 2023: Portugal Report*. Brussels.

EY. (2019). *How Robotic Process Automation (RPA) is Transforming Tax Functions*. Retrieved from https://www.ey.com

Eze, S. C., & Okafor, C. (2023). The impact of cognitive diversity on financial team decision-making and performance. *Journal of Financial Management*, *12*(3), 205–223.

Fama, E. F. (1970). Efficient capital markets: A review of theory and empirical work. *The Journal of Finance*, *25*(2), 383–417. DOI: 10.2307/2325486

Favre, L., & Galeano, J. A. (2002). Mean-modified value-at-risk optimization with hedge funds. *Journal of Alternative Investments*, *5*(2), 21–25. DOI: 10.3905/jai.2002.319052

Feng, G., & Zheng, M. (2022). Economic policy uncertainty and renewable energy innovation: International evidence. *Innovation and Green Development.*, *100010*(2), 100010. Advance online publication. DOI: 10.1016/j.igd.2022.100010

Feng, Z., Zeng, B., & Ming, Q. (2018). Environmental regulation, two-way foreign direct investment, and green innovation efficiency in China's manufacturing industry. *International Journal of Environmental Research and Public Health*, *15*(10), 2292. DOI: 10.3390/ijerph15102292 PMID: 30347639

Ferhi, A., & Helali, K. (2024). The impact of renewable energy on the environment and socio-economic welfare: Empirical evidence from OECD countries. *Journal of the Knowledge Economy*, *15*(1), 4776–4799. DOI: 10.1007/s13132-023-01320-x

Fernando, C. S., Sharfman, M. P., & Uysal, V. B. (2009, August). Do investors want firms to be green? Environmental performance, ownership and stock market liquidity. In *Academy of Management Proceedings* (Vol. 2009, No. 1, pp. 1-6). Briarcliff Manor, NY 10510: Academy of Management. DOI: 10.5465/ambpp.2009.44248481

Fiaschi, D., Giuliani, E., & Nieri, F. (2020). Overcoming the liability of origin by doing no-harm: Emerging country firms' social irresponsibility as they go global. *Journal of World Business*, *55*(4), 101094. DOI: 10.1016/j.jwb.2016.09.001

Fraenkel, J., & Filer, C. (2022). Prisoners of a distant past? Linguistic diversity and the time-depth of human settlement in Papua New Guinea. *World Development*, *157*, 105921. Advance online publication. DOI: 10.1016/j.worlddev.2022.105921

Friede, G., Busch, T., & Bassen, A. (2015). ESG and financial performance: Aggregated evidence from more than 2000 empirical studies. *Journal of Sustainable Finance & Investment*, *5*(4), 210–233. DOI: 10.1080/20430795.2015.1118917

Gaivoronski, A. A., & Pflug, G. (2005). Value-at-risk in portfolio optimization: Properties and computational approach. *The Journal of Risk*, *7*(2), 1–31. DOI: 10.21314/JOR.2005.106

Galloway, L., & Mochrie, R. (2005). The use of ICT in rural firms: A policy-oriented literature review. *Info*, *7*(3), 33–46. DOI: 10.1108/14636690510596784

García-Sánchez, I. M., Ortiz-Martínez, E., Marín-Hernández, S., & Aibar-Guzmán, B. (2023). How does the European Green Deal affect the disclosure of environmental information? *Corporate Social Responsibility and Environmental Management*, *30*(6), 2766–2782. DOI: 10.1002/csr.2514

Gartner. (2020). *How to Overcome Legacy Systems in Digital Transformation*. Gartner Research Brief.

Ghobakhloo, M., & Iranmanesh, M. (2021). Digital transformation success under Industry 4.0: A strategic guideline for manufacturing SMEs. *Journal of Manufacturing Technology Management*, *32*(8), 1533–1556. DOI: 10.1108/JMTM-11-2020-0455

Gobierno de México. (2021). *Programa Especial de la Transición Energética 2021-2024*. Secretaría de Energía.

González-Hernández, L., Ramírez-Montoya, M. S., & García-Peñalvo, F. J. (2019). Energy literacy among Mexican university students: A cross-sectional study. *Sustainability*, *11*(24), 7143.

Gray, R. (2010). Is Accounting for Sustainability Actually Accounting for Sustainability…and How Would We Know? *An Exploration of Narratives of Organisations and the Planet. Accounting, Organizations and Society*, *35*(1), 47–62. DOI: 10.1016/j.aos.2009.04.006

Hall, J. A. (2011). *Accounting Information Systems* (7th ed.). South-Western College Publishing.

Harmawan, B. N., & Ridho, W. F. (2024). Determinants influencing SMEs in E-commerce adoption through local government facilities in Indonesia: Mixed methods approach. *The Electronic Journal on Information Systems in Developing Countries*, *90*(2), e12301. DOI: 10.1002/isd2.12301

Harris, L., Johnson, K., & Martinez, D. (2024). Behavioral training and inclusive culture: Enhancing decision quality in financial organizations. *Journal of Organizational Behavior*, *45*(1), 78–94.

Hashim, H. T. (2022). Impact of quality and management in accounting information systems on decision making for smes enterprises. *Academy of Accounting and Financial Studies Journal*, *26*(6), 1–11.

He, C., Jia, F., Wang, L., Chen, L., & Fernandes, K. (2023). The impact of corporate social responsibility decoupling on financial performance: The role of customer structure and operational slack. *International Journal of Operations & Production Management*, *43*(12), 1859–1890. DOI: 10.1108/IJOPM-08-2022-0521

Hendricks, S., & Mwapwele, S. D. (2023). A systematic literature review on the factors influencing e-commerce adoption in developing countries. *Data and Information Management*, *8*(3), 100045. DOI: 10.1016/j.dim.2023.100045

Hennessy, C. A. (2004). Tobin's Q, debt overhang, and investment. *The Journal of Finance*, *59*(4), 1717–1742. DOI: 10.1111/j.1540-6261.2004.00677.x

Hernández-Terrones, L. M., Rodríguez-Hernández, O., & Martínez-Rodríguez, M. (2021). Energy literacy and renewable energy adoption in Mexican households: A regional analysis. *Energy Policy*, *156*, 112415.

Hla, D., & Teru, S. P. (2015). Efficiency of accounting information system and performance measures – Literature Review. *International Journal of Multidisciplinary and Current Research*, *3*, 976–984.

Hong, L. J., Hu, Z., & Liu, G. (2014). Monte Carlo methods for value-at-risk and conditional value-at-risk: A review. [TOMACS]. *ACM Transactions on Modeling and Computer Simulation*, *24*(4), 1–37. DOI: 10.1145/2661631

Hong, W., & Zhu, K. (2006). Migrating to Internet-based e-commerce: Factors affecting e-commerce adoption and migration at the firm level. *Information & Management*, *43*(2), 204–221. DOI: 10.1016/j.im.2005.06.003

Huang, K., & Etienne, X. (2021). Do natural hazards in the Gulf Coast still matter for state-level natural gas prices in the US? Evidence after the shale gas boom. *Energy Economics*, *98*, 105267. Advance online publication. DOI: 10.1016/j.eneco.2021.105267

Hu, J., Hu, X., Peng, Y., & Zhang, Y. (2024). The Green Costs of Debt Overhang: Evidence from Local Government Debt Restructuring. *Available at SSRN* 5076456.

Hull, J. (2009). *Options, Futures, and Other Derivatives* (Vol. 2). Pearson Education.

Hussein, L. A., & Baharudin, A. S. (2017). Factors affecting small and medium enterprises (SMEs) continuance intention to adopt e-commerce in Jordan. *International Journal of Advanced and Applied Sciences*, *4*(4), 110–117. DOI: 10.21833/ijaas.2017.04.016

IAPMEI. (2023). *Digital Decade Country Report – Portugal.* Agência para a Competitividade e Inovação. Retrieved from https://www.iapmei.pt

IFAC. (2019). *Enabling the Accountant's Role in Effective Enterprise Risk Management*. International Federation of Accountants.

IFAC. (2022). *Accountancy and Cybersecurity: Professional Responsibilities and Challenges*. International Federation of Accountants.

Infosys. (2021). *Transforming Finance with Intelligent Automation*. Infosys Whitepaper. Retrieved from https://www.infosys.com

Instituto Nacional de Estadística y Geografía. (2024). *Censos Económicos 2023: Resultados preliminares*. INEGI. https://www.inegi.org.mx/programas/ce/2024/

International Energy Agency. (2023). *Mexico Energy Outlook 2023*. IEA Publications.

International Energy Agency. (2023). *World Energy Outlook 2023*. IEA Publications. https://www.iea.org/reports/world-energy-outlook-2023

Istiyana, A. N., Nurniah, N., Fatmawati, F., & Rahman, A. (2025). Factors Influencing the Success of E-Commerce-Based Accounting Information System (Study on MSMEs in Makassar). *American Journal of Commerce and Technology Applications*, *10*(1), 45–57.

Javed, S., & Husain, U. (2021). Impact of Financial Factors on Social and Financial Sustainability in Banking Sector: A Mediating Role of Financial Literacy. In Singh, D. (Ed.), *S., A*. Financial Inclusion in Emerging Markets., DOI: 10.1007/978-981-16-2652-4_13

Jiming, L., Chengqin, S., & Zhaohua, W. (2010, August). An empirical analysis of debt financing on firm investment behavior: evidence from China. In *2010 International Conference of Information Science and Management Engineering* (Vol. 2, pp. 356-359). IEEE. DOI: 10.1109/ISME.2010.17

Jorion, P. (1996). Risk2: Measuring the risk in value at risk. *Financial Analysts Journal, 52*(6), 47–56. DOI: 10.2469/faj.v52.n6.2039

Kahneman, D. (2011). *Thinking, fast and slow*. Farrar, Straus and Giroux. https://ia800603.us.archive.org/10/items/DanielKahnemanThinkingFastAndSlow/Daniel%20Kahneman-Thinking%2C%20Fast%20and%20Slow%20%20.pdf

Kahneman, D., & Tversky, A. (1979). Prospect theory: An analysis of decision under risk. *Econometrica, 47*(2), 263–291. DOI: 10.2307/1914185

Kalemli-Ozcan, S., Laeven, L., & Moreno, D. (2015). *Debt overhang, rollover risk and investment in Europe.*

Kalemli-Özcan, Ş., Laeven, L., & Moreno, D. (2022). Debt overhang, rollover risk, and corporate investment: Evidence from the European crisis. *Journal of the European Economic Association, 20*(6), 2353–2395. DOI: 10.1093/jeea/jvac018

Khan, K., & Su, C.-W. (2022). Does policy uncertainty threaten renewable energy? Evidence from G7 countries. *Environmental Science and Pollution Research International, 29*(24), 34813–34829. DOI: 10.1007/s11356-021-16713-1 PMID: 35040056

Khin, S., & Ho, T. C. F. (2019). Digital technology, digital capability and organizational performance: A mediating role of digital innovation. *International Journal of Innovation Science, 11*(2), 177–195. DOI: 10.1108/IJIS-08-2018-0083

Klapper, L., & Panos, G. A. (2011). Financial literacy and retirement planning: The Russian case. *Journal of Pension Economics and Finance, 10*(4), 599–618. DOI: 10.1017/S1474747211000503

Kotter, J. P. (1996). *Leading Change*. Harvard Business Press.

KPMG. (2021). *Clara: The Future of Audit*. KPMG Insights. Retrieved from https://home.kpmg

Kraus, S., Palmer, C., Kailer, N., Kallinger, F. L., & Spitzer, J. (2021). Digital transformation: An overview of the current state of the art of research. *SAGE Open*, *11*(3), 1–14. DOI: 10.1177/21582440211047576

Kuchler, A. (2020). Leverage, investment, and recovery from a financial crisis: The role of debt overhang. *Studies in Economics and Finance*, *37*(1), 143–159. DOI: 10.1108/SEF-04-2019-0158

Kuester, K., Mittnik, S., & Paolella, M. S. (2006). Value-at-risk prediction: A comparison of alternative strategies. *Journal of Financial Econometrics*, *4*(1), 53–89. DOI: 10.1093/jjfinec/nbj002

Kurtzman, R., & Zeke, D. (2015). *The gains from resolving debt overhang: Evidence from a structural estimation*. Working Paper.

Lacity, M., & Willcocks, L. (2016). Robotic Process Automation: The Next Transformation Lever for Shared Services. *Journal of Information Technology Teaching Cases*, *6*(2), 1–12.

Lal, K. (2002). E-business and manufacturing sector: A study of small and medium-sized enterprises in India. *Research Policy*, *33*(1), 111–127. DOI: 10.1016/S0048-7333(01)00191-3

Lawrence, J. E., & Tar, U. A. (2010). Barriers to e-commerce in developing countries. Information. *Society and Justice Journal*, *3*(1), 23–35.

Lee, S., & Kim, J. (2022). Nudging investor behavior: Behavioral finance and regulatory strategies. *Journal of Policy Analysis*, *37*(4), 456–478.

Looi, H. C. (2005). E-commerce adoption in Brunei Darussalam: A quantitative analysis of factors influencing its adoption. *Communications of the Association for Information Systems*, *15*, 61–81. DOI: 10.17705/1CAIS.01503

Loo, M. K., Ramachandran, S., & Raja Yusof, R. N. (2024). Systematic Review of Factors and Barriers Influencing E-Commerce Adoption among SMEs over the Last Decade: A TOE Framework Perspective. *Journal of the Knowledge Economy*, *16*(2), 1–25. DOI: 10.1007/s13132-024-02257-5

Lusardi, A., & Mitchell, O. (2023). The Importance of Financial Literacy: Opening a New Field. Working Paper 31145 *NBER WORKING PAPER SERIES*. https://www.nber.org/system/files/working_papers/w31145/w31145.pdf DOI: DOI: 10.3386/w31145

Lusardi, A., & Mitchell, O. S. (2011). Financial literacy around the world: An overview. *Journal of Pension Economics and Finance*, *10*(4), 497–508. DOI: 10.1017/S1474747211000448 PMID: 28553190

Lu, Y., Cao, B., Hua, Y., & Ding, L. (2020). Efficiency Measurement of Green Regional Development and Its Influencing Factors: An Improved Data Envelopment Analysis Framework. *Sustainability (Basel)*, *12*(11), 4361. DOI: 10.3390/su12114361

Maji, S. G., & Haloi, A. (2025). Corporate Sustainable Practices, Institutional Factors, and Sustainable Development Goals: Evidence From Asian Emerging Markets. *Sustainable Development (Bradford)*, sd.70006. Advance online publication. DOI: 10.1002/sd.70006

Manda, H. M., Abidin, Z., & Jusman, I. A. (2024). *The Impact of Using E-Commerce and Accounting Information Systems on Financial Performance in MSMEs*. Jurnal Ekonomi, Manajemen dan Akuntansi, 15(3), 112–126.

Maroufkhani, P., Ismail, W. K. W., & Ghobakhloo, M. (2020). Big data analytics adoption model for small and medium enterprises. *Journal of Science and Technology Policy Management*, *11*(2), 285–309. DOI: 10.1108/JSTPM-02-2020-0018

Martínez-Rodríguez, M., & López-Pérez, C. (2020). Household energy literacy and renewable energy investment decisions in Mexico. *Energy and Building*, *225*, 110324.

Martinez, T., Smith, P., & Chen, R. (2021). Assessing behavioral nudges in financial regulation: Evidence from multiple jurisdictions. *Regulation & Governance*, *15*(3), 298–317.

Mehmann, J., Teuteberg, F., 2016. The fourth-party logistics service provider approach to support sustainable development goals in transportation - a case study of the German agricultural bulk logistics sector. *J. Clean. Prod. 126*, 382e393. DOI: 10.1016/j.jclepro.2016.03.095

Michael, S. (2017). *United Nations Development Programme (UNDP)*. Max Planck Encyclopedia of Public International Law., DOI: 10.1093/law:epil/9780199231690/e550

Molla, A., & Licker, P. S. (2005). E-commerce adoption in developing countries: A model and instrument. *Information & Management*, *42*(6), 877–899. DOI: 10.1016/j.im.2004.09.002

Moll, J., & Yigitbasioglu, O. M. (2019). The Role of Internet-Related Technologies in Shaping the Work of Accountants: New Directions for Accounting Research. *The British Accounting Review*, *51*(6), 100833. DOI: 10.1016/j.bar.2019.04.002

Monteiro, A. P., Cepêda, C., Borges, A. P., & Vieira, E. (2024). Does CSR committee presence, stakeholder engagement, gender equality (SDG 5) and firm value influence ESG performance reporting? An EU pre and during Covid-19 analysis. Measuring Business Excellence, (ahead-of-print). https://doi.org/DOI: 10.1108/MBE-03-2024-0034

Moullin, M. (2017). Improving and evaluating performance with the public sector scorecard. *International Journal of Productivity and Performance Management*, *66*(4), 442–458. DOI: 10.1108/IJPPM-06-2015-0092

Moyen, N. (2007). How big is the debt overhang problem? *Journal of Economic Dynamics & Control*, *31*(2), 433–472. DOI: 10.1016/j.jedc.2005.10.008

Mundlak, Y. (1978). On the pooling of time series and cross section data. *Econometrica*, *46*(1), 69–85. DOI: 10.2307/1913646

Myers, S. C. (1977). Determinants of corporate borrowing. *Journal of Financial Economics*, *5*(2), 147–175. DOI: 10.1016/0304-405X(77)90015-0

Ncube, L. B. (2020). The Evolution of Management Accounting: A Review of the Evidence. *Journal of Accounting and Finance in Emerging Economies*, *6*(3), 775–784.

Nguyen, T. H., & Waring, T. S. (2013). The adoption of customer relationship management (CRM) technology in SMEs: An empirical study. *Journal of Small Business and Enterprise Development*, *20*(4), 824–848. DOI: 10.1108/JSBED-01-2012-0013

Nguyen, T., & Tran, L. (2022). Cognitive biases and audit quality: The role of behavioral training. *Accounting, Organizations and Society*, *101*, 101247. Advance online publication. DOI: 10.1016/j.aos.2022.101247

Nicolas, T. (2021). Short-term financial constraints and SMEs' investment decision: Evidence from the working capital channel. *Small Business Economics*. Advance online publication. DOI: 10.1007/s11187-021-00488-3 PMID: 38624861

Nicolo, G., Zampone, G., De Iorio, S., & Sannino, G. (2024). Does SDG Disclosure Reflect Corporate Underlying Sustainability Performance? Evidence From UN Global Compact Participants. *Journal of International Financial Management & Accounting*, *35*(1), 214–260. DOI: 10.1111/jifm.12194

OECD. (2018). *Digital Government Review of Estonia: Reinventing the Public Sector*. OECD Digital Economy Papers.

OECD. (2021). *The Digital Transformation of SMEs*. OECD Publishing., DOI: 10.1787/bdb9256a-

OECD. (2024). *SME Digitalisation in 2024: Managing Shocks and Transitions*. OECD SME and Entrepreneurship Papers, OECD Publishing.

Oliveira, T., Thomas, M., Baptista, G., & Campos, F. (2020). Mobile payment: Understanding the determinants of customer adoption and intention to recommend the technology. *Computers in Human Behavior*, *61*, 404–414. DOI: 10.1016/j.chb.2016.03.030

Opoku, A. (2016, September). SDG2030: A sustainable built environment's role in achieving the post-2015 United Nations Sustainable Development Goals. In *Proceedings of the 32nd Annual ARCOM Conference* (Vol. 2, pp. 1149-1158). Manchester, UK: Association of Researchers in Construction Management.

Palm, J., & Eriksson, L. (2013). Residential solar electricity adoption: How households in Sweden search for and use information. *Energy Policy*, *62*, 1024–1030. DOI: 10.1016/j.enpol.2013.07.115

Pattasani, S., Mohapatra, S., & Jyoti, A. (2025). IoT-Based Social Device Network with Cloud Computing Architecture. *Systematic Reviews*.

Pearce, D., & Turner, R. K. (1990). *Economics of natural resources and the environment*. Johns Hopkins University Press.

Pineda-Escobar, M. A. 2019. Moving the 2030 agenda forward: SDG implementation in Colombia. *Corp. Govern. Internatl. J. Bus. Soc. 19* (1), 176e188. DOI: 10.1108/CG-11-2017-0268

Pizzi, S., Caputo, A., Corvino, A., & Venturelli, A. (2020). Management research and the UN sustainable development goals (SDGs): A bibliometric investigation and systematic review. *Journal of Cleaner Production*, *276*, 124033. DOI: 10.1016/j.jclepro.2020.124033

Pizzi, S., Rosati, F., & Venturelli, A. (2021). The determinants of business contribution to the 2030 Agenda: Introducing the SDG Reporting Score. *Business Strategy and the Environment*, *30*(1), 404–421. DOI: 10.1002/bse.2628

Poddar, P., Bhattacharya, R., & Bhatt, R. (2025). Algorithmic trading and behavioral finance: An integrated approach. *Journal of Financial Technology*, *10*(1), 34–56.

Porter, M. E., & Millar, V. E. (1985). How Information Gives You Competitive Advantage. *Harvard Business Review*, *63*(4), 149–160.

Portugal, B. C. S. D. (2023). *SDG Compass*. Lisboa, Portugal. https://bcsdportugal.org/wp-content/uploads/2020/12/SDG-Compass.pdf

Probst, G., Raub, S., & Romhardt, K. (1999). *Managing knowledge: Building blocks for success*. John Wiley & Sons.

PwC. (2022). *Global Digital Trust Insights Survey 2022*. Retrieved from https://www.pwc.com

Quinn, M. (2014). Stability and Change in Management Accounting Over Time—A Century or So of Evidence from Guinness. *Management Accounting Research*, *25*(1), 76–92. DOI: 10.1016/j.mar.2013.06.001

Rahayu, R., & Day, J. (2015). Determinant factors of e-commerce adoption by SMEs in developing country: Evidence from Indonesia. *Procedia: Social and Behavioral Sciences*, *195*, 142–150. DOI: 10.1016/j.sbspro.2015.06.423

Ramos Farroñán, E. V., Farfán Chilicaus, G. C., Cruz Salinas, L. E., Correa Rojas, L., Chuquitucto Cotrina, L. K., Licapa-Redolfo, G. S., Vera Zelada, P., & Vera Zelada, L. A. (2025). Green Finance and the Energy Transition: A Systematic Review of Economic Instruments for Renewable Energy Deployment in Emerging Economies. *Energies*, *18*(17), 4560. DOI: 10.3390/en18174560

Reddy, P. R., & Kumar, A. S. (2022). Credit Card Fraudulent Transactions Prediction Using Novel Sequential Transactions by Comparing Light Gradient Booster Algorithm Over Isolation Forest Algorithm. 2022 2nd International Conference on Innovative Practices in Technology and Management (ICIPTM)

Richins, G., Stapleton, R., Stratopoulos, T., & Wong, C. (2017). Big Data Analytics: Opportunity or Threat for the Accounting Profession? *Journal of Information Systems*, *31*(3), 63–79. DOI: 10.2308/isys-51805

Rogers, E. M. (2003). *Diffusion of innovations* (5th ed.). Free Press.

Rom, A., & Rohde, C. (2007). Management accounting and integrated information systems: A literature review. *International Journal of Accounting Information Systems*, *8*(1), 40–68. DOI: 10.1016/j.accinf.2006.12.003

Rosati, F., & Faria, L. G. D. (2019a). Addressing the SDGs in sustainability reports: The relationship with institutional factors. *Journal of Cleaner Production*, *215*, 1312–1326. DOI: 10.1016/j.jclepro.2018.12.107

Rosati, F., & Faria, L. G. D. (2019b). Business contribution to the Sustainable Development Agenda: Organizational factors related to early adoption of SDG disclosure. *Corporate Social Responsibility and Environmental Management*, *26*(3), 588–597. DOI: 10.1002/csr.1705

Sachs, J., Schmidt-Traub, G., Kroll, C., Lafortune, G., Fuller, G., & Woelm, F. (2021). *Sustainable Development Report 2021*. Cambridge University Press. DOI: 10.1017/9781009106559

Sadiq, U., Khan, A. F., Ikhlaq, K., & Mujtaba, B. G. (2012). The impact of information systems on the performance of human resources department. *Journal of Business Studies Quarterly*, *3*(4), 77–91.

Safiullah, M., Houqe, M. N., Ali, M. J., & Azam, M. S. (2024). Debt overhang and carbon emissions. *International Journal of Managerial Finance*, *20*(4), 1069–1093. DOI: 10.1108/IJMF-06-2023-0305

Sajady, H., Dastgir, M., & Nejad, H. H. (2008). Evaluation of the effectiveness of accounting information systems. *International Journal of Information Science and Technology*, *6*(2), 49–59.

Santoro, G., Vrontis, D., Thrassou, A., & Dezi, L. (2018). The Internet of Things: Building a knowledge management system for open innovation and knowledge management capacity. *Technological Forecasting and Social Change*, *136*, 347–354. DOI: 10.1016/j.techfore.2017.02.034

Sari, W., Setiawan, A., & Reswari, R. A. (2025). *Implementation of E-Commerce and Accounting Information Systems Towards Successful SMEs Performance.* Jurnal Ilmiah Manajemen dan Bisnis, 25(1), 88–100.

Scapens, R. W., & Jazayeri, M. (2003). ERP Systems and Management Accounting Change: Opportunities or Impacts? *European Accounting Review*, *12*(1), 201–233. DOI: 10.1080/0963818031000087907

Scupola, A. (2003). The adoption of Internet commerce by SMEs in the south of Italy: An environmental, technological and organizational perspective. *Journal of Global Information Technology Management*, *6*(1), 52–71. DOI: 10.1080/1097198X.2003.10856343

Secretaría de Energía. (2023). *Balance Nacional de Energía 2022*. Gobierno de México.

Secretaría de Energía. (2024). *Estrategia Nacional de Energía 2024-2038*. SENER. https://www.gob.mx/sener/articulos/la-secretaria-de-energia-publica-el-programa-de-desarrollo-del-sistema-electrico-nacional-2024-2038

Secretaría de Medio Ambiente y Recursos Naturales. (2022). *Estrategia Nacional de Cambio Climático: Visión 10-20-40*. SEMARNAT. https://dsiappsdev.semarnat.gob.mx/datos/portal/publicaciones/2025/ENCC_2025_SEMARNAT.pdf

Sen, A. (2017). *Collective choice and social welfare* (Expanded ed.). Harvard University Press.

Sen, A. (1999). *Development as freedom*. Oxford University Press.

Simon, H. A. (1955). A behavioral model of rational choice. *The Quarterly Journal of Economics*, *69*(1), 99–118. DOI: 10.2307/1884852

Sokołowski, M., & Heffron, R. (2022, February). Defining and conceptualising energy policy failure: The when, where, why, and how. *Energy Policy*, *161*, 112745. DOI: 10.1016/j.enpol.2021.112745

Solomon, J. F., Solomon, A., Joseph, N. L., & Norton, S. D. (2013). Impression management, myth creation and fabrication in private social and environmental reporting: Insights from Erving Goffman. *Accounting, Organizations and Society*, *38*(3), 195–213. DOI: 10.1016/j.aos.2013.01.001

Soni, M. (2023). The impact of ESG practices on financial performance: Evidence from emerging markets. *Investment Management and Financial Innovations*, *20*(3), 150–163. DOI: 10.1016/j.jclepro.2017.02.180

Soni, M., & Dayal, V. (2023). Assessing ESG performance through SDG disclosure: A study of European listed firms. *Proceedings of the International Conference on Business Excellence*, 17(1), 749–762. https://doi.org/DOI: 10.2478/picbe-2023-0072

Soto-Acosta, P., Popa, S., & Martinez-Conesa, I. (2018). Information technology, knowledge management and environmental dynamism as drivers of innovation adoption in SMEs. *Journal of Knowledge Management*, *20*(4), 824–849. DOI: 10.1108/JKM-10-2017-0448

Soudani, S. N. (2012). The usefulness of an accounting information system for effective organizational performance. *International Journal of Economics and Finance*, *4*(5), 136–145. DOI: 10.5539/ijef.v4n5p136

Sovacool, B. K., & Blyth, P. L. (2015). Energy and environmental attitudes in the green state of Denmark: Implications for energy democracy, low carbon transitions, and energy literacy. *Environmental Science & Policy*, *54*, 304–315. DOI: 10.1016/j.envsci.2015.07.011

Sun, H., Edziah, B. K., Sun, C., & Kporsu, A. K. (2019). Institutional quality, green innovation and energy efficiency. *Energy Policy*, *135*, 111002. DOI: 10.1016/j.enpol.2019.111002

Teece, D. J. (2014). A dynamic capabilities-based entrepreneurial theory of the multinational enterprise. *Journal of International Business Studies*, *45*(1), 8–37. DOI: 10.1057/jibs.2013.54

Thaler, R. H. (1999). Mental accounting matters. *Journal of Behavioral Decision Making*, *12*(3), 183–206. DOI: 10.1002/(SICI)1099-0771(199909)12:3<183::AID-BDM318>3.0.CO;2-F

Topaloglou, N., Vladimirou, H., & Zenios, S. A. (2008). A dynamic stochastic programming model for international portfolio management. *European Journal of Operational Research*, *185*(3), 1501–1524. DOI: 10.1016/j.ejor.2005.07.035

Tornatzky, L. G., & Fleischer, M. (1990). *The Processes of Technological Innovation*. Lexington Books.

UNDP. (2019). *Integrating the SDGs into Corporate Reporting: A Practical Guide*. United Nations Development Programme.

Unilever. (2021). *Sustainable Living Plan: Annual Progress Report*. Retrieved from https://www.unilever.com

United Nations (UN). (2015) Transforming our world by 2030: A new agenda for global action Zero. Draft of the outcome document for the UN Summit to adopt the Post-2015 Development Agenda. New York: United Nations.

United Nations Development Programme (UNDP). (2017). *SDG Integration: UNDP and the Sustainable Development Goals*. https://sdgintegration.undp.org/

United Nations Environment Programme (UNEP). (2013) *Embedding the Environment in Sustainable Development Goals, UNEP Post-2015 Discussion Paper 1, Version 2*. Nairobi: United Nations Environment Programme.

Van Weele, A. J., & Van Raaij, E. M. (2014). The future of purchasing and supply management research: About relevance and rigor. *The Journal of Supply Chain Management, 50*(1), 56–72. DOI: 10.1111/jscm.12042

Vanlaer, W., Picarelli, M., & Marneffe, W. (2021). Debt and private investment: Does the EU suffer from a debt overhang? *Open Economies Review, 32*(4), 789–820. DOI: 10.1007/s11079-021-09621-x

Vasarhelyi, M. A., Kogan, A., & Tuttle, B. (2015). Big Data in Accounting: An Overview. *Accounting Horizons, 29*(2), 381–396. DOI: 10.2308/acch-51071

Vilaseca, J., Torrent-Sellens, J., & Guillen, M. (2007). ICT use in marketing as innovation success factor: Enhancing cooperation in new product development processes. *European Journal of Innovation Management, 10*(2), 268–288. DOI: 10.1108/14601060710745297

Warren, J. D.Jr, Moffitt, K. C., & Byrnes, P. (2015). How Big Data Will Change Accounting. *Accounting Horizons*, *29*(2), 397–407. DOI: 10.2308/acch-51069

Wilburn, K., & Wilburn, R. (2020). ESG Reporting Using UN Sustainable Development Goals. *Journal of Strategic Innovation & Sustainability*, *15*(2).

Wittry, M. D. (2021). (Debt) overhang: Evidence from resource extraction. *Review of Financial Studies*, *34*(4), 1699–1746. DOI: 10.1093/rfs/hhaa070

World Bank. (2021). *Digital Public Financial Management: Toward Transparency and Inclusion*. World Bank Publications.

World Bank. (2021). *Digital Transformation for Development*. World Bank Publications.

Wymer, S. A., & Regan, E. A. (2005). Factors influencing e-commerce adoption and use by small and medium businesses. *Electronic Markets*, *15*(4), 438–453. DOI: 10.1080/10196780500303151

Xero. (2023). *Annual Report and Global Impact*. Retrieved from https://www.xero.com

Yoon, K., Hoogduin, L., & Zhang, L. (2020). Cloud Computing and Accounting: A Framework for Cloud-Based Accounting Information Systems. *Journal of Accounting and Organizational Change*, *16*(4), 617–643.

Zampone, G., & Guidi, M. (2024). Sustainability reporting and assurance practices contribution to SDG disclosure: Evidence from communication on progress (CoP). *Meditari Accountancy Research*, *32*(7), 236–265. DOI: 10.1108/MEDAR-09-2023-2165

Zhao, T., & Liu, Z. (2022). Drivers of CO2 emissions: A debt perspective. *International Journal of Environmental Research and Public Health*, *19*(3), 1847. DOI: 10.3390/ijerph19031847 PMID: 35162869

Zhu, K., & Kraemer, K. L. (2005). Post-adoption variations in usage and value of e-business by organizations: Cross-country evidence from the retail industry. *Information Systems Research*, *16*(1), 61–84. DOI: 10.1287/isre.1050.0045

Zhu, K., Kraemer, K. L., & Xu, S. (2006). The process of innovation assimilation by firms in different countries: A technology diffusion perspective on e-business. *Management Science*, *52*(10), 1557–1576. DOI: 10.1287/mnsc.1050.0487

About the Contributors

Ana Pinto Borges holds a PhD in Economics, Faculty of Economics, University of Porto, in 2009. Since 2010 is Coordinating Professor at ISAG - European Business School specializing on the areas of Economics, Management, and Finance, and since 2015 Coordinator of the Master's Degree in Business Management and President of the Pedagogical Council of ISAG. She is Scientific Coordinator of Research Centre in Business Sciences and Tourism (CICET – FCVC) since 2021 and coordinated the ISAG Research Centre (NIDISAG) between 2015 and 2021. Since 2018, she is researcher of the Centre for Research in Organizations, Markets and Industrial Management (COMEGI). She supervised 2 PhD theses and is now supervising other 2, in addition to having supervised more than 40 master's theses. She published more than 180 publications (around 120 indexed in Scopus/WoS databases) in journals/book chapters/proceedings and 5 books (3 indexed in Scopus). She is associate editor at the Eurasian Business Review (indexed by Scopus/WoS – Q1) and editor and one of the founding members of the European Journal of Applied Business and Management (EJABM). She founded, integrated the organizer and scientific committees, and did the co-editor of the proceedings of International Conference in Applied Business and Management (ICABM – 5 eds since 2016), International Workshop in Tourism and Hospitality Management (IWTHM – 3 eds since 2017), and in Accounting and Taxation (IWAT – 3 eds since 2021). All these academic events have been indexed or are in evaluation by WoS and by EBSCO, among others. Furthermore, she is the coordinator and co-author of several applied projects financed by external entities (companies, municipalities, among others). She is Economist at the Portuguese Health Regulatory Authority since 2010 with the main function of carrying out sectoral studies and issuing opinions in the scope of access, quality and competition. Member of the Associação Portuguesa de Economia da Saúde (since 2005).

Albertina Paula Moreira Monteiro. She has a PhD in Economics and Business, specialising in accounting (University of Santiago de Compostela) and a PhD in Marketing and Strategy (University of Minho), a Master's degree in Accounting and Auditing (University of Minho) and a degree in Accounting and Business Management (Polytechnic Institute of Porto). She is a Senior Lecturer at Porto Accounting and Business School of the Polytechnic Institute of Porto (ISCAP-IPP) in the scientific area of Accounting. She is an integrated researcher at the Centre for Organizational and Social Studies of the Polytechnic Institute of Porto (CEOS.PP) and a collaborating researcher at the CICF (Polytechnic Institute of Cávado and Ave) and OSEAN (University of Madeira). She has been involved in several research projects in accounting area. Furthermore, She has published numerous scientific articles in indexed international journals and in the proceedings of international conferences.

Elvira Vieira holds a PhD in Applied Economics at the University of Santiago de Compostela, in 2007. Since 2012, serves as Dean of ISAG - European Business School, where she is also Principal Coordinating Lecturer, Member of the Technical-Scientific Council and Coordinator of the Scientific Area of Economics, since 2009. Also, invited Lecturer at the Polytechnic Institute of Viana do Castelo - School of Business Sciences, since 2009. With a research affiliation as integrated member at the Applied Management Research Unit (UNIAG) since 2010, and collaborator member at the Research Centre in Business Sciences and Tourism (CICET - FCVC) since 2021, she's author of more than 160 publications in scientific journals with peer review, some indexed in various international databases (WoS - Clarivate Analytics, Scopus and others) and published 22 book chapters and 5 books. Supervised 4 doctoral theses and 25 master's dissertations. Has participated as a researcher in more than 30 projects and has been the lead researcher on 15. Her key area of expertise include Social Sciences with an emphasis on Human Capital, Economics, Management, Tourism, Regional and

Cross-border Development, Innovation and Entrepreneurship, Information and Communication Technologies and Corporate Governance. Received 2 awards/honours - 1st Euroregion Research Award and Diploma of Honorary Member of the European Higher Council of Honorary Doctors from ESERP Business School.

***

Csongor Czipf, Ph.D. Honorary Associate Professor, Assistant Professor Széchenyi István University, Győr, Hungary Gyula Kautz Faculty of Economics, Department of International Applied Economics Ongoing teaching experience at Széchenyi István University since 1999. Appointed as Regional Economic Manager of the Piarist Order Hungarian Province in Budapest as of January 2022. Master's degree in Religious Education and Dormitory Teaching obtained from the College of Theology in Győr in 2017. Doctoral degree awarded in 2011 by Janus Pannonius University of Pécs. Research specialization: corporate evaluation from a human resources perspective. Bachelor's degree in Economics with a specialization in Comparative Economic Policy completed in 1999 at Széchenyi István College.

Amir Ahmad Dar is the Faculty in the Department of Mathematics at Lovely Professional University Punjab. The area of interest: Financial mathematics, financial economics, statistics and business mathematics.

Sasswat G MBA Finance student currently pursuing his postgraduate studies at Saveetha School of Management, SIMATS University (2024–2026). Possesses a strong foundation in financial analysis, investment research, and data interpretation, complemented by academic credentials in commerce with a focus on Bank Management from Madras University. I actively participates in business summits, and various academic and extracurricular activities.

Dhiwakar Gandhi is pursuing an MBA (2024–2026) at Saveetha School of Management, SIMATS University, Chennai, with academic exposure across multiple management specializations including Hospital Management, Finance, and Business Analytics. He completed his schooling at Government Higher Secondary School, Chennai, where he was a topper in both SSLC and HSC. A graduate in Commerce from Ramakrishna Mission Vivekananda College, Chennai, Dhiwakar has strong research interests in artificial intelligence, analytics, sustainable management, and interdisciplinary business studies. He aims to contribute to knowledge creation and innovative management practices that foster sustainability and value across diverse industries.

Orlando Manuel Lima Rua Assistant Professor of Management at the School of Accounting and Administration (ISCAP) of the Polytechnic of Porto (Portugal). Researcher at Center of Business and Legal Studies (CECEJ) (Polytechnic of Porto – ISCAP) and at Management Applied Research Unit (UNIAG) of the Association of Polytechnic Institutes of Northern Portugal (APNOR).

Mohamed Musthakeem S is an MBA graduate from Saveetha School of Management, Chennai, with a B.E. in Electrical and Electronics Engineering from M.I.E.T. Engineering College, Tiruchirapalli. He has professional experience as a Maintenance Engineer (Electrical & Facility Management) at Sri Kousalya Construction Limited, Chennai, and as an Electrical Maintenance Engineer at VAGUS Technologies, Tiruchirapalli. He is skilled in leadership, critical thinking, problem solving, human resource management, and logistics. Fluent in English and Tamil, Mohamed is currently conducting active research at Saveetha School of Management to further his expertise and contribute

Patricia Orozco Quijano is an Associate Professor in the School of Business Administration at Laurentian University, Canada. She specializes in entrepreneurship, International business, and sustainable development, with research spanning work-integrated learning, capability building, and heritage-based innovation. Her recent work focuses on renewable energy adoption in emerging economies. Dr. Orozco has extensive experience in curriculum leadership, bilingual program development, and community–industry partnerships, connecting academic research with practice to foster inclusive and sustainable growth.

Carlos Rodríguez-Maillard With more than 25 years of experience in diverse industries such as logistics, shared services centers, construction products and banking. Working in countries like Brazil, Colombia and México. I am a process and transformation leader at Grupo DEACERO, a leading steel producer in Mexico and America. My mission is to improve the business strategy across the organization, using my skills in Digital Transformation, problem-solving, change management and business management. I am also a professor at EGADE Business School (Tecnológico de Monterrey). I share my knowledge in Organizational Performance Management, User-Centered Design, and Project Management classes with MBA and MBM students. I have a PhD in business administration, an MBA, a master's in finance and technology administration and multiple articles and book chapters published in academic and business journals. I am fluent in Spanish, English, and Portuguese and enjoy learning new things and facing new challenges.

Index

P

R

S

T

www.ingramcontent.com/pod-product-compliance
Lightning Source LLC
LaVergne TN
LVHW081525300926
849161LV00006B/1295

Digital Governance, Democracy, and Inclusion in Developing Countries

Andrew Enaifoghe
https://orcid.org/0000-0003-4890-9179
University of Zululand, South Africa

IGI Global
Scientific Publishing
Publishing Tomorrow's Research Today

Vice President of Editorial Melissa Wagner
Director of Acquisitions Mikaela Felty
Director of Book Development Jocelynn Hessler
Production Manager Mike Brehm
Cover Design Jose Rosado

Published in the United States of America by
IGI Global Scientific Publishing
701 East Chocolate Avenue
Hershey, PA, 17033, USA
Tel: 717-533-8845 | Fax: 717-533-7115
Website: https://www.igi-global.com E-mail: cust@igi-global.com

Library of Congress Cataloging-in-Publication Data

(CIP Data Pending)
ISBN13: 979-8-2600-1618-3
Isbn13Softcover: 979-8-2600-1619-0
EISBN13: 979-8-2600-1620-6
British Cataloguing in Publication Data
A Cataloguing in Publication record for this book is available from the British Library.

This volume is dedicated to all those who continue to champion the cause of democratic governance and inclusive citizen participation in the face of adversity.

To the tireless advocates, civil society leaders, educators, and public servants across the Global South who work daily to uphold the principles of transparency, accountability, and justice, your commitment inspires this work.

To the youth, women, and marginalised communities whose voices are often unheard but whose aspirations shape the future of democracy, this book is for you.

And to the scholars and thinkers who believe in the transformative power of informed civic engagement, may this volume serve as a resource and a reaffirmation of your efforts.

This book is also dedicated to those who advocate for democratic government and citizen empowerment, frequently amidst challenges, and who recognise the transformational power of informed and active civic participation.

Table of Contents

Detailed Table of Contents

The modern vocabulary of authority and legitimacy pretends to universality while carrying the weight of its parochial European past. From Hobbes's Leviathan to Habermas's public sphere, theories fashioned in Europe parade as global truths. Yet, when imposed upon India, they obscure more than they illuminate. Colonial consciousness entrenched this distortion, making Indians see themselves through alien eyes. Against this backdrop, the chapter retrieves India's civilizational grammar—dharma, seva, rajadharma, and plural community orders—as alternative grounds for legitimacy. Authority here rests not on a contract among atomized individuals, but on duties within a cosmic and moral order. The aim is not civilizational chauvinism but conceptual pluralism: a call for political theory that allows multiple traditions to speak in their own voices, rather than repeating the conceit of one history masquerading as universal truth.

Nationality law defines belonging but often serves as a political tool of exclusion. In developing democracies, it institutionalizes discrimination through restrictive jus soli and jus sanguinis principles, marginalizing minorities and reinforcing social hierarchies. Such exclusion leads to statelessness, disenfranchisement, and weakened democracy. By transforming citizenship into privilege, these laws erode equality and cohesion. Reforming nationality law toward inclusive citizenship is vital to ensure belonging becomes a universal right and to strengthen democratic participation and legitimacy.

The paper analyses the changing dimensions of media and regulations, focusing on the transition from traditional to digital in light of its role as the fourth pillar of democracy in India. The authors argue that the effect of digital media on democracy is two-fold. As much as it has increased free speech, civic engagement, and accountability, it has also created the dangers of manipulated information, hate speech, loss of trust in institutions, and the dangers of polarisation. In this paper we tracks down historical regulation as far back as colonial days to the present IT Rules, focusing on judicial interventions that have been strengthening the freedom of the media and the optics of regulation versus constitutional guarantees. The authors have referred to the European model of regulation to argue that India is now in need of transparent, inclusive, and judicially reviewed governance in order to maintain democratic discourse in the digital age.

Enhancing democratic governance in India through amendments in public policies requires a multi-faceted approach that strengthens transparency, accountability, inclusivity, and citizen participation. There are certain points that can be put into consideration to make viable amendments related to public policies of India; policy amendments can be introduced to improve democratic governance. By amending public policies to enhance transparency, accountability, and participation, India can deepen its democratic governance. A combination of legal reforms, institutional strengthening, and technological integration can ensure a more responsive and inclusive democracy. Diving deeper into the area, electoral reforms, criminalization of politics, proportional representation, inner-party democracy, citizens' awareness, voter empowerment & turnout, independent election commission strengthening a fair representation of nation and its citizen would be expected. This in the long run would add to the enhancement of existing public policies of India.

Professionalizing public service has been the topic of scholarly debate for many years. Such debates have focused more on local government; hence they are identified as main looters of public funds. Poor service delivery in local government continues to be a major issue in South Africa; hence, many citizens find themselves in serious poverty and unfavored living circumstances. In 2020 the Minister of Public Service and Administration has adopted and approved the new national framework for professionalizing the public sector. The framework also emphasizes that the public officials must comply with Section 195 principles of the South African Constitution, Batho Pele principles, and Public Service Chater while also ensuring that qualified and competent staff are appointed for the positions. Therefore, this chapter analyzes the role of this new professional framework in the delivery of local government services.

The focus of this chapter is on how citizens can get involved in the digital government transformation. A systematic literature review (SLR) approach is employed to provide

This paper presents a comparative study examining the relationship between access to digital infrastructures and electronic participation in four countries: Ghana, Senegal, Nigeria, and others. The study compares the participation rates and institutional structures amongst urban and rural respondents (2019-2024), reviewed through a mixed-method approach on 2,847 respondents. Results show diverse effectiveness in e-participation, with Ghana recording a 68 percent increase in citizen initiatives, Senegal 45 percent, and Nigeria 31 percent. The Quality of the infrastructure, e-literacy schemes, and the government's interest are predictive of the successful implementation of e-participation. The study aims to address a knowledge gap regarding digital inequalities and their impact on democratic processes, exploring potential solutions for digital inclusion within democratic governance in sub-Saharan Africa.

This chapter examines the intricate relationship between economic participation and sustainable development in South Africa following the end of apartheid. Economic development has been boosted by trade and empowerment initiatives, but the gains have remained concentrated in capital-intensive industries, widening racial and regional disparities. Due to structural obstacles in employment, land distribution, and education, more than 50% of South Africans continue to live in poverty, and high inequality (Gini > 0.63) endures. At the same time, reliance on resource extraction and carbon-intensive businesses has led to environmental costs that disproportionately impact impoverished people. To balance economic, social, and ecological objectives, the study suggests an integrated framework of policies. These include: (1) trade policies that give priority to inclusive value chains; (2) green

Preface

INTRODUCTION

The accelerating pace of digital transformation has redefined the contours of governance, democracy, and inclusion across the globe, with particularly profound implications for developing countries. Digital technologies have introduced new modalities of state-citizen interaction, reshaped institutional accountability, and expanded opportunities for participation. Yet, these transformations are not without tension. Persistent inequalities, uneven access to digital infrastructure, and competing normative frameworks challenge the promise of inclusive digital governance. This volume, *Digital Governance, Democracy, and Inclusion in Developing Countries*, seeks to critically interrogate these dynamics while foregrounding voices and contexts that are often underrepresented in mainstream discourse.

This edited collection emerges from the recognition that governance in the digital age cannot be understood through a singular theoretical or geographical lens. Instead, it demands a pluralistic approach that accounts for historical legacies, cultural specificities, and socio-economic realities. Across diverse regional contexts—from India and Indonesia to South Africa and West Africa—the contributors examine how digital systems intersect with democratic institutions and practices. The chapters collectively emphasize that while digital tools can enhance transparency, participation, and service delivery, they can also reproduce exclusion, deepen divides, and strain democratic norms if not carefully governed.

The aim of this book is therefore twofold: first, to advance scholarly and policy-oriented debates on digital governance in developing contexts; and second, to offer grounded insights that can inform more equitable and inclusive governance frameworks. By bringing together interdisciplinary perspectives, this volume contributes to a more nuanced understanding of how digital transformation can be aligned with democratic values and social justice.

CHAPTER OVERVIEW

Chapter 1, *Whose Authority? What Legitimacy?*, challenges the universality of dominant Western political theories by examining their limitations in the Indian context. It reclaims indigenous conceptual frameworks such as *dharma* and *rajadharma* to argue for a pluralistic understanding of authority and legitimacy that is rooted in civilizational traditions.

Chapter 2, *Nationality Law as an Instrument of Exclusion in Developing Democracies*, explores how citizenship laws can function as mechanisms of marginalization. It highlights the ways in which restrictive legal frameworks contribute to statelessness and democratic erosion, advocating for reforms that prioritize inclusivity and equal belonging.

Chapter 3, *The Fourth Pillar in the Digital Age*, analyzes the evolving role of media within India's democratic framework. It examines the dual impact of digital media in enhancing free speech while simultaneously introducing risks such as misinformation, polarization, and regulatory overreach.

Chapter 4, *Enhancing Democratic Governance Through Amendments in Existing Public Policies of India*, focuses on the need for policy reforms to strengthen transparency, accountability, and citizen participation. It emphasizes electoral reforms, institutional strengthening, and technological integration as pathways to deepening democratic governance.

Chapter 5, *New Professional Framework as a Catalyst to Improve Service Delivery in Local Government*, turns attention to South Africa, assessing how professionalization of the public sector can address inefficiencies and improve service delivery at the local level.

Chapter 6, *Citizen Engagement in Digital Government Transformation*, provides a systematic literature review with insights from Indonesia. It maps varying levels of citizen participation and identifies key challenges such as digital literacy and infrastructure gaps, offering strategies for more inclusive engagement.

Chapter 7, *Integration of UMEGA Model and Cultural Theory*, presents an empirical study of e-government adoption in Indonesia. By integrating technical and cultural perspectives, it underscores the importance of environmental and social factors in shaping user behavior.

Chapter 8, *Digital Divides and Democratic Dividends*, offers a comparative analysis of e-participation across West African democracies. It highlights how disparities in infrastructure and digital access influence democratic participation outcomes.

Chapter 9, *Economic Participation and Sustainable Development in South Africa*, broadens the discussion by linking economic inclusion with governance and environmental sustainability. It proposes integrated policy approaches to address inequality, poverty, and ecological challenges.

CONCLUSION

Taken together, the chapters in this volume illuminate the complex and often contradictory nature of digital governance in developing countries. While digital technologies hold transformative potential, their impact is mediated by existing institutional structures, socio-economic inequalities, and cultural contexts. The contributions demonstrate that without deliberate efforts to address these underlying conditions, digitalization may reinforce rather than reduce exclusion.

A recurring theme across the book is the importance of contextual sensitivity. Whether in the realm of legal frameworks, public policy, or technological adoption, solutions must be tailored to local realities rather than imported wholesale from different contexts. This calls for a rethinking of dominant paradigms and a greater openness to alternative epistemologies and governance models.

Ultimately, this volume underscores that the pursuit of inclusive digital governance is not merely a technical challenge but a deeply political and ethical one. It requires sustained commitment from policymakers, scholars, practitioners, and citizens alike to ensure that digital transformation advances democratic values, fosters participation, and promotes equitable development. It is our hope that this book will serve as both a critical resource and a catalyst for ongoing dialogue and action in this vital field.

Acknowledgement

The completion of this edited volume would not have been possible without the invaluable contributions, support, and encouragement of many individuals and institutions.

First and foremost, I extend my deepest gratitude to the chapter contributors—distinguished scholars, practitioners, and policy experts—whose rigorous research, insightful analyses, and commitment to democratic ideals have enriched this work. Their diverse perspectives and dedication to advancing governance and citizen participation in developing contexts form the intellectual backbone of this volume.

I am also grateful to the peer reviewers and editorial advisors who provided constructive feedback and helped refine the quality and coherence of the chapters. Their scholarly guidance has been instrumental in shaping the final product.

Special thanks go to the academic institutions and research centres, especially the University of Zululand, that supported these endeavours, whether through funding, access to resources, or intellectual collaboration. Their commitment to fostering critical inquiry and policy-relevant scholarship is deeply appreciated.

To my colleagues and students who offered encouragement and engaged in thoughtful dialogue throughout the development of this book, I am sincerely thankful. Your insights and enthusiasm have been a source of inspiration.

Finally, I acknowledge the broader community of advocates, civil society actors, and public servants who continue to work tirelessly to strengthen democratic governance and empower citizens across the Global South. This volume is dedicated to your efforts and your vision for a more just, inclusive, and participatory world.

Introduction

The rapid proliferation of digital technology is profoundly transforming governance structures, political engagement, and social inclusion in emerging nations. Digitalisation has generated new potential to improve state capacity, democratic accountability, and citizen inclusion through e-government platforms, digital identities, social media-driven civic participation, and data-enabled public service delivery. Simultaneously, it has produced significant issues, such as inequitable access to technology, algorithmic bias, inadequate regulatory frameworks, cybersecurity threats, and the marginalisation of under-represented groups from digital public spaces. Comprehending these opportunities and risks is crucial for researchers, policymakers, and practitioners focused on inclusive and democratic development in the Global South.

The book argued that democratic governance in developing countries is undergoing a profound transformation as governments, citizens, and institutions increasingly integrate digital technologies into public life. Over the past two decades, digital governance—also referred to as e-governance—has emerged as a powerful mechanism for strengthening transparency, accountability, and participation within democratic systems. This transformation is driven by rapid technological advancements, widespread mobile connectivity, and the growing expectation that governments should provide efficient, accessible, and citizen-centred services. As a result, digital governance is not merely a technical innovation; it has become a critical catalyst for reimagining the relationship between states and their citizens in the Global South.

Many developing countries face persistent governance challenges, including weak institutional capacity, limited citizen engagement, bureaucratic inefficiencies, corruption, and socio-economic inequalities. These challenges often impede the realisation of inclusive democratic governance. Digital tools, such as online service portals, open data platforms, mobile government applications, social media engagement channels, and blockchain-based systems, offer promising pathways for addressing such governance deficits. When strategically implemented, digital governance can enhance administrative efficiency, expand access to public services, foster participatory decision-making, and strengthen public trust in government institutions.

Yet, the digital turn also introduces new complexities. Issues such as the digital divide, cyber-security risks, inadequate infrastructure, limited digital literacy, and the politicisation of online spaces pose significant barriers to inclusive democratic participation. While technology can enhance governance, it can also reproduce or even deepen existing inequalities if implementation lacks a citizen-centric and context-sensitive approach. For many developing countries, the challenge lies not only in adopting technological solutions but in ensuring that such solutions are equitable, sustainable, and aligned with democratic values.

Against this backdrop, this edited volume brings together interdisciplinary perspectives, empirical research, and case studies to examine how digital governance can serve as a transformative force for strengthening democratic governance and citizen participation in developing nations. The chapters explore a wide range of themes, including digital inclusion, e-participation platforms, public sector innovation, data governance, digital rights, civic technology, government transparency, and the socio-political impact of emerging technologies. By engaging both theoretical and practical insights, the book provides a comprehensive understanding of how digital governance is reshaping governance landscapes across Africa, Asia, Latin America, and other regions of the Global South.

Ultimately, this volume argues that enhancing democratic governance in developing countries requires more than the adoption of digital tools. It demands an integrated approach that combines technological innovation with inclusive policy design, institutional reform, and active citizen engagement. Digital governance holds immense potential to democratise public administration, empower citizens, and create more resilient and responsive democratic systems. However, realising this potential depends on the political will of governments, the capacity of institutions, and the vibrancy of civil society in shaping a digital future that is participatory, transparent, and just.

By offering scholarly insights and practical recommendations, this book aims to contribute to global discourse on digital transformation and democratic development. It invites policymakers, academics, civil society actors, and practitioners to reflect on how digital governance can be leveraged to build stronger democracies and more engaged citizenries in developing nations.

Andrew Enaifoghe
University of Zululand, South Africa

Chapter 1
Whose Authority? What Legitimacy?
Global Norms, Indian Traditions, and the Conceptual Crisis

Keerthiraj
http://orcid.org/0000-0002-2536-8579
GFGC Punjalakatte, Mangalore University, India

Prashanth S. P.
http://orcid.org/0000-0002-6812-3950
M.S. Ramaiah College of Arts, Science, and Commerce, India

Apoorva Misra
http://orcid.org/0009-0009-0476-8125
Alliance University, India

ABSTRACT

The modern vocabulary of authority and legitimacy pretends to universality while carrying the weight of its parochial European past. From Hobbes's Leviathan to Habermas's public sphere, theories fashioned in Europe parade as global truths. Yet, when imposed upon India, they obscure more than they illuminate. Colonial consciousness entrenched this distortion, making Indians see themselves through alien eyes. Against this backdrop, the chapter retrieves India's civilizational grammar—dharma, seva, rajadharma, and plural community orders—as alternative grounds for legitimacy. Authority here rests not on a contract among atomized individuals, but on duties within a cosmic and moral order. The aim is not civiliza-

DOI: 10.4018/979-8-2600-1618-3.ch001

tional chauvinism but conceptual pluralism: a call for political theory that allows multiple traditions to speak in their own voices, rather than repeating the conceit of one history masquerading as universal truth.

INTRODUCTION

Political theorists have long treated their concepts of authority and legitimacy as universally applicable truths. From the social contract philosophers of early-modern Europe to contemporary liberal-democratic models enshrined in international norms, a singular story about what makes power legitimate has been projected onto the globe. Article 21 of the Universal Declaration of Human Rights, for example, proclaims that "the will of the people shall be the basis of the authority of government", an unambiguous statement of a particular Western liberal understanding of legitimacy now presented as a global ideal (United Nations, 1948). Yet when such theories travel beyond their native soil, especially into a civilization as historically and conceptually distinct as India's, they often distort more than they reveal. This chapter offers a civilizationally grounded critique of authority and legitimacy in global politics, adopting an assertive and strategically critical tone. We will expose the limitations and even distortions that arise when Western political theories are uncritically applied to Indian contexts, and sketch the outlines of an alternative perspective rooted in India's own conceptual world (Koppell, 2007; Bernstein, 2004).

At the outset, let us be clear: the aim is not to reject the Western intellectual tradition in toto or to indulge in mere civilizational chauvinism. Rather, it is to interrogate the epistemic arrogance that often accompanies Western universalism – the presumption that concepts forged in the historical experience of Europe (like the social contract, secularism, or the nation-state) have a natural authority to define political reality everywhere. This arrogance was once buttressed by colonial power; today it survives as colonial consciousness – a mindset in which even formerly colonized societies continue to see themselves through the conceptual lenses of the West. The result is a pervasive intellectual dependency: Indian intellectuals have often merely reproduced Western descriptions of India, accepting theories of authority, social structure, and legitimacy developed elsewhere as the normative yardstick for their own society.

In doing so, they frequently misunderstand or ignore the indigenous bases of authority that have sustained Indian communities for ages.

This chapter argues that we can no longer afford such a one-sided approach. A truly global political theory – one responsive to a call for "Rethinking Authority and Legitimacy in Global Politics" – must be willing to learn from multiple civilizations. It must acknowledge that concepts like "state", "power", "legitimacy", and "authority" do not carry identical meanings across cultures. The Indian context provides a prime example of a rich, non-Western conceptual matrix that challenges universalist assumptions. India's civilizational experience, from ancient Dharma-shastric kingship to modern democratic experiments, offers alternative ways of grounding political authority – ways that emphasize duties over rights, cosmic order (Rta/Dharma) over social contract, spiritual guidance alongside temporal power, and community relationships over atomized individualism. These differences are not just quaint historical footnotes; they directly bear on contemporary issues of governance, legitimacy, and order in India and other non-Western polities (Hurd, 2018).

Using a mix of polemic and satire – for sometimes a dose of irony is the best antidote to complacent universalism – we will critique the canonical Western theories and their application to India. Along the way, we will invoke major thinkers (Plato, Aristotle, Hobbes, Locke, Rousseau, Weber, Foucault, Habermas, Schmitt, among others) and engage them from this Indian vantage point. The tone will be unapologetically assertive: where Western theory has been imperious, we respond with incisive critique; where it has been blind to its own parochialism, we shine a light; where it has been patronizing toward Indian traditions, we answer with a bit of satirical reversal. The goal is not mere confrontation but correction – to identify misunderstandings about Indian traditions not to assign blame, but to highlight deep civilizational differences in conceptual grounding. Only by appreciating these differences can we begin to imagine a pluralistic global political ontology that does not simply default to Western assumptions (Ficek, 2023).

In what follows, we first summarize the dominant Western theories of authority and legitimacy – a necessary step to understand what is being "universalized." Next, we unpack the universalist assumptions and colonial legacies embedded in these theories, showing how they have been internalized in Indian political discourse (often with counterproductive results). We then pivot to the Indian civilizational context: outlining indigenous conceptions of authority (rooted in dharma, spiritual-temporal synthesis, and community autonomy) and illustrating how Western framings have misread or undermined these. Specific case studies – from the misinterpretation of caste and caste-based authority, to the transplanted notion of secularism, to the colonial-era characterization of Indian kingship as "Oriental despotism" – will reveal the scale of misunderstanding. Finally, we propose the contours of an alternative approach to authority and legitimacy, one that is civilizationally sensitive and therefore better equipped to deal with global diversity. In doing so, we call to "theorize the Indian problem of living together in a different way rather than simply modifying Western political theories." (De Roover, Claerhout, & Rao, 2011).

The stakes are high. As global politics grapples with crises of legitimacy – from failing states to the alienation of citizens in ostensibly "successful" democracies – the need to rethink these concepts is urgent. A one-size-fits-all model, born of one historical trajectory, is clearly inadequate in a world of many histories and cultures. By the end of this chapter, the hope is to have sketched the beginnings of a truly pluralistic framework for understanding authority and legitimacy: one that can accommodate, say, an Indian village council's moral influence, a Chinese ruler's "Mandate of Heaven," an African community's Ubuntu-based consensus, alongside the familiar institutions of Western governance. Such a framework would not only be more inclusive and just in an academic sense; it could foster more legitimate politics on the ground, because it would resonate with peoples' own civilizational values rather than forcing them into a Procrustean bed of alien concepts.

Let us begin, then, by revisiting what the Western tradition actually says about authority and legitimacy – and noting, with a critical eye, the assumptions built into that narrative.

THE CANONICAL WESTERN THEORIES: A BRIEF OVERVIEW

Plato and Aristotle: Reason and the Common Good as Foundations of Authority.

Western political thought begins in ancient Greece, where Plato and Aristotle shaped ideas of legitimate authority. In The Republic, Plato grounds authority in knowledge of the Good (Plato, 380 BCE). He envisions philosopher-kings—educated in truth and uniquely suited to govern justly. Since ordinary people's judgments are clouded by ignorance and passions, only the wise can rule in the common interest. The philosopher-king's legitimacy rests on epistemic superiority: having escaped the "cave" of illusions, he alone grasps reality. For Plato, knowledge—not consent—confers the right to rule. Plato's model is elitist yet driven by a genuine concern: how can authority serve justice rather than oppression? His answer is meritocratic, paternalistic, and decidedly un-democratic. Legitimacy comes not from popular approval but from alignment with moral order—accessible only to the few. This standard framed authority as serving the common good rather than rulers' self-interest, setting a benchmark later challenged by liberals who emphasized consent, but echoed in ideas like rulers' "moral obligation" today.

Aristotle, Plato's student, brought a somewhat more empirical and pluralistic approach. In his Politics, Aristotle analyzed different forms of government and introduced the idea that regimes can be judged by whether they serve the common good or the selfish interest of rulers. For Aristotle, a monarchy (rule by one) or aristocracy (rule by few) can be legitimate if it aims at the common good, whereas even a democracy (rule by many) would be illegitimate if it descends into serving the crowd's whims, what he calls ochlocracy, or mob rule (Aristotle, trans). In a sense, Aristotle gave us the first systematic notion of legitimacy in Western thought: the right to rule depends on serving justice and the community's welfare. Authority is justified only when oriented toward the telos (end) of human flourishing in the polis. He favored what he called a "polity," a mixed government balancing elements of democracy and oligarchy, as the most stable and just form – an early anticipation of the idea that checks and balances contribute to legitimacy by preventing any single interest from dominating. We might say Aristotle's take on legitimacy is proto-constitutional: authority must be bound by the purpose of governance (the good life for the citizens) and by laws.

Hobbes, Locke, Rousseau: The Social Contract and the Birth of the Modern "Legitimate" State.

Fast-forward to early modern Europe, and we encounter a dramatic shift in thinking about authority. The Wars of Religion and the collapse of medieval feudal order had thrown Europe into turmoil. In response, thinkers like Thomas Hobbes, John Locke, and Jean-Jacques Rousseau developed social contract theories to explain how legitimate political authority can arise from a pre-political "state of nature." Their writings – Hobbes' Leviathan (1651), Locke's Two Treatises of Government (1689), Rousseau's Social Contract (1762) – became foundational for Western political ontology, centering the individual and their consent as key.

Hobbes portrayed the state of nature as a war of all against all, where life was "solitary, poor, nasty, brutish, and short" (Hobbes, 1651) Because individuals enjoy natural liberty and equal power to harm, insecurity reigns—a "continual fear and danger of violent death." Authority arises not from divine right or moral truth but from necessity: rational individuals surrender their powers to a sovereign in exchange for peace. The social contract thus unites many wills into one, producing the Leviathan—an absolute ruler or assembly holding a monopoly on coercive force. For Hobbes, sovereignty must be near-absolute, since division invites chaos. Legitimacy is de facto: as long as the sovereign preserves life and order, rule is justified. Rebellion is warranted only if protection fails—for instance, when the sovereign endangers subjects' lives. Hobbes's logic, forged amid England's civil war, elevates order above morality: security is the only morality. This sharply contrasts Indian political thought, where dharma (moral order) grounds authority. India rarely resembled a Hobbesian "state of nature"; stability often rested on customary law, caste panchayats, and shared authority between rulers and religion. Hobbes, from a Eurocentric lens, ignored such sources of order, assuming only a singular sovereign could impose peace. This blind spot had real consequences when the British, implicitly Hobbesian, viewed India as desperately in need of the Pax Britannica.

Locke, writing a few decades later, offered a more optimistic and liberal vision. The state of nature, for him, is not a war of all against all but a condition where natural rights—life, liberty, property—exist without impartial enforcement. For Locke, consent of the governed is paramount: "no one can be put out of this estate, and subjected to the political power of another, without his own consent," he argues, hence "the consent of the governed" is the basis of all lawful government (Locke, 1689). This contract is revocable: if government fails to protect rights or becomes abusive, the people may rebel. Legitimacy is thus conditional—political power is rightful only while serving its entrusted ends and retaining consent. Locke's theory challenged divine right and inspired revolutions, and indeed he was often invoked in resistance to colonialism (consent of the governed being a stark criterion that empires did not meet). It's ironic, however, that British colonial administrators seldom applied Locke's criteria to their own rule in India – where was the Indian consent? As one historical footnote, the American Declaration of Independence (1776) invoked the Lockean principle to justify throwing off British rule i.e. "governments... derive their just powers from the consent of the governed" and when such consent is violated, it is the people's right to alter or abolish (U.S. Continental Congress, 1776). Yet colonial practice revealed a double standard. British rule in India invoked Locke rhetorically but ignored Indian consent; in 1857, demands for self-rule were crushed as mutiny. This selective application highlights an epistemic gap. Today, Locke's consent principle still underpins global norms of legitimate governance—elections, referendums, "rule by the people." But consent itself is culturally contingent. In India, village assemblies (panchayats) practiced consensus long before liberal democracy, though in forms rooted in group identity. The Westminster model, imposed through Lockean rhetoric, produced a hybrid: vigorous elections entwined with caste and community blocs. Consent, then, operates differently across civilizations—something Locke's universalism overlooked.

Rousseau radicalized the social contract by declaring: "Man is born free, and everywhere he is in chains.". His question: how to construct a polity where people obey only themselves and thus remain free? His answer is the notion of the general will: through the contract, individuals merge into a collective sovereign whose laws aim at the common good. In obeying these laws, citizens obey only themselves—free through self-legislation. The general will is not the sum of private desires but an orientation toward the public good. Hence Rousseau's paradox: those resisting it must be "forced to be free" (Rousseau, 1762). Here we see the seeds of both democratic idealism and totalitarian danger. On one hand, Rousseau legitimized authority as based on the collective autonomy of a people; on the other, he sanctioned a kind of moral authoritarianism in the name of that collective good. In practice, Rousseau inspired the French Revolution and modern republicanism: sovereignty resides in the people, and legitimacy comes from laws expressing the general will. Today, his influence is visible in ideas of popular sovereignty, national self-determination, and participatory democracy. But consider applying Rousseau in India: Who is the people of India, in a land of such internal diversity? What is the "general will" in a subcontinent of a thousand communities? The post-colonial Indian state attempted a Rousseauian unification – speaking of "We, the People of India" in the Constitution – but skeptics might argue this was a fiction overlaid on deeply plural realities. India has hardly produced noticeable tracts on 'social contract' or explicit theories of the state – not because Indians lacked politics, but because their political life was organized on different premises. Indeed, Indian tradition rarely conceived society as an aggregation of free individuals making a joint will; rather, it was understood as an organic web of duties (dharma) and inherited roles. The concept of Swadharma (one's own duty) meant each person had an obligation determined by their context (family, caste, stage of life), and legitimacy was about everyone doing their duty, including rulers doing Rajdharma. The idea of explicitly forging a collective "national will" was largely absent – perhaps until modern nationalism imported that notion. Modern India therefore fused Rousseauian form with indigenous substance: universal franchise and national sovereignty alongside Gandhian ideals of consensus and village self-rule. The tension between collective will and plural duties has shaped Indian democracy ever since.

Max Weber: Legitimacy in Sociological Perspective

Enter the 20th century, and we find Max Weber offering a descriptive typology of authority that has become classic. Weber wasn't trying to prescribe the best form of legitimacy; he wanted to understand why people obey power – what makes them believe authority is rightful. He identified three "ideal types" of legitimate authority: traditional, charismatic, and rational-legal (Weber, 1978). In Weber's words, authority is nothing other than "power accepted as legitimate by those subjected to it".

1. Traditional authority rests on established belief in the sanctity of age-old customs and lineage. The classic example is a hereditary monarch or a feudal lord – people obey because that's how it's always been, the right of the ruler is anchored in tradition and often religion. Many pre-modern Indian polities exemplified this: the Maharajas, Nawabs, village headmen, etc., commanded obedience largely because tradition (often intertwined with notions of sacred duty) demanded it. The authority of a Brahmin priest or a caste elder in India is similarly "traditional" in Weber's sense – it's not codified in law or necessarily charismatic, but it's accepted due to social custom. The British, coming from a society that was itself transitioning to rational-legal authority, often misinterpreted India's traditional authorities as either despotic or irrational, failing to see the internal

logic and legitimacy those figures had in the eyes of their people. For instance, a village might accept the arbitration of a local headman because tradition vested him with that role – this was genuine legitimacy in context, though a British officer might see it as "ignorant natives following superstition" rather than lawful authority.

2. Charismatic authority arises from the personal magnetism or heroism of an individual leader, and the devotion they inspire. Weber had in mind figures like prophets, revolutionaries, or great warriors – think of a Joan of Arc, a Napoleon, or in the Indian context, perhaps a Guru Nanak, a Shivaji, or even a Mahatma Gandhi. Charismatic authority is inherently unstable (since it's tied to one person's qualities) and often revolutionary, in that it breaks from tradition and established rules. In Indian history, charismatic authority has repeatedly been a force for change – whether a saint challenging ritual orthodoxy by sheer spiritual presence, or a charismatic political leader mobilizing masses (Gandhi's own authority during the freedom struggle was notably charismatic-traditional: people followed him with near-religious fervor, seeing him as a Mahatma or great soul). Weber's insight is that charisma routinized can lead to new forms of order – for example, after a charismatic leader dies, their authority might be "routinized" into either traditional authority (creating a new custom or dynasty) or rational-legal authority (institutionalizing the leader's ideas into laws). The emergence of the Indian Republic had a bit of this: the charisma of the independence movement leaders was transferred into a constitutional order, giving initial legitimacy to what was otherwise a transplant of Western institutional forms.
3. Rational-legal authority is the hallmark of modern bureaucratic states: Weber, the hallmark of modern states is rational-legal authority: rule based on impersonal laws and procedures rather than personal power. Legitimacy stems from lawful rules and proper appointment—people obey office, not individual. Prime ministers, judges, or police officers in constitutional democracies derive authority in this way. Weber argued that societies evolve from traditional to charismatic to rational-legal authority, with the bureaucratic nation-state as its highest form. Colonial India complicates this picture. The British portrayed their rule as rational-legal—codified law, civil services, "rule of law"—but for most Indians it lacked legitimacy. It could not be justified within local beliefs about justice or moral order, relying instead on coercion. Sociologist David Beetham later clarified: "a power relationship is not legitimate because people believe in its legitimacy, but because it can be justified in terms of their beliefs" (Beetham, 1991). By that standard, British rule failed. Even today, rational-legal authority in India coexists uneasily with traditional and charismatic sources. A villager may respect both the magistrate's order and a local priest's word—or follow a

charismatic leader over written law. When these clash, legitimacy depends less on formal legality than on resonance with community beliefs. This illustrates a broader lesson: governance reforms that stress legality without attending to local values often struggle for acceptance.

Weber's framework is extremely useful as a descriptive lens – it helps us see that what counts as legitimacy can vary: in one context, pedigree and custom, in another, divine aura, in another, formal legality. However, even Weber arguably assumed an evolutionary schema (from traditional to rational-legal) that mirrored the Western experience of modernization. In the colonial narrative, Europe considered itself advanced in rational-legal authority while casting colonies as stuck in tradition or prone to charismatic rebellions. This teleology fed into the justification for imperial "tutelage": the idea that colonized peoples needed to be taught rational administration. This entire narrative – of linear progress from primitive/traditional authority to modern/legal authority – is itself a product of Western culture's self-description. It fails to consider that a civilization like India's did not necessarily valorize the legal-bureaucratic form of authority as the highest. Indeed, Indian political thought may value the fusion of the ethical and political (dharma and danda) more than the separation of the two under impersonal legality.

Foucault and Habermas: Power, Discourse, and Legitimation Crises.

The 20th century also produced more critical or nuanced takes on how power operates and how legitimacy is sustained or lost in complex societies. Michel Foucault turned the focus away from the centralized sovereign and toward the diffuse ways power permeates society through discourse, knowledge, and institutions. Foucault infamously said, "Power is everywhere; not because it embraces everything, but because it comes from everywhere… Power is not an institution, nor a structure, nor a possession. It is the name we give to a complex strategic situation in a particular society" (Foucault, 1978). This means that legitimacy is not just a matter of official doctrines or explicit consent; it's embedded in what people take for granted as truth or normal. A state's authority might be buttressed by scientific discourses (e.g. ideas of racial hierarchy or development economics) that make its rule seem "necessary" or "rational" beyond question. Foucault would have us see that Western political theory itself – the knowledge that proclaims what is legitimate – is part of a power/knowledge regime. It's not coincidental that the colonial project was accompanied by an Orientalist discourse that consistently portrayed Indians as incapable of self-rule due to their "caste superstition," "Oriental despotism," or "religious fanaticism." These were Foucauldian discourses that manufactured the "truth" of Indian inferiority, thereby legitimizing colonial authority as the bringer of reason and progress. In effect, colonial power operated not just through guns but through knowledge, creating a narrative wherein Western modes of authority (the bureaucrat, the missionary, the law court) were automatically valid and Indian ones (the guru, the caste council, the ritual king) were not. This power of discourse survives today in subtler forms. Consider international development narratives that dub certain countries "failed states" or "corrupt regimes" – often based on benchmarks that presume a single valid model of governance rooted in Western liberal norms (Keerthiraj & Vang-Phu, 2025). Such labeling exerts pressure on those countries to accept external intervention or wholesale import of Western institutional templates as the path to "legitimacy." A Foucauldian lens encourages us to be skeptical: whose interests and worldview are embedded in these supposedly universal benchmarks? Epistemic hegemony can itself be seen as a form of authority.

Habermas sought new foundations of legitimacy in an age where religion and tradition no longer commanded universal assent. In Legitimation Crisis (1973), he argued that modern capitalist states face tension: their functional demands—consumerism, technocratic governance, austerity—often erode the cultural lifeworld that sustains meaning and social integration (Habermas, 1973). Legitimacy falters when policies cannot be justified in terms citizens recognize as their own values. His solution was deliberative democracy. Legitimacy, he claimed, requires rational-critical discourse in which all affected can participate, and where laws gain assent through public reasoning, not merely formal legality. For Habermas, legitimacy is an ongoing communicative achievement, not a one-time act of consent. Yet this ideal rests on a Eurocentric faith in reasoned debate. Habermas envisioned something like the European coffee-house public sphere—rational, secular, linguistically uniform. In India, however, legitimacy claims often rest on passions, traditions, or religious idioms. Parliamentary or media debates are less Habermasian deliberation than identity-driven contestation. Policies like cow slaughter prohibition cannot be settled by secular argument alone; cultural sentiments weigh heavily. From an Indian perspective, this need not signal democratic "deficit." Thinkers like Ashis Nandy suggest India's traditions of tolerance—accommodating difference without forcing abstract consensus—may offer an alternative legitimacy resource. Habermas rightly insists that authority requires justification, but the forms of justification may extend beyond rationalist debate to include narratives, symbols, and cultural meanings that resonate locally.

Carl Schmitt: The Political and the Myth of Universal Norms.

As a counter-voice within the Western canon, Carl Schmitt offers a bracing critique of liberal pretensions. Schmitt, a controversial figure (and a Nazi jurist, it must be noted), nonetheless made enduring points about sovereignty and the nature of politics. In Political Theology (1922), he famously asserted, "The sovereign is he who decides on the exception" (Schmitt, 1922). That is, the true authority is revealed not by routine law-making, but by who can suspend the law in a crisis – who can declare a state of emergency and act outside the legal norm to protect the polity. This was a direct challenge to liberal constitutionalism: Schmitt argued that every legal order is ultimately based on a sovereign decision, an act of power that is prior to law. Moreover, he claimed "all significant concepts of the modern theory of the state are secularized theological concepts" – meaning ideas like sovereignty, miracle (state of exception), etc., have their roots in Christian theological reasoning (e.g. God's miracles as exceptions to natural law). For our purpose, Schmitt is valuable in highlighting that Western political concepts carry theological baggage and are not as universal as they seem. He would likely smirk at the idea of a universally valid liberal order – to him, politics was fundamentally about the friend-enemy distinction, about collective identities defining themselves against others. Liberal talk of universal humanity or universal norms, he thought, often masks a will to dominate: "Whoever invokes humanity wants to cheat," Schmitt quipped, implying that claims of acting for "humanity" often serve to de-humanize one's enemies and justify one's own expansion. In global politics, one can see Schmitt's point play out: powerful nations invoking "human rights" or "international community" to legitimize interventions that curiously align with their strategic interests, effectively designating some regime as the "enemy of humanity" to be eliminated. Schmitt would not be surprised that the language of universal legitimacy can cloak a new imperialism.

Applying Schmitt's lens to our theme: The imposition of Western political ontology in places like India can be seen as a kind of "global liberal exception" – where, in the name of universal values (democracy, secularism, etc.), very specific institutional forms and ideologies were pushed upon societies regardless of local context, and any resistance was labeled as irrational or fanatical (the new enemy of progress). Schmitt, might agree that behind the façade of universal principles lies the friend-enemy logic of coloniality: the "civilized" versus the "backward," the secular versus the fanatical, etc. That said, Schmitt's own alternative – a mythic homogenous people under a decisive sovereign – is not what we seek for India. India's reality is plural and defies homogeneity; any attempt to enforce one (whether a Hindu rashtra or a secular monolith) is likely to produce unrest. But Schmitt at least gives us a warning: beware of liberal universalism's righteous mask – it may demand of India an artificial uniformity (e.g. one law for all, one notion of nationhood) thatdoesn't fit, and thus will always require states of exception to maintain (like emergency laws, suspensions of democratic process when the populace votes "the wrong way," etc.).

Having toured these Western theories, what emerges is that each is a product of its time and place: Plato's Athens, Aristotle's polis, Hobbes' war-torn Christendom, Locke's constitutional England, Rousseau's Geneva and Paris, Weber's industrializing Germany, Foucault's post-1968 France, Habermas' late-modern West, Schmitt's Weimar Germany. Yet each tends to present itself in abstract form, inviting later generations to apply it broadly. This context-stripping is where distortions begin. If we treat these theories as an arsenal of ready-made templates and measures, we risk what Habermas himself called "the historical injustice of general theories" – they become "peculiarly abstract in relation to the historical forms of legitimate domination". In other words, the general theory might ignore how legitimacy actually operates in a given society at a given time.

Nowhere is this risk more evident than in the encounter between Western political thought and Indian socio-political reality. We now turn to that encounter: how Western assumptions met Indian traditions, what misunderstandings ensued, and how colonialism cemented some of these distortions into the mainstream discourse. This will set the stage for us to articulate an alternative perspective grounded in India's civilizational ethos.

UNIVERSALIST ASSUMPTIONS AND COLONIAL LEGACIES

When the British (and other Europeans) began describing Indian society and politics in the colonial era, they did so through the categories of their own intellectual tradition – the one we've just outlined. This yielded a picture of India that was often unrecognizable to Indians themselves, yet it became the dominant narrative, both in colonial policy and in post-colonial Indian elite discourse. Edward Said called this process Orientalism: the West's self-serving way of structuring its experience of the East (Said, 1978). Western descriptions of India told us more about the West than about India. Crucially, these descriptions had real power – they made reality on the ground by influencing education, law, and self-perception of Indians (the colonial consciousness effect). Here, we dissect some key universalist assumptions that Western thinkers (explicitly or implicitly) carried into their analysis of Indian authority and legitimacy, and the colonial legacies that resulted. The tone will now sharpen – there is something darkly comedic about some of these endeavors, and a touch of satire will help underscore the absurdity of imposing certain frames on a vastly different culture.

The Myth of the Social Contract in India: Were Indians Ever Individuals Seeking a Contract?

Western assumption #1: Society is fundamentally an aggregation of individuals who at some point (implicitly or explicitly) agree on a form of government – hence political authority must ultimately trace its legitimacy to such an agreement or consent of individuals (à la Hobbes/Locke/Rousseau).

The colonial British were quite perplexed that they could find no Indian Magna Carta, no equivalent of a social contract or a Parliament in India's long history. This absence was quickly interpreted not as a sign of a different ontology, but as a lack – Indians must have been living in a Hobbesian state of despotism because they "failed" to invent contractual governance. James Mill's influential History of British India (1817) argued that India had always been despotic, with the people oppressed by arbitrary rulers and Brahmins, until the British introduced the rule of law (Mill, 1817). This fit the Hobbesian narrative: only an absolute sovereign (in this case the East India Company, later the British Crown) could rescue Indians from their own anarchic or tyrannical past. The reality was far more complex: Indian polity was often decentralized, with village communities and guilds enjoying autonomy, and rulers bound by the expectations of Raj Dharma (the duty of kings) and threatened with loss of legitimacy (even revolt) if they egregiously violated norms of justice. There was no single "contract" moment, but a continuous negotiation – implicit contracts embedded in tradition. For example, a king's duty to protect cows or Brahmins was not written as a contract signed by subjects, but if he violated it, he could face uprisings or ostracism by society.

The Western social contract myth in India thus distorted two ways: it failed to see indigenous forms of consent/legitimation, and it failed to appreciate that Indian society was not built on the primacy of the individual. The very question "Did individuals consent to this king?" might have seemed nonsensical in a context where social roles were so embedded that the modern individual-as-political-agent was absent. People saw themselves as families, castes, sects first, not as abstract individuals. Authority was often mediated through those layers – e.g., a caste council might endorse the king, and that sufficed for members of that caste. The British insisted on dealing with atomized subjects under a uniform law, which undermined these intermediate structures, ironically creating more legitimacy problems (the colonial state had to employ a lot of coercion, as we noted, because it cut off the channels of consent that ran through communities).

The Secular-State Paradigm: Universal Separation or Colonial Imposition?

Western assumption #2: A legitimate modern polity is a secular nation-state – meaning the state stands apart from religion, exercising authority through secular law and reason, while religion is confined to private faith or voluntary association. This assumption traces to European experiences (the Wars of Religion, the Enlightenment) that made separation of church and state seem the obvious solution for social peace and rational governance (as seen in Locke's letters on toleration or later in the U.S. First Amendment and French laïcité).

In the colonial gaze, India's mixing of religion and polity – e.g., Hindu kings performing religious rites as state ceremonies, the caste system entangled with governance, personal laws based on religion – was seen as a mark of civilizational backwardness. "Oriental despotism" was often code for a regime where the ruler was either deemed semi-divine or where priests held sway over governance (the stereotype was that Brahmin priests controlled superstitious kings, keeping the masses oppressed – essentially a theocracy). The British firmly believed they were instituting a proper separation: Queen Victoria's 1858 proclamation assured her Indian subjects that the Raj would not interfere with their religion and that all would be equal before law regardless of creed (Victoria, 1858). This sounded noble and indeed introduced a kind of secular principle in governance. But it was shot through with colonial consciousness: the British simultaneously codified "religious law" for Hindus and Muslims (freezing certain interpretations as the law, e.g., in matters of marriage or inheritance), which was paradoxical – the secular state was administrating religious law. They did it because they couldn't ignore the reality that Indians lived in religiously defined communities. The result was an enduring legal pluralism that independent India inherited: different personal laws for Hindus, Muslims, etc. – a direct outcome of trying to force-fit the secular state model onto a plural society in a hurry.

Secularism in India has been a conceptual muddle from the start, a solution to a problem that was defined through Western categories rather than Indian realities. In Europe, separating church and state made sense because Christianity had a corporate church structure with political power; in India, "religion" was not analogous – there was no monolithic Hindu church, nor a clear demarcation of religion vs. social custom vs. law in pre-modern times. By turning dharma into "religion" and then asserting the state must be "secular," colonial discourse introduced distortions: it created Indian "religions" (the British legally constructed Hinduism, Sikhism, etc., as separate religions with set doctrines, whereas previously the boundaries were fluid). Then it imposed the secularism doctrine, which in practice meant the state had to juggle the sensitivities of these newly hardened religious identities while claiming neutrality. The story of Indian secularism post-1947 is one of continuous strain: far from resolving conflicts, it sometimes exacerbated them by forcing issues into a rigid majority-minority framework borrowed from Westphalian nation-state logic. For example, treating Hinduism as equivalent to a dogmatic "religion" led to policies like a uniform civil code being seen as a majoritarian imposition on minorities, whereas personal law reform within communities became politically charged. The secular state ideal, in a sense, mis-framed what Indian pluralism needed. Traditional Indian polities managed plurality through tolerance and layering – e.g., different communities followed their own norms under the umbrella of a kingdom that patronized multiple sects. The British insisted on a single legal order (except where they kept separate religious laws), thus making identity a zero-sum game in politics (if law favors X's sentiments, Y feels discriminated, etc.).

Satirically put, the Western secularist came to India like a doctor with a hammer seeing everything as a nail: "You have a Hindu majority and Muslim minority? Ah, a potential religious conflict! The cure is secularism – let's banish religion to the private sphere." But religion in India was not just private belief; it was intertwined with culture, art, social norms, and identity in a way far different from the dogmatic Church-versus-State battles of Europe. Thus, the secularist "cure" often rang hollow or even seemed an attack on deeply held ways of life (leading to the ironic phenomenon that secularism in India got equated by many with being anti-Hindu or overly pro-minority – a distortion of the original principle, but arising from how it was implemented).

Indian thinkers used Indian terms to interpret Western topoi, leading to distortions of both problem and solution. In case of secularism, the "problem" of communal conflict was framed in terms drawn from Europe (as a religious intolerance issue akin to Protestant-Catholic strife), and the "solution" was also drawn from Europe (state neutrality, equal legal citizenship abstracted from community). But the actual Indian problem might have been different – perhaps one of addressing historical grievances and reforming inter-community relations without erasing community identities. Because the terms were misaligned, the discourse seesawed between rigid Western secularism and its critics who often slid into apologism for religious communalism. Both sides in India – secularists and Hindu traditionalists – ended up accepting the colonial narrative that Hinduism = an antiquated religion with an invidious caste system, etc., they just differed on whether to reform it (secularist stance) or glorify it (reactionary stance). Either way, the frame was set by the West. So, the entire debate on what makes authority legitimate in India – a secular constitution vs. a theocratic or ethnoreligious state – has been happening on imported theoretical terrain, often to the detriment of more indigenous ways of imagining political community.

RETHINKING AUTHORITY AND LEGITIMACY

How might one articulate a theory of authority and legitimacy rooted in the Indian civilizational experience, yet intelligible in global discourse? This is a challenging question, but we can outline some key principles and compare them with Western assumptions as we go. The tone here will be assertive but also aspirational – pointing towards alternatives not in a spirit of parochialism, but with a conviction that India's differences hold lessons of general value for reimagining politics in the 21st century.

Dharma, Not (Just) Contract: A Duty-Centered Ontology of Authority

A cornerstone of Indian thought is Dharma – a complex concept encompassing righteousness, duty, law, and cosmic order. Unlike Western theories that often start with rights or contracts, an Indian perspective might start with duties and roles. Authority, in this view, is legitimate when it fulfills Dharma – the specific duties attached to one's role as a ruler, official, elder, etc., and the general duty of upholding cosmic/social order.

For example, the ancient text Shantiparva of the Mahabharata (in the form of Bhishma's counsel to Yudhishthira) elaborates on Raja Dharma (the duty of kings): to protect the people, to discipline evildoers, to be impartial and compassionate, to follow advice of wise counselors (often Brahmins), and so on (Vyasa, 400 BCE). A contemporary application: In Indian political culture, even today, leaders are often evaluated in moral terms – "mera neta paapi hai ya punya?" ("Is my leader sinful or virtuous?") – rather than strictly by legal or efficiency terms. Scandals that involve moral turpitude (sexual impropriety, irreverence to religion, etc.) can destroy a politician's career as much as, or more than, technical failures. This is sometimes scoffed at as "irrational" by Westernized commentators ("why should private life matter?"), but it harks back to the dharmic expectation that an authority figure must be a role model (like Rama Rajya ideal – the ruler as virtuous). Instead of dismissing this as pre-modern, a civilizational approach would embrace it: yes, public authority entails an ethical exemplarity in Indian context (Chi, 2012; Negi et al., 2024). Thus, legitimacy involves a character component. We might formalize this: beyond constitutional legality and performance indices, an Indian theory of legitimacy could include "ethical credibility" – does the person in authority command moral respect?

Compare this to Weber's charismatic authority – there it's about personal heroism. The Indian version is less about charisma (though that plays a part) and more about character (Guna). Dharma as a basis of authority also means legitimacy is context-sensitive and plural. There isn't one secular law that fits all, but rather each context, community, or season of life might have its appropriate guiding norms. In classical India, law (neeti or vidhi) was not entirely uniform; there were allowances that different jatis or regions might have different customs (this was formalized in the British notion of "personal laws" by religion, but earlier it was more fluid by locality and caste). A king's dharma included respecting local norms. This suggests a concept of polycentric legitimacy: multiple sources of authority can co-exist (village council, caste elders, royal decree, guild regulations), each legitimate in its domain so long as aligned to the overall dharmic order. The king was Chakravartin (wheel-turner) – ideally, he harmonized these spheres rather than micromanaged them. Global politics today might learn from this model: instead of insisting on one hierarchy of authority (like nation-state sovereignty as absolute), we could see a layering – local communities, nations, international bodies each have authority in different realms, needing balance rather than total supremacy of one level. India historically thrived without a unitary Leviathan; perhaps in a globalized yet fragmented world, a network of overlapping authorities (tribal councils, city governments, national states, UN agencies, etc.) could be more resilient and legitimate collectively than any attempt at a one-world Leviathan. The Indian concept that dharma is one but duties are many could undergird a pluralistic governance idea: various authorities justified by their service to common dharma (human well-being, justice), not by a formal contract linking them all.

Civilizational Grounding: A Global Call for Plural Political Ontologies

In offering these Indian perspectives – dharma-centric legitimacy, spiritual-temporal synergy, authority as service, pluralistic tolerance – the aim is not parochial but potentially universal in a deeper sense. They challenge Western political ontology to expand: from homo economicus or rights-bearing individual to duty-bearing relational self; from secular disenchantment to re-infusing ethical purpose; from uniformity to federated diversity. One might worry: would this mean going back to monarchy or caste? No, it means taking the underlying principles that once informed those and reimagining them for today. For example, the concept of Varna (social function) without the birth-based hierarchy could inspire a system where different talents and roles are all respected (a bit like how some argue we should not look down on vocational careers versus white-collar – an echo of the dignity-of-labor principle implicit in the ideal that all varnas have their necessary place). Likewise, a Raja today could be a democratically elected leader but still behave like the ancient ideal king by listening to sages (scientists maybe, or genuine cultural elders) and protecting the weak.

Indian civilization often specialized in synthesis. We see attempts now to synthesize Western and Indian: e.g., Integral Humanism (the philosophy of Deendayal Upadhyaya adopted by some Indian political streams) tries to marry modern polity with dharmic social vision. It posits that individual, society, and spiritual reality are integrated – thus economic and political decisions must factor in cultural and spiritual well-being, not just material progress. Such thinking hasn't yet fully translated into policy beyond slogans, but it shows the direction. At a global scale, adopting a civilizationally grounded alternative means creating space for different regions to contribute their ethos to the global order. Instead of one-size-fits-all indices of "good governance" (usually biased to Western liberal norms), we might have multi-criteria that include, say: harmony index (how well a society maintains social cohesion, an Asian strength often) alongside freedom index, participation index, sustainability index, and so on. India might score better on harmony than on Western freedom metrics, which might correct an otherwise skewed picture and suggest different remedies (Misra & Keerthiraj, 2024; Wenner, 2020).

Imagine Plato, Hobbes, and Locke on one side of a table, and Yudhishthira, Gandhi or a common person with Indian experience on the other. They debate how to govern a village. Plato demands a philosopher-king exam for the headman; Hobbes wants to impose a strict penal code; Locke says hold a vote. Yudhishthira says, "First, let's see what dharma the villagers follow and who among them has lived it best – that person will be our guide." Gandhi says, "Find the one who calls himself the greatest servant, and he is the leader." The Western trio looked puzzled – this wasn't in their playbook. But maybe, just maybe, they then nod in thoughtful consideration.

CONCLUSION

To rewrite authority and legitimacy in global politics, as we set out to do, is to enlarge the canvas. The old narrative, dominated by Western political theory, is painted in bold primary colors – state vs. individual, church vs. state, consent vs. coercion, legal vs. illegal. The Indian civilizational palette adds shades and hues in between: duties alongside rights, spiritual alongside secular, community alongside individual, harmony alongside freedom, moral charisma alongside legal-rational authority. The resulting picture is richer, more textured, and arguably more representative of the human experience across cultures. We exposed how a careless universalism distorted understanding, especially of Indian realities, turning nuanced traditions into caricatures of despotism, fanaticism, or barbarism. We also exposed how colonial lenses were internalized, leading Indians to doubt their own legacy and mimic models not always suited to their context – a condition remedied only by conscious decolonization of social sciences. But exposure is only half the task. We then proposed an alternative view, drawing on classical and contemporary Indian thought: one that sees legitimacy as rooted in dharma (a shared moral order) and seva (service), moderated by pluralism and guided by the insight that no single worldview has a monopoly on truth.

In practice, moving toward a civilizationally grounded politics means fostering confidence among non-Western societies to voice their paradigms. It also means urging Western institutions to reform. For example, the UN might benefit from less top-down lecture and more cultural brokerage – maybe have "Civilizational caucuses" that bring insights (already, concepts like Gross National Happiness from Bhutan or Ubuntu from Africa have gained some international traction; more such ideas could flourish). On national levels, countries like India can innovate democratic forms that include traditional councils (as some North-East Indian hills do, blending modern councils with chieftains). These experiments, if documented and theorized, can contribute back to global knowledge – perhaps informing even Western communities looking for more communitarian or spiritually fulfilling governance models amid their own crises of alienation. We set a polemical tone in parts, using satire to call out the epistemic arrogance of believing Westminster or Washington had nothing to learn from Varanasi or Beijing. But that polemic was not to dismiss Western achievements, rather to humble and broaden the conversation. Likewise, we did not shy from criticizing Indian failings – the point is not that Indian tradition was utopian (it wasn't; it had rigidities and injustices) – but that its fundamental worldview offers correctives to the blind spots of a purely West-centric narrative. In a sense, India's message to global political theory might echo what Krishna told Arjuna in the Bhagavad Gita when imparting wisdom: "Think not that this is new – it is the ancient truth I rekindle for your present need" (Vyasa, 400 BCE). Similarly, the idea that leadership is a sacred trust, or that pluralism is strength, are ancient truths

The chapter's assertive tone has been deliberate. Too often non-Western ideas have been presented apologetically, as if seeking validation. Here we spoke with strategic aggression – to signal confidence in our intellectual inheritance and to jolt the complacent universalist out of his haze. If a bit of exaggeration or caricature of Western thought occurred, it was in service of making a point sharply – a mirror to how Eastern ideas have been caricatured historically. Now, at least, the playing field of critique is leveled. In concluding, we return to the original provocation: Authority and legitimacy in global politics need rethinking. This rethinking is not a one-time seminar exercise; it is an ongoing negotiation as humanity faces new challenges that no single tradition can solve. Climate change, digital surveillance, pandemics – each raises ethical and authority questions that transcend old frameworks. A globally legitimate solution will likely draw on technological rationality (West), community solidarity (East), respect for nature (Indigenous), and spiritual humility (universal religious) all together. No single compass is enough; we need all hands-on deck, all wisdom traditions in counsel.

REFERENCES

Aristotle. (350). Politics (C. D. C. Reeve, Trans.). Hackett Publishing.

Beetham, D. (1991). *The Legitimation of Power*. Palgrave Macmillan. DOI: 10.1007/978-1-349-21599-7

. Bernstein, S. (2004). The Elusive Basis of Legitimacy in Global Governance: Three Conceptions.

. Chi, Z. (2012). Transition of Origin of Old Indian Kingship's Legitimacy.

De Roover, J., Claerhout, S., & Rao, B. (2011). Liberal political theory and the cultural migration of ideas: The case of secularism in India. *Political Theory*, *39*(5), 571–599. DOI: 10.1177/0090591711413545

Ficek, R. (2023). *Legitimacy in the Context of the Global Institutions of Power and the Contemporary Determinants of International Politics*. Teka Komisji Politologii i Stosunków Międzynarodowych., DOI: 10.17951/teka.2022.17.1.23-36

Foucault, M. (1978). The History of Sexuality: Vol. 1. *An Introduction* (Hurley, R., Trans.). Pantheon Books.

Habermas, J. (1973). *Legitimation Crisis* (McCarthy, T., Trans.). Beacon Press.

Hobbes, T. (1651). *Leviathan* (Malcolm, N., Ed.). Oxford University Press.

Hurd, I. (2018). Legitimacy and contestation in global governance: Revisiting the folk theory of international institutions. *The Review of International Organizations*, *14*(4), 717–729. DOI: 10.1007/s11558-018-9338-z

Keerthiraj, M. A., & Vang-Phu, T. (2025). India's BRICS Engagement: A Strategic Lever in South Asia and the Indian Ocean. In A. Gedikli, S. Erdogan, & H. Çalışkan Terzioğlu (Eds.), Changing the Global Political Economy: BRICS Countries and Alternative Relations Strategies (pp. 189-214). IGI Global Scientific Publishing. https://doi.org/DOI: 10.4018/979-8-3693-7393-4.ch006

Koppell, J. (2007). Global Governance Organizations: Legitimacy and Authority in Conflict. *Journal of Public Administration: Research and Theory*, *18*(2), 177–203. DOI: 10.1093/jopart/mum041

Locke, J. (1689). *Two Treatises of Government* (Laslett, P., Ed.). Cambridge University Press.

Mill, J. (1817). The History of British India (W. Thomas, Ed.). Routledge/Thoemmes Press.

. Misra, A. & Keerthiraj. (2024). Integrating Sustainability in India's Tourism Sector: An Uphill Battle. In S. Poddar, B. Paul, & M. Luperi (Eds.), Sustainable Business Ecosystems and Social Perspectives (pp. 359-386). IGI Global Scientific Publishing. https://doi.org/DOI: 10.4018/979-8-3693-8437-4.ch016

Negi, A., Irshad, M., & Luthviati, R. (2024). *Deconstructing Attributes of Constitutional Legitimacy: A Case Study of Indian Constitution. Journal of Human Rights*. Culture and Legal System., DOI: 10.53955/jhcls.v4i1.114

. Plato. (380 BCE). The Republic (B. Jowett, Trans.). Dover Publications.

Rousseau, J.-J. (1762). *The Social Contract* (Cress, D. A., Trans.). Hackett Publishing.

Said, E. W. (1978). *Orientalism*. Pantheon Books.

Schmitt, C. (1922). *Political Theology: Four Chapters on the Concept of Sovereignty* (Schwab, G., Trans.). University of Chicago Press.

United Nations. (1948). Universal Declaration of Human Rights. United Nations. https://www.un.org/en/about-us/universal-declaration-of-human-rights

U.S. Continental Congress. (1776). The Declaration of Independence (P. Force, Ed.). Dover Publications.

Victoria, Q. (1858). Proclamation of 1858 to the Princes, Chiefs, and People of India. In Philips, C. H. (Ed.), *The Evolution of India and Pakistan, 1858 to 1947* (pp. 1–3). Oxford University Press.

Vyasa. (400 BCE). The Bhagavad Gita (E. Easwaran, Trans.). Nilgiri Press.

Vyasa. (400 BCE). The Mahabharata of Krishna-Dwaipayana Vyasa, Book 12: Shanti Parva (K. M. Ganguli, Trans.). Munshiram Manoharlal.

Weber, M. (1978). *Economy and Society: An Outline of Interpretive Sociology* (Roth, G., & Wittich, C., Eds.). University of California Press.

Wenner, M. (2020). Trajectories of Hybrid Governance: Legitimacy, Order and Leadership in India. *Development and Change*. Advance online publication. DOI: 10.1111/dech.12624

Chapter 2
Nationality Law as an Instrument of Exclusion in Developing Democracies:
Systematic Discrimination and Minority Marginalization

Cassadee Orinthia Yan
http://orcid.org/0009-0005-2737-3434
Maslow Quest Foundation, New Zealand

ABSTRACT

Nationality law defines belonging but often serves as a political tool of exclusion. In developing democracies, it institutionalizes discrimination through restrictive jus soli and jus sanguinis principles, marginalizing minorities and reinforcing social hierarchies. Such exclusion leads to statelessness, disenfranchisement, and weakened democracy. By transforming citizenship into privilege, these laws erode equality and cohesion. Reforming nationality law toward inclusive citizenship is vital to ensure belonging becomes a universal right and to strengthen democratic participation and legitimacy.

INTRODUCTION

Democracy rests upon the principle of popular sovereignty; yet the very delineation of *who* constitutes "the people" is neither automatic nor politically neutral. Nationality law furnishes the juridical framework by which the state determines who

DOI: 10.4018/979-8-2600-1618-3.ch002

shall be recognized as a member of the political community and who shall remain outside its fold. As such, it operates as the legal threshold for rights, representation, and civic recognition. Beyond the formal entitlements of suffrage and other rights, the concept of citizenship is built on a profound sense of belonging and accountability in the relationship between the state and the individual. Indeed, as Safran (1997) and Lister (2007) have persuasively argued, the meaning of citizenship relates to one's relationship not only with government but also with other individuals within the shared political sphere.

Although often presented as a dry matter of legal classification, nationality law's impacts are inherently political. In many developing democracies—where institutions may be fragile, populations heterogeneous, and the legacies of colonial rule deeply entrenched—rules governing membership serve as instruments of boundary-making and power consolidation. Such laws are deployed not merely to define identity in the abstract but also to reward loyal constituencies, solidify ruling coalitions, and exclude or weaken perceived rivals. In practice, regimes with exclusionary nationality laws have deprived disfavored minorities of basic services, stigmatized them as outsiders, and silenced their voices in the political arena.

Over time, these legal and administrative exclusions corrode trust in public institutions and destabilize social cohesion, as observers of African nationality practices have documented. Manby's (2016) comparative research on African citizenship laws, for example, chronicles how ostensibly neutral provisions have been manipulated to marginalize certain ethnic groups, thereby eroding institutional legitimacy. Likewise, Schmid's (2020) analysis of boundary regimes underscores such effects, demonstrating that when large segments of a population are relegated to second-class status, the very fabric of democratic society is weakened. In sum, nationality law in such contexts becomes a formidable tool of political engineering—defining insiders and outsiders in ways that reinforce the dominance of those who control the legal narrative of citizenship.

Hence, this chapter examines how nationality law functions as an instrument of systematic discrimination in developing democracies, with particular focus on the marginalization of minority groups. It is contended here that exclusion is not an inadvertent by-product of nationality policy but a deliberately engineered facet of the architecture of nationality law itself. Such design is evident in five interlocking mechanisms: (1) the imposition of restrictive *jus soli* and *jus sanguinis* rules that narrowly circumscribe birthright membership; (2) onerous and protracted naturalization processes that deter or bar long-term residents from acquiring citizenship; (3) gender-discriminatory provisions that deny women equal capacity to transmit nationality; (4) the bureaucratic manipulation of civil registration and identity documentation to deny recognition to minorities; and (5) the normalization of denationalization as a governmental prerogative. By tracing the operation of these mechanisms, the chapter shows how law can transform social cleavages into enduring structures of inequality. Put simply, the legal criteria for citizenship—far from being neutral determinants of status—often crystallize political agendas of inclusion or exclusion, codifying societal biases into formal stratifications that persist across generations.

In order to substantiate this thesis, the full discussion proceeds as follows. First, it develops a theoretical framework for understanding nationality law as both a legal status and a political practice, elucidating how the very *language* of citizenship law can serve as a foundation for nation-building or for exclusion. Second, it situates contemporary exclusionary regimes in their historical context, examining how colonial legacies and postcolonial power struggles have shaped the boundaries of national belonging. Third, it analyzes the legal texts and administrative practices through which exclusion is effectuated—ranging from the wording of statutes to the chokeholds of bureaucratic procedure. Finally, it assesses the consequences of these exclusionary regimes for democratic governance, surveys comparative experiences of reform, and, on that basis, advances a set of policy recommendations for constructing a more inclusive model of citizenship.

The central claim that emerges is that nationality law is not a peripheral technicality of governance; it is a fundamental component of democracy itself. The design of a nation's citizenship regime fundamentally determines the breadth of the *demos*—those entitled to partake in self-government. Inclusive citizenship laws enlarge the *demos* or *populace,* buttress the principle of equality, strengthen accountability between rulers and ruled, and lay the groundwork for meaningful popular participation in public life (Lister, 2007; Safran, 1997). Conversely, exclusionary laws contract the political community and create hierarchies of belonging; they delegitimize the ideal of equal citizenship, weaken governance by estranging segments of the population, and ultimately undermine the integrity of democratic institutions (Manby, 2016; Schmid, 2020). For developing democracies in particular, the imperative is clear—to transform nationality law from a mechanism of exclusion into an instrument of democratic inclusion, thereby ensuring that the promise of popular sovereignty genuinely extends to all those who reside within the state's territory and jurisdiction. Only by broadening the base of citizenship and securing it as a universal status can emerging democracies hope to achieve stable institutions, cohesive societies, and accountable governance in the long run.

SECTION I – ON THE LEGAL NATURE OF MEMBERSHIP AND THE CONSTRUCTION OF THE POLITICAL COMMUNITY

Citizenship, though written into law in modern times, is an old idea. It has always meant more than a legal status; citizenship defines how a person relates to the state and to others with whom it is shared. In law, citizenship gives people civil and political rights such as voting, owning property, going to court, and taking part in public life. However, it also involves duties of loyalty, service, and participation in perpetuating the common good. To be a citizen, therefore, is not just to live in a country but to belong to it in a recognized, mutual way. Together, citizenship and nationality law determine who is included in this relationship—and who is left out (Lister, 2007; Safran, 1997; Manby, 2016).

Nationality law generally relies on two main ideas: *jus soli* ("right of the soil") and *jus sanguinis* ("right of blood"). Each claims ancient origins, but both concepts took on their modern shape only in the nineteenth century. The first confers citizenship based on birthplace, i.e., being born in a country; the second, on descent from parents who are citizens. The *jus soli* tradition—rooted in Roman and later English law—reflects a civic view of belonging: anyone born on the territory is a member of it. *Jus sanguinis*, common in continental Europe, ties citizenship to ancestry and culture, imagining the state as a family of shared blood and heritage. As modern scholars note, these are not timeless principles but political inventions that grew out of migration, empire, and fears of population change (Bertocchi & Strozzi, 2010; Perl-Rosenthal et al., 2024; Schmid, 2020).

Neither principle is as neutral as it appears. Some countries that once offered automatic citizenship by birth have since added restrictions—for example, requiring that a parent be legally resident before a child born within the territory can be recognized as a citizen. Britain's Nationality Act of 1981 is a well-known case, having replaced unconditional birthright with conditional citizenship. Other states, especially those emerging from colonial rule, have used *jus sanguinis* to favor "indigenous" populations, excluding groups viewed as foreign. In this way, law evolves from a set of rules to a political instrument for defining identity and controlling who "belongs" (Manby, 2016; Safran, 1997).

Seen in this light, nationality law is more than a formal institution—it is a tool of governance. The categories it creates—citizen, alien, stateless person—shape who receives rights and protection from the state. Governments, particularly those still forming democratic systems, often use these laws to decide who counts as loyal and who can be ignored. In many developing countries, citizenship is linked to ethnic or religious patronage: granting it can be a reward for political support, while withholding it punishes dissent (Manby, 2016; Schmid, 2020).

It is within the bureaucracy that administers nationality—civil registries, immigration departments, ministries of the interior—that these ideas are put into practice. In such offices, people are accepted or delayed, their documents questioned or rejected. Research has shown that eak or biased civil registration systems can make entire communities effectively invisible, denying them citizenship in practice even when the law seems inclusive (Badewa, 2022; Herberholz, 2022; Loganathan et al.,

2023; Warria, 2020). What appears to be simple inefficiency often hides systematic discrimination, allowing exclusion to continue behind the façade of legal procedure.

Ultimately, nationality law should be seen as a foundation of power, not a neutral set of rules. It reflects the balance between civic and ethnic ideas of the nation, between inclusion and control. Encompassing the ability to both protect and exclude, citizenship law remains one of the most influential—and most contested—parts of modern public law. It defines the edges of the political community, deciding not only who belongs, but, perhaps more importantly, who does not (Lister, 2007; Safran, 1997).

SECTION II – HISTORICAL ANTECEDENTS: COLONIAL LEGACIES AND THE POSTCOLONIAL BOUNDARIES OF CITIZENSHIP

The modern politics of nationality cannot be separated from the long shadows of empires. Colonial rule did more than redraw maps—it constructed hierarchies of belonging that have endured well beyond the end of formal domination. Through law, bureaucracy, and racial ideology, colonial powers divided populations into the privileged and the governed, the visible and the invisible. Those divisions, once etched into legal codes, became the raw material from which postcolonial states later built their own citizenship regimes (Manby, 2016).

Colonial administrators treated nationality not as a shared civic bond but as a means of organizing control. People were classified by race, tribe, religion, and gender, and those categories determined everything from taxation and land ownership to the right to move freely. In British colonies, for example, "natives" were governed through indirect rule and denied the rights of imperial citizens, while settlers enjoyed full political recognition. The French system went further, offering citizenship only to a narrow elite who met cultural and educational tests, thereby institutionalizing the idea that political belonging had to be earned through assimilation. Across Africa and Asia, the message was the same: nationality was not a universal entitlement but a mark of proximity to the ruling power (Drissa, 2021; Manby, 2016).

When independence came, these hierarchies did not vanish. The new states inherited colonial borders that bore little relationship to linguistic, cultural, or ethnic realities. People who had long moved, traded, and intermarried across regions suddenly found themselves separated by newly sovereign frontiers. In these settings, leaders sought to forge unity out of diversity—and often did so by narrowing the meaning of citizenship. In many countries, nationality became tied to "authentic" origin or ancestral belonging, rather than to residence or contribution. What had once been an imperial boundary between ruler and ruled became an internal line between the citizen and the outsider (Babo, 2018; Drissa, 2021).

Côte d'Ivoire offers a clear example of this effect. At independence, the country's founding laws promised inclusion, recognizing the diversity created by decades of regional migration. Yet as political competition intensified in the late twentieth century, this inclusive vision collapsed. The ideology of *Ivoirité* redefined the Ivorian as someone whose parents—and often grandparents—were of "pure" Ivorian origin. Hence, entire communities, particularly those of Burkinabé descent, were stripped of political rights and treated as foreigners in the land of their birth. What began as a cultural debate over identity became a weapon of political exclusion, fueling social division and even civil conflict (Babo, 2018; Drissa, 2021).

The Dominican Republic followed a parallel logic, shaped by its own colonial and racial history. For most of the twentieth century, the country granted citizenship to anyone born on its soil, reflecting the *jus soli* principle. Nevertheless, long-standing prejudice against Haitians, rooted in centuries of plantation labor and racial hierarchy, gave rise to legal reinterpretations. In 2013, the Constitutional Tribunal ruled that people born to undocumented Haitian parents—stretching back several generations—had never been citizens. Consequently, thousands were rendered stateless overnight, stripped of their nationality in a single judicial act (Hannam, 2014; Sagás & Román, 2017).

Similarly, Myanmar's 1982 Citizenship Law reveals the same dynamic in a different setting. Colonial Burma's borders had drawn together an extraordinary mix of communities, and migration under British rule blurred distinctions between ethnic groups. After independence was declared, the new government sought to reclaim sovereignty through a highly exclusive definition of national identity. The law recognized 135 "national races," a list that deliberately excluded the Rohingya. By creating multiple tiers of citizenship—full, associate, and naturalized—it turned ethnic hierarchy into legal "fact." In doing so, the state not only denied the Rohingya legal recognition but also laid the groundwork for decades of persecution and statelessness (Haque, 2017; Kyaw, 2017).

These cases illustrate a recurring truth: exclusionary nationality laws exclusionary nationality laws rarely emerge arbitrarily. They grow out of inherited systems of classification that once served empires. Postcolonial governments, often facing economic strain and political insecurity, found in those systems a ready-made language for defining belonging and loyalty. Restrictive citizenship rules offered a means of drawing boundaries around power—of deciding who could claim the benefits of the state and who could be denied them. Citizenship, once imagined as a universal bond, became a form of political capital, granted or withheld according to the shifting calculations of those in power (Manby, 2016; Schmid, 2020).

Even today, administrative traces of colonialism remain visible. Civil registration and identity systems, which are introduced to manage labor, taxation, and surveillance, still serve as the gatekeepers of citizenship. In many countries, obtaining proof of birth or nationality requires ancestral documentation that entire communities simply do not have. For people whose forebears migrated, intermarried, or were excluded from recordkeeping, proving "belonging" becomes almost impossible. The result is a quiet but enduring exclusion, where those without papers exist within the nation yet remain outside its protection (Badewa, 2022; Warria, 2020).

The past, in this sense, is not concluded. The colonial logic of inclusion and exclusion continues to shape who can claim citizenship today. Postcolonial states have replaced imperial authority with national sovereignty, but the underlying structures of inequality often remain intact. The challenge for modern democracies, therefore, is not only to reform their laws but to reckon with their histories—to recognize that the boundaries of citizenship were never neutral, and that true equality requires dismantling the hierarchies inherited from empire (Manby, 2016; Schmid, 2020).

SECTION III – THE ARCHITECTURE OF EXCLUSION: LAW, BUREAUCRACY, AND THE CODIFICATION OF INEQUALITY

The power of nationality law lies both in its broad principles and its everyday application. Legal texts may speak in the neutral language of equality and procedure, but the way those texts are designed and implemented often produces—and legitimizes—exclusion. Beneath the surface of citizenship policy lies a layered architecture of legal provisions, bureaucratic practices, and administrative habits that determine who can claim belonging and who cannot.

At the core of this system are the two doctrines that have long structured citizenship: *jus soli* (citizenship by birthplace) and *jus sanguinis* (citizenship by descent). While these frameworks appear to offer simple, logical rules, they have proved remarkably flexible in the service of political agendas. *Jus soli* is often praised as the more inclusive approach—citizenship based on where one is born rather than who one's parents are. Yet even countries that follow this principle have frequently seen the scope narrowed in the hands of lawmakers. For instance, Britain's 1981 Nationality Act transformed unconditional birthright citizenship into a conditional one, requiring that at least one parent be legally settled in the country. The change, like many others, was justified as a response to immigration and social pressure; yet, in practice, it reinforced boundaries of race and class (Bertocchi & Strozzi, 2010).

Jus sanguinis, on the other hand, ties belonging to ancestry. It can preserve cultural continuity, but it also carries an exclusionary logic—especially in postcolonial states that equate "true" citizenship with ethnic origin. In such systems, whole communities are labelled as perpetual outsiders because their ancestors came from elsewhere, even if their inhabitants have lived in that country for generations (Manby, 2016). By applying this approach, governments have been able to define who is "indigenous" and, by implication, who is not—a distinction that has been most persistently used as a tool of exclusion in developing democracies.

Nationality law also establishes hierarchies through naturalization. The process is often presented as a path to inclusion, and yet it is, in many cases, deliberately obstructive. Lengthy residency requirements, arbitrary "good character" tests, and complex documentation demands turn naturalization into a privilege for the few who can afford it—financially, socially, and politically. States justify these hurdles as necessary to protect sovereignty or cultural cohesion, but the effect is to create a permanent class of residents who live in the country but remain legally marginal (Schmid, 2020).

Moreover, the exclusion does not end with the law; it extends into the bureaucratic systems that make citizenship "real." Birth registration, identification cards, and residency certificates are the everyday documents that transform the abstract idea of nationality into a practical reality. Yet access to these documents is far from equal. For example, civil registration systems in much of Africa and Asia remain weak, underfunded, and, in some cases, openly discriminatory. Officials may require impossible proofs of ancestry, reject names associated with minority groups, or delay processing applications indefinitely. These decisions often go unrecorded and unchallenged, yet they have life-altering consequences. People who cannot obtain papers cannot attend school, travel freely, or work in the formal economy (Badewa, 2022; Warria, 2020).

This bureaucratic exclusion is particularly visible in Kenya, where members of the Nubian community—a group descended from Sudanese soldiers settled during the colonial era—face recurring discrimination in the citizenship process. To receive an identity card, Nubians must undergo extra "vetting" procedures, present multiple witnesses, and prove familial ties dating back decades. Such practices create what one scholar calls *"citizenship by discretion"*—a system in which belonging depends less on law than on the attitude of local officials (Balaton-Chrimes, 2024). In effect, the bureaucratic gatekeepers of the state determine who is allowed to exist as a legal person.

Even where nationality laws appear gender-neutral, discrimination can persist through practice. In several countries, women still cannot pass nationality to their children or foreign spouses on equal terms with men. Some laws make a child's citizenship dependent on the father's status, leaving children of single mothers or of unknown fathers stateless. The social impact of this inequality is immense. It traps women and their families in cycles of dependency and insecurity, reducing their access to education, employment, and inheritance rights (Bellizzi & Nivoli,

2023; Fisher, 2016). In these cases, the private realm of family becomes a domain wherein the state can enforce exclusion.

Finally, in recent years, many states—both developing and developed—have expanded their powers of *denationalization,* as they can strip individuals of their citizenship on grounds such as "disloyalty" or "fraud." Governments claim this authority is necessary for national security, yet they often employ it against minorities and dissidents who lack political protection. When citizenship can be taken away by administrative order, it ceases to be a right and becomes a conditional privilege (Birkvad, 2023; Pillai & Williams, 2017; Tripkovic, 2023).

Collectively, these mechanisms form what might be called the *infrastructure of exclusion.* Through a mix of legal design and bureaucratic discretion, states continually redraw the line between insiders and outsiders. The law provides the justification, the bureaucracy enforces it, and together they create a system that appears lawful even as it undermines equality. This is how nationality law—an institution meant to express belonging—becomes a tool for marginalization.

SECTION IV – JURIDICAL AND COMPARATIVE ILLUSTRATIONS OF EXCLUSION

The power of nationality law often becomes clearest not in theory but in the stories of those it excludes. Across different regions, legal systems that appear neutral on paper have been turned into instruments for drawing boundaries around belonging. The details vary—some are rooted in ethnicity, others in race, ancestry, or bureaucracy—but the logic is remarkably consistent: citizenship is withheld from those who fall outside the dominant vision of the nation. Examining cases from Myanmar, the Dominican Republic, Côte d'Ivoire, Kenya, Nepal, and the Gulf States reveals how these laws operate in practice, producing distinct yet eerily similar forms of statelessness.

Myanmar offers one of the most devastating examples of how law can be used to erase entire communities. The 1982 Citizenship Law, introduced by the military government, divided the population into three categories—full, associate, and naturalized citizens—each defined by increasingly restrictive documentation requirements. Beneath the bureaucratic language of classification lay a clear message about who belonged: Only members of the 135 officially recognized "national races" were entitled to full citizenship. The Rohingya, a Muslim community with centuries of history in Rakhine State, were deliberately left off that list. Stripped of recognition, they became foreigners in their own homeland (Haque, 2017; Kyaw, 2017).

The consequences have been catastrophic. Deprived of identity cards, the Rohingya were excluded from education, healthcare, and mobility. When the military launched brutal "clearance operations" in 2017, more than 700,000 fled to Bangladesh. Their lack of citizenship allowed the state to deny responsibility, framing the violence as the removal of "illegal immigrants" rather than an attack on its own people (Alam, 2018). What Myanmar demonstrates, in stark clarity, is the way in which the law's technical vocabulary—when infused with ethnonationalist ideology—can be used to provide moral and bureaucratic cover for persecution.

As Myanmar's exclusionary system was built through ethnic categorization, the Dominican Republic's was sustained through race and history. For decades, Dominican nationality followed *jus soli*—citizenship by birth within the territory. Yet the deep racial divide between Dominicans and neighboring Haitians gradually reshaped this legal principle. In 2013, the country's Constitutional Tribunal ruled that anyone born to parents deemed "in transit" was never entitled to citizenship, even if their families had lived in the country for generations (Hannam, 2014). The decision extended back to 1929, effectively revoking citizenship from tens of thousands of Dominicans of Haitian descent. Those who had been voters, workers, and students suddenly became stateless.

The government justified this as a matter of national sovereignty, but the subtext was racial hierarchy: blackness and foreignness were conflated to redraw the boundaries of belonging. The Dominican case demonstrates how easily citizenship can be reinterpreted when prejudice masquerades as constitutional principle. As Sagás and Román (2017) and Blake (2014) argue, the law became a means of policing racial identity, reinforcing the colonial narrative that whiteness and citizenship were synonymous.

Côte d'Ivoire presents a different, though equally revealing, manifestation of the same impulse. After independence, the Ivorian state adopted an inclusive model of citizenship, shaped by the region's long history of migration. However, as political competition deepened in the 1990s, the government turned to exclusionary nationalism as a strategy for power. Under the banner of *Ivoirité*, political leaders redefined citizenship around "authentic" origin, requiring proof of Ivorian parentage. The policy effectively disenfranchised northern and Sahelian communities, many of whom had migrated generations earlier from neighboring states (Babo, 2018; Drissa, 2021).

This narrowing of belonging had immediate political repercussions. Opposition leader Alassane Ouattara was barred from running for president on the grounds that one of his parents was not "Ivorian by birth." The doctrine of *Ivoirité* turned citizenship into a weapon—dividing communities, legitimizing discrimination, and ultimately contributing to civil conflict. Here, nationality law did not just mirror ethnic divisions; it deepened them, transforming identity into a fault line for political struggle.

In Kenya, the exclusionary logic operates more quietly but no less effectively. Rather than dramatic court rulings or explicit racial decrees, it is bureaucracy that enforces the boundary. The Nubian community, descendants of Sudanese soldiers settled during the colonial period, have long lived as Kenyans in every practical sense. Yet today, when they apply for national identification cards—a requirement for education, employment, or even travel—they are subjected to a "vetting" process unique to their community. Committees demand proof of ancestry stretching back generations, which is often impossible to provide (Balaton-Chrimes, 2024).

This slow, procedural denial illustrates how power may not reside in the law itself but in the administration of that law. For the Nubians, citizenship exists in theory but not in practice; their lives are defined by waiting, paperwork, and the quiet authority of officials who decide who counts as Kenyan. As one observer remarked, "The file, the form, and the waiting room have replaced the frontier post as the new border of belonging."

A similar story is playing out today in Nepal, though its roots lie in geography and gender. The Madhesi community, concentrated along the border with India, shares language and culture with families across the frontier. These cross-border ties have made them targets of suspicion within Kathmandu's political establishment. Despite constitutional guarantees of citizenship by birth or descent, Madhesi applicants are routinely denied documents on the grounds of "uncertain loyalty." Women, in particular, suffer doubly: Nepal's nationality law still restricts their ability to pass citizenship to their children or spouses. The result is a bureaucracy of exclusion that combines patriarchy and nationalism into a single, self-perpetuating system (Kyaw, 2017; Warria, 2020).

The Gulf States offer a final and striking contrast. In Kuwait and other wealthy monarchies, the Bidoon—whose name literally means "without"—represents a population left behind by the state's creation. When nationality registers were compiled at independence, thousands of long-term residents were omitted, often for political or tribal reasons. Despite living their entire lives in these countries, the Bidoon remain officially classified as "illegal residents," barred from most forms of work, education, and healthcare. Their existence exposes a deep contradiction: even in states of immense wealth, citizenship remains a scarce and strategic privilege, reserved for those who fit the ruling narrative of nationhood (Manby, 2016).

Across these diverse contexts, a pattern emerges. Whether exclusion is justified through ethnicity, race, ancestry, or administrative discretion, its intent and effect is the same: to draw a line between insiders and outsiders, between those recognized by law and those rendered invisible. Nationality law, at its best, protects and integrates; however, at its worst, it divides and expels. The boundary is enforced through ethnicity in Myanmar, through race in the Dominican Republic, and, in Kenya and Nepal, through bureaucracy and gender. Each of these systems practices exclusion but cloaks it in the language of legality, turning what should be a universal status into a selective privilege.

This shared logic reveals the paradox at the heart of modern citizenship. The same legal frameworks that claim to define equality often conceal the tools of inequality. Citizenship can be both a shield and a sword—a means of protection for some and exclusion for others. In every case, it reflects the same uneasy truth: that the law's promise of belonging is always mediated by power, and that the boundary between inclusion and exclusion remains, even today, a matter of political choice (Manby, 2016; Schmid, 2020).

SECTION V – THE CONSEQUENCES OF LEGAL DISCRIMINATION: POLITICAL, ECONOMIC, AND INTERGENERATIONAL MARGINALIZATION

The exclusion created by nationality laws does not end at the point of legal recognition. Once a person is denied citizenship—or forced to live under its constant uncertainty—the effects ripple through every part of life. What begins as a matter of paperwork becomes a crisis of survival, dignity, and belonging. The political, social, and psychological costs accumulate, shaping not only individual fates but also the democratic and economic life of entire societies.

Citizenship is the foundation of political voice. Without it, people are shut out of decision-making, unable to vote, to stand for office, or to engage fully in civic life. In countries where documentation determines eligibility, thousands are excluded from elections simply because they lack identity cards or birth certificates. The consequence is not just silence, but political invisibility, as communities without recognition have no representatives to defend their interests and no institutional channel to challenge injustice. This political marginalization weakens democracy itself, shrinking the public sphere to include only those already privileged by law. Côte d'Ivoire's history of *Ivoirité*, where entire groups were stripped of voting rights by questioning their ancestry, offers a vivid reminder of how easily law can be used to redraw the boundaries of the nation's electorate (Zilla, 2022).

Moreover, political exclusion quickly transforms into economic deprivation. Legal identity is the key that unlocks opportunity—the right to attend school, to work legally, to open a bank account, or to own property. Without it, individuals are left at the margins of the formal economy, confined to informal labor with little protection or security. Across regions, from the Rohingya in Myanmar to Dominicans of Haitian descent, the denial of citizenship has pushed communities into poverty, dependency, and exploitation (Herberholz, 2022; Loganathan et al., 2023; Sagás & Román, 2017). Statelessness strips away not only legal rights but also the means to improve one's circumstances. Without recognition, effort itself loses reward. The result is a cycle where poverty and exclusion reinforce each other, binding generations to a condition of permanent precarity.

Furthermore, this exclusion is not gender neutral. In many states, nationality law still privileges fathers over mothers, treating women as secondary transmitters of citizenship. When a mother cannot pass her nationality to her child or foreign spouse, her family's legal existence becomes conditional on a man's status. For women whose partners are absent, deceased, or of uncertain nationality, this rule creates an impossible burden. The consequences are not merely symbolic: children grow up without papers, unable to enroll in school or receive medical care, while their mothers live with the daily anxiety of bureaucratic rejection. In these families, inequality under the law is lived as emotional exhaustion and social invisibility (Bellizzi & Nivoli, 2023; Beninger & Manjoo, 2022; Fisher, 2016).

Over time, this legal and social exclusion produces deep psychological scars. Citizenship, at its core, is recognition—it is the state's way of saying "you belong here." When that recognition is denied, the absence becomes an emotional wound. Stateless individuals often describe feeling like ghosts within their own societies—present but unseen, tolerated but never accepted. They live with a persistent fear of detention, deportation, or humiliation at the hands of officials. Uncertainty corrodes self-worth and trust in institutions, leading to isolation and despair. As one stateless youth in Malaysia described, "Without papers, it's like you don't exist." These are not merely personal tragedies but collective losses, as a society that allows its members to vanish from civic life also loses part of its moral and human foundation (UNHCR, 2014).

The harshest truth is that these effects are rarely temporary. Exclusion reproduces itself through generations. Parents without citizenship cannot register the births of their children, passing on their own invisibility. Each unregistered child marks another link in a chain of inherited marginalization. In Kenya, Côte d'Ivoire, and elsewhere, such patterns have persisted for decades, leaving entire communities effectively outside the state's protection. Statelessness, once entrenched, becomes self-sustaining—an invisible caste system that outlasts the governments that created it (Manby, 2016).

Together, these layers of harm—political silence, economic poverty, gendered dependency, psychological suffering, and generational exclusion—form a single story: the story of how law, once meant to define equality, can become an engine of inequality. Exclusionary nationality systems do not simply deny rights; they reconfigure the moral order of citizenship itself. They teach societies to see some of their own as strangers. In doing so, they hollow out democracy from within, leaving behind institutions that appear stable but, in fact, rest on foundations of exclusion and fear. The struggle for inclusive citizenship, therefore, is not only a legal project but a democratic one—a test of whether the state can still recognize all who live within it as part of "the people."

SECTION VI – TOWARD THE RECONSTRUCTION OF CITIZENSHIP: LEGAL REFORM AND THE DEMOCRATIC STATE

The history of nationality law shows how power can turn inclusion into exclusion. Yet it also reveals that the same legal systems that marginalize can, if reimagined, become instruments of equality. Reforming citizenship is not merely a matter of technical correction; it is an act of democratic reconstruction. To rethink who belongs is to rethink what the nation itself stands for.

Meaningful reform begins with an acknowledgment that citizenship is more than a bureaucratic status—it is a public trust. Laws that define nationality must do more than manage population registries; they must embody a commitment to equality. For developing democracies, this means embedding non-discrimination directly into constitutional or quasi-constitutional frameworks. Guaranteeing that women and men have equal rights to confer nationality, and that children are protected from statelessness at birth, affirms the state's duty to recognize everyone within its borders as part of its collective life (Bellizzi & Nivoli, 2023; Beninger & Manjoo, 2022; Fisher, 2016).

However, rights on paper are not enough. Reform must reach the administrative heart of citizenship—the civil registration and documentation systems through which belonging is confirmed. In many countries, the first step toward inclusion is practical: ensuring that every birth is registered, that fees are abolished, and that documentation is accessible in all languages. Investing in digital registration and mobile outreach may seem mundane, yet these simple measures restore the state's promise of recognition to those long excluded. A citizen who can finally hold an identity card, send a child to school, or apply for a job experiences democracy not as an abstract idea but as a tangible fact (Badewa, 2022; Warria, 2020).

Reform also requires limiting the state's power to revoke citizenship. In recent years, governments have expanded denationalization powers in the name of security, creating a class of citizens whose status depends on political favor. Restoring due process—judicial review, transparent criteria, and the prohibition of statelessness—reasserts the idea that citizenship is a right, not a privilege to be withdrawn at will (Birkvad, 2023; Pillai & Williams, 2017; Tripkovic, 2023). The democratic state must reject the temptation to treat belonging as conditional, for that logic ultimately erodes trust between rulers and ruled.

Equally vital is addressing the quiet, everyday discrimination that persists within bureaucracies. Bias in administrative decision-making—often justified as "procedure"—is one of the most insidious forms of exclusion. Regular audits, independent oversight, and community representation in civil-registration bodies can make these systems more transparent. When minorities participate in administering citizenship, the process itself becomes an act of reconciliation.

Regional and international cooperation can further sustain reform. As statelessness and migration often transcend national boundaries, peer review and shared standards are essential. Mechanisms such as the African Union's draft protocol on nationality, or UNHCR's post-#IBelong initiatives, provide frameworks for states to align domestic law with international norms and to learn from each other's progress (Manby, 2016). In an age where borders are porous but inequality is not, such collaboration strengthens the moral fabric of global governance.

Ultimately, the reconstruction of citizenship is a political and ethical project. A nation that defines itself narrowly will always fear difference; one that embraces inclusion gains both stability and legitimacy. Inclusive nationality laws expand the *demos*, deepen accountability, and make democratic participation real. They remind governments that sovereignty derives from recognition, not exclusion.

Democracy, in its truest form, begins with belonging. When every person who lives under a state's authority is acknowledged as part of its people, citizenship ceases to be a gate and becomes a bridge—a connection between the ideals of equality and the everyday realities of life. Reforming nationality law is therefore not only about correcting injustice; it is about completing the democratic promise itself.

CONCLUSION – CITIZENSHIP AS THE FIRST PRINCIPLE OF DEMOCRATIC ORDER

At its core, nationality law is far more than an administrative tool. It is a mirror of how a society understands itself—who belongs, who is trusted, and who is seen. The choices that states make in defining citizenship reveal their most fundamental values. Inclusive laws express confidence in the idea of a shared future; exclusionary laws, by contrast, expose the fragility of nations still governed by fear and hierarchy.

Throughout history, citizenship has functioned as both a promise and a test. It promises equality, protection, and participation to all who make up the political community. Yet it also tests the willingness of that community to live up to its ideals. When states design nationality laws that divide rather than unite, they turn that promise inward, using the law not to bind people together but to separate them. Over time, these divisions weaken the very institutions that depend on shared trust and mutual recognition.

The cases examined in this chapter—from Myanmar's ethnic exclusions to the Dominican Republic's racial denials, from Côte d'Ivoire's politicization of identity to the everyday bureaucratic discrimination in Kenya and Nepal—illustrate the same underlying truth. When law becomes a means of managing belonging instead of ensuring it, democracy falters. Statelessness and exclusion do not simply affect individuals; they erode the moral authority of the state. A government that denies recognition of some of its people cannot claim to represent them.

The inverse is also true. Nationality law is rooted in equality and strengthens every other part of the democratic order. Recognizing citizenship as a right—secured by birth, residence, or participation—expands the *demos*, making political life more representative and resilient. Inclusion breeds stability, because people who are recognized as citizens have a stake in defending the institutions that protect them. This is why reforming nationality law must be seen not as a peripheral policy issue but as a central democratic task.

Citizenship is the first principle of democracy because it defines the boundaries of accountability. It determines who counts when power is exercised, whose voices are heard, and whose lives are safeguarded by the rule of law. A democracy that narrows its citizenry narrows its conscience; one that opens its definition of belonging strengthens both its legitimacy and its humanity.

The lesson of this inquiry is therefore simple, though its implementation is not: the path to stronger democracies runs through inclusive citizenship. When law ceases to treat belonging as privilege and begins to recognize it as the foundation of political equality, the state transforms. It becomes not a fortress of exclusion but a house large enough to hold all its people.

Nationality law, thus, is not just a technical framework—it is the architecture of belonging itself. And how a nation builds that architecture will determine not only who its citizens are, but what kind of democracy it will become.

REFERENCES

Alam, M. J. (2018). The Rohingya minority of Myanmar: Surveying their status in international law. *International Journal on Minority and Group Rights*, *25*(2), 157–182. DOI: 10.1163/15718115-02503002

Babo, A. (2018). Ivoirité and citizenship in Ivory Coast: The controversial policy of Ivorian authenticité. In *The Politics of Social Inclusion in Africa* (pp. 245–267). Duke University Press.

Badewa, A. A. (2022). Statelessness, development, and protection of 'disadvantaged groups': Bridging the post-2030 sustainable development gaps. *African Human Mobility Review*, *8*(3), 56–74. DOI: 10.14426/ahmr.v8i3.1151

Balaton-Chrimes, S. (2024). Jus tribalis: Statelessness, ethnicity and registration in Kenya. *Statelessness & Citizenship Review*, *6*(2), 127–151. DOI: 10.35715/SCR6001.114

Bellizzi, S., & Nivoli, A. (2023). Gender discrimination in nationality laws: A systemic type of violence against women. *International Journal of Gynaecology and Obstetrics : The Official Organ of the International Federation of Gynaecology and Obstetrics*, *163*(1), 3–6. DOI: 10.1002/ijgo.14986 PMID: 37408521

Beninger, C., & Manjoo, R. (2022). The impact of gender discrimination on statelessness: Causes, consequences and legal responses. *African Human Mobility Review*, *8*(3). Advance online publication. DOI: 10.14426/ahmr.v8i3.1125

Bertocchi, G., & Strozzi, C. (2010). The evolution of citizenship: Economic and institutional determinants. *The Journal of Law & Economics*, *53*(1), 95–136. DOI: 10.1086/600080

Birkvad, S. R. (2023). "Citizenship cheaters" before the law: Reading fraud-based citizenship-stripping cases. *International Political Sociology*, *17*(1), 1–18. DOI: 10.1093/ips/olad006

Blake, J. (2014). (Forthcoming). Haiti, the Dominican Republic, and race-based statelessness. *Georgetown Journal of International Law and Modern Critical Race Perspectives*, *46*, 499–526.

Drissa, K. (2021). The concept of "Ivoirité": An identity, nationalism, and citizenship in a postcolonial state. *Revue Akofena*, *2*(21), 217–228.

Fisher, B. L. (2016). Gender discrimination and statelessness in the Gulf Cooperation Council states. *Michigan Journal of Gender & Law*, *23*(2), 269–341. DOI: 10.36641/mjgl.23.2.gender

Hannam, M. A. (2014). "Soy dominicano": The status of Haitian descendants born in the Dominican Republic and measures to protect their right to a nationality. *Vanderbilt Journal of Transnational Law*, *47*(4), 1123–1175.

Haque, M. M. (2017). Rohingya ethnic Muslim minority and the 1982 Citizenship Law in Burma. *Journal of Muslim Minority Affairs*, *37*(4), 454–469. DOI: 10.1080/13602004.2017.1399600

Herberholz, C. (2022). 'We are inferior, we have no rights': Statelessness and mental health among ethnic minorities in Northern Thailand. *SSM - Population Health*, *19*, 101138. DOI: 10.1016/j.ssmph.2022.101138 PMID: 35711727

Kyaw, N. N. (2017). Unpacking the presumed statelessness of Rohingyas. *Journal of Immigrant & Refugee Studies*, *15*(3), 269–286. DOI: 10.1080/15562948.2017.1330981

Lister, R. (2007). Inclusive citizenship: Realizing the potential. *Citizenship Studies*, *11*(1), 49–61. DOI: 10.1080/13621020601099856

Loganathan, T., Ong, Z. L., Hassan, F., Chan, Z. X., & Majid, H. A. (2023). Barriers and facilitators to education access for marginalised non-citizen children in Malaysia: A qualitative study. *PLoS One*, *18*(6), e0286793. DOI: 10.1371/journal.pone.0286793 PMID: 37267412

Manby, B. (2016). *Citizenship law in Africa: A comparative study* (2nd ed.). Open Society Foundations. DOI: 10.47622/9781936133291

Perl-Rosenthal, N., & Erman, S. (2024). Inventing birthright: The nineteenth-century fabrication of *jus soli* and *jus sanguinis*. *Law and History Review*, *42*(3), 421–448. DOI: 10.1017/S0738248024000221

Pillai, S., & Williams, G. (2017). Twenty-first-century banishment: Citizenship stripping in common law countries. *The International and Comparative Law Quarterly*, *66*(3), 1–35. DOI: 10.1017/S0020589317000021

Safran, W. (1997). Citizenship and nationality in democratic systems: Approaches to defining and acquiring membership in the political community. *International Political Science Review*, *18*(3), 313–335. DOI: 10.1177/019251297018003006

Schmid, S. D. (2020). The architecture of national boundary regimes: Mapping immigration and citizenship policies in 23 democracies 1980–2010. *Comparative Migration Studies*, *8*(1), 1–19. DOI: 10.1186/s40878-020-00182-5

Tripkovic, M. (2023). Renouncing criminal citizens: Patterns of denationalization. *Punishment & Society*, *25*(6), 1351–1371. DOI: 10.1177/14624745221080705

Warria, A. (2020). Stateless transnational migrant children in South Africa: Implications and opportunities for social work intervention. *African Human Mobility Review*, *6*(2), 6–24. DOI: 10.14426/ahmr.v6i2.795

Zilla, C. (2022). Defining democratic inclusion from the perspective of democracy and citizenship theory. *Democratization*, *29*(8), 1518–1538. DOI: 10.1080/13510347.2022.2090929

ADDITIONAL READINGS

Shachar, A. (2009). *The Birthright Lottery: Citizenship and Global Inequality. Harvard University Press. Brubaker, R. (1992). Citizenship and Nationhood in France and Germany*. Harvard University Press.

Soysal, Y. N. (1994). Limits of Citizenship: Migrants and Postnational Membership in Europe. University of Chicago Press. Carens, J. H. (2013). The Ethics of Immigration. Oxford University Press. Bloemraad, I. (2017). Understanding Membership in a World of Global Migration. *AJS; American Journal of Sociology*, *122*(6).

Yan, C. O. (2023). Nationality Law and Labor Migration: A Comparative Analysis of Legal Frameworks and Economic Outcomes in the United Arab Emirates and United Kingdom. *Migration Letters : An International Journal of Migration Studies*, *20*(5), 59–83. Advance online publication. DOI: 10.59670/ml.v20i5.3019

Yan, C. O. (2024). Manufacturing Statelessness Through Exclusionary Citizenship Law: A Comparative Study on Kenya and South Africa. *International Comparative Jurisprudence*, *6*(1). Advance online publication. DOI: 10.13165/j.icj.2024.06.007

KEY TERMS AND DEFINITIONS

Colonial Legacies: Structural inequalities and legal frameworks inherited from colonial rule that persist post-independence.

Denationalization: The administrative or legal revocation of a person's citizenship.

Gender Discrimination: Unequal treatment in nationality laws preventing women from transmitting citizenship equally.

Inclusive Citizenship: A democratic ideal ensuring equal recognition and participation for all residents.

Jus Sanguinis: Citizenship based on descent or ancestry ("right of blood"). Statelessness – The condition of not being recognized as a citizen by any country's legal system.

Jus Soli: The principle granting citizenship by birthplace ("right of the soil").

Marginalization: The systemic exclusion of certain groups from full participation and recognition in society.

Nationality Law: The legal framework determining state membership and defining who belongs to the nation. Citizenship – A legal and social status granting rights, duties, and recognition within a political community.

Chapter 3 The Fourth Pillar in the Digital Age: Free Speech, Media Regulations, and Democracy in India's Legal Framework

Pallav Pallav
http://orcid.org/0009-0005-1753-9891
The West Bengal National University of Juridical Sciences, Kolkata, India

S. M. Aamir Ali
http://orcid.org/0000-0002-8686-0217
Vinayaka Mission's Law School, Vinayaka Mission's Research Foundation (Deemed to be) University, Chennai, India

Akash Dixit
http://orcid.org/0009-0004-8468-9542
Dr. Vishwanath Karad MIT-World Peace University, India

Anuttama Ghose
http://orcid.org/0000-0002-7210-4074
Vinayaka Mission's Law School, Vinayaka Mission's Research Foundation (Deemed to be) University, Chennai, India

ABSTRACT

The paper analyses the changing dimensions of media and regulations, focusing on the transition from traditional to digital in light of its role as the fourth pillar of democracy in India. The authors argue that the effect of digital media on democracy is two-fold. As much as it has increased free speech, civic engagement, and

DOI: 10.4018/979-8-2600-1618-3.ch003

accountability, it has also created the dangers of manipulated information, hate speech, loss of trust in institutions, and the dangers of polarisation. In this paper we tracks down historical regulation as far back as colonial days to the present IT Rules, focusing on judicial interventions that have been strengthening the freedom of the media and the optics of regulation versus constitutional guarantees. The authors have referred to the European model of regulation to argue that India is now in need of transparent, inclusive, and judicially reviewed governance in order to maintain democratic discourse in the digital age.

INTRODUCTION

The media have evolved alongside technology, hence increasing their significance. Examining the media's status quo in its capacity to facilitate speech and expression is imperative, as it is regarded as the cornerstone of a strong democracy. It is impossible to exaggerate the importance of free media in promoting an informed citizenry, holding public officials accountable, and facilitating the open exchange of information essential for effective democratic governance. It is referred to as the fourth pillar, which is responsible for overseeing the government's actions, disseminating information to the public, and maintaining checks and balances within the political system. These functions are crucial for developing a robust democracy (Lorenz-Spreen et al., 2023). The evolution may be traced from ancient writings through the advancement of printing technology, which facilitated the emergence of print media in newspapers, magazines, and books. Subsequently, electronic communication led to the creation of electronic media, including radio and television, culminating in the advent of the Internet and digital media.

Technological advancement has facilitated the growth of digital media, which is still in the process of evolving. Even though it is presently in the process of being adequately defined and regulated, we may adopt a simple meaning of the term "digital media", which may be defined as media that operate on a digital platform via the Internet (Section 2 of The Information Technology (Intermediary Guidelines and Digital Media Ethics Code) Rules, 2021). Digital media has surmounted the constraint of conventional media, which is that the public is merely a spectator. The public's function has evolved into that of a content creator, regardless of whether it pertains to entertainment or news (Stone & Dohel, 2013). The active role of disseminating information, ideas and creations has promoted the individual right of free speech and expression; further, the ability to criticise governmental actions and present opinions and viewpoints promotes the collective rights of the society (Balkin, 2004). It is palpable that the barriers of traditional media, i.e. print and electronic, have been bypassed by digital technology, which facilitates democratic discourse.

Even though digital technology has increased the scope of media, it comes with challenges, like the dissemination of manipulated information and political polarisation (Ghose et al., 2025). Although wide information availability is provided by it, the genuineness remains questionable. Similarly, issues like vulgarity, obscenity, hate speech, propaganda promotion and attempts to manipulate public discourse have become common. Unlike traditional media regulation, the essence of regulations has transformed digital media. One of the reasons is that the proliferation of digital media is based on the concept that it gives wider freedom of speech and expression. The minimal regulation of the digital media attracted participants' engagement. A dualist or dyadic system of speech control was previously prevalent. The speaker and the state were the sole participants for the most part (Balkin, 2018). The state enforced regulations on all forms of mass media, such as newspapers, cinema theatres, radio stations, television stations, and publishing firms. However, a third set of players, which consists of businesses that support and regulate the digital public sphere that individuals use to communicate, is now becoming increasingly important in ensuring freedom of speech (Balkin, 2018). The role of industry-based self-regulation has been an important option, but its effectiveness and decisions have always been questioned. So, the paper attempts to unfold the democratic and legal framework developments with the transformation of media to digital media.

THE FOURTH PILLAR: DIGITAL MEDIA AS A WATCHDOG AND BRIDGE

The media has unparalleled significance in democracy as it is the educator of society and watchdog on governmental functions (Francke, 1995). Media not only disseminates information from the government but also brings to light the societal issues and fills the communication gap between the government and the people (Francke, 1995). Media as a cornerstone of democracy originated during the Enlightenment, when intellectuals such as John Locke (1689/1988) defended press freedom and freedom of expression. During the American and French Revolutions, independent newspapers played a crucial role in influencing political discourse and public opinion, and the idea gained popularity (John, 2019). However, this media nomenclature as the fourth pillar is generally attached to Edmund Burke, who pointed at the reporters' gallery in Parliament as "Fourth Estate" more significant than the three conventional estates of the realm (Bulla, 2022). As mass communication technology developed during the 20th century, the media's position as the Fourth Pillar became more established in the contemporary era.

Newspapers, radio, television, and finally the internet allowed information to be widely disseminated and citizens to participate in democratic processes. The watchdog role is the media's most fundamental and distinctive role in a democracy. This may be defined as the media's responsibility to keep a close eye on individuals in positions of authority, including governments, political parties, institutions, and companies, and to hold them accountable so that society continues to hold them accountable. These functions are also the fulcrum of media rights in a democracy. Freedom of the media originates from freedom of speech and expression. It functions on both individual rights and collective rights of society. Although press freedom is fundamental to a democratic state, it does not include immunity for every act and publication. Absolute rights have no place in a progressive society, and a balanced approach is imperative. Therefore, we find that the free press has restrictions and limitations.

We may refer to the words of Blackstone, who states, "Allowing the press to be subject to censorship would limit all freedom of expression to the whims of one individual and make him the final arbiter of all contentious issues in government, religion, and education. However, to penalise any harmful or offensive work that, upon publication, must be decided upon a poisonous tendency after a fair and impartial adjudication. This is required to maintain peace and good order in government and religion, which are the only firmly established pillars of liberty" (Blackstone, 1765, p. 152). Similar to Blackstone, Dicey defines freedom of the press as "the right of an individual to publish anything they choose in books or newspapers, but English law does not acknowledge any particular privileges granted to the press" (Dicey, 2010, p. 239). According to Justice Holmes, one of the primary goals of the constitutional provision was to prohibit all prior restrictions on publications that other governments had implemented. However, it usually does not stop punishment for actions that may be judged against the public interest, and the preliminary freedom applies to both the true and the false (*Pattern v. Colorado*, 1938). It freely expresses one's beliefs, opinions, and ideas by any visual manifestation, including gestures, songs, and the like. It refers to expressing what a free citizen feels in front of the general public (*Lovell v. City of Griffin*, 1937). We may refer to the *Life Insurance Corporation of India v. Manubhai D. Shah* (1993), where the SC explained the relevance of the media.

It noted: "Any democratic system depends on the freedom to express one's opinions, and any attempt to restrict, suppress, or gag this privilege would be fatal to democracy and would aid users in autocracies or dictatorships."

Technological advances have made the media increasingly important in democracy. Event information from one region can now be communicated globally in minutes (Berg & Hofmann, 2021). Books and newspapers were once printed on large, expensive presses and distributed only to a limited percentage of the population, usually within a country or state. Even when the electronic media took over, radio and television transmission used expensive equipment, satellites, and studios to reach a nation, region, or the world. Recent advances in digital media have changed how individuals communicate, whether privately through chats and debates or publicly through news and other information. Digital media enables access to information at any time and location, unlike conventional media, that was limited by time and space (Gil de Zúñiga, Weeks, & Ardèvol-Abreu, 2019). Digitisation has also made live reporting and faster information transmission possible. Digital media changed the role of people in public debate by removing conventional media's limits on information recipients. Digital media allow everyone to share their ideas and highlight issues, which is crucial in a democracy. Digital media platforms like "X" and "Meta" have diminished the role of traditional media as gatekeepers and allowed government officials to directly communicate with the public, promoting unbiased, uncoloured raw information, which is essential in a democracy. Citizen journalism has also emerged, shattering the hegemony of a few companies in traditional media (Yujie et al., 2022). Thus, digital technology has transformed media.

INDIA'S COMMITMENT TO FREE SPEECH & EXPRESSION: STRONG ROOTS, FRAGILE BRANCHES

Global media systems differ from one another based on the political, religious, cultural, and economic aspects of many civilisations. There were restrictions on what the media could say about the government in countries practising communism and totalitarianism, such as China and the former USSR. For fear of revolutions, nearly anything spoken against the state was suppressed. However, in bourgeois democracies like the USA, practically anything is acceptable (Post, 2024). In India, it was sheer serendipity that brought the printing press. The Portuguese printing press, along with the necessary personnel, happened to stop in Goa, and the person in charge of the delivery never reached the destination (De Souza, 2008). The press remained in Goa and thrived there after material intended for missionary work was printed there (De Souza, 2008).

Media and its regulation started during the British era in India, while the press was the prominent mode of information dissemination for independence. Regulations were aimed at controlling and curbing any such actions. The British strategy towards the growing press in the late nineteenth century included state persecution, costly litigation, and the deportation of editors (Dhavan, 1984). Regulations adopted during 1797 demanded, among other things, the pre-inspection of all periodicals under pain of expulsion. During the 19th century, the British deployed two different models for control (Dhavan, 1984). One technique delegated responsibilities to editors while requiring critical information about the owner, editor, and printer. The second method involved a complete licensing scheme (Dhavan, 1984). We find similar regulation strategies being used throughout the colonial period. It must be highlighted that even though these regulations were intended to curb freedom, India adopted such methods even after independence and the declaration of fundamental rights of free speech and expression as media regulation. We may cite the instance of national emergency during 1975-77, which revived the forfeited deposit system under even stricter conditions, along with pre-censorship. The period may be the darkest times for media freedom in Independent India (Nair, 1999; Gupta, 2007).

Post-Independence India safeguarded the right to "free speech and expression" by Article 19 (1) (a) of the Constitution. However, the phrase "freedom of the press or media freedom" remains missing under Article 19. In contrast to the American Constitution, press freedom) neither expressly nor independently guaranteed by Article 19 (1). However, Dr. Ambedkar clarified the omission by pointing out that the press does not have any unique rights that citizens should grant or use in their individual capacities. No specific declaration was required since the editor or management is just expressing their right to free expression. Still, the omission of explicit mention resulted in the press not getting institutional rights as opposed to the American Constitution (Sajid, 2023). It was only by the judicial interpretation that the rights of the media were read under the broad meaning of speech and expression. Undoubtedly, media freedom has long been considered a prerequisite for a democratic system of governance. Still, it is equally true that there can be no absolute right, and the constitution's framers were conscious of this and reasonable limitations on the right in the interest of several factors were listed in Article 19(2). What must be highlighted is that the recognition of these rights under the constitution has now changed the nature of media regulation; it is now mandated to facilitate a democratic society rather than suppressing freedom.

Judicial Foundations of Media Freedom

The Supreme Court (SC) of India judgments in the case of Romesh Thapper v. State of Madras (1950) established the rights of the media. It was laid that "Without a doubt, freedom of speech and expression encompasses the freedom to propagate ideas, and this freedom is guaranteed by freedom of circulation, which is just as crucial to that freedom as freedom of publication. In fact, without circulation, the publication's worth would be minimal." Similarly, in *Bennet Coleman v. Union of India* (1973), it was decided that forcing a newspaper to cut back on advertising space would directly impact circulation because it would inevitably result in price increases. Such an attempt would amount to an unreasonable restriction on the right to free expression, or it would restrict circulation, which would limit the amount of information that could be disseminated, or it would restrict its freedom to choose how to exercise the right, or it would weaken its independence by encouraging it to seek government assistance. In yet another noteworthy decision, *Indian Express Newspapers (Bombay) Pvt. Ltd. v. Union of India* (1985), the SC went further to clarify the significance and meaning of this freedom: "The phrase freedom of the press refers to the absence of governmental meddling, which could potentially affect newspaper readership and content. That freedom cannot be restricted for the sake of the general welfare. The press promotes the public interest by disseminating information and viewpoints necessary for a democratic electorate to make informed decisions. The foundation of social and political interactions is press freedom".

The scope of commercial statements or advertisements was clarified in the *Tata Press v. Mahanagar Telephone-Nigam Limited* (1995), where it was expressed that the protection of free speech will also cover such speech and expression. The SC clarified that "The advertisement as a 'Commercial Speech' has two facts,". "Even though advertising is merely a business transaction, it disseminates information about the marketed goods. The information provided by the adverts benefits the general public. The open exchange of business information is essential in a democracy. Without the general population being educated by the information in commercials, there can be no honest and cost-effective marketing. Without "Commercial speech" freedom, a democracy's economic system would be severely hampered. The commercial speech has a right to be heard by the general audience. In addition to guaranteeing freedom of speech and expression, Article 19(1)(a) of the Constitution safeguards a person's rights to hear, read, and receive the aforementioned speech." The Supreme Court held that the freedom given by Article 19(1)(a) could only be restricted for the reasons listed in Article 19(2) and could not be denied by creating a monopoly for the government's advantage. Even though the judiciary laid down the jurisprudence of electronic media, we may look at the case of *The Secretary, Ministry of Information and Broadcasting v. Cricket Association of Bengal & Anr.* (1995), the SC stated that the government did not have a monopoly on electronic media and that any citizen has the right, under Article 19(1)(a), to livestream and broadcast any significant event to the public via electronic media. To free the electronic media from the constraints of government control, the court ordered the union to set up an impartial and independent body to oversee "Doordarshan" and "AIR". The court also expressed that "the ability to communicate effectively and widely, both domestically and internationally, is a basic right to freedom of speech".

The Role of the Judiciary in Safeguarding Digital Media

The Indian judiciary has even explored and developed the fulcrum of digital media rights and regulation, which we must look at this juncture as well. Police detained two women for reportedly making inappropriate and disrespectful remarks on "Facebook" over the appropriateness of closing Mumbai following the passing of a political figure. Under section 66A of the Information Technology Act, 2000 (IT) which penalised "anyone who transmits information through a computer resource or communication device that is blatantly offensive or that is sent with the knowledge that it is false with the intent to cause annoyance, inconvenience, danger, insult, injury, hatred, or ill will", the police made the arrests. The episode received much media attention and criticism, even though the charges were dropped later. The women subsequently petitioned, arguing that the section infringes their right to free speech and is therefore unconstitutional. The case, *Shreya Singhal v. Union of India* (2013), became a landmark judgment for upholding freedom of speech and expression and digital media rights. The judgment delivered by Justices Chelameswar and Nariman answered whether the section infringed upon the freedom of expression protected by Article 19(1)(a). The fact that section 66A intended protection against annoyance, inconvenience, danger, obstruction, insult, injury, criminal intimidation, or ill-will falls outside the scope of the listed grounds under Article 19(2), it was argued to be unconstitutional.

Additionally, it was claimed that the statute's failure to explain prohibitions precisely has a "chilling effect" on the right to free speech. The government maintained that courts should only get involved in the legislative process when "a statute is clearly violative of the rights conferred on the citizen under Part III of the Constitution," as the legislature is best suited to meet the people's demands. Further, it was argued that a provision may not always be deemed unconstitutional based just on instances of abuse. Additionally, the government believed that since the law deals with new ways to violate people's rights online, its ambiguous wording could not be a reason for invalidity. The government claims that "if the statute is otherwise legislatively competent and non-arbitrary," ambiguity cannot be used to declare it unconstitutional.

The Court began by going over three key ideas in interpreting the right to free speech: incitement, advocacy, and discussion. It asserts that "the core" of the right is "mere discussion or even advocacy of a particular cause, however unpopular." Furthermore, the law can only restrict freedom when a debate or advocacy qualifies as incitement (Scanlon, 2024). Since the provision does not distinguish "between mere discussion or advocacy of a particular point of view, which may be annoying or inconvenient or grossly offensive to some and incitement by which such words lead to an imminent causal connection with public disorder, etc.," it was determined that the provision has the potential to restrict all forms of internet communications. The Court expressed that sending a communication intended to irritate or insult someone constitutes a full violation of the section. Therefore, without requiring that the message have a definite tendency to disturb public order, the law does not distinguish between dissemination to a large audience and dissemination to a single individual.

Regarding whether the section was a legitimate endeavour to shield people from online communications that contain defamatory remarks, the court pointed out that "injury to reputation" is the primary component of defamation. It concluded that it does not apply to this goal because the legislation also forbids insulting remarks that could irritate or inconvenience a person without harming their reputation. Regarding the petitioners' argument regarding vagueness, the Court upheld United States of America (US) judicial precedent, which states that "where no reasonable standards are laid down to define guilt in a section which creates an offence, and where no clear guidance is given to either law-abiding citizens or to authorities and courts, a section which creates an offence and which is vague must be struck down as being arbitrary and unreasonable" (*Grayned v. City of Rockford*, 1972). The court determined the section is unconstitutional for vagueness since it leaves many terms unclear and open-ended (Chemerinsky, 2019).

The next judicial development we must examine is the *Anuradha Basin v. Union of India* (2020). The SC examined that the internet is the foundation of digital media and that individuals have the fundamental right to access it. The case is significant as it was in the backdrop of the change in constitutional statutes of the state of Jammu and Kashmir. Other than all the measures taken, we may focus on a limited part of our research, the administration suspended landline and internet services, including mobile services, on 4th August 2019 until further directives. Anuradha Bhasin filed a petition before the SC in response to these limitations. One issue pertinent to our study was whether the Constitution's fundamental rights, including the freedom of speech and expression, extend online. According to the court, the state's limits did not amount to repression or infringement on the petitioner's right to free speech. The court also noted in its ruling that the concept of inherent limitations served as the foundation for the constitutional liberties protected by the Indian Constitution (Juyal, 2023). In light of this, it was observed:

"According to Dworkin, rights are the ultimate goal, and they cannot be altered because they are the highest standard established by the Constitution. This would suggest that if the legislature or executive branch takes a specific action that violates a right to further the public good, they will not be allowed to do so if doing so would restrict a right. Although American courts frequently adopt this strategy, given Part III's structure and inherent limitations, it might not be entirely appropriate in the Indian context (*Anuradha Basin v. Union of India*, 2020)"

However, the court pointed out that press freedom is still vital for a democratic country to function effectively. It emphasised that media freedom is a fundamental right and, in this regard, it reaffirmed that the constitution has always protected it since it is one of the essential rights (Baxi, 1990). It was decided, highlighting that:

"Press freedom is unquestionably a fundamental and valuable right protected by Article 19 (1) (a) of the Constitution. Any contemporary democracy must have this right for knowledge to be shared and for necessary dialogue to take place (*Anuradha Bhasin v. Union of India*, 2020)"

The petitioner contended that a number of state-imposed press limitations inadvertently violated press freedom in J&K. The court examined the jurisprudence of the chilling impact of press limitations, acknowledging the seriousness of the situation and the significance of Media freedom. Given its vital role in bolstering democracy, it instructed the state to protect media freedom constantly. Additionally, the court decided that "there is no justification for allowing a sword of Damocles to hang over the media indefinitely and that journalists are to be accommodated in reporting." Therefore, the court acknowledged the state's duty to guarantee media freedom at all times and upheld its fundamentally inherent nature in a democracy while resolving the aforementioned question. Nevertheless, it is important to remember that the court decision does not give the administration complete authority to impose excessive press limitations. Rather, the court has clarified that such limitations must be appropriate, reasonable, and required given the particular facts. The court's ruling warns that any attempt to restrict press freedom must be carefully considered because it is an essential and fundamental part of a democratic society (Hudson, 1996).

DIGITAL MEDIA GOVERNANCE PRIORITISES CONTROL OVER DEMOCRATIC DIALOGUE

The effect of the digital media on democracy is two-fold. It enables new venues of interaction, education, and accountability, but also adds issues like polarisation, misinformation, hate speech, and distrust in institutions, which require careful regulation and public understanding (Pallav et al., 2025). Digital media must use their democratic potential and integrate a risk-reduction plan to preserve or increase democracy in the digital age. Recent legislative developments may clarify India's digital media regulatory approach. Digital media legislation in India combines self-regulation and state oversight. Rules, 2021 (IT (Guidelines for Intermediaries and Digital Media Ethics Code)) tend to legislate both. In keeping with section 87 of the IT Act, the rules include intermediary guidelines and content restriction requirements. The Rules replace previous provisions and considerably increase the ability to impose extra requirements on digital media corporations and social media intermediaries (Guha, 2023). The MIB (Ministry of Information and Broadcasting) oversees the Code of Ethics and related protections and standards for digital media firms in compliance with regulations. The Ministry of Electronics and Information Technology (MeitY) will also evaluate intermediary due diligence rules, notably social media actors. These rules apply to "intermediaries and social media intermediaries (including significant social media intermediaries)", "publishers of news and current affairs content, including news aggregators, news agencies, and individual news reporters to the extent they are transmitting content in the course of a systematic business, professional, or commercial activity" and "publishers o The guideline has three parts. Part 1 covers the definition, Part 2 covers the Grievance Redressal Mechanism and Due Diligence standards the intermediary must follow, and Part 3 covers digital media regulations, processes, and safeguards (OTT platforms and online news portals). Rule 2 covers the definition. The Rule defined "social media intermediary" and "significant social media intermediary" based on the government's declared user count (Abhishek, 2022).

Intermediaries will only be eligible for safe harbour protections from liability with regard to any third-party information, data, or communication link that they host or make available if they comply with the due diligence requirements and also meet the content neutrality requirements of section 79 of the IT Act (Gupta & Srinivasan, 2023). The Rules incorporate the requirements of the Old Intermediary Guidelines, including the requirement to post the terms of use, privacy policy, and user agreement. The intermediaries are required to adhere to specific due diligence responsibilities as outlined in Rule 3. According to the rule, every intermediary is responsible for publishing the user agreement, privacy policy, and rules and regulations. According to the rule, the intermediary will cease granting access to that user if they fail to follow the rules and terms of the agreement as mandated in the provision. Rule 3(1) (d) covers the mandate of the content takedown. It elaborates that any information pertaining to the "security of the State", "the sovereignty and integrity of India", etc., that is unlawful under the law must be deleted by the intermediary within 36 hours of obtaining a court order or notification from a government agency. The Rules of 2021 also refer to the Grievance Redressal Mechanism, which mandates that the grievance officer take action within 24 hours of the issue and address it within 15 days. In addition to providing a route for the complainant to submit the complaint details or a communication link, the intermediary must take the necessary steps to receive this complaint. Also, the designation of the Chief Compliance Officer, Nodal Contact Person, and Resident Grievance Officer is mentioned in the Due Diligence requirements. According to the Rules, the intermediary must produce a monthly compliance report detailing the steps they have taken in response to complaints (Devadasan, 2024).

The Rules also mandate Information and user registration records must be kept by intermediaries for 180 days after (i) the date on which any unlawful information is removed or access to it is disabled due to actual knowledge, voluntary action, or grievances received by the intermediary, and (ii) additionally if a user withdraws or their registration is cancelled (Kumar Srivastava, 2021). The Rules require that information be provided to authorised government agencies within 72 hours of receiving the order, even though this has always been necessary for identity verification, preventing, detecting, investigating, or prosecuting illegal offences, or cybersecurity incidents. One of the controversial provisions is that social media sites providing messaging services are required to identify the message's original sender (Guha, 2023). If required by a court order or other authority as laid down by the Rules, this becomes mandatory when read with section 69 of the IT Act. A copy of the initial originator's material in electronic format must be given to the court or government agency. Though the grounds like protection of public order, security, integrity and sovereignty, defamation, etc, are mentioned, they are of wide amplitude and can cover almost any request (Thomas, 2023).

Additionally, automated filtering is also a requirement under the Rules. SSMIs shall make an effort to proactively detect and eliminate illegal content, including any representation of rape or child sexual abuse, using automated technologies. In the process, it must ensure that its users' interests, such as their right to privacy and freedom of speech, are weighed against the use of such tools. To assess the frequency and accuracy of these tools, their potential for bias and discrimination, and their potential effects on privacy and security, SSMIs must also implement the proper procedures to provide human oversight (Thomas, 2023). Other than this, the SSMI must also make it obvious that the information is being promoted, sponsored, or directed solely at the recipient if it transmits or performs services on behalf of someone else for whom it has a copyright or with whom it has a contractual agreement for exclusive licensing or exclusivity, for direct financial gain, or both. It's unclear how an organisation engaging in this targeting will satisfy Section 79 of the IT Act's requirements for content neutrality (Kumar Srivastava, 2021).

Additionally, it's unclear if this need would be satisfied by properly marking the information or if it would necessitate the publication of general or specific declarations for each sponsored or marketed content item. User verification is also mandated in the Rules. People who register for SSMI services from India or use their services there must be able to voluntarily verify themselves using methods such as a user's active mobile number. A tangible mark of verification visible to all other service users must be given to the user upon completion of such verification (Guha, 2023). So, we find that digital media platforms require detailed compliance.

One of the most controversial parts is regulating the publisher of news and current affairs content and online curated content. Part 2 of the rules governs that, and we may lay down the essential features of the part. Publishers of online curated content, news, and current affairs content that work in India or regularly distribute their work within its borders must follow the Code of Ethics outlined in the Rules of 2021. For example, under Rule 13, the news and current affairs content publishers must adhere to the Press Council of India's Norms of Journalistic Conduct. Also, under part 3 of the Rules of 2021, the publishers of online curated content are required to self-classify such content based on factors like context, impact, target audience, etc., and to place appropriate access control measures in place to prevent children from accessing "A-rated" content. Moreover, a publisher operating in India is required under the Rules of 2021 within 30 days of publication to provide the MIB with specific information, including the entity's details. They must also release monthly compliance reports that include the specifics of the complaints they have received (Guha, 2023).

The Rules of 2021 foresee a three-tiered regulatory structure for the grievance redressal framework for OTT and other content curators (rules 9–13). The first level (self-regulation) requires that each publisher set up a grievance redressal procedure, designate a Grievance Officer in India, and post the officer's name and contact information on its website. All concerns pertaining to the Code of Ethics will be directed to the Grievance Officer, who will also serve as the liaison between the MIB, the self-regulating organisation, and the complainant. The development of a self-regulating body is the second level. The Rules call for establishing one or more self-regulating organisations comprising publishers and business professionals. These organisations would be registered with the MIB and led by a former Supreme Court or High Court judge. The MIB will publish codes of practice and a charter for these self-regulating organisations. The publisher is required to join one of the self-regulating organisations and follow its rules and regulations. The self-regulatory organisation can accept complaints from complainants, handle complaints that the publisher does not address within 15 days, and provide publishers with advice or guidelines mandating that they apologise, restrict the content, or post warning cards or disclaimers.

Furthermore, the self-regulating organisation will ensure that the publication complies with the Code of Ethics. The publisher has 15 days to file a complaint with the government-established oversight mechanism (Oversight Mechanism) if they disregard any guidelines or advisories provided by the self-regulating body. The self-regulating body can only submit illegal content to the Oversight Mechanism; it cannot give instructions for its removal or change (Guha, 2023).

The MIB has been empowered to form an Interdepartmental Committee (Committee) to hear and investigate complaints at the third level (Government Oversight). This Committee cannot give the publisher any orders or directives; it can only provide suggestions to the MIB. MIB can also provide orders, advice, assistance, and direction to ensure that the publishers follow the Code of Practice. After reviewing the grievance, the Committee may suggest to the MIB during the hearing stage that the content be removed or modified on the grounds listed. If the Committee makes recommendations about removing or modifying content, the MIB-appointed authorised officer must present the recommendation to the MIB for review. On approval, the officer may then direct the publisher or other intermediary to remove or modify the pertinent content. According to the Rules, the Authorised Officer's commands and directives may only pertain to a particular piece of content and cannot compel any organisation to stop operating. The Authorised Officer will examine the content in an "emergency," where there can be no delay, and decide whether it violates the listed grounds stipulated in Section 69A of the IT Act. It may then recommend that the content be removed from the MIB. On satisfaction, it may, without providing a hearing, make an interim order under Section 69A to immediately prohibit this content. The MIB could exert significant regulatory control over publishers and the content published on online platforms while posing as self-regulation. The provisions of the Rules 2021 indicate that India is adopting a model of strictly state-regulated media, which might not be in line with its constitutional protections of free speech and expression (Guha, 2023). As we have already seen, the judiciary has applied the principles of limited restriction on the grounds listed, ambiguity, and chilling effect in the protection of media freedom in India. How far these provisions will pass such a test will have to be seen.

Overview of the 2022 Amendment to the Intermediary Guidelines and Digital Media Ethics Code

Before these modifications, intermediaries had to prominently post rules and regulations, privacy policies, etc., on their website or mobile application as part of their due diligence duties under Rule 3(1)(a). These duties are now further enhanced by the Amendment Rules, which mandate that intermediaries not only publish the rules and regulations, etc., but also make sure that they are complied with and that (i) they are published in English or any of the 22 regional Indian languages listed in the Eighth Schedule of the Indian Constitution, depending on the user's preferred language. Further, Under Rule 3(1)(b)- Intermediaries are now legally required by the Amendment to not only notify users of their rules, regulations, privacy policy, etc., but also to take reasonable steps to prevent users from hosting, displaying, uploading, changing, publishing, transmitting, storing, updating, or sharing any information that is, among other things, pornographic, unlawful, etc. Additionally, the intermediary must notify its users of these regulations in English or any other language chosen by the user and listed in the Eighth Schedule of the Indian Constitution. This additional clause has been added to ensure that the intermediary's duty to comply is more than just a formality and that they take proactive steps to guarantee compliance (Panjiar & Waghre, 2022). However, because intermediaries may be required to take additional steps (like implementing technology-based protocols, automated tools, algorithms, or introducing content moderation, filtration, and detection mechanisms, among other things) to ensure that users comply with this provision, this amendment may increase compliance for intermediaries and expand their role in relation to their users.

Also, we find that the word "misinformation" has been added to Rule 3(1)(b)(vi). It is illegal for an intermediary to give its users false information purposefully. Although there is no definition for the phrase "misinformation," it significantly impacts third-party content that is made accessible on an intermediary's website or mobile application. The same was challenged before the judiciary, which we will deal with subsequently. In the past, intermediaries were required by Rule 3(1)(b)(ii) to make sure that "defamatory" and "libellous" content was not hosted on their platform. The terms "defamatory" and "libellous," however, have been eliminated from this clause in accordance with the Amendment. According to the press release, the modification aims to rationalise this clause by relieving an intermediary of the burden of determining whether the content is "defamatory" or "libellous," as a court review should be used to make this conclusion. Additionally, content that can instigate violence between other castes or religions has now been added to the list of forbidden content that an intermediary is not allowed to publish or share (Kakkar et al., 2025).

What must be highlighted is that the role of 3 party regulation of content has been emphasised, as we argued in the initial sections of the paper, that now the regulation of media is not limited to the state. The role of private players is equally important. It must also be brought to light that even though the relevance of third-party regulation is increasing, the concern that them being the gatekeepers of public discourse is evident, which was bypassed by the digital media (Ali et al., 2024).

The Controversy and Judicial Review of the Fact-Checking Unit in India

The Rules of 2021 and Amendment 2022 are under judicial review for several provisions. After the 2023 revision, one of the Rules was disputed, and we must read the legal ruling to understand its ramifications. According to the MEIT's Information Technology (Intermediary Guidelines and Digital Media Ethics Code) Amendment Rules, 2023 (IT Rules 2023), social media sites like "Facebook" and "Twitter" had to remove any "business of the Central Government" news that was deemed "fake, false, or misleading" by a government-established "fact-checking unit". In April 2023, observational comedian "Kunal Kamra" petitioned the Bombay HC, arguing that the Central Government's fact-checking unit violated section 79 of the IT Act (Vora, 2023). Section 79 protects intermediary social media firms from user-generated content. Intermediaries must remove information after government notification under Section 79(3). The petitioner claimed that intermediaries may lose safe harbour status if they violate the IT Rules under Rule 7 of the Rules

2021. The "News Broadcasters and Digital Association", "Association of Indian Magazines", and "Editors Guild of India" also contested the clause. After grouping the petitions, the Bombay High Court Division Bench decided (Global Freedom of Expression, 2024). State actions that affect parties' rights must pass fairness criteria and be compatible with the statutes, or they must be just, fair, and reasonable, the court ruled. Democracy relies on government accountability and transparency, and Article 19(1)(a) protects reporting, opinion, criticism, and analysis that serve the public interest. It is against the rule of law for the FCU to be obliged to use any approach that violates this civil right, including a fair one. The updated Rule 3(1)(b)(v) exempts the State from Rule 3(2)'s information removal process. Ambiguity about the FCU's legality threatens its fairness without a process (Kakkar et al., 2025).

To maintain the "safe harbour" protection granted by section 79(1) of the IT Act, the intermediary whose platform contains the flagged information must remove it in accordance with rule 3(1)(b)(v). In this sense, the FCU's flagging of information suggests that it be removed; the intermediary is not required by the rules to do as much. According to a joint interpretation of section 79(2)(c) of the IT Act and rule 7 of the IT Rules, the intermediary may decline to take action on such identification and forfeit its safe harbour protection. Therefore, the State's regulations require the intermediary to remove content that the FCU deems "fake, false, or misleading"; otherwise, the intermediaries' safe harbour protections would be revoked. The nature of the provision is that it creates a "chilling effect" (Jain, 2024).

Only under the eight grounds of Article 19(2) may the fundamental right to freedom of speech and expression under Article 19(1)(a) of the Indian Constitution be reasonably restricted, and even then, the restriction must be justified based on necessity rather than expediency or convenience. It is incorrect to argue that fraudulent, inaccurate, or deceptive information is exempt from these limitations. However, as Article 19(2) does not list "fake, false, or misleading" material as a reasonable restriction, it is equally incorrect to argue that any such information falls within these restrictions (Yadav & Bajpai, 2024). The court also highlighted that the constitution not only recognises the right to truthful speech but also the limitation of the state in determining the same.

FRAMEWORKS AND POLICIES SHAPING DIGITAL MEDIA GOVERNANCE IN EUROPE

Even though a comparison of the EU would rather raise the question of it not being a nation, its developments in digital media regulation require consideration. Further, its applicability and acceptance are unparalleled, making it vital in developing the global media regulation framework. Pluralism and media freedom are essential components of democracy and EU members' fundamental rights. Without a free press that can critically examine those in authority, true democracy is impossible. One of the main pillars of the checks and balances that support democratic governance is the media (European Commission, 2025). This is why targeting independent media frequently marks the beginning of the slide towards authoritarian control. Many governments throughout the world have followed this course in recent decades, persecuting media organisations and individual journalists by intimidation and frequent violence. "Pluralism" and "media freedom" are among the four pillars included in the rule of law report from the European Commission, which focuses on several important topics, such as openness of media ownership and the autonomy of media regulating bodies, transparency and equity in the distribution of public advertising, journalist safety, and information availability (European Commission, 2025).

Freedom of Expression Under Article 10 of the European Convention on Human Rights

This article does not prohibit state licensing requirements for film, television, and broadcasting. Every person has the right to free speech, which includes the right to express opinions and receive and distribute information without government intervention. Exercise of these freedoms may be subject to legal obligations or penalties that are necessary in a democracy to protect national security, territorial integrity, or public safety; stop disorder or criminal activity; protect morals or health; protect others' rights or reputations; stop the disclosure of confidential information; or maintain the judiciary's authority and impartiality (Brogi et al., 2023). Ratification of the ECHR requires participation in the Council of Europe (ECHR); however, all present Member States are Contracting States (Brogi et al., 2023). To join the Council of Europe, governments must uphold the rule of law, human rights, and fundamental freedoms. The ECHR applies only to Contracting States, and to be enforceable, it must be incorporated into national law. States may stipulate how international treaties are incorporated.

Because additional protocols are only required for states that have ratified them, each state may have a different range of protection with regard to the specific guarantees in the Convention.3 In addition, Contracting States may express reservations about any specific provision in the Convention at the time of signature (Article 57(1) ECHR). First and foremost, the right to freedom of expression is protected by Article 10 ECHR, as stated in paragraph 1. The European Court of Human Rights (ECtHR) determined in its Handyside case that "One of the fundamental pillars of a democratic society and a prerequisite for both its advancement and each person's personal growth is the right to free speech (*Handyside v. United Kingdom*, 1976)."

But Art. 10 ECHR covers not just the "freedom of communication," but the entire communication process, which includes at least six subareas: freedom of expression and information, freedom of the press and broadcasting, freedom of art and science, and freedom of religion. Given that there are multiple ways to communicate, the freedom of expression serves as the foundation for the protection of the freedom of communication. A review of the ECHR's jurisprudence reveals that it is challenging to distinguish between the freedom of expression and the freedom of the press, with journalists who make statements potentially protected by either the freedom of broadcasting or the freedom of expression, as this right is involved in the majority of cases (Fenwick & Phillipson, 2011).

Governing Digital Media and Online Content: A European Perspective

Keeping this brief, we may discuss digital media regulation and the union's position. The union further regulates online entertainment platforms, prioritising user protection, privacy, and content standards. "Data Protection Regulation" (GDPR) and "Audiovisual Media Services Directive" (AVMSD) are two key EU laws. Online platforms had to observe many broadcast requirements, including minors' protection, hate speech bans, and a minimum quota for European content, after the 2018 AVMSD modification (European Commission, 2025). The law mandated online entertainment platforms to contain a certain percentage of European content in their libraries to balance foreign influences and promote home media and culture. Because each union member state can apply the AVMSD according to its own laws, enforcement varies (European Commission, 2025). The GDPR greatly enhances data privacy by regulating how Over-the-Top (OTT) platforms collect, store, and handle user data. GDPR requires OTT platforms to obtain users' consent before collecting personal data, be open about how it is used, and guarantee their rights to data access, rectification, and erasure (Voigt & Von dem Bussche, 2017). These regulations have pushed OTT services to change their data processing methods to comply with GDPR. Other countries are considering similar privacy regulations due to the GDPR's global precedence. These regulations have pushed OTT services to change their data processing methods to comply with GDPR. Other countries are considering similar privacy regulations due to the GDPR's global precedence. Although member states have various interpretations and implementations, the EU's GDPR and AVMSD focus on user privacy and content regulation, which has actually made OTT platforms more controlled (George et al., 2019). While countries like Germany have strong data privacy laws that augment GDPR, France has added content requirements for OTT providers. This variation shows the EU's complex yet strong OTT regulation, which mixes member-state-specific details with centralised rules (Garg & Ghuman, 2024).

Europe "fit for the digital age" was a von der Leyen Commission priority. To make the internet safer and fairer, the EU government and Parliament passed the Digital Markets Act (European Commission, 2022). "What is illegal offline should be illegal online," is the idea. The Digital Markets Act levels the playing field for digital companies, making it easier for smaller businesses and startups to compete. The measure sets clear rules for huge platforms, or "gatekeepers," to protect them from overburdening enterprises and customers. These platforms can no longer favour their own products and services above others. Customers must be able to delete pre-installed software and apps to switch platforms and apps (Van Den Boom, 2023). The approach will also boost compatibility with communications platforms. This means users may send messages, share files, and make video chats between messaging apps, regardless of size. These measures encourage user data sharing and break the monopoly. It is palpable that even though the European model promotes statute-based regulations, it differs from India in the context that it limits the state's interventions while allowing freedom of expression of the media and citizens.

CONCLUSION

Digital media has revolutionised free expression, media legislation, and other democratic and legal procedures in India. Digital platforms have transformed what was once a physical limitation and order of pure gatekeeping by traditional print and broadcast media to give the ordinary citizen a voice and to participate in the process of rationality driven by educated citizens. The revolution has expanded free speech and expression, creating a more participatory and alive democratic culture. It has allowed people from different backgrounds to voice their thoughts, question government actions, and contribute to the marketplace of ideas.

However, this levelling out of information creation and dissemination raises regulatory and ethical difficulties. Traditional regulation methods for print and broadcast media don't fit the global digital media's rapid, interactive dynamics. Genuine voices and misinformation, hate speech, and propaganda have increased online, which must be dealt with promptly and thoughtfully. Regulatory excess or imprecise laws can limit useful expression and impede the democratic fabric they are designed to defend. The unanticipated independence of digital actors challenges the Indian government's political and developmental desire to regulate the media. Although minimal government regulation can promote accountability and prevent harm, it should not be used to oppress. Using James Madison's warning against insidious encroachments on liberty, the writers caution against sneaky attacks on liberty made in the name of regulation. We may further lay out a few suggestions which are apparent through the research, such as:

1. India should adapt its laws and institutions to regulate digital media and preserve freedom of expression while addressing abuses. Transparent, targeted, and judicially reviewable regulations are needed.
2. Digital literacy will help citizens navigate the internet responsibly; thus, the government must promote it. An intelligent public can better distinguish between reputable sources, contribute to democracy, and avoid manipulation, especially in India, where rural people are readily misled.
3. The state, independent monitors, technology firms, the media, and the public must collaborate to create and enforce digital media regulations. An inclusive strategy can boost platform legitimacy, accountability, and self-regulation. Stakeholders are criticising the IT guidelines 2021 for lacking public consultation.
4. Finally, the role of the judiciary must be highlighted; it must be vigilant to protect against overregulation. The expedited resolution of cases involving fundamental rights will increase trust on the part of people and safeguard democracy.

We may conclude that the future of public discourse and Indian democracy lies in the balance between citizen expression enabled by digital media and the carefully designed, more robust but less invasive protections that ensure the free expression and consequences of the people, as well as the digitalisation of civic engagement. Such a proactive balance will be core in enabling perpetuity and further enhancement of any democratic system in the digital era.

REFERENCES

Abhishek, A. (2022). The State Deputising Citizens to Discipline Digital News Media: The Case of the IT Rules 2021 in India. *Digital Journalism (Abingdon, England), 11*(10), 1769–1787. DOI: 10.1080/21670811.2022.2134163

Ali, S. M. A., Ghose, A., & Iqbal, S. M. U. (2024). Media bias and "othering": A critical discourse on news framing of the Rohingya crisis settlement in Bangladesh and India. In Kir Elitaş, S. (Ed.), (pp. 264–277). Advances in Media, Entertainment, and the Arts. IGI Global., DOI: 10.4018/979-8-3693-3459-1.ch016

Balkin, J. M. (2004). Digital speech and democratic culture: A theory of freedom of expression for the information society. *New York University Law Review, 79*(1), 1–55.

Balkin, J. M. (2018). Free speech in the algorithmic society: Big data, private governance, and new school speech regulation. *University of California, Davis, Law Review, 51*(3), 1149–1210. https://lawreview.law.ucdavis.edu/issues/51/3/Essays/51-3_Balkin.pdf

Balkin, J. M. (2018). Free speech is a triangle. *Columbia Law Review, 118*(7), 2011–2056.

Baxi, U. (1990). The Indian Supreme Court and media freedom: From the untrammelled press to the responsible press. *International Journal of Constitutional Law, 8*(3), 574–591. DOI: 10.1093/iccn/8.3.574

Berg, S., & Hofmann, J. (2021). Digital democracy. *Internet Policy Review, 10*(4). Advance online publication. DOI: 10.14763/2021.4.1612

Blackstone, W. (1765). []. Clarendon Press.]. *Commentaries on the Laws of England, 4*, 152.

Brogi, E., Borges, D., Carlini, R., Nenadić, I., Bleyer-Simon, K., Kermer, J. E., Reviglio, U., Trevisan, M., & Verza, S. (2023, July). *The European Media Freedom Act: Media freedom, freedom of expression and pluralism* (Study No. PE 747.930). Policy Department for Citizens' Rights and Constitutional Affairs, Directorate-General for Internal Policies, European Parliament. https://www.europarl.europa.eu/RegData/etudes/STUD/2023/747930/IPOL_STU(2023)747930_EN.pdf

Bulla, D. (2022). Fourth estate. In *The SAGE encyclopedia of journalism* (Vol. 4, pp. 675–679). SAGE Publications, Inc., DOI: 10.4135/9781544391199.n164

Chemerinsky, E. (2019). *Constitutional law: Principles and policies* (6th ed.). Aspen Publishers.

De Souza, T. R. (2008). Portuguese India, the Politics of Print and a Questionable Modernity [Review of *Between Empires: Print and Politics in Goa*, by R. Pinto]. *Economic and Political Weekly*, *43*(33), 31–33.

Devadasan, V. (2024). Conceptualising India's safe harbour in the era of platform governance. *Indian Journal of Law and Technology*, *19*(1), 7–52. DOI: 10.55496/NBQQ3956

Dhavan, R. (1984). On the law of the press in India. *Journal of the Indian Law Institute*, *26*(3), 288–332. https://www.jstor.org/stable/43953869

Dicey, A. V. (2010). *Introduction to the study of the law of the constitution* (8th ed.). Oxford University Press.

European Commission. (2022). Digital Markets Act and Digital Services Act. https://digital-strategy.ec.europa.eu/en/policies/digital-markets-act-and-digital-services-act

European Commission. (2025). Media freedom and pluralism. https://digital-strategy.ec.europa.eu/en/policies/media-freedom

European Commission. (2025). Revision of the Audiovisual Media Services Directive (AVMSD). https://digital-strategy.ec.europa.eu/en/policies/revision-avmsd

Fenwick, H., & Phillipson, G. (2011). Media freedom and freedom of expression: An analysis of the European Court of Human Rights jurisprudence. *Human Rights Law Review*, *11*(1), 135–163.

Francke, W. (1995). The Evolving Watchdog: The Media's Role in Government Ethics. *The Annals of the American Academy of Political and Social Science*, *537*(1), 109–121. DOI: 10.1177/0002716295537000010

Garg, N., & Ghuman, D. P. K. (2024). Regulatory frameworks for OTT platforms: Global and Indian context. *Library Progress International*, *44*(3), 7880–7895.

George, D., Reutimann, K., & Tamò-Larrieux, A. (2019). GDPR bypass by design? Transient processing of data under the GDPR. *International Data Privacy Law*, *9*(4), 285–298. DOI: 10.1093/idpl/ipz017

Ghose, A., Pallav, P., & Ali, S. M. A. (2025). AI and political polarisation: Analysing the impact of algorithmic bias on governance in diverse political systems. In Günar, A. (Ed.), (pp. 135–160). Advances in Finance, Accounting, and Economics. IGI Global., DOI: 10.4018/979-8-3693-7036-0.ch007

Gil de Zúñiga, H., Weeks, B. E., & Ardèvol-Abreu, A. (2019). Digital media and politics: Effects of the great information equality and participation. *Journal of Broadcasting & Electronic Media*, *63*(2), 286–301. DOI: 10.1080/08838151.2019.1662019

Global Freedom of Expression. (2024). Kunal Kamra v. Union of India. Columbia University. https://globalfreedomofexpression.columbia.edu/cases/kunal-kamra-v-union-of-india/

Guha, S. (2023). Information technology (intermediary guidelines and digital media ethics code) rules, 2021: An analytical approach. *NUJS Law Review*, *16*(1), 1–45.

Gupta, I., & Srinivasan, L. (2023). Evolving scope of intermediary liability in India. *International Review of Law Computers & Technology*, *37*(3), 294–324. DOI: 10.1080/13600869.2022.2164838

Gupta, N. (2007). The Emergency and the press in India: A dark chapter. *Journal of Southeast Asian Studies*, *30*(1), 1–15.

Hudson, D. L. (1996). Prior Restraint and the Press: The Continuing Battle Over Freedom of Expression. *Communications and the Law*, *1*(3), 54–67.

Jain, A. (2024). *The Bombay High Court dismisses the Ministry of Truth*. Verfassungsblog., DOI: 10.59704/a561364a8208abeb

John, R. R. (2019). Freedom of expression in the digital age: A historian's perspective. *Church. Communication and Culture*, *4*(1), 25–38. DOI: 10.1080/23753234.2019.1565918

Juyal, R. (2023). Constitutional Liberties and Cyberspace: Analysing the Anuradha Bhasin v Union of India case and its impact on fundamental rights. *Legal Information Management*, *23*(4), 276–281. DOI: 10.1017/S1472669623000622

Kakkar, J. M., Mohan, S., & Devadasan, V. (2025). Safe Harbour and Content Moderation Regulation in India. In Chakravorti, B., & Trachtman, J. P. (Eds.), *Defeating Disinformation: Digital Platform Responsibility, Regulation and Content Moderation on the Global Technological Commons* (pp. 60–84). Cambridge University Press.

Kumar Srivastava, A. (2021). India's reading regulation as a prohibition: A critical review of the new it rules 2021 in relation to social media networks and messaging applications. *European Data Protection Law Review*, *7*(3), 450–455. DOI: 10.21552/edpl/2021/3/14

Locke, J. (1988). *Two treatises of government* (Laslett, P., Ed.). Cambridge University Press. (Original work published 1689) DOI: 10.1017/CBO9780511810268

Lorenz-Spreen, P., Oswald, L., Lewandowsky, S., & Hertwig, R. (2023). A systematic review of worldwide causal and correlational evidence on digital media and democracy. *Nature Human Behaviour*, *7*(1), 74–101. DOI: 10.1038/s41562-022-01460-1 PMID: 36344657

Nair, P. (1999). Media and democracy in India. *Economic and Political Weekly*, *34*(5), 238–244.

Pallav, P., Ali, S. M. A., & Ghose, A. (2025). Combating misinformation, disinformation, and fake news: A comparative study of the USA, UK, and India. In G. Ilik, M. Karadjoski, I. Ilijevski, & B. Nenovski (Eds.), *Combatting Misinformation and Global Nations' False Narratives Through Education* (pp. 195–222). IGI Global. https://doi.org/DOI: 10.4018/979-8-3693-9601-8.ch008

Panjiar, T., & Waghre, P. (2022, November 10). A public brief on the IT Amendment Rules, 2022, a.k.a. 'how the government is trying to moderate online speech'. *Internet Freedom Foundation*. https://internetfreedom.in/public-brief-on-the-it-amendment-rules-2022/

Post, R. C. (2024, January 8). The press and American democracy: Identifying four distinct constitutional functions of "the press". *Knight First Amendment Institute Blog*. https://knightcolumbia.org/blog/the-press-and-american-democracy

Sajid, A. (2023). Dr. B. R. Ambedkar and freedom of the press. [IJRAR]. *International Journal of Research and Analytical Reviews*, *2*(4), 47–49. https://academicjournal.ijraw.com/media/post/IJRAW-2-4-16.1.pdf

Scanlon, T. M. (2024). Freedom of speech. In Zalta, E. N. (Ed.), *The Stanford Encyclopedia of Philosophy* (Spring 2024 Edition). Stanford University., https://plato.stanford.edu/entries/freedom-speech/

Stone, M., & Dohel, I. (Eds.). (2013). *From traditional to online media: Best practices and perspectives: 14th Central Asia Media Conference, Ashgabat, Turkmenistan, 5–6 July 2012* (OSCE Representative on Freedom of the Media). Organisation for Security and Co-operation in Europe. https://www.osce.org/files/f/documents/8/3/102312.pdf

Thomas, K. M. (2023). A game not played well: A critical analysis of the draft amendment to the Information Technology (Intermediary Guidelines and Digital Media Ethics Code) Rules, 2021. *Tech Law Forum @ NALSAR*. https://techlawforum.nalsar.ac.in/a-game-not-played-well-a-critical-analysis-of-the-draft-amendment-to-the-information-technology-intermediary-guidelines-and-digital-media-ethics-code-rules-2021/

Van Den Boom, J. (2023). What does the Digital Markets Act harmonise? – Exploring interactions between the DMA and national competition laws. *European Competition Journal*, *19*(1), 57–85. DOI: 10.1080/17441056.2022.2156728

Voigt, P., & Von dem Bussche, A. (2017). *The EU General Data Protection Regulation (GDPR): A Practical Guide*. Springer. DOI: 10.1007/978-3-319-57959-7

Vora, A. (2023, June 26). Challenge to the IT Rules 2023. *Supreme Court Observer*. https://www.scobserver.in/journal/challenge-to-the-it-rules-2023/

Yadav, A., & Bajpai, R. (2024). Analysing *Kunal Kamra v. Union of India* in light of the vires of IT (Amendment) Rules, 2023 - Part II. *NLIU Law Review*. https://nliulawreview.nliu.ac.in/blog/analysing-kunal-kamra-v-uoi-in-light-of-the-vires-of-it-amendment-rules-2023-part-ii/

Yujie, Z., Al Imran Yasin, M., Alsagoff, S. A. B. S., & Hoon, A. L. (2022). The mediating role of new media engagement in this digital age. *Frontiers in Public Health*, *10*, 879530. DOI: 10.3389/fpubh.2022.879530 PMID: 35586011

KEY TERMS AND DEFINITIONS

Citizen Journalism- The process in which citizens can develop: disseminate, and comment on news or opinion online without media gatekeeping.

Digital Literacy: The ability of citizens to critically access, evaluate, and responsibly interact with digital content, as critical to deter manipulation and bolster democratic engagement.

Digital Media: Digital media, where anyone may consume and create information, has expanded participatory communication beyond print and electronic media.

Freedom of Speech and Expression: Article 19 1(a) of the Indian Constitution grants citizens the right to think, express, publish, discuss, and debate freely, subject to reasonable constraints under Article 19 (2).

Self-Regulation: A system where digital platforms, publishers, or industry organisations build their own rules, conventions, laws, and grievance redressal mechanisms without state involvement.

Chapter 4
Enhancing Democratic Governance Through Amendments in Existing Public Policies of India

Tarun Dwivedi
http://orcid.org/0009-0005-5288-7154
Amity University, Jaipur, India

Avinash Kumar
Amity University, Jaipur, India

Rahul Tripathi
http://orcid.org/0000-0002-2479-8585
Amity University, Jaipur, India

Parul Mishra
http://orcid.org/0000-0002-7287-6939
Amity School of Languages, Amity University, Jaipur, India

ABSTRACT

Enhancing democratic governance in India through amendments in public policies requires a multi-faceted approach that strengthens transparency, accountability, inclusivity, and citizen participation. There are certain points that can be put into consideration to make viable amendments related to public policies of India; policy amendments can be introduced to improve democratic governance. By amending public policies to enhance transparency, accountability, and participation, India can deepen its democratic governance. A combination of legal reforms, institutional strengthening, and technological integration can ensure a more responsive and in-

DOI: 10.4018/979-8-2600-1618-3.ch004

clusive democracy. Diving deeper into the area, electoral reforms, criminalization of politics, proportional representation, inner-party democracy, citizens' awareness, voter empowerment & turnout, independent election commission strengthening a fair representation of nation and its citizen would be expected. This in the long run would add to the enhancement of existing public policies of India.

I. INTRODUCTION

Democratic governance is categorised by transparency, accountability, and citizen participation (Dahl, 1989). In India, public policies play a decisive part in determining governance, however, there are many policies that entail amendments to familiarise to contemporary challenges. Policy reforms aim to augment governance by improving service delivery, reducing corruption, and ensuring inclusive growth (World Bank, 2017). Applicable democratic governance stimulates as to which extent existing associations and nations advance and thrive. It has been observed that numerous groups in expanding and post-socialist countries, the action and influence of democratic governance materialise through sector based reforms. Attempts to enhance democratic governance aims to hold bright influences on sectoral improvements, how these are employed, who are the target contributors in them at different boards, and what envisaged outcomes are accomplished. In opposition, sector based policy amendments and program interpolations can provide to upgrade and increase democratic governance. The impression of democratic governance syndicates structures of a political administration in which citizens embrace the right to administer themselves (democracy) with forms and methods that are implied to succeed public dealings rendering to putative guidelines and measures (governance). Democratic administrations hire a set of techniques that guarantees expressive battle amongst individuals and groups for political power, visible contribution in the optimal of leaders and policies, and in the distribution of societal roles. Analytical studies and the existing sources imply that there are two focal approaches that advanced democratic governance that can influence sectoral reforms. The initial one, and most comprehensively, democratic governance has the power to establish a progressive facilitating environment for reforms. Second, it can boost the productivity and efficiency of reform consequences and conclusions.

Managerial Implications of Policy Amendments

The efficiency of administration visible in amended policies like, NEP 2020 SDG4 out of 17 SDG of UN agenda 2030, for upgradation of system, plays a noticeable role in democratic enhancement, in the long run. For instance, stakeholder organised and unorganised including direct and indirect coordination, and participatory governance models lead to profitable implication of policies- Inclusion of academics with Industry for instance, aims at bridging the gap between academics and Industry promoting entrepreneurship culture. The stakeholders, Vice Chancellors, Principals, Directors/Deans, are suggested to inculcate courses like AI and Skill development in the programme structure. According to the organization for economic co-operation and development (OECD), the industry conducts around two-thirds of R&D in science and technology studies. The remaining 20% of R&D work is carried out by universities, while 10% is carried out by the government (Organisation for Economic Co-operation and Development (OECD, 2017). The world's top-ranking universities attract industry funding for their projects and innovations. The pharmaceutical industry is one of the most prominent investors in universities (Shehatta and Mahmood, 2016). The IT industry has also started investing in academies because it has concluded that it is beneficial to spend on students and academia. Exactly 26,355 universities from all over the world are included in a survey carried out in July 2016 that lists the countries arranged by the number of universities in the top rankings (Shattock, 2017). With this statistical data, it can be concluded that collaboration between the industry and academia is on the rise.

This paper explores how amendments in existing public policies can strengthen democratic governance in India by analysing key legislative and administrative reforms. Although there has been plethora of study/analysis conducted in regard to academia bridging with industry, there still exists criticism of academic research. Various patterns and frameworks that need to be addressed remain unaddressed in information science, which includes professional/client collaboration and the right of each stakeholder (Birdsall, 2009). The reason behind this gap is the lack of agencies cooperating with the challenges of the academics. A policy offering substantial collaboration in form of paid internships through government can pave the way for better learning and earning.

II. UNDERSTANDING DIRECT VS. INDIRECT PUBLIC POLICY

It is prevalent that the large number of policies (especially schemes) have a direct influence and an even larger number (frameworks, strategies, regulations, reforms) have a primarily indirect influence on the public in India and both enhances democratic governance appropriately. The cumulative effect of both types shapes the lives of citizens. However, we can understand the nature of this influence:

- **Sheer Volume & Scope:** Democratic governance holds formidable influences on sector based reforms. While Governance in India spans countless sectors (economy, health, education, environment, infrastructure, agriculture, defence, social justice, technology, internal security, foreign policy, etc.). Each sector has numerous policies at different levels.

- **Federal System of Governance:** Indian constitution consists federal governance system and at every level the authority makes policies for its effective governance. This includes:
  - **Union (Central) Government:** The Government who is responsible for running country as per democratic governance creates national-level policies which is applicable across India. For instance, National Education Policy, National Health Policy, Industrial Policy, Agricultural Export Policy, Digital India, National Cyber Security Policy).
  - **State Governments:** The state government ensures the democracy through their separate policy formulation right's. The ruling government formulate their own policies within the framework set by the Constitution and central laws, tailored to state-specific needs (e.g., State Industrial Policies, State Health Missions, State Agricultural Policies, State IT Policies).
  - **Local Governments:** Panchayat and Municipalities ensure democracy, implement policies and create localized rules and plans influencing governance at the grassroots level.
- **Dynamic Nature:** Policies are constantly being introduced, revised, merged, superseded, or allowed to lapse to handle the contemporary circumstances. There's no single, static registry containing all active policies across all levels and different sectors.
- **"Directly Influence" is Subjective:** It is fact that almost any government policy influences governance to some degree at all levels, either by setting goals, allocating resources, or changing administrative processes.

Direct Influence: The Policies that deliver tangible benefits, services, rights, obligations, or restrictions *immediately* and *visibly* to individual citizens or specific, identifiable groups are responsible for direct influence. Its characteristic often involves cash transfers, subsidies, service delivery, specific entitlements, or clear regulations affecting daily life.

Examples

- **Schemes**: PM-KISAN (cash to farmers), Pradhan Mantri Awas Yojana (housing), Ayushman Bharat (health insurance), Mahatma Gandhi National Rural Employment Guarantee Act (MGNREGA) (guaranteed work/wages), Old Age Pensions, Mid-Day Meal Scheme etc.

- **Regulations**: Traffic rules, building codes, pollution control norms (affecting local residents), food safety standards etc.
- **Entitlements**: Right to Information Act, Right to Education Act provisions, Public Distribution System (ration cards) etc.
- **Tax Policies**: Specific exemptions or rebates directly impacting disposable income (e.g., standard deduction in income tax) etc.

Indirect Influence: These Policies shape the broader economic, social, institutional, or infrastructural environment. Their impact on the public is mediated through market forces, long-term development, changes in service providers, or overall systemic improvements/declines. It Focus on frameworks, institutions, macro-level interventions, or foundational changes whose effects trickle down over time.

Examples

- **Macro-Economic Policies**: Monetary Policy (interest rates set by RBI), Fiscal Policy (overall government spending/taxation structure), Foreign Trade Policy, FDI policies.
- **Sectoral Development Policies**: National Education Policy (NEP - framework for long-term systemic change), National Health Policy (setting goals/strategies), National Manufacturing Policy, National Agriculture Policy.
- **Infrastructure Policies**: National Infrastructure Pipeline, National Highways Development Program, Sagarmala (ports), Bharatmala (roads). (Benefit is indirect via improved connectivity/efficiency).
- **Institutional Reforms**: Insolvency and Bankruptcy Code (IBC), Goods and Services Tax (GST - simplifies system but indirect price effect), Ease of Doing Business reforms.
- **Research & Innovation Policies**: National Policy on Research & Development, Science & Technology policies.
- **Defence & Foreign Policy**: National Security Strategy, international treaties.

Vast Majority Involve Indirect Influence: Most policies formulated at the Union and State levels are broad frameworks, strategies, regulations for industries/sectors, or institutional reforms. Their impact on the public is fundamentally indirect and long-term. Think of policies setting standards for industries, promoting investment in sectors, or reforming administrative processes.

Significant Number with Direct Influence: A large subset, particularly government schemes and entitlements administered by both Union and State governments, are designed for direct impact. This includes hundreds of Central Sector Schemes, Schemes sponsored by central government, and thousands of State-specific schemes.

Regulations directly governing public behaviour (like environmental norms affecting local communities) also fall here.

The Blurred Middle: Many policies have elements of both direct influence and indirect.

- An agricultural policy might set indirect market frameworks and include direct subsidy components.
- An industrial policy might offer indirect tax benefits to companies and mandate direct skill development programs for workers.

III. POLICY FORMULATION IN INDIA

Public policy in India involves a comprehensive set of guiding principles, goals, and initiatives devised by the centre to address the country's diverse social, financial, and political issues (Singh et al., 2023). Public policies are essentially governmental decisions and the result of collective activities undertaken to pursue specific goals (Vedantham & Kamruddin, 2017). Distinguishing essential problems, regulating policy substitutes, anticipating and assessing the consequences of different alternatives, and finally, selecting the preferred course of action steps. Birkland examines that 'policy process' is a method that transforms policy planning into interpretation, completion, evaluating actual policies that are executed and hold confident consequences (Birkland, 2011). Fig 1 describes the policy formulation process in India.

Figure 1.

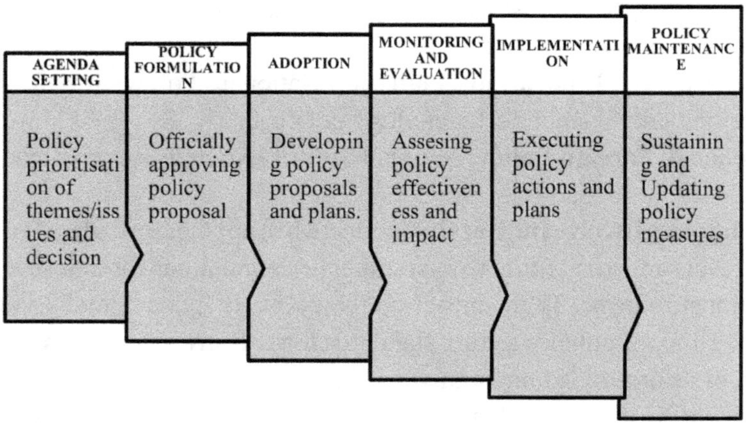

1. **Constitutional and Legal Framework:** The constitution governs deeply the Policy-making in India, it is characterized by the autonomous and sovereign republic, a system approved by parliament, and a centralised structure. The over-arching socio-economic philosophy embedded in the Preamble, Fundamental Rights, and Directive Principles of State Policy also significantly shapes this framework. The key actors and institutions in policy formulation in India is multi-level and multi-dimensional, involving a wide array of stakeholders. This method combines constituent requirements, recognized supports, and autonomous theories to construct strategies that counter collective requirements, however enactment of such suggestions time and again encounters substantial disputes in practice. The various stake holders are as follows:

   (a) **Governmental Institutions:** These institutions are different levels where the policy idea formulates and through different phases and opinion comes in effect. These levels are as follows:

      (i) **Legislature (Parliament):** In Indian federal governmental system parliament holds the sovereign power of policy-making, it decrees laws that make policies into power and legitimizes government decisions. While it influences policies and their amendment through debates, most legislation originates from the executive.

      (ii) **Executive:** The executive comprises the President, the Council of Ministers (Cabinet), and the governmental machinery. They are constitutionally tasked with formulating policies and their amendment to be presented to the Parliament. The Prime Minister holds a significant position in guiding Cabinet decision-making. Administrative secretaries and ministries play a crucial role by providing essential data and advising ministers during policy formulation and its amendments.

      (iii) **Judiciary:** The judiciary influences policy through its authority of judicial analysis. The judiciary assess the constitutional behavior of legislative and administrative actions, and through its judgments in Public Interest Litigation (PIL) arguments.

      (iv) **NITI Aayog (formerly known as Planning Commission):** National Institution for Transforming India (NITI) provides policy recommendations to the government. It is a think tank, replaced planning commission and comprise experts in the concerned field for efficient policy formulation and its execution.

      (v) **Non-Governmental Institutions:** These informal participants play vital role to the policy process and support in different manner deeply for data input and ground level knowledge for perfect policy decision.

   (b) **Political Parties and Pressure Groups:** These groups exert influence through their election manifestoes, by mobilizing public support, and through lobbying efforts. The "group theory" speculates that public policy emerges from the conflict between various groups, with influence depending on factors like mammon, managerial dexterity, governance attribute, negotiating competence, and entrance to competent authorities.

(c) **Individual Citizens and Media:** Citizens initiate policy engagement by voting, though direct individual participation in policy-making is often limited. The media significantly impacts public opinion and policy debates.

(d) **Research Organizations and Think Tanks:** These contribute to policy formation by conducting research, analysing data, and offering evidence-based proposals.

(e) **Non-Governmental Organizations (NGOs) and Civil Society:** These sects aggressively advocate for specific social concerns, represent diverse interests, and influence policy decisions. They also function as a connect linking the government and the public, facilitating dialogue and input.

(f) **External Agencies:** International bodies such as the United Nations and its organizations (WHO, ILO, UNDP), the World Bank, and the International Monetary Fund significantly influence policy outcomes, particularly in developing countries like India.

Challenges in Policy Formulation: Despite a well-structured framework, policy formulation in India faces several constraints. These include inadequate expertise and skills among personnel involved, lack of clarity in defining goals, an overemphasis on short-term benefits, and insufficient involvement of socially enlightened groups. Decision-makers' ideologies, caste, class interests, or regional and ethnic loyalties can also influence policy choices. Furthermore, the complexity of formulating policies in a multi-ethnic and multicultural nation makes it challenging to balance diverse interests and avoid competing agendas. There can also be issues like lack of reliable data and inadequate policy research which hinder effective formulation.

The public policies of India persist to encounter arguments, involving active enactment, distortion, and supply restrictions. Management relating to state and central governments continues to be a main reason, as does confirming that policies reach downgraded inhabitants. Nevertheless, the embryonic attitude of public policies in India echoes the country's exertions to stabilize pecuniary evolution with societal impartiality and ecofriendly sustainability, directing to accomplish a comprehensive and affluent future through amendments in existing public policies.

IV. BASIC PUBLIC POLICY IN INDIA

Basic public policy in India refers to the set of general principles, goals, and actions adopted by the government to address the needs of the people and promote the country's development and welfare. These policies in India are shaped by constitutional values like justice, equality, liberty, and fraternity. The constitution of India governs its democratic phenomena. It covers areas like welfare, economy, education, health, security, environment, and governance. These policies are vibrant and advance with the varying demands of society. While, the basic public policy in Indian constitution is explicitly, but it establishes the "foundational principles, objectives, and directives" that guide all the public policy in India. These are embedded in several key parts which are as follows:

1. **The Preamble**: The soul of the Constitution, declaresIndia as a:
    - **Sovereign**: Independent authority.
    - **Socialist**: Committed to reducing inequalities (interpreted as social and economic justice, not state ownership of all means of production).
    - **Secular**: Equal respect and protection for all religions; no state religion.
    - **Democratic**: Government based on the will of the people.
    - **Republic:** Head of state (President) is elected, not hereditary.
    - It secures for all citizens:
    - **Justice**: Social, economic, and political.
    - **Liberty**: Of thought, expression, belief, faith, and worship.
    - **Equality**: Of status and opportunity.
    - **Fraternity**: Assuring the dignity of the individual and the unity and integrity of the nation.
2. **Fundamental Rights (Part III - Articles 12-35)**: These are justiciable (enforceable in court) rights guaranteeing individual freedoms and protections against state arbitrariness. Any Public policy being formulated or amended cannot violate these rights. Key rights include:
    - Right to Equality (Articles 14-18)
    - Right to Freedom (Articles 19-22)
    - Right against Exploitation (Articles 23-24)
    - Right to Freedom of Religion (Articles 25-28)
    - Cultural and Educational Rights (Articles 29-30)
    - Right to Constitutional Remedies (Article 32)
3. **Directive Principles of State Policy (DPSP) (Part IV - Articles 36-51)**: This is the "core blueprint for public policy" in India. While not directly enforceable in courts (unlike Fundamental Rights), they tend to be structural in the governance of the country and its responsibility of the State to employ this doctrine

in drafting laws and policies. They outline the socio-economic goals the state should strive to achieve:

- **Social Justice**: Promoting welfare, minimizing inequalities (Art. 38), securing equal pay, humane work conditions, livelihood (Art. 39, 41, 42, 43), raising nutrition/living standards (Art. 47).
- **Gandhian Principles**: Organizing village panchayats (Art. 40), promoting cottage industries (Art. 43), prohibiting intoxicants (Art. 47).
- **Economic Welfare**: Equitable distribution of resources (Art. 39(b)&(c)), preventing wealth concentration.
- **Environmental Protection**: Safeguarding forests/wildlife (Art. 48A), protecting the environment (interpreted by courts).
- International Peace & Security (Art. 51).
- Uniform Civil Code (Art. 44 - aspirational goal).
- Education (Art. 45, 46).

4. **Fundamental Duties (Part IVA - Article 51A):** Public participation Added later (42nd Amendment), these outline the moral obligations of general public to maintain the Constitution, national unison, and contribute to the country's progress. Public policy aims to foster an environment where these duties can be fulfilled.

These parts of constitution are guiding framework for all laws and government actions. It performs as balancing act during policy formulation. Policy often involves balancing potentially conflicting goals (e.g., individual liberty vs. social justice, rapid development vs. environmental protection). The Constitution provides the reference points for this balancing. Judicial review holds the power to strike down any policy during the violation of any basic public policy (e.g., Right to Life under Art. 21 now includes right to health, education, clean environment, etc., drawing from DPSPs). Public policy evolves as society changes, but it must always operate within the constitutional framework. This can be judge through landmark policies (like land reforms, right to education, MGNREGA, environmental regulations, affirmative action) are deeply rooted in DPSPs and Fundamental Rights interpretations.

V. PUBLIC POLICY NEED

The democracy ensures judicial distribution of resources available or arranged by ruling government for the people of the nation. Governance discusses all approaches of employing limit and authorization in the provision of resources (World Bank,1994). Public policy is the source through which this judicial distribution comes into reality. Public policy in India covers a wide range of sectors and is shaped by the Constitution, legislation, political ideologies, judicial decisions, and administrative processes. The core elements which are required ever and important always for the people of any nation are as follows:

1. **Welfare and Social Justice:** India follows a welfare state model, as directed by the Directive Principles of State Policy (Part IV of the Constitution). Public policies aim to reduce inequality, support disadvantaged groups (like Scheduled Castes, Scheduled Tribes, and women), and provide access to basic necessities. Mahatma Gandhi National Rural Employment Guarantee Act (MGNREGA)/ (VB-G RAM G) The Viksit Bharat-Guarantee For Rojgar and Ajeevika Mission, Public Distribution System (PDS), PM Awas Yojana (housing) etc are few successful policies which ensures welfare and social justice for the people of nation.
2. **Economic Development:** Policies focus on inclusive economic growth, industrial development, and poverty reduction. The government uses policies to balance private sector participation and public sector responsibility. The main focus is growth of every individual of the nation. Make in India, Start-up India, Atmanirbhar Bharat (self-reliant India) etc are several policies which is need of India for future growth.
3. **Education and Health:** Education and healthcare are top priorities to ensure human development. The government aims for universal access and improvement in quality. Policies like National Education Policy (NEP) 2020, Ayushman Bharat (health insurance scheme), Midday Meal Scheme etc are the need of the nation for better health and education for the people. These policies have given new momentum to the growth of the nation.
4. **Environmental Sustainability:** Indian policy aims to balance development with environmental protection. The participation of government in global climate change conferences and its policy for National Action Plan on Climate Change, Swachh Bharat Mission (Clean India), National Electric Mobility Mission etc reflects its mandate for environmental sustainability.
5. **Law and Order & National Security:** The Indian government also focuses on ensuring internal security, border safety, and law enforcement through various public policy measures. These policies are National Cyber Security Policy, Anti-terrorism laws, Police and judicial reforms etc.
6. **Governance and Digital India:** Improving transparency, accountability, and efficiency in governance is a major policy objective. This all can be achieved through awareness of its nation's people. The Indian government policies that ensure the awareness of its people are Digital India, e-Governance initiatives, Right to Information Act (RTI) etc.

The Public policy need ensures fundamental rights, objectives and directive principle. "In essence, the "Public policy" mandated by the Indian Constitution is the pursuit of a just, egalitarian, and humane society where individual freedoms are protected, socio-economic inequalities are minimized, and the dignity of every citizen is upheld, all within a democratic, secular, and republican framework." The DPSPs provide the most direct roadmap for this policy direction.

VI. PUBLIC POLICY AMENDMENT

The existing policy amendment comes in to action when the policy goal changes or existing problem need contemporary solution as per resources available. Public policy needed in India refers to the new or reformed policies that are essential to address emerging challenges and to improve governance, equity, and development outcomes in the country. The key areas where public policy is urgently needed to draft or needs to keep in mind when drafting any public policy or amendment in any existing policy to strengthening the democratic governance in India are as follows:

1. **Employment and Skilling Policy:** The high youth unemployment, jobless growth, and skills mismatch in India needs to focus on policies like
   - Vocational and digital skill development aligned with industrial needs
   - Creation of green jobs and formal sector employment for its youth
   - Encouragement of entrepreneurship and MSMEs for national GDP
2. **Healthcare Policy Reform:** Inadequate public healthcare infrastructure, high out-of-pocket costs, rural-urban disparity require policy or amendment in existing policy needs to focus like:
   - Increased public investment in healthcare
   - Strengthening primary and preventive healthcare
   - Mental health and elderly care
   - Universal health coverage
3. **Education System Overhaul:** Poor learning outcomes, rote learning, and digital divide require policy or amendment in existing policy needs to focus like:
   - Implementing National Education Policy (NEP) fully
   - Access to quality education in rural areas
   - Digital education infrastructure
   - Teacher training and accountability
4. **Climate Change and Environment:** Rising pollution, climate vulnerability, water scarcity require policy or amendment in existing policy needs to focus like:
   - Renewable energy policy reforms

- Strict enforcement of environmental regulations
- Climate-resilient agriculture
- Urban climate action plans

5. **Agriculture and Rural Development:** Agrarian distress, low farmer incomes, climate impacts. require policy or amendment in existing policy needs to focus like:
   - Agricultural marketing reforms (like MSP overhaul)
   - Investment in irrigation, storage, and rural logistics
   - Crop diversification and sustainable practices
   - Direct income support and crop insurance
6. **Urban Governance and Infrastructure:** Unplanned urbanization, poor infrastructure, rising slums require policy or amendment in existing policy needs to focus like:
   - Affordable housing and public transport
   - Smart and sustainable urban planning
   - Waste management and water supply systems
7. **Digital Policy and Cybersecurity:** Data privacy concerns, increasing cyber threats, digital divide require policy or amendment in existing policy needs to focus like:
   - Strong data protection legislation to secure citizens of the nation.
   - Cybersecurity awareness and defence capabilities to counter the cyber-attacks.
   - Affordable digital access in rural India
8. **Judicial and Police Reforms:** Delay in justice, police accountability, overcrowded jails require policy or amendment in existing policy needs to focus like:
   - Fast-track courts and judicial infrastructure
   - Police training, accountability, and depoliticization
   - Alternate dispute resolution mechanisms
9. **Social Security and Inclusion:** Vulnerability of informal sector workers, elderly, disabled, and minorities require policy or amendment in existing policy needs to focus like:
   - Universal social security coverage
   - Pension and insurance for gig and informal workers
   - Gender-sensitive and inclusive policy design
10. **Policy on Artificial Intelligence and Emerging Tech:** Lack of regulation, potential job loss, ethical concerns require policy or amendment in existing policy needs to focus like:
    - National AI and emerging tech strategy
    - Ethics and regulation of AI applications

- Promoting innovation while safeguarding rights

VII. SIGNIFICANCE OF THE STUDY

The findings showcase the significance of national contribution, institutional strengthening, and addressing inequalities to enhance democracy of governance. Positive environment for reforms and to enrich the effect of policy is core significance of this study. Several studies focus on the impact of electoral reforms, participatory governance models, and the task of public in promoting accountability and competent governance. Furthermore, research emphasizes the need for policies that foster trust in government, promote transparency, and ensure fair treatment, particularly in the context of public services and benefit claims. This research shall prove to be significant because it not only critiques existing policies but also provides actionable recommendations to enhance democratic governance through structured, inclusive, and transparent amendments as per public need. It serves as a valuable resource for governments, researchers, and activists working toward more accountable and people-centric governance in India and beyond. It addresses critical vulnerabilities in modern democratic systems while unlocking pathways to resilience, equity, and legitimacy. In an era marked by polarization, distrust in institutions, and complex global challenges. The study on holds substantial importance for policymakers, academics, civil society, and citizens due to the following reasons:

1. Strengthening Democratic Governance

Autonomous governance thrives on obviousness, culpability, and citizen contribution. Policy amendments can reinforce these principles by making governance more responsive and inclusive. Institutional integrity, Transparency & Accountability, decentralisation, civic engagement, ethical political culture and inclusive government are few factors through which the Indian stakeholders are strengthening its democracy. By analysing reforms like the RTI Act, GST, and NEP 2020, the research provides insights into how structured policy changes can improve governance efficiency and public trust. Strengthening democratic governance in India requires multi-faceted efforts:

a. **Institutional Integrity:** The Indian constitution ensures democracy in every form of its Governance system. Institutions play crucial role in any policy process in India. The steps like bolster the independence, capacity, and resources of key institutions like Election Commission, Judiciary, Comptroller & Auditor

General (CAG), Chief Vigilance Commissioner (CVC)) and ensure transparent appointments gives strength to the democracy.

b. **Transparency & Accountability:** The existing policy's which are responsible for increasing transparency and accountability of every stakeholder in policy making are act which hinder the confidentiality of corruption. Article 368 of the Indian constitution gives power to the Parliament to amend any provision of the Constitution if needed. These amendment gives strength to the transparency and accountability. In India the rigorously implement the Right to Information Act, enforce asset declaration, and enact robust anti-corruption mechanisms (including campaign finance reform) achieve this goal judiciously.

c. **Decentralization:** The participation of citizen comes in to reality when their involvement includes at grassroot level. 73rd and 74th Constitutional amendments to the Indian Constitution on strengthening the local democracy and participation of citizen has achieved this goal successfully. Local democracy in India urges citizen contribution and engagement in community decision-making processes. It offers a political platform for citizens to raise their interests, contribute in public meetings, and make selected delegates responsible for their acts (Heller, 2009). Empower community governments (Panchayati Raj Institutions, Urban Local Bodies) fiscally and administratively for effective grassroots service delivery.

d. **Civic Engagement:** Civic engagement is the lifeblood of democracy. It transforms passive residents into active citizens. It refers to the active participation of individuals and groups in public life to address community issues, influence decision-making, and contribute to the common good. It promotes active citizen participation through accessible grievance redressal, participatory budgeting and protecting civil society space and media freedom. Civic engagement, the active participation of citizens in shaping public affairs, is a cornerstone of a vibrant democracy (Polizzi, 2019).

e. **Inclusive Governance:** It is a system of governing that actively ensures all members of society especially marginalized, vulnerable, and underrepresented groups. It arranges & manages meaningful opportunities to participate in decision-making processes, access public services, and hold power-holders accountable. It goes beyond formal equality to address structural barriers and power imbalances, aiming for genuine equity and representation. It also ensures equitable representation and participation of every marginalized group like woman, minorities, schedule cast, schedule tribe, other backward cast) at all levels of decision-making.

f. **Ethical Political Culture:** The democratic governance fosters ethical conduct among elected representatives and strengthen intra-party democracy. An ethical political culture refers to a system of shared values, norms, attitudes, and practices within a society that prioritizes integrity, justice, accountability, and the common good in political life. It shapes how authority is applied, choices are made, and population engage with their government and each other. It builds trusts, ensures good and democratic governance, protect rights, encourage economic and social development, proceed as per rule of law.

2. Addressing Implementation Gaps

Many policies in India face challenges in execution due to bureaucratic delays, corruption, and lack of public awareness. By identifying key obstacles in policy implementation and suggesting amendments that can bridge these gaps, ensuring that laws achieve their intended outcomes.

First, improve policy design through realistic goal-setting, adequate resource allocation (financial, human, technological), and robust stakeholder consultation, especially with sub-national governments and communities.

Second, strengthen bureaucratic capacity and accountability via specialized training, clearer role definitions, performance-linked incentives, and reduced political interference in routine administration.

Third, enhance monitoring & evaluation (M&E) using real-time digital systems (like PFMS, e-Gov) for tracking progress, coupled with independent third-party audits and social audits to ensure transparency and course correction.

Fourth, empower local governance (Panchayati Raj Institutions/Urban Local Bodies) through genuine devolution of funds, functions, and functionaries, recognizing their critical role in last-mile delivery.

Finally, foster political commitment across parties for sustained focus on outcomes rather than announcements, ensuring policies survive electoral cycles. Closing the gap requires tackling bureaucratic inertia, resource constraints, weak M&E, and fragmented accountability simultaneously

3. Promoting Evidence-Based Policymaking

The research emphasizes the need for data-driven and participatory policy amendments rather than politically motivated changes. Advocating for evidence-based reforms, the study contributes to more rational and effective governance. The key strategies are strengthening data infrastructure, building analytical capacity, fostering research-based link, promoting a culture of evidence and institutionalize the evaluation. The evidence-based policy making reduces time and increases efficiency of policy to achieve its maximum goal.

4. Enhancing Citizen Engagement

A core aspect of democratic governance is citizen involvement in decision-making. The study examines how policy amendments can foster greater public participation through consultations, digital governance tools, and grievance redressal mechanisms thereby making democracy more participatory. Truly robust democratic governance demands moving beyond periodic elections to foster continuous, meaningful citizen engagement in public policy. This may accomplish through following strategies:

(a) **Digital Tool:** Leveraging accessible technology is crucial, user-friendly online platforms for information dissemination, feedback collection (e.g., e-petitions, policy simulations), and virtual consultations can significantly lower barriers, reaching broader demographics, including youth and geographically dispersed populations.

(b) **Diverse Participation:** Deliberate diversification of participation methods is essential to maximise civic engagement. Complementing digital tools with proven offline mechanisms like participatory budgeting, citizen juries, deliberative polls, and well-publicized local town halls ensures inclusion for those less digitally connected and allows for deeper, more nuanced dialogue on complex issues.

(c) **Inclusive Outreach:** Prioritizing inclusivity is non-negotiable to increase participation. Proactive outreach using trusted community organizations, multilingual materials, childcare provisions, and varied meeting times is vital to engage marginalized groups often excluded from traditional processes, ensuring policy reflects diverse societal needs.

(d) **Trust Building:** The clear communication that how citizen input influenced final decisions (or why not) through accessible reports and feedback loops demonstrates respect and encourages future engagement.

(e) **Cultural Flexibility:** Shifting from mere consultation to empowering citizens as partners in identifying problems, brainstorming solutions, and co-designing policies supported by capacity-building initiatives – unlocks collective intelligence and enhances policy legitimacy and effectiveness. Implementing these interconnected approaches strengthens democracy by making policymaking more responsive, representative, and grounded in the lived experiences of the populace.

5. Policy Learning for Future Reforms

By evaluating past amendments (e.g., GST rate rationalizations, RTI modifications, NEP restructuring), the study offers lessons for future reforms in areas like healthcare, environmental governance, and digital rights. This can guide policymakers in designing more effective laws. The focus is on building adaptable, evidence-informed policies ready for tomorrow's challenges. It enhances policy resilience, identify early opportunities, mitigate long term risk and improve adaptability. It opens way for researchers and experts to work more deeply in the field to gives effective participation for future policy generation.

6. Comparative Relevance for Other Democracies

While focused on India, the findings have broader implications for developing democracies facing similar governance challenges. The study's framework can be adapted to assess policy reforms in other nations striving for better governance. It gives the real ground experience before promulgation of any policy.

VIII. LITERATURE REVIEW

Democratic governance relies on the continuous evolution of public policies to address emerging socio-political and economic challenges. In India, policy amendments play a crucial role in strengthening governance by improving transparency, accountability, and citizen participation. This literature review synthesizes existing research on public policy reforms in India, focusing on key legislative and administrative changes that have shaped democratic governance. The review is structured around three core themes: (1) theoretical foundations of democratic governance and policy amendments, (2) empirical studies on major policy reforms in India, and (3) gaps and future directions for research.

1. Theoretical Foundations of Policy Amendments in Democratic Governance

Democratic Governance and Public Policy

Citizen centric governance has virtue to check the changing nature of the modern state and leads to do amendment in existing public policies to overpower the dangers assumed for the democracy. Democratic governance is characterized by institutions that ensure transparency, accountability, and citizen engagement (Dahl, 1989). According to Grindle (2004), effective governance requires policies that are inclusive, adaptable, and enforceable. Policy amendments serve as a mechanism to correct inefficiencies, incorporate public feedback, and align laws with contemporary needs (Howlett & Ramesh, 2003).

Self-governing governance can be well-defined as the happenings of the state and citizens or political society to form businesses, links, management, compromise, interchange, agreement and addition in the development of framing and applying public policies (Bevir, 2006; Ingrams, 2019; Strebel et al., 2019).

Brown (2003) explained that responsibility and obviousness of state organizations in executing social and economic improvement would add to the independent governance.

Institutional Theory and Policy Change

North's (1990) institutional theory posits that well-designed policies reduce transaction costs and enhance governance efficiency. In the Indian context, Kapur & Mehta (2005) argue that path dependency and bureaucratic resistance often hinder necessary reforms, necessitating structured amendments to overcome institutional inertia.

Participatory Governance and Policy Reforms

Fung (2006) emphasizes that citizen participation in policymaking enhances legitimacy and effectiveness. Studies on India's Panchayati Raj system (Mathew, 2002) and the Right to Information Act (RTI) (Peisakhin & Pinto, 2010) demonstrate that policies incorporating public input lead to better implementation and trust in governance.

2. Empirical Evidence on Policy Amendments in India

Right to Information (RTI) Act (2005) and Amendments

The RTI Act is widely regarded as a landmark in India's democratic governance for empowering citizens to hold authorities accountable (Singh, 2020). However, the RTI (Amendment) Act, 2019, which altered the tenure and salary of Information Commissioners, faced criticism for potentially weakening transparency (Chakraborty, 2021). Empirical studies suggest that while RTI remains effective, bureaucratic delays and political interference hinder its full potential (Roberts, 2010).

Goods and Services Tax (GST) Reforms

The introduction of GST in 2017 aimed to unify India's fragmented tax system, reducing compliance burdens and improving revenue collection (Rao, 2019). Subsequent amendments, such as rate rationalizations and e-invoicing, improved compliance but also highlighted challenges like complexity for small businesses (Ministry of Finance, 2021). Research indicates that GST's success depends on further simplification and stakeholder consultations (Jain, 2018).

National Education Policy (NEP) 2020

The NEP replaced the outdated 1986 policy, emphasizing multilingual education, digital learning, and vocational training (MHRD, 2020). Studies suggest that while the policy is progressive, its implementation faces hurdles such as lack of funding, teacher training gaps, and regional disparities (Tilak, 2021).

Digital Governance and Aadhaar Reforms

India's push for digital governance through Aadhaar and Direct Benefit Transfers (DBT) has improved service delivery but raised concerns about privacy and exclusion errors (Drèze & Khera, 2017). Amendments strengthening data protection laws (e.g., Digital Personal Data Protection Act, 2023) are critical for balancing efficiency and rights (Sharma, 2023).

3. Gaps in Existing Literature and Future Research Directions

1. Limited studies on long-term impacts of policy amendments (e.g., GST's effect on informal sectors).
2. Need for comparative analyses between states on policy implementation effectiveness.
3. Role of civil society and media in shaping policy amendments remains underexplored.
4. Digital governance reforms require more research on privacy-security trade-offs.

This literature review highlights how policy amendments in India have enhanced democratic governance but also identifies persistent challenges such as bureaucratic inefficiencies, lack of public consultation, and implementation gaps. Future research should focus on participatory amendment processes, impact assessments, and cross-country comparisons to strengthen evidence-based policymaking.

IX. THEORETICAL FRAMEWORK

Democratic governance relies on the theories of contribution, accountability, and the rule of law (Grindle, 2004). Policy amendments should align with these principles to ensure legitimacy and effectiveness. The *institutional theory* (North, 1990) suggests that well-structured policies reduce transaction costs and enhance governance efficiency. Similarly, the *participatory governance model* (Fung, 2006) emphasizes citizen involvement in policymaking to improve outcomes.

1. Key Policy Amendments and Their Impact on Governance

Right to Information (RTI) Act (2005) and Subsequent Reforms

The RTI Act empowers citizens to seek information from public authorities, enhancing transparency (Peisakhin & Pinto, 2010). However, amendments such as the RTI (Amendment) Act, 2019, which altered the tenure and salary of Information Commissioners, raised concerns about weakening accountability (Singh, 2020). Despite this, RTI remains a cornerstone of democratic governance in India. As per mechanism Citizens can file requests; Public Information Officers (PIOs) are mandated to provide information within 30 days. It has become a powerful tool for citizens to expose corruption, redress grievances, and monitor government functioning. The most significant amendment came in **2019**, which had a major impact on the autonomy of the Information Commissions, the act's appellate bodies.

- **RTI (Amendment) Act, 2019:**
- **Changed Service Conditions:** It empowered the central government to set the tenure, salaries, and allowances for the Chief Information Commissioner (CIC) and Information Commissioners (ICs) at both central and state levels.
- **Diluted Autonomy:** Previously, these were statutorily fixed to be equivalent to Election Commissioners, ensuring high independence. The amendment is criticized for potentially undermining the autonomy of these watchdogs by making them dependent on the government.
- **Impact on Governance**

  The RTI Act has profoundly improved governance by:
- **Enhancing Transparency:** Making government processes and spending more open to public scrutiny.
- **Curbing Corruption:** Acting as a deterrent and a tool to expose malfeasance.
- **Promoting Citizen-Centric Governance:** Making administration more responsive.

However, the 2019 amendment poses a challenge by potentially weakening the institutional independence of Information Commissions, which could dilute the Act's long-term effectiveness as a check on governmental power. The ongoing struggle is to protect the RTI's core spirit from dilution.

Goods and Services Tax (GST) Reforms

The GST (2017) unified India’s fragmented tax system, improving economic governance (Rao, 2019). Subsequent amendments, like rate rationalizations and the introduction of e-invoicing, enhanced compliance and reduced tax evasion (Ministry of Finance, 2021). These reforms demonstrate how policy adjustments can improve governance efficiency. It is one of India's most significant fiscal reforms. It subsumed a complex web of multiple central and state taxes into a single, unified tax regime, creating a common national market.

- **Key Features of the Reform:**
- **One Nation, One Tax:** Replaced over a dozen central and state levies (like VAT, excise duty, service tax) with a single GST.
- **Dual Structure:** A unique dual GST model where both the Central and State governments levy tax on a common base.
- **IT-Driven System:** The GST Network (GSTN) provides a shared IT infrastructure for registration, return filing, and tax payment, minimizing human interface.
- **Impact on Governance:**
- **Cooperative Federalism:** The GST Council, a constitutional body with representation from the Centre and all states, embodies a new culture of decision-making through consensus. This has strengthened fiscal federalism.
- **Enhanced Transparency and Ease of Doing Business:** The unified tax system dismantled inter-state check-posts, reducing logistics time and costs. The transparent, online system has made compliance clearer and reduced harassment.
- **Formalization of Economy:** By bringing a vast number of businesses into the formal tax net through its compliance chain, GST has increased the tax base and boosted government revenue in the long run.
- **Efficiency in Tax Administration:** The input tax credit mechanism discourages tax evasion by creating an auditable trail of transactions. Data analytics on GSTN data improves compliance monitoring.
- **Challenges & Subsequent Refinements:**

  Initial implementation faced issues like technical glitches and complex multi-tier rate structure. Subsequent reforms have focused on simplifying return filing (e.g., introduction of GST ANX-1 & 2) and rationalizing tax slabs.

Overall, GST has been a transformative governance reform, making the tax system more efficient, transparent, and cooperative, despite initial transitional challenges.

National Education Policy (NEP) 2020

The NEP 2020 replaced the outdated 1986 policy, emphasizing inclusivity and digital learning (MHRD, 2020). Amendments promoting multilingual education and vocational training aim to democratize access to quality education, aligning with democratic governance goals.

- **Key Policy Amendments:**
- **Structural Change:** Replaces the 10+2 structure with a 5+3+3+4 pedagogical model, integrating Early Childhood Care and Education (ECCE) and strengthening foundational learning.
- **Multidisciplinary & Flexibility:** Breaks down rigid separations between streams, allowing students flexible subject choices and promoting a holistic, multidisciplinary education across schools and higher education.
- **Regulatory Overhaul:** Establishes a single, overarching regulator—the Higher Education Commission of India (HECI)—to replace multiple bodies, reducing fragmentation and focusing on standard-setting and accreditation rather than control.
- **Internationalization & Language:** Promotes the internationalization of Indian campuses and emphasizes instruction in mother tongue/regional languages until at least Grade 5.
- **Impact on Governance:**
- **Decentralization and Empowerment:** The policy empowers schools, colleges, and universities with greater autonomy in designing curricula and awarding degrees, shifting governance from a top-down model to a more collaborative one.
- **Outcome-Based Accreditation:** The focus shifts from input-based regulation to outcome-based accreditation, governed by a single regulator (HECI), aiming to improve accountability and quality.
- **Technology Integration:** Mandates the creation of a National Educational Technology Forum (NETF) to facilitate technology-based infrastructure, planning, and administration, making educational governance more data-driven and efficient.

- **Cooperative Federalism:** As education is a concurrent subject, the NEP's implementation requires extensive consultation and coordination between the Centre and states, testing and strengthening the framework of cooperative federalism.

By restructuring the educational architecture and its regulatory philosophy, NEP 2020 seeks to transform educational governance from a command-and-control system to an enabling and facilitative one, fostering greater innovation and inclusivity.

X. CHALLENGES IN POLICY AMENDMENTS

Despite Progress, Challenges Persist

- **Bureaucratic resistance** slows implementation (Jain, 2018).
- **Lack of stakeholder consultation** leads to policy gaps (Chakraborty, 2021).
- **Political interference** undermines evidence-based reforms (Kapur & Mehta, 2005).

Recommendations for Strengthening Democratic Governance

1. **Enhance public participation** in policymaking through consultations and digital platforms.
2. **Strengthen oversight mechanisms** to ensure accountability in policy implementation.
3. **Adopt evidence-based amendments** using data analytics and impact assessments.

XI. CONCLUSION

The journey of democratic governance in India is a continuous process of evolution, negotiation, and reform. As this paper has argued, the vitality of this democracy is intrinsically linked to the dynamism of its public policies. The static nature of any policy in a society as complex and rapidly changing as India's is a recipe for obsolescence and governance failure. Therefore, amendments in existing public policies are not merely administrative adjustments; they are the essential lifeblood of a responsive and robust democratic system. This research has demonstrated that structured, inclusive, and evidence-based policy amendments are a decisive mechanism for strengthening the core tenets of democratic governance: transparency, accountability, and citizen participation.

The analysis began by establishing the foundational relationship between democratic governance and public policy, drawing from theoretical frameworks that emphasize the state's duty to be both effective and legitimate. The Indian Constitution, with its profound commitment to justice, liberty, equality, and fraternity enshrined in the Preamble, Fundamental Rights, and Directive Principles of State Policy, provides the immutable moral and legal compass for all policy action. Any amendment, whether to the RTI Act or the GST framework, must be evaluated against this constitutional bedrock to ensure it enhances, rather than diminishes, democratic values. The distinction between policies with direct and indirect influence further illuminates the multifaceted nature of governance, where both immediate welfare schemes and long-term strategic frameworks collectively shape the citizen-state relationship and the quality of democracy.

The examination of key legislative and administrative reforms—the Right to Information Act, the Goods and Services Tax, and the National Education Policy—serves as a powerful testament to the transformative potential of policy amendments. The RTI Act emerged as a landmark intervention that fundamentally altered the power dynamic between the citizen and the state, embedding transparency as a non-negotiable component of governance. However, its subsequent amendment in 2019 also serves as a cautionary tale, highlighting how changes perceived to dilute institutional autonomy can trigger legitimate concerns about accountability. This underscores a critical lesson: the *process* and *intent* behind an amendment are as crucial as the amendment itself. A reform that weakens checks and balances, even if framed as an efficiency measure, can erode democratic trust.

Conversely, the implementation of GST exemplifies how a policy amendment, despite initial complexities, can strengthen democratic governance by fostering cooperative federalism. The GST Council, as a sustained forum for negotiation between the Centre and states, has institutionalized a new form of political and fiscal dialogue. This has not only economic but profound democratic significance, as it moves inter-governmental relations beyond zero-sum politics towards collaborative problem-solving. Similarly, the NEP 2020, with its emphasis on decentralization, flexibility, and inclusivity, represents a paradigmatic shift in educational governance. Its success, however, hinges on amendments that empower local institutions and address implementation gaps, proving that a progressive policy on paper requires a congruent administrative culture on the ground.

Despite these significant strides, the path of policy reform in India is fraught with persistent challenges. Bureaucratic inertia, political short-termism, inadequate stakeholder consultation, and the sheer complexity of balancing diverse interests in a federal polity often act as formidable barriers. The gap between policy intent and implementation remains a chasm where governance failures often occur, disproportionately affecting the most marginalized populations. Furthermore, emerging challenges—from the ethical dilemmas of artificial intelligence and data privacy to the existential threat of climate change—demand a new generation of agile, forward-looking policies. The areas identified as needing urgent policy attention, such as employment, healthcare, and social security, are not just sectoral issues; they are the very arenas where the legitimacy of Indian democracy will be tested.

To navigate these challenges and harness the full potential of policy amendments, the paper proposes a multi-pronged approach rooted in the principles of democratic governance:

1. **Deepening Participatory Amendment Processes:** Policy formulation and amendment must transition from a top-down, bureaucratic exercise to a collaborative endeavour. This requires institutionalizing pre-legislative consultations, making greater use of digital platforms for public feedback, and actively engaging civil society organizations and grassroots representatives. The goal is to move from token participation to meaningful co-creation, ensuring policies are grounded in the lived realities of citizens.
2. **Championing Evidence-Based Policymaking:** The era of policy-making driven solely by political ideology or expediency must give way to a culture of evidence. This necessitates investing in robust data infrastructure, strengthening independent policy research institutions, and mandating rigorous impact assessments for all major amendments. Data-driven decisions are inherently more transparent and less susceptible to capture by vested interests.
3. **Strengthening the Ecosystem of Accountability:** Amendments should be designed to reinforce, not weaken, accountability mechanisms. This includes protecting the autonomy of regulatory institutions like the Information Commissions, enhancing the capacity of audit bodies, and promoting social audits, particularly for schemes directly impacting local communities. The Right to Information Act itself must be safeguarded as a master key for unlocking other accountability tools.
4. **Building Adaptive and Future-Ready Governance:** The policy amendment process itself needs to become more agile and iterative. Policies should be designed as living documents with built-in review clauses and sunset provisions, allowing for regular course correction based on monitoring and evaluation. This is especially critical for managing the disruptions of new technologies and the evolving climate crisis.

In final words, the task of strengthening democratic governance in India through policy amendments is a continuous and collective enterprise. It demands vigilance from citizens, integrity from institutions, and foresight from political leadership. The amendments analysed in this paper reveal a clear pattern: when reforms are guided by constitutional morality, informed by public deliberation, and implemented with a commitment to equity, they fortify the democratic edifice. When they are rushed, opaque, or serve narrow interests, they risk creating cracks in its foundation. As India continues its journey as the world's largest democracy, the wisdom with which it amends its public policies will ultimately determine its ability to secure justice, liberty, and dignity for all its citizens, thereby fulfilling the profound promise of its Constitution. The work of perfecting the union through thoughtful reform is never finished, but it is the most vital work a democracy can undertake.

REFERENCES

Aiyar, Y., & Samji, S. (2009). *Citizen participation in public services: The experience of NREGA in India*. World Bank.

Bevir, M. (2006). Democratic governance: Systems and radical perspectives. *Public Administration Review*, *66*(3), 426–436. DOI: 10.1111/j.1540-6210.2006.00599.x

Birdsall, W. F. (2009). The role of the client in informing science: To be informed and to inform. Informing Science. *The International Journal of an Emerging Transdiscipline*, *12*, 147–157. DOI: 10.28945/432

Birkland, T. A. (2011). *An introduction to the policy process: Theories, concepts, and models of public policy making* (3rd ed.). PHI Learning.

Brown, M. M. (2003). Democratic governance: Toward a framework for sustainable peace. *Global Governance*, *9*(2), 141–146. DOI: 10.1163/19426720-00902003

Chakraborty, P. (2021). *Public policy in India: Participation and accountability*. Oxford University Press.

Dahl, R. A. (1989). *Democracy and its critics*. Yale University Press.

Drèze, J., & Khera, R. (2017). Recent social security initiatives in India. *World Development*, *98*, 555–572. DOI: 10.1016/j.worlddev.2017.05.010

Fung, A. (2006). Varieties of participation in complex governance. *Public Administration Review*, *66*(S1), 66–75. DOI: 10.1111/j.1540-6210.2006.00667.x

Grindle, M. S. (2004). Good enough governance: Poverty reduction and reform in developing countries. *Governance: An International Journal of Policy, Administration and Institutions*, *17*(4), 525–548. DOI: 10.1111/j.0952-1895.2004.00256.x

Heller, P. (2009). Making citizens from below: India's emerging local government. In *Democratic deficits: The governance of India's public institutions* (pp. 57–82). Cambridge University Press.

Ingrams, A. (2019). Big data and Dahl's challenge of democratic governance. *The Review of Policy Research*, *36*(3), 357–377. DOI: 10.1111/ropr.12331

Kapur, D., & Mehta, P. B. (2005). *Public institutions in India: Performance and design*. Oxford University Press.

Kumar, A., & Narain, V. (2015). Public policy and governance in India. *Vision (Basel)*, *18*(4), 257–260. DOI: 10.1177/0972262914555815

Ministry of Finance. (2021). GST reforms and economic growth. Government of India. https://www.finmin.nic.in

North, D. C. (1990). *Institutions, institutional change and economic performance*. Cambridge University Press.

Peisakhin, L., & Pinto, P. (2010). Is transparency an effective anti-corruption strategy? Evidence from a field experiment in India. *Regulation & Governance*, *4*(3), 261–280. DOI: 10.1111/j.1748-5991.2010.01081.x

Polizzi, G. (2019). Information literacy in the digital age: Why critical digital literacy matters for democracy. In *Media and information literacy in higher education* (pp. 1–24). DOI: 10.29085/9781783303922.003

Shattock, M. (2017). The "world class" university and international ranking systems: What are the policy implications for governments and institutions? *Policy Reviews in Higher Education*, *1*(1–2), 4–21. DOI: 10.1080/23322969.2016.1236669

Shehatta, I., & Mahmood, K. (2016). Correlation among top 100 universities in the major six global rankings: Policy implications. *Scientometrics*, *109*(2), 1231–1254. DOI: 10.1007/s11192-016-2103-3

Strebel, M. A., Kübler, D., & Marcinkowski, F. (2019). The importance of input and output legitimacy in democratic governance: Evidence from a population-based survey experiment in four West European countries. *European Journal of Political Research*, *58*(2), 488–513. DOI: 10.1111/1475-6765.12293

Tilak, J. B. G. (2021). *Education policy in India: Challenges and prospects*. Routledge.

World Bank. (1994). *Governance: The World Bank's experience*. World Bank.

World Bank. (2017). *World Development Report 2017: Governance and the law*. World Bank. DOI: 10.1596/978-1-4648-0950-7

Chapter 5

New Professional Framework as a Catalyst to Improve Service Delivery in Local Government

Mandisi Matyana
http://orcid.org/0000-0001-6928-4724
University of Zululand, South Africa

Xolani Thusi
http://orcid.org/0000-0001-7316-6165
University of Johannesburg, South Africa

ABSTRACT

Professionalizing public service has been the topic of scholarly debate for many years. Such debates have focused more on local government; hence they are identified as main looters of public funds. Poor service delivery in local government continues to be a major issue in South Africa; hence, many citizens find themselves in serious poverty and unfavored living circumstances. In 2020 the Minister of Public Service and Administration has adopted and approved the new national framework for professionalizing the public sector. The framework also emphasizes that the public officials must comply with Section 195 principles of the South African Constitution, Batho Pele principles, and Public Service Chater while also ensuring that qualified and competent staff are appointed for the positions. Therefore, this chapter analyzes the role of this new professional framework in the delivery of local government services.

DOI: 10.4018/979-8-2600-1618-3.ch005

1. INTRODUCTION

Improved service delivery remains the main purpose or reason we have a local government in South Africa. However, this is not always the case in most of the municipalities hence their service provision tends to be poor and confronted with many dysfunctionalities. According to Thusi et al. (2023a), the South African local government is confronted with issues such as lack of political will, corruption, lack consequence management, lack of accountability, cadre deployment, etc. These issues are caused by various issues and practices within local government such as political interference in administration, comradeship that hinders proper accountability and proper management, improper appointment of staff to position, more especially in senior management positions, compromised community participation in governance platforms such as Integrated Development Plans (Matyana & Mthethwa, 2022b; Mamokhere & Meyer, 2023). Over these identified issues or practices, the communities have been affected. Their freedoms have been infringed and compromised. They have been complaining to the government that the local government is not doing well with the provision of services to their communities (Matyana & Thusi, 2023). Their cry has been in the form of vandalism of some of the public goods, violent strikes, and refusal to participate in general elections (Schulz-Herzenberg, 2020; Chauke, 2020; Mamokhere, 2021).

Since 1994, numerous academics have debated local administration, especially municipalities. Some of these scholars include Matlala & Uwizeyimana (2020); Thusi et al. (2023); and Matyana & Thusi (2023a). These academics believe that the area of government most impacted by mishandled public finances is local government. Stated differently, this branch of government is thought to be the primary pilferer of public monies, particularly from the municipalities. The majority of officials participate in corrupt acts, unauthorized and irregular spending, wasteful spending, etc. Concerns have also been raised by Auditor General of South Africa regarding the rising number of South African municipalities that are not receiving clean audit results. According to Auditor General of South Africa out of 257 municipalities only 27 have received a clean audit in the financial year of 2020/2021 and because of such a failure, billions were lost in local government.

Again, in 2020 over this issue and other practices facing the public sector, the minister Public Service and Administration saw the need to make the situation and intervened. The minister has signed and promulgated the new national framework for professionalizing the public sector. This framework aims to ensure that proper service delivery is achieved throughout the public sector. The standard of service delivery is being improved and the public and ordinary citizens of South Africa are happy with the provision of services by public sector institutions including the local government, particularly municipalities. To be specific, this framework has the following key objectives:

- 'Entrenching a dynamic professionalisation system in the public service.
- Strengthening and enabling the legal and policy instruments to professionalise categories of occupations in the public service.
- Enhancing and building partnerships and relationships with professional bodies.
- Ensuring meritocracy in the recruitment and career management of public servants, which are in line with the National Development Plan and the Medium-Term Strategic Framework.
- Initiating consequence management for material irregularities through the transgression mechanisms available to professional bodies and the Public Audit Amendment Act of (Act 5 of 2018) '.

Although these objectives may be different, the main purpose is to ensure that only ethical, competent and qualified staff are appointed in senior or authority positions and to support the continuous learning of all public sector employees. This framework further supports the professionalization of all public servants. It is important that public servants always maintain professional behavior as they are given authority to take crucial decisions for the state and for the state funds. This assertion is also supported by Aliushyna et al. (2022) that professionalisation promotes effective and efficient use of resources in the public sector. Based on the background mentioned above, particularly poor service delivery in local government and the importance of professionalising public servants to improve their ability to provide better services to communities and ordinary citizens of South Africa, this chapter aims to evaluate the new professional policy framework in local government. The objective is to make sure that local government, particularly the municipalities, implement this framework effectively and that their employees are professional and committed to providing effective service delivery.

2. BACKGROUND

The South African Constitution outlines the foundational rights for all citizens. These rights include the entitlement to basic services such as water, housing, education, and health, which some of these services are mandated to the local government to provide. Therefore, the Constitution of South Africa sought the local government to be professional. This assertion is also supported by Kaizer (2022) that the Constitution remains the backbone of public sector professionalism. It provides relevant chapters and sections that force the public servants to be professional. The word professionalization is best defined by Section 195 of the Constitution. To be specific, Section 195 (1) outlines the fundamental ideals and principles of public administration. These include a shared ethos and set of values that are intended to foster "a high standard of professional ethics." Professional conduct encompasses various aspects such as developing policies in a participatory and people-centered manner, providing services with transparency, efficiency, and impartiality, and managing and governing institutions with responsibility and integrity. To maximize human potential, public administration also requires the cultivation of effective career development and human resource management strategies. To be more specific, Section 195 of the Constitution outlines these principles as follows:

Table 1. Principles of Section 195 of the Constitution

A high level of professional ethics must be promoted and maintained	This implies that public servants must be ethical. They must be able to differentiate what is right or wrong in each practice they do. Ethics plays a crucial role in ensuring that everyone behaves appropriately. Mostafa & Abed El-Motalib (2020) observe ethics as a viable vehicle for effective service delivery which requires employees to not do things, they would not appreciate to be done to them so they should "treat others in a manner that they would also like to be treated".
The promotion of effective, efficient, and economic use of resources	According to Thusi et al (2023) governments do face some scarcity in the provision of goods and services; therefore, it is important for the public servants to manage the available resources in a most effective, efficient, and economical manner. This assertion is in line with this principle. It requires the public servants to use money for the specific requirement. They must also avoid risks with taxpayer money. In support of this statement, Christensen et al. (2020) states that the effective, efficient, and economical use of public funds improve the lives of citizens as they tend to live better.
Public administration must be development oriented	This principle requires the public servants to be transformative in their practices. They must always keep in mind that society is changing, and different socio-economic issues are arising as well. Such economic issues include poverty, unemployment, and inequality, so they must be able to provide programs and agendas that respond to these socioeconomic issues.
Services must be provided impartially, fairly, equitably, and without bias	The study findings of Matyana & Mthethwa (2022) have noted that some of the public services they are provided in a bias manner by the officials, of which such biasness is caused by various reasons such as political dynamics, geographical positioning of the village, council tensions, etc. However, such practices conflict with this principle. This principle requires public servants to provide services in a manner that they value human lives. They must always be fair and impartial in providing goods and services. They must also meet specific quality and quantity requirements. If they fail to do so, it causes unnecessary service delivery backlogs and disparities (Matyana & Mthethwa, 2022; Mamokhere, 2023; Yende, 2023).

continued on following page

Table 1. Continued

People's needs must be responded to, and public participation must be encouraged	Public participation remains the cornerstone of democracy. According to Matyana and Mthethwa (2022), it is a viable vehicle towards good governance. Hügel & Davies (2020) supports this by stating that public participation is also about empowering and engaging the citizens in decisions affecting them to achieve transformed governance. Therefore, this principle requires public servants to be involved with ordinary affected citizens when it comes to governance. It discourages the fat that government must assume the needs of the citizens of the community; rather there should be an engagement of understanding what is really expected by the citizens and community. This helps to ensure that people's needs are being effectively addressed and public servants do not waste money on unnecessary and less important goods and services (Wahlund & Palm, 2022).
Public accountability and transparency	Transparency and accountability cannot be separated in the discipline of public administration and in practice. They are vital tools towards good governance. They force the public servants to be open about their practices and also give accounts of the actions taken. Transparency and accountability help to avoid inaccuracy, inequity, and misconduct in governance (Winker et al., 2023).

Source: Designed by the authors.

In professionalization of public servants, the Batho-Pele principles still play a huge role. They are outlined in terms of the White Paper on Transforming Service Delivery (1997). Mojapelo et al. (2023) observes the Batho Pele principles as a tool for ensuring reliable and customer-oriented service. Basically, these principles guide public servants towards providing effective and efficient customer services to the citizens of South Africa. There are eight, and each principle addresses a specific requirement expected form public servants and public institutions. First, they are required to consult the citizens when it comes to the quantity and caliber of public services that they receive; citizens ought to be consulted and, if feasible, given a choice in what services they receive. Secondly, they are required to public servants to maintain services standards for the services they provide to the citizens. Third, public servants must allow citizens to have access to services they are entitled to. Fourth, public servants are also expected to give full accurate information to the citizens with regard to the services they are entitled to. Fifthly, public servants are also expected to be open and transparent when it comes to service delivery, they must be able to give information to the citizens of South Africa on how they charge the costs and who is doing the service. Sixthly, public servants are also expected to redress where it is necessary; they must be able to apologize and give an explanation about the mistake they have committed and indicate the cover-up plan. Again, they must treat all citizens with courtesy. Lastly, public servants must promote value for money in their practices. They must be able to use the available budgets in a most economical and efficient manner and further give the necessary information on their spendings.

This professionalization framework is also supported by five pillars, which are regarded as a strategic plan of action on how to implement this professionalization framework in the public sector. These include, Pre-entry, recruiting, and selection, Induction and on-boarding, Planning, and performance management, continually leaning and development, Career progression and career incidents. These pillars are just briefly explained in this section; they will be explained more in Section 4 as the researcher will be linking the application of these pillars in local government of which that is the main purpose of this paper. The focus is to explain more what these pillars mean to local government and what are the implementation expectations to enhance service delivery.

3. METHODOLOGY

A qualitative method was used to collect data. This method was used due to its flexibility to get more in-depth information for the study. Systematic review was used as a tool to collect data. A systematic review employs critical methodologies to identify, describe, and assess pertinent research in order to provide an academic synthesis of the evidence that is currently accessible on a topic that has been presented in an understandable manner. Before distilling opinions into a well-informed conclusion backed by substantial evidence, a systematic review collects, analyses, and assesses data from published research on the topic (Omazic & Zunk, 2021). Zunder (2021) provides support for this method by stating that it includes guidelines for organizing a written literature discussion that can be used in the research process. The researchers have only focused on service delivery, professionalisation published articles and related reports and document published in the last five years. The ones with relevant information were selected in this study but the ones that were ill-relevant were filtered out.

4. RESULTS AND DISCUSSION

The results and discussion of this study are discussed and presented below. They are primarily looking at two main factors, namely, why the South African local government must be professionalized (current challenges facing local government), and Strategies for enforcing professionalization in local government, of which these strategies are in line with the new professional framework on professionalizing public sector.

Why Professionalize Local Government (Current Challenges)

The need to professionalize local government comes from various challenges that are currently facing local government. These challenges include cadre deployment, shortages of proper skills, failure to comply with minimum entry requirements, etc. These challenges tend to reduce the capacity for municipal service delivery and lead to many managerial dysfunctionalities. The following are discussed:

Cadre Deployment

According to Thusi et al. (2023a), the deployment of cadres is one of the factors that has the biggest negative impact on the effective administration of local government budgets. According to these scholars, cadre deployment promotes poor service performance and is related to a number of managerial issues, including delegating inexperienced staff to handle service delivery. Cadre deployment is the term used to describe the process by which the ruling party chooses and employs party members or supporters. The deployment of a cache impedes transparency and trustworthy governance, since it is associated with insufficient accountability. Because cadre deployment encourages them to avoid responsibilities, employees can cover for one another due to their friendship. Matyana & Mthethwa (2022b) provide evidence to support the aforementioned claim, stating that cadre deployment has a detrimental effect on communities and ordinary citizens in addition to affecting service delivery performance and status. Due to inadequate service delivery and financial mismanagement on the part of municipal officials, communities and their residents often find themselves in challenging circumstances. Furthermore, these challenging circumstances prevent individuals from taking advantage of opportunities for social and economic development, as well as higher living standards (Zulu et al., 2022). It is evident that when cadre deployment is embraced and employed as a successful means of providing services, there is a risk of misappropriation of public monies because of related problems, including a lack of responsibility in governance, a lack of transparency, and a comradeship relationship.

Shortage of Skills

Local government employees must have a variety of financial skills to handle public finances responsibly. These abilities include problem solving, financial planning, risk assessment, financial analysis, and budgeting, among others. Jumanne (2021) asserts that having sound financial management skills is crucial to ensure that municipalities provide better services. They help to ensure that workers consistently make wise choices regarding available funds. In order to provide better service delivery, this helps to guarantee that municipal finances are open and transparent. According to Enwereji (2022), most South African municipalities receive clean audits from the South African Auditor General because they lack the necessary expertise to manage funds well. Enwereji claims that a lack of financial literacy leads to further problems including poor consequence management and responsibility. The Auditor General of South Africa supports this assertion in the MFMA report for 2020–2021, stating that the majority of South African municipalities perform poorly or handle their finances inefficiently as a result of 'Limited skills and capacity in finance, information technology, and technical units (which are responsible for infrastructure projects) led municipalities to rely heavily on consultants. Vacancies and instability in key positions, such as municipal manager and chief financial officer, contributed to the limited improvement in audit results and delays in dealing with material irregularities and other transgressions. '

Failure to Comply With Entry Requirements and Experience

The Minister of Cooperative Governance and Traditional Affairs (COGTA) is authorized by the Municipal Systems Act to establish the minimum qualifications for entrance and the required work experience to fill positions, particularly those involving management. This covers jobs such as chief financial officers, department heads, and municipal managers, among others. However, it is clear that several municipalities across the nation do not adhere to the minimal admission requirements and experience requirements set forth by the COGTA minister. According to Olvera and Avellaneda (2019), there is a favorable correlation between performance and effective work experience. These academics claim that an employee's performance usually improves or vice versa once they get job experience. It has been noted that because local government employs cadres, work experience and minimal qualifications are frequently compromised or avoided in South African municipalities (Masuku & Jili, 2019). Political parties aim to assign their supporters to important municipal jobs, such municipal administrators, even though these candidates lack the necessary training and expertise. The claim that certain municipalities persist in selecting municipal administrators and senior managers who do not possess the necessary qualifications for their positions is corroborated by COGTA (2020).

Only 31 of the 57 senior management appointments made in all provinces in South Africa in 2020, according to the COGTA minister, were suitable and in compliance with the Municipal Systems Act and its regulations. A total of 26 posts were unfilled or were not in compliance with the Municipal Systems Act and its rules. In the end, these illegitimate senior post fillings have an impact on the towns' financial management; as a result, the hired personnel will not have the ability or knowledge to properly manage the municipal finances.

Political Interference

One of the main problems is political interference in South African towns. Political interference in administrative matters is becoming more and more obstinate in South African municipalities (Matyana & Mthethwa, 2022a). Municipalities struggle greatly, according to Mngomezulu (2020), to manage interactions between officials and politicians. Tensions between influential political and administrative figures in the towns appear to be the standard, as is improper political meddling in administrative matters. Political interference is the process by which the municipality's political leaders, such as the mayor and council members, encroach on administrative responsibilities that were not initially assigned to them. Political figures lack the ability and expertise to carry out such tasks because they are not included in administrative procedures. Political interference is not good for service delivery; therefore, it compromised the performance and the proper financial management of the municipality (Eja & Ramegowda, 2020). Masuku and Jili (2019) also support that "the political interface in local municipalities greatly affects effective and efficient administration, as well as growth opportunities. Administrators therefore have the important function of ensuring that explicit assignments of objectives and administrative functions are wholly separate from the policymaking activities of government. '

Lack of Consequence Management

In South Africa, officials who have been proven guilty or unethical in the course of their work are not subject to consequence management in government or public organizations. Both political and appointed authorities are affected by this issue. It is now commonplace for authorities to misuse or steal public funds without facing consequences or being held accountable for their actions. This issue has a big impact on local government, especially municipalities. The lack of consequence management undermines the requirements of the South African Constitution and other governmental financial acts, especially the Public Finance Management Act and the Municipal Finance Management Act. In addition to the breach of these legal frameworks, the primary victims of this money loss are regular South Africans who are waiting for efficient service delivery. Because there is a lack of consequence management, which results in waste of public funds and corruption, government officials are aware that they will not be held accountable for their improper activities (Bergeron, 2015). As a result, the government needs to speak up in favour of consequence management in public institutions.

Lack of Political Will

One of the negative consequences that affects South Africa's service delivery is a lack of effective political leadership. According to Thusi et al. (2023a), a lack of political will is the inability of politicians to make decisions that will have a beneficial influence on the institutions they manage and the provision of services. These academics see politicians as having a negative impact on the provision of services in South Africa. These failures include poor consequence management, lack of dedication, corruption, and lack of public accountability. Any of these setbacks impair the public sector institution's performance and capabilities, in addition to creating certain dysfunctions within the organization. Municipalities are classified as the primary sites of government theft because it has been found that these setbacks occur more frequently in local government (Amundsen, 2019). Baum et al. (2022) agrees with this statement, stating that a lack of political will stems from the political leadership abusing their position, which in turn disrupts the regular or systematic course of events. Therefore, it is crucial to ensure that politicians continue to have strong political will to ensure improved service delivery to the public and provide strategic leadership capable of handling a wide range of governance-related concerns.

Lack of Accountability

Transparency and accountability cannot be separated. They are moving in the same direction, even if they appear to be taking different paths (Sibanda et al., 2020). These scholars also demonstrate how accountability and openness improve value for money as cornerstones of effective government. To be transparent and responsible, public institutions and officials must take ownership of the results of financial expenditures and report on, defend, and explain their activities. In addition to ensuring that communities and citizens obtain the necessary proof, accountability also improves justice in the provision of services, according to Shin & Park (2019). The assertion that successful accountability leads to better decision-making in service delivery is further reinforced by McKenzie et al. (2023). This is a result of authorities' fear of making decisions that aren't optimal for growth and the public interest or for sound governance.

Combating corruption is one of the main functions of accountability in the provision of services (Ejiogu et al., 2019; Kohler & Dimancesco, 2020; Thusi et al. (2023b). Over the years, allegations and reports of corruption have been directed towards South African authorities. When the Auditor General releases the audit report each year, there has been mismanagement or theft of public funds as a result of corrupt activities. According to BusinessTech's 2022 report, South Africa is among the nations with the highest rates of public sector corruption. Of which these corruption practices take place in a form of maladministration, procurement corruption, abuse of authority, bribery, extortion, fraud, employment corruption, misappropriate of resources. Whatever form of corruption exists in the public sector or inside the government, it is bad and needs to be stopped because it erodes accountability and hinders transparency. The South African Auditor General agrees that the government needs a clear, effective, and efficient framework for holding people accountable (Matyana & Sibiya, 2024). The Auditor General goes on to explain that accountability transforms the lives of ordinary people and promotes constructive change in the public sector.

Strategies for Enforcing Professionalization in Local Government

According to the New Professional Framework, the above challenges can be improved by enforcing the professionalization, particularly at local government. This framework focuses on five key practices that must be applied in the public sector. They include pre-entry, recruiting and selection, induction and on-boarding, planning and performance management, continually learning development, career progression and career incidents.

Pre-Entry, Recruiting and Selection

To professionalise the public sector, pre-entry procedures must be tightened to ensure meritocratic appointments at all levels (NSG,2022). The most prominent problem in recruiting and selecting employees in South African local government is cadre deployment and nepotism conducted by political elites, which undermines municipalities' mandates and impedes service delivery. In Support, Mphahlele & Zandamela (2021) noted that political elites' involvement in hiring underqualified people and individuals with personal value interests hinders the development of service delivery structures and programmes. Political elitism, which prioritises personal interests, has a negative impact on human resource management techniques. Local government appointments made based on meeting pre-entry conditions, such as matching the applicant's qualifications, expertise, and abilities to the job description, can assist improve the professionalism of the local government sector and public service delivery. According to AGSA (2022), the Limpopo premier's office failed to reduce consultant costs by 60% as planned due to a lack of skills and capacity among finance officials to address internal control deficiencies. This is one of the examples of personnel who gained access to the systems due to a lack of strict pre-entry procedures in local government, which threatens long-term public service delivery. The Professionalisation Framework has been adopted, making it generally applicable to everybody, particularly at pre-entry assessments (NSG, 2022). The application of the framework has several potential benefits for the local government sector as an instrument of service delivery. One of the most noticeable benefits is the hiring of qualified personnel for crucial positions in local government. AGSA (2022) agreed that hiring qualified candidates for open jobs and professionalising local government according to the recently approved professionalisation framework are essential for sustainability.

Induction and On-Boarding

Onboarding, also known as induction, is the process of training new employees to understand the organization's norms, rules, and internal dynamics, allowing them to function effectively as members and stakeholders (Iguodala-Cole, Anto & Jawondo,2020). A workplace orientation helps individuals learn the culture and dynamics of their work environment. Induction to the public sector and workplace orientation must occur simultaneously. The existing method of inducting new staff months or years following their appointment lacks merit (NSG,2022). As shown by the NSG, the existing induction strategy in the public sector is ineffective, limiting the capacity of the South African public sector to carry out a seamless and progressive induction to quickly profit from recruited. Joseph & Sridevi (2015) alluded that accelerating the transition of new employees into their responsibilities gives organizations a competitive advantage by allowing them to reap benefits sooner. To reap the benefits of newly employed individuals, the South African local government sector must strengthen their induction process and adapt them to the organisational culture. To make this possible, NSG (2022) suggested the following:

Participate in induction programs before assuming duty

Induction programs are mandatory for all public personnel, including those in Local Government, SOE Boards, Military, State Security, Police, and Correctional Services, before starting work. Political leaders, advisors, and traditional leaders must complete induction programs within 90 days after their employment.

Compulsory Participation in the Reorientation Program

All public sector employees, including local government, SOE boards, the military, state security, police and correctional services, traditional institutions of leadership, political office staff, and advisors, must participate in mandatory reorientation programmes. Provide coaching and mentoring programs for senior management, specialists, and technical positions during onboarding within the first six months of employment.

Planning and Performance Management

Performance management involves creating and effectively managing organisational goals to achieve desired outcomes (Poister,2010). NSG (2022) indicated that professionalization should be prioritized in planning, performance management, and appraisal systems, with specific performance criteria and assessment tools for different types of personnel. According to Broadbent and Laughlin (2009), performance management involves planning work and setting expectations, continually monitoring performance, developing the capacity to perform, periodically rating performance in a summary fashion, and rewarding good performance. To evaluate whether employees meet the criteria, the local government should review their performance and compare it to the expected performance. When a local government discovers that its personnel are failing to meet the defined criteria, it must devise measures to improve and develop their performance. This procedure will improve professionalism, organisational performance, and service delivery. According to AGSA (2022), municipalities with clean audits demonstrate strong financial and performance management practices and comply with relevant legislation. They provide proper planning, competent implementation, and reliable performance reporting. Performance evaluation is an important instrument for measuring the frameworks established by any organisation for its personnel. This tool tracks individual contributions and performance against organisational goals, identifies strengths and areas for improvement, and assesses whether the goals are met. It also acts as a foundation for future planning and development (Daoanis,2012). The local government must ensure that employee performance reviews are conducted properly, as employees may be discouraged if they perceive that the appraisals were biased. This is significant because performance appraisal is a technique that compares individual performance to desired performance and rewards those who perform well. When properly implemented, it has the potential to increase professionalisation in local government and improve municipalities' ability to provide effective and efficient services.

Continually Learning and Development (CPD)

Lifelong learning, often known as CPD, helps individuals retain their professional knowledge and abilities. CPD can take many different forms, including formal educational courses and learning through ordinary work practices. CPD refers to upgrading professional knowledge through structured, short courses for occupational groups including physicians, attorneys, and teachers (Collin, Van der Heijden & Lewis, 2012). Continuing professional development (CPD) helps maintain and improve knowledge, abilities, and attitudes in various jobs (Namaganda,2020).

According to NSG (2022), improving continuous learning and professional development interventions is crucial to the successful professionalisation of the public sector. The proposals are as follows:

- Identify suitable training and learning pathways to help employees become more professional.
- The NSG will launch an executive education programme to professionalise executives in institutions and refresh their skills. Improve current knowledge and skills using lifetime learning programs.
- Fully implement the 2014 Cabinet resolution to modernise supply chain management (SCM) and the formation of an SCM council.
- Create an HRM&D council to coordinate interests and professionalise human resource management and development in the public sector.
- Create and apply CPD frameworks and policies. A framework for CPD activities should incorporate significant developments in education and training, including the use of technology to promote learning and ensure quality instructional interventions.
- Collaborate with HEIs and SAQA-recognized professional bodies to enhance the CPD program as a capacity development tool for employees at all levels.

Career Progression and Career Incidents

Employees are an asset to every organization and contribute significantly to its success. Career progression is a reward system used by organizations to increase employee productivity via a series of connected job experiences and activities across a lifetime (Mugaa, Guyo & Otieno, 2018). The local government should not maintain personnel at the same employment level for an extended period. Routine tasks that are repeated over an extended period may discourage and inhibit employee performance and professionalism. The local government must devise strategies to ensure that qualified staff who meet the standards for the next level advance to the next level or grade. Career progression can be defined as the progress of a person throughout their career. Career development refers to the good outcomes of a person's professional experience. Junior employees see senior management positions as opportunities for progression due to a lack of comparable technical positions (Agyekum, Kissi, Danku, Ampratwum & Amegatsey,2020). To improve career progression and career incidents, the NSG (2022) recommended the following:

- Career Management must align with South Africa's National Policy for an Integrated Career Development System. This includes career guidance, education, and adaptation to support public servants throughout their careers.

Establish a minimum number of years of service for advancement from one level to the next.

Introduce a public sector exam for promotion from junior to middle management, or a required course in relevant subjects of study designed by the NSG.

Identify public sector occupations based on job content, entry requirements, promotion, career progression, mobility, and professional development.

Rewrite the rotating door policy (2008) to allow public personnel to shift between the corporate, academic, and public sectors to promote "fresh and current" practices.

Revise and improve the Recognition of Prior Learning (RPL) policy to reduce its numerous interpretations. Consider targeted recruitment to optimise its use in the public sector.

5. CONCLUSION

In conclusion, this chapter has analyzed the new Professionalization Framework, and its application in the public service. However, the researchers were more interested in the implementation and application of this framework at the local government level. It has been noted that this framework could play a crucial role in local government if it is properly applied. This is because the local government is faced with various challenges that automatically affect service delivery at the end of the day. These challenges include lack of political will, high levels of corruption, lack of transparency and accountability, failure to comply with necessary skills and experience. These challenges cause some incompetence within the local government. Therefore, the researchers discussed how five key objectives of the new professionalization framework could be effectively applied in local government. These include pre-entry, recruiting, and selection; Induction and on-boarding; Continually leaning and development (CPD); Career progression and career incidents. The purpose of this discussion is to advise and ensure that the local government is professional and committed to making South Africa a better place for its inhabitants.

Study Limitations

This research was limited with to service delivery and professionalization information within the South African public sector, particularly, for local government. The new professional framework for the public sector was used as a specific point of departure and leading stick for this study.

Recommended Future Studies

This study recommends the future study that will look at the establishment of a professional body for all public sector employees. Such a professional body must admit, accept, and take removal actions of the public sector employees. In other words, all public sector employees must apply to that professional body and be accepted before they can start practicing or taking part in service delivery management. The body must have specific regulations and guidelines on regulating the behavior of public sector employees, and there must be clear communication on how the body will deal with non-complying employees. Such employees could be involved in illegal practices such as corruption, therefore, the body can remove them from the system and not be allowed to serve anymore in service delivery.

REFERENCES

Agyekum, K., Kissi, E., Danku, J. C., Ampratwum, G., & Amegatsey, G. S. (2020). Factors driving the career progression of construction project managers. *Journal of Engineering, Design and Technology, 18*(6), 1773–1791. DOI: 10.1108/JEDT-09-2019-0242

Aliushyna, N., Boiko, O., Hzhybovska, T., & Rak, Y. (2022). Professionalisation of public servants in the context of implementing public administration reforms. *Public Policy and Administration, 21*(5).

Amundsen, I. (Ed.). (2019). *Political corruption in Africa: Extraction and power preservation*. Edward Elgar Publishing. DOI: 10.4337/9781788972529

Baum, F., Townsend, B., Fisher, M., Browne-Yung, K., Freeman, T., Ziersch, A., & Friel, S. (2022). Creating political will for action on health equity: Practical lessons for public health policy actors. *International Journal of Health Policy and Management, 11*(7), 947. PMID: 33327689

Bergeron, W. P. (2015). Considering culture in evacuation planning and consequence management. *Journal of Emergency Management (Weston, Mass.), 13*(2), 87–92. DOI: 10.5055/jem.2015.0222 PMID: 25902292

Broadbent, J., & Laughlin, R. (2009). Performance management systems: A conceptual model. *Management Accounting Research, 20*(4), 283–295. DOI: 10.1016/j.mar.2009.07.004

Chauke, T. A. (2020). Youth apathy in an electoral democracy: A critical discourse on civil participation in South Africa. *African Journal of Gender. Social Development, 9*(3), 35.

Christensen, T., Yamamoto, K., & Aoyagi, S. (2020). Trust in local government: Service satisfaction, culture, and demography. *Administration & Society, 52*(8), 1268–1296. DOI: 10.1177/0095399719897392

Collin, K., Van der Heijden, B., & Lewis, P. (2012). Continuing professional development. *International Journal of Training and Development, 16*(3), 155–163. DOI: 10.1111/j.1468-2419.2012.00410.x

Daoanis, L. E. (2012). Performance Appraisal System: It's Implication to Employee Performance. *International journal of economics and management sciences, 2*(3), 55-62.

Eja, K. M., & Ramegowda, M. (2020). Government project failure in developing countries: A review with particular reference to Nigeria. *Global Journal of Social Sciences*, *19*, 35–47. DOI: 10.4314/gjss.v19i1.4

Ejiogu, A., Ejiogu, C., & Ambituuni, A. (2019). The dark side of transparency: Does the Nigeria extractive industries transparency initiative help or hinder accountability and corruption control? *The British Accounting Review*, *51*(5), 100811. DOI: 10.1016/j.bar.2018.10.004

Enwereji, P. C. (2022). Enhancing financial accountability in south African local municipalities: a consequence management viewpoint. Financial Studies, 26(4).

Hügel, S., & Davies, A. R. (2020). Public participation, engagement, and climate change adaptation: A review of the research literature. *Wiley Interdisciplinary Reviews: Climate Change*, *11*(4), e645. DOI: 10.1002/wcc.645 PMID: 35859618

Iguodala-Cole, H. I., Anto, J. B., & Jawondo, A. I. (2020). Effects of induction as an adjustment mechanism of recruits in industrial organizations in Nigeria. *International Journal of Development and Management Review*, *15*(1), 83–95.

Joseph, D., & Sridevi, M. S. (2015). Effective onboarding as a talent management tool for employee retention. *International Journal of Management and Social Sciences*, *3*(7), 175–186.

Jumanne, D. (2021). The Effects of Effective Management of Funds on Financial Institutions Service Delivery in Tanzania: A Case of Manungu SACCOS in Kigoma Municipality (Doctoral dissertation, The Open University of Tanzania).

Kaizer, R. M. (2022). From Cadre Deployment to Professionalizing Public Service in South Africa: A Reflective Approach to Service Delivery Improvement. *African Journal of Development Studies*, *2022*(si1), 21.

Kohler, J. C., & Dimancesco, D. (2020). The risk of corruption in public pharmaceutical procurement: how anti-corruption, transparency and accountability measures may reduce this risk. Global health action, 13(sup1), 1694745.

Mamokhere, J. (2021). Evaluating the impact of service delivery protests in relation to socio-economic development: a case of Greater Tzaneen local Municipality, South Africa. *African Journal of Development Studies (formerly AFFRIKA Journal of Politics, Economics and Society)*, *2021*(si1), 79-96.

Mamokhere, J. (2023). Sending a message to the top: The influence of service delivery protests on service delivery planning in South African municipalities. *Insights into Regional Development*, *5*(2), 60–71. DOI: 10.9770/IRD.2023.5.2(4)

Mamokhere, J., & Meyer, D. F. (2023). Towards an Exploration of the Significance of Community Participation in the Integrated Development Planning Process in South Africa. *Social Sciences (Basel, Switzerland)*, *12*(5), 256. DOI: 10.3390/socsci12050256

Masuku, M. M., & Jili, N. N. (2019). Public service delivery in South Africa: The political influence at local government level. *Journal of Public Affairs*, *19*(4), e1935. DOI: 10.1002/pa.1935

Matlala, L. S., & Uwizeyimana, D. E. (2020). Factors influencing the implementation of the auditor general's recommendations in South African municipalities. *African Evaluation Journal*, *8*(1), 1–11. DOI: 10.4102/aej.v8i1.464

Matyana, M., & Mthethwa, R. M. (2022a) community Participation Conundrum in the Winnie Madikizela Mandela Local Municipality Integrated Development Plan: Exploration of an EnhancedFuture.

Matyana, M. and Mthethwa, R.M., (2022b) Service Delivery Disparities at Winnie Madikizela Mandela Local Municipality: Prospect and Challenges.

Matyana, M., & Sibiya, L. M. (2024). Reviving Ethics in Service Delivery: South African Local Government Perspective. In *Challenges of Public Administration Management for Higher Education* (pp. 175-194). IGI Global.

Matyana, M., & Thusi, X. (2023). Making public service delivery more accessible to people with disabilities: The South African government narrative. *International Journal of Research in Business and Social Science (2147-4478)*, *12*(7), 413-418.

McKenzie, C., Brophy, K., Konstanta, G., & Webster, L. (2023). A vision for change leadership: Trust, transparency and accountability at University of Wollongong Library. *Journal of Academic Librarianship*, *49*(3), 102710. DOI: 10.1016/j.acalib.2023.102710

Mngomezulu, S. (2020). Political interference in the administration of service delivery in Umlalazi local municipality of KwaZulu-Natal, South Africa. *Journal of Economics and Behavioral Studies*, *12*(1 (J)), 38–45. DOI: 10.22610/jebs.v12i1(J).3003

Mojapelo, M., Modiba, M., & Saurombe, N. (2023). Applying Batho Pele principles in South African public archives–Do public programming initiatives count? *Information Development*, *39*(2), 357–375. DOI: 10.1177/02666669211049382

Mostafa, A. M. S., & Abed El-Motalib, E. A. (2020). Ethical leadership, work meaningfulness, and work engagement in the public sector. *Review of Public Personnel Administration*, *40*(1), 112–131. DOI: 10.1177/0734371X18790628

Mphahlele, M., & Zandamela, H. (2021). Local government capacity development: A case study of a South African district municipality. *Journal of Public Administration and Governance*, *11*(2), 156177–156177.

Mugaa, L. G., Guyo, W., & Otieno, R. O. (2018). Influence of Career Progression on Employee Performance in Large Commercial Banks in Nairobi City County in Kenya.

Namaganda, A. (2020). Continuing professional development as transformational learning: A case study. *Journal of Academic Librarianship*, *46*(3), 102152. DOI: 10.1016/j.acalib.2020.102152

Olvera, J. G., & Avellaneda, C. N. (2019). Subnational government performance: Testing multiple dimensions of governors' experience. *Public Administration Review*, *79*(3), 383–398. DOI: 10.1111/puar.13035

Omazic, A., & Zunk, B. M. (2021). Semi-systematic literature review on sustainability and sustainable development in higher education institutions. *Sustainability (Basel)*, *13*(14), 7683. DOI: 10.3390/su13147683

Poister, T. H. (2010). The future of strategic planning in the public sector: Linking strategic management and performance. *Public Administration Review*, *70*(s1), s246–s254. DOI: 10.1111/j.1540-6210.2010.02284.x

Schulz-Herzenberg, C. (2020). The Decline of Partisan Voting and the Rise in Electoral Uncertainty in South Africa's 2019 General Elections. In *Reflections on the 2019 South African General Elections* (pp. 98–116). Routledge. DOI: 10.4324/9781003031345-7

Shin, D., & Park, Y. J. (2019). Role of fairness, accountability, and transparency in algorithmic affordance. *Computers in Human Behavior*, *98*, 277–284. DOI: 10.1016/j.chb.2019.04.019

Thusi, X., Mahlatse, R., & Matyana, M. (2023b). Innovation as a Tool to Improve Public Service Delivery: South African Government Perspective. *INTERDISCIPLINARY JOURNAL ON LAW, SOCIAL SCIENCES AND HUMANITIES*, *4*(2), 175–189. DOI: 10.19184/idj.v4i2.39165

Thusi, X., Matyana, M., & Jili, N. (2023a). Lack of political will: A barrier to public service delivery in South Africa and a high cost for citizens. *Journal of Studies in Social Sciences and Humanities (JSSSH). E-ISSN*, *9*(2), 137–147.

Wahlund, M., & Palm, J. (2022). The role of energy democracy and energy citizenship for participatory energy transitions: A comprehensive review. *Energy Research & Social Science*, *87*, 102482. DOI: 10.1016/j.erss.2021.102482

Winker, M. A., Bloom, T., Onie, S., & Tumwine, J. (2023). Equity, transparency, and accountability: Open science for the 21st century. *Lancet*, *402*(10409), 1206–1209. DOI: 10.1016/S0140-6736(23)01575-1 PMID: 37805196

Yende, N. E. (2023). Towards Sustainable Service Delivery by South African Local Authorities: A Community Participation Strategy. *African Journal of Development Studies*, *13*(1), 197.

Zulu, P., Yalezo, B., & Mutambara, E. (2022). An assessment of cadre deployment practices in KwaZulu-Natal local government. *Academy of Strategic Management Journal*, *21*, 1–22.

Zunder, T. H. (2021). A semi-systematic literature review, identifying research opportunities for more sustainable, receiver-led inbound urban logistics flows to large higher education institutions. *European Transport Research Review*, *13*(1), 1–14. DOI: 10.1186/s12544-021-00487-1

Chapter 6

Citizen Engagement in Digital Government Transformation:

A Systematic Literature Review With Insights From Indonesia

Andrari Grahitandaru
National Research and Innovation Agency, Indonesia

Ekawati Marlina
http://orcid.org/0000-0002-9754-3460
National Research and Innovation Agency, Indonesia

Nimas Ayu Untariyati
National Research and Innovation Agency, Indonesia

Budi Nugroho
http://orcid.org/0000-0002-2919-1731
National Research and Innovation Agency, Indonesia

Hengki Muradi
National Research and Innovation Agency, Indonesia

Zain Saifullah
National Research and Innovation Agency, Indonesia

Rival Adrian Juliansyah
National Research and Innovation Agency, Indonesia

Armita Widyasuri
http://orcid.org/0009-0004-6956-8419
National Research and Innovation Agency, Indonesia

Rezzy Eko Caraka
National Research and Innovation Agency, Indonesia

DOI: 10.4018/979-8-2600-1618-3.ch005

ABSTRACT

The focus of this chapter is on how citizens can get involved in the digital government transformation. A systematic literature review (SLR) approach is employed to provide a comprehensive overview of citizen role models, challenges, and strategies for strengthening public participation in e-government. Particular attention is devoted to the Indonesian experience, which is used as a case study. The literature review reveals that citizen engagement spans a range from passive to transformative. Various challenges, such as the digital literacy gap, limited infrastructure, and data privacy issues, need to be addressed through inclusive and sustainable strategies. Indonesia's platforms—LAPOR!, JAKI, Sapawarga, and e-Musrenbang—demonstrate how citizens participate, while the Satu Data Desa initiative serves as an example of community engagement in practice. Thus, this chapter contributes a conceptual mapping of citizen engagement models, offering practical implications for digital government designers, managers, and developers.

INTRODUCTION

Digital transformation in government (e-government) has become a key element in achieving Sustainable Development Goals (SDGs), especially in developing countries. Digital transformation refers to changes in how governments provide services to citizens through digital technology and information (Zhang, 2023). In this context, digital technology enables two-way dialogue between the government and the public, speeds up service delivery, and increases public trust in government institutions (Guo et al., 2024). The transformation process is related to the adoption of technology and an evolution towards a more open, efficient, and participatory government. Digital transformation enables more efficient, transparent, and responsive public services. E-government is not only seen as a technical innovation but also as an inclusive and sustainable development strategy.

E-government encompasses four main models of service delivery, namely Government-to-Government (G2G), Government-to-Employees (G2E), Government-to-Business (G2B), and Government-to-Citizens (G2C) (Wadesango et al., 2023). Among the four models, G2C is often considered the main objective of e-government because it focuses directly on improving the community's quality of life. Examples of G2C services include population services portals such as ID cards and birth certificates, digital health services, online tax payments, and public complaint applications. Through these services, the public is a recipient of services and an important actor in creating more open and responsive governance.

The public has an important role in shaping the direction and pace of digital government evolution (Guo et al., 2024). Public participation is key in ensuring technological transformation aligns with social needs (Jose, 2022). Therefore, establishing an inclusive participation mechanism is an important prerequisite for successfully implementing sustainable e-government.

The public plays an important role in the digital transformation of government; therefore, this chapter aims to explore models of public engagement in e-government systematically. The focus of this study includes identifying models of public roles, challenges faced in implementing digital participation, and strategies that can be used to increase public engagement in digital governance. Additionally, this paper will provide insights from the Indonesian context as a case study to understand the dynamics of public engagement in digital transformation within government in developing countries.

Researchers used a method called the Systematic Literature Review (SLR) to achieve the study's goals. SLR involved finding, studying, and combining different studies related to digital transformation in government. Using the SLR process, publications were identified and selected based on specific criteria. Information was collected and the main results were studied to see what they mean. To identify the publication, the Scopus database was used.

The most important part of this study is that it helps people understand how society affects the digital transformation of government (e-government). Findings from this study add to the existing knowledge in this area by combining different ideas about roles, challenges, and strategies for how communities can get involved in changing how the government uses digital technology. By examining and organizing information from different academic publications, this study helps us understand more about how people's participation fits into the digital governance framework. The study offers insights based on facts that policymakers, digital public service managers, and platform developers can use to design more inclusive and relevant programs. By adding case studies from Indonesia, researchers can also learn about local dynamics and the challenges of implementing e-government in developing countries. These insights are important for making decisions based on the specific situation.

DIGITAL TRANSFORMATION IN E-GOVERNMENT

Evolution of Digital Government

These days, the idea of e-government has grown to include not only online services, but also interactive platforms that allow citizens to participate in decisions that affect them. The "Government-as-a-Service (GaaS) approach," which was introduced by Orgeron et al., (2025), focuses on flexibility, openness, and collaboration between the government and citizens. The model shows citizens as active users who not only receive services but also help design and evaluate policies.

In South Africa, Ayodele et al. (2025) showed how a simple technology that anyone with a mobile device can use successfully got more people involved in digital participation, especially in places with limited digital infrastructure. Digital transformation should include everyone to avoid creating new gaps in access to public services. Research on the development of digital government in ten representative provinces and cities in China, applying resource dependency theory and platform governance theory, has been conducted by Guo et al. (2024). There are three different models: the platform monopoly model, the service delivery model, and the internal management model. Local governments depend on external resources, and these resources influence how power is shared, how rules are made, and who owns what in digital government management.

To date, the study of digital government has generally focused on theoretical dimensions, institutional design, technological transformation, and service delivery models. However, most of this study uses a static approach that fails to capture the dynamic nature of the evolution of digital government. The study proposes a three-stage model of China's digital government evolution (Figure 1): 1996–2006: Technology-Oriented Digital Government, 2007–2015: Mutual Transparency-Oriented Digital Government, 2016–present: People-Oriented Digital Government.

Figure 1. The evolution of Chinese digital government (Guo et al., 2024)

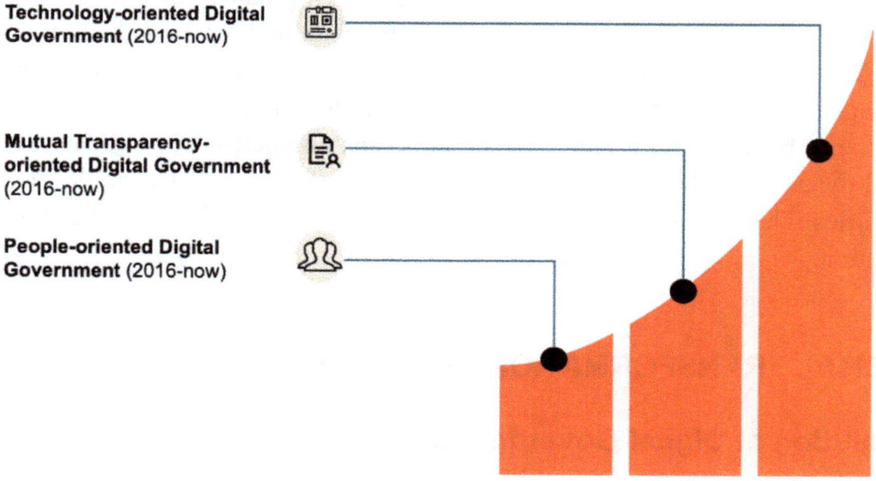

The stages in the evolution of digital government can be described as follows.

The Technology-Oriented Digital Government.

The technology-oriented phase of China's digital government (pre-2006) emphasized efficiency, productivity, and technical expertise in decision-making, marked by initiatives such as the *Three Golden Projects*. This phase was characterized by four main features: (1) prioritization of network infrastructure to enhance administrative efficiency, though still rudimentary; (2) initial use of digital platforms for one-way information disclosure to the public; (3) broad-based yet early-stage construction of digital government across various departments; and (4) heightened attention to security concerns, leading to preliminary protective measures.

The Mutual Transparency-Oriented Digital Government.

From 2007 to 2015, China's digital government changed from a one-way dependence on technology and information to a transparent and mutually beneficial model of information. These changes highlighted the need for a continuous flow of information between the government and citizens. It became essential for the government to be transparent and responsive to public opinion. Citizens can see how the government works on the inside. At the same time, the government can watch what the public thinks of it and what it needs.

The interactive transparency model has several key features: information flows in both directions, openness and accountability, citizen participation in policy-making, privacy protection, and transparency that can be measured to assess performance. All of these things help to build trust, get more people involved, and create a system for running things that balances being open with being effective and keeping things private. The idea is based on addressing information imbalances and reducing the knowledge gap between the government and citizens through digital platforms and analytical tools.

The People-Oriented Digital Government

Since 2016, China has been working on a plan to use technology to manage its government in a way that is focused on people. At first, this plan was all about technology and being open about what it was doing. Now, it is all about putting citizens first. During this phase, efficiency, productivity, and inclusiveness are emphasized. The public is actively involved as users and contributors to public services. Digital platforms allow for communication in both directions, making information more clear and fair while reducing information gaps. The approach shows a change where technology is not only a tool but also a way to make governance more responsive, fair, and focused on the people it serves.

Significant reforms support this evolution, including the "Once-Only" policy and the development of the National Integrated eGovernment Platform. Each of these changes makes it easier to manage the company, reduce costs, and combine digital services. Important milestones include the 2016 guidelines for integrating digital services, development of the national platform from 2018 to 2019, and State approval of the digital governance plan in 2021 as part of the 14th Five-Year Strategic Plan. Because of these reforms, digital governance is now more organized, services are more accessible to the public, and responsiveness has improved.

Reimagining Public Engagement in the Digital Era

Digital transformation in e-government involves more than technology. Governments are using ICT to interact, serve, and engage citizens differently. Information and Communication Technology (ICT) has made it necessary for governments to be more responsible, honest, and welcoming in today's digital era. Digital technology has created ways for people to take part in government and created complex challenges.

E-government's foundation is in strategies, citizen roles and the challenges they face. Five aspects work together to adapt governments to the digital age: digital services, citizen engagement, data management, organizational capabilities, and policies. Technology can improve public services, engage citizens, and strengthen a government's ability to support digital initiatives.

Systematic Literature Review

The study used a method called a "systematic literature review" to thoroughly examine how citizens are involved in the transformation of digital government. The systematic approach ensured rigorous identification and analysis of relevant scholarly works that address the multifaceted nature of citizen participation in e-government initiatives. SLR process was conducted by the Preferred Reporting Items for Systematic Reviews and Meta-Analyses (PRISMA) guidelines. Literature searches were conducted using the Scopus database with relevant keywords related to the research focus, namely citizen engagement, public participation, community involvement, digital transformation, digitalisation, e-governance, digital governance, and electronic governance. The initial search yielded 40 articles. The first stage involved selecting articles based on titles and abstracts, where those that did not meet the inclusion criteria or were duplicates were excluded. After this stage, 32 articles remained for further review. The next stage was full-text assessment. Of the 32 articles, 11 were eliminated because their discussions were outside the scope of this study. Thus, 21 articles met the final criteria and were used as the basis for analysis and synthesis in the study. Figure 2 illustrates the step-by-step process of the SLR, showing how the review was conducted.

Figure 2. PRISMA flow diagram used for selection process

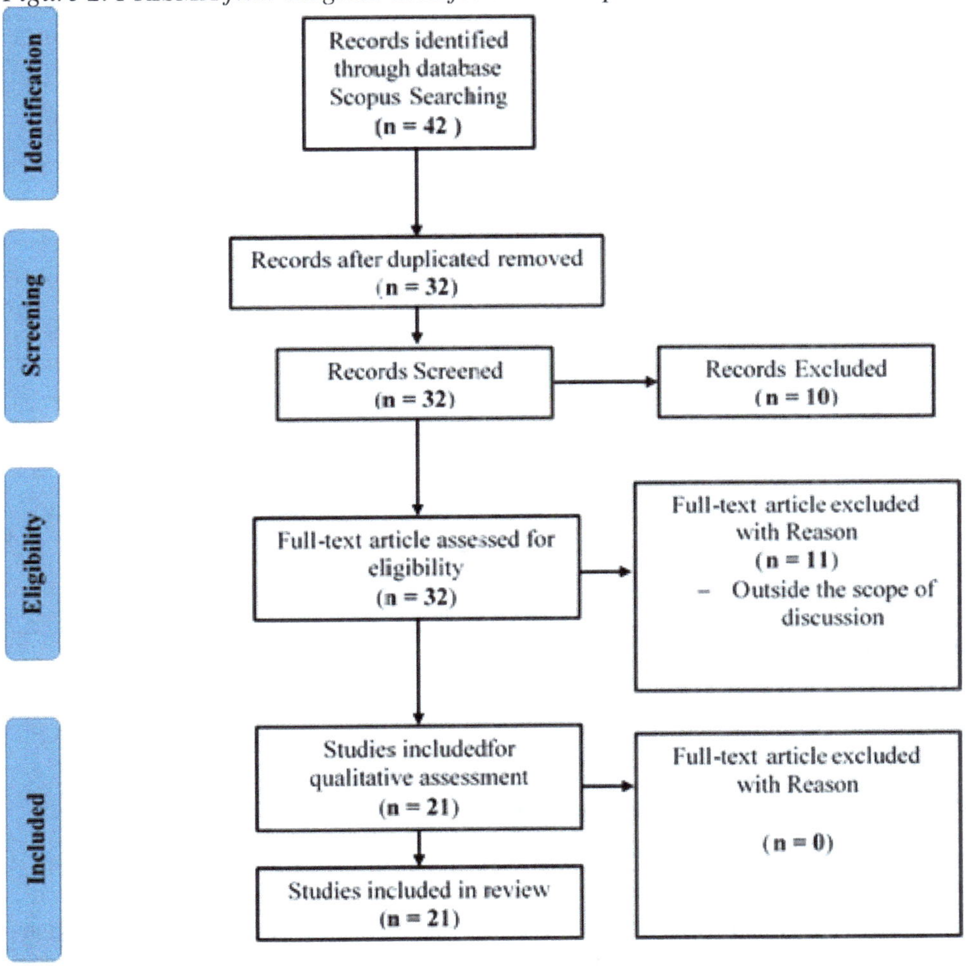

The 21 articles analyzed are listed in *Table 1*. From these articles, data was extracted with a focus on three main aspects: citizen role models, various challenges faced, and community engagement strategies in the digital transformation of government.

Table 1. Analytical findings from the literature review

Citation	Country (Case study)	Model	Challenges	Strategies
(Abbas et al., 2024)	Pakistan	v		v
(Al-Ansi et al., 2024)	-	v	v	v
(Alam et al., 2025)	Bangladesh	v	v	v
(Ayodele et al., 2025)	Afrika selatan	v		v
(Balaskas et al., 2022)	Yunani		v	v
(Daßler et al., 2024)	-	v	v	v
(Faruque et al., 2025)	Bangladesh	v	v	v
(Hien et al., 2024)	Vietnam	v		v
(Hujran et al., 2023)	Uni Emirat Arab	v		v
(Karachay et al., 2020)	Rusia	v		v
(Kuppelwieser and Klaus, 2024)		v		v
(Lestari et al., 2025)	Indonesia	v	v	v
(Mahmood, 2016)		v	v	v
(Moskvych et al., 2025)		v	v	
(Orgeron et al., 2025)		v	v	v
(Popescu et al., 2024)	Romania	v	v	v
(Rittl et al., 2025)		v		v
(Santolamazza et al., 2024)	Italia	v	v	v
(Sarkar, 2022)	Selandia Baru	v	v	v
(Vasylchyshyn et al., 2024)		v	v	v
(Zhang, 2023)	China		v	v

Citizen Engagement Models in Digital Government Transformation

The digital transformation has given rise to various models of citizen engagement, ranging from passive participation to active collaboration. Moskvych et al. (2025) identified five types of digital participation: the intermediary model, the co-development model, the consumer report model, the knowledge base model, and the media production model. There are many ways to get involved, from reporting issues to creating content and helping to develop policies.

Arnstein's Ladder is a well-known and widely used framework for classifying levels of public engagement (Kotus, 2013). It is used to evaluate and improve citizen participation processes in various contexts. Community involvement is essential, and this model clarifies its definition and the accomplishments that can be attained via varying degrees of community engagement (Nilson et al., 2024). There are three levels of participation, and Arnstein's Ladder has eight steps grouped into these levels. The first level is non-participation, which includes therapy and manipulation. The second level is tokenism, which includes informing, consultation, and placation. The third level is citizen power, which includes partnership, delegated power, and citizen control. Sherry Arnstein first presented her "Ladder of Citizen Participation" in 1969, and it is still important today.

Designed as a basic guide for assessing and designing participation processes, this framework has been criticized and changed. The program has been criticized for oversimplifying participation and failing to show the complicated power dynamics involved. Experts often find this framework too simplistic because it fails to consider the importance of context and details in the relationship between engagement and power (Nilson et al., 2024).

Related to community engagement practices, another framework is that developed by the International Association for Public Participation (IAP2). Designed to help organizations and governments involve the community in decision-making processes, IAP2 includes five levels of public participation, each with increasing impact on the community: informing, consulting, involving, collaborating, and empowering (Legacy et al., 2023). The IAP2 framework includes five levels of public participation, each with an increasing impact on the community: informing, consulting, involving, collaborating, and empowering.

Both Arnstein's Ladder and the IAP2 framework are ways of thinking about how people are involved in digital government transformation. According to these frameworks, there are six levels of participation: passive, transactional, responsive, cooperative, collaborative, and transformative. The explanation and illustrations for each level are provided here.

Passive

During this time, the community's role is mostly limited to receiving or accessing information from the government. Interaction is one-way, with a primary focus on public socialisation or education. Public access to information and services is conducted online, for example, through the national portal (www.pakistan.gov.pk), where users can read government announcements and programmes (Abbas et al., 2024), or receive policy updates and security information through the e-government platform (Alam et al., 2025).

Transactional

At the transactional stage, the public uses government digital services for administrative purposes or specific public services, characterised by a one-way interaction pattern aimed at completing their tasks or obligations. Access and utilisation of services are carried out through the Government-as-a-Service (GaaS) platform, which provides convenience and efficiency (Orgeron et al., 2025). To create more personalised, proactive, adaptive, and citizen-centric e-government services, the government is developing a service model based on artificial intelligence, big data, and automation, thereby placing citizens at the centre of an evolving digital service ecosystem.

Within the framework of smart government, the public plays an active role as users of electronic services, interacting directly with the government (Hujran et al., 2023). This role is transactional, where citizens access and use digital services directly, but their involvement in decision-making or collaboration with the government remains limited. For example, in the case of e-participatory budgeting in Rome, citizens use digital tools to participate in the public budgeting process (Santolamazza et al., 2024). Furthermore, in the context of Romania's digital transformation of public services, people utilise digital platforms to access and meet their needs (Popescu et al., 2024). Meanwhile, in Pakistan's digital transformation of e-governance, people utilise cloud computing-based services that provide ease of access, scalability, and cost efficiency (Abbas et al., 2024).

Responsive

At the responsive stage, the public participates by providing input, feedback, or reporting issues, which are then responded to by the government. Communication is two-way and ongoing, with the government following up on public input, even though strategic collaboration has not yet been established. The public acts as active users of e-government services that utilise AI and IoT technology to interact with the government (Al-Ansi et al., 2024). In addition to accessing and using these digital services, the public also provides feedback and responses that help the government evaluate and improve the quality of its services. In the context of e-government as a mediator in building public trust, the public plays a responsive role by providing feedback on digital services, expecting transparency, accountability, and service quality. However, their participation and trust are hindered by a lack of knowledge about digital transformation and concerns regarding privacy and security (Mahmood, 2016). In the context of digital transformation in e-governance in Pakistan, the public not only utilises the services but also provides feedback that helps the government improve them (Abbas et al., 2024). People in Bangladesh play an active role in e-governance and cybersecurity. How they engage with government digital services depends on how they perceive threats, how much they trust the system, and how well the system works. These factors affect how much people comply with security measures (Alam et al., 2025).

Cooperative

In these communities, people start working together with the government on certain activities or projects. Participation is planned and will require more intensive information exchange to achieve common goals. The community collaborates in a planned and active manner in implementing the Smart City programme and e-government services in Christchurch, New Zealand (Sarkar, 2022). The community participates in a planned and structured budgeting process and is involved in evaluating the effectiveness of projects, demonstrating systematic cooperation with the government or Smart City managers (Karachay et al., 2020).

Collaborative

At the collaborative level, the community plays an active role in planning, decision-making, and implementation of government programmes through partnerships that involve the sharing of responsibilities and resources. For example, digital government in Ho Chi Minh City not only provides services but also strengthens public engagement and trust through active partnerships between citizens and the government in designing and implementing solutions (Hien et al., 2024). This active participation is also evident when the community, together with the government and other supporting parties, designs, tests, and adapts e-participation mechanisms to suit local needs and conditions (Ayodele et al., 2025).

Community involvement in public policy through online geographic information systems (WebGIS) reveals that their role extends beyond being mere recipients of information to also include data collection, digital tool usage, and collaboration with government in designing waste management solutions (Rittl et al., 2025). Additionally, wiki-government, collaborative democracy, and crowdsourcing are utilised to encourage active community involvement in decision-making, policy formulation, and the provision of joint solutions (Moskvych et al., 2025). Other forms of engagement include citizenship experience, where citizens participate in the design and development of public services, mobility, digital health, urban design, and tax policy (Kuppelwieser & Klaus, 2024), including the case of the online queueing system at Sawerigading Palopo City Hospital, which was developed based on citizen input (Lestari et al., 2025), as well as collaboration in innovation labs for the co-production of public service innovations (Daßler et al., 2024).

Transformative

Participation is at its highest level, a transformative level, with the community becoming an integral part of the government's innovation and digital transformation process, acting as a strategic partner in creating systemic and sustainable change. The community acts as an agent of change in the transition to a circular economy paradigm and a zero-waste city (Rittl et al., 2025). Through social media and the e-government ecosystem, the public is involved in the process of transforming government systems and public governance (Vasylchyshyn et al., 2024). The public contributes to the development of electronic democracy, enhances transparency, and participates in public decision-making processes.

Challenges in Engaging Citizen in Digital Government Transformation

Citizens are increasingly involved in digital government transformation, not only as service users but also in policy-making, service design, and governance. Participation ranges from simply receiving information to driving major changes (Moskvych et al., 2025). However, social, institutional, and technological challenges often hinder this involvement. These challenges directly affect the success of digital initiatives while also influencing democratic participation, equity, and public trust in the digital era.

Societal Challenges

Social challenges in citizen engagement include digital literacy and skill gaps, unequal digital access, and cultural as well as behavioral resistance. A major challenge in digital government transformation is unequal digital literacy across population groups. Digital literacy goes beyond basic computer use to include evaluating online information, protecting privacy, and navigating complex interfaces (Orgeron et al., 2025). Older adults, people with health conditions, rural residents, and low-income groups are particularly affected, often lacking the skills to use services like online forms, document uploads, or digital signatures. Since e-government systems are complex, insufficient skills may discourage use or increase the need for support, reducing efficiency. Moreover, as technology evolves, literacy requirements keep changing, creating a constant demand for skills development that many citizens struggle or refuse to pursue, especially if they see little benefit from going online.

The digital divide remains a key barrier to inclusive digital government (Faruque et al., 2025). Contributing factors include limited access to devices, internet connectivity, and digital infrastructure, particularly in rural and remote areas (Orgeron et al., 2025). Economic constraints also play a major role, as low-income households often cannot afford reliable internet or high-quality devices. This results in unequal access, where wealthier groups benefit from efficient digital services while poorer groups rely on slower, traditional channels. Furthermore, access quality differs widely; some citizens enjoy fast connections and multiple devices, while others depend only on shared or limited mobile access, restricting their ability to fully engage with e-government platforms.

Citizens' attitudes toward technology and government strongly influence their engagement in digital transformation. Many remain hesitant to use digital services, preferring face-to-face interactions due to cultural norms that value personal contact and physical documents (Mahmood, 2016). Generational differences also pose challenges, as older citizens—more familiar with traditional processes—may feel excluded or view digital initiatives as burdensome. Moreover, trust is critical: concerns about data use, surveillance, and algorithmic decision-making often discourage participation, especially where governments have histories of intrusive monitoring.

Institutional Challenges

Institutional challenges refer to challenges related to organizational culture and change management, bureaucratic structures and processes, as well as administrative readiness and capacity. Government institutions often resist change and innovation, making it difficult to use digital technology effectively for citizen engagement (Balaskas et al., 2022). Traditional bureaucratic cultures emphasize hierarchy, procedures, and risk avoidance, which can limit flexibility and responsiveness. Managing change is challenging due to political pressures, multiple stakeholders, and limited expertise, often resulting in technology-focused initiatives that neglect human and organizational factors. Performance systems prioritizing efficiency over citizen engagement create weak incentives for user-centered design, digital inclusion, and proactive participation, reducing the effectiveness of digital transformation.

Bureaucracy often limits citizen participation in digital government. Poor coordination and lack of integration between departments force citizens to use multiple platforms, duplicate information, and navigate disconnected processes, contrasting with seamless private-sector digital experiences. Traditional bureaucratic workflows—long approvals, paper-based procedures, and rigid steps—are often replicated digitally, creating inefficiencies and user frustration. Additionally, outdated regulations on privacy, procurement, and administration can restrict the use of digital tools like real-time feedback, co-design platforms, and open data, limiting citizen engagement and reducing service effectiveness.

Many government institutions lack the staff, digital skills, funding, and training needed to support citizen participation in digital transformation (Balaskas et al., 2022). Administrative readiness also requires the ability to respond to citizen feedback and adapt services accordingly, but many agencies are slow or inflexible, resulting in digital services that fail to meet user needs. Without proper support for using digital platforms, solving technical issues, and understanding new processes, citizen engagement may decline.

Technological and Security Challenges

Privacy and data security remain key barriers to citizen adoption of digital government services. Rising awareness of data breaches has made people cautious about sharing personal information, especially when trust in government protection is low (Orgeron et al., 2025). Complex data collection practices, along with technical and unclear privacy policies, create confusion and mistrust. Cross-border data flows and cloud computing further raise concerns, as varying legal frameworks complicate how governments safeguard privacy while still ensuring efficient service delivery.

Cybersecurity issues undermine public trust in digital government. Limited resources, outdated legacy systems, and increasing cyber threats make it difficult for governments to ensure security without reducing accessibility. Data breaches or service disruptions reinforce the perception that governments cannot adequately protect citizens' data, leading to declining trust.

Government digital services remain difficult to access due to outdated, isolated systems that limit integration and efficiency. Citizens expect seamless, one-stop services, but poor interoperability forces them to repeat information and switch platforms, causing frustration. Rapidly evolving technology, combined with limited resources and expertise, leaves many systems outdated, reducing performance, compatibility, and user satisfaction—ultimately hindering digital transformation.

Strategies to Enhance Citizen Engagement

Digital transformation in government requires a comprehensive strategic approach to ensure broad and sustained public engagement. Addressing these challenges requires comprehensive strategies that recognize the interconnected nature of societal, institutional, and technological barriers to citizen engagement. Government institutions must invest in public capacity and digital literacy programs, improve access to and inclusion of technology, transparency, accountability, and public trust, collaboration and learning between regions.

Public Capacity and Digital Literacy

One of the main strategies is to strengthen public capacity and digital literacy (Orgeron et al., 2025); Hien et al., 2024; Balaskas et al., 2022; Al-Ansi et al., 2024). Public capacity refers to how well citizens understand policy issues, how well they can participate in decision-making processes, and how well they can use the available channels for participation. Digital literacy refers to people's ability to access, evaluate, and use technology-based information in a smart and productive way. Digital literacy is becoming more important as more people use online platforms, such as e-consultations, public reporting applications, and virtual discussion forums. If people don't know how to use technology well, they might be left out of the process because they can't take full advantage of it. Therefore, governments and stakeholders need to invest resources in training programs, the provision of inclusive technology infrastructure, and the development of educational materials that various community groups can easily understand. This approach increases the number of people who can participate and makes sure that citizens' contributions to the democratic process are more meaningful, based on information, and represent the diversity of society.

Improve Access to and Inclusion of Technology

Another strategy to enhance engagement is ensuring technology is accessible and inclusive (Faruque et al., 2025; Hujran et al., 2023; Vasylchyshyn et al., 2024). Equal access to devices, the internet, and digital tools is essential, especially for remote communities, low-income groups, and people with disabilities. Digital divides—both physical (limited connectivity) and socio-economic (cost and digital skills)—remain major barriers. Addressing these requires comprehensive efforts, such as free public internet, affordable devices, and network expansion. Public technologies like smart kiosks, Wi-Fi hotspots, and interactive information screens, integrated with urban design, can broaden access and foster active participation (Kuppelwieser & Klaus, 2024; Santolamazza et al., 2024).

Beyond infrastructure, the design of digital tools (DTs) is crucial. Rome's participatory budgeting in 2019 showed that while DTs enabled information sharing, they lacked deeper engagement functions such as deliberation or monitoring. Effective platforms should be user-friendly and collaborative, empowering citizens to co-create public value. Collaboration between governments, private sectors, and civil society can build an inclusive digital ecosystem. This not only increases participation but also reduces inequality, strengthens trust, and ensures policies reflect broader societal needs.

Transparency, Accountability, and Public Trust

Transparency, accountability, and trust are essential for encouraging public participation in digital government (Hien et al., 2024; Zhang, 2023). Transparency means making government budgets, policies, and performance data openly available and easy to understand. When citizens can monitor and evaluate government actions, misuse of power is reduced. Accountability mechanisms such as audits, oversight, evaluations, and complaint channels further strengthen this process. Participation in innovation labs also helps design citizen-focused services while reinforcing transparency and trust (Daßler et al., 2024).

Trust grows when citizens feel their voices matter and decisions benefit them. A lack of openness, however, leads to skepticism and disengagement. In digital transformation, innovative and responsive service design must prioritize inclusiveness—such as multilingual access, disability-friendly formats, and user-friendly platforms (Sarkar, 2022). Responsiveness also means adapting to feedback, as shown in initiatives like digital waste governance using WebGIS or citizen co-designed apps for hospitals (Lestari et al., 2025; Rittl et al., 2025).

Effective feedback tools—like chatbots, dashboards, and online reporting—allow governments to adapt quickly and improve service quality. Success requires trained officials, secure technology, and an organizational culture open to change. By embedding transparency and accountability into digital services, governments can build legitimacy, strengthen trust, and create a more democratic, inclusive, and citizen-centered ecosystem.

Collaboration and Learning between Regions

Strengthening collaboration and learning between regions is a key strategy for improving citizen engagement (Orgeron et al., 2025). Regional collaboration allows the exchange of ideas, innovations, and best practices, enabling governments to avoid repeated mistakes, save resources, and adapt successful methods to different contexts. Mechanisms such as interregional partnerships, national forums, and international cooperation (e.g., OECD, UNDP) support this process, while digital platforms make information sharing faster and cheaper. Effective collaboration, however, requires strong political commitment, supportive policies, and sufficient resources from both central and local governments.

This strategy complements three others: improving digital literacy, expanding access and inclusion, and strengthening transparency and accountability. Together, these four approaches form a comprehensive ecosystem for participation. Effective engagement requires not only technology but also citizen skills, motivation, and trust. Governments must invest in infrastructure, design user-friendly and inclusive services, and build credibility through transparency, oversight, and responsive feedback systems.

Research shows that successful e-participation depends on three dimensions: technological (ease, security, compatibility), organisational (support, resources, capacity), and environmental (regulation, culture, social pressure) (Ninčević Pašalić & Ćukušić, 2024). Participatory budgeting and co-production also illustrate how citizen involvement can increase trust, accountability, and inclusiveness (Broadhurst, 2024; Buele et al., 2020). When adapted to local realities and supported by continuous feedback, these approaches strengthen governance.

In short, digital transformation requires an integrated strategy—linking literacy, inclusion, trust, collaboration, and adaptive participation models—to build a more democratic, citizen-centered, and responsive government.

Citizen Engagement in the Various Online Indonesian Platforms

The digital transformation of government in Indonesia has created new ways for citizens to get involved in public governance processes. In the past, people could only get involved by going to meetings in person or by dealing with official government offices. Now, there are more ways to get involved, and they are more active and open to new ideas. Technology has made it easier for people to get involved in public services and decision-making. There are seven examples of platforms in Indonesia that help citizens get involved in different areas.

The seven platforms to be reviewed are LAPOR!, JAKI (Jakarta Kini), Sapawarga, Open Data Indonesia, e-Musrenbang, SIPD, and Petabencana. Each platform has different characteristics, community role models, and sectors. A comparison of each platform is listed in Table 2.

Table 2. Comparative analysis of citizen engagement applications in Indonesia

Platform	Sector	Level of engagement	Url
LAPOR! (Layanan Aspirasi dan Pengaduan Online Rakyat)	Public scrutiny	Responsive	https://www.lapor.go.id/
JAKI (Jakarta Kini)	Public service	Cooperative	https://jaki.jakarta.go.id
Sapawarga	Public service	Cooperative	https://sapawarga.jabarprov.go.id
Open Data Indonesia	Data	Collaborative	https://data.go.id

continued on following page

Table 2. Continued

Platform	Sector	Level of engagement	Url
e-Musrenbang	Development planning	Collaborative	https://musrenbang.jakarta.go.id (One example is the Jakarta e-Musrembang)
SIPD (Sistem Informasi Pemerintah Daerah)	Local government administration	Passive	https://sipd.kemendagri.go.id
Petabencana	Disaster management	Collaborative	https://petabencana.id

Launched in 2013, LAPOR! is Indonesia's national platform for citizen complaints and feedback on public services. Citizens submit reports, and the government responds, making the platform a symbol of openness and accountability, though follow-up and digital adoption remain challenges (Susniwati et al., 2024). LAPOR! centralizes complaints, routing them to the appropriate agency and integrating with local systems via APIs for efficient information flow (Abbas, 2019). The platform enables data analysis, categorization, and sentiment analysis to identify key issues and public opinion. For example, feedback on social assistance programs like KPS and BLSM helps improve distribution (Surjandari et al., 2016; Tulili et al., 2023).

At the regional level, JAKI (Jakarta) and Sapawarga (West Java) are provincial digital platforms that integrate multiple public services into single "super apps." JAKI allows citizens to access city information, report environmental issues, monitor traffic, and use healthcare services, supporting Jakarta's smart city goals and the digital economy while ensuring data security. Both platforms foster cooperative participation, enabling two-way engagement where citizens submit reports and ideas. Studies show these apps enhance government–citizen interactions, though their effectiveness depends on interface design and system responsiveness (Kencono, 2025).

Open Data Indonesia is a government open data portal that provides cross-sector access for the public. Within this platform, citizen participation takes place at a collaborative level. Open data initiatives in Indonesia are part of broader e-government and digital transformation efforts, aimed at enhancing transparency, public engagement, and government accountability. Findings from the literature indicate that citizen involvement in Open Government Data (OGD) initiatives is influenced by factors such as social altruism and the perceived urgency of issues. Interestingly, low data quality does not always act as a barrier to participation. On the contrary, in some cases, it may actually stimulate higher levels of community engagement (Purwanto et al., 2018).

E-Musrenbang is Indonesia's digital platform for public participation in urban development planning, serving as an online version of the traditional Musrenbang (Development Planning Deliberation Forum). It enhances transparency, accountability, and citizen involvement by allowing residents to submit proposals, verify information, and collaborate with local governments on development priorities (Anindito et al., 2022). While the government retains final decision-making authority, the platform facilitates broader participation, enabling citizens to identify local issues and contribute solutions that reflect community needs.

The Sistem Informasi Pemerintah Daerah (SIPD), or Regional Government Information System, serves as an essential platform for managing and enhancing the efficiency of regional government operations. It integrates various types of information, including regional development, regional finance, and other government-related data, to support the implementation of regional development. In this system, the public can only access the available information, placing citizens at a passive level of participation.

Petabencana is a disaster management platform that leverages community participation and real-time data to enhance disaster response and preparedness. Petabencana emphasizes the importance of community involvement in disaster preparedness and response. This approach aligns with findings that community-based initiatives are more effective in enhancing disaster resilience compared to top-down governmental strategies (Sugiana et al., 2025). In the case of Petabencana, citizens contribute real-time disaster information, which is then integrated with government systems, illustrating community participation at a collaborative level.

Community Roles in the Implementation of Satu Data Desa (One Village Data): A Study of Tabanan and Jembrana

Indonesia's digital government is advancing One Data Indonesia through structured data governance under Bappenas, the official data trustee. Key regulations supporting this effort include Presidential Regulation No. 39/2019, Bappenas Regulations No. 16/2020 and 17/2020, and the latest Ministerial Regulation No. 7/2025, which governs the sharing of national social and economic data. Responsibilities for data management are divided into mandatory, required, and optional measures, covering data accuracy, interoperability, validation, security, coordination, and capacity-building, with optional measures enhancing usability and access through APIs, dashboards, and collaborative innovation.

This study examines Jembrana and Tabanan regencies in Bali, both developing village-level one data systems but using different approaches. Despite differences, both aim for integrated regional data yet face challenges in fulfilling regulatory requirements. The analysis focuses on program strategies, public involvement in data collection, and implementation challenges.

Village Program Precision (OpenSID) from Tabanan Regency, Bali Province.

The explanation of the Precision Village Program in Tabanan Regency focuses on the strategy for its implementation, the forms of public involvement in data collection, and the challenges encountered during the process, as described in this subsection. The program's primary objective is to establish One Village One Data across 133 villages in Tabanan, ensuring that the information is accurate, up-to-date, and integrated. This initiative is designed to strengthen development planning by relying on actual and reliable data.

Community Participation

The One Village One Data initiative in Tabanan involves multiple stakeholders to ensure accurate, up-to-date, and integrated data across 133 villages, supporting evidence-based planning (Figure 3). Citizens act as primary data providers, supplying information on population, social conditions, health, and education. Village governments, including SID operators and staff, input and verify this data in the Precision Village Information System (SIDP).

Figure 3. Flow of role in OpenSID

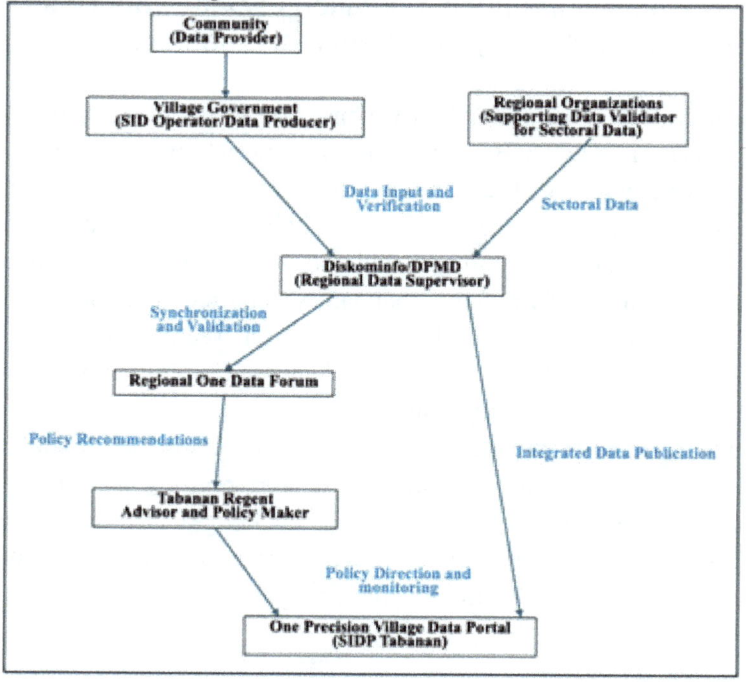

At the regency level, OPDs provide sectoral data and validate relevant information, while Diskominfo and village community empowerment offices supervise data synchronization and validation. The regional One Data Forum reviews and further validates data, offering policy recommendations to the Regent, who sets policy directions. The result is an integrated data portal that consolidates village-level information for reliable, data-driven development planning.

Citizen Engagement Challenges in Village Data Systems

Limited human resources and low digital literacy continue to pose significant challenges, as many citizens are not yet accustomed to using technology, making intensive training and ongoing guidance essential. Enhancing community literacy as data producers is a crucial factor for success, alongside the regulatory and budgetary commitment of the District Government and the village's capacity to adapt to technological changes.

Tabanan Regent's Strategy to Realize One Precision Data from Village.

The first strategy establishes regent regulations as legal guidelines for precision village data and One Regional Data, requiring villages to update data at least every six months. In Tabanan, this aligns with Regional Regulation No. 12/2022 and Regent Regulation No. 17/2024, supporting a digital program under the local Communication and Information Technology Department.

The second strategy focuses on infrastructure centralization. Cloud servers, villages.id domains, and SIDP dashboards are provided to all 133 villages, eliminating the need for local setups. The Precision Village Program uses OpenSID/OpenKab applications, integrated with OpenDesa, a legally recognized non-profit, to ensure sustainability and strengthen village and supra-village data governance. The integration between OpenSID and OpenKab is illustrated in Figure 4.

Figure 4. Connection OpenSID and OpenKab

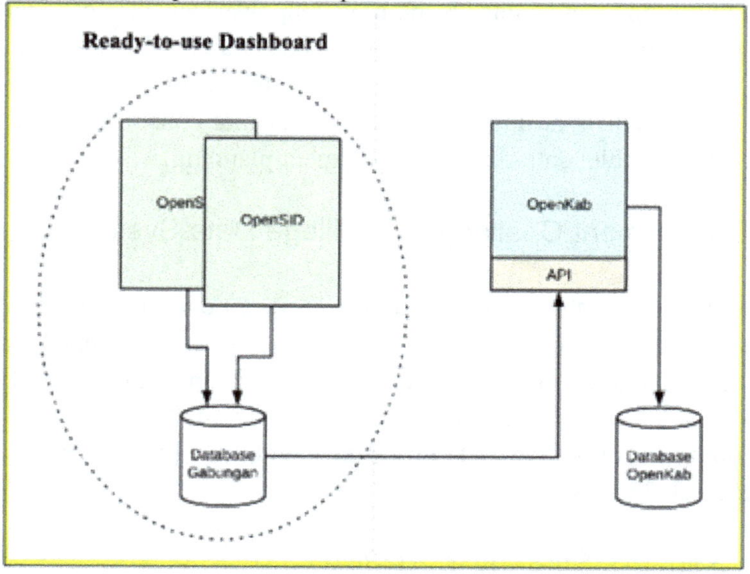

OpenDesa develops the OpenVillage ecosystem, including OpenSID (villages), OpenDK (sub-districts), and OpenKab (districts), all open-source, free, and continuously updated based on local needs. OpenSID is widely adopted, with over 6,500 villages using it daily. OpenDesa reinvests all revenue to sustain development and collaborates with local governments to optimize application use.

OpenSID Premium allows villages to fund advanced features, such as a shared database for integrated village data while retaining customization options. It includes population management tools, mobile services, and automated updates via a Ready-to-Use Dashboard. OpenKab extracts and visualizes data from OpenSID for regency-level planning. In regencies with 100+ OpenSID Premium subscribers, OpenDesa provides dedicated programming support at no extra cost.

Additional strategies involve infrastructure provision (cloud servers, domains, dashboards, licenses), collaboration with external agencies (OpenDesa, BPS, social security), and capacity-building through technical guidance and digital literacy programs to strengthen village data management and accountability.

Jembrana One Data From Village (JSDDD) Program

The Jembrana Satu Data dari Desa (JSDDD) program implements Presidential Regulation No. 39/2019 locally, creating a standardized village data system for all OPDs in Jembrana Regency to support SDG-based micro-development. Launched on September 20, 2022, by the Minister of Villages and the Regent of Jembrana, it is Indonesia's first integrated SDG-focused village data initiative. Backed by Regent Regulation 7/2022, 800 trained surveyors, and a digital platform, JSDDD enables precise, effective, and data-driven local development policies.

Regent's Strategy Jembrana Realizing One Village Data

The Regent issued a regulation governing One Regional Data. Jembrana Regent Regulation Number 7 of 2022 concerning One Regional Data, enacted on February 25, 2022, serves as the legal framework for the implementation of the JSDDD in Jembrana. This regulation establishes the governance framework, institutional roles, coordination flow, and mechanisms for data collection, verification, storage, and dissemination. The implementation of the JSDDD is based on Jembrana Regent Regulation No. 7 of 2022 concerning Regional Data Governance, which aligns with Presidential Regulation 39/2019. The JSDDD was launched after Regent I Nengah Tamba issued a local legal framework for One Regional Data, and is directly supported by the central Statistics Agency (BPS) to validate its implementation in the field. Essentially, this regulation positions village communities as crucial actors, not simply data objects. Challenges are addressed through regulations, forums, and data portals, while sustainability is ensured through the obligations of all regional officials (including villages), funding, and integration into the national system.

The implementation strategy for SDG-based village-level data collection in Jembrana district exemplifies a digitally integrated and multi-stakeholder governance model aimed at enhancing micro-regional planning. Intensive training programs were conducted by the National Statistics Agency, the Jembrana district government, and the Regional Planning Agency to equip village officials and surveyors with standardized procedures for SDG-aligned data collection. This capacity-building initiative ensures the reliability and granularity of village-level data, which is essential for targeted development interventions (Permatasari et al., 2021). Institutional collaboration plays a pivotal role, with Central BPS providing technical oversight, Bappeda acting as the coordinator, and the Ministry of Communication and Information serving as the data steward, while villages function as the primary data collectors. As shown in Figure 5, all the data are gathered together in the JSDDD (Jembrana Satu Data Dari Desa) application, a website that allows us to examine poverty, happiness, infrastructure, and the potential of villages from many different angles. The digital system makes it easy for different agencies to work together and share data. The system helps people make plans and policies based on facts (Hasudungan et al., 2024). Using subjective well-being indicators (like happiness) along with objective metrics (such as the Multidimensional Poverty Index) shows a forward-thinking approach to development analytics. This approach acknowledges the complex relationship between material poverty and perceived quality of life (Strotmann & Volkert, 2018). All of these plans show how digital transformation, working together at an institutional level, and local data management can help villages in Indonesia achieve the Sustainable Development Goals more quickly.

Figure 5. JSDDD application for village data collection

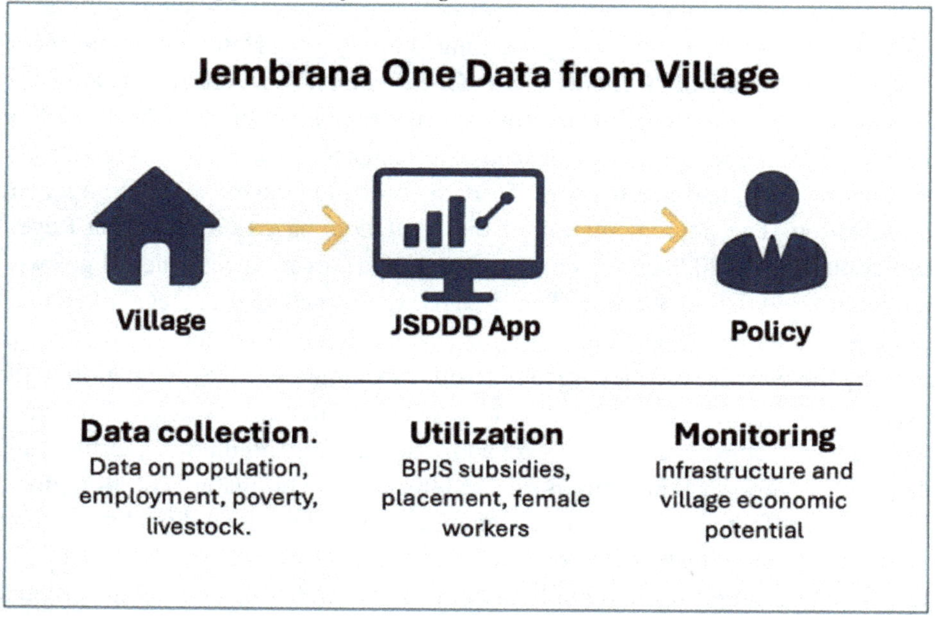

Community engagement in Jembrana Regency is crucial for village-level data aligned with the SDGs. Villages and sub-districts act as both data producers and users, collecting micro-level socio-economic, spatial, infrastructure, and well-being data through 800 trained local surveyors. Residents' active participation ensures primary data meets SDG standards, which is verified and uploaded to the JSDDD digital platform. This system supports accurate data entry, validation, and localized planning for economic, social, infrastructure, and happiness indicators. By serving as both data generators and beneficiaries, villages promote a participatory, decentralized data governance approach, improving policy relevance and responsiveness.

Challenge Realizing One Regional Data

The realization of One Regional Data at the village level faces significant human resource challenges that hinder its implementation. As shown in Figure 6, a lack of digital skills, a weak understanding of data management standards, a shortage of trained statisticians, and an overwhelming workload for village officials all together limit data quality and consistency. Solving these problems is important to make villages stronger, make sure data is collected correctly, and support good policies in different areas. This diagram shows the urgent need for interventions to build strategic capacity.

Figure 6. Challenge Village Human Resource Capacity to Realize One Regional Data

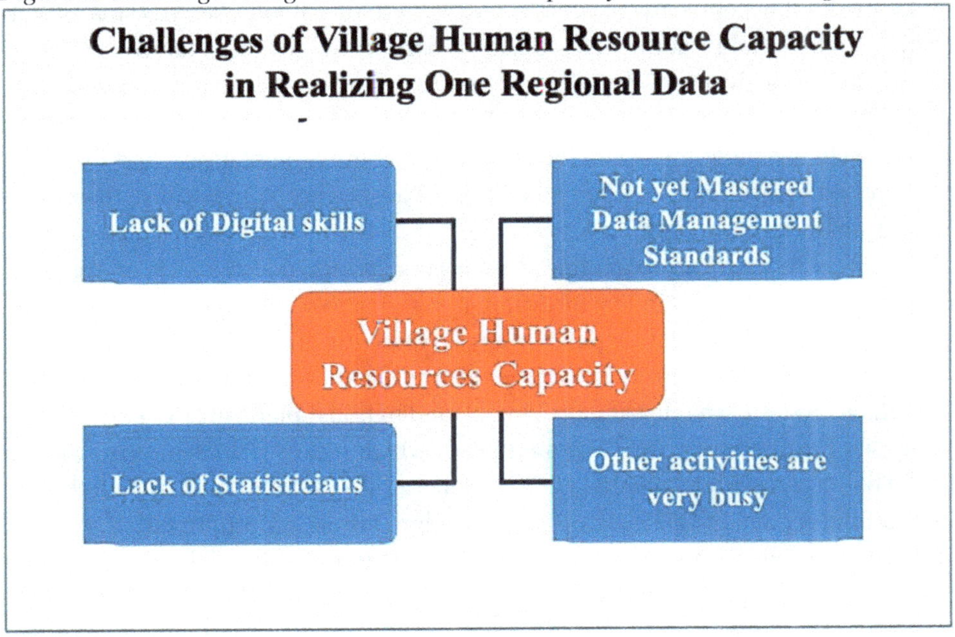

Collecting centralized data in Indonesia faces multiple challenges. There is a shortage of trained personnel, especially surveyors, who often lack formal skills in survey methodology, data classification, and national indicator interpretation, leading to errors (Singer, 2018). Limited digital literacy also causes mistakes when using mobile or tablet-based survey apps (Akbar & Wijaya, 2024). Surveyors may have differing interpretations of key categories such as employment, poverty, and housing, while low incentives reduce motivation and data quality (Lipps et al., 2019).

The JSDDD (Jembrana Satu Data Dari Desa) initiative faces institutional hurdles. Local government departments (OPDs) operate in silos, sharing little data, while villages lack dedicated statistical teams (Bernot et al., 2024). Inconsistent definitions—for instance, of poverty—complicate data integration (Kurniawati et al., 2024). Budget limitations hinder servers, applications, training, and maintenance, slowing data quality and integration. Although Regent Regulation No. 7/2022 provides legal support, lack of detailed technical guidance hampers implementation. Additional issues include inconsistent data formats, weak inter-agency collaboration, poor IT infrastructure in remote areas, and reliance on regional leaders' priorities. Strengthened institutions, unified governance protocols, and inclusive digital infrastructure are crucial for sustainable regional data integration.Challenge main from side social data and economic data

Collecting economic data in Jembrana's villages is also difficult due to certain limitations. Many people in the economy work in informal jobs, such as small-scale farming, fishing, and trading. This makes it hard to collect and analyze economic data (Castellano-Álvarez et al., 2024). Many small businesses and home-based businesses do not have formal registration, which makes it hard to know how much they contribute to the economy. Also, the data on agriculture, plantations, and livestock are recorded in different ways across villages. This is a problem because these data are very important for the region.

Problems in both the social and economic areas include the lack of standard measurements and the inability of different systems to work together. Definitions of village-level issues, such as poverty levels, often differ from national standards. Data from different administrative levels can be difficult to compare because of this. The village systems and district, provincial, and national platforms (e.g., One Data Indonesia, Regsosek) are not fully integrated, which makes it difficult to exchange data. The long-term sustainability of data operations is threatened by two things: limited funding and the absence of long-term institutional commitment. Surveyors who change often without learning more disrupts the quality of the data. To deal with these challenges, we need to invest in standardization, digital infrastructure, and developing human resources. This will make sure that regional data systems are reliable and relevant (Cao & Iansiti, 2023).

REFERENCES

Abbas, A. E. (2019). API integration of national complaint handling system in Indonesia: A state of the art review. *2019 International Conference on ICT for Smart Society (ICISS)*, pp. 1–5. DOI: 10.1109/ICISS48059.2019.8969837

Abbas, Q., Alyas, T., Alghamdi, T., Alkhodre, A. B., Albouq, S., Niazi, M., & Tabassum, N. (2024). Redefining governance: A critical analysis of sustainability transformation in e-governance. *Frontiers in Big Data*, *7*, 1349116. DOI: 10.3389/fdata.2024.1349116 PMID: 38638340

Akbar, M., & Wijaya, G. (2024). Digital literacy of rural areas in Indonesia: Challenges and opportunities. *Proceedings of the 4th International Conference on Rural Socio-Economic Transformation, RUSET 2023,* 1 November 2023, Bogor, Indonesia. DOI: 10.4108/eai.1-11-2023.2344347

Al-Ansi, A. M., Garad, A., Jaboob, M., & Al-Ansi, A. (2024). Elevating e-government: Unleashing the power of AI and IoT for enhanced public services. *Heliyon*, *10*(23), e40591. DOI: 10.1016/j.heliyon.2024.e40591 PMID: 39654738

Alam, M. S., Ahmed, S., Dhali, M., & Alam, S. S. (2025). Citizens' engagement with cybersecurity measures in Bangladesh: A cross-sectional study. *International Journal of Information Security*, *24*(1), 4. DOI: 10.1007/s10207-024-00918-9

Anindito, D. B., Sagala, S. A. H., & Tarigan, A. K. M. (2022). E- *musrenbang*: A digital framework for local participatory planning at the community level. *International Development Planning Review*, *44*(2), 191–216. DOI: 10.3828/idpr.2021.5

Ayodele, O., Plantinga, P., Sanchez-Bentacourt, D., Dlamini, S., & Dlamini, N. (2025). How do researchers and public officials co-navigate e-participation implementation? An action-research experience with South African municipalities. *Systems*, *13*(2), 125. DOI: 10.3390/systems13020125

Balaskas, S., Panagiotarou, A., & Rigou, M. (2022). The influence of trustworthiness and technology acceptance factors on the usage of e-government services during COVID-19: A case Study of post COVID-19 Greece. *Administrative Sciences*, *12*(4), 129. DOI: 10.3390/admsci12040129

Bernot, A., Tjondronegoro, D., Rifai, B., Hasan, R., Liew, A. W.-C., Verhelst, T., & Tiwari, M. (2024). Institutional dimensions in open government data: A deep dive into Indonesia's *Satu Data* initiative and its implications for developing countries. *Public Performance & Management Review*, *47*(6), 1399–1429. DOI: 10.1080/15309576.2024.2377609

Broadhurst, K. (2024). Contextualising co-production and complex needs: Understanding the engagement of service users with severe and multiple disadvantages. *Public Policy and Administration*, *39*(2), 259–277. DOI: 10.1177/09520767221122277

Buele, I., Vidueira, P., Yagüe, J. L., & Cuesta, F. (2020). The participatory budgeting and its contribution to local management and governance: Review of experience of rural communities from the Ecuadorian Amazon rainforest. *Sustainability (Basel)*, *12*(11), 4659. DOI: 10.3390/su12114659

Cao, R., & Iansiti, M. (2023). *Data governance, interoperability and standardization: Organizational adaptation to privacy regulation*. Data Governance.

Castellano-Álvarez, F. J., Robina-Ramírez, R., & Silva, F. (2024). Rural areas facing the challenge of economic diversification: Threats and opportunities. *Agriculture*, *14*(4), 623. DOI: 10.3390/agriculture14040623

Daßler, L., Hein, A., & Krcmar, H. (2024). Innovating public services: Drivers and challenges of Innovation Labs in the Co-Production of E-Government Services. *Proceedings of the 25th Annual International Conference on Digital Government Research*, 711–720. DOI: 10.1145/3657054.3657138

Faruque, M., Amin, A., Sharmin, M., & Rahman, M. M. (2025). Fostering sustainable digital governance: Citizen acceptance of web-portal-based integrated platforms in Bangladesh through A TAM-TPB approach. *Journal of Risk Analysis and Crisis Response*, *15*(1), 19. DOI: 10.54560/jracr.v15i1.551

Guo, Y., Zhang, T., & Deng, Y. (2024). Past, present, and future of digital government: Insights from Chinese practices. *Public Administration Issues*, *0*(5), 6–24. DOI: 10.17323/1999-5431-2024-0-5-6-24

Hasudungan, R. G., Galistya, T. M., Solana, A., Aini, N., Ngurah Diksa, I. G. B., & Sri Jayanti, D. A. (2024). Rekomendasi skema sistem satu data daerah. *Seminar Nasional Official Statistics*, *2024*(1), 735–744. DOI: 10.34123/semnasoffstat.v2024i1.2203

Hien, B. N., Tuyen, N. T. K., Lan, N. T., Ngan, N. T. K., & Thanh, N. N. (2024). The impact of digital government initiatives on public value creation: Evidence from Ho Chi Minh City, Vietnam. *Revista de Gestão Social e Ambiental*, *18*(2), e04892. DOI: 10.24857/rgsa.v18n2-092

Hujran, O., Al-Debei, M. M., Al-Adwan, A. S., Alarabiat, A., & Altarawneh, N. (2023). Examining the antecedents and outcomes of smart government usage: An integrated model. *Government Information Quarterly*, *40*(1), 101783. DOI: 10.1016/j.giq.2022.101783

Jose, R. (2022). Future scenarios as a tool for citizen engagement in smart cities. *2022 7th International Conference on Smart and Sustainable Technologies (SpliTech)*, 1–6. DOI: 10.23919/SpliTech55088.2022.9854333

Karachay, V., Chugunov, A., & Neustroeva, R. (2020). Participatory budgeting and e-participation in smart cities: Comparative overview. *Proceedings of the 13th International Conference on Theory and Practice of Electronic Governance*, 835–838. DOI: 10.1145/3428502.3428634

Kencono, D. S.Dewi Sekar Kencono. (2025). Exploring public sentiment toward regional e-government apps: A case study of Sapawarga and Jaki in Indonesia. *Journal of Information Systems Engineering & Management*, *10*(15s), 285–298. DOI: 10.52783/jisem.v10i15s.2458

Kotus, J. (2013). Position of the Polish city on the ladder of public participation: Are we going the right way? The case of Poznań. *Cities (London, England)*, *35*, 226–236. DOI: 10.1016/j.cities.2013.08.001

Kuppelwieser, V. G., & Klaus, P. (2024). Future research directions: Enhancing the citizenship experience. *Journal of Retailing and Consumer Services*, *81*, 103973. DOI: 10.1016/j.jretconser.2024.103973

Kurniawati, M. V., Zulmy, M. F., & Ruldeviyani, Y. (2024). The optimizing data quality in interagency data sharing: A framework. *Jurnal Ilmu Komputer Dan Informasi*, *18*(1), 47–66. DOI: 10.21609/jiki.v18i1.1310

Legacy, C., Barry, J., Novacevski, M., & Boyco, M. (2023). "Shared language" Or "Straitjacket"? The hidden costs of legitimising participation through standardised frameworks. *Planning Theory & Practice*, *24*(3), 325–341. DOI: 10.1080/14649357.2023.2214530

Lestari, I., Abdullah, M. T., Hasniati, H., & Nara, N. (2025). Enhancing public services through agile governance: A case study of the online queue application at RSUD Sawerigading Palopo city. *Edelweiss Applied Science and Technology*, *9*(3), 1466–1472. DOI: 10.55214/25768484.v9i3.5561

Lipps, O., Herzing, J. M. E., Pekari, N., Ernst-Staehli, M., Pollien, A., Riedo, G., & Reveilhac, M. (2019). Incentives in surveys. *FORS Guide N°8*, Version 1.1. DOI: 10.24449/FG-2019-00008

Mahmood, M. (2016). Enhancing citizens' trust and confidence in government through digital transformation. *International Journal of Electronic Government Research*, *12*(1), 99–110. DOI: 10.4018/IJEGR.2016010105

Nilson, R., Rand, J., Hoen, B., & Elmallah, S. (2024). Halfway up the ladder: Developer practices and perspectives on community engagement for utility-scale renewable energy in the United States. *Energy Research & Social Science*, *117*, 103706. DOI: 10.1016/j.erss.2024.103706

Ninčević Pašalić, I., & Ćukušić, M. (2024). Understanding E-participation adoption: Exploring technological, organizational, and environmental factors. *Technological Forecasting and Social Change*, *207*, 123633. DOI: 10.1016/j.techfore.2024.123633

Orgeron, C. P., Rials, W., & Druchyna, S. (2025). The AI-driven state: How government-as-a-service is transforming public service. *International Journal of Electronic Government Research*, *21*(1), 1–24. DOI: 10.4018/IJEGR.381327

Permatasari, P., Ilman, A. S., Tilt, C. A., Lestari, D., Islam, S., Tenrini, R. H., Rahman, A. B., Samosir, A. P., & Wardhana, I. W. (2021). The village fund program in Indonesia: Measuring the effectiveness and alignment to sustainable development goals. *Sustainability (Basel)*, *13*(21), 12294. DOI: 10.3390/su132112294

Popescu, M. A. M., Barbu, A., Moiceanu, G., Costea-Marcu, I.-C., Militaru, G., & Simion, P. C. (2024). Citizens' perception of digital public services: A case study among Romanian citizens. *Administrative Sciences*, *14*(10), 259. DOI: 10.3390/admsci14100259

Purwanto, A., Zuiderwijk, A., & Janssen, M. (2018). Citizen engagement in an open election data initiative: A case study of Indonesian's "Kawal Pemilu." *Proceedings of the 19th Annual International Conference on Digital Government Research: Governance in the Data Age*, 1–10. DOI: 10.1145/3209281.3209305

Rittl, L. G. F., Zaman, A., & De Oliveira, F. H. (2025). Digital transformation in waste management: Disruptive innovation and digital governance for zero-waste cities in the global south as keys to future sustainable development. *Sustainability (Basel)*, *17*(4), 1608. DOI: 10.3390/su17041608

Santolamazza, V., Mattei, G., & Grandis, F. G. (2024). Citizens' role and digitalisation in the participatory budgeting to create public value: The case of Rome. *International Journal of Public Sector Management*. Advance online publication. DOI: 10.1108/IJPSM-05-2023-0165

Sarkar, A. (2022). Smart city digital transformation journey: An investigation of stage models. *28th Americas Conference on Information Systems*. https://aisel.aisnet.org/ukais2022

Singer, E. (2018). The use and effects of incentives in surveys. In Vannette, D. L., & Krosnick, J. A. (Eds.), *The palgrave handbook of survey research* (pp. 63–70). Springer International Publishing., DOI: 10.1007/978-3-319-54395-6_9

Strotmann, H., & Volkert, J. (2018). Multidimensional poverty index and happiness. *Journal of Happiness Studies, 19*(1), 167–189. DOI: 10.1007/s10902-016-9807-0

Sugiana, D., Suryana, A., Wirakusumah, T. K., & Subekti, P. (2025). Communication innovations for adaptation to climate change and increased disaster risk. *International Journal of Safety and Security Engineering, 15*(03), 465–477. DOI: 10.18280/ijsse.150306

Surjandari, I., Megawati, C., Dhini, A., & Sanditya Hardaya, I. B. N. (2016). Application of text mining for classification of textual reports: A study of Indonesia's national complaint handling system. *Proceedings of the International Conference on Industrial Engineering and Operations Management.*

Susniwati, S., Kurniawati, K., & Susilawati, S. (2024). Public policy innovation in Indonesia: Enchancing citizen engagement through E-government initiatives. *PINISI Discretion Review, 8*(1), 1. DOI: 10.26858/pdr.v8i1.66364

Tulili, T. R., Nurcahyono, D., Rijal, S., Kurniawan, A., & Saleh, M. T. R. (2023). Classification of public opinion on news presentation at lapor website using Naïve Bayes classifier (NBC) algorithm method. In *Proceedings of the 3rd International Conference of Bio-Based Economy for Application and Utility* (020228). DOI: 10.1063/5.0135542

Vasylchyshyn, O., Storozhenko, L., Babkova, T., Kuchmenko, V., & Kovalchuk, V. (2024). Social media as a factor in the transformation of public administration, justice and legality. *Multidisciplinary Reviews, 7*(Special Issue), 2024spe039. Advance online publication. DOI: 10.31893/multirev.2024spe039

Wadesango, N., Jori, A. K., & Lovemore, S. (2023). Literature review of the relationship between E-procurement and cost reduction. *Multidisciplinary Science Journal, 5*, 2023ss0316. DOI: 10.31893/multiscience.2023ss0316

Zhang, Y. (2023). Citizens' trust and digital attitudes: Evidence from city digital transformation in Shanghai, China *Public Administration and Policy, 26*(3), 258–271. DOI: 10.1108/PAP-01-2023-0014

KEY TERMS AND DEFINITION

Citizen Engagement: using digital platforms and technologies to allow for communication between the government and the people.

Digital Transformation in Government (E-Government): the use of information and communication technologies (ICT) by government agencies to transform relationships with citizens, businesses, and other government entities

Government-to-Business (G2B): a model of government service delivery that emphasizes the interactions between government agencies and business entities.

Government-to-Citizens (G2C): a model of e-government service delivery that functions in a direct manner, serving individual citizens through the utilization of digital platforms and channels.

Government-to-Employees (G2E): the model of e-government under consideration is one that prioritizes internal government operations and the services provided to public sector employees.

Government-to-Government (G2G): a model of e-government that facilitates interactions and information sharing between different government agencies, departments, and levels of government (local, regional, and national).

Systematic Literature Review (SLR): a rigorous research methodology that involves the comprehensive identification, evaluation, and synthesis of all relevant research evidence on a specific topic or research question.

Transparency: ghe principle and practice of making government information, processes, and decision-making visible and accessible to citizens.

Chapter 7
Integration of UMEGA Model and Cultural Theory to Analyze Citizens' Use of E-Government:
A Case Study of Disdukcapil Smart Bantul Application

Eliza Meiyani
Government Affairs and Administration, Universitas Muhammadiyah Yogyakarta, Indonesia

Rindi Kosasi
Universitas Muhammadiyah Yogyakarta, Indonesia

Muhammad Younus
http://orcid.org/0000-0001-9654-1546
Universitas Muhammadiyah Yogyakarta, Indonesia

Fadhil Hayan Mochammad
University Muhammadiyah Palu, Indonesia

ABSTRACT

This study aims to examine the factors that influence the use of the Disdukcapil Smart Bantul application in Bantul, Indonesia, by integrating the Unified Model of E-Government Adoption (UMEGA) with Cultural Theory. Through this approach,

DOI: 10.4018/979-8-2600-1618-3.ch007

the research seeks to gain a deeper understanding of how attitudes, intentions, social norms, and environmental support shape people's behavior in adopting e-government services. A quantitative method was employed using SmartPLS 4, with survey data collected from randomly selected users of the application. The findings reveal that social norms and environmental conditions, such as internet access and technical assistance, play a more significant role in encouraging the use of e-government services than psychological factors. This highlights the importance of practical and contextual support in driving adoption. The novelty of this research lies in its integrated perspective, combining both technical and cultural dimensions to provide a more comprehensive view of user behavior, while emphasizing that a supportive environment is essential for success

INTRODUCTION

Integrating e-government services is essential to improve public administration and service delivery to the public by utilizing digital tools and systems. E-Government enables the creation of a new paradigm in public administration that is more modern, by significantly improving efficiency, transparency and accessibility of services. In Indonesia, the quality of e-services including information quality, data security and privacy, plays a major role in influencing public satisfaction and trust in the public services provided (Mulyana & Jamaludin, 2023). E-governance provides many benefits, such as helping to reduce corruption, save budgets, and improve the quality of public services-all of which are essential to creating a more efficient and transparent government in this modern era (Storozhenko, 2023). The quality of e-services, such as information accuracy, data security, and privacy protection, greatly affects people's satisfaction and trust in digital-based public services. When these services feel safe and the information is reliable, citizens will feel more trusting and satisfied using them (Mulyana & Jamaludin, 2023).

The implementation of e-government, such as providing online services and enabling digital participation, has helped curb corruption. By reducing direct contact between citizens and civil servants and distributing authority more evenly, e-government promotes transparency and ensures public services are more open and accountable (Martins et al., 2023). People are increasingly optimistic about e-government services, especially with innovations such as the Disdukcapil (Population and Civil Registry Office) Smart Bantul service at Population and Civil Registry Office (Disdukcapil) Bantul. However, in order to fully benefit from e-government, there are still challenges to overcome, such as gaps in digital infrastructure and improving human resource capabilities. Some common obstacles that arise in e-government implementation include low digital literacy, limited internet access, lack of trust in digital services, and issues related to privacy and data security. A major challenge in digital literacy is that many citizens and government employees still need to develop the skills necessary to use digital platforms well. These skills are important so that they can make the most of e-government services, making public services easier to access and use (Kanaan et al., 2023). To provide easier and more efficient services for its citizens, the Bantul Regency Government has launched the Disdukcapil (Population and Civil Registry Office) Smart Bantul application. This application is designed so that the people of Bantul can take care of various administrative needs more simply and quickly, right from the palm of their hands.

Figure 1. Display and menu options of the Disdukcapil (Population and Civil Registry Office) Smart Bantul Application

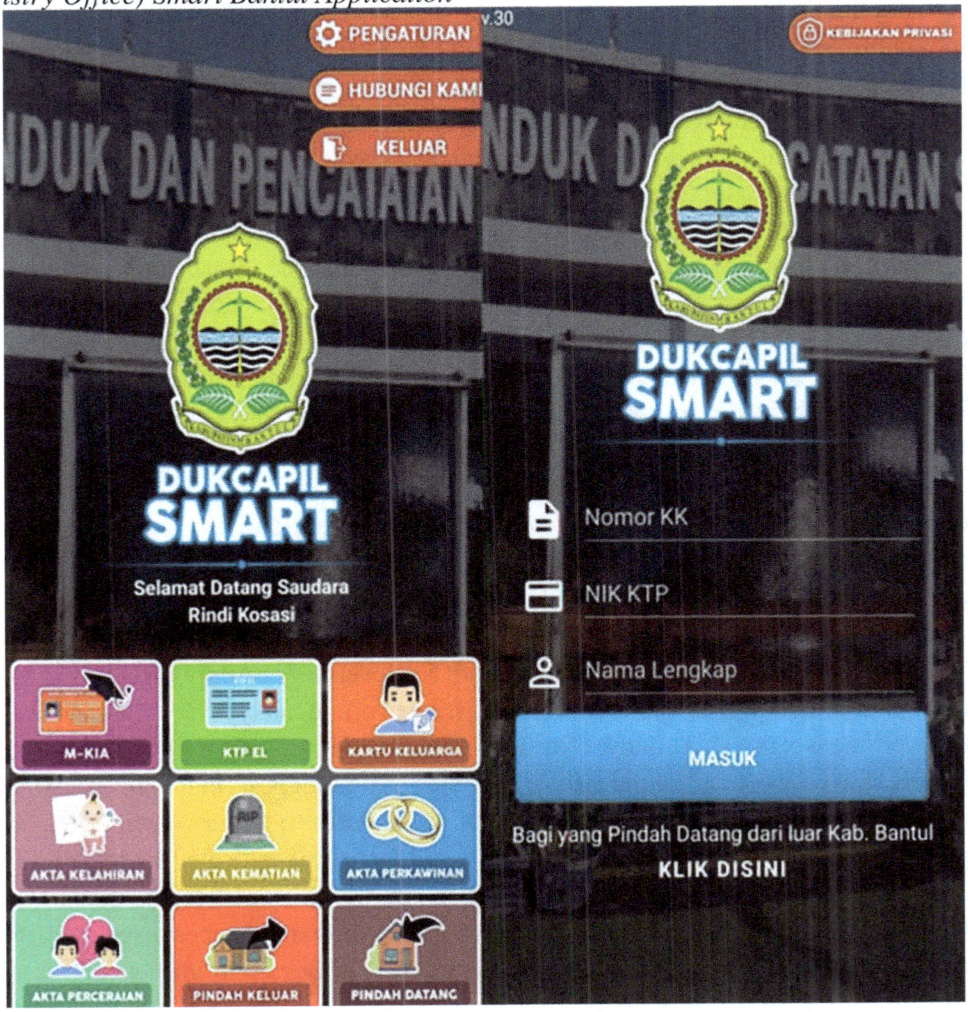

In early 2019, the Population and Civil Registration Office (Disdukcapil) of Bantul Regency introduced a public service application called Disdukcapil (Population and Civil Registry Office) Smart Bantul. The Disdukcapil (Population and Civil Registry Office) Smart Bantul application is a digital platform developed by the Population and Civil Registry Office of Bantul Regency. This application aims to make it easier for people to access population administration services online, such as making or changing ID cards, family cards (KK), birth certificates, death certificates, and other documents. This application is designed to help the community in managing population administration more easily. Disdukcapil (Population and Civil Registry Office) Smart Bantul is an e-government innovation that aims to improve the efficiency, effectiveness and transparency of administrative services in Bantul, Indonesia. This move is also in line with trends in Indonesia, where Information and Communication Technology (ICT) is increasingly being integrated into public services to improve access and user satisfaction (Darmawan & Nugroho, 2020). The Disdukcapil (Population and Civil Registry Office) Smart Bantul app is an important advancement in the digitization of public services, leveraging technological innovation to address evolving user needs. While the app offers many conveniences, the adoption rate among the public is still low, indicating that there are barriers to its use.

Based on user reviews, there are some who feel that the information provided in the app is not clear enough. They often have difficulty in understanding the requirements of the documents that need to be uploaded or the steps that need to be followed. Therefore, this study aims to analyze the factors that influence people's intention and behavior to use the Disdukcapil (Population and Civil Registry Office) Smart Bantul application. By integrating the Unified Model of E-Government Adoption (UMEGA) and Cultural Theory, it is hoped that this research can provide deeper insight into user behavior and the challenges faced. The results of this study are expected to provide recommendations for application developers and policy makers to improve e-government adoption in Bantul, as well as contribute to the literature on technology adoption in the context of public services.

The combination of the Unified Model of E-Government Adoption (UMEGA) and cultural theory offers a more thorough framework to analyze how citizens use e-government services. A number of studies, including by T. T. T. Nguyen (2023), highlight the importance of the artistic approach as this suggests that e-government services need to be more culturally sensitive in order to better match people's expectations. Moreover, by integrating external factors as indicated by the PEST (Political, Economic, Social, and Technological) framework together with UMEGA, the understanding of e-government adoption can be further enhanced, especially in developing countries, where external factors play a large role in influencing user behavior (T. T. T. Nguyen, 2023). S. Avazov and S. Lee, PhD (2020), reveal that by combining these models and theories, policymakers can design more effective strategies to encourage e-government adoption as well as ensure its sustainable use. This is done by addressing the various factors, both from within citizens and external conditions, that influence their behavior (Avazov & Lee, PhD., 2020). Y. Guo (2023) explains that the UMEGA Model, which includes factors such as performance expectations, ease of use, social influence, perceived risk, available support, and attitudes, has proven effective in predicting e-government adoption. For example, in Uzbekistan, people's expectations of service performance are the main factor driving their intention to use e-government (Guo, 2023).

Combining the UMEGA model with an artistic approach can help us better understand and improve e-government adoption, especially in developing countries. This approach makes e-government services more adaptable to user needs and creates more effective policies to support user behavior. The novelty of this research is highlighted by emphasizing its unique approach that combines the Unified Model of E-Government Adoption (UMEGA) with Cultural Theory. This integration provides a comprehensive understanding of user behavior towards the Disdukcapil (Population and Civil Registry Office) Smart Bantul application, which has not been addressed in previous studies that typically focus separately on technical or cultural aspects. This research aims to illustrate how combining these perspectives can improve e-government adoption, especially in the context of developing countries such as Indonesia, thus making e-government services more adaptable to user needs and increasing public service innovation in a modern context. This new framework is expected to provide insights that align e-government services with user expectations, thus addressing the gaps that exist in previous research.

Therefore, this study aims to analyze the factors that influence people's intention and behavior in using the Disdukcapil (Population and Civil Registry Office) Smart Bantul application. By integrating the Unified Model of E-Government Adoption (UMEGA) and Cultural Theory, this research is expected to provide deeper insights into user behavior and challenges faced. The results of this study are expected to provide recommendations for application developers and policy makers to improve e-government adoption in Bantul, as well as contribute to the literature on technology adoption in the context of public services.

LITERATURE REVIEW AND THEORETICAL FRAMEWORK

Citizen Use Of E-Government

Various things affect how often citizens utilize e-government services, such as how they see the usefulness of the service, their level of trust, the quality of the existing system, and the influence of their social environment. In a study conducted by T. P. U. Siwi and Z. Nawawi (2023), it was found that perceptions of e-service quality including core services, facilities, and support had a positive impact on trust and perceived usefulness. This all led to increased satisfaction and use of e-government services among the public (Siwi & Nawawi, 2023). Citizens' use of e-government involves the application of information and communication technology (ICT) to facilitate interaction with government agencies. This not only increases transparency and efficiency, but also encourages active participation from the public. The development of ICT is therefore crucial in reducing corruption and increasing transparency and accountability, all of which are essential elements for a democratic government (Mikhalchenko, 2021). E-government makes it easier for citizens to access various public services online, such as registering births, paying taxes, renewing licenses, and obtaining health services. In this way, services become more accessible, save time, and reduce costs. In addition, digital technology opens up opportunities for citizens to consult, provide input on policies, and participate in elections online. These all help to strengthen democracy and encourage active citizen engagement in governance. In addition, e-government also makes government operations more efficient by reducing bureaucracy, speeding up administrative processes, and improving the quality of services provided to the public.

UMEGA THEORY - *Attitude*

The view that e-government services can significantly improve efficiency and effectiveness strongly influences positive attitudes towards their use. Research in Indonesia shows that belief in the benefits of these services has a major impact on the intention to use them. In addition, trust in government and the internet are also important factors that influence people's attitudes towards e-government. When citizens feel trust, they are more likely to adopt and use these services, as seen in studies in South Africa and Pakistan (Khurshid et al., 2019). Attitudes towards e-government reflect how aware and interested citizens are in the digital services offered by the government. This includes their understanding of the existence and benefits of such services, as well as their interest in learning more and using them. With structural and regulatory guarantees in place from the government, perceptions of the ease of use of these services will increase, which in turn can foster positive attitudes towards technology and encourage more people to utilize e-government services (Borazon & Nguyen, 2022). Some of the factors that influence attention to e-government services include government efforts in promotion and education, positive experiences experienced by users, and support from the media and the community. When people's awareness of e-government services increases, they will be more motivated to explore and utilize them in their daily lives.

Behavioral Intention

Behavioral intention towards e-government focuses on how individuals are able or willing to use e-government services in the future. E-government service quality, public trust, and leadership have a positive effect on public opinion which in turn affects the effectiveness of service quality and leadership in influencing user behavior (Hariguna et al., 2023). This is influenced by individuals' views on the benefits derived from public services, such as efficiency and ease of access. Users are more attracted to e-government technology due to the fact that it is easy to use and does not require much effort. Ease of use and social influence are essential to drive e-government adoption (T. T. U. Nguyen et al., 2024). Policymakers and service providers should concentrate on making these platforms easier to use and use social influence to attract users' attention (Warsono et al., 2023). By addressing these issues, governments can improve the efficiency, transparency and accessibility of their services. Ultimately, this will result in increased public trust and increased participation in e-government (Fikri et al., 2023). Social factors such as friends and family encouraging e-government use are also important. In addition, externally derived elements, such as the availability of adequate infrastructure and technical support that facilitate access to these services, can increase people's desire to use e-government and increase their confidence in data security and privacy. Overall, by considering these factors, the desire to use e-government services will increase.

Effort Expectancy

E-government effort expectancy refers to how people perceive the use of e-government technology. Effort expectancy, which measures how easy or difficult e-government services are, also has a positive impact on people's perception of these services (Muhammad & Kaya, 2023). Research in Indonesia shows that the perception of e-government services can improve efficiency and effectiveness significantly affects the intention to use them (Malodia et al., 2021). This includes the belief that the use of e-government services can be regulated and supervised. This perception is influenced by an easy-to-understand user interface, clear instructions, and ease of access to the e-government platform. The less effort required to access and use e-government services, the more likely it is that people will use them regularly. Expectations for effort are also linked to improvements in the quality of public services. Simplifying e-government systems can increase their effectiveness, make them more accessible, and make them more user-friendly (Aritonang, 2017). A study shows that effort expectancy significantly influences citizens' desire to use e-government services in Indonesia. The research suggests that ease of use and other components, such as performance expectancy and social influence, play an important role in e-government service uptake (Afrizal & Wallang, 2021).

Facilitating Conditions

To increase e-government adoption in Indonesia, it is important to address constraints such as poor ICT infrastructure, inadequate human resources, and lack of citizen readiness (Sabani et al., 2019). To ensure fairness and equality, the availability of electronic public services enables the government to meet various legal needs and overcome traditional barriers such as organizational difficulties and geographical distance (Rudanetska, 2023). Conditions that support e-government include external conditions that enable or prevent people from using e-government services, such as adequate technological infrastructure, fast and stable internet connection, and available technical support. Policies and regulations that support the use of e-government are also included in these conditions (Mensah et al., 2020). These conditions are important in creating an enabling environment for effective and efficient adoption and use of e-government services by the public. This is important because e-government is technically available and provides a positive and secure user experience. By creating an enabling environment for the adoption of these technologies, governments can maximize the potential of e-government to improve the efficiency of public administration and public services.

CULTURAL THEORY - *Beliefs and Values*

Citizens' beliefs and values re critical in shaping the adoption and use of e-government services; their perceptions of benefits, security and reliability influence their intentions and satisfaction. Trust is a key factor that influences citizens' intention and satisfaction in using e-government services. Citizen trust and participation in services can increase with improved security and privacy (Ahmed & Musa Ahmed, 2023). It is important to increase e-government service adoption and value creation: increase public trust in the internet, improve infrastructure conditions, and provide significant value in terms of time savings and ease of use (Aranyossy, 2022). Quality-safety systems and environmental policies increase public trust in citizen-centered e-governance systems. However, access to information may not always have the greatest impact (Jafari et al., 2022). Trust is a major factor that determines social media acceptance of e-government services. Factors such as individual characteristics, government factors, risk factors, and social media attributes influence this trust (Khan et al., 2023).

Social Norms

Social norms play an important role in citizens' adoption and use of e-government services, societal expectations, perceived social benefits, and individual desires influence their behavior. Social norms are informal rules that individuals follow because they believe that others act in the same way and expect sanctions if they deviate, which can lead to a mismatch between personal preferences and expressed preferences (Valentim, 2023). Social influence and perceived trust are critical when receiving government services online. Everywhere, familiarity and connections influence social influence (Liu, 2022). As citizens expect interactive services, online consultation, and the ability to self-manage their social benefits and services, increasing the transparency of social welfare information and services through digital transformation is essential (Gasumova et al., 2022). Therefore, social norms, including societal expectations, perceived social benefits, and individual desires, significantly influence the adoption and use of e-government services. This means that different methods are needed to increase people's engagement with digital government platforms.

Social Intentions

Perceived value, behavioral control, and social influence shape citizens' perceptions of e-government portals. Cost, convenience, and accuracy of information are the main factors (Yap et al., 2019). In addition, the two main predictors of citizen participation in e-government are trust in e-government and transparency of good governance aspects. To spread information about e-government through social media, it is important to see how easy and useful it is (Avazov & Lee, PhD., 2020). Social intention is the social reason that drives people to use e-government services. E-government offers many conveniences, such as faster access to public information, more transparent administrative processes, and more efficient public services. People in countries with social intentions tend to use e-government to increase their participation in government activities, support government transparency and accountability, and help build a more intelligent and engaged society. In addition, social intentions also include increasing digital inclusion so that more people can use technology in their interactions with the government and benefit from it. Thus, in the context of e-government, social intentions reflect people's aspirations to build a society that is more connected, transparent, and responsive to public needs.

Figure 2. Research Design

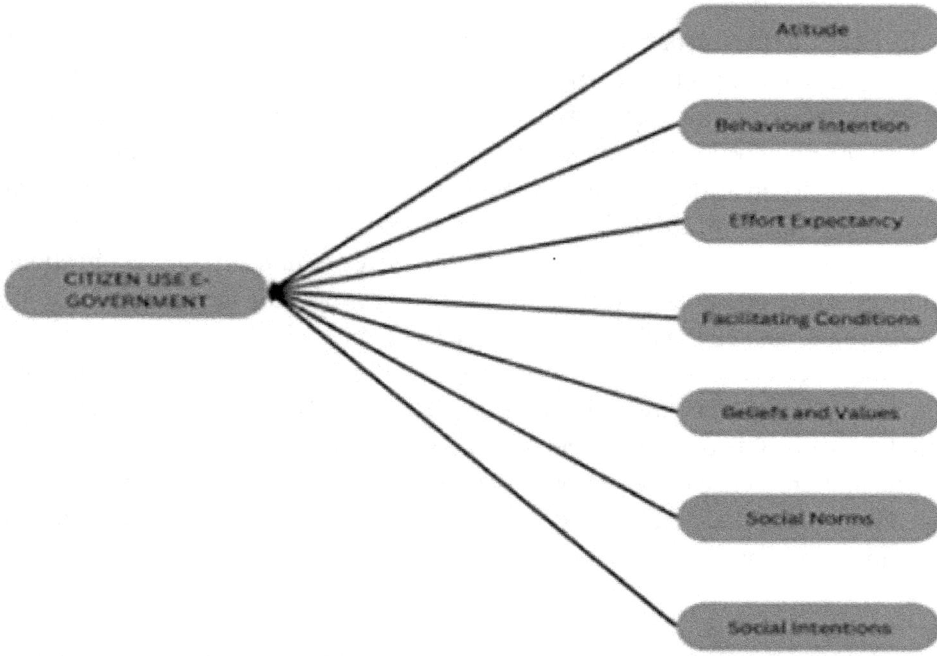

H.1= Attitude has a positive and significant effect on citizen use of government
H.2= Behaviour intention positively and significantly towards citizen use of government
H.3= Effort Expectancy positively and significantly towards citizen use of government
H.4= Facilitating Conditions positively and significantly towards citizen use of government
H.5= Beliefs and Values positively and significantly towards citizen use of government
H.6= Social Norms positively and significantly towards citizen use of government
H.7= Social institutions positively and significantly towards citizen use of government

The seven hypotheses were designed using the Technology Acceptance Model (TAM) and the DeLone and McLean information system success models, which have proven effective in explaining technology adoption behavior. This research offers a new approach by combining the UMEGA Model and Cultural Theory, namely the

Technology Acceptance Model (TAM) developed by Davis (1989) which explains that two main factors, namely 'perceived ease of use' and 'perceived usefulness', influence users' intention to adopt technology. In the context of e-government, an understanding of TAM is essential to analyze how users respond to applications such as Disdukcapil (Population and Civil Registry Office) Smart Bantul which has never been done in the context of using e-government applications in Indonesia. Previously, research focused more on technical or cultural aspects separately, while this study integrates both aspects to provide a more comprehensive understanding of user behavior. DeLone and McLean (1992) identified six dimensions of information system success, including system quality, information quality, and user satisfaction.

This model is relevant in the context of this study because the success of the Disdukcapil (Population and Civil Registry Office) Smart Bantul application is highly dependent on the quality of services provided and user satisfaction with the application. Research by Siwi and Nawawi (2023) shows that e-government service quality has a positive effect on user trust and satisfaction, which supports the hypothesis that service quality will increase users' intention to use the Disdukcapil (Population and Civil Registry Office) Smart Bantul application (Siwi & Nawawi, 2023). This study aims to understand more deeply the factors that encourage or hinder the use of e-government services by Bantul residents through hypothesis testing. The research results are expected to help policymakers design implementations to increase the acceptance of e-government services.

METHODOLOGY

Research Design

This research uses quantitative methods with data collection through questionnaires distributed to 100 respondents, who were selected using the Slovin formula. The questionnaire was designed with closed answer options and used a Likert scale to measure respondents' opinions and attitudes towards e-government services. The collected data were then analyzed using Structural Equation Modeling (SEM) with Partial Least Square (PLS) technique through SmartPLS-4 software. The data analysis process included validity and reliability testing, as well as interpretation of relationships between variables to gain a deeper understanding of the factors influencing the use of the Disdukcapil (Population and Civil Registry Office) Smart Bantul application.

Population and Sampling Technique

The population that is the focus of this study includes the people of Bantul City who have used or have access to e-government services, especially online community services known as Disdukcapil (Population and Civil Registry Office) Smart Bantul. To determine the number of respondents from the total users of the Disdukcapil (Population and Civil Registry Office) Smart Bantul application, which reached 5000 people, the researcher utilized a respondent sample table by applying the Slovin formula. The Slovin formula was used in this study to determine a representative sample size from a larger population. The advantage of using the Slovin formula is its ability to provide an appropriate sample size with an acceptable error rate. By using this formula, researchers can ensure that the sample taken is large enough to represent the population, so that the results of the study can be generalized. In addition, this formula is simple and easy to apply, making it easier for researchers to determine the number of respondents needed to achieve valid and reliable results. The Slovin formula calculates the sample size needed in a study, considering the population size and the acceptable error rate. The formula is as follows:

$$\frac{N}{1 + N(e)^{\wedge 2}}$$

n = sample size

N = population size

e = the desired error rate (usually in decimal form).

Using data from this study, where the total population (N) is 5000 users and the permissible error rate (e) is 10% (0.1), the calculation of the sample size (n) is as follows:

$$n\frac{5000}{1 + 5000(0.1)^2}$$

$$n\frac{5000}{1 + 5000 \times 0.1}$$

$$n\frac{5000}{1 + 50}$$

$$n\frac{5000}{51}$$

= 98.04

n rounded into 100 respondents with a total population of 5000 users of the Disdukcapil (Population and Civil Registry Office) Smart Bantul application.

Data Collection Techniques

The research data was collected through questionnaires distributed to one hundred respondents, the sample size was calculated using the Slovin formula. To facilitate effective data collection, the questionnaire was distributed via WhatsApp and Google Forms. This method enabled the collection of data regarding the use of Disdukcapil (Population and Civil Registry Office) Smart Bantul e-government services in Bantul. Using a Google Form-based questionnaire, researchers can optimize the data collection process efficiently and reach respondents faster. Distribution through WhatsApp also allows researchers to reach respondents directly and facilitate their participation in the study. This study involved various community groups regarding gender, age, and education level. The criteria for respondents included in this study are citizens who have used e-government services, especially the Disdukcapil (Population and Civil Registry Office) Smart Bantul application. By analyzing these demographic characteristics, we can get a clearer picture of the respondents' profiles and how demographic variations can affect respondents' views and experiences of the services studied. The following table illustrates the demographic characteristics of respondents in Table 1.

Table 1. Respondents demographic

Respondent Characteristic	Category	Percentage (%)
Gender	Man	46%
	Woman	56%
Age	20-30 Years	71%
	31-40 Years	21%
	41-50 Years	8%
	51-60 Years	
	>60 Years	
Education	Elementary School/Junior High School	2%
	Senior High School/Vocational High School	46%
	Associate Degree (Diploma 3)	12%
	Bachelor's Degree (S1)	37%
	Master's Degree	2%
	Doctoral Degree (Ph.D.)	1%

The respondent characteristics table shows the distribution based on gender, age, and education level. Regarding gender, 46% of respondents were male and 56% female, indicating higher female participation in this study. Based on age, most respondents were in the young age group, namely 20-30 years, which reached 71%. This was followed by the 31-40 age group, with a percentage of 21%, and the 41-50 age group, which contributed 8%. There were no respondents over 50 years old. Regarding education, respondents with high school or vocational high school education dominated with a percentage of 46%, indicating that almost half of the respondents had a secondary education background.

As many as 37% of respondents were D4 or S1 graduates, suggesting that more than a third of respondents had higher education. Only 1% of respondents had a doctorate or doctoral degree. Respondents with primary (elementary/middle school) and postgraduate (master's) education accounted for 2% each. This data provides a complete picture of the demographics of the research respondents. This description of demographic statistics provides a complete picture of the demographics of the research respondents. By knowing the demographics of the respondents, we can find out how variables such as age, gender and education level can influence their perceptions and experiences with the Disdukcapil (Population and Civil Registry Office) Smart Bantul application.

Research Data Instruments and Measurements

This study uses a closed questionnaire with pre-prepared answers, so that respondents only need to choose one of the available answer options. This method has several advantages, including ease of data processing as the answers received are uniform and the fact that respondents do not need to formulate their own answers, which reduces the possibility of bias. To ensure that all answer options cover the full range of possibilities related to the research questions, the closed questionnaire was carefully designed.

Using a Likert scale, which usually consists of five or seven grades, respondents can determine how much they agree or disagree with a statement. These grades range from "strongly disagree" to "strongly agree". This scale was chosen because it can provide an in-depth picture of respondents' opinions, attitudes, or perceptions towards various aspects of the e-government services under study. In addition, because each level has a numerical value that can be calculated and processed statistically, this scale makes it easier for researchers to categorize and analyze data quantitatively. This study uses a Likert scale to measure the data collected.

Table 2. Likert Scale

Value	Information
1	Strongly disagree
2	Disagree
3	Neutral
4	Seven
5	Strongly agree

Table 2 presents the Likert scale used in the study to measure respondents' opinions and perceptions of the Disdukcapil Smart Bantul e-government service application. This scale consists of five rating levels, ranging from "Strongly Disagree" (score 1) to "Strongly Agree" (score 5), which allows respondents to express their level of agreement with the given statements. By using this scale, researchers can categorize and analyze data quantitatively, providing a more in-depth picture of user satisfaction and areas that need to be improved to enhance the user experience of using the app.

Data Analysis

Data analysis includes grouping and organizing data into patterns, categories, and basic descriptive units collected from field notes, documentation, and interviews. The data analysis method used was Structural Equation Modeling (SEM), with Partial Least Square (PLS) techniques, supported by SmartPLS-4 software. SEM-PLS-4 is a popular and effective variance-based methodology for analyzing complex and interrelated data. It is suitable for small data samples and does not follow the normal distribution assumption. SEM-PLS uses a two-stage method. The measurement model assesses the reliability and validity of the constructs, and the structural model assesses the relationships between the constructs. Some of the important processes that will be followed during this data analysis include:

Figure 3. Data Analysis Flow

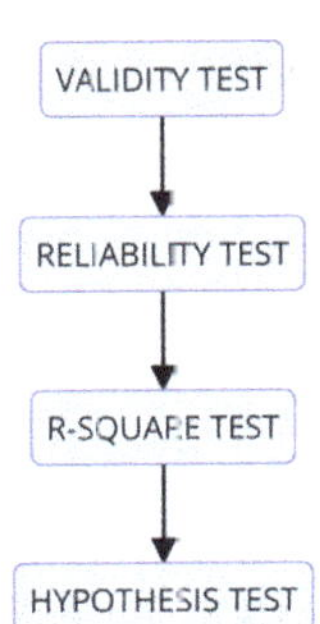

The validity test is the first step to ensuring that the measurement device accurately shows the intended idea. How well the indicators used measure the variables to be studied is determined by this test. Reliability tests also evaluate the consistency of metric results. If instruments are used repeatedly under the same conditions, they will give the same results, indicating the presence of internal consistency. In SEM-PLS, composite reliability and Cronbach's Alpha are used to evaluate dependability. An acceptable composite value is usually above 0.70, and a reasonable Cronbach's Alpha value is also considered to be above 0.70. This test retests the measurement results under the same conditions. In this study, the validity and reliability of the instruments are critical to ensure that the data collected is reliable and reflects the variables being measured. Validity refers to the extent to which an instrument measures what it is supposed to measure. To test validity, the authors used factor analysis to ensure that the items in the questionnaire correlate with the expected constructs. Reliability refers to the consistency of the results obtained from the instrument. In this study, we used two methods to test reliability: Composite Reliability and Cronbach's Alpha. The expected Composite Reliability value is above 0.70, and a good Cronbach's Alpha value is also expected above 0.70. Thus, the instruments used in this study can be considered valid and reliable, which provides confidence that the research results can be trusted.

Furthermore, the R-Square test is conducted to determine how well the model explains the variation in the data. The R-Square value indicates the proportion of variance in the dependent variable that can be explained by the independent variables in the model; the higher the R-Square value, the better the model's description of the relationship between variables. Hypothesis testing is the final step. The aim is to find out if there is a significant relationship between the research variables. If the p-value is less than 0.05 or the t-statistic value is greater than 1.96, then the hypothesis is important. To ensure that there is a hypothesized relationship between variables in a model, hypothesis testing is used. The results of data analysis allow this test to help researchers determine the validity of the hypothesis.

Figure 4. Research Flow

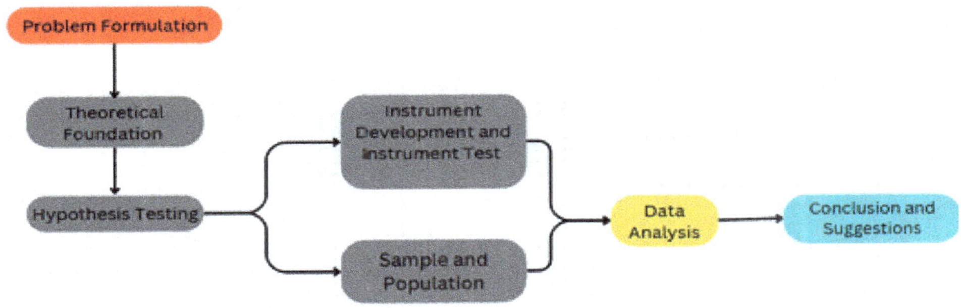

The SEM-PLS method allows researchers to thoroughly analyze data to find relationships between variables, test theoretical models, and ensure that research results can be applied to other populations. This method allows researchers to discover patterns and relationships that are not visible with conventional analysis methods. This helps them gain a deeper understanding of the phenomenon under study. The figure summarizing the research flow helps to understand the methods used in this study. Figure 4 shows the steps used in the research, including problem formulation, creation of a theoretical framework, instrument development and testing, hypothesis testing, and data analysis. After that, results are drawn, and recommendations are given.

RESULT AND DISCUSSION

Structural Equation Modeling (SEM) was used to conduct this study, and the Partial Least Square (PLS) technique was used. The analysis results include hypothesis testing, interpretation of the relationship between variables in the Umega Model, and interpretation of the Cultural Theory used in this study.

Figure 5. Validated Research Model

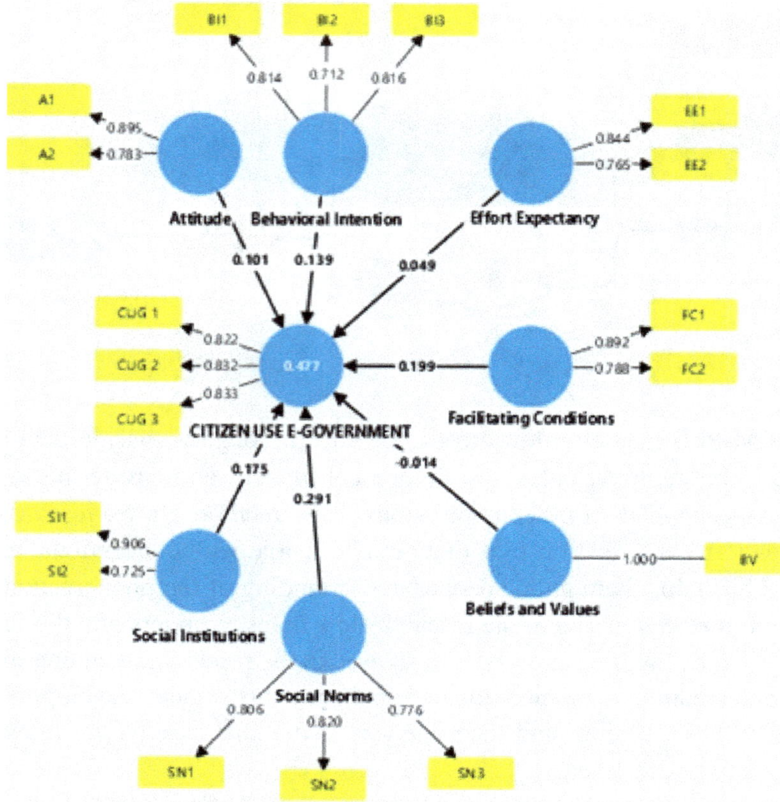

Source: processed using SmartPLS 4

Figure 5 is a structural model that describes the factors that affect the use of e-government by citizens. The model consists of several primary constructs, including Attitude measured by two indicators, A1 with a value of 0.895 and A2 with 0.783. This Attitude influences Behavioral Intention with a path value of 0.101. Behavioral Intention itself is measured by three indicators, namely BI1 (0.814), BI2 (0.712), and BI3 (0.816), and influences the use of e-government with a tracking value of 0.139. Effort Expectancy, measured by two indicators, EE1 (0.844) and EE2 (0.785), influences the use of e-government with a tracking value of 0.045. Facilitating Conditions, measured by two indicators, FC1 (0.892) and FC2 (0.788), affect the use of e-government with a tracking value of 0.199. Citizen Use E-Government is measured by three indicators: CUG1 (0.822), CUG2 (0.832), and CUG3 (0.833). This construct is influenced by various factors such as behavioral intentions, business expectations, and supporting conditions.

In addition, Social Institutions, as measured by two indicators, SI1 (0.906) and SI2 (0.725), affect the use of e-government with a tracking value of 0.175. Social Norms, measured by three indicators, SN1 (0.806), SN2 (0.820), and SN3 (0.776), influence the use of e-government with a track value of 0.291. Finally, beliefs and values, measured by one indicator, BV (1,000), do not directly affect citizens' use of e-government. This model shows the relationship between constructs with arrow lines and path coefficient values that indicate the strength of influence between each construct. This model helps to understand how various factors affect citizens' use of e-government. Robertson and Evans (2020) explained that Cronbach's alpha is the most widely used statistic to indicate the internal reliability of a scale, with a value higher than 0.70 indicating good reliability (Robertson & Scott Evans, 2020).

Table 3. Reliability Results

	Cronbach's alpha	Composite reliability (rho_a)	Composite reliability (rho_c)	Average variance extracted (AVE)
Attitude	0.895	0.833	0.828	0.707
Behavioral Intention	0.691	0.718	0.825	0.812
Citizen Use E-Government	0.773	0.778	0.888	0.887
Effort Expectancy	0.462	0.471	0.787	0.649
Facilitating Conditions	0.598	0.633	0.829	0.708
Social Institutions	0.536	0.619	0.803	0.873
Social Norms	0.72	0.72	0.843	0.642

Source: primary questionnaire data (processed using SmartPLS 4)

The table 3 above shows the reliability test results for various variables in the study, with values higher than 0.70 indicating good reliability. The Attitude variable has a Cronbach's alpha value of 0.895 and a composite reliability (rho_c) of 0.828, indicating good internal consistency. Behavioral intention shows a Cronbach's alpha value of 0.691, slightly below the standard, but the rho_c value reaches 0.825, indicating adequate reliability. The Citizen Use E-Government variable has a Cronbach's alpha value of 0.773 and a rho_c of 0.888, indicating strong reliability. Effort Expectancy has a low Cronbach's alpha value of 0.462 but a composite reliability (rho_c) of 0.787, indicating better consistency. For the Facilitating Conditions variable, Cronbach's alpha value is 0.598, but the rho_c reaches 0.829, thus still indicating good internal consistency. Social Institutions have a Cronbach's alpha of 0.536, which is low, but the composite reliability of 0.803 still indicates adequate reliability. Finally, Social Norms show a Cronbach's alpha value of 0.720 and a rho_c of 0.843, indicating strong reliability. Most variables meet or approach the expected reliability standards, except for a few variables that require improvement to improve internal consistency. The findings of this study indicate that the assessment tool used has good validity and reliability in measuring public acceptance of e-government services. The next step is to assess the extent to which the structural model can explain the public's use of e-government services using a reliable instrument. The R-square value provides an overview of how much the model can explain the dependent variable. The table shows the R square and modified R square values for the citizen e-government utilization variable:

Table 4. R-Square

	R-square	R-square adjusted
CITIZEN USE E-GOVERNMENT	0.477	0.437

The CITIZEN USE E-GOVERNMENT variable has an R-square value of 0.477, meaning that about 47.7% of the variation in using e-government services can be explained by the variables or factors in the model or analysis. The adjusted R-square value is 0.437. The R-square against the number of independent variables in the model shows that considering the number of independent variables used in the analysis, the model can explain about 43.7% of the variation in e-government services. This fairly high R-square value indicates that the variables or factors included in the model significantly correlate with the use of e-government services. Therefore, the variable of citizen e-government use is an important factor in determining how much e-government services are used by the public. The results of this study can help the government make plans to increase the use and adoption of digital services by citizens.

The hypothesis is tested using the R-squared value to determine how effective the structural model is in showing how citizens use e-government services. This study analyzes the influence of independent factors, such as effort expectancy, supporting conditions, performance expectancy, and social influence, on the use of e-government by the public. The table below presents the results of the hypothesis testing, including the original sample size (O), sample mean (M), standard deviation (STDEV), T statistic (|O/STDEV|), and p-value. This p-value determines whether the hypothesis will be accepted or rejected.

Table 5. Hypotheses Test

	Original sample (O)	Sample mean (M)	Standard deviation (STDEV)	T statistics (|O/ STDEV|)	P values	
Attitude -> CITIZEN USE E-GOVERNMENT	0.101	0.089	0.098	1.049	0.294	Rejected
Behavioral Intention -> CITIZEN USE E-GOVERNMENT	0.139	0.151	0.113	1.228	0.220	Rejected
Beliefs and Values -> CITIZEN USE E-GOVERNMENT	-0.014	-0.023	0.08	0.176	0.860	Rejected
Effort Expectancy -> CITIZEN USE E-GOVERNMENT	0.049	0.05	0.09	0.551	0.582	Rejected
Facilitating Conditions -> CITIZEN USE E-GOVERNMENT	0.189	0.195	0.105	1.985	0.047	Accepted
Social Institutions -> CITIZEN USE E-GOVERNMENT	0.175	0.188	0.09	1.934	0.053	Rejected
Social Norms -> CITIZEN USE E-GOVERNMENT	0.291	0.289	0.115	2.531	0.011	Accepted

Source: primary questionnaire data (processed using SmartPLS 4)

Based on the analysis of the paths presented in the table, the constructs that affect citizens' use of e-government are analyzed using T-statistics and P-value values. It can be valid if the T-statistic value is more than 1.96 and the P-value is less than 0.05. In this case, only two pathways meet the validity criteria. First, the Facilitating Conditions for using e-government showed a T-statistical value of 1,985 and a P-value of 0.047, so it was declared valid. Second, Social Norms for using e-government have a T-statistical value of 2.531 and a P-value of 0.011, which is also declared valid. Meanwhile, other pathways need to meet the validity criteria. The path from Attitude to the use of e-government has a T-Statistic value of 1,049 and a P-Value of 0.294, Behavioral Intention has a T-Statistic value of 1,228 and a P-Value of 0.220, Beliefs and Values has a T-Statistic value of 0.176 and a P-Value of 0.860, Effort Expectancy has a T-Statistic value of 0.551 and P-Value 0.582, and Social Institutions has a T-Statistic value of 1,934 and a P-Value of 0.053. These pathways are declared invalid because they do not meet the requirements of a T-statistic value of more than 1.96 and a P-value of less than 0.05.

There are only two factors that have a significant influence on citizens' use of e-government: social norms and facilitating conditions. These two factors met the validity criteria with a T-statistic value of more than 1.96 and a P-value of less than 0.05, which indicates that their relationship with the use of e-government is statistically significant. Social Norms have a strong influence because they reflect social pressures and expectations that encourage individuals to use e-government services. The Supporting Conditions are essential because they include resources and infrastructure that facilitate access and use of e-government, such as internet availability and technical assistance. In this study, the results show that social norms and environmental conditions have a significant influence on the use of e-government services, which is in line with the findings by Siwi and Nawawi (2023) who also found that the perceived quality of e-government services contributes to user satisfaction and trust (Siwi & Nawawi, 2023).

However, in contrast to the study by Mulyana and Jamaludin (2023), which emphasizes the importance of psychological factors in e-government adoption, this study shows that practical and environmental factors are more dominant in influencing user behavior (Mulyana & Jamaludin, 2023). These findings add to our understanding of the dynamics of e-government application usage, especially in the context of culture and digital infrastructure in Indonesia. On the other hand, other factors such as Attitude, behavioral intention, beliefs and values, effort expectancy, and social institutions did not significantly influence the use of e-government.

Effort Expectancy has a positive effect on user intention in using the Disdukcapil (Population and Civil Registry Office) Smart Bantul application. However, the results showed that there was no significant effect of effort expectations on user intentions. Research by Darmawan Napitupulu et al (2024) found that effort expectations have a significant influence on user intentions in the context of e-government (Napitupulu et al., 2024). The study shows that the easier users find it to use technology, the greater their intention to adopt the service. The insignificance of the results in this study may be due to the high level of digital literacy among respondents, which makes them feel comfortable and have no difficulty in using the application. The beliefs and values that users have towards the app will have a positive effect on their intention to use the app. However, the results showed that this hypothesis was not significant. Research by Cho Sang Hyun. et al (2019) shows that beliefs and values have a significant effect on user intention to use e-government services (Cho et al., 2019).

The study emphasizes the importance of positive perceptions of the benefits and value of the services offered. In the context of this study, the insignificance of the results can be caused by a lack of clear understanding or information about the benefits offered by the Disdukcapil (Population and Civil Registry Office) Smart Bantul application, so that respondents do not feel a significant added value. Social influence from the surrounding environment (e.g., friends, family) has a positive effect on user intentions. However, the results showed that social influence was not significant. Research by Cioc et al (2023) found that social influence has a significant impact on user intention to adopt new technology (Cioc et al., 2023). The study shows that support from close people can increase user confidence in using technology. The insignificance of the results in this study may be due to other more dominant factors, such as the accessibility and ease of use of the application, which have more influence on user decisions. (Behavioral Intentions to Use Energy Efficiency Smart Solutions under the Impact of Social Influence: An Extended TAM Approach)

A variety of logical reasons can cause this. Attitudes and Behavioral Intentions may play a small role because although individuals have positive intentions, they still need adequate supporting conditions to implement them. Beliefs and Values may not be directly relevant to using certain technologies, such as e-government, as they are more general and not specific to technology. Business Expectations may not be significant because citizens may feel that using e-government does not require a considerable effort or because they are already familiar with similar technologies. Social institutions may not provide direct encouragement because their influence can be more macro and do not directly influence individual decisions to use e-government. Thus, these results suggest that more practical and environmental factors, such as Social Norms and Supporting Conditions, are more influential in encouraging the use of e-government than individual or psychological factors.

To increase the significance of the hypothesis that is not significant in the research on the use of the Disdukcapil (Population and Civil Registry Office) Smart Bantul application, it is recommended that the application manager conduct a more intensive education and socialization program regarding the benefits and ease of use of the application. In addition, involving community leaders or local influencers in promotional campaigns can help increase public trust and interest in using the application. Improving the user interface and user experience is also important to ensure the app is easy to use. With these steps, it is expected to encourage wider adoption and improve users' intention and behavior in utilizing e-government services.

CONCLUSION

This study aims to analyze the factors that influence the use of Disdukcapil (Population and Civil Registry Office) Smart Bantul application in Bantul, Indonesia, by integrating the Unified Model of E-Government Adoption (UMEGA) and Cultural Theory. Through this approach, this research successfully identifies and explores the various elements that influence people's intention and behavior in using e-government applications. The results show that there are several key factors that contribute to the adoption of the Disdukcapil (Population and Civil Registry Office) Smart Bantul application. First, social norms were shown to have a significant influence. People tend to be more motivated to use the app if they see that people around them, such as family, friends or coworkers, are also using the service. This suggests that social support and neighborhood influence are crucial in encouraging the use of new technologies. This study notes that social factors and practical environment are more influential compared to individual psychological factors, which is in line with previous findings that social norms can increase trust and intention to use e-government services.

Secondly, practical environmental conditions, such as adequate internet access and technical support, also play an important role. This study found that users who have good access to the internet and receive technical assistance when experiencing difficulties are more likely to use the Disdukcapil (Population and Civil Registry Office) Smart Bantul application. The data shows that 98% of respondents have good internet access, which contributes to the ease of use of the application. Therefore, improving internet infrastructure and providing effective technical support services are necessary to increase e-government adoption. Third, this study underscores the importance of perceived service quality. Users who feel that the application provides clear benefits, such as ease in accessing administrative services, are more likely to continue using the application. Previous research shows that perceptions of e-government service quality, including core and support services, have a positive impact on satisfaction and service usage. Therefore, it is important for app developers to continuously improve service quality and ensure that the app meets users' needs.

While this study provides valuable insights, there are some limitations that need to be noted. First, the unbalanced demographic distribution of respondents may affect the generalizability of the results. Most of the respondents were from a younger age group, so their views and experiences may not be representative of the entire population. Future research is recommended to involve a more diverse sample in terms of age, education, and socio-economic background. Secondly, this study used a survey method which may not fully capture the nuances of user behavior. Therefore, qualitative approaches, such as in-depth interviews or focus group discussions, may provide a deeper understanding of the experiences and challenges users face in using the Disdukcapil (Population and Civil Registry Office) Smart Bantul application. As a recommendation, the government and relevant stakeholders are advised to:

1. Improving Internet Infrastructure: Ensure better internet access throughout Bantul, especially in underserved areas, to support the use of e-government applications.
2. Provide Technical Support: Develop a technical support program that can help users, especially those less familiar with technology, to overcome problems they may face when using the applications.
3. Conduct Awareness Campaigns: Organize campaigns to raise public awareness about the benefits and how to use Disdukcapil (Population and Civil Registry Office) Smart Bantul application, so that more people are motivated to use them.
4. Improving Service Quality: Continue to evaluate and improve the application to ensure that the services provided meet users' expectations and needs.

With these measures, it is expected that the use of the Disdukcapil (Population and Civil Registry Office) Smart Bantul application will increase, making public administration services more efficient, transparent and accessible to all the people of Bantul. This research provides a solid foundation for further development in the field of e-government and is expected to serve as a reference for future research exploring factors that influence technology adoption in a government context. This research presents a novelty by combining the UMEGA Model and Cultural Theory to analyze the user behavior of the e-government application "Disdukcapil (Population and Civil Registry Office) Smart Bantul" in Bantul. Unlike previous studies that only focus on technical or cultural aspects, this research combines both perspectives to understand the factors that influence the use of e-government.

REFERENCES

Afrizal, D., & Wallang, M. (2021). Attitude on intention to use e-government in Indonesia. *Indonesian Journal of Electrical Engineering and Computer Science, 22*(1), 435. DOI: 10.11591/ijeecs.v22.i1.pp435-441

Ahmed, M. M., & Musa Ahmed, A. (2023). Citizens' Data Protection in E-government System. *International Journal of Innovative Computing, 13*(2), 1–9. DOI: 10.11113/ijic.v13n2.389

Aranyossy, M. (2022). User adoption and value of e-government services (Citizen-centric empirical study from Hungary). *Acta Oeconomica, 72*(4), 477–497. DOI: 10.1556/032.2022.00032

Aritonang, D. M. (2017). The Impact of E-Government System on Public Service Quality in Indonesia. *European Scientific Journal, 13*(35), 99. DOI: 10.19044/esj.2017.v13n35p99

Avazov, S., & Lee, PhD., S. (2020). E-Government Adoption in Uzbekistan: Empirical validation of the Unified Model of Electronic Government Acceptance (UMEGA). *The 21st Annual International Conference on Digital Government Research*, 338–339. DOI: 10.1145/3396956.3397008

Borazon, E. Q., & Nguyen, H. T. T. (2022). E-government Use in Vietnam: Do External Variables Drive a Positive Attitude Towards Technology? DOI: 10.21203/rs.3.rs-2191455/v1

Cho, S. H., Oh, S. Y., Rou, H. G., & Gim, G. Y. (2019). A Study on The Factors Affecting The Continuous Use of E-Government Services—Focused on Privacy and Security Concerns-. *2019 20th IEEE/ACIS International Conference on Software Engineering, Artificial Intelligence, Networking and Parallel/Distributed Computing (SNPD)*, 351–361. DOI: 10.1109/SNPD.2019.8935693

Cioc, M. M., Popa, . C., Olariu, A. A., Popa, C. F., & Nica, C.-B. (2023). Behavioral Intentions to Use Energy Efficiency Smart Solutions under the Impact of Social Influence: An Extended TAM Approach. *Applied Sciences (Basel, Switzerland), 13*(18), 10241. DOI: 10.3390/app131810241

Darmawan, A. B., & Nugroho, R. A. (2020). Factors that Affect User Satisfaction of Dukcapil Application (Dukcapil Dalam Genggaman) in Surakarta Regency. *JAKPP (Jurnal Analisis Kebijakan & Pelayanan Publik)*, 154–175. DOI: 10.31947/jakpp.vi.11588

Fikri, R., Purnomo, E. P., Pribadi, U., & Binti Mohammad, N. (2023). Technology Readiness of e-Government in the Use of Poverty Data for Social Assistance in Indonesia. In Stephanidis, C., Antona, M., Ntoa, S., & Salvendy, G. (Eds.), *HCI International 2023 Posters* (Vol. 1835, pp. 195–202). Springer Nature Switzerland., DOI: 10.1007/978-3-031-36001-5_25

Gasumova, S. E., & Starshinova, A. V. Perm State University, Bezrukov, A. V., & Ural Federal University named after the first President of Russia B.N. Yeltsin. (2022). Citizens' expectations from digitalization in the sphere of social welfare and social services. *Вестник Пермского Университета. Философия. Психология. Социология, 2*, 315–328. DOI: 10.17072/2078-7898/2022-2-315-328

Guo, Y. (2023). How Does Culture Influence Chinese People's Views and Actions on e-Government Websites? A Study on Citizens' Continuous Use of e-Government Websites Based on Cultural Model. *Proceedings of the 24th Annual International Conference on Digital Government Research*, 135–143. DOI: 10.1145/3598469.3598484

Hariguna, T., Rahardja, U., & Aini, Q. (2023). The antecedent e-government quality for public behaviour intention, and extended expectation-confirmation theory. *Computer Science and Information Technologies, 4*(1), 33–42. DOI: 10.11591/csit.v4i1.pp33-42

Jafari, S. M., Nikbakhsh, S., Komijani, P., & Karimi, F. (2022). Identifying the Antecedents of Public Trust in the Citizen-Centric E-Governance. *The Eurasia Proceedings of Science Technology Engineering and Mathematics, 17*, 129–135. DOI: 10.55549/epstem.1176069

Kanaan, A., AL-Hawamleh, A., Abulfaraj, A., Al-Kaseasbeh, H. M., & Alorfi, A. (2023). The effect of quality, security and privacy factors on trust and intention to use e-government services. *International Journal of Data and Network Science, 7*(1), 185–198. DOI: 10.5267/j.ijdns.2022.11.004

Khan, S., Umer, R., Uddin, N., Muhammad, J., & Ahmed, N. (2023). Identifying the factors affecting individuals' trust to use social media for e-government services: A conceptual model. *Mehran University Research Journal of Engineering and Technology, 42*(1), 109. DOI: 10.22581/muet1982.2301.11

Khurshid, M. M., Zakaria, N. H., Rashid, A., Ahmed, Y. A., & Shafique, M. N. (2019). Adoption of Transactional Service in Electronic Government – A Case of Pak-Identity Service. In Pappas, I. O., Mikalef, P., Dwivedi, Y. K., Jaccheri, L., Krogstie, J., & Mäntymäki, M. (Eds.), *Digital Transformation for a Sustainable Society in the 21st Century* (Vol. 11701, pp. 439–450). Springer International Publishing., DOI: 10.1007/978-3-030-29374-1_36

Liu, D. (2022). Factors Affecting Digital Government Adoption: Empirical Study of Trust and Social Influences on Extended TAM. *International Journal of Business Studies and Innovation*, *2*(3), 38–48. DOI: 10.35745/ijbsi2022v02.03.0004

Malodia, S., Dhir, A., Mishra, M., & Bhatti, Z. A. (2021). Future of e-Government: An integrated conceptual framework. *Technological Forecasting and Social Change*, *173*, 121102. DOI: 10.1016/j.techfore.2021.121102

Martins, J., Veiga, L., & Fernandes, B. (2023). Are electronic government innovations helpful to deter corruption? Evidence from across the world. *Economics and Politics*, *35*(3), 1177–1203. DOI: 10.1111/ecpo.12255

Mensah, I. K., Zeng, G., & Luo, C. (2020). E-Government Services Adoption: An Extension of the Unified Model of Electronic Government Adoption. *SAGE Open*, *10*(2), 215824402093359. DOI: 10.1177/2158244020933593

Mikhalchenko, A. (2021). ELECTRONIC GOVERNANCE IN THE PROCESS OF MAKING MANAGEMENT DECISIONS. *Scientific Notes of Taurida National V.I. Vernadsky University. Series. Economy and Management*, *71*(3). Advance online publication. DOI: 10.32838/2523-4803/71-3-7

Muhammad, A. S., & Kaya, T. (2023). Factors affecting the citizen's intention to adopt e-government in Nigeria. *Journal of Information. Communication and Ethics in Society*, *21*(3), 271–289. DOI: 10.1108/JICES-05-2022-0054

Mulyana, Y., & Jamaludin, M. (2023). Effects of government electronic service quality on citizen satisfaction with integrated service delivery in urban areas. *International Journal of Public Policy and Administration Research*, *10*(1), 24–33. DOI: 10.18488/74.v10i1.3293

Napitupulu, D., Usino, W., Azmi, N. A., Kartika, R. S., Supratikta, H., Suhendra, A., Yohanitas, W. A., Saksono, H., Halik, A., & Suhandojo, S. (2024). Understanding the key driver of e-government services continuance usage intention: An integrated model of Expectation Confirmation Model and Technology Acceptance Model. *Journal of Infrastructure. Policy and Development*, *8*(12), 7957. DOI: 10.24294/jipd.v8i12.7957

Nguyen, T. T. T. (2023). Citizens' intentions to use e-government during the COVID-19 pandemic: Integrating the technology acceptance model and perceived risk theory. *Kybernetes*, *52*(7), 2329–2346. DOI: 10.1108/K-07-2022-1023

Nguyen, T. T. U., Nguyen, P. V., Huynh, H. T. N., Vrontis, D., & Ahmed, Z. U. (2024). Identification of the determinants of public trust in e-government services and participation in social media based on good governance theory and the technology acceptance model. *Journal of Asia Business Studies*, *18*(1), 44–61. DOI: 10.1108/JABS-04-2023-0160

Robertson, O., & Scott Evans, M. (2020). Just how reliable is your internal reliability? An overview of Cronbach's alpha (α). *PsyPag Quarterly*, *1*(115), 23–27. DOI: 10.53841/bpspag.2020.1.115.23

Rudanetska, O. (2023). International access level to administrative services in electronic format. *Analytical and Comparative Jurisprudence*, *1*(1), 380–383. DOI: 10.24144/2788-6018.2023.01.64

Sabani, A., Deng, H., & Thai, V. (2019). Evaluating the Development of E-Government in Indonesia. *Proceedings of the 2nd International Conference on Software Engineering and Information Management*, 254–258. DOI: 10.1145/3305160.3305191

Siwi, T. P. U., & Nawawi, Z. (2023). Building Citizen Satisfaction Towards E-Government Services: A Conceptual Framework. *Jurnal Manajemen Pelayanan Publik*, *6*(2), 253. DOI: 10.24198/jmpp.v6i2.46471

Storozhenko, L. (2023). ELECTRONIC GOVERNMENT AS A TOOL FOR NETOCRATIC MANAGEMENT: BENEFITS AND CAPABILITIES. *Grail of Science*, *26*(26), 78–81. DOI: 10.36074/grail-of-science.14.04.2023.010

Valentim, V. (2023). *Norms (Entry for the Encyclopedia of Political Sociology)*. DOI: 10.31219/osf.io/erfpg

Warsono, H., Yuwono, T., & Putranti, I. R. (2023). Analyzing technology acceptance model for collaborative governance in public administration: Empirical evidence of digital governance and perceived ease of use. *International Journal of Data and Network Science*, *7*(1), 41–48. DOI: 10.5267/j.ijdns.2022.12.008

Yap, C. S., Ahmad, R., Newaz, F. T., & Mason, C. (2019). Continuous Use Intention of E-Government Portals the Perspective of Older Citizens. *International Journal of Electronic Government Research*, *15*(1), 1–16. DOI: 10.4018/IJEGR.2019010101

Chapter 8
Digital Divides and Democratic Dividends:
Comparing E-Participation Outcomes Across Three West African Democracies

Soumi Ghosh
http://orcid.org/0000-0003-2764-5944
Maharaja Agrasen Institute of Technology, India

Ritik Raj
http://orcid.org/0009-0001-1812-8112
Maharaja Agrasen Institute of Technology, India

ABSTRACT

This paper presents a comparative study examining the relationship between access to digital infrastructures and electronic participation in four countries: Ghana, Senegal, Nigeria, and others. The study compares the participation rates and institutional structures amongst urban and rural respondents (2019-2024), reviewed through a mixed-method approach on 2,847 respondents. Results show diverse effectiveness in e-participation, with Ghana recording a 68 percent increase in citizen initiatives, Senegal 45 percent, and Nigeria 31 percent. The Quality of the infrastructure, e-literacy schemes, and the government's interest are predictive of the successful implementation of e-participation. The study aims to address a knowledge gap regarding digital inequalities and their impact on democratic processes, exploring potential solutions for digital inclusion within democratic governance in sub-Saharan Africa.

DOI: 10.4018/979-8-2600-1618-3.ch008

1. INTRODUCTION

Modern democracy increasingly utilizes digital technologies to enhance interaction with citizens, facilitate consultations on practices, and promote state transparency. Yet, the potential of automated democratic involvement through technology faces a serious problem in developing countries, where the digital divide forms inequalities in obtaining electronic participation opportunities (Norris, 2001). Such an imbalance is particularly sharp in sub-Saharan Africa as infrastructural limitations, economic and social disparities, and unevenly strong governments introduce multi-dimensional diversion and access to digital inclusion and exclusion. A region that forms a persuasive situation to explore these developments is West Africa, as it includes a variety of countries that have some experience with democracy, but have varying technologies and adoption of technology in the use of digital forms. The democratic environment of the region is diverse in terms of the colonial heritage of countries, the system used in their economy, and the level of technology adoption, which results in creating natural laboratories to compare the results of participation. This research paper will fill a significant gap in comparative research in terms of digital democracy studies by taking a systematic approach in explaining how the digital divide impacts the effectiveness of e-participation in three strategic comparative West Africa democracies about Ghana, Senegal, and Nigeria. These countries reflect a spectrum of democratic regulations and technological embedment, which provides information regarding the Impact of the various institutional, economic, and social settings on the outcomes of digital participation. The relevance of the research extends beyond academia, as it offers policymakers, development professionals, and international agencies a practical framework for promoting democratic governance through technology. Understanding the mechanisms through which digital divides influence democratic participation enables more effective interventions and resource allocation strategies.

1.1 Research Objectives

This investigation pursues four primary objectives:

1. **Comparative Analysis**: Systematically compare e-participation implementation strategies, outcomes, and challenges across Ghana, Senegal, and Nigeria.
2. **Digital Divide Assessment**: Examine how varying levels of digital infrastructure, literacy, and access influence citizen engagement with electronic participation platforms.

3. **Institutional Framework Evaluation**: Analyze the role of governmental policies, regulatory frameworks, and institutional capacity in shaping e-participation effectiveness.
4. **Democratic Impact Measurement**: Assess the relationship between e-participation initiatives and broader democratic outcomes, including transparency, accountability, and citizen satisfaction.

1.2 Research Questions

The study addresses three central research questions:

RQ1: How do variations in digital divide characteristics across Ghana, Senegal, and Nigeria influence citizen participation rates and engagement quality in e-participation initiatives?
RQ2: What institutional and policy factors contribute to differential e-participation outcomes across these three democracies?
RQ3: To what extent do e-participation programs enhance democratic governance quality and citizen satisfaction with governmental responsiveness?

2. LITERATURE REVIEW

2.1 Theoretical Foundations

The intersection of digital technology and democratic governance has generated extensive scholarly attention, with researchers developing various theoretical frameworks to understand e-participation phenomena. The digital divide concept, initially articulated by Norris (2001), has evolved from simple access-based definitions to more nuanced understandings encompassing skills, usage, and outcomes disparities.

Democratic theory provides additional theoretical grounding, particularly deliberative democracy frameworks emphasizing citizen engagement and participatory governance (Habermas, 1996). According to these theoretical considerations, technology has the potential to foster democratic legitimacy by increasing opportunities for participation and responsiveness within governments, aligning with citizen preferences (Dahl, 2020).

2.2 E-Participation in Developing Countries

In the case of developing countries, the studies on e-participation indicate the existence of multifaceted patterns of adoption, implementation, and outcomes. The

Latin American evidence shows that to be successful, a combination of approaches focusing on infrastructure, capacity building, and institutional reform is the only solution to e-participation (Sandoval-Almazan & Gil-Garcia, 2021). The Asian example highlights the importance of cultural aspects and social trust in enhancing e-participation efficacy.

The e-Participation implementation has its challenges and opportunities in the African context. According to the studies by Manda and Backhouse (2017), the rate of mobile technology penetration is higher than that of traditional internet access, and there are other avenues through which people can conduct digital participation. Nonetheless, researchers also find out that there are still barriers in the form of linguistic divide, literacy, and economic limitations (Fuchs & Horak, 2008).

2.3 Digital Divides in Sub-Saharan Africa

In the digital divide literature, specific emphasis is given to the sub-Saharan Africa region, which focuses on various aspects of technological inequality. Inequalities in the telecommunications sphere are reflected in the unfairness of the development of infrastructure related to the project; rural regions are underinvested relative to large cities (Gillwald et al., 2018). The socioeconomic gaps interact with gender, age, and wealth disparities, leaving some population groups with a compound disadvantage (Deen-Swarray et al., 2020).

Recent academic literature also notes new trends in the digital adoption of mobile-first strategies, in which people use their smartphones instead of accessing the internet through a computer (Porter et al., 2018). This leapfrogging condition surfaces new possibilities in the inclusive e-participation design practices, along with the setbacks of the platforms that would need a high rate of digital literacy.

2.4 Comparative Democratic Governance in West Africa

The modes of institutional arrangements and indicators of governance quality are varied in West African democracies, which makes them implementable in comparative analysis. Ghana has experienced relatively stable institutionalized forms of the democratic process obtained through the transition in 1992; however, the country has issues with economic inequality as well as inequity in its regions (Gyimah-Boadi, 2015).

The example of Senegal as a multi-democratic country shows peculiarities such as a well-established civil society and the absence of violence in the process of political changes. However, in the country, there continues to be the issue of youth unemployment and a lack of development in many regions (Beck, 2017). The current federal system and high density of ethnic groups in Nigeria bring the intriguing dynamics of governance, and this concept holds relevance to the implementation of national e-participation programs (Ikelegbe & Umukoro, 2014).

2.5 Research Gaps and Contributions

Although there is a trend towards digital democracy and e-participation, corresponding to a high interest in those fields of study, there are still significant research gaps in the African context. There are a limited number of studies that consider rigorous comparative designs to estimate cross-national differences in the consequences of e-participation. Likewise, few studies have systematically examined the nexus between various facets of digital divides and specific features of e-participation programs. The study bridges these gaps by coming up with several new things:

1. **Methodological Innovation:** A combination of methodologies enables comparative research, such as a mixed-methods approach, allowing for the use of standardized measures across countries to conduct excellent cross-national analysis.
2. **Theoretical Integration:** Integrating the digital divide theory with democratic governmental structures will provide a more in-depth analysis.
3. **Exhaustiveness Empirical:** Using both quantitative measurement of the participation and a qualitative analysis of the institution is a method of getting more deeply into the causal processes.
4. **Policy Relevance:** Advising the formulators of the practice and policies on how to ensure a positive contribution to the system of democratic governance by using technological innovations.

3. METHODOLOGY

3.1 Research Design

The proposed research is a mixed-method comparative case study that will be used to analyze the results of e-participation in Ghana, Senegal, and Nigeria. The structure of the study combines quantitative measurement of participation indicators with a qualitative evaluation of the frameworks and experiences at both the institutional and individual citizen levels. Through such methodological practice, it is possible to complexify the knowledge relative to the measurable consequences coupled with the causal mechanism underlying the same.

The timeframe spans from 2019 to 2024, aiming to cover e-participation projects that occurred during this period and represent aspects of technological progress and organizational evolution. This period provides us with sufficient data to conduct a trend analysis that remains current in significance.

3.2 Case Selection

The three case studies-Ghana, Senegal, and Nigeria have been selected as part of a strategic sampling based on the following factors:

Democratic Institutional Variation: countries have different responses to democratic governance; namely, Ghana with its institutional settlement, Senegal with civil society penetration, and Nigeria with its federal complexity.
Economic Diversity: The countries also have different financial structures and forms of development, and this provides the potential to study the economic factors in e-participation implementation.
Digital Infrastructure Difference: The three nations exhibit significant variations in their adopted telecommunications infrastructure and the pace at which they have implemented these, providing a natural basis for comparison across countries.
Regional Representation: The cases embody the two biggest West African Anglophone and Francophone cultures of democracy.

3.3 Data Collection Strategy

The data collection was carried out were conducted using various sources and means to ascertain sufficient coverage and triangulation of methods:

3.3.1 Quantitative Data Collection

Government Platform Analytics: Official data on national e-participation portals, such as the number of user registrations, the time spent on the same, as well as the rate of comment submission, and the demographic aspects of the e-participants.
Survey Data: Original survey research conducted with 2,847 respondents across urban and rural constituencies in all three countries, measuring digital access, usage patterns, and satisfaction with e-participation experiences.
Infrastructure Metrics: Secondary data from telecommunications authorities, international organizations, and private sector sources measuring internet penetration, mobile phone adoption, and broadband quality indicators.

3.3.2 Qualitative Data Collection

Elite Interviews: Semi-structured interviews with 48 government officials, civil society leaders, and technology sector representatives across the three countries, exploring institutional perspectives on e-participation implementation.
Focus Group Discussions: 12 focus groups with citizens who have participated in e-participation initiatives, examining user experiences, barriers, and suggestions for improvement.
Document Analysis: Systematic analysis of policy documents, legislative frameworks, and official reports related to digital governance and e-participation implementation.

3.4 Analytical Framework

The analytical framework integrates multiple theoretical perspectives to examine the relationship between digital divides and e-participation outcomes:

3.4.1 Digital Divide Assessment model

Digital Divide Index = f(Infrastructure Access, Device Availability, Digital Skills, Usage Patterns, Socioeconomic Factors)

Where:

- Infrastructure Access: Broadband availability, mobile coverage
- Device Availability: Smartphone/computer ownership rates
- Digital Skills: Basic and advanced digital literacy measures
- Usage Patterns: Frequency and sophistication of digital tool usage
- Socioeconomic Factors: Income, education, age, gender, location

3.4.2 E-Participation Effectiveness Framework

E-participation effectiveness assessment incorporates four dimensions:

Reach: Proportion of the eligible population engaging with e-participation platforms
Depth: Quality and sophistication of citizen contributions and interactions
Impact: Evidence of citizen input influencing policy decisions and governmental responses
Sustainability: Continuity of participation over time and across different policy issues

3.5 Measurement Indicators

Standardized measurement indicators enable cross-national comparison:

3.5.1 Digital Divide Indicators

Dimension	Indicator	Measurement Method
Infrastructure	Internet penetration rate	ITU/national statistics
Infrastructure	Mobile broadband coverage	Telecommunications authorities
Access	Device ownership rates	Household surveys
Access	Internet Affordability Index	Relative cost analysis
Skills	Digital literacy rates	Standardized assessments
Skills	Advanced usage capabilities	Behavioral observation
Usage	Active internet users	Platform analytics
Usage	E-government service adoption	Official statistics

3.5.2 E-Participation Outcome Indicators

Dimension	Indicator	Measurement Method
Reach	Registration rates	Platform analytics
Reach	Geographic distribution	Spatial analysis
Depth	Comment/contribution quality	Content analysis
Depth	Deliberative interaction patterns	Network analysis
Impact	Policy incorporation rates	Document analysis
Impact	Government responsiveness	Response time analysis
Sustainability	Repeat participation rates	Longitudinal tracking
Sustainability	Cross-platform engagement	Multi-platform analysis

3.6 Algorithm for Cross-National Comparison

Algorithm: Comparative E-Participation Assessment

Input:

- Digital divide metrics for countries A, B, and C
- The facts used to support E-participation in the three countries, A, B, and C.

- Institutional context variables for countries A, B, and C

Step 1: Normalize all metrics to 0-100 scale Step 2: Calculate composite digital divide scores Step 3: Calculate composite e-participation effectiveness scores Step 4: Perform a correlation analysis between the variables and outcomes Step 5: Control for institutional and socioeconomic variables Step 6: Generate comparative rankings and performance gaps Step 7: Identify best practices and improvement opportunities

Output:

- Comparative performance matrix
- Correlation coefficients and significance levels
- Policy recommendation framework

3.7 Ethical Considerations

This is a study where its ethics are followed thoroughly:

Informed consent: All survey respondents and interview participants signed informed consent, and it was clearly explained to the participants about the purpose of the research and the use of data.
Confidentiality: Responses of the individual are confidential, and the data will be reported in an aggregated form.
Cultural Sensitivity: Research instruments and procedures have been localized, and local partners have been consulted.
Data Protection: All forms of data protection, collection, and storage follow international standards of data protection and national policy.

4. COUNTRY PROFILES AND CONTEXT ANALYSIS

4.1 Ghana: Democratic Consolidation and Digital Innovation

As part of West Africa, Ghana has one of the most stable democracies because there have been successful democratic transitions in Ghana since 1992, and institutional work that promotes transparency in governance. Such institutional maturity is evident in the country's approach to participation, as a systematic attempt has been made to elaborate on the use of digital technologies in the course of democratization.

4.1.1 Digital Infrastructure Landscape

Ghana's telecommunications sector has experienced significant development over the past decade, driven by both public investment and private sector competition. The National Communications Authority reports internet penetration rates of 71% as of 2024, with mobile internet comprising the primary access method for most citizens. The government's digitalization agenda, anchored by the Digital Ghana Initiative, has prioritized expanding broadband infrastructure to underserved areas.

Key infrastructure indicators include:

- Mobile phone penetration: 137% (multiple SIM ownership)
- Internet users: 18.96 million (71% of population)
- Broadband subscriptions: 15.2 million
- 4G coverage: 85% of populated areas

4.1.2 E-Participation Implementation

Ghana's e-participation framework centers on the "Citizen App" platform, launched in 2020 as a comprehensive digital engagement tool. The platform is also a combination of various functionalities, such as consultation of policies, service feedback, and direct contact with the elected representatives. The Ministry of Communications and Digitalisation is in charge of the platform development and maintenance and acts in collaboration with the local technology companies.

The highlights of the strategy of Ghana can be observed as follows:

- Multi-language support (English, Twi, Ewe, Dagbani)
- SMS-based participation options for low-bandwidth users
- Integration with existing government service platforms
- Regular virtual town halls with ministers and local officials

4.1.3 Institutional Framework

Ghana's e-participation initiatives operate within a supportive legal and institutional environment. The Electronic Transactions Act has established the legal basis for electronic transactions of government services, and the Right to Information Act ensures transparency in government activities. The National Information Technology Agency is the government regulatory agency that facilitates the digital government initiatives, as well as provides technical standards and oversight.

4.2 Senegal: Civil Society Engagement and Digital Inclusion

The democratic tradition of Senegal has become noticeable through very high civil society values and nonviolent transitions of political regimes. E-participation in the country has concentrated on cascading down the involvement to the grassroots and plugging the communities through digital inclusion initiatives.

4.2.1 Digital Infrastructure Development

Senegal has achieved significant progress in telecommunication development, but the gap between urban and rural areas of the country remains substantial. The nation has a plan called Digital Senegal 2025, in which priority is given to equal access to digital services and developing digital literacy. Internet penetration was at 58 percent in 2024, with mobile internet being the primary access method.

The characteristics of infrastructures entail the following:

- Mobile phone penetration: 119%
- Internet users: 10.23 million (58% of population)
- Broadband subscriptions: 8.7 million
- 4G coverage: 78% of populated areas

4.2.2 E-Participation Mechanisms

There are different means of e-participation in the Senegal e-participation ecosystem. The app, "Sunu Gox" (Our City), will enable residents to report local issues in their town and participate in regional planning. There is also the Dialogue National platform, which allows the national policy consultation on significant matters of governance.

Distinctive aspects of Senegal's approach:

- Community mediator programs bridging digital divides
- Integration with traditional governance structures
- Youth-focused digital participation initiatives
- Civil society partnership in platform management

4.2.3 Governance and Regulatory Environment

Senegal's regulatory framework for digital governance reflects the country's commitment to transparency and citizen engagement.

4.3 Nigeria: Federal Complexity and Digital Challenges

The situation in Nigeria presents both a challenge and an opportunity for e-participation, given the country's federal arrangement and diverse populations. The country's large population and significant economic status make it crucial for understanding the scale of participation in the African environment.

4.3.1 Digital Infrastructure Realities

Nigeria faces significant challenges with its digital infrastructure, despite being Africa's largest economy. As of 2024, internet penetration stands at 51%, with substantial variations between states and between urban and rural areas. The Nigerian Communications Commission has initiated several programs to address these disparities.

Current infrastructure status:

- Mobile phone penetration: 104%
- Internet users: 109.2 million (51% of population)
- Broadband subscriptions: 85.9 million
- 4G coverage: 65% of populated areas

4.3.2 E-Participation Initiatives

Nigeria's federal structure necessitates multi-level e-participation approaches. The "Open Government Partnership" commitment has driven the development of consultation platforms at the federal and state levels. However, implementation varies significantly across different states and federal agencies.

Key platforms and initiatives include:

- Federal Ministry consultation portals
- State-level citizen engagement platforms
- Local government digital service centers
- Civil society-led monitoring platforms

4.3.3 Institutional Challenges and Opportunities

Nigeria's complex institutional environment presents both challenges and opportunities for e-participation. Federal-state coordination issues can impede nationwide implementation, while the diversity of local contexts enables experimentation with different approaches. The National Information Technology Development Agency provides coordination and technical support, though resource constraints limit comprehensive implementation.

5. DATA ANALYSIS AND RESULTS

5.1 Digital Divide Characterization

The analysis reveals significant variations in digital divide characteristics across the three countries, with important implications for e-participation implementation effectiveness.

5.1.1 Infrastructure Divide Analysis

Table 1. Digital Infrastructure Comparison (2024)

Indicator	Ghana	Senegal	Nigeria	Regional Average
Internet Penetration (%)	71.2	58.4	51.1	60.2
Mobile Broadband Coverage (%)	85.3	78.1	65.4	76.3
Average Internet Speed (Mbps)	15.7	12.3	8.9	12.3
Broadband Affordability Index	2.1	3.4	4.7	3.4
Rural Internet Access (%)	45.2	32.8	28.1	35.4

The data demonstrates Ghana's leadership in digital infrastructure development, with the highest internet penetration and mobile broadband coverage rates. Nigeria, despite its economic size, shows the lowest infrastructure development indicators, particularly in rural areas. Senegal occupies an intermediate position, with targeted improvements in urban centers but persistent rural challenges.

5.1.2 Access and Affordability Patterns

Cost barriers represent significant impediments to digital participation across all three countries. Analysis of telecommunications spending as a proportion of average income reveals substantial affordability challenges, particularly for rural and low-income populations.

Figure 1. Digital Access Patterns by Income Quintile

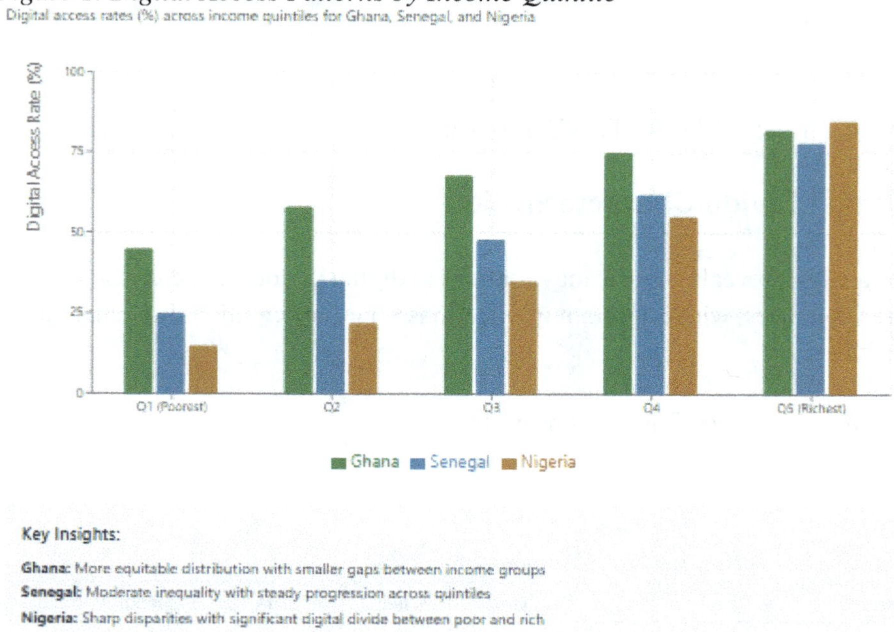

5.1.3 Digital Skills Assessment

Primary research data reveals substantial variation in digital literacy levels across countries and demographic groups. Standardized digital literacy assessments administered to survey participants indicate:

Table 2. Digital Literacy Scores by Country and Demographic

Demographic	Ghana	Senegal	Nigeria	Significance
Overall Average	67.3	54.1	48.7	$p < 0.001$
Urban Residents	74.2	62.8	57.3	$p < 0.001$
Rural Residents	52.4	38.9	32.1	$p < 0.001$
Youth (18-35)	78.9	68.2	61.4	$p < 0.001$
Adults (36-55)	58.7	45.3	39.8	$p < 0.001$
Seniors (56+)	34.1	28.7	22.3	$p < 0.01$
Higher Education	82.4	71.6	65.9	$p < 0.001$

continued on following page

Table 2. Continued

Demographic	Ghana	Senegal	Nigeria	Significance
Secondary Education	61.2	48.7	43.1	$p < 0.001$
Primary/No Education	28.9	21.4	18.7	$p < 0.01$

These results demonstrate consistent patterns across all three countries, with urban residents, younger populations, and more educated individuals exhibiting higher digital literacy levels. However, Ghana maintains advantages across all demographic categories.

5.2 E-Participation Implementation Analysis

5.2.1 Platform Reach and Adoption

Quantitative analysis of e-participation platform usage reveals substantial differences in citizen engagement across the three countries:

Table 3. E-Participation Platform Performance Metrics (2019-2024)

Metric	Ghana	Senegal	Nigeria
Total Registered Users	2,847,291	1,523,674	5,429,183
Active Monthly Users	1,936,438	687,052	1,681,148
Participation Rate (% of internet users)	68.2	44.8	30.9
Average Session Duration (minutes)	12.7	8.9	6.3
Policy Consultation Submissions	485,729	156,341	294,876
Government Response Rate (%)	73.4	52.1	28.7
User Satisfaction Score (1-10)	7.8	6.4	5.1

Ghana demonstrates superior performance across all platform metrics, achieving the highest participation rates and user engagement levels. Nigeria, despite having the most significant absolute number of registered users due to population size, shows the lowest participation rates relative to internet user populations.

5.2.2 Geographic Distribution Patterns

Spatial analysis of e-participation reveals significant urban-rural disparities in all three countries:

Table 4. E-Participation by Geographic Location

Location Type	Ghana Participation Rate	Senegal Participation Rate	Nigeria Participation Rate
Capital Cities	84.7%	67.3%	45.2%
Other Urban Centers	71.2%	48.9%	32.1%
Semi-Urban Areas	58.3%	35.7%	24.8%
Rural Areas	42.1%	26.4%	15.3%

These disparities reflect underlying digital divide patterns, with rural populations facing compounded barriers to e-participation engagement.

5.2.3 Demographic Participation Patterns

Analysis of participant demographics reveals important patterns regarding inclusivity and representation:

Table 5. E-Participation Demographics by Country

Demographic	Ghana (%)	Senegal (%)	Nigeria (%)	National Population (%)
Age Groups				
18-25 years	28.4	34.7	41.2	22.1
26-35 years	31.7	29.8	28.6	18.7
36-45 years	22.9	19.4	16.3	15.4
46-55 years	12.1	11.2	9.7	12.8
56+ years	4.9	4.9	4.2	31.0
Gender				
Male	57.8	63.2	68.4	49.8
Female	42.2	36.8	31.6	50.2
Education				
Higher Education	34.7	28.9	25.3	8.2
Secondary	47.8	45.1	43.9	34.6
Primary/None	17.5	26.0	30.8	57.2

The data reveals consistent patterns of youth over-representation, male dominance, and educational bias across all three countries. These patterns indicate significant representation gaps that limit the democratic inclusivity of e-participation initiatives.

5.3 Institutional Effectiveness Assessment

5.3.1 Government Responsiveness Analysis

Qualitative analysis of government responses to citizen inputs through e-participation platforms reveals varying levels of institutional responsiveness:

Table 6. Government Responsiveness Indicators

Indicator	Ghana	Senegal	Nigeria
Average Response Time (days)	8.3	14.7	28.4
Substantive Response Rate (%)	67.2	45.8	22.1
Policy Integration Rate (%)	23.4	12.7	6.8
Follow-up Communication (%)	78.9	52.3	31.2
Citizen Satisfaction with Responses (1-10)	7.2	5.8	4.1

Ghana's institutional responsiveness significantly exceeds that of Senegal and Nigeria, with faster response times and higher rates of substantive engagement with citizen inputs.

5.3.2 Policy Integration Assessment

Document analysis examining the integration of citizen inputs into actual policy decisions reveals limited but varying success across countries:

Ghana: Policy consultation processes demonstrate systematic integration of citizen feedback, with 23.4% of substantive suggestions being incorporated into final policy documents. The National Development Planning Commission has established formal procedures for reviewing and incorporating e-participation inputs.

Senegal: Moderate success in policy integration, with 12.7% of citizen suggestions being reflected in policy outcomes. Civil society organizations play essential roles in advocating for citizen input consideration.

Nigeria: Limited policy integration success, with only 6.8% of citizen inputs being incorporated into policy decisions. Federal-state coordination challenges and institutional capacity limitations contribute to low integration rates.

5.4 Democratic Outcomes Assessment

5.4.1 Citizen Satisfaction and Trust

Survey data examining citizen satisfaction with democratic processes and governmental responsiveness reveal significant cross-national differences:

Table 7. Democratic Satisfaction Indicators

Indicator	Ghana	Senegal	Nigeria
Government Responsiveness (1-10)	6.8	5.4	4.2
Democratic Satisfaction (1-10)	7.1	6.2	5.1
Trust in Government (1-10)	6.4	5.8	4.7
Perceived Transparency (1-10)	6.9	5.9	4.5
E-Participation Value (1-10)	7.6	6.7	5.8

Ghana consistently demonstrates higher citizen satisfaction across all democratic governance indicators, while Nigeria shows the lowest satisfaction levels.

5.4.2 Correlation Analysis

Statistical analysis examining relationships between digital divide characteristics and e-participation outcomes reveals significant correlations:

Table 8. Correlation Matrix - Digital Divides and E-Participation Outcomes

Variables	Correlation Coefficient	Significance Level
Internet Access × Participation Rate	0.847	$p < 0.001$
Digital Literacy × Platform Engagement	0.723	$p < 0.001$
Infrastructure Quality × User Satisfaction	0.681	$p < 0.001$
Government Responsiveness × Repeat Usage	0.759	$p < 0.001$
Income Level × Platform Access	0.634	$p < 0.001$
Education × Contribution Quality	0.592	$p < 0.01$

These correlations confirm strong relationships between digital divide characteristics and e-participation effectiveness, supporting the theoretical framework underlying this research.

6. DISCUSSION

6.1 Digital Divides as Determinants of E-Participation Success

The empirical findings provide compelling evidence that digital divide characteristics serve as primary determinants of e-participation effectiveness across West African democracies. The excellent outcome of the e-participation initiatives in Ghana is consistent with the country's more advanced digital network, improvements in internet penetration, and enhanced digital literacy among its citizens.

The infrastructure gap poses another significant limitation for nations with limited broadband access and slow internet connections, which struggle to achieve more robust citizen participation through online channels. The conundrum of Nigeria in this context is indicative of larger developmental constraints, as the lack of proper telecommunication infrastructure hinders both urban and rural community ascendance in the application of digital democracy.

In addition to the mere accessibility questions, the discussion indicates that digital literacy is an equally important segment. Differences in digital skills across countries and within specific groups can be so significant as to create substantial barriers to e-participation. People without advanced skills in digital literacy can use the platforms; however, they can hardly participate in deeper policy consultation processes or user-intensive e-participation platforms.

6.2 Institutional Capacity and Government Responsiveness

The study shows that technological infrastructure is not the only factor that leads to the success of e-participation. The capacity of institutions to process citizen inputs, provide responsive feedback, and incorporate participation results into policy decisions is equally important. Ghana's high scores in government responsiveness measures are due to systematic investments in institutional infrastructure for digital governance capacity.

This dynamic comes to the fore when one compares the scale of platform adoption in Nigeria with the low level of responsiveness by the government. Although the number of registered users is vast, the absence of an institutionalized system for handling and responding to citizen inputs diminishes the value of e-participatory schemes in terms of democracy. When citizens feel the government is unresponsive in giving feedback, they are less prone to continue the engagement process, thus generating negative feedback loops that will make the platform ineffective in the long run.

The medium performance of Senegal demonstrates how civil society organizations can help moderate the low governmental capacity by prioritizing citizen attention and maintaining pressure on institutional responsiveness. Such a finding implies that non-governmental actors can play significant roles in mediating e-participation effectiveness.

6.3 Demographic Representation and Democratic Inclusivity

The fact that the three countries exhibit the same trends in demographic bias regarding e-participation is quite alarming. It serves as a good indicator of concern over the democratic quality of projects oriented towards e-participation. Systematic misrepresentation of younger, male, educated, and urban demographics precludes the inclusion of key demographic groups, leading to a possible bias in policy inputs and lessening the legitimacy of the e-participation results.

Underlying digital divides can cause these gaps in representation. Still, they can also be caused by the choices that go into the design of a platform and in the outreach policies that are set in place, which incidentally discriminate against the representatives of other demographic groups. The domination of youth leadership cannot be processed positively in terms of introducing progressive views, which can undermine the experience and preferences of older citizens who make up an immense proportion of the nation.

Actual gender differences in participation rates in all three countries suggest e-participation initiatives may do nothing to democratically enhance the lives of potential citizens, instead of perpetuating existing trends of political exclusion. There are multiplying disadvantages to rural women with little formal education due to the intersectional effects of gender, education, and location.

6.4 Urban-Rural Divides and Geographic Representation

Participation differences between urban and rural environments, recorded in all three countries, also indicate inherent problems in achieving representative e-participation in predominantly rural-based societies. Rural dwellers face several limitations, including poor infrastructure, low levels of digital literacy, and possibly differing aspirations for political participation.

Such geographical asymmetries are significant when considering the consequences of policy making because city-based involvement could potentially lead to policy discourse that is biased about urban concerns and interests. The needs of rural development, the preferences of agricultural policies, and the traditional arrangements of governance may be underrepresented in participatory processes, as most urban dwellers dominate these processes.

This observation that participation in rural areas remains very low, even in Ghana, which has the most advanced digital infrastructure compared to the other two countries, suggests that infrastructure development alone may not be sufficient to reduce and overcome urban-rural participation imbalances. Attention may be required regarding cultural aspects, other communication preferences, and how to integrate with the traditional governance system.

6.5 Policy Integration and Democratic Impact

The fact that the input made by citizens was limited in its application to real decision-making is a significant problem of e-participation legitimacy and efficacy. At the same time, even Ghana, which shows the best performance in this respect, turns out to incorporate only 23.4 percent of more quotable citizen suggestions into policy outcomes. This weak level of integration gives doubts about the real democratic value of the e-participation activities.

These challenges in policy integration can be indicative of multiple factors, including institutional inertia to citizen participation, technical issues in handling the vast amount of submissions, and the sheer complexity of constructing a unified policy framework that effectively accounts for the diverse preferences of citizens. Moreover, the quality and certainty of citizen contributions can vary significantly, ranging from being relatively high to being too general or uninformed to have a meaningful impact on sophisticated policy making. However, all the positive correlations between government responsiveness and repeat usage following the platform indicate that even trim levels of policy integration should help generate higher citizen engagement.

Citizens who feel their inputs are taken seriously and sometimes make a difference in policy outcomes are more likely to stay active.

6.6 Cross-National Learning and Best Practices

The comparative analysis shows several proposed promising learning practices that can be transformed in the context of different nations:

The Multi-Language Strategy in Ghana: The availability of e-participation sites with multiple local language options also offers much better access to people who do not speak English. This would go a long way in having nations like Nigeria, which are visibly diverse.

Integration of Civil Society in Senegal: The existence of formal collaboration between government agencies and civil society organizations in operating e-participatory platforms introduces more accountability channels, ensuring that the differences between citizen contributions and governance processes are bridged.

Community Mediator Programs: Senegal's innovative and skills-based approaches incorporate trained community mediators to help citizens with limited digital literacy access e-participation platforms.

Federal-State Coordination: In a federal system, the e-participation imperative is a collaborative effort of both Federal and State governments. Nigeria has been one of the countries affected by this aspect, presenting both challenges and opportunities. The coordination barriers not only impede effectiveness but also facilitate experimentation and learning through various strategies that apply in different states.

6.7 Theoretical Implications

The findings of the research add rich contributions to the theoretical knowledge about digital democracy in several crucial ways:

Digital Divide Complexity: As proven by the results, digital divides work through a variety of overlapping scales that combine to form complexified structures of inclusion and exclusion. Simple binary distinctions between "connected" and "unconnected" populations fail to capture the nuanced reality of differential digital capabilities and outcomes.

Institutional Mediation: The strong correlation between institutional responsiveness and e-participation effectiveness confirms that technological deterministic approaches to digital democracy are insufficient. Institutional capacity and political will serve as crucial mediating factors between technological capabilities and democratic outcomes.

Representation Paradox: The finding that e-participation initiatives may reinforce rather than reduce existing patterns of political exclusion suggests significant limitations to technological solutions for democratic inclusion. Without deliberate attention to representation issues, digital democracy may exacerbate rather than ameliorate democratic deficits.

6.8 Methodological Contributions

This research makes several methodological contributions to comparative digital democracy research:

Standardized Metrics: The development of standardized metrics for cross-national comparison of e-participation outcomes enables more rigorous comparative analysis and facilitates replication in other regional contexts.

Mixed-Methods Integration: The combination of quantitative platform analytics with qualitative institutional analysis provides a comprehensive understanding of both measurable outcomes and underlying causal mechanisms.
Longitudinal Perspective: The five-year timeframe enables analysis of trends and changes over time, providing insights into the evolution of e-participation initiatives and their democratic impacts.

7. POLICY RECOMMENDATIONS

7.1 Infrastructure Development Strategies

There are several priorities concerning infrastructure development according to the findings of the research:

7.1.1 Rural Connectivity Enhancement

Universal Service Obligations: Governments must enhance the universal service obligations of telecommunications service operators, which should extend to include rural and underserved markets as requirements for operating licenses. Such regulatory strategies can be seen as a response to Ghana's success in increasing internet access rates in the countryside.
Public-Private Partnerships: Strategic partnerships are one way to enhance telecommunications in rural areas, as they involve an exchange of costs and risks between government agencies and private telecommunications companies. Other developing countries have modeled revenue-sharing arrangements that have proven to be viable in terms of covering rural areas.
Community Networks: Community-owned and operated networks: Supporting these initiatives may provide long-term connections to isolated areas that cannot sustain commercial networks through financially unsustainable processes. Communities, with the option of flexibility in regulations the technical support, can come up with the proper connectivity solutions.

7.1.2 Affordability Interventions

Programs of Subsidized Access: Subsidies can be provided to low-income categories, reducing the financial constraints of internet access. Such programs should be structured to prevent market distortions and ensure sustainable funding mechanisms.

Device Financing Schemes: Smartphones and other digital devices have innovative finance systems that could be used to resolve the situation of capital limitation that has limited digital accessibility. Collaborations with lending entities and making companies can generate readily available sources of financing.
Public Access Points: This can be achieved by creating well-equipped communities with limited private access, providing shared access, and developing a digital literacy target to be realized through guided use.

7.2 Digital Literacy and Capacity Building

7.2.1 Comprehensive Digital Literacy Programs

Life-Long Learning strategies: Digital literacy programs must consider the aged bracket, ranging from the different levels of skill and the fact that digital skills needs are dynamic. This can be incorporated into current adult education programs to enhance their effectiveness and relevance.
Context-Relevant Curricula: It should be made clear that digital literacy training must focus on skills pertinent to e-participation and digital citizenship: provision of critical judgment of online information, assessment of privacy and online security, and proficient online communication.
Gender-Sensitive Programming: Emphasizing the role of females in the digital literacy programme can help bridge gender gaps in e-participation. Women have certain limitations that should be considered in programs, including time availability, cultural factors, and applications.

7.2.2 Institutional Capacity Development

Government Official Training: This level of responsiveness and effectiveness can be supplemented with systematic training for government officials in managing the e-participation platform. It must be trained on the technical management of the platform, citizen engagement strategy, and process of policy integration.
Civil Society Capacity Building: By helping to develop digital engagement capacity at the civil society organizations' level, it is possible to establish new avenues of citizen engagement and also establish accountability mechanisms around e-participation projects.

7.3 Platform Design and Implementation

7.3.1 Inclusive Design Principles

Multi-Modal Access: To cater to the needs of all population categories based on technology capacity and preferences, e-participation systems should provide various methods of access, including web interfaces, mobile phone applications, SMS systems, and voice calls.
Accessibility Standards - Platforms must adhere to international web accessibility standards to ensure usability by individuals with disabilities and those with limited digital literacy skills.
Linguistic Diversity: A wider use of local language would enable more people to consume, but it would be very costly since consuming it would require extensive use of the translation and localization solutions.

7.3.2 User Experience Optimization

Intuitive Platforms: The platform s interfaces are designed to be simple and easy to navigate, ensuring that even users with limited digital knowledge can easily navigate around the platform. One of the methods of encountering and solving such usability issues involves user testing of representative groups.
Progressive Disclosure: Everything must be provided through progressive disclosure mechanisms so that users can acquire more and more complexity, depending on the acquisition of skills and confidence.
Offline Capabilities: Where feasible, platforms should support offline interaction capabilities, allowing users to prepare contributions without continuous internet connectivity and submit when connections are available.

7.4 Institutional Reform and Governance

7.4.1 Responsiveness Mechanisms

Formal Response Requirements: Establishing formal requirements for government agencies to respond to citizen inputs within specified timeframes can improve institutional responsiveness. These requirements should include both acknowledgment and substantive response obligations.
Transparency in Policy Integration: Clear processes for considering citizen inputs in policy development, with public documentation of how inputs are evaluated and integrated, can enhance citizen confidence in e-participation value.

Performance Monitoring: Regular monitoring and public reporting of e-participation platform performance, including responsiveness metrics and policy integration outcomes, creates accountability incentives for government agencies.

7.4.2 Inter-Governmental Coordination

Federal-State Alignment: In federal systems like Nigeria, coordination mechanisms between federal and state-level e-participation initiatives can prevent duplication, share best practices, and ensure consistent citizen experiences across government levels.
Regional Cooperation: West African countries can benefit from regional cooperation in e-participation development, sharing experiences, technical resources, and best practices. Regional organizations like ECOWAS could facilitate such collaboration.

7.5 Addressing Representation Gaps

7.5.1 Targeted Outreach Strategies

Demographic-Specific Engagement: reinforcement of participation gaps through specific outreach programmes focused on the unrepresented demographics, such as women, people of older age, the rural population, and people with disabilities. Such programs ought to include group-related barriers and preferences.
Integration with traditional media: Integrating e-participation projects with conventional media, such as radio, television, and print, creates the potential to reach populations without internet access and to increase participation among connected users.
Community Leader Involvement: Traditional and religious leaders, as well as community organizations, may be involved to enhance outreach effectiveness and trust in e-participation efforts.

7.5.2 Alternative Participation Modalities

Hybrid Methods: Just as we may apply the digital platforms to low digital literacy population, we can employ both the digital platforms and traditional forms of engagement e.g. town halls, focus groups, community meetings, and these could be used as an engagement strategy which may offer more than one point of entry to less experienced citizens, thus providing an incentive to learn more about digital engagement in the long term.

Assisted Participation: In the short term, it is possible to fill the skills deficit through training community volunteers or government personnel. These individuals can then assist citizens with low digital literacy abilities in using e-participation facilities, thereby building stronger abilities in the long run.

7.6 Monitoring and Evaluation Framework

7.6.1 Comprehensive Metrics

Multi-Dimensional Assessment: Monitoring and evaluation systems ought to review e-participation achievement in more than a single dimension, reach, representativeness, the quality of engagement, responsiveness of the institutions, and policy influence.

Longitudinal Tracking: Citizen satisfaction, patterns of platform usage, and overall democratic outcomes could be tracked in the long term to understand e-participation development and sustainability.

Comparative Analysis: Periodic comparison with regional and international best practices can provide the areas that can be improved and used to design adaptive management

7.6.2 Citizen Feedback Integration

User Experience Research: Regularly undertaking user experience research through surveys, focus groups, and usability testing can identify areas for improvement in the platform and enable iterative development to address these issues.

Participatory Evaluation: Involving citizens in evaluating e-participation initiative effectiveness creates additional engagement opportunities while ensuring that success metrics reflect user perspectives and priorities.

8. LIMITATIONS AND FUTURE RESEARCH DIRECTIONS

8.1 Research Limitations

8.1.1 Temporal Constraints

This study's five-year timeframe, while substantial for technology research, may be insufficient to capture long-term democratic impacts of e-participation initiatives. Democratic consolidation and institutional change processes often require decades to mature, suggesting that longer-term studies may reveal different patterns of relationship between digital divides and democratic outcomes.

The rapid pace of technological change also means that findings regarding specific platforms and technologies may become outdated quickly. Future research should consider how emerging technologies, including artificial intelligence, blockchain, and improved mobile connectivity, might alter the dynamics examined in this study.

8.1.2 Geographic Scope

The focus on three West African countries, while enabling deep comparative analysis, limits generalizability to other African regions and developing country contexts. Different colonial legacies, economic structures, and cultural contexts may create different patterns of digital divide impacts on e-participation effectiveness.

The selection of relatively stable democracies also means that findings may not apply to countries experiencing political instability, conflict, or authoritarian governance. E-participation dynamics in fragile state contexts may differ substantially from those observed in consolidated democracies.

8.1.3 Methodological Constraints

Self-Selection Bias: E-participation platform users represent self-selected populations that may differ systematically from non-users in ways that affect research findings. Survey-based approaches to understanding non-user perspectives, while included in this study, may not fully capture the experiences and preferences of citizens who choose not to engage with digital platforms.

Language and Cultural Barriers: Despite efforts to address linguistic diversity through multilingual survey instruments and local research partnerships, subtle cultural factors and communication preferences may have influenced data collection and interpretation.

Technology Evolution: The rapid evolution of digital technologies during the study period may have created inconsistencies in platform capabilities and user experiences that complicate longitudinal analysis.

8.2 Future Research Directions

8.2.1 Expanded Geographic Analysis

Continental Comparative Studies: Future research should expand geographic scope to include countries from different African regions, enabling analysis of how diverse institutional, economic, and cultural contexts influence e-participation outcomes. East African countries with different colonial legacies and West African countries with varying endowments of resources could provide valuable comparative insights.
Global South Comparisons: Comparative studies including countries from Asia, Latin America, and other developing regions could identify universal patterns versus context-specific factors in digital divide impacts on democratic participation.
Conflict and Post-Conflict Contexts: Research in countries experiencing political instability or post-conflict reconstruction could examine how e-participation initiatives function under different governance conditions and contribute to peace-building and democratic consolidation processes.

8.2.2 Technological Innovation Studies

Artificial Intelligence Integration: Future research should examine how artificial intelligence technologies, including natural language processing, automated translation, and intelligent content analysis, might address some of the barriers to effective e-participation identified in this study.
Blockchain and Distributed Technologies: Studies of blockchain-based voting and participation systems could examine whether distributed technologies can enhance trust, transparency, and security in e-participation initiatives.
Mobile-First Approaches: Given the mobile-first nature of internet adoption in Africa, research focusing specifically on mobile-optimized e-participation platforms could provide insights into more effective design approaches for developing country contexts.

8.2.3 Institutional Analysis

Policy Integration Mechanisms: Detailed process-tracing studies examining how citizen inputs are considered, processed, and integrated into policy decisions could identify specific institutional innovations that enhance e-participation effectiveness.
Multi-Level Governance: Research examining e-participation implementation across different levels of government, from local to national, could provide insights into optimal institutional arrangements and coordination mechanisms.
Civil Society Roles: Studies focusing specifically on civil society organization roles in e-participation could examine how non-governmental actors can complement government efforts and enhance democratic accountability.

8.2.4 Long-Term Impact Assessment

Democratic Consolidation Effects: Longitudinal studies examining whether e-participation initiatives contribute to broader democratic consolidation processes could provide insights into their fundamental democratic value.
Generational Change Analysis: Research tracking how digital natives who grow up with e-participation opportunities differ in their political engagement patterns and democratic expectations could inform long-term democratic development strategies.
Social Capital Formation: Studies examining whether e-participation contributes to social capital formation and civic engagement beyond formal political processes could assess broader social impacts.

8.2.5 Methodological Innovations

Big Data Analytics: Future research could leverage big data analytics approaches to analyze large-scale e-participation platform data, potentially identifying patterns and relationships not visible through traditional analytical methods.
Experimental Designs: Randomized controlled trials testing different e-participation platform features, outreach strategies, or institutional response mechanisms could provide more rigorous causal identification of practical approaches.
Mixed Reality Studies: Research examining how virtual and augmented reality technologies might enhance e-participation experiences could identify new possibilities for immersive democratic engagement.

8.3 Theoretical Development Opportunities

8.3.1 Digital Democracy Theory

Representation Theory Integration: Future theoretical work should more systematically integrate digital democracy research with representation theory, examining how digital technologies alter traditional concepts of political representation and accountability.

Deliberative Democracy Extensions: Research examining whether and how e-participation platforms can support genuine deliberative democracy processes could contribute to both theoretical understanding and practical platform design.

Democratic Quality Frameworks: Development of more sophisticated frameworks for assessing democratic quality in digital contexts could provide better analytical tools for evaluating e-participation impacts.

8.3.2 Development Theory Connections

Digital Development Integration: Theoretical work connecting digital divide research with broader development theory could provide a more comprehensive understanding of how technological factors interact with economic, social, and political development processes.

Capability Approach Applications: Applying the capability approach to digital democracy could provide normative frameworks for evaluating whether e-participation initiatives enhance human capabilities and freedoms.

9. CONCLUSION

The analysis of the role played by virtual divisions and e-participation in the effects of democracies in Ghana, Senegal, and Nigeria has demonstrated a strong argument that the availability of technology gives the scales of democracy in West African communities a clear edge over the inaccessibility of technology. The study proves that practical implementations of e-participation involve holistic measures to ensure that the infrastructure is developed, the digital literacy is advanced, institutional capacity is built, and representation disparities are being addressed with a purpose.

9.1 Key Findings Summary

The critical findings highlighted in the analysis have significant implications both for the theory and practice of digital democracy:

Digital Divides as Democratic Determinants: The high correlation between the quality of digital infrastructure, the rate of internet access, the level of digital literacy, and the effectiveness of e-participation proves that technological inequalities lead to unequal chances for people to use their democratic rights. Countries with more developed digital infrastructure and higher rates of digital literacy tend to perform better in terms of e-participation across various aspects.

Criticality of Institutional Capacity: Beyond technology, the capacity of institutions to handle citizen inputs, their responsiveness in providing feedback, and the incorporation of participation results into policy-making processes are equally critical in determining e-participation success. Ghana's well-formed involvement in investing in digital governance capacity is evident in its better results compared to Nigeria. Problems in Nigeria suggest that institutional limitations can hinder technological investment.

Representation Gaps Lingering: Despite the promise of democratic inclusion in e-participation projects, representation gaps persist in all three nations, particularly in areas such as youth inclusion, men's participation, higher education, and urban areas. Such tracks suggest that digital democracy can exacerbate existing tendencies of political exclusion unless proactive efforts are made to overcome barriers faced by less privileged groups.

Policy Integration: Little success has been achieved in translating citizen inputs into tangible policy decisions, which significantly undermines the legitimacy and effectiveness of e-participation. The top-ranking country incorporates fewer than a quarter of all substantive suggestions made by citizens into its policy outcomes, highlighting the issue of genuine democracy in current practices.

9.2 Theoretical Contributions

This study has several contributions to the digital democracy theory:

Multi-Dimensional Digital Divide Framework: The results indicate that digital divides are served out in several dimensions interacting with each other, such as access to infrastructure, availability of devices, ability to utilize and use digital platforms, and socioeconomic status. This kind of complexity requires less binarity of theory in terms of connected and unconnected populations.

Institutional Mediation Theory: The study affirms that the effect of technological capability on democratic outcomes is mediated by the fact that the same is institutional. Theories that focus on digital democracy and technological determinism remain incomplete until they address institutional capacity and political will.

Democratic Representation Paradox: The discovery that e-participation can contribute more significantly to bad than good democratic representation disparities is reason enough to signify significant shortcomings in the technological fix of democratic inclusion. Such a paradox can be addressed theoretically concerning how digital technologies relate to the pre-existing patterns of power and inequality.

9.3 Policy Implications

The study comes up with several practical policy implications:

Whole-of-Government Infrastructure Investment: Governments are encouraged to prioritize universal broadband access, particularly for rural areas that are currently poorly served. Novel financing tools and interest in the form of public-private partnerships in infrastructure development can promote faster infrastructure creation while addressing the limitations of public resources.
Digital Literacy Civic Education: Digital literacy programs should be reconceptualized as civic education programs, enabling citizens to be well-coached in their democratic practices within the digital age. Such programs are to focus more on critical thinking competencies, privacy privacy and viable online communication as well as technical skills.
Institutional Responsiveness Systems: Legitimacy and effectiveness of e-participation can be brought about through the formalization of the requirements imposed on government responses to citizen inputs, as well as by the introduction of transparency into policy integration processes. Accountability of government agencies through performance monitoring and reporting to the general populace serves as an incentive.

9.4 Regional and International Significance

The experience of the implementation of e-participation in West Africa also gives tips to other developing regions and even the outside development organizations:

Regional Cooperation Opportunities: Systematic regional cooperation can help accelerate the development of e-participation within West African countries by laying the groundwork for technical resources, best practices, and lessons learned. Such collaboration could be provided with the assistance of regional bodies such as ECOWAS, which would help in the process of democratic consolidation.

Program Design in Development: International development organizations must consider the digital divide in their democracy promotion programs, recognizing that technological inequality creates unequal opportunities for engagement with democracy. The multidimensionality of programs should also focus on infrastructure, skills, and capacity building at the institutional level and not on a single component.

Sustainable Development Goal Compatibility: The studies provide the basis of a more substantial alignment between SDG 16 (Peace, Justice and Strong Institutions) and SDG 9 (Industry, Innovation and Infrastructure), as the curbing of corruption, abuse of power, social, and economic structures is taken into account as technology development and democratic governance are mutually reinforcing in present-day environments.

9.5 Academic Research Contributions

The research provides several contributions to the study of comparative political science and the analysis of digital democracy:

Methodological Innovation: The comparative mixed-methods framework, with its essential cross-national value, enables rigorous research to provide a detailed forecasting of outcome parameters as well as the causal process behind them. The given approach can be transferred to other regional scenarios and applied to other nations. The extensive collection of quantitative and qualitative data gathered as part of this study lends itself to being used as an empirical base of evidence upon which maturation and policy analysis are conducted in the future. The longitudinal approach enables the study of trends and alterations over time.

Interdisciplinary Integration: The study has successfully integrated the know-how of political science, development studies, information systems, and public administration, thereby highlighting the advantages of multidisciplinary research on informative social phenomena.

9.6 Future Outlook

This rapid pace of technological advancements and emerging democratic exigencies demonstrates that e-participation remains a substantial area of research inquiry and policy-oriented activity. Several trends will become more likely to dominate the future:

Technological Convergence: Recent technologies, including artificial intelligence, blockchain, and enhanced mobile connectivity, will open new avenues for learning how to make e-participation more effective, but may also generate new types of digital divides.

Generational Change: Digital natives are now a significant number of adult citizens, and their expectations for digital government services and participation opportunities are likely to increase. This pressure may lead to a rise in the e-participation opportunities offered.

Global Learning Networks: Enhancing learning further involves sharing international knowledge and facilitating technical cooperation on e-participation, thereby accelerating knowledge gathering and reducing the risk of international failure.

9.7 Final Reflections

Tensions between the potential of technology and social reality are reflected in the dynamics of West African digital divides and democratic dividends, further exacerbating the long-term tensions between prerequisite and post-facto paradigms in development processes. Although digital technologies offer new opportunities to enhance democratic participation and government responsiveness, these opportunities can only be realized through holistic measures that address societal inequalities and the shortcomings of existing institutions.

The situation in Ghana, Senegal, and Nigeria provides an example of the possibilities for implementing e-participation, as well as the issues associated with this phenomenon in developing countries. The comparative success of Ghana demonstrates what can be achieved when a country focuses on building digital infrastructure, strengthening institutions, and implementing acceptable governance. The experience of Senegal underscores the importance of civil society organizations in bridging the gap between technological advancements and citizens' needs. The issues Nigeria is facing demonstrate how institutional boundaries and other communication impediments can even hinder significant technological investments.

Lastly, the question of how democratic or not a measure of a project aimed at raising e-participation is not a question of the technical savvy of the project in question, but rather is a question of institutional promises of democracy and responsiveness and real commitments to granting citizens sovereign power.

The digital technologies may supplement these democratic values; however, they cannot replace the political will and power of institutions needed to get democracy to work well with every citizen.

The way ahead entails the need to give more focus on reducing the digital divide without losing the focus of ensuring our institutions are equipped with the capacity to deliver on the governance of the same democracy. Such simultaneous attention on the technological inclusion and institutional capabilities is most promising for achieving the possibilities of the democratic promise of the digital technologies in West African societies at large.

REFERENCES

Beck, L. J. (2017). The roots of popular protest in Mali and Senegal. *Journal of Democracy*, *28*(3), 143–158.

Dahl, R. A. (2020). *On democracy*. Yale University Press.

Deen-Swarray, M., Adeya, C. N., & Ndung'u, N. S. (2020). *Digital pathways for development: The benefits of expanding broadband access in sub-Saharan Africa*. Brookings Institution.

Fuchs, C., & Horak, E. (2008). Africa and the digital divide. *Telematics and Informatics*, *25*(2), 99–116. DOI: 10.1016/j.tele.2006.06.004

. Gillwald, A., Mothobi, O., & Rademan, B. (2018). *The state of ICT in South Africa* (Research ICT Africa Policy Paper Series No. 5).

Gyimah-Boadi, E. (2015). Africa's waning democratic commitment. *Journal of Democracy*, *26*(1), 101–113. DOI: 10.1353/jod.2015.0000

Habermas, J. (1996). *Between facts and norms: Contributions to a discourse theory of law and democracy*. MIT Press. DOI: 10.7551/mitpress/1564.001.0001

Ikelegbe, A., & Umukoro, N. (2014). Exclusion and the challenges of democratic governance in Nigeria. *Journal of Developing Societies*, *30*(1), 1–26.

Manda, M. I., & Backhouse, J. (2017). Towards a smart society through digital inclusion: A proposal for an inclusive growth framework. In *International Conference on Social Implications of Computers in Developing Countries* (pp. 130–141). Springer.

Norris, P. (2001). *Digital divide: Civic engagement, information poverty, and the internet worldwide*. Cambridge University Press. DOI: 10.1017/CBO9781139164887

Porter, G., Hampshire, K., De Lannoy, A., Bango, A., Munthali, A., Robson, E., & Abane, A. (2018). Mobile phones and education in sub-Saharan Africa: From youth practice to public policy. *Journal of International Development*, *30*(1), 22–39. DOI: 10.1002/jid.3116

Sandoval-Almazan, R., & Gil-Garcia, J. R. (2021). Digital government and public participation in Latin America: A comparative analysis. *Government Information Quarterly*, *38*(3), 101573.

APPENDICES

Appendix A: Survey Instrument - Citizen E-Participation Survey

Section A: Demographic Information

1. Age: _____ years
2. Gender: Male ☐ Female ☐ Other ☐ Prefer not to say ☐
3. Highest level of education completed:
    - o No formal education ☐
    - o Primary education ☐
    - o Secondary education ☐
    - o Tertiary/University education ☐
    - o Postgraduate education ☐
4. Primary occupation: ________________
5. Monthly household income (local currency): ________________
6. Location: Urban ☐ Semi-urban ☐ Rural ☐
7. Region/State: ________________

Section B: Digital Access and Usage

8. Do you own or have regular access to:
    - o Mobile phone: Yes ☐ No ☐
    - o Smartphone: Yes ☐ No ☐
    - o Computer/laptop: Yes ☐ No ☐
    - o Tablet: Yes ☐ No ☐
9. How do you primarily access the internet?
    - o Mobile data ☐
    - o Home broadband ☐
    - o Public Wi-Fi ☐
    - o Internet café ☐
    - o Other: ________________ ☐
10. How often do you use the internet?
    - o Daily ☐
    - o Several times per week ☐
    - o Weekly ☐
    - o Monthly ☐
    - o Rarely ☐
    - o Never ☐

Section C: Digital Literacy Assessment

11. Rate your ability to perform the following tasks (1=Cannot do, 5=Very confident):
    - o Send and receive emails: 1 2 3 4 5
    - o Use social media platforms: 1 2 3 4 5
    - o Download and install apps: 1 2 3 4 5
    - o Conduct online banking: 1 2 3 4 5
    - o Search for information online: 1 2 3 4 5
    - o Participate in online discussions: 1 2 3 4 5

Section D: E-Participation Experience

12. Are you aware of government e-participation platforms in your country? Yes ☐ No ☐
13. Have you ever participated in online government consultations or platforms? Yes ☐ No ☐ (If No, skip to Question 20)
14. Which platforms have you used? (Check all that apply)
    - o National government consultation portals ☐
    - o Local government platforms ☐
    - o Social media government pages ☐
    - o Mobile government apps ☐
    - o Other: _________________ ☐
15. How frequently do you participate in e-participation activities?
    - o Weekly ☐
    - o Monthly ☐
    - o Several times per year ☐
    - o Rarely ☐
16. What types of activities have you engaged in? (Check all that apply)
    - o Policy consultations ☐
    - o Service feedback ☐
    - o Community reporting ☐
    - o Direct communication with officials ☐
    - o Online petitions ☐
    - o Virtual town halls ☐

Section E: Barriers and Challenges

17. What barriers have you experienced in e-participation? (Check all that apply)
    - o Poor internet connectivity ☐
    - o High data costs ☐

- o Lack of digital skills ☐
- o The platform is challenging to use ☐
- o Language barriers ☐
- o Lack of time ☐
- o Distrust of government ☐
- o Privacy concerns ☐
- o Lack of awareness ☐
- o No government response ☐

Section F: Satisfaction and Impact

18. Rate your satisfaction with e-participation experiences (1=Very dissatisfied, 5=Very satisfied):
    - o Ease of platform use: 1 2 3 4 5
    - o Government responsiveness: 1 2 3 4 5
    - o Quality of information provided: 1 2 3 4 5
    - o Overall experience: 1 2 3 4 5
19. Do you believe your participation has influenced government decisions? Yes, significantly ☐ Yes, somewhat ☐ No impact ☐ Unsure ☐

Section G: Democratic Attitudes

20. Rate your agreement with the following statements (1=Strongly Disagree, 5=Strongly Agree):
    - o The government is responsive to citizens' needs: 1 2 3 4 5
    - o Citizens can influence government decisions: 1 2 3 4 5
    - o E-participation improves democracy: 1 2 3 4 5
    - o I trust government digital platforms: 1 2 3 4 5
    - o Digital technology enhances transparency: 1 2 3 4 5

Appendix B: Interview Guide - Government Officials

Opening Questions

1. Please describe your role in e-participation implementation in your organization.
2. What are the primary objectives of your e-participation initiatives?

    Implementation Experience 3. What challenges have you encountered in implementing e-participation platforms? 4. How do you measure the success of e-participation initiatives? 5. What technical or resource constraints have affected implementation?

Citizen Engagement 6. How do you reach different demographic groups through e-participation? 7. What strategies do you use to encourage citizen participation? 8. How do you handle citizen inputs that are received through the platforms?
Institutional Factors 9. How does your organization process and respond to citizen feedback? 10. What mechanisms exist for integrating citizen inputs into policy decisions? 11. How do you coordinate e-participation across different government levels?
Outcomes and Impact 12. What evidence do you have of e-participation's Impact on policy outcomes? 13. How has e-participation affected citizen-government relationships? 14. What improvements would you make to current approaches?

Appendix C: Focus Group Discussion Guide

Introduction (10 minutes)

- Welcome and introductions
- Explanation of research purpose
- Ground rules for discussion

Digital Access and Experience (15 minutes)

1. How do participants typically access and use digital technologies?
2. What challenges do they face in using government digital services?
3. What support would help them use digital platforms more effectively?

E-Participation Awareness and Usage (20 minutes) 4. What do participants know about government e-participation opportunities? 5. Who has participated in online government consultations or platforms? 6. What motivated participation, or what prevents participation?
Platform Experience (20 minutes) 7. For participants: Describe your experience using e-participation platforms 8. What worked well and what was problematic? 9. How could platforms be improved to meet user needs?
Democratic Impact (15 minutes) 10. Do participants believe their online inputs influence government decisions? 11. How has e-participation affected their relationship with the government? 12. What would increase their confidence in e-participation value?
Recommendations (10 minutes) 13. What advice would participants give to the government about e-participation? 14. What would encourage more people to participate online?

Appendix D: Digital Divide Index Calculation Methodology

The Digital Divide Index (DDI) combines multiple indicators across four dimensions:

Dimension 1: Infrastructure Access (Weight: 30%)

- Internet penetration rate (10%)
- Mobile broadband coverage (10%)
- Average connection speed (5%)
- Rural connectivity rate (5%)

Dimension 2: Device Availability (Weight: 25%)

- Smartphone ownership rate (15%)
- Computer/laptop ownership rate (10%)

Dimension 3: Digital Skills (Weight: 25%)

- Introductory digital literacy rate (15%)
- Advanced digital skills rate (10%)

Dimension 4: Usage Patterns (Weight: 20%)

- Active internet users (10%)
- Government digital service adoption (10%)

Calculation Formula: DDI = (Infrastructure $\times$ 0.30) + (Device $\times$ 0.25) + (Skills $\times$ 0.25) + (Usage $\times$ 0.20)

Where each component is normalized to a 0-100 scale.

Interpretation:

- 80-100: Low digital divide
- 60-79: Moderate digital divide
- 40-59: High digital divide
- 0-39: Very high digital divide

Appendix E: E-Participation Effectiveness Framework

Reach Indicators (25%)

- Registration rate: (Registered users / Internet users) × 100
- Geographic distribution: Herfindahl index of regional participation
- Demographic representation: Deviation from population demographics

Depth Indicators (25%)

- Average session duration
- Comments per user per session
- Policy document downloads per user
- Repeat participation rate

Impact Indicators (25%)

- Government response rate to citizen inputs
- Average response time (days)
- Policy integration rate: (Inputs integrated / Total substantive inputs) × 100
- Citizen satisfaction with government responses

Sustainability Indicators (25%)

- User retention rate over 12 months
- Cross-platform engagement rate
- Platform usage trend (increasing/decreasing)
- Long-term participation commitment

Overall E-Participation Effectiveness Score: EPES = (Reach × 0.25) + (Depth × 0.25) + (Impact × 0.25) + (Sustainability × 0.25)

Appendix F: Statistical Analysis Details

Table 9. Correlation Analysis Results

Variable Pair	Pearson r	Significance	Confidence Interval
Internet Access × Participation Rate	0.847***	$p < 0.001$	[0.789, 0.892]
Digital Literacy × Platform Engagement	0.723***	$p < 0.001$	[0.654, 0.781]
Infrastructure Quality × User Satisfaction	0.681***	$p < 0.001$	[0.607, 0.744]
Government Responsiveness × Repeat Usage	0.759***	$p < 0.001$	[0.694, 0.814]
Income Level × Platform Access	0.634***	$p < 0.001$	[0.554, 0.704]
Education × Contribution Quality	0.592**	$p < 0.01$	[0.507, 0.667]
Age × Digital Skills	-0.456**	$p < 0.01$	[-0.534, -0.369]
Rural Location × Participation Rate	-0.523***	$p < 0.001$	[-0.597, -0.439]

Note: *** $p < 0.001$, ** $p < 0.01$, * $p < 0.05$

Table 10. Regression Analysis - Determinants of E-Participation

Predictor	B	SE B	β	t	p
Constant	12.45	3.21	-	3.88	< 0.001
Internet Access	0.68	0.09	0.42	7.56	< 0.001
Digital Literacy	0.34	0.07	0.28	4.86	< 0.001
Government Responsiveness	0.45	0.08	0.31	5.63	< 0.001
Income Level	0.12	0.05	0.14	2.40	< 0.05
Education	0.23	0.09	0.16	2.56	< 0.05
Age	-0.08	0.03	-0.15	-2.67	< 0.01
Urban Location	8.34	2.12	0.19	3.93	< 0.001

Model Summary: $R^2 = 0.73$, Adjusted $R^2 = 0.71$, $F(7, 284) = 109.4$, $p < 0.001$

Algorithm G.1: Cross-National E-Participation Comparison

Algorithm: Comparative E Participation Analysis

INPUT: CountryData[3], Indicators[20], TimeSpans[5] OUTPUT: ComparativeReport, PolicyRecommendations

STEP 1: Data Preprocessing FOR each country in CountryData: Normalize indicators to 0-100 scale Handle missing values using multiple imputation Calculate composite scores for each dimension END FOR

STEP 2: Digital Divide Assessment FOR each country: Calculate DDI = Σ(dimension_score × weight) Rank countries by overall DDI score Identify specific dimension strengths/weaknesses END FOR

STEP 3: E-Participation Effectiveness Analysis FOR each country: Calculate EPES using a four-dimensional framework Analyze temporal trends and patterns Identify correlation patterns with DDI scores END FOR

STEP 4: Statistical Testing Perform ANOVA tests for cross-national differences Calculate correlation matrices for key relationships Conduct a regression analysis for causal inference Test for statistical significance at $\alpha = 0.05$

STEP 5: Gap Analysis Identify performance gaps between countries Calculate the improvement potential for each dimension Prioritize intervention areas based on impact potential

STEP 6: Best Practice Identification Extract successful practices from top performers Analyze contextual factors enabling success Assess transferability across different contexts

STEP 7: Policy Recommendation Generation Generate targeted recommendations for each country Prioritize interventions based on cost-benefit analysis Develop implementation timelines and milestones

RETURN comparative_analysis_report

Chapter 9
Economic Participation and Sustainable Development in South Africa:
Interlinking Trade, Poverty, Inequality, and the Environment

Leonard Agwuna
http://orcid.org/0000-0002-8425-4811
University of KwaZulu-Natal, South Africa

Bruce Rhodes
University of KwaZulu-Natal, South Africa

Shaun Mowat
http://orcid.org/0000-0002-4643-140X
University of KwaZulu-Natal, South Africa

ABSTRACT

This chapter examines the intricate relationship between economic participation and sustainable development in South Africa following the end of apartheid. Economic development has been boosted by trade and empowerment initiatives, but the gains have remained concentrated in capital-intensive industries, widening racial and regional disparities. Due to structural obstacles in employment, land distribution, and education, more than 50% of South Africans continue to live in poverty, and high inequality (Gini > 0.63) endures. At the same time, reliance on resource extraction and carbon-intensive businesses has led to environmental costs that

DOI: 10.4018/979-8-2600-1618-3.ch009

disproportionately impact impoverished people. To balance economic, social, and ecological objectives, the study suggests an integrated framework of policies. These include: (1) trade policies that give priority to inclusive value chains; (2) green industrial strategies to reduce carbon emissions from growth; (3) redistributive measures to address resource inequality; and (4) environmental justice interventions.

INTRODUCTION

It's critical to distinguish between persistent structural inequality and South Africa's liberal progress (Shifa et al., 2023). The country's social, economic, and environmental systems are still being impacted by apartheid's lasting repercussions (Shifa et al., 2023). Although political democracy and economic stability are significant achievements, problems still need to be fixed. For example, there are still shocking disparities in wealth and income, millions of people live in poverty, unemployment is among the highest in the world, and environmental degradation is accelerating. These issues all threaten sustainable and equitable development (Shifa et al., 2023).

Economic participation, which is defined as substantial involvement in economic activities through employment, entrepreneurship, or asset ownership, is at the heart of these issues. In South Africa, there are still notable differences in engagement by gender, race, and area. This is because apartheid's exclusionary policies and post-apartheid reforms' inability to adequately advance equality is to blame (Bhorat et al., 2017). Despite moderate economic improvement and incorporation into international trade networks, the exclusion of large masses from the formal sector has contributed to poverty and inequality. Unemployment disproportionately affects Black South Africans, women, and youth, impeding overall socioeconomic growth and sustaining cycles of marginalization (Nattrass & Seekings, 2018).

Since the 1990s, South Africa's economic strategy has been based on trade liberalization, which includes involvement in international markets, export-led development, and tariff reductions (Edwards & Lawrence, 2012). Trade has made it easier to access global value chains and diversify the economy, but the rewards have not been distributed fairly. Capital-intensive industries like manufacturing and mining have dominated growth, sometimes displacing poor populations (Rodrik, 2008). Additionally, the economy is susceptible to changes in commodity prices and environmentally harmful activities like coal mining and deforestation because of its reliance on resource-based exports (Sovacool et al., 2021).

Trade and environmental sustainability have an especially complicated relationship. According to Grossman and Krueger (1995), the Environmental Kuznets Curve (EKC) suggests that environmental deterioration may worsen with economic expansion at first before getting better as incomes increase and regulatory frameworks get stronger. The trajectory of South Africa, however, casts doubt on this theory because economic expansion is nevertheless accompanied by significant carbon emissions, water stress, and biodiversity loss (Dasgupta et al., 2002). The disproportionate burden of degradation in the environment falls on impoverished and rural communities, who are caught in a vicious cycle where environmental damage increases poverty and limits adaptive capacity (Duraiappah, 1998).

In South Africa, poverty is still widespread and complex. More than 50% of people live below the upper-bound poverty line, even with the growth of social subsidies and the enhancement of access to essential services (Stats SA, 2023). Because there is a lack of infrastructure and economic prospects in rural areas, informal settlements, and historic homelands, poverty is geographically concentrated there. According to Chambers and Conway (1992) and the FAO (2018), impoverished communities often turn to unsustainable resource usage, such as deforestation for fuel, which worsens environmental degradation and increases vulnerability.

With a Gini coefficient surpassing 0.63, South Africa has among of the highest levels of inequality in the world (Shifa et al., 2023). Disparities in wealth, education, employment, and service accessibility are all included in this inequality, which goes beyond wealth. These divisions are maintained by structural impediments such as concentrated capital, spatial segregation, and insufficient assistance for small and medium-sized businesses (SMEs) and informal workforce. Through prioritizing skilled labor and capital-intensive industry, trade and globalization have occasionally made inequality worse (Rodrik, 2018), weakening social mobility and inclusive growth.

A comprehensive strategy to sustainable development is necessary if South Africa is to address the interconnected problems of trade, poverty, inequality, and environmental degradation. The Sustainable Development Goals (SDGs) state that development must be ecologically sustainable, commercially viable, and socially inclusive. This necessitates a drastic shift away from extractive, uneven, and carbon-intensive development patterns and toward ones that prioritize equity, resilience, and ecological stewardship (UNCTAD, 2024).

The Triple-Bottom-Line (Elkington, 2018) and Doughnut Economics (Raworth, 2017) are two ideas that highlight the necessity of balancing economic efficiency, environmental restrictions, and social justice. These theories provide useful guidance. Implementing these ideas entails aligning trade and investment plans with environmental goals while enabling marginalized populations to participate in and benefit from economic growth. Although South Africa's National Development Plan (NDP 2030) reflects these objectives, execution has been hampered by institutional, political, and competency constraints (Gumede, 2017).

The study examines the intricate relationship between economic participation and sustainable development in South Africa, with a focus on the connections between trade, poverty, inequality, and the environment. It identifies significant policy gaps and looks at the structural, economic, and social changes required to develop a more equitable and sustainable growth strategy. If these problems are properly resolved, South Africa may be one step closer to realizing its objective of equitable progress within the framework of the global community.

Economic Participation in Post-Apartheid South Africa

Economic participation, which encompasses the ability of individuals and communities to access productive resources like capital, land, infrastructure, and skills as well as to engage in income-generating activities, is a crucial element of inclusive and sustainable development. This concept is important in South Africa since apartheid purposefully excluded the Black majority and other non-white communities from official economic systems. Even though the democratic transition of 1994 promised political and economic progress (Seekings & Nattrass, 2008), the history of exclusion continues to shape current problems.

In order to remedy historical injustices and advance inclusion, post-apartheid administrations have implemented a number of policies, including employment equity, land reform, affirmative procurement, and Black Economic Empowerment (BEE). For example, land reform programs seek to address racially uneven ownership patterns, whereas BEE seeks to improve Black ownership, management, and control of productive assets (Matyana & Thusi, 2023). Economic prejudice persists despite these attempts. Despite the official unemployment rate of over 32%, young unemployment surpassed 60% as of early 2023 (Statistics South Africa, 2023). Black South Africans, women, and rural areas are all negatively impacted by these disparities, which are a reflection of a labor market that is still exclusive and segregated (Bhorat et al., 2021). Structural barriers, such as reliance on exports of primary commodities, capital-intensive industries, skill gaps, and subpar educational outcomes, have hampered further advancement (Hall, 2015).

For individuals who are unable to obtain work, especially women, those living in rural regions, and migrants, the informal sector provides an essential safety net (Rogan & Skinner, 2019). Domestic duties, street vending, and small-scale farming are examples of both business endeavors and survival tactics. On the other hand, factors including inconsistent income, restricted credit availability, and a lack of social protection make informal workers more vulnerable. These issues are made worse by the sector's exclusion from urban planning and policy (Skinner, 2018). Entrepreneurship is frequently hailed as a means of achieving economic inclusion, however it is hampered for Black-owned SMEs by structural hurdles. Growth is hampered by a lack of support systems, legal restrictions, poor infrastructure, and restricted access to funding (Charman et al., 2017). Despite the creation of organizations such as the Small Enterprise Development Agency (SEDA), corruption and bureaucratic inefficiencies undermine its efficacy (Herrington et al., 2017).

One of the main pillars of post-apartheid reparations, land reform, has had difficulty producing revolutionary outcomes. The state's three-pronged strategy of tenure reform, redistribution, and reparation hasn't done much to improve rural livelihoods or change ownership patterns (Hall, 2015). Due to a lack of post-transfer assistance, a large portion of redistributed land remains fallow, and investment is deterred by tenure insecurity in slums and communities. Agricultural production and gender parity are undermined by the additional obstacles that women experience because of administrative and patriarchal practices (Walker, 2005). BEE has produced a range of results. Critics contend that, although fostering a diverse corporate leadership and a Black middle class, it has largely benefited a politically connected elite rather than facilitating widespread empowerment (Southall, 2007). Additionally, small enterprises are frequently burdened by regulatory obligations, which unintentionally discourage expansion.

Inequalities in education also limit labor market participation. Township and rural schools often lack infrastructure, competent instructors, and resources despite improvements, which perpetuates a skills gap (Spaull, 2013). Despite the expansion of Technical and Vocational Education and Training (TVET) programs, issues with curriculum relevancy, employer relationships, and social attitudes still exist (Akoojee, 2016). These problems are exacerbated by gender inequality. According to Posel and Casale (2020), women are overrepresented in low-wage, informal, and care-based occupations. These disparities were made worse by the COVID-19 epidemic, as many women left the workforce as a result of job losses in industries with a high female labor force and caregiving responsibilities. In order to promote women's economic involvement, gender-responsive policies like childcare assistance, equal pay legislation, and focused enterprise growth are essential (Statistics South Africa, 2023).

Unequal access to finance persists, especially for the impoverished and those living in rural areas. Although fintech and mobile banking present viable remedies, disparities in infrastructure, affordability, and digital literacy run the risk of escalating already-existing differences (Demirgüç-Kunt et al., 2018). Formal employment, informal work, unpaid care, and alternative livelihoods must all be included in a comprehensive definition of economic involvement. Expanding people's actual freedoms to live the lives they value is crucial, according to a capabilities-based approach influenced by Sen and Nussbaum's work (Sen, 1999).

Even though South Africa's policies have advanced significantly since 1994, there is still disparity in the country's development toward equitable economic participation. Inclusive development is nevertheless hindered by structural unemployment, marginalization of the informal sector, unequal access to resources, and delayed transition. To tackle these issues, comprehensive policies that eliminate structural obstacles, encourage fair access to opportunities, and cultivate sustainable livelihoods for all South Africans are needed.

Trade and Development Dynamics

A middle-income country with a varied trading portfolio, South Africa has a special position in the international trading system. Its advantageous geographic location, comparatively sophisticated infrastructure, and wealth of natural resources endow it with strong trade relations with major international economies, such as China, the European Union (EU), the United States, and regional partners within the Southern African Development Community (SADC). Since the end of apartheid, trade policy has been impacted by trade openness, tariff reductions, and a commitment to regional and continental integration, particularly through frameworks like the African Continental Free Trade Area (AfCFTA) and the SADC Free-Trade Area. The fact that trade liberalization has had uneven impacts on employment, inequality, and sectoral development despite its beneficial benefits on macroeconomic growth raises questions about how it may support sustainable development (Bhorat et al., 2017).

The liberalization of trade in the 1990s, initiated under the General Agreement on Tariffs and Trade (GATT) and later institutionalized through the World Trade Organization (WTO), marked a significant shift toward a more open trade regime. This openness facilitated South Africa's integration into the global economy, boosting exports particularly in capital-intensive sectors such as mining and finance (Edwards & Lawrence, 2012). Mineral exports, including gold, platinum, and coal, continue to play a central role in the country's trade balance. Simultaneously, the financial sector has flourished in a globally connected environment, attracting foreign investment and expanding South African capital across the continent. However, this growth has been largely capital-intensive and has not translated into broad-based employment gains. The phenomenon of "jobless growth" remains a defining feature of South Africa's post-liberalization economy (Rodrik, 2008). The disconnect between trade-driven economic expansion and labor market absorption underscores a key developmental challenge: how to ensure that trade contributes not only to GDP growth but also to inclusive and sustainable livelihoods.

Manufacturing and agriculture sectors historically associated with labor absorption and poverty reduction have struggled under liberalized trade regimes. The manufacturing sector, once a cornerstone of the apartheid-era economy, has experienced deindustrialization and a decline in its contribution to GDP and employment since the 1990s (Tregenna, 2016). Increased competition from imports, especially from low-cost producers like China, has undermined domestic manufacturing firms, particularly in clothing, textiles, and electronics. While export-oriented manufacturing such as vehicle assembly and machinery has shown resilience, it has remained highly capital-intensive and geographically concentrated in urban industrial hubs, limiting broader employment benefits.

In agriculture, trade liberalization has led to increased exposure to volatile global markets and has widened the divide between large-scale commercial farmers and smallholder or subsistence producers. Although South Africa remains a net exporter of agricultural products such as citrus, wine, and maize these gains have primarily accrued to well-capitalized farms with access to irrigation, storage, and export logistics (Kirsten et al., 2012). Small-scale farmers, particularly in former homeland areas, continue to face barriers to market access, finance, and infrastructure, which undermines their ability to benefit from trade integration. This dichotomy illustrates the dual nature of South Africa's economy, where formal, export-linked enterprises operate alongside marginalized informal producers and workers (Aliber & Hall, 2012).

Trade-related growth has also reinforced spatial and class inequalities. Urban areas such as Johannesburg, Cape Town, and Durban have reaped the benefits of global investment, logistics hubs, and export-oriented services. In contrast, rural provinces—home to large numbers of the poor and underemployed—remain disconnected from global markets and investment flows (Bhorat et al., 2017). This spatial disparity is further compounded by unequal access to skills and technology, which limits the ability of rural populations and township-based entrepreneurs to engage competitively in trade-related activities. Thus, the geography of trade in South Africa has reproduced rather than resolved developmental divides.

One of the most critical weaknesses in South Africa's trade-driven development model is its failure to stimulate intensive employment growth. The capital-intensive nature of mining and finance, along with the automation of many manufacturing processes, has contributed to declining labor intensity in core sectors (Rodrik, 2008). Moreover, the rigid duality of the South African labor market marked by a protected, high-wage formal sector and a precarious, low-wage informal sector has limited job creation even in times of export booms. This has perpetuated high unemployment, particularly among youth and low-skilled workers, who are unable to transition into growing sectors of the economy.

Sustainability issues and trade policies also interact. Significant environmental degradation, such as land destruction, water pollution, and greenhouse gas emissions, are caused by South Africa's reliance on resource exports. In addition to being one of the biggest consumers of water and carbon emissions, the mining industry accounts for a significant portion of foreign exchange profits (Sovacool et al., 2021). The nation is among the top 15 carbon emitters in the world due to its substantial reliance on coal for both export and domestic energy generation, which puts trade objectives and climate pledges under international agreements like the Paris Accord at odds (UNEP, 2024).

The Environmental Kuznets Curve (EKC) concept states that after initially rising with economic development, environmental degradation may progressively decline as income levels increase, and more environmental laws and cleaner technology become available (Grossman & Krueger, 1995). However, in South Africa's case, there is a noticeable break from this pattern. Long-term inequality, a heavy reliance on fossil fuels, particularly coal, and a lack of institutional capacity have all played a part in delaying or preventing the anticipated environmental turning point. Ecological inequality has been made worse by trade liberalization without adequate environmental restrictions, which has disproportionately impacted communities close to extractive industries, where pollution exposure and resource depletion are most severe (Dasgupta et al., 2002).

Considering these challenges, South Africa has attempted to align its trade policy with sustainable development objectives. The National Trade Policy Framework (2021) places a high importance on inclusive trade that fosters industrialization, supports SMEs, and fortifies regional connectivity. The nation has also launched programs to encourage green exports, such as goods made from sustainable agriculture, biodiversity, and advances in renewable energy. Policy discrepancies continue to be a significant barrier, nevertheless. While support for small-scale producers and inclusive industrialization is still poorly planned and underfunded, ongoing incentives for mining growth and the export of fossil fuels frequently undercut sustainability goals (Dinc & Otkur, 2021).

There is a strategic chance to change South Africa's trade strategy in the direction of more sustainable and equitable results through regional economic integration, especially through the African Continental Free Trade Area (AfCFTA). Increasing intra-African trade might support labor-intensive industries like light manufacturing and agro-processing, diversify export markets, and create robust regional value chains. However, substantial expenditures in institutional reforms, infrastructure, and skill development are needed to realize this promise. To fully benefit from regional trade integration, it is imperative to remove non-tariff obstacles, increase logistical effectiveness, and resolve intra-African business constraints (Hartzenberg, 2011).

Although South Africa's trade policy has benefited the economy overall, its effects on development have been mixed. While providing only modest improvements in employment and poverty alleviation, the existing trade-growth relationship has strengthened trends of inequality and environmental stress. Reconfiguring trade to support inclusive and sustainable development requires a dual strategy: first, deepening support for sectors and regions currently marginalized in the trade regime; and second, embedding environmental and social considerations into trade policy frameworks. Doing so will ensure that trade contributes not only to growth, but also to broader developmental goals in South Africa.

Poverty and Inequality: Persistent Structural Challenges

South Africa's development trajectory is fundamentally constrained by deep-rooted poverty and one of the highest levels of inequality in the world. These challenges are not merely statistical anomalies; they are the structural legacies of colonial dispossession, apartheid-era exclusion, and the uneven implementation of post-apartheid reforms. Despite the progress made through social protection systems and redistributive policies, a significant portion of the population remains trapped in poverty, and wealth continues to be highly concentrated in the hands of a few. These persistent disparities obstruct the goals of inclusive growth and sustainable development (Stats SA, 2023; Shifa et al., 2023).

According to Statistics South Africa (2023), over 55% of South Africans live below the upper-bound national poverty line, while extreme poverty (measured by the food poverty line) still affects over 20% of the population. Social grants, which reach over 18 million South Africans, have been instrumental in preventing destitution and ensuring basic consumption among vulnerable groups, especially children, the elderly, and people with disabilities (Black et al., 2020). However, while these grants are effective at alleviating extreme poverty, they are not designed to fundamentally alter structural inequalities or create pathways to sustainable economic inclusion.

Income inequality in South Africa remains exceptionally high, with a Gini coefficient exceeding 0.63, according to the World Bank (2022). This reflects stark disparities in earnings, wealth accumulation, and access to productive assets. The top 10% of earners account for more than 60% of total income, while the bottom 50% earn less than 8% (Chatterjee et al., 2021). These inequalities are particularly pronounced along racial lines: on average, White South Africans continue to earn significantly more than their Black counterparts and hold a disproportionately large share of wealth and capital assets. Post-apartheid economic policies, while progressive in intent, have not sufficiently disrupted the racially skewed ownership patterns that were entrenched by apartheid's spatial and economic planning (Seekings & Nattrass, 2008).

Inequality in South Africa is not only about income—it is multidimensional, encompassing education, health, housing, land, and employment. Geographic disparities further compound these inequalities. Rural provinces such as the Eastern Cape, Limpopo, and parts of KwaZulu-Natal continue to face chronic underdevelopment due to historical neglect and contemporary governance failures. These areas often lack basic infrastructure such as roads, electricity, and clean water, and suffer from poor access to quality education, healthcare, and economic opportunities (Turok & Visagie, 2018). As a result, people in these provinces are more likely to be unemployed, food insecure, and reliant on social grants for survival.

Education plays a central role in either breaking or reinforcing the cycle of poverty. In South Africa, access to quality education remains highly unequal, with former Model C and private schools outperforming township and rural schools by significant margins (Spaull, 2013). Although basic education is widely accessible, the quality gap undermines the capacity of learners from disadvantaged backgrounds to transition into higher education or the formal labour market. The poor performance of the education system, particularly in mathematics and science, contributes to a persistent skills mismatch in the economy, thereby reinforcing labour market exclusion for the majority (Van der Berg, 2008).

Persistent poverty is also largely caused by asset inequality. Even after decades of post-apartheid land reform, there is still a great deal of inequality in land ownership. Many beneficiaries lack the resources or capital necessary to make profitable use of the land they acquire as a result of the state's sluggish, frequently bureaucratic, and inadequately funded land redistribution and restitution initiatives (Hall, 2015). Additionally, informal settlements are growing in metropolitan areas as a result of fast urbanization and the state's inability to provide sufficient and reasonably priced housing, thus entrenching housing inequality (Turok & Borel-Saladin, 2016). An additional layer of exclusion for the urban poor is created by their inability to obtain credit, formal employment, and basic services due to their lack of solid tenure and sufficient housing.

Another important factor causing inequality and poverty is structural unemployment. The labor market in South Africa is characterized by a strict dichotomy: a sizable, unstable informal sector and a tiny, well-paid formal sector. While the informal sector is under supported, characterized by fragility and low productivity, the formal industry is capital-intensive and finds it difficult to hire low-skilled people (Rogan & Skinner, 2019). The youth have been disproportionately affected by this labor market structure, which has led to ongoing unemployment. Over 60% of young people were unemployed in 2023, a statistic that indicates both economic stagnation and the shortcomings of the education-to-employment pipeline (Stats SA, 2023)

Gender inequality intersects deeply with poverty and labour market exclusion. Women, particularly Black and rural women, are disproportionately represented in low-paid, informal, and care-based employment. They are also more likely to bear the burden of unpaid domestic responsibilities, which limits their ability to participate in economic activities and access educational or entrepreneurial opportunities (Posel & Casale, 2020). Despite progressive legal frameworks aimed at gender equality, implementation gaps and patriarchal norms continue to restrict women's empowerment and inclusion.

Although the state has implemented a range of redistributive policies including free basic services, housing subsidies, and black economic empowerment (BEE) many of these initiatives have not significantly altered structural inequality. BEE, for example, has helped create a Black middle class and fostered some degree of corporate diversity. However, it has also been criticized for enabling elite enrichment rather than broad-based empowerment, with limited trickle-down effects for the poor majority (Southall, 2007). Without more inclusive forms of economic empowerment that reach rural, unemployed, and informal populations, redistributive efforts will continue to fall short.

Addressing poverty and inequality in South Africa requires a shift in policy thinking from compensatory measures to transformative strategies. This includes investing in universal, quality education; expanding public employment programs; promoting land reform and asset redistribution; and supporting the informal sector as a legitimate component of the economy. In addition, macroeconomic policy must be aligned with redistributive goals assuring that fiscal policy, trade, and industrial strategies are explicitly pro-pocr and employment-generating (Bhorat et al., 2017).

Sustainable development theory argues that reducing poverty and inequality is both financially and morally necessary. High inequality hinders investment and long-term growth by lowering demand, undermining social cohesion, and increasing the likelihood of unrest. Poverty also contributes to a vicious cycle of ecological degradation and loss of livelihood, sometimes pushing populations to engage in ecologically harmful practices such informal mining, overgrazing, and deforestation (Duraiappah, 1998). Coordination of policies that promote sustainable development and economic inclusiveness is necessary to end this cycle.

Environmental Degradation and Ecological Limits

Growing degradation of the environment and overuse of natural resources are major obstacles to South Africa's road to sustainable development. South Africa must strike a difficult balance between the environment and its aspirations for growth. Despite making up only 0.8% of the world's population, South Africa is one of the continent's leading emitters of greenhouse gases, contributing roughly 1.3% of global emissions due to its strong reliance on coal, making it one of the continent's most carbon-intensive economies (DOEFF and TO, I.R., 2022). The energy industry, industrial operations, and an economy that has historically relied on resource extraction are the main drivers of this carbon intensity.

The environmental pollution in South Africa is rooted in the country's energy system. About 85% of the nation's electricity is produced from coal, which dominates the power generating industry (Calitz and Wright, 2021). While coal has historically supported industrialization and employment in mining-dependent communities, it has also led to severe environmental consequences, including air pollution, acid mine drainage, and widespread greenhouse gas emissions. These emissions undermine South Africa’s commitments to the Paris Agreement and place pressure on national and subnational governments to transition toward renewable energy sources. However, the transition remains sluggish due to infrastructural bottlenecks, vested interests in the coal industry, and insufficient investment in green technologies.

The ecological footprint in South Africa continues to rise, particularly in urban centers such as Johannesburg, Cape Town, and Durban, where consumption patterns and industrial expansion have exceeded the biocapacity of local ecosystems (Street, 2023). The ecological footprint, a measure of the demand placed on nature by individuals and economies, reflects the extent to which human activity outpaces the planet's capacity to regenerate resources and absorb waste. South Africa's growing ecological deficit points to unsustainable levels of consumption, poor waste management, and unplanned urban sprawl.

Urbanization, though central to economic participation and access to services, is straining environmental systems. Unchecked urban growth often leads to the conversion of green spaces into informal settlements and industrial zones, placing pressure on water supplies, waste infrastructure, and biodiversity. In many communities, waste management is still lacking, especially when it comes to plastic and toxic industrial waste. Urban air quality is also declining as a result of increased car use and emissions from unauthorized energy sources, such as paraffin and coal stoves, which are utilized by low-income households (DEA, 2020). These environmental challenges are closely linked to poverty and inequality because disadvantaged communities often reside in environmentally degraded regions and are less equipped to adapt to climate-related concerns.

Deforestation, land erosin, and overgrazing are examples of environmental degradation in rural areas. Natural resources are the main source of food, fuel, and income for a large number of people living in rural areas. However, because of poverty, precarious tenure, and restricted access to extension services, unsustainable land use practices have decreased agricultural output and depleted soil fertility (Schreiner et al., 2018). The decline of community rangelands, which include pollinators and medicinal plants, and biodiversity loss are threatening the environmental foundations of rural economies (Street, 2023)

The primary reasons of South Africa's increasing water scarcity are pollution, climate change, excessive water consumption, and deteriorating infrastructure. The country's water supply is under a lot of stress since several areas have been classified as water limited. Droughts like the one that hit the Western Cape in 2018 have highlighted the vulnerability of water security and its importance for social stability and economic continuity (Ziervogel, 2019). Mining, agriculture, and urban consumption all contribute to water stress through overuse and contamination, particularly of surface and groundwater resources. Acid mine drainage and agricultural runoff have contaminated many river systems, posing a health risk to people and decreasing aquatic biodiversity.

The Environmental Kuznets Curve (EKC) theory provides a useful but controversial perspective in the context of South Africa. According to this theory, environmental deterioration first rises in tandem with wealth growth before progressively decreasing due to more robust regulatory frameworks and rising public demand for environmental quality (Grossman & Krueger, 1995). Even if it could be accurate in many high-income countries, the EKC has come under fire for assuming a linear trend of environmental improvement without accounting for local institutional and governance variables.

The "turning point" of the EKC model is being hampered by institutional inconsistencies, fragmented policy execution, and weak environmental laws, according to evidence from South Africa (Dasgupta et al., 2002). Particularly at the local level, the nation's progressive environmental laws, such the National Environmental Management Act (NEMA), are not always applied. Towns usually lack the capacity, means, and political will necessary to effectively implement environmental regulations. Environmental impact assessments (EIAs), which are legally required for development projects, are either conducted in a hurry or are not adequately enforced, particularly in areas where the private sector has substantial interests.

Furthermore, policy misalignments between environmental goals and economic priorities hinder sustainable development. For instance, the government's continued investment in fossil fuel-based infrastructure, such as the Medupi and Kusile coal-fired power stations, conflicts with the National Development Plan's commitment to a low-carbon economy. In a similar vein, the mining sector remains vital to South Africa's export strategy despite its high environmental costs and minimal impact on employment (Bhorat et al., 2017). This disparity reflects the political economics of environmental governance, where short-term growth imperatives are prioritized above long-term sustainability considerations.

Climate change makes it more complicated. South Africa is especially vulnerable to the effects of climate change, which include rising temperatures, altered rainfall patterns, and severe weather events. These changes are putting food production, water supply, and public health at risk. The poor are disproportionately impacted, especially in rural areas and informal settlements, because of their low ability to adapt and susceptibility to environmental hazards (Ziervogel et al., 2014). Initiatives for economic inclusion must address climate change, which is a developmental and environmental issue, in order to boost resilience among the underprivileged.

Despite these challenges, South Africa has the opportunity to shift its environmental worldview toward sustainability and equity. The Renewable Energy Independent Power Producer Procurement Program (REIPPPP) has successfully attracted investments in wind and solar energy, resulting in lower emissions and job creation. However, to guarantee that the energy transition benefits local communities and workers who are displaced from fossil fuel businesses, more size and inclusion are required (Baker et al., 2014). Achieving a balance between economic activity and environmental integrity may be accomplished through green industrial practices, such as energy efficiency measures, sustainable agriculture, and circular economic projects.

The concept of environmental equality is particularly relevant in South Africa, where environmental problems frequently have a detrimental effect on the underprivileged and impoverished. Examples of sustainable development movements that highlight the link between ecological deterioration and social injustice include those that promote clean air in Mpumalanga or oppose coal mining in the Wild Coast. The pillars of sustainable development in South Africa include equity, participatory governance, and recognizing communities as active players in environmental decision-making (Cock, 2011).

Interlinkages: Trade, Poverty, Inequality, and the Environment

In South Africa, what Rittel and Webber (1973) call "wicked problems" are a complicated network of interconnected socioeconomic problems that are challenging to resolve and call for systemic solutions. These issues include poverty, inequality, global trade dynamics, and environmental degradation. This country's distinctive environment—which was shaped by the legacy of apartheid, continued socioeconomic disparity, a resource-dependent trade economy, and growing ecological concerns—makes it especially challenging to achieve inclusive sustainable development. Developing policies that simultaneously advance social justice, economic inclusivity, and environmental sustainability require an understanding of these intricate relationships.

In order to foster development and modernization, the post-apartheid economic strategy gave trade liberalization and global integration first priority. Despite the fact that sectors like mining and banking have significantly increased both foreign investment and national revenue, the benefits have been unevenly distributed (Bhorat et al., 2017). Minerals (coal, gold, platinum, etc.) make up the majority of South Africa's exports, but doing so comes at a high social and environmental cost (Bond, 2018). Examples of how mining-adjacent communities frequently experience land dispossession, environmental contamination, and health hazards while having limited access to the money created include acid mine drainage and heavy metal pollution in Mpumalanga and Limpopo (Humby, 2016). Poor populations that rely on subsistence farming and natural resources are particularly affected since declining soil and water quality endanger livelihoods and worsen poverty.

This scenario is a prime illustration of the "poverty-environment trap" that Duraiappah (1998) defined as a vicious cycle in which poverty exacerbates environmental degradation. Unsustainable firewood gathering and informal mining are common practices among rural and periurban families that depend on natural resources for their sustenance, which hastens deforestation and soil erosion. Richer groups are the ones least affected by environmental effects, illustrating Raworth's (2017) concept of "environmental injustice." They also cause the most ecological harm because of their high energy and consumption levels (Street, 2023).

Climate change exacerbates these gaps, since droughts, heat waves, and floods disproportionately affect disadvantaged people that lack adequate housing, insurance, and climate-resilient livelihoods (Ziervogel et al., 2014). While large commercial operations often benefit from export-oriented strategies in areas like horticulture, agricultural liberalization has undermined local food systems and weakened small farmers against subsidized global competition. Often, these trade policies exacerbate gaps (Greenberg, 2013).

Integrating social protection with economic and environmental policies such as concentrating public works projects on green infrastructure and ecological restoration is essential to addressing these interconnected problems (Phillips, 2004). bringing back land reform to rectify historical injustices and support sustainable land use and food sovereignty. Training in green skills and environmental education should be increased to encourage participation in the green economy. Using alternate frameworks for growth, like the Triple-Bottom-Line (Elkington, 2018) and Doughnut-Economics (Raworth, 2017), that balance ecological limitations and societal demands

Breaking the existing patterns of exclusion need coordinated, cross-sectoral policies that put people and the environment first in order to achieve sustainable development in South Africa. This necessitates switching from growth models that are centered on GDP to strategies that balance social justice, ecological sustainability, and economic participation (Elkington, 2018).

Inclusive Trade Policies

Development may be greatly aided by trade, but only if it is conducted within inclusive and equitable frameworks. Trade liberalization has historically given capital-intensive industries like banking and mining precedence over labor-intensive industries like agriculture and small-scale manufacturing in South Africa (Bhorat et al., 2017). This structural mismatch has hampered the larger developmental advantages of trade and led to chronic economic inequality. To solve these challenges, trade agreements must be backed by comprehensive social protection programs and inclusive economic policies that seek to minimize adverse consequences and promote equitable participation.

A robust system of social safety nets, such as conditional cash transfers, food assistance programs, and unemployment insurance, is necessary to shield underprivileged groups from trade-related economic shocks. Strategic investments in education, vocational training, and the development of digital skills are essential for empowering historically deprived communities and giving them the chance to actively participate in regional and global value chains. Because of these complementary measures, the advantages of trade are distributed more fairly across society (Ziervogel, 2019).

In order to promote inclusive growth, South Africa should prioritize local policy initiatives that actively encourage small and medium-sized firms (SMEs) to enter export-oriented industries, with a concentration on Black-owned and women-led businesses. Comprehensive support systems that include firm incubation centers, export credit facilities, and improved financial access may significantly boost small enterprises' competitiveness. Infrastructure development in historically disadvantaged areas, particularly provinces like the Eastern Cape and Limpopo, should be a focus of trade facilitation projects in order to reduce regional inequities in trade participation (Edwards & Lawrence, 2012).

Aligning trade policy with sustainable development principles, as envisioned by the African Continental Free Trade Area (AfCFTA), is one way to ensure that trade fosters social progress and economic transformation. Trade agreements must support regional value chains, integrate labor and environmental standards, and encourage green industrialization models that prioritize ecological sustainability and fair economic participation in order to accomplish this alignment. By employing this comprehensive approach, South Africa may utilize trade as a powerful tool to attain more equitable and sustainable development outcomes (Bhorat et al., 2017).

Green Industrialization

An inclusive, innovative, and ecologically friendly industrial strategy must take the place of South Africa's carbon-intensive one. Green industrialization, which is based on circular economy models, sustainable tourism, and renewable energy, provides a route to economic diversification and environmental resilience. The nation is well-positioned for investments in renewable energy because of its abundance of solar and wind resources, which may lessen reliance on coal while also creating jobs and boosting local economies (Baker et al., 2014).

Investment in the renewable energy sector can be accelerated by government incentives such as feed-in tariffs, green bonds, and public-private partnerships. Waste-to-energy technology, recycling, and sustainable product design are a few examples of circular economy activities that ought to be incorporated into industrial strategy. In addition to creating new markets and job opportunities, these tactics lessen environmental externalities, especially for small recyclers and unorganized garbage pickers. Furthermore, ecotourism and nature-based enterprises may promote conservation and offer sustainable livelihoods in rural areas when local people actively participate in ownership and benefit-sharing agreements (Cock, 2011).

Research and development, training in green skills, and institutional changes should be given top priority in industrial policy in order to facilitate the green transition. Institutions of technical and vocational education and training (TVET) must change their focus to offer degrees that are applicable to low-carbon industries. This will guarantee that no one is left behind in the transition to sustainability and that South Africa's workforce is equipped to meet the needs of a shifting global economy.

Redistributive Reforms

Reducing inequality and expanding economic participation require deep structural reforms that redistribute access to productive assets and essential services. Land reform remains a central pillar in redressing apartheid-era dispossession and enabling economic inclusion in agriculture and land-based enterprises. However, land reform must be accompanied by post-settlement support, such as extension services, irrigation infrastructure, and access to markets, to ensure the sustainability of land transfers (Hall, 2010).

Progressive taxation, including wealth taxes and environmental levies, can be used to fund universal basic services in education, healthcare, and housing. These services are foundational to enhancing individual capabilities and reducing barriers to economic participation. In the long term, universal access to quality education is the most powerful tool for breaking intergenerational cycles of poverty. Targeted education reforms should address early childhood development, teacher training, and curricula that include environmental literacy and entrepreneurship.

Housing policy should focus not only on shelter but on integrating marginalized communities into economic hubs through improved transportation, internet connectivity, and social infrastructure. Such spatial transformation is essential in dismantling the apartheid geography that still limits economic opportunities for the majority of South Africans.

Environmental Justice Frameworks

Environmental concern must be the cornerstone of South Africa's framework for sustainable development. While wealthy elites continue to benefit financially from industrialization and resource exploitation, disadvantaged populations experience negative environmental effects such pollution, water scarcity, and land degradation (Bond, 2018). To stop growth from making ecological damage or social inequities worse, strong environmental management and fair distribution of environmental benefits are crucial.

The Department of Forestry, Fisheries, and the Environment (DFFE) must enforce environmental protections more strictly. This entails upholding climate mitigation pledges, strictly enforcing air and water quality rules, and applying environmental impact assessments (EIAs). Accountability measures including severe fines, mandatory rehabilitation, and making emissions data publicly available should be put in place to deter violations and ensure corporate responsibility.

Community-driven conservation efforts, such indigenous stewardship programs and community-managed protected areas, must be supported. Legal recognition, technical support, and ongoing funding can encourage ecological preservation and socioeconomic resilience by empowering local people to assume the role of stewards of natural resources (Schreiner et al., 2018). Local governments must integrate climate adaptation into their planning processes to ensure that decisions regarding land use, infrastructure, and service delivery take environmental hazards into account. Expanding community views in environmental governance and fostering equitable and responsive policy outcomes need inclusive participatory approaches (Schreiner et al., 2018). By putting environmental justice first, South Africa may work toward development that safeguards ecosystems and communities that are at risk.

Data and Monitoring Systems

The foundation of effective policymaking in South Africa is timely, harsh, and disaggregated information. The country's statistics systems need to be improved in order to adequately represent the complex reality of regional poverty patterns, environmental issues, and informal businesses. The informal sector, which provides vital job and income opportunities, particularly for women and young people, is still significantly underrepresented, according to official data (Rogan & Skinner, 2019). Improved data collection and analysis may enable more targeted support mechanisms, such as better social protection programs and regulatory frameworks that permit the progressive formalization of informal economic activity. Environmental monitoring systems must prioritize accessibility and integration with national planning procedures. Critical data on ecological footprints, carbon emissions, and environmental health indicators should be made publically available, as should spatial mapping tools that track climatic vulnerabilities, resource consumption, and infrastructure shortages at the local level (Schreiner et al., 2018). This data democratization is necessary to promote evidence-based decision-making in government, academia, and civil society.

The measurement of poverty has to be adjusted to account for its complex character. The entire spectrum of poverty is not well represented by conventional income-based indicators. The Multidimensional Poverty Index (MPI), which considers housing, health, education, and environmental challenges, provides a more comprehensive assessment tool to guide policy actions (Schreiner et al., 2018). South Africa's sustainable development agenda advocates for ground-breaking policies that strike a balance between economic inclusion, environmental preservation, and social justice. This necessitates combining trade policy with socioeconomic goals and inclusive industrialization initiatives. using skill development and integrated planning to capitalize on green industrialization for job creation and ecological resilience (Bhorat et al., 2017). This integrated approach might help South Africa reach its objectives of equitable, inclusive, and sustainable development (Bhorat et al., 2017). In order to transform data insights into creative policies that protect South Africa's natural heritage and benefit all South Africans, the future demands both political will and technological know-how.

CONCLUSION

The relationship between economic participation and sustainable development in South Africa is shaped by the intricate interactions of trade dynamics, poverty, inequality, and environmental limits. - The country's economic development is influenced by its historical foundation, political decisions, and international economic integration. Growth in trade has increased GDP, but it has also exacerbated structural inequalities and made people more vulnerable to shifts in the global market. Despite significant legislative efforts, enduring poverty and deeply rooted inequality continue to impede inclusive transformation.

Environmental elements play an equal role in South Africa's development equation. The nation's natural resource wealth has fueled economic expansion at a significant ecological cost. The need to balance economic expansion with environmental protection has changed from being a goal to a need. Government agencies, civil society organizations, and commercial companies must work together to maintain this delicate balance. Furthermore, South Africa's chances of making lasting growth depend on finding solutions to these interrelated problems. Success will need stringent monitoring protocols, effective implementation plans, and creative policy frameworks grounded in empirical evidence. Strategic international partnerships will be necessary to support domestic development goals.

Limitations and Prospects for Further Study

Notwithstanding its thoroughness, this study's reliance on secondary data sources limits its timeliness, accuracy, and comprehensiveness. The validity of the conclusions and recommendations that take into consideration South Africa's changing circumstances may be impacted by inconsistent data.

The research's focus on trade, poverty, inequality, and environmental issues always ignores other vital factors including institutional efficacy, social cohesion dynamics, and governance capacity, despite the fact that these topics are significant to the discussion of sustainable development. The technique, which mostly draws on current literature, emphasizes the necessity of supplementary primary research that uses quantitative tools to produce localized, granular insights and qualitative methods to collect stakeholder viewpoints.

Future studies ought to focus on a few important areas:

Global Economic Interactions: Examining how South Africa's growth path is impacted by changing trade patterns, financial institutions, and technology upheavals.

Policy Impact Assessment: Methodical assessment of the efficacy of current policies in tackling environmental sustainability, poverty, and inequality, including identification of implementation gaps and creative substitutes

Social-Ecological Systems: Examination of how social networks, community resilience, and collective action mediate economic participation and environmental outcomes, with particular attention to intersecting inequalities.

Integrated Methodologies: Development of interdisciplinary research frameworks that synthesize economic, environmental, social, and political perspectives to generate holistic sustainable development solutions.

This study advances understanding of South Africa's sustainable development challenges by elucidating the complex interdependencies between economic systems, social equity, and environmental sustainability. However, sustained research efforts remain crucial to address knowledge gaps, refine analytical frameworks, and inform policy innovation. Through continued scholarly engagement and evidence-based policymaking, South Africa can progress toward a future characterized by inclusive growth, social justice, and ecological resilience

REFERENCES

Africa, S. S. (2023). [Pretoria: StatsSA.]. *Quarterly Labour Force Survey, Q1*, 2023.

Akoojee, S. (2016). Private TVET in Africa: Understanding the context and managing alternative forms creatively. *Journal of Technical Education and Training*, *8*(2).

Aliber, M., & Hall, R. (2012). Support for smallholder farmers in South Africa: Challenges of scale and strategy. *Development Southern Africa*, *29*(4), 548–562. DOI: 10.1080/0376835X.2012.715441

Baker, L., Newell, P., & Phillips, J. (2014). The political economy of energy transitions: The case of South Africa. *New Political Economy*, *19*(6), 791–818. DOI: 10.1080/13563467.2013.849674

Bhorat, H., Kanbur, R., & Stanwix, B. (2017). Minimum wages in Sub-Saharan Africa: A primer. *The World Bank Research Observer*, *32*(1), 21–74.

Bhorat, H., Lilenstein, A., & Stanwix, B. (2021). *The impact of the National Minimum Wage in South Africa: Early quantitative evidence*. Development Policy Research Unit, University of Cape Town.

Black, S., Spreen, C. A., & Vally, S. (2020). Education, Covid-19 and care: Social inequality and social relations of value in South Africa and the United States. *Southern African Review of Education with Education with Production*, *26*(1), 40–61.

Bond, P. (2018). Ecological-economic narratives for resisting extractive industries in Africa. In *Environmental impacts of transnational corporations in the global South* (pp. 73–110). Emerald Publishing Limited. DOI: 10.1108/S0161-723020180000033004

Calitz, J. R., & Wright, J. G. (2021). *Statistics of utility-scale power generation in South Africa in 2020.*

Chambers, R., & Conway, G. (1992). *Sustainable rural livelihoods: Practical concepts for the 21st century.*

Charman, A. J., Petersen, L. M., Piper, L. E., Liedeman, R., & Legg, T. (2017). Small area census approach to measure the township informal economy in South Africa. *Journal of Mixed Methods Research*, *11*(1), 36–58. DOI: 10.1177/1558689815572024

Chatterjee, A., Czajka, L., & Gethin, A. (2021). Can redistribution keep up with inequality? Evidence from South Africa, 1993–2019.

Cock, J. (2011). Labour's response to climate change. *Global Labour Journal*, *2*(3). Advance online publication. DOI: 10.15173/glj.v2i3.1109

Dasgupta, S., Laplante, B., Wang, H., & Wheeler, D. (2002). Confronting the environmental Kuznets curve. *The Journal of Economic Perspectives, 16*(1), 147–168. DOI: 10.1257/0895330027157

Demirguc-Kunt, A., Klapper, L., Singer, D., Ansar, S., & Hess, J. (2018). *The Global Findex Database 2017: Measuring financial inclusion and the fintech revolution.* World Bank Publications. DOI: 10.1596/978-1-4648-1259-0

Dinc, A., & Otkur, M. (2021). Emissions prediction of an aero-piston gasoline engine during surveillance flight of an unmanned aerial vehicle. *Aircraft Engineering and Aerospace Technology, 93*(3), 462–472. DOI: 10.1108/AEAT-09-2020-0196

Duraiappah, A. K. (1998). Poverty and environmental degradation: A review and analysis of the nexus. *World Development, 26*(12), 2169–2179. DOI: 10.1016/S0305-750X(98)00100-4

Edwards, L., & Lawrence, R. (2012). *South African trade policy and the future global trading environment.*

Elkington, J. (2018). 25 years ago I coined the phrase "triple bottom line." Here's why it's time to rethink it. *Harvard Business Review, 25*(2–5), 2–5.

Food and Agriculture Organization of the United Nations. (2018). *FAOSTAT.* Rome. https://www.fao.org/faostat

Greenberg, S. (2013). The disjunctures of land and agricultural reform in South Africa: Implications for the agri-food system.

Grossman, G. M., & Krueger, A. B. (1995). Economic growth and the environment. *The Quarterly Journal of Economics, 110*(2), 353–377. DOI: 10.2307/2118443

Gumede, V. (2017). Presidencies and policy in post-apartheid South Africa. *Politeia, 36*(1), 1–17.

Hall, C. M. (2010). Changing paradigms and global change: From sustainable to steady-state tourism. *Tourism Recreation Research, 35*(2), 131–143. DOI: 10.1080/02508281.2010.11081629

Hall, R. (2015). Rural resource grabs or necessary inward investment? The politics of land and water in Africa.

Hartzenberg, T. (2011). *Regional integration in Africa* (ERSD-2011-14). WTO Staff Working Paper.

Herrington, M., Kew, P., & Mwanga, A. (2017). *South Africa report.*

Humby, T. L. (2016). Redressing mining legacies: The case of the South African mining industry. *Journal of Business Ethics*, *135*(4), 653–664. DOI: 10.1007/s10551-014-2380-8

Matyana, M., & Thusi, X. (2023). Unemployment and poverty in South Africa: Assessing the National Development Plan 2030 predictions. *International Journal of Development and Sustainability*, *12*(6), 212–226.

Nattrass, N., & Seekings, J. (2018). Employment and labour productivity in high unemployment countries. *Development Policy Review*, *36*(S2), O769–O785. DOI: 10.1111/dpr.12313

Phillips, A. (2004). Defending equality of outcome. *Journal of Political Philosophy*, *12*(1), 1–19. DOI: 10.1111/j.1467-9760.2004.00188.x

Posel, D., Casale, D., & Grapsa, E. (2020). Household variation and inequality: The implications of equivalence scales in South Africa. *African Review of Economics and Finance*, *12*(1), 102–122.

Raworth, K. (2017). *Doughnut economics: Seven ways to think like a 21st century economist.* Chelsea Green Publishing.

Rittel, H. W., & Webber, M. M. (1973). Dilemmas in a general theory of planning. *Policy Sciences*, *4*(2), 155–169. DOI: 10.1007/BF01405730

Rodrik, D. (2008). Understanding South Africa's economic puzzles. *Economics of Transition*, *16*(4), 769–797. DOI: 10.1111/j.1468-0351.2008.00343.x

Rodrik, D. (2018). An African growth miracle? *Journal of African Economies*, *27*(1), 10–27.

Rogan, M., & Skinner, C. (2019, December 12). South Africa's informal sector creates jobs, but shouldn't be romanticised. *The Conversation*. https://theconversation.com/south-africas-informal-sector-creates-jobs-but-shouldnt-be-romanticised-128931

Schreiner, G. O., Snyman-van der Walt, L., De Jager, M., Dludla, A., Lochner, P. A., Wright, J., Scholes, R. J., Atkinson, D., & Hardcastle, P. (2018). Advancing a participatory and science-based approach to policy formulation for shale gas development in South Africa. In *Citizen and other stakeholder participation in unconventional fossil fuel land use decision-making, policy formation, regulatory practice or other governance mechanisms*.

Seekings, J., & Nattrass, N. (2008). *Class, race, and inequality in South Africa.* Yale University Press.

Sen, A. (1999). *On ethics and economics*. Oxford University Press.

Shifa, M., Mabhena, R., Ranchhod, V., & Leibbrandt, M. V. (2023). *An assessment of inequality estimates for the case of South Africa* (WIDER Working Paper No. 2023/90).

Skinner, C. (2018). *Digital human: The fourth revolution of humanity includes everyone*. John Wiley & Sons.

Southall, R. (2007). Ten propositions about black economic empowerment in South Africa. *Review of African Political Economy*, *34*(111), 67–84. DOI: 10.1080/03056240701340365

Sovacool, B. K., Turnheim, B., Hook, A., Brock, A., & Martiskainen, M. (2021). Dispossessed by decarbonisation: Reducing vulnerability, injustice, and inequality in the lived experience of low-carbon pathways. *World Development*, *137*, 105116. DOI: 10.1016/j.worlddev.2020.105116

Spaull, N. (2013). South Africa's education crisis: The quality of education in South Africa 1994–2011. *Centre for Development and Enterprise*, *21*(1), 1–65.

Street, K. (2023). *Sustainable Development Goals: Country report 2023*.

TO, I. R. (2022). *Submission to the Department of Forestry, Fisheries and the Environment (DFFE)*.

Tregenna, F. (2016). Sectoral dimensions of employment intensity. In *Towards employment-intensive growth in South Africa* (pp. 108–125).

Turok, I., & Borel-Saladin, J. (2016). Backyard shacks, informality and the urban housing crisis in South Africa: Stopgap or prototype solution? *Housing Studies*, *31*(4), 384–409. DOI: 10.1080/02673037.2015.1091921

Turok, I., & Visagie, J. (2018). *Inclusive urban development in South Africa: What does it mean and how can it be measured?* The Institute of Development Studies and Partner Organisations.

UNEP. (2024). *Climate risks in the power generation sector*.

Van der Berg, S. (2008). How effective are poor schools? Poverty and educational outcomes in South Africa. *Studies in Educational Evaluation*, *34*(3), 145–154. DOI: 10.1016/j.stueduc.2008.07.005

Walker, L. (2005). Men behaving differently: South African men since 1994. *Culture, Health & Sexuality*, *7*(3), 225–238. DOI: 10.1080/13691050410001713215 PMID: 16864199

World Bank Group. (2022). *Global economic prospects, January 2022*. World Bank Publications.

Ziervogel, G. (2019). *Unpacking the Cape Town drought: Lessons learned*. African Centre for Cities.

Ziervogel, G., New, M., Archer van Garderen, E., Midgley, G., Taylor, A., Hamann, R., Stuart-Hill, S., Myers, J., & Warburton, M. (2014). Climate change impacts and adaptation in South Africa. *Wiley Interdisciplinary Reviews: Climate Change*, *5*(5), 605–620. DOI: 10.1002/wcc.295

Compilation of References

Abbas, A. E. (2019). API integration of national complaint handling system in Indonesia: A state of the art review. *2019 International Conference on ICT for Smart Society (ICISS)*, pp. 1–5. DOI: 10.1109/ICISS48059.2019.8969837

Abbas, Q., Alyas, T., Alghamdi, T., Alkhodre, A. B., Albouq, S., Niazi, M., & Tabassum, N. (2024). Redefining governance: A critical analysis of sustainability transformation in e-governance. *Frontiers in Big Data*, *7*, 1349116. DOI: 10.3389/fdata.2024.1349116 PMID: 38638340

Abhishek, A. (2022). The State Deputising Citizens to Discipline Digital News Media: The Case of the IT Rules 2021 in India. *Digital Journalism (Abingdon, England)*, *11*(10), 1769–1787. DOI: 10.1080/21670811.2022.2134163

Africa, S. S. (2023). [Pretoria: StatsSA.]. *Quarterly Labour Force Survey*, *Q1*, 2023.

Afrizal, D., & Wallang, M. (2021). Attitude on intention to use e-government in Indonesia. *Indonesian Journal of Electrical Engineering and Computer Science*, *22*(1), 435. DOI: 10.11591/ijeecs.v22.i1.pp435-441

Agyekum, K., Kissi, E., Danku, J. C., Ampratwum, G., & Amegatsey, G. S. (2020). Factors driving the career progression of construction project managers. *Journal of Engineering, Design and Technology*, *18*(6), 1773–1791. DOI: 10.1108/JEDT-09-2019-0242

Ahmed, M. M., & Musa Ahmed, A. (2023). Citizens' Data Protection in E-government System. *International Journal of Innovative Computing*, *13*(2), 1–9. DOI: 10.11113/ijic.v13n2.389

Aiyar, Y., & Samji, S. (2009). *Citizen participation in public services: The experience of NREGA in India*. World Bank.

Akbar, M., & Wijaya, G. (2024). Digital literacy of rural areas in Indonesia: Challenges and opportunities. *Proceedings of the 4th International Conference on Rural Socio-Economic Transformation, RUSET 2023,* 1 November 2023, Bogor, Indonesia. DOI: 10.4108/eai.1-11-2023.2344347

Akoojee, S. (2016). Private TVET in Africa: Understanding the context and managing alternative forms creatively. *Journal of Technical Education and Training*, *8*(2).

Alam, M. J. (2018). The Rohingya minority of Myanmar: Surveying their status in international law. *International Journal on Minority and Group Rights*, *25*(2), 157–182. DOI: 10.1163/15718115-02503002

Alam, M. S., Ahmed, S., Dhali, M., & Alam, S. S. (2025). Citizens' engagement with cybersecurity measures in Bangladesh: A cross-sectional study. *International Journal of Information Security*, *24*(1), 4. DOI: 10.1007/s10207-024-00918-9

Al-Ansi, A. M., Garad, A., Jaboob, M., & Al-Ansi, A. (2024). Elevating e-government: Unleashing the power of AI and IoT for enhanced public services. *Heliyon*, *10*(23), e40591. DOI: 10.1016/j.heliyon.2024.e40591 PMID: 39654738

Aliber, M., & Hall, R. (2012). Support for smallholder farmers in South Africa: Challenges of scale and strategy. *Development Southern Africa*, *29*(4), 548–562. DOI: 10.1080/0376835X.2012.715441

Ali, S. M. A., Ghose, A., & Iqbal, S. M. U. (2024). Media bias and "othering": A critical discourse on news framing of the Rohingya crisis settlement in Bangladesh and India. In Kir Elitaş, S. (Ed.), (pp. 264–277). Advances in Media, Entertainment, and the Arts. IGI Global., DOI: 10.4018/979-8-3693-3459-1.ch016

Aliushyna, N., Boiko, O., Hzhybovska, T., & Rak, Y. (2022). Professionalisation of public servants in the context of implementing public administration reforms. *Public Policy and Administration*, *21*(5).

Amundsen, I. (Ed.). (2019). *Political corruption in Africa: Extraction and power preservation*. Edward Elgar Publishing. DOI: 10.4337/9781788972529

Anindito, D. B., Sagala, S. A. H., & Tarigan, A. K. M. (2022). E- *musrenbang*: A digital framework for local participatory planning at the community level. *International Development Planning Review*, *44*(2), 191–216. DOI: 10.3828/idpr.2021.5

Aranyossy, M. (2022). User adoption and value of e-government services (Citizen-centric empirical study from Hungary). *Acta Oeconomica*, *72*(4), 477–497. DOI: 10.1556/032.2022.00032

Aristotle. (350). Politics (C. D. C. Reeve, Trans.). Hackett Publishing.

Aritonang, D. M. (2017). The Impact of E-Government System on Public Service Quality in Indonesia. *European Scientific Journal, 13*(35), 99. DOI: 10.19044/esj.2017.v13n35p99

Avazov, S., & Lee, PhD., S. (2020). E-Government Adoption in Uzbekistan: Empirical validation of the Unified Model of Electronic Government Acceptance (UMEGA). *The 21st Annual International Conference on Digital Government Research*, 338–339. DOI: 10.1145/3396956.3397008

Ayodele, O., Plantinga, P., Sanchez-Bentacourt, D., Dlamini, S., & Dlamini, N. (2025). How do researchers and public officials co-navigate e-participation implementation? An action-research experience with South African municipalities. *Systems, 13*(2), 125. DOI: 10.3390/systems13020125

Babo, A. (2018). Ivoirité and citizenship in Ivory Coast: The controversial policy of Ivorian authenticité. In *The Politics of Social Inclusion in Africa* (pp. 245–267). Duke University Press.

Badewa, A. A. (2022). Statelessness, development, and protection of 'disadvantaged groups': Bridging the post-2030 sustainable development gaps. *African Human Mobility Review, 8*(3), 56–74. DOI: 10.14426/ahmr.v8i3.1151

Baker, L., Newell, P., & Phillips, J. (2014). The political economy of energy transitions: The case of South Africa. *New Political Economy, 19*(6), 791–818. DOI: 10.1080/13563467.2013.849674

Balaskas, S., Panagiotarou, A., & Rigou, M. (2022). The influence of trustworthiness and technology acceptance factors on the usage of e-government services during COVID-19: A case Study of post COVID-19 Greece. *Administrative Sciences, 12*(4), 129. DOI: 10.3390/admsci12040129

Balaton-Chrimes, S. (2024). Jus tribalis: Statelessness, ethnicity and registration in Kenya. *Statelessness & Citizenship Review, 6*(2), 127–151. DOI: 10.35715/SCR6001.114

Balkin, J. M. (2004). Digital speech and democratic culture: A theory of freedom of expression for the information society. *New York University Law Review, 79*(1), 1–55.

Balkin, J. M. (2018). Free speech in the algorithmic society: Big data, private governance, and new school speech regulation. *University of California, Davis, Law Review, 51*(3), 1149–1210. https://lawreview.law.ucdavis.edu/issues/51/3/Essays/51-3_Balkin.pdf

Balkin, J. M. (2018). Free speech is a triangle. *Columbia Law Review, 118*(7), 2011–2056.

Baum, F., Townsend, B., Fisher, M., Browne-Yung, K., Freeman, T., Ziersch, A., & Friel, S. (2022). Creating political will for action on health equity: Practical lessons for public health policy actors. *International Journal of Health Policy and Management, 11*(7), 947. PMID: 33327689

Baxi, U. (1990). The Indian Supreme Court and media freedom: From the untrammelled press to the responsible press. *International Journal of Constitutional Law, 8*(3), 574–591. DOI: 10.1093/icon/8.3.574

Beck, L. J. (2017). The roots of popular protest in Mali and Senegal. *Journal of Democracy, 28*(3), 143–158.

Beetham, D. (1991). *The Legitimation of Power*. Palgrave Macmillan. DOI: 10.1007/978-1-349-21599-7

Bellizzi, S., & Nivoli, A. (2023). Gender discrimination in nationality laws: A systemic type of violence against women. *International Journal of Gynaecology and Obstetrics : The Official Organ of the International Federation of Gynaecology and Obstetrics, 163*(1), 3–6. DOI: 10.1002/ijgo.14986 PMID: 37408521

Beninger, C., & Manjoo, R. (2022). The impact of gender discrimination on statelessness: Causes, consequences and legal responses. *African Human Mobility Review, 8*(3). Advance online publication. DOI: 10.14426/ahmr.v8i3.1125

Bergeron, W. P. (2015). Considering culture in evacuation planning and consequence management. *Journal of Emergency Management (Weston, Mass.), 13*(2), 87–92. DOI: 10.5055/jem.2015.0222 PMID: 25902292

Berg, S., & Hofmann, J. (2021). Digital democracy. *Internet Policy Review, 10*(4). Advance online publication. DOI: 10.14763/2021.4.1612

Bernot, A., Tjondronegoro, D., Rifai, B., Hasan, R., Liew, A. W.-C., Verhelst, T., & Tiwari, M. (2024). Institutional dimensions in open government data: A deep dive into Indonesia's *Satu Data* initiative and its implications for developing countries. *Public Performance & Management Review, 47*(6), 1399–1429. DOI: 10.1080/15309576.2024.2377609

Bertocchi, G., & Strozzi, C. (2010). The evolution of citizenship: Economic and institutional determinants. *The Journal of Law & Economics, 53*(1), 95–136. DOI: 10.1086/600080

Bevir, M. (2006). Democratic governance: Systems and radical perspectives. *Public Administration Review, 66*(3), 426–436. DOI: 10.1111/j.1540-6210.2006.00599.x

Bhorat, H., Lilenstein, A., & Stanwix, B. (2021). *The impact of the National Minimum Wage in South Africa: Early quantitative evidence*. Development Policy Research Unit, University of Cape Town.

Bhorat, H., Kanbur, R., & Stanwix, B. (2017). Minimum wages in Sub-Saharan Africa: A primer. *The World Bank Research Observer*, *32*(1), 21–74.

Birdsall, W. F. (2009). The role of the client in informing science: To be informed and to inform. Informing Science. *The International Journal of an Emerging Transdiscipline*, *12*, 147–157. DOI: 10.28945/432

Birkland, T. A. (2011). *An introduction to the policy process: Theories, concepts, and models of public policy making* (3rd ed.). PHI Learning.

Birkvad, S. R. (2023). "Citizenship cheaters" before the law: Reading fraud-based citizenship-stripping cases. *International Political Sociology*, *17*(1), 1–18. DOI: 10.1093/ips/olad006

Black, S., Spreen, C. A., & Vally, S. (2020). Education, Covid-19 and care: Social inequality and social relations of value in South Africa and the United States. *Southern African Review of Education with Education with Production*, *26*(1), 40–61.

Blackstone, W. (1765). []. Clarendon Press.]. *Commentaries on the Laws of England*, *4*, 152.

Blake, J. (2014). (Forthcoming). Haiti, the Dominican Republic, and race-based statelessness. *Georgetown Journal of International Law and Modern Critical Race Perspectives*, *46*, 499–526.

Bond, P. (2018). Ecological-economic narratives for resisting extractive industries in Africa. In *Environmental impacts of transnational corporations in the global South* (pp. 73–110). Emerald Publishing Limited. DOI: 10.1108/S0161-723020180000033004

Borazon, E. Q., & Nguyen, H. T. T. (2022). E-government Use in Vietnam: Do External Variables Drive a Positive Attitude Towards Technology? DOI: 10.21203/rs.3.rs-2191455/v1

Broadbent, J., & Laughlin, R. (2009). Performance management systems: A conceptual model. *Management Accounting Research*, *20*(4), 283–295. DOI: 10.1016/j.mar.2009.07.004

Broadhurst, K. (2024). Contextualising co-production and complex needs: Understanding the engagement of service users with severe and multiple disadvantages. *Public Policy and Administration*, *39*(2), 259–277. DOI: 10.1177/09520767221122277

Brogi, E., Borges, D., Carlini, R., Nenadić, I., Bleyer-Simon, K., Kermer, J. E., Reviglio, U., Trevisan, M., & Verza, S. (2023, July). *The European Media Freedom Act: Media freedom, freedom of expression and pluralism* (Study No. PE 747.930). Policy Department for Citizens' Rights and Constitutional Affairs, Directorate-General for Internal Policies, European Parliament. https://www.europarl.europa.eu/RegData/etudes/STUD/2023/747930/IPOL_STU(2023)747930_EN.pdf

Brown, M. M. (2003). Democratic governance: Toward a framework for sustainable peace. *Global Governance*, *9*(2), 141–146. DOI: 10.1163/19426720-00902003

Buele, I., Vidueira, P., Yagüe, J. L., & Cuesta, F. (2020). The participatory budgeting and its contribution to local management and governance: Review of experience of rural communities from the Ecuadorian Amazon rainforest. *Sustainability (Basel)*, *12*(11), 4659. DOI: 10.3390/su12114659

Bulla, D. (2022). Fourth estate. In *The SAGE encyclopedia of journalism* (Vol. 4, pp. 675–679). SAGE Publications, Inc., DOI: 10.4135/9781544391199.n164

Calitz, J. R., & Wright, J. G. (2021). *Statistics of utility-scale power generation in South Africa in 2020.*

Cao, R., & Iansiti, M. (2023). *Data governance, interoperability and standardization: Organizational adaptation to privacy regulation*. Data Governance.

Castellano-Álvarez, F. J., Robina-Ramírez, R., & Silva, F. (2024). Rural areas facing the challenge of economic diversification: Threats and opportunities. *Agriculture*, *14*(4), 623. DOI: 10.3390/agriculture14040623

Chakraborty, P. (2021). *Public policy in India: Participation and accountability*. Oxford University Press.

Chambers, R., & Conway, G. (1992). *Sustainable rural livelihoods: Practical concepts for the 21st century.*

Charman, A. J., Petersen, L. M., Piper, L. E., Liedeman, R., & Legg, T. (2017). Small area census approach to measure the township informal economy in South Africa. *Journal of Mixed Methods Research*, *11*(1), 36–58. DOI: 10.1177/1558689815572024

Chatterjee, A., Czajka, L., & Gethin, A. (2021). Can redistribution keep up with inequality? Evidence from South Africa, 1993–2019.

Chauke, T. A. (2020). Youth apathy in an electoral democracy: A critical discourse on civil participation in South Africa. *African Journal of Gender. Social Development*, *9*(3), 35.

Chemerinsky, E. (2019). *Constitutional law: Principles and policies* (6th ed.). Aspen Publishers.

Cho, S. H., Oh, S. Y., Rou, H. G., & Gim, G. Y. (2019). A Study on The Factors Affecting The Continuous Use of E-Government Services—Focused on Privacy and Security Concerns-. *2019 20th IEEE/ACIS International Conference on Software Engineering, Artificial Intelligence, Networking and Parallel/Distributed Computing (SNPD)*, 351–361. DOI: 10.1109/SNPD.2019.8935693

Christensen, T., Yamamoto, K., & Aoyagi, S. (2020). Trust in local government: Service satisfaction, culture, and demography. *Administration & Society*, *52*(8), 1268–1296. DOI: 10.1177/0095399719897392

Cioc, M. M., Popa, . C., Olariu, A. A., Popa, C. F., & Nica, C.-B. (2023). Behavioral Intentions to Use Energy Efficiency Smart Solutions under the Impact of Social Influence: An Extended TAM Approach. *Applied Sciences (Basel, Switzerland)*, *13*(18), 10241. DOI: 10.3390/app131810241

Cock, J. (2011). Labour's response to climate change. *Global Labour Journal*, *2*(3). Advance online publication. DOI: 10.15173/glj.v2i3.1109

Collin, K., Van der Heijden, B., & Lewis, P. (2012). Continuing professional development. *International Journal of Training and Development*, *16*(3), 155–163. DOI: 10.1111/j.1468-2419.2012.00410.x

Dahl, R. A. (1989). *Democracy and its critics*. Yale University Press.

Dahl, R. A. (2020). *On democracy*. Yale University Press.

Daoanis, L. E. (2012). Performance Appraisal System: It's Implication to Employee Performance. *International journal of economics and management sciences*, *2*(3), 55-62.

Darmawan, A. B., & Nugroho, R. A. (2020). Factors that Affect User Satisfaction of Dukcapil Application (Dukcapil Dalam Genggaman) in Surakarta Regency. *JAKPP (Jurnal Analisis Kebijakan & Pelayanan Publik)*, 154–175. DOI: 10.31947/jakpp.vi.11588

Dasgupta, S., Laplante, B., Wang, H., & Wheeler, D. (2002). Confronting the environmental Kuznets curve. *The Journal of Economic Perspectives*, *16*(1), 147–168. DOI: 10.1257/0895330027157

Daßler, L., Hein, A., & Krcmar, H. (2024). Innovating public services: Drivers and challenges of Innovation Labs in the Co-Production of E-Government Services. *Proceedings of the 25th Annual International Conference on Digital Government Research*, 711–720. DOI: 10.1145/3657054.3657138

De Roover, J., Claerhout, S., & Rao, B. (2011). Liberal political theory and the cultural migration of ideas: The case of secularism in India. *Political Theory, 39*(5), 571–599. DOI: 10.1177/0090591711413545

De Souza, T. R. (2008). Portuguese India, the Politics of Print and a Questionable Modernity [Review of *Between Empires: Print and Politics in Goa*, by R. Pinto]. *Economic and Political Weekly*, *43*(33), 31–33.

Deen-Swarray, M., Adeya, C. N., & Ndung'u, N. S. (2020). *Digital pathways for development: The benefits of expanding broadband access in sub-Saharan Africa.* Brookings Institution.

Demirguc-Kunt, A., Klapper, L., Singer, D., Ansar, S., & Hess, J. (2018). *The Global Findex Database 2017: Measuring financial inclusion and the fintech revolution.* World Bank Publications. DOI: 10.1596/978-1-4648-1259-0

Devadasan, V. (2024). Conceptualising India's safe harbour in the era of platform governance. *Indian Journal of Law and Technology*, *19*(1), 7–52. DOI: 10.55496/NBQQ3956

Dhavan, R. (1984). On the law of the press in India. *Journal of the Indian Law Institute*, *26*(3), 288–332. https://www.jstor.org/stable/43953869

Dicey, A. V. (2010). *Introduction to the study of the law of the constitution* (8th ed.). Oxford University Press.

Dinc, A., & Otkur, M. (2021). Emissions prediction of an aero-piston gasoline engine during surveillance flight of an unmanned aerial vehicle. *Aircraft Engineering and Aerospace Technology*, *93*(3), 462–472. DOI: 10.1108/AEAT-09-2020-0196

Drèze, J., & Khera, R. (2017). Recent social security initiatives in India. *World Development*, *98*, 555–572. DOI: 10.1016/j.worlddev.2017.05.010

Drissa, K. (2021). The concept of "Ivoirité": An identity, nationalism, and citizenship in a postcolonial state. *Revue Akofena*, *2*(21), 217–228.

Duraiappah, A. K. (1998). Poverty and environmental degradation: A review and analysis of the nexus. *World Development*, *26*(12), 2169–2179. DOI: 10.1016/S0305-750X(98)00100-4

Edwards, L., & Lawrence, R. (2012). *South African trade policy and the future global trading environment.*

Eja, K. M., & Ramegowda, M. (2020). Government project failure in developing countries: A review with particular reference to Nigeria. *Global Journal of Social Sciences*, *19*, 35–47. DOI: 10.4314/gjss.v19i1.4

Ejiogu, A., Ejiogu, C., & Ambituuni, A. (2019). The dark side of transparency: Does the Nigeria extractive industries transparency initiative help or hinder accountability and corruption control? *The British Accounting Review*, *51*(5), 100811. DOI: 10.1016/j.bar.2018.10.004

Elkington, J. (2018). 25 years ago I coined the phrase "triple bottom line." Here's why it's time to rethink it. *Harvard Business Review*, *25*(2–5), 2–5.

Enwereji, P. C. (2022). Enhancing financial accountability in south African local municipalities: a consequence management viewpoint. Financial Studies, 26(4).

European Commission. (2022). Digital Markets Act and Digital Services Act. https://digital-strategy.ec.europa.eu/en/policies/digital-markets-act-and-digital-services-act

European Commission. (2025). Media freedom and pluralism. https://digital-strategy.ec.europa.eu/en/policies/media-freedom

European Commission. (2025). Revision of the Audiovisual Media Services Directive (AVMSD). https://digital-strategy.ec.europa.eu/en/policies/revision-avmsd

Faruque, M., Amin, A., Sharmin, M., & Rahman, M. M. (2025). Fostering sustainable digital governance: Citizen acceptance of web-portal-based integrated platforms in Bangladesh through A TAM-TPB approach. *Journal of Risk Analysis and Crisis Response*, *15*(1), 19. DOI: 10.54560/jracr.v15i1.551

Fenwick, H., & Phillipson, G. (2011). Media freedom and freedom of expression: An analysis of the European Court of Human Rights jurisprudence. *Human Rights Law Review*, *11*(1), 135–163.

Ficek, R. (2023). *Legitimacy in the Context of the Global Institutions of Power and the Contemporary Determinants of International Politics*. Teka Komisji Politologii i Stosunków Międzynarodowych., DOI: 10.17951/teka.2022.17.1.23-36

Fikri, R., Purnomo, E. P., Pribadi, U., & Binti Mohammad, N. (2023). Technology Readiness of e-Government in the Use of Poverty Data for Social Assistance in Indonesia. In Stephanidis, C., Antona, M., Ntoa, S., & Salvendy, G. (Eds.), *HCI International 2023 Posters* (Vol. 1835, pp. 195–202). Springer Nature Switzerland., DOI: 10.1007/978-3-031-36001-5_25

Fisher, B. L. (2016). Gender discrimination and statelessness in the Gulf Cooperation Council states. *Michigan Journal of Gender & Law*, *23*(2), 269–341. DOI: 10.36641/mjgl.23.2.gender

Food and Agriculture Organization of the United Nations. (2018). *FAOSTAT*. Rome. https://www.fao.org/faostat

Foucault, M. (1978). The History of Sexuality: Vol. 1. *An Introduction* (Hurley, R., Trans.). Pantheon Books.

Francke, W. (1995). The Evolving Watchdog: The Media's Role in Government Ethics. *The Annals of the American Academy of Political and Social Science*, *537*(1), 109–121. DOI: 10.1177/0002716295537000010

Fuchs, C., & Horak, E. (2008). Africa and the digital divide. *Telematics and Informatics*, *25*(2), 99–116. DOI: 10.1016/j.tele.2006.06.004

Fung, A. (2006). Varieties of participation in complex governance. *Public Administration Review*, *66*(S1), 66–75. DOI: 10.1111/j.1540-6210.2006.00667.x

Garg, N., & Ghuman, D. P. K. (2024). Regulatory frameworks for OTT platforms: Global and Indian context. *Library Progress International*, *44*(3), 7880–7895.

Gasumova, S. E., & Starshinova, A. V. Perm State University, Bezrukov, A. V., & Ural Federal University named after the first President of Russia B.N. Yeltsin. (2022). Citizens' expectations from digitalization in the sphere of social welfare and social services. *Вестник Пермского Университета. Философия. Психология. Социология, 2*, 315–328. DOI: 10.17072/2078-7898/2022-2-315-328

George, D., Reutimann, K., & Tamò-Larrieux, A. (2019). GDPR bypass by design? Transient processing of data under the GDPR. *International Data Privacy Law*, *9*(4), 285–298. DOI: 10.1093/idpl/ipz017

Ghose, A., Pallav, P., & Ali, S. M. A. (2025). AI and political polarisation: Analysing the impact of algorithmic bias on governance in diverse political systems. In Günar, A. (Ed.), (pp. 135–160). Advances in Finance, Accounting, and Economics. IGI Global., DOI: 10.4018/979-8-3693-7036-0.ch007

Gil de Zúñiga, H., Weeks, B. E., & Ardèvol-Abreu, A. (2019). Digital media and politics: Effects of the great information equality and participation. *Journal of Broadcasting & Electronic Media*, *63*(2), 286–301. DOI: 10.1080/08838151.2019.1662019

Global Freedom of Expression. (2024). Kunal Kamra v. Union of India. Columbia University. https://globalfreedomofexpression.columbia.edu/cases/kunal-kamra-v-union-of-india/

Greenberg, S. (2013). The disjunctures of land and agricultural reform in South Africa: Implications for the agri-food system.

Grindle, M. S. (2004). Good enough governance: Poverty reduction and reform in developing countries. *Governance: An International Journal of Policy, Administration and Institutions*, *17*(4), 525–548. DOI: 10.1111/j.0952-1895.2004.00256.x

Grossman, G. M., & Krueger, A. B. (1995). Economic growth and the environment. *The Quarterly Journal of Economics*, *110*(2), 353–377. DOI: 10.2307/2118443

Guha, S. (2023). Information technology (intermediary guidelines and digital media ethics code) rules, 2021: An analytical approach. *NUJS Law Review*, *16*(1), 1–45.

Gumede, V. (2017). Presidencies and policy in post-apartheid South Africa. *Politeia*, *36*(1), 1–17.

Guo, Y. (2023). How Does Culture Influence Chinese People's Views and Actions on e-Government Websites? A Study on Citizens' Continuous Use of e-Government Websites Based on Cultural Model. *Proceedings of the 24th Annual International Conference on Digital Government Research*, 135–143. DOI: 10.1145/3598469.3598484

Guo, Y., Zhang, T., & Deng, Y. (2024). Past, present, and future of digital government: Insights from Chinese practices. *Public Administration Issues*, *0*(5), 6–24. DOI: 10.17323/1999-5431-2024-0-5-6-24

Gupta, I., & Srinivasan, L. (2023). Evolving scope of intermediary liability in India. *International Review of Law Computers & Technology*, *37*(3), 294–324. DOI: 10.1080/13600869.2022.2164838

Gupta, N. (2007). The Emergency and the press in India: A dark chapter. *Journal of Southeast Asian Studies*, *30*(1), 1–15.

Gyimah-Boadi, E. (2015). Africa's waning democratic commitment. *Journal of Democracy*, *26*(1), 101–113. DOI: 10.1353/jod.2015.0000

Habermas, J. (1973). *Legitimation Crisis* (McCarthy, T., Trans.). Beacon Press.

Habermas, J. (1996). *Between facts and norms: Contributions to a discourse theory of law and democracy*. MIT Press. DOI: 10.7551/mitpress/1564.001.0001

Hall, R. (2015). Rural resource grabs or necessary inward investment? The politics of land and water in Africa.

Hall, C. M. (2010). Changing paradigms and global change: From sustainable to steady-state tourism. *Tourism Recreation Research*, *35*(2), 131–143. DOI: 10.1080/02508281.2010.11081629

Hannam, M. A. (2014). “Soy dominicano”: The status of Haitian descendants born in the Dominican Republic and measures to protect their right to a nationality. *Vanderbilt Journal of Transnational Law*, *47*(4), 1123–1175.

Haque, M. M. (2017). Rohingya ethnic Muslim minority and the 1982 Citizenship Law in Burma. *Journal of Muslim Minority Affairs*, *37*(4), 454–469. DOI: 10.1080/13602004.2017.1399600

Hariguna, T., Rahardja, U., & Aini, Q. (2023). The antecedent e-government quality for public behaviour intention, and extended expectation-confirmation theory. *Computer Science and Information Technologies*, *4*(1), 33–42. DOI: 10.11591/csit.v4i1.pp33-42

Hartzenberg, T. (2011). *Regional integration in Africa* (ERSD-2011-14). WTO Staff Working Paper.

Hasudungan, R. G., Galistya, T. M., Solana, A., Aini, N., Ngurah Diksa, I. G. B., & Sri Jayanti, D. A. (2024). Rekomendasi skema sistem satu data daerah. *Seminar Nasional Official Statistics*, *2024*(1), 735–744. DOI: 10.34123/semnasoffstat.v2024i1.2203

Heller, P. (2009). Making citizens from below: India’s emerging local government. In *Democratic deficits: The governance of India’s public institutions* (pp. 57–82). Cambridge University Press.

Herberholz, C. (2022). ‘We are inferior, we have no rights’: Statelessness and mental health among ethnic minorities in Northern Thailand. *SSM - Population Health*, *19*, 101138. DOI: 10.1016/j.ssmph.2022.101138 PMID: 35711727

Herrington, M., Kew, P., & Mwanga, A. (2017). *South Africa report*.

Hien, B. N., Tuyen, N. T. K., Lan, N. T., Ngan, N. T. K., & Thanh, N. N. (2024). The impact of digital government initiatives on public value creation: Evidence from Ho Chi Minh City, Vietnam. *Revista de Gestão Social e Ambiental*, *18*(2), e04892. DOI: 10.24857/rgsa.v18n2-092

Hobbes, T. (1651). *Leviathan* (Malcolm, N., Ed.). Oxford University Press.

Hudson, D. L. (1996). Prior Restraint and the Press: The Continuing Battle Over Freedom of Expression. *Communications and the Law*, *1*(3), 54–67.

Hügel, S., & Davies, A. R. (2020). Public participation, engagement, and climate change adaptation: A review of the research literature. *Wiley Interdisciplinary Reviews: Climate Change*, *11*(4), e645. DOI: 10.1002/wcc.645 PMID: 35859618

Hujran, O., Al-Debei, M. M., Al-Adwan, A. S., Alarabiat, A., & Altarawneh, N. (2023). Examining the antecedents and outcomes of smart government usage: An integrated model. *Government Information Quarterly*, *40*(1), 101783. DOI: 10.1016/j.giq.2022.101783

Humby, T. L. (2016). Redressing mining legacies: The case of the South African mining industry. *Journal of Business Ethics*, *135*(4), 653–664. DOI: 10.1007/s10551-014-2380-8

Hurd, I. (2018). Legitimacy and contestation in global governance: Revisiting the folk theory of international institutions. *The Review of International Organizations*, *14*(4), 717–729. DOI: 10.1007/s11558-018-9338-z

Iguodala-Cole, H. I., Anto, J. B., & Jawondo, A. I. (2020). Effects of induction as an adjustment mechanism of recruits in industrial organizations in Nigeria. *International Journal of Development and Management Review*, *15*(1), 83–95.

Ikelegbe, A., & Umukoro, N. (2014). Exclusion and the challenges of democratic governance in Nigeria. *Journal of Developing Societies*, *30*(1), 1–26.

Ingrams, A. (2019). Big data and Dahl's challenge of democratic governance. *The Review of Policy Research*, *36*(3), 357–377. DOI: 10.1111/ropr.12331

Jafari, S. M., Nikbakhsh, S., Komijani, P., & Karimi, F. (2022). Identifying the Antecedents of Public Trust in the Citizen-Centric E-Governance. *The Eurasia Proceedings of Science Technology Engineering and Mathematics*, *17*, 129–135. DOI: 10.55549/epstem.1176069

Jain, A. (2024). *The Bombay High Court dismisses the Ministry of Truth.* Verfassungsblog., DOI: 10.59704/a561364a8208abeb

John, R. R. (2019). Freedom of expression in the digital age: A historian's perspective. *Church. Communication and Culture*, *4*(1), 25–38. DOI: 10.1080/23753234.2019.1565918

Jose, R. (2022). Future scenarios as a tool for citizen engagement in smart cities. *2022 7th International Conference on Smart and Sustainable Technologies (SpliTech)*, 1–6. DOI: 10.23919/SpliTech55088.2022.9854333

Joseph, D., & Sridevi, M. S. (2015). Effective onboarding as a talent management tool for employee retention. *International Journal of Management and Social Sciences*, *3*(7), 175–186.

Jumanne, D. (2021). The Effects of Effective Management of Funds on Financial Institutions Service Delivery in Tanzania: A Case of Manungu SACCOS in Kigoma Municipality (Doctoral dissertation, The Open University of Tanzania).

Juyal, R. (2023). Constitutional Liberties and Cyberspace: Analysing the Anuradha Bhasin v Union of India case and its impact on fundamental rights. *Legal Information Management, 23*(4), 276–281. DOI: 10.1017/S1472669623000622

Kaizer, R. M. (2022). From Cadre Deployment to Professionalizing Public Service in South Africa: A Reflective Approach to Service Delivery Improvement. *African Journal of Development Studies, 2022*(si1), 21.

Kakkar, J. M., Mohan, S., & Devadasan, V. (2025). Safe Harbour and Content Moderation Regulation in India. In Chakravorti, B., & Trachtman, J. P. (Eds.), *Defeating Disinformation: Digital Platform Responsibility, Regulation and Content Moderation on the Global Technological Commons* (pp. 60–84). Cambridge University Press.

Kanaan, A., AL-Hawamleh, A., Abulfaraj, A., Al-Kaseasbeh, H. M., & Alorfi, A. (2023). The effect of quality, security and privacy factors on trust and intention to use e-government services. *International Journal of Data and Network Science, 7*(1), 185–198. DOI: 10.5267/j.ijdns.2022.11.004

Kapur, D., & Mehta, P. B. (2005). *Public institutions in India: Performance and design*. Oxford University Press.

Karachay, V., Chugunov, A., & Neustroeva, R. (2020). Participatory budgeting and e-participation in smart cities: Comparative overview. *Proceedings of the 13th International Conference on Theory and Practice of Electronic Governance*, 835–838. DOI: 10.1145/3428502.3428634

Keerthiraj, M. A., & Vang-Phu, T. (2025). India's BRICS Engagement: A Strategic Lever in South Asia and the Indian Ocean. In A. Gedikli, S. Erdogan, & H. Çalışkan Terzioğlu (Eds.), Changing the Global Political Economy: BRICS Countries and Alternative Relations Strategies (pp. 189-214). IGI Global Scientific Publishing. https://doi.org/DOI: 10.4018/979-8-3693-7393-4.ch006

Kencono, D. S.Dewi Sekar Kencono. (2025). Exploring public sentiment toward regional e-government apps: A case study of Sapawarga and Jaki in Indonesia. *Journal of Information Systems Engineering & Management, 10*(15s), 285–298. DOI: 10.52783/jisem.v10i15s.2458

Khan, S., Umer, R., Uddin, N., Muhammad, J., & Ahmed, N. (2023). Identifying the factors affecting individuals' trust to use social media for e-government services: A conceptual model. *Mehran University Research Journal of Engineering and Technology*, *42*(1), 109. DOI: 10.22581/muet1982.2301.11

Khurshid, M. M., Zakaria, N. H., Rashid, A., Ahmed, Y. A., & Shafique, M. N. (2019). Adoption of Transactional Service in Electronic Government – A Case of Pak-Identity Service. In Pappas, I. O., Mikalef, P., Dwivedi, Y. K., Jaccheri, L., Krogstie, J., & Mäntymäki, M. (Eds.), *Digital Transformation for a Sustainable Society in the 21st Century* (Vol. 11701, pp. 439–450). Springer International Publishing., DOI: 10.1007/978-3-030-29374-1_36

Kohler, J. C., & Dimancesco, D. (2020). The risk of corruption in public pharmaceutical procurement: how anti-corruption, transparency and accountability measures may reduce this risk. Global health action, 13(sup1), 1694745.

Koppell, J. (2007). Global Governance Organizations: Legitimacy and Authority in Conflict. *Journal of Public Administration: Research and Theory*, *18*(2), 177–203. DOI: 10.1093/jopart/mum041

Kotus, J. (2013). Position of the Polish city on the ladder of public participation: Are we going the right way? The case of Poznań. *Cities (London, England)*, *35*, 226–236. DOI: 10.1016/j.cities.2013.08.001

Kumar Srivastava, A. (2021). India's reading regulation as a prohibition: A critical review of the new it rules 2021 in relation to social media networks and messaging applications. *European Data Protection Law Review*, *7*(3), 450–455. DOI: 10.21552/edpl/2021/3/14

Kumar, A., & Narain, V. (2015). Public policy and governance in India. *Vision (Basel)*, *18*(4), 257–260. DOI: 10.1177/0972262914555815

Kuppelwieser, V. G., & Klaus, P. (2024). Future research directions: Enhancing the citizenship experience. *Journal of Retailing and Consumer Services*, *81*, 103973. DOI: 10.1016/j.jretconser.2024.103973

Kurniawati, M. V., Zulmy, M. F., & Rukdeviyani, Y. (2024). The optimizing data quality in interagency data sharing: A framework. *Jurnal Ilmu Komputer Dan Informasi*, *18*(1), 47–66. DOI: 10.21609/jiki.v18i1.1310

Kyaw, N. N. (2017). Unpacking the presumed statelessness of Rohingyas. *Journal of Immigrant & Refugee Studies*, *15*(3), 269–286. DOI: 10.1080/15562948.2017.1330981

Legacy, C., Barry, J., Novacevski, M., & Boyco, M. (2023). "Shared language" Or "Straitjacket"? The hidden costs of legitimising participation through standardised frameworks. *Planning Theory & Practice*, *24*(3), 325–341. DOI: 10.1080/14649357.2023.2214530

Lestari, I., Abdullah, M. T., Hasniati, H., & Nara, N. (2025). Enhancing public services through agile governance: A case study of the online queue application at RSUD Sawerigading Palopo city. *Edelweiss Applied Science and Technology*, *9*(3), 1466–1472. DOI: 10.55214/25768484.v9i3.5561

Lipps, O., Herzing, J. M. E., Pekari, N., Ernst-Staehli, M., Pollien, A., Riedo, G., & Reveilhac, M. (2019). Incentives in surveys. *FORS Guide N°8*, Version 1.1. DOI: 10.24449/FG-2019-00008

Lister, R. (2007). Inclusive citizenship: Realizing the potential. *Citizenship Studies*, *11*(1), 49–61. DOI: 10.1080/13621020601099856

Liu, D. (2022). Factors Affecting Digital Government Adoption: Empirical Study of Trust and Social Influences on Extended TAM. *International Journal of Business Studies and Innovation*, *2*(3), 38–48. DOI: 10.35745/ijbsi2022v02.03.0004

Locke, J. (1689). *Two Treatises of Government* (Laslett, P., Ed.). Cambridge University Press.

Locke, J. (1988). *Two treatises of government* (Laslett, P., Ed.). Cambridge University Press. (Original work published 1689) DOI: 10.1017/CBO9780511810268

Loganathan, T., Ong, Z. L., Hassan, F., Chan, Z. X., & Majid, H. A. (2023). Barriers and facilitators to education access for marginalised non-citizen children in Malaysia: A qualitative study. *PLoS One*, *18*(6), e0286793. DOI: 10.1371/journal.pone.0286793 PMID: 37267412

Lorenz-Spreen, P., Oswald, L., Lewandowsky, S., & Hertwig, R. (2023). A systematic review of worldwide causal and correlational evidence on digital media and democracy. *Nature Human Behaviour*, *7*(1), 74–101. DOI: 10.1038/s41562-022-01460-1 PMID: 36344657

Mahmood, M. (2016). Enhancing citizens' trust and confidence in government through digital transformation. *International Journal of Electronic Government Research*, *12*(1), 99–110. DOI: 10.4018/IJEGR.2016010105

Malodia, S., Dhir, A., Mishra, M., & Bhatti, Z. A. (2021). Future of e-Government: An integrated conceptual framework. *Technological Forecasting and Social Change*, *173*, 121102. DOI: 10.1016/j.techfore.2021.121102

Mamokhere, J. (2021). Evaluating the impact of service delivery protests in relation to socio-economic development: a case of Greater Tzaneen local Municipality, South Africa. *African Journal of Development Studies (formerly AFFRIKA Journal of Politics, Economics and Society), 2021*(si1), 79-96.

Mamokhere, J. (2023). Sending a message to the top: The influence of service delivery protests on service delivery planning in South African municipalities. *Insights into Regional Development, 5*(2), 60–71. DOI: 10.9770/IRD.2023.5.2(4)

Mamokhere, J., & Meyer, D. F. (2023). Towards an Exploration of the Significance of Community Participation in the Integrated Development Planning Process in South Africa. *Social Sciences (Basel, Switzerland), 12*(5), 256. DOI: 10.3390/socsci12050256

Manby, B. (2016). *Citizenship law in Africa: A comparative study* (2nd ed.). Open Society Foundations. DOI: 10.47622/9781936133291

Manda, M. I., & Backhouse, J. (2017). Towards a smart society through digital inclusion: A proposal for an inclusive growth framework. In *International Conference on Social Implications of Computers in Developing Countries* (pp. 130–141). Springer.

Martins, J., Veiga, L., & Fernandes, B. (2023). Are electronic government innovations helpful to deter corruption? Evidence from across the world. *Economics and Politics, 35*(3), 1177–1203. DOI: 10.1111/ecpo.12255

Masuku, M. M., & Jili, N. N. (2019). Public service delivery in South Africa: The political influence at local government level. *Journal of Public Affairs, 19*(4), e1935. DOI: 10.1002/pa.1935

Matlala, L. S., & Uwizeyimana, D. E. (2020). Factors influencing the implementation of the auditor general's recommendations in South African municipalities. *African Evaluation Journal, 8*(1), 1–11. DOI: 10.4102/aej.v8i1.464

Matyana, M. and Mthethwa, R.M., (2022b) Service Delivery Disparities at Winnie Madikizela Mandela Local Municipality: Prospect and Challenges.

Matyana, M., & Mthethwa, R. M. (2022a) community Participation Conundrum in the Winnie Madikizela Mandela Local Municipality Integrated Development Plan: Exploration of an EnhancedFuture.

Matyana, M., & Sibiya, L. M. (2024). Reviving Ethics in Service Delivery: South African Local Government Perspective. In *Challenges of Public Administration Management for Higher Education* (pp. 175-194). IGI Global.

Matyana, M., & Thusi, X. (2023). Making public service delivery more accessible to people with disabilities: The South African government narrative. *International Journal of Research in Business and Social Science (2147-4478), 12*(7), 413-418.

Matyana, M., & Thusi, X. (2023). Unemployment and poverty in South Africa: Assessing the National Development Plan 2030 predictions. *International Journal of Development and Sustainability, 12*(6), 212–226.

McKenzie, C., Brophy, K., Konstanta, G., & Webster, L. (2023). A vision for change leadership: Trust, transparency and accountability at University of Wollongong Library. *Journal of Academic Librarianship, 49*(3), 102710. DOI: 10.1016/j.acalib.2023.102710

Mensah, I. K., Zeng, G., & Luo, C. (2020). E-Government Services Adoption: An Extension of the Unified Model of Electronic Government Adoption. *SAGE Open, 10*(2), 215824402093359. DOI: 10.1177/2158244020933593

Mikhalchenko, A. (2021). ELECTRONIC GOVERNANCE IN THE PROCESS OF MAKING MANAGEMENT DECISIONS. *Scientific Notes of Taurida National V.I. Vernadsky University. Series. Economy and Management, 71*(3). Advance online publication. DOI: 10.32838/2523-4803/71-3-7

Mill, J. (1817). The History of British India (W. Thomas, Ed.). Routledge/Thoemmes Press.

Ministry of Finance. (2021). GST reforms and economic growth. Government of India. https://www.finmin.nic.in

Mngomezulu, S. (2020). Political interference in the administration of service delivery in Umlalazi local municipality of KwaZulu-Natal, South Africa. *Journal of Economics and Behavioral Studies, 12*(1 (J)), 38–45. DOI: 10.22610/jebs.v12i1(J).3003

Mojapelo, M., Modiba, M., & Saurombe, N. (2023). Applying Batho Pele principles in South African public archives–Do public programming initiatives count? *Information Development, 39*(2), 357–375. DOI: 10.1177/02666669211049382

Mostafa, A. M. S., & Abed El-Motalib, E. A. (2020). Ethical leadership, work meaningfulness, and work engagement in the public sector. *Review of Public Personnel Administration, 40*(1), 112–131. DOI: 10.1177/0734371X18790628

Mphahlele, M., & Zandamela, H. (2021). Local government capacity development: A case study of a South African district municipality. *Journal of Public Administration and Governance, 11*(2), 156177–156177.

Mugaa, L. G., Guyo, W., & Otieno, R. O. (2018). Influence of Career Progression on Employee Performance in Large Commercial Banks in Nairobi City County in Kenya.

Muhammad, A. S., & Kaya, T. (2023). Factors affecting the citizen's intention to adopt e-government in Nigeria. *Journal of Information. Communication and Ethics in Society*, *21*(3), 271–289. DOI: 10.1108/JICES-05-2022-0054

Mulyana, Y., & Jamaludin, M. (2023). Effects of government electronic service quality on citizen satisfaction with integrated service delivery in urban areas. *International Journal of Public Policy and Administration Research*, *10*(1), 24–33. DOI: 10.18488/74.v10i1.3293

Nair, P. (1999). Media and democracy in India. *Economic and Political Weekly*, *34*(5), 238–244.

Namaganda, A. (2020). Continuing professional development as transformational learning: A case study. *Journal of Academic Librarianship*, *46*(3), 102152. DOI: 10.1016/j.acalib.2020.102152

Napitupulu, D., Usino, W., Azmi, N. A., Kartika, R. S., Supratikta, H., Suhendra, A., Yohanitas, W. A., Saksono, H., Halik, A., & Suhandojo, S. (2024). Understanding the key driver of e-government services continuance usage intention: An integrated model of Expectation Confirmation Model and Technology Acceptance Model. *Journal of Infrastructure. Policy and Development*, *8*(12), 7957. DOI: 10.24294/jipd.v8i12.7957

Nattrass, N., & Seekings, J. (2018). Employment and labour productivity in high unemployment countries. *Development Policy Review*, *36*(S2), O769–O785. DOI: 10.1111/dpr.12313

Negi, A., Irshad, M., & Luthviati, R. (2024). *Deconstructing Attributes of Constitutional Legitimacy: A Case Study of Indian Constitution. Journal of Human Rights*. Culture and Legal System., DOI: 10.53955/jhcls.v4i1.114

Nguyen, T. T. T. (2023). Citizens' intentions to use e-government during the COVID-19 pandemic: Integrating the technology acceptance model and perceived risk theory. *Kybernetes*, *52*(7), 2329–2346. DOI: 10.1108/K-07-2022-1023

Nguyen, T. T. U., Nguyen, P. V., Huynh, H. T. N., Vrontis, D., & Ahmed, Z. U. (2024). Identification of the determinants of public trust in e-government services and participation in social media based on good governance theory and the technology acceptance model. *Journal of Asia Business Studies*, *18*(1), 44–61. DOI: 10.1108/JABS-04-2023-0160

Nilson, R., Rand, J., Hoen, B., & Elmallah, S. (2024). Halfway up the ladder: Developer practices and perspectives on community engagement for utility-scale renewable energy in the United States. *Energy Research & Social Science*, *117*, 103706. DOI: 10.1016/j.erss.2024.103706

Ninčević Pašalić, I., & Ćukušić, M. (2024). Understanding E-participation adoption: Exploring technological, organizational, and environmental factors. *Technological Forecasting and Social Change*, *207*, 123633. DOI: 10.1016/j.techfore.2024.123633

Norris, P. (2001). *Digital divide: Civic engagement, information poverty, and the internet worldwide*. Cambridge University Press. DOI: 10.1017/CBO9781139164887

North, D. C. (1990). *Institutions, institutional change and economic performance*. Cambridge University Press.

Olvera, J. G., & Avellaneda, C. N. (2019). Subnational government performance: Testing multiple dimensions of governors' experience. *Public Administration Review*, *79*(3), 383–398. DOI: 10.1111/puar.13035

Omazic, A., & Zunk, B. M. (2021). Semi-systematic literature review on sustainability and sustainable development in higher education institutions. *Sustainability (Basel)*, *13*(14), 7683. DOI: 10.3390/su13147683

Orgeron, C. P., Rials, W., & Druchyna, S. (2025). The AI-driven state: How government-as-a-service is transforming public service. *International Journal of Electronic Government Research*, *21*(1), 1–24. DOI: 10.4018/IJEGR.381327

Pallav, P., Ali, S. M. A., & Ghose, A. (2025). Combating misinformation, disinformation, and fake news: A comparative study of the USA, UK, and India. In G. Ilik, M. Karadjoski, I. Ilijevski, & B. Nenovski (Eds.), *Combatting Misinformation and Global Nations' False Narratives Through Education* (pp. 195–222). IGI Global. https://doi.org/DOI: 10.4018/979-8-3693-9601-8.ch008

Panjiar, T., & Waghre, P. (2022, November 10). A public brief on the IT Amendment Rules, 2022, a.k.a. 'how the government is trying to moderate online speech'. *Internet Freedom Foundation*. https://internetfreedom.in/public-brief-on-the-it-amendment-rules-2022/

Peisakhin, L., & Pinto, P. (2010). Is transparency an effective anti-corruption strategy? Evidence from a field experiment in India. *Regulation & Governance*, *4*(3), 261–280. DOI: 10.1111/j.1748-5991.2010.01081.x

Perl-Rosenthal, N., & Erman, S. (2024). Inventing birthright: The nineteenth-century fabrication of *jus soli* and *jus sanguinis*. *Law and History Review*, *42*(3), 421–448. DOI: 10.1017/S0738248024000221

Permatasari, P., Ilman, A. S., Tilt, C. A., Lestari, D., Islam, S., Tenrini, R. H., Rahman, A. B., Samosir, A. P., & Wardhana, I. W. (2021). The village fund program in Indonesia: Measuring the effectiveness and alignment to sustainable development goals. *Sustainability (Basel)*, *13*(21), 12294. DOI: 10.3390/su132112294

Phillips, A. (2004). Defending equality of outcome. *Journal of Political Philosophy*, *12*(1), 1–19. DOI: 10.1111/j.1467-9760.2004.00188.x

Pillai, S., & Williams, G. (2017). Twenty-first-century banishment: Citizenship stripping in common law countries. *The International and Comparative Law Quarterly*, *66*(3), 1–35. DOI: 10.1017/S0020589317000021

Poister, T. H. (2010). The future of strategic planning in the public sector: Linking strategic management and performance. *Public Administration Review*, *70*(s1), s246–s254. DOI: 10.1111/j.1540-6210.2010.02284.x

Polizzi, G. (2019). Information literacy in the digital age: Why critical digital literacy matters for democracy. In *Media and information literacy in higher education* (pp. 1–24). DOI: 10.29085/9781783303922.003

Popescu, M. A. M., Barbu, A., Moiceanu, G., Costea-Marcu, I.-C., Militaru, G., & Simion, P. C. (2024). Citizens' perception of digital public services: A case study among Romanian citizens. *Administrative Sciences*, *14*(10), 259. DOI: 10.3390/admsci14100259

Porter, G., Hampshire, K., De Lannoy, A., Bango, A., Munthali, A., Robson, E., & Abane, A. (2018). Mobile phones and education in sub-Saharan Africa: From youth practice to public policy. *Journal of International Development*, *30*(1), 22–39. DOI: 10.1002/jid.3116

Posel, D., Casale, D., & Grapsa, E. (2020). Household variation and inequality: The implications of equivalence scales in South Africa. *African Review of Economics and Finance*, *12*(1), 102–122.

Post, R. C. (2024, January 8). The press and American democracy: Identifying four distinct constitutional functions of "the press". *Knight First Amendment Institute Blog*. https://knightcolumbia.org/blog/the-press-and-american-democracy

Purwanto, A., Zuiderwijk, A., & Janssen, M. (2018). Citizen engagement in an open election data initiative: A case study of Indonesian's "Kawal Pemilu." *Proceedings of the 19th Annual International Conference on Digital Government Research: Governance in the Data Age*, 1–10. DOI: 10.1145/3209281.3209305

Raworth, K. (2017). *Doughnut economics: Seven ways to think like a 21st century economist*. Chelsea Green Publishing.

Rittel, H. W., & Webber, M. M. (1973). Dilemmas in a general theory of planning. *Policy Sciences*, *4*(2), 155–169. DOI: 10.1007/BF01405730

Rittl, L. G. F., Zaman, A., & De Oliveira, F. H. (2025). Digital transformation in waste management: Disruptive innovation and digital governance for zero-waste cities in the global south as keys to future sustainable development. *Sustainability (Basel)*, *17*(4), 1608. DOI: 10.3390/su17041608

Robertson, O., & Scott Evans, M. (2020). Just how reliable is your internal reliability? An overview of Cronbach's alpha (α). *PsyPag Quarterly*, *1*(115), 23–27. DOI: 10.53841/bpspag.2020.1.115.23

Rodrik, D. (2008). Understanding South Africa's economic puzzles. *Economics of Transition*, *16*(4), 769–797. DOI: 10.1111/j.1468-0351.2008.00343.x

Rodrik, D. (2018). An African growth miracle? *Journal of African Economies*, *27*(1), 10–27.

Rogan, M., & Skinner, C. (2019, December 12). South Africa's informal sector creates jobs, but shouldn't be romanticised. *The Conversation*. https://theconversation.com/south-africas-informal-sector-creates-jobs-but-shouldnt-be-romanticised-128931

Rousseau, J.-J. (1762). *The Social Contract* (Cress, D. A., Trans.). Hackett Publishing.

Rudanetska, O. (2023). International access level to administrative services in electronic format. *Analytical and Comparative Jurisprudence*, *1*(1), 380–383. DOI: 10.24144/2788-6018.2023.01.64

Sabani, A., Deng, H., & Thai, V. (2019). Evaluating the Development of E-Government in Indonesia. *Proceedings of the 2nd International Conference on Software Engineering and Information Management*, 254–258. DOI: 10.1145/3305160.3305191

Safran, W. (1997). Citizenship and nationality in democratic systems: Approaches to defining and acquiring membership in the political community. *International Political Science Review*, *18*(3), 313–335. DOI: 10.1177/019251297018003006

Said, E. W. (1978). *Orientalism*. Pantheon Books.

Sajid, A. (2023). Dr. B. R. Ambedkar and freedom of the press. [IJRAR]. *International Journal of Research and Analytical Reviews*, *2*(4), 47–49. https://academicjournal.ijraw.com/media/post/IJRAW-2-4-16.1.pdf

Sandoval-Almazan, R., & Gil-Garcia, J. R. (2021). Digital government and public participation in Latin America: A comparative analysis. *Government Information Quarterly*, *38*(3), 101573.

Santolamazza, V., Mattei, G., & Grandis, F. G. (2024). Citizens' role and digitalisation in the participatory budgeting to create public value: The case of Rome. *International Journal of Public Sector Management*. Advance online publication. DOI: 10.1108/IJPSM-05-2023-0165

Sarkar, A. (2022). Smart city digital transformation journey: An investigation of stage models. *28th Americas Conference on Information Systems*. https://aisel.aisnet.org/ukais2022

Scanlon, T. M. (2024). Freedom of speech. In Zalta, E. N. (Ed.), *The Stanford Encyclopedia of Philosophy* (Spring 2024 Edition). Stanford University., https://plato.stanford.edu/entries/freedom-speech/

Schmid, S. D. (2020). The architecture of national boundary regimes: Mapping immigration and citizenship policies in 23 democracies 1980–2010. *Comparative Migration Studies*, *8*(1), 1–19. DOI: 10.1186/s40878-020-00182-5

Schmitt, C. (1922). *Political Theology: Four Chapters on the Concept of Sovereignty* (Schwab, G., Trans.). University of Chicago Press.

Schreiner, G. O., Snyman-van der Walt, L., De Jager, M., Dludla, A., Lochner, P. A., Wright, J., Scholes, R. J., Atkinson, D., & Hardcastle, P. (2018). Advancing a participatory and science-based approach to policy formulation for shale gas development in South Africa. In *Citizen and other stakeholder participation in unconventional fossil fuel land use decision-making, policy formation, regulatory practice or other governance mechanisms*.

Schulz-Herzenberg, C. (2020). The Decline of Partisan Voting and the Rise in Electoral Uncertainty in South Africa's 2019 General Elections. In *Reflections on the 2019 South African General Elections* (pp. 98–116). Routledge. DOI: 10.4324/9781003031345-7

Seekings, J., & Nattrass, N. (2008). *Class, race, and inequality in South Africa*. Yale University Press.

Sen, A. (1999). *On ethics and economics*. Oxford University Press.

Shattock, M. (2017). The "world class" university and international ranking systems: What are the policy implications for governments and institutions? *Policy Reviews in Higher Education*, *1*(1–2), 4–21. DOI: 10.1080/23322969.2016.1236669

Shehatta, I., & Mahmood, K. (2016). Correlation among top 100 universities in the major six global rankings: Policy implications. *Scientometrics*, *109*(2), 1231–1254. DOI: 10.1007/s11192-016-2103-3

Shifa, M., Mabhena, R., Ranchhod, V., & Leibbrandt, M. V. (2023). *An assessment of inequality estimates for the case of South Africa* (WIDER Working Paper No. 2023/90).

Shin, D., & Park, Y. J. (2019). Role of fairness, accountability, and transparency in algorithmic affordance. *Computers in Human Behavior, 98*, 277–284. DOI: 10.1016/j.chb.2019.04.019

Singer, E. (2018). The use and effects of incentives in surveys. In Vannette, D. L., & Krosnick, J. A. (Eds.), *The palgrave handbook of survey research* (pp. 63–70). Springer International Publishing., DOI: 10.1007/978-3-319-54395-6_9

Siwi, T. P. U., & Nawawi, Z. (2023). Building Citizen Satisfaction Towards E-Government Services: A Conceptual Framework. *Jurnal Manajemen Pelayanan Publik, 6*(2), 253. DOI: 10.24198/jmpp.v6i2.46471

Skinner, C. (2018). *Digital human: The fourth revolution of humanity includes everyone*. John Wiley & Sons.

Southall, R. (2007). Ten propositions about black economic empowerment in South Africa. *Review of African Political Economy, 34*(111), 67–84. DOI: 10.1080/03056240701340365

Sovacool, B. K., Turnheim, B., Hook, A., Brock, A., & Martiskainen, M. (2021). Dispossessed by decarbonisation: Reducing vulnerability, injustice, and inequality in the lived experience of low-carbon pathways. *World Development, 137*, 105116. DOI: 10.1016/j.worlddev.2020.105116

Spaull, N. (2013). South Africa's education crisis: The quality of education in South Africa 1994–2011. *Centre for Development and Enterprise, 21*(1), 1–65.

Stone, M., & Dohel, I. (Eds.). (2013). *From traditional to online media: Best practices and perspectives: 14th Central Asia Media Conference, Ashgabat, Turkmenistan, 5–6 July 2012* (OSCE Representative on Freedom of the Media). Organisation for Security and Co-operation in Europe. https://www.osce.org/files/f/documents/8/3/102312.pdf

Storozhenko, L. (2023). ELECTRONIC GOVERNMENT AS A TOOL FOR NETOCRATIC MANAGEMENT: BENEFITS AND CAPABILITIES. *Grail of Science, 26*(26), 78–81. DOI: 10.36074/grail-of-science.14.04.2023.010

Strebel, M. A., Kübler, D., & Marcinkowski, F. (2019). The importance of input and output legitimacy in democratic governance: Evidence from a population-based survey experiment in four West European countries. *European Journal of Political Research, 58*(2), 488–513. DOI: 10.1111/1475-6765.12293

Street, K. (2023). *Sustainable Development Goals: Country report 2023.*

Strotmann, H., & Volkert, J. (2018). Multidimensional poverty index and happiness. *Journal of Happiness Studies, 19*(1), 167–189. DOI: 10.1007/s10902-016-9807-0

Sugiana, D., Suryana, A., Wirakusumah, T. K., & Subekti, P. (2025). Communication innovations for adaptation to climate change and increased disaster risk. *International Journal of Safety and Security Engineering, 15*(03), 465–477. DOI: 10.18280/ijsse.150306

Surjandari, I., Megawati, C., Dhini, A., & Sanditya Hardaya, I. B. N. (2016). Application of text mining for classification of textual reports: A study of Indonesia's national complaint handling system. *Proceedings of the International Conference on Industrial Engineering and Operations Management.*

Susniwati, S., Kurniawati, K., & Susilawati, S. (2024). Public policy innovation in Indonesia: Enchancing citizen engagement through E-government initiatives. *PINISI Discretion Review, 8*(1), 1. DOI: 10.26858/pdr.v8i1.66364

Thomas, K. M. (2023). A game not played well: A critical analysis of the draft amendment to the Information Technology (Intermediary Guidelines and Digital Media Ethics Code) Rules, 2021. *Tech Law Forum @ NALSAR.* https://techlawforum.nalsar.ac.in/a-game-not-played-well-a-critical-analysis-of-the-draft-amendment-to-the-information-technology-intermediary-guidelines-and-digital-media-ethics-code-rules-2021/

Thusi, X., Mahlatse, R., & Matyana, M. (2023b). Innovation as a Tool to Improve Public Service Delivery: South African Government Perspective. *INTERDISCIPLINARY JOURNAL ON LAW, SOCIAL SCIENCES AND HUMANITIES, 4*(2), 175–189. DOI: 10.19184/idj.v4i2.39165

Thusi, X., Matyana, M., & Jili, N. (2023a). Lack of political will: A barrier to public service delivery in South Africa and a high cost for citizens. *Journal of Studies in Social Sciences and Humanities (JSSSH). E-ISSN, 9*(2), 137–147.

Tilak, J. B. G. (2021). *Education policy in India: Challenges and prospects.* Routledge.

TO, I. R. (2022). *Submission to the Department of Forestry, Fisheries and the Environment (DFFE).*

Tregenna, F. (2016). Sectoral dimensions of employment intensity. In *Towards employment-intensive growth in South Africa* (pp. 108–125).

Tripkovic, M. (2023). Renouncing criminal citizens: Patterns of denationalization. *Punishment & Society, 25*(6), 1351–1371. DOI: 10.1177/14624745221080705

Tulili, T. R., Nurcahyono, D., Rijal, S., Kurniawan, A., & Saleh, M. T. R. (2023). Classification of public opinion on news presentation at lapor website using Naïve Bayes classifier (NBC) algorithm method. In *Proceedings of the 3rd International Conference of Bio-Based Economy for Application and Utility* (020228). DOI: 10.1063/5.0135542

Turok, I., & Borel-Saladin, J. (2016). Backyard shacks, informality and the urban housing crisis in South Africa: Stopgap or prototype solution? *Housing Studies*, *31*(4), 384–409. DOI: 10.1080/02673037.2015.1091921

Turok, I., & Visagie, J. (2018). *Inclusive urban development in South Africa: What does it mean and how can it be measured?* The Institute of Development Studies and Partner Organisations.

U.S. Continental Congress. (1776). The Declaration of Independence (P. Force, Ed.). Dover Publications.

UNEP. (2024). *Climate risks in the power generation sector.*

United Nations. (1948). Universal Declaration of Human Rights. United Nations. https://www.un.org/en/about-us/universal-declaration-of-human-rights

Valentim, V. (2023). *Norms (Entry for the Encyclopedia of Political Sociology).* DOI: 10.31219/osf.io/erfpg

Van Den Boom, J. (2023). What does the Digital Markets Act harmonise? – Exploring interactions between the DMA and national competition laws. *European Competition Journal*, *19*(1), 57–85. DOI: 10.1080/17441056.2022.2156728

Van der Berg, S. (2008). How effective are poor schools? Poverty and educational outcomes in South Africa. *Studies in Educational Evaluation*, *34*(3), 145–154. DOI: 10.1016/j.stueduc.2008.07.005

Vasylchyshyn, O., Storozhenko, L., Babkova, T., Kuchmenko, V., & Kovalchuk, V. (2024). Social media as a factor in the transformation of public administration, justice and legality. *Multidisciplinary Reviews*, *7*(Special Issue), 2024spe039. Advance online publication. DOI: 10.31893/multirev.2024spe039

Victoria, Q. (1858). Proclamation of 1858 to the Princes, Chiefs, and People of India. In Philips, C. H. (Ed.), *The Evolution of India and Pakistan, 1858 to 1947* (pp. 1–3). Oxford University Press.

Voigt, P., & Von dem Bussche, A. (2017). *The EU General Data Protection Regulation (GDPR): A Practical Guide*. Springer. DOI: 10.1007/978-3-319-57959-7

Vora, A. (2023, June 26). Challenge to the IT Rules 2023. *Supreme Court Observer*. https://www.scobserver.in/journal/challenge-to-the-it-rules-2023/

Vyasa. (400 BCE). The Bhagavad Gita (E. Easwaran, Trans.). Nilgiri Press.

Vyasa. (400 BCE). The Mahabharata of Krishna-Dwaipayana Vyasa, Book 12: Shanti Parva (K. M. Ganguli, Trans.). Munshiram Manoharlal.

Wadesango, N., Jori, A. K., & Lovemore, S. (2023). Literature review of the relationship between E-procurement and cost reduction. *Multidisciplinary Science Journal, 5*, 2023ss0316. DOI: 10.31893/multiscience.2023ss0316

Wahlund, M., & Palm, J. (2022). The role of energy democracy and energy citizenship for participatory energy transitions: A comprehensive review. *Energy Research & Social Science*, *87*, 102482. DOI: 10.1016/j.erss.2021.102482

Walker, L. (2005). Men behaving differently: South African men since 1994. *Culture, Health & Sexuality*, *7*(3), 225–238. DOI: 10.1080/13691050410001713215 PMID: 16864199

Warria, A. (2020). Stateless transnational migrant children in South Africa: Implications and opportunities for social work intervention. *African Human Mobility Review*, *6*(2), 6–24. DOI: 10.14426/ahmr.v6i2.795

Warsono, H., Yuwono, T., & Putranti, I. R. (2023). Analyzing technology acceptance model for collaborative governance in public administration: Empirical evidence of digital governance and perceived ease of use. *International Journal of Data and Network Science*, *7*(1), 41–48. DOI: 10.5267/j.ijdns.2022.12.008

Weber, M. (1978). *Economy and Society: An Outline of Interpretive Sociology* (Roth, G., & Wittich, C., Eds.). University of California Press.

Wenner, M. (2020). Trajectories of Hybrid Governance: Legitimacy, Order and Leadership in India. *Development and Change*. Advance online publication. DOI: 10.1111/dech.12624

Winker, M. A., Bloom, T., Onie, S., & Tumwine, J. (2023). Equity, transparency, and accountability: Open science for the 21st century. *Lancet*, *402*(10409), 1206–1209. DOI: 10.1016/S0140-6736(23)01575-1 PMID: 37805196

World Bank Group. (2022). *Global economic prospects, January 2022*. World Bank Publications.

World Bank. (1994). *Governance: The World Bank's experience*. World Bank.

World Bank. (2017). *World Development Report 2017: Governance and the law*. World Bank. DOI: 10.1596/978-1-4648-0950-7

Yadav, A., & Bajpai, R. (2024). Analysing *Kunal Kamra v. Union of India* in light of the vires of IT (Amendment) Rules, 2023 - Part II. *NLIU Law Review*. https://nliulawreview.nliu.ac.in/blog/analysing-kunal-kamra-v-uoi-in-light-of-the-vires-of-it-amendment-rules-2023-part-ii/

Yap, C. S., Ahmad, R., Newaz, F. T., & Mason, C. (2019). Continuous Use Intention of E-Government Portals the Perspective of Older Citizens. *International Journal of Electronic Government Research, 15*(1), 1–16. DOI: 10.4018/IJEGR.2019010101

Yende, N. E. (2023). Towards Sustainable Service Delivery by South African Local Authorities: A Community Participation Strategy. *African Journal of Development Studies, 13*(1), 197.

Yujie, Z., Al Imran Yasin, M., Alsagoff, S. A. B. S., & Hoon, A. L. (2022). The mediating role of new media engagement in this digital age. *Frontiers in Public Health, 10*, 879530. DOI: 10.3389/fpubh.2022.879530 PMID: 35586011

Zhang, Y. (2023). Citizens' trust and digital attitudes: Evidence from city digital transformation in Shanghai, China. *Public Administration and Policy, 26*(3), 258–271. DOI: 10.1108/PAP-01-2023-0014

Ziervogel, G. (2019). *Unpacking the Cape Town drought: Lessons learned*. African Centre for Cities.

Ziervogel, G., New, M., Archer van Garderen, E., Midgley, G., Taylor, A., Hamann, R., Stuart-Hill, S., Myers, J., & Warburton, M. (2014). Climate change impacts and adaptation in South Africa. *Wiley Interdisciplinary Reviews: Climate Change, 5*(5), 605–620. DOI: 10.1002/wcc.295

Zilla, C. (2022). Defining democratic inclusion from the perspective of democracy and citizenship theory. *Democratization, 29*(8), 1518–1538. DOI: 10.1080/13510347.2022.2090929

Zulu, P., Yalezo, B., & Mutambara, E. (2022). An assessment of cadre deployment practices in KwaZulu-Natal local government. *Academy of Strategic Management Journal, 21*, 1–22.

Zunder, T. H. (2021). A semi-systematic literature review, identifying research opportunities for more sustainable, receiver-led inbound urban logistics flows to large higher education institutions. *European Transport Research Review, 13*(1), 1–14. DOI: 10.1186/s12544-021-00487-1

About the Contributors

Andrew Enaifoghe (PhD) is an author, publisher and enthusiastic emerging academic researcher. He is a passionate lecturer/educator with experience developing and implementing diverse curricula covering various subjects related to my specialisation. He is highly skilled at motivating students through positive encouragement and re-enforcement of concepts through interactive classroom instruction and observation. He thrives in both independent and collaborative work environments.

***

S. M. Aamir Ali is presently working as an Assistant Professor at Vinayaka Mission's Law School, Vinayaka Mission's Research Foundation (Deemed University), Chennai, India. He is currently pursuing his PhD from West Bengal National University of Juridical Sciences (WBNUJS), Kolkata, and has completed his LL.M from National Law School of India University (NLSIU), Bengaluru, with a specialization in Human Rights Law. Mr Ali has been teaching across specializations in Constitutional Law, Human Rights and Criminal Law at UG and PG levels since 2019.

Rezzy Eko Caraka (SENIOR IEEE MEMBER) is an accomplished academic with a diverse range of roles and experiences. Currently, he serves as a Researcher at the Research Center for Data and Information Sciences within the Research Organization for Electronics and Informatics, National Research and Innovation Agency (BRIN), Indonesia, a position he has held since February 2022. Alongside this, he holds the position of Professor at the Department of Information Management, Chaoyang University of Technology on March 2024. Before his current positions, Caraka has held various roles in prestigious institutions. He was a Post-doctoral Researcher with the Department of Statistics at Seoul National University from

2019 to December 2021. Subsequently, he served as a Post-Doctoral Researcher with the Department of Nuclear Medicine at Seoul National University Hospital from January 2021 to January 2022. Following this, he assumed the role of Research Assistant Professor at the Department of Statistics, Seoul National University, from January to April 2022. Caraka's academic engagements are not limited to his research roles. He has also been actively involved in teaching and mentoring. He has been an Adjunct Lecturer with the Faculty of Economics and Business at Universitas Indonesia since 2021 and an Adjunct Lecturer at the Graduate School, Department of Statistics at Padjadjaran University since 2021 as well. Furthermore, he has served as a Senior Research Fellow with the Department of Mathematics at Ulsan National Institute of Science and Technology, South Korea, from 2022 to June 2024. Caraka has recently taken up the position of Senior Lecturer at Telkom University starting in 2024, which indicates his continued dedication to academia and his commitment to fostering learning and research in his field. Caraka has been recognized for his contributions to the field, being acknowledged as a top 2% researcher in AI and Machine Learning by Stanford University. His diverse research interests encompass statistics, Large-Scale Optimization, Machine Learning, Big Data Analytics, Data Science, and Sustainable Development Goals.

Akash Dixit is an Assistant Professor of law at the School of Law, MIT-World Peace University, Pune. He holds an LL.M. in Business Laws from the National Law University, Delhi, and a B.A. LL.B. (Hons.) in Energy Laws from UPES, Dehradun. He qualified the UGC-NET in 2022. His research interests include Constitutional Law, Banking Laws, and Insolvency Law.

Anuttama Ghose is an Associate Professor of Law Dr. Anuttama Ghose is an Associate Professor of Law at Vinayaka Mission's Law School (VMLS), Chennai. She has completed her B.A LL.B (IPR Hons.) from the School of Law, KIIT University, Bhubaneshwar and LL.M with specialisation in the field of Intellectual Property Laws from Symbiosis Law School, Pune, India. She has previously worked as Vice-Principal and Assistant Professor of Law at Indian Institute of Legal Studies, Darjeeling, West Bengal. Apart from being an IPR enthusiast, she is a very keen researcher and has over 50 academic publications in National and International Journals to her credit.

Andrari Grahitandaru received her Bachelor of Physics degree from Bandung Institute of Technology, Indonesia, in 1983 and her Master of Optoelectrotechnics degree from the University of Indonesia, Indonesia, in 1992. Her research interests include Electronic Election Systems, Digital Government, Information Systems, Digital Government Architecture, especially Digital Service Management Data

Architecture. She works at the Data and Information Science Research Center, National Research and Innovation Agency (BRIN) as a Senior Researcher in the Digital Government Research Group. She is also an active Vice Chairman of the Technology Auditors Association and an active member of the Indonesian Researchers Association.

Rival Adrian Juliansyah Received a Bachelor of Informatics Engineering degree from the College of Informatics and Computer Management in Sumedang, Indonesia,in 2019 . His research interests include e-government, application audit and infrastructure for electronic-based government systems (SPBE). As a member of the Digital Government Research Group, he works at the Data and Information Science Research Center (PR SDI), National Research and Innovation Agency (BRIN).

Keerthiraj is currently with the Department of Political Science, GFGC Punjalakatte (affiliated with Mangalore University) and has previously served at the School of Law & Liberal Arts, Alliance University, Bengaluru. His journey is not one of overcoming odds but of discovering how knowledge emerges in places the academy rarely sees. Born in a forest village of coastal Karnataka, in a family untouched by formal education, he worked as a coolie, quarry labourer, salesman etc. to support his studies and family. These experiences are the ground on which his thinking grew. He completed his BA in History, Economics, and Political Science, followed by an MA in Political Science from Mangalore University. His PhD at Kuvempu University focused on Media, Public Policy, Public Perceptions, and Politics. His work spans political ideologies, diplomacy, public policy, strategy, and international relations. His teaching and research are driven not by trend but by a deeper question: how do we make sense of the world around us? For him, scholarship is not a career but a form of responsibility—to rethink, unlearn, and make knowledge that speaks from lived experiences and scientific inquiry.

Ekawati Marlina earned her Ph.D. in Computer Science from the University of Indonesia in 2023. She currently serves as a researcher at the Research Centre for Data Science and Information, National Research and Innovation Agency (PRSDI BRIN). Her research activities focus on e-government, research data management, and information systems.

Parul Mishra is a Professor of English at Amity School of Languages, Amity University Rajasthan since 2016. Prior to Amity she has served in reputed HEIs of government of India. Prof Mishra holds 26 years of teaching and research experience with 5 books and 48 research papers published nationally/internationally.

Apoorva Misra is a legal scholar specializing in international law, public policy, environmental law, and sustainable development. She holds a Doctorate of Philosophy in Law from Guru Gobind Singh Indraprastha University, Delhi (2023) for her thesis titled "Locating Environment in the Application of Sustainable Development: A Critical Analysis of Environmental Jurisprudence", and a Master of Law from TERI School of Advanced Studies, New Delhi (2018). She is serving as Assistant Professor of Law at Alliance University and has published widely in peer-reviewed journals and edited volumes.

Shaun Mowat is a lecturer in the Department of Economics in the School of Commerce at the University of KwaZulu-Natal, South Africa. His research interests are mainly in the area of ecological and environmental economics, with a specific interest in ecosystem services.

Hengki Muradi, born in Kepahiang on April 5, 1988, earned his bachelor's degree in Mathematics from Bengkulu University, a master's degree in Mathematics from the University of Indonesia, and a doctoral degree in Statistics and Data Science from IPB University. He is currently a researcher at the Research Center for Data and Information Science, National Research and Innovation Agency (BRIN), with research interests in mathematics, statistics, and machine learning. Since 2007, through his initiative Greatstat, he has supported hundreds of researchers in research methodology and data analysis, while continuously contributing to the advancement of statistical science and data-driven innovation in Indonesia.

Budi Nugroho received his Bachelor's degree in Mathematics and Natural Science from the University of Padjadjaran, Indonesia, in 2002 and his Master's degree in Informatics from the Bandung Institute of Technology, Indonesia, in 2011. In 2019, he received his Dr. Eng. in Computer Science from Kumamoto University, Japan. His research interests include informetrics, socio-informatics, digital government, and information systems. He serves the Research Center for Data Science and Information, Research and Innovation National Agency (BRIN) as a Senior Researcher in the Digital Government Research Group. He is also an active member of the Association of Computing and Machinery (ACM) and the Indonesian Researcher

Prashanth S. P. is an Assistant Professor of Political Science in the Department of Humanities at M S Ramaiah College of Arts, Science and Commerce-Autonomous, Bangalore. He has seven years of teaching experience and has taught courses on political theory, political thought, comparative politics, and public administration. His current research focuses on linguistic politics and nation-building in India, exploring the intersection of language, identity, and state policy. His broader research interests include constitutional law, Western and Indian political thought, governance, and democratic processes. He has participated in national conferences and workshops on political science and public policy.

Pallav is a Junior Research Fellow (UGC) and Ph.D Scholar at The West Bengal National University of Judicial Sciences (NUJS), Kolkata. He has completed a PG Diploma in Media Laws from NALSAR, Hyderabad. He has qualified Prestigious UGC NET with JRF. He has practical experience as an Advocate at the Patna High Court. He has also completed an LLM. He has completed BBA LL.B. (Constitutional Law Hons.) from the School of Law, KIIT University, Bhubaneswar.

Zain Saifullah is a researcher at the Research Center for Society and Culture, the National Research and Innovation Agency (BRIN), Indonesia. After graduating from the Oklahoma State University in 1995, working as a System Analyst; and now his research focuses on e-government audit.

Armita Widyasuri earned a Bachelor's degree in Computer Science from Gunadarma University, Indonesia, in 2017, and a Master's degree in Information Systems Management from Gunadarma University, Indonesia, in 2020. Her research interests include digital government, data science, and information systems. She is currently working at the Deputy for Research and Innovation Utilization, National Research and Innovation Agency (BRIN) as a junior engineer in the Directorate of Technology Transfer and Audit Systems.

Muhammad Younus graduated in 2019 from the Karachi Institute of Economics and Technology University in Karachi, Pakistan, and got a Bachelor's degree in Computer Science. The four-year undergraduate program in Computer Science formed the basis of Younus's perseverance towards achieving an in-depth knowledge in the field. After graduation, Younus worked for the past few years as a business IT analyst in the product and research development of a logistics startup in Pakistan called TPL Logistics. They aim to Digitize Logistics Operations in Pakistan from the First Mile to the Last Mile. After this, Younus graduated in 2024 from the Universitas Muhammadiyah Yogyakarta in Yogyakarta, Indonesia, and got a Master's Degree in Government Science. Younus's research interest is transforming governance and the public sector through technology. This experience has given Younus the confidence and also kindled a desire to do research. The interdisciplinary nature has convinced Younus in taking this decision as it is the ideal choice for an exciting research career. At the same time, I am confident of contributing originally to the ongoing work. By working under the guidance of distinguished Team, Younus shall certainly be able to exploit my potential to the fullest.

Index

www.ingramcontent.com/pod-product-compliance
Lightning Source LLC
LaVergne TN
LVHW081524300926
849161LV00006B/1282